THE NATION'S HEALTH

JONES AND BARTLETT PUBLISHERS
SERIES IN HEALTH

Becoming an Addictions Counselor: A Comprehensive Text, Myers/Salt
Cases in Sport Marketing, McDonald/Milne
Clinical Decision Making from Theory to Practice, Eddy
Community Health Promotion Ideas That Work, Kreuter, et al.
Concepts of Athletic Training (Second Edition), Pfeiffer/Mangus
Drug Abuse Prevention, Wilson/Kolander
Drugs and Society (Sixth Edition), Hanson/Venturelli
Dying Death and Bereavement, Corless
*EMPOWER: Enabling Methods of Planning and Organizing Within Everyone's
    Reach,* Gold/Green/Kreuter
Explorations in Women's Health, Howley/Edwards
Exploring the Dimensions of Human Sexuality, Greenberg/Bruess/Haffner
Essentials for Health and Wellness (Second Edition), Edlin/Golanty/McCormack
    Brown
Fostering Emotional Well-Being in the Classroom (Second Edition), Page/Page
Health and Welfare for Families in the 21st Century, Wallace, et al.
Health and Wellness (Sixth Edition), Edlin/Golanty/McCormack Brown
Health Education: A Cognitive Behavioral Approach, Read
Health Education: Creating Strategies for School and Community Health
    (Second Edition), Gilbert/Sawyer
Health Policy: Crisis and Reform in the U.S. Health Care Delivery System
    (Second Edition), Harrington/Estes
Healthy People 2010, U.S. Department of Health and Human Services
An Introduction to Community Health (Third Edition), McKenzie/Pinger/Kotecki
Introduction to Epidemiology (Second Edition), Timmreck
Managing Stress: Principles and Strategies for Health and Wellbeing (Second
    Edition), Seaward
The Nation's Health (Sixth Edition), Lee/Estes
New Dimensions in Women's Health (Second Edition), Alexander/LaRosa/Bader
Perspectives on Death and Dying, Fulton/Melress
Physical Activity and Health: A Report of the Surgeon General, U.S. Department
    of Health and Human Services
Practicing the Application of Health Education Skills, Keyser, et al.
Skill Building Activities for Alcohol and Drug Education, Bates/Wigtil
Sport Marketing: Managing the Exchange Process, Milne/McDonald
Teaching Health Science (Fourth Edition), Bender, et al.

Sixth Edition

The Nation's Health

Edited by

PHILIP R. LEE
Institute for Health Policy Studies
School of Medicine
University of California, San Francisco
and
Program in Human Biology
Stanford University, Stanford

CARROLL L. ESTES
Institute for Health and Aging
School of Nursing
University of California, San Francisco

FATIMA M. RODRIGUEZ
Assistant Editor
Program in Human Biology
Stanford University, Stanford

JONES AND BARTLETT PUBLISHERS

Sudbury, Massachusetts
BOSTON   TORONTO   LONDON   SINGAPORE

World Headquarters
Jones and Bartlett Publishers
40 Tall Pine Drive
Sudbury, MA 01776
978-443-5000
info@jbpub.com
www.jbpub.com

Jones and Bartlett Publishers Canada
2406 Nikanna Road
Mississauga, Ontario
CANADA L5C 2W6

Jones and Bartlett Publishers International
Barb House, Barb Mews
London W6 7PA
UK

Production Credits
Sponsoring Editor: Suzanne Jeans
Associate Editor: Amy Austin
Senior Production Editor: Lianne Ames
Manufacturing Buyer: Therese Bräuer
Design: Clarinda Publication Services
Editorial Production Service: Clarinda Publication Services
Typesetting: The Clarinda Company
Cover Design: Anne Spencer
Printing and Binding: Malloy Lithographing
Cover Printing: Malloy Lithographing
Cover Photos: PhotoDisc

Library of Congress Cataloging-in-Publication Data
The nation's health / edited by Philip R. Lee, Carroll L. Estes.
     p. cm.
  Includes bibliographical references and index.
  ISBN 0-7637-1286-8
    1. Public Health—United States. 2. Medical policy—United States. 3. Health care
reform—United States. I. Lee, Philip R. (Philip Randolph), 1924– II. Estes, Carroll L.
RA445.N36 2001
362.1′0973—dc21   00-022254

Printed in the United States of America

04 03 02 01 00   10 9 8 7 6 5 4 3 2 1

CONTENTS

PREFACE

The nation's health is a continuing concern, yet a source of great pride because of the improvement in the health of the American people during the 20th century. This volume—edited by two top health policy analysts—includes a practical, in-depth guide to the factors affecting the health of Americans and the role of public health and medical care in ensuring the nation's health.

Health care reform was the top domestic priority when the fourth edition was published. President Clinton's proposal to provide universal health insurance and contain the rapidly rising costs of care was never acted on by Congress after more than two years of debate and discussion. Despite the failure of Congress to act on health care reform, progress has been made in a host of areas affecting health: tobacco, immunization, HIV/AIDS, environmental health (e.g., water, pesticides), dietary guidelines, physical activity, and food safety. There are a continuing set of questions related to health care, including those related to managed competition, capitation, global budgets, the medical-industrial complex, rationing of care, specialist versus generalist practice of medicine, and forces that continue to drive costs upward. The question is often asked whether or not it is possible to expand access to care and at the same time control relentlessly rising costs. Former senator Bradley, a candidate for the Democratic Party's nomination for President in 2000, raised the issue of health care as a right with his proposal in the Fall of 1999 for federally guaranteed health insurance for at least 95 percent of the population. In addition, Medicare has again risen to the top of the health policy agenda. Special attention in this edition is given to Medicare reform issues.

Other important questions addressed in this volume are: what is the relationship of socioeconomic class to health? How important are clinical preventive services? Why do Americans spend over twice as much per capita for health care than people in most other industrial countries and yet rank far behind in infant mortality, life expectancy, and other measures of health status? How do we eliminate medical care that is wasteful, inefficient, and unnecessary and improve the quality of health care?

In this book, a number of the nation's leading health policy experts look at the complex web of issues, policies, controversies, and proposed solutions that surround health policy, public health, and health care in the United States.

The sixth edition of *The Nation's Health* represents part of a multidisciplinary program for advanced training and education in health policy and health services research that is conducted by the Institute for Health Policy Studies, School of Medicine, and the Institute for Health and Aging, School of Nursing, University of California, San Francisco, and the Program in Human Biology, Stanford University.

During 1999, when this book was being prepared, Philip Lee served as an active Emeritus Professor of Social Medicine on the UCSF faculty and as Consulting Professor, Human Biology Program, Stanford University, where he teaches undergraduate students about health care, health policy, federal health programs, and international health care systems and policies. While serving as Assistant Secretary for Health/DHHS in the Clinton Administration from 1993 to 1997, he played a key role in the national effort to restate the nation's health care agenda in response to many of the problems and issues described in this book and in keeping with many of its themes.

Professor Carroll Estes was serving as Professor of Sociology and Director of the Institute for Health & Aging (Emeritus), UCSF. She has recently served as a Consultant for Social Science Research for the Social Security Administration, as President of the Gerontological Society of America, and as a member of the "Notch" Commission dealing with Social Security retirement benefits.

Special appreciation goes to Fatima Rodriguez, who served as assistant editor of the sixth edition and as research assistant to Dr. Lee. She coordinated work efforts between the editors, the research assistants, and the publisher; reviewed and helped select articles; organized the book; and assisted with the editing. Thanks also to Tracy Weitz and Brian Kaskie, who served as research assistants to Professor Estes, for their critical role in the review, selection, and editing of articles. Special appreciation also to Samantha Collins, a research assistant at the Institute for Health Policy Studies, who has provided editorial assistance.

Although *The Nation's Health* is a project of the Institute for Health Policy Studies and the Institute for Health and Aging, UCSF, and the Program in Human Biology, Stanford University, the views expressed are those of the authors only and do not necessarily reflect those of the University of California or Stanford University.

INTRODUCTION

The sixth edition of *The Nation's Health* continues the emphasis of earlier editions on the precarious set of circumstances faced by the nation's public health and health care systems as we stand on the verge of the 21st century. As such, the nation's health is viewed both individually and collectively. At the individual level, health is very often a high priority, but it must often compete with many other priorities. Collectively views are mixed, often complicated by the fact that health is often equated with access to medical care, which primarily meets the needs of individuals. While the public supports many public health measures (i.e., immunizations, food safety), there is little understanding among the general populace of the terms *public health* and *population health*. We intend this book to represent a range of views about factors affecting health status, the current state of public health and health care, and the future of the health system, with particular emphasis on the current issues and proposals for change. In order to make some sense of the massive literature on health, public health, and health care, we have organized the material into five parts, with one to four chapters per part. The five parts are:

1. Health of the Nation and Determinants of Health
2. Health Policy and the Politics of Health
3. Public Health, Clinical Preventive Services, and the Emerging Collaboration of Medicine and Public Health
4. Health Insurance and Health Care Systems
5. Women's Health and Aging

In addition to the material included in the chapters (over 50 articles—excerpts of book chapters, chart books, and issue briefs), we have included an appendix containing a list of recommended readings.

While there is broad agreement about the importance of health, there is much less agreement about the definition of health. While the World Health Organization's (WHO) definition of health as a "state of complete physical, mental and social well being and not merely the absence of disease or infirmity" has been in use for more than 50 years, it has often proved difficult to measure and apply to a population (WHO, 1968). Many other definitions, which range from adaptation to wholeness, have been proposed, but none have found universal acceptance (Breslow, 1990). At the time of the WHO definition, the germ theory was the dominant paradigm, and most of the emphasis was on measures to control infectious diseases. Navarro has noted that the WHO definition on health "was an enormous break with the traditional understanding of health and medicine, putting both in their proper context." (Navarro, 1998). While broadening the conceptual basis for defining health, the WHO definition still presents a challenge in its practical application. How can we, as a society, go about ensuring the health, so defined, of each of our members?

The absence of a clear framework within which to develop policies that focused on the nation's health has resulted in an overemphasis on the role of medical care and a serious fragmentation of public health programs. Indeed in 1988, a report by the Institute of Medicine, *The Future of Public Health* noted "a growing perception . . . that this nation has lost sight of its public health goals and has allowed the system of public health activities to fall into disarray" (IOM, 1988).

Corrective measures, particularly the effort to develop a health policy framework, had begun prior to our first edition and almost a decade ahead of the IOM Report. The concept of the determinants of health was to play a critical role in the shaping of a new health policy framework. Canada had preceded the United States with the 1974 Lalonde Report *A New Perspective on the Health of Canadians* (1974), published by the Canadian Department of National Health and Welfare. The Lalonde Report marked a very important step in shaping the current understanding about health. It made very clear that health does not equal medical care. The document helped to clarify thinking about how to apply the concept of the determinants of health to policy, and it proposed five intervention strategies: (1) health promotion; (2) regulation; (3) research; (4) health care; and (5) goal setting. Then in the United States, the *Surgeon General's Report on Health Promotion and Disease Prevention* (DHHS, 1977) set goals to reduce mortality among infants, children, adolescents, and adults and increase independence among older adults. A process was thereby set in motion to establish a more balanced health policy. *Surgeon General's Report on Promoting Health/Preventing Disease: Objectives for the Nation in the U.S. Public Health Service* (DHHS, 1980) was published in 1980, setting goals for 1990. *Healthy People 2000: National Health Promotion and Disease Prevention* followed in 1991 (DHHS, 1990). In 1991, the Centers for Disease Control and Prevention (CDC) published a set of eighteen health status indicators and encouraged their use by federal, state and local health agencies. The indicators ranged from race/ethnicity, infant mortality, and total deaths per 100,000 population, to proportion of persons living in counties exceeding U.S. Environmental Protection Agency standards for air quality during the previous year. Most recently in this evolving chapter of the nation's health policy, *Healthy People 2010* has been drafted, and objectives were released in January of 2000 (DHHS, 2000).

A second concept that is gaining wider acceptance and is contributing to the development of a new framework for health policy is the idea of population health. In his book, *Population Health: Concepts and Methods* (1998), T.K. Young used the term *population health* as a less cumbersome substitute for the health of populations. He noted:

> ". . . In the 1990s the phrase has taken on a new connotation, especially in Canada and the United Kingdom. It refers to a conceptual framework for thinking about why some people are healthier than others as well as the policy development, research agenda, and the resource allocations that flow from it. The difference between 'population health' and terms such as community health and public health, which have been around a long time, is subtle" (p. 4).

We agree with others that the term *population health* is broader than traditional public health and includes greater attention to the determinants of health and the social inequities (e.g. income, occupation, education) that are important contributors to the health status of populations. In his book, *Purchasing Population Health,* (1997) Kindig draws on many different disciplines to propose a different approach to purchasing health care services. Kindig drew primarily on the work of the Canadian Institute for Advanced Research's (CIAR) Multidisciplinary group in Population Health based at the University of British Columbia, but overall included faculty from a half dozen Canadian institutions. The product of their efforts, *Why Are Some People Healthy and Others Not? The Determinants of Health of Populations,* summarized a great deal of what is known, but it virtually ignored the importance of traditional public health programs in improving the health status of populations (Evans, Barer, & Marmor, 1994).

In this volume, as in the fifth edition, we give a great deal of attention to population health, the determinants of health, and the evolving role of public health. In this edition, we begin with a review of improvements in the health of the nation during this century and the factors that contributed to this improvement. Special attention is given to minority health, disparities in health status, and the *Healthy People 2010 Objectives* (2000). As the *Healthy People* targets demonstrate, a problem that requires particular attention in the near future is the disparity in health status related to socioeconomic status. This is especially true among minorities. Infant mortality related to lack of access to appropriate health services is considerably higher for blacks than for whites, largely because of the continuing prevalence of low-birthweight infants among blacks; it is higher for the poor than for the rich; and it is higher in the United States than in twenty-one other countries. Furthermore, sophisticated treatments such as coronary artery bypass graft surgery, coronary angioplasty, and total hip replacement are less available to many poor people, even when insured. Other services often less available or unavailable to the poor are clinical preventive services and management of chronic conditions. These services are often critical to good health, and to the functional capacity and well being of the individual.

At the same time that the health care delivery crisis is playing out, a number of health and social problems are decimating the lives of many and straining the capacity of the public health and health care systems. At issue are the problems of violence, substance abuse, HIV/AIDS, homelessness, chronic mental illness, and unintended pregnancy, as well as the growing problem of asthma, particularly among African American children and the increasing burden of type II diabetes. All of these issues or burdens are expensive in terms of human health and well being, each with a high price tag. These problems require the combined efforts of both public health and health care, as well as the community, if they are to be dealt with effectively. Some health issues that have begun to be dealt with in a more promising, systematic manner include tobacco use, immunization, HIV/AIDS, food safety, newly emerging infections, unintended pregnancy, especially among adolescents, and certain chronic illnesses such as asthma and diabetes mellitus. Yet concurrent with these advances, the number of chronically ill elderly continues to increase, highlighting the lack of provision in our system for serving their special needs.

After opening with consideration of these prominent issues to the health of the nation, and the determinants of health, we introduce a new section on health policy and the politics of health. In Chapter 3, Health Policy, are overview pieces by Longest (1998), Barr, Lee, and Benjamin (1999), and a section from Professor Sherry Glied's book on health care reform, *Chronic Condition: Why Health Reform Fails* (1997). Also included is a very important paper by Estes and Linkins "Decentralization, Devolution, and the Deficit: the Changing Role of the State and the Community (1991)," because it deals with one of the central issues in the shortcomings of the current health policy debate. We follow this chapter with a new chapter on values, ethics, and ideology, dealing with the ethics of managed care, health care, and the key issue of whether health care and long-term care are market goods or social goods.

The issue of health care as a social or market good has been given new life not only by the power of the patient's rights movement but also by recent proposal by former senator Bradley, a candidate for the Democratic party's nomination for president in the 2000 elections. The former senator has moved to make health insurance available to virtually all Americans and has called good health care a solemn right and not a luxury.

The position advocated by former senator Bradley, and many others, that health care is a social (or public) good, is based on the concept that all members to society benefit when the health care of all individuals is provided for. This pertains to not only preventive care but acute and rehabilitative treatment as well. This view, that health care is a social good, is widely accepted in other Western, industrialized democracies, and is indeed prevalent among the nations of the Organization of Economic Cooperation and Development (OECD). Every other country in the OECD, except the United States, bases the provision and financing of health care for their populations on this premise.

In the United States, in contrast, health care is considered a normal commodity. It is supplied by competitive, profit-maximizing firms and is ideally purchased by informed buyers, whose demand for health care is a function of the price of the services. The result of this view of health care as a market good has been the growth of managed care, the growth of for-profit health plans, hospitals, and health systems, and what has been described as the "medical-industrial complex." The corporate transformation of health care, predicted in many of its dimensions by Paul Starr in his book *The Social Transformation of Medicine* (1982), has been updated by Brad Gray in *The Profit Motive and Patient Care: The Changing Accountability of Doctors and Hospitals* (1991). The predominance of the idea within American society that health care is a market good, and not a social good, has been dramatically illustrated in health care financing, organization, and delivery in the U.S. over the past 30 years.

In The Politics of Health (Chapter 5) we add a new article by Hacker and Skocpol, "The New Politics of U.S. Health Policy" (1997). They describe the formidable obstacles that stand in the way of even incremental reforms. Many of these obstacles are based on strongly held values, including the antigovernment ideologies that have been a recurrent theme in American politics over the past several years (see also Barr, Lee, and Benjamin's article in Chapter 4). Interest groups, often reflecting these antigovernment sentiments, also exert a strong influence on health policy. In our Recommended Reading we included Professor Nestle's paper, "Food Lobbyists, the Food Pyramid and Nutrition Policy" (1993), because it illustrates the role of interest groups in shaping health policies. This involvement, too, has only increased in recent years.

Next, we devote considerably more attention to public health and prevention than in the past. We have added Part III, on prevention and public health examined from both an historical and current perspective. We add a particularly important set of readings from Lasker's monograph on medicine and public health that stresses the increasing importance of collaboration between medicine and public health in achieving the nation's health goals for the future (Lasker and Associates, 1997). In spite of significant advances in the past 20 years, serious problems remain in public health. Among these, of prominent concern is the serious underinvestment in the nation's public health infrastructure (e.g., information systems) and a continued emphasis on categorical disease control programs. These need to be rectified if goals such as those set in *Healthy People 2010* are to be met.

In addition to the materials from Dr. Lasker's monograph, the chapter includes a series of short reprints from the Centers for Disease Control and Prevention on the great advances in public health during the 20th century.

Despite a huge investment of resources, the problems in health care are equally serious. We devote Part IV to these issues, including a great deal of new material on Medicare, medical markets, and managed care.

The transformation of the health care system in the past 30 years has been described by Starr (1982), Gray (1991), Salmon (1995), and others. In his book, *The Social Transformation of American Medicine,* Starr describes the evolution of the role of the medical profession and health care system in the 20th-century as follows:

> "In the 20th century not only did physicians become a powerful, prestigious, and wealthy profession, but they succeeded in shaping the basic organization and financing structure of American medicine. More recently, that system has begun to slip from their control, as power has moved away from the organized profession towards complexes of medical schools and hospitals, financing and regulatory agencies, health insurance agencies, prepaid health plans, and other health care chains, conglomerates, holding companies, and other corporations" (p. 8).

Today, in view of the failure of Congress to enact the major health care reforms proposed by President Clinton in 1993, more and more people are looking for incremental reforms in health care policy at the federal level, while managed care is being pushed aggressively in the private sector by employers and the health insurance industry as a means of controlling health care costs. Yet there are growing complaints about managed care, and the number of uninsured persons continues to increase. Moreover, although more slowly than in the past, health care costs continue to rise, even in the face of expanding managed care structures.

The 1980s and 1990s also saw a nationwide increase in the number and types of corporate for-profit providers and insurers, including managed care plans. The developments in managed care and organized delivery systems are described in detail by Gray (1991) and Shortell (1995), included in our Recommended Readings. Although Shortell's review is comprehensive, it is now 5 years old and a number of the integrated systems have collapsed—both among for-profit as well as non-profit models. In addition, there have been major conversions of nonprofit health entities to for-profit corporations, such as with Blue Cross of California, which have raised serious questions of the disposition and control of assets as well as access to care. This hotly debated phenomenon has resulted in the proprietary ownership of many hospitals, surgicenters, urgent care centers, clinical laboratories, and imaging facilities. Hospitals and other providers have become increasingly competitive and, as a result, they have begun to operate more like businesses, using techniques such as advertising, marketing, specialization, and productivity monitoring. The effects of this trend are just beginning to be understood.

Most observers and participants in public health and health care agree that there is need for fundamental change and restructuring of the health care system, but change is incremental at best. In 1993, President Clinton proposed a restructuring of the nation's health care system through a plan that would have provided comprehensive health insurance coverage to all Americans. Designed to be phased in gradually by the year 2000, the plan was debated in Congress, but eventually was not even voted upon by the full Senate or House of Representatives. The failure of this approach to comprehensive reform has been described in books by Skopcol (1996), Johnson and Broder (1996) and Glied (1997). Moreover, the demise of the Clinton plan has led to a good deal of soul searching about how best to address the serious health problems confronting the nation and to emphasize incremental change. Demonstrating this incremental approach to reform are the Health Insurance Portability and Accountability Act (Kennedy–Kassebaum) of 1996, the Balanced Budget Act of 1997, including the Child Health Initiative and reforms in Medicare to stimulate greater participation in managed care, and, most recently, the enactment of different bills by the U.S. Senate and House of Representatives to establish a patient's "Bill of Rights." The legislation provides for federal regulation of health plans, an area long left to the states. More than twenty states have enacted state laws to provide greater patient protections in managed care plans. At the state level, more and more states are mandating enrollment of Medicaid beneficiaries in managed care, often exempting the aged (also covered by Medicare) and the disabled.

Many contributors to this volume argue that the nation is confronted by an outmoded personal health care system that is the result of failed policies and continued technological expansion at the expense of the provision of sound basic care for all and effective nationwide programs of disease prevention, health protection, and health promotion. Those who are well insured are the lucky benefactors of a comprehensive delivery system. Meanwhile, those who suffer most from a lack of adequate public health protection and access to personal health care are poor children, some of whom are unable to obtain even basic care, such as immunizations. Also victimized are the disabled and those who suffer from debilitating chronic illness. Finally, across all age groups and geographic areas, the working poor are consistently disadvantaged by our current system.

The irony is that at a time when the working poor have been victimized by society's disparities, a large segment of society has come to expect access to almost unlimited medical care. Along with the benefits of high-priced care come the pitfalls of overtreatment, overprescribing, unnecessary surgery, and neglect of emphasis on sound preventive measures. Thus issues related to quality of care are being examined anew. We devote Chapter 10 (Part IV) to these issues. Measuring the effects of medical interventions is a complex and imprecise science. Increasingly, clinicians are asked to interpret medical findings that they are ill-equipped to evaluate. This causes vastly differing treatments from one clinician to another, and the end result is that new issues related to inappropriate care are being investigated today.

Finally, Part V deals with the long-neglected issues of women's health, aging, and long-term care. These issues will continue to grow in importance with the aging of the population. The chapter highlights the contribution that gender and age play in determining the health of individuals and the population. The chapter begins with an examination of the role of gender in health with a review of the Institute of Medicine's report on women. It advances three themes: women have different biologies and physiologies, divergent life courses, and unequal social status (Benderley, 1997a). There are themes that form the background for the articles included on women's health and how women are treated in the health care system (e.g., Oppenheimer and Schultz, 1999). Dr. Susan Blumenthal, who has been a leader on women's health issues, strikes a more optimistic note, emphasizing the progress that has been made but pointing out the current problems and what needs to be done (Blumenthal, 1997).

The importance of health insurance coverage for women is emphasized in The Commonwealth Fund 1998 Survey of Women's Health (Collins et al., 1999). Consistent with many other works in this volume, low-income and less educated women are less likely than higher income, more educated women to receive needed health care services.

Similar to the health status of women, the health status of older individuals is a mixed story. Improvements in health status, described in Chapter 1, have extended life, but the advances have been experienced unevenly. Because of the importance of aging in our society, we have included a substantial section on aging. There has been anxiety among federal policy makers about the impact of the aging population on federal entitlement programs, but the issues are more complex. In addition, aging is not gender neutral. Equally important, from a policy perspective, is Dorothy Rice's article, "Medicare: A Women's Issue" (1999). As a function of their greater longevity, women comprise a larger percentage of the Medicare beneficiaries than men; consequently, they rely on Medicare for more years. They also bear a greater burden of chronic illness and are more likely to have lower incomes and to be living alone in their later years.

The chapter concludes with an article by Estes and Weitz, advocating a new paradigm that incorporates the contents of earlier articles in this chapter. This new model recognizes the complex interaction of medical, social, and economic factors that affect women's wellness as they age and bridges the gap between concerns about women and aging.

In this book, we critically examine the nation's health; the determinants of health; the roles of both public health (population-based intervention); personal health care; and the collaboration between medicine, public health, and the community in protecting and ensuring the health of the population. Rather than merely emphasizing the care of the sick, the financing of care and public health, we look at the complex web of issues, policies, controversies, hazards, problems, and proposed solutions to protect and promote the nation's health, with special emphasis on women's health and the aging of the population. Despite improvements in health behaviors and the overall environment, (with concomitant increases in life expectancy and reduced mortality) that the advances of science, medical care, and public health have occasioned as we head into the 21st century, America must confront critical issues if it is to maintain its leadership role in science and become a world leader in public health and health care. We believe the message of the first edition is as relevant today as it was twenty years ago:

"Despite the complexity of the issues, one clear message rings through: Americans over the decades have abdicated a large portion of responsibility for their health to physicians, drugs, hospitals and modern technology. Individuals and health professionals in our society have pursued an imbalanced approach to well being that is rapidly heading toward a dead end. We have distorted the relationship between medicine and health.

"Health is not just a matter for science and medicine: it also involves social, economic, philosophical, and ethical issues—issues that cut to the core of American values and institutions" (Lee, 1981, pp. xix–xx).

BIBLIOGRAPHY

Barr, D.A., Lee, P.R., and Benjamin, A.E. Health care and health care policy in a changing world. In Wallace, H., Green, G., Jaros, K.J., et al. (Eds.). *Health and Welfare for Families in the 21st Century,* Editors: Boston: Jones & Bartlett, 1999; 13–29.

Breslow, L. The future of public health. Prospects for the 1990s. *Ann Review Public Health,* 1990; 11:1–28.

Estes, C. & Linkins, K.W. Decentralization, devolution and the deficit: The changing role of the state and the community. In Ghoyna, J.G. (Ed.): *Resecuring Social Security and Medicare: Understanding Privatization and Risk.* Washington, DC: The Gerontological Society, 1991; 37–44.

Estes, C.E., Harrington, C., & Pellow. Medical industrial complex *Enc. Sociology,* (In press.)

Evans, R.G., Barer, M.L., & Marmor, T.R. (Eds). *Why Are Some People Healthy and Others Not? The Determinants of Health of Populations.* New York: Aldine De Gruyter, 1994.

Dubos, R. *Mirage of health: Utopias, Progress, and Biological Change.* New York: Harper & Row, 1959.

Glied, S. *Chronic Condition: Why Health Reform Fails.* Cambridge, MA: Harvard University Press, 1997; 1–16.

Gray, B. *The Profit Motive and Patient Care: The Changing Accountability of Doctors and Hospitals.* Cambridge, MA: Harvard University Press, 1991.

Hacker, J.S., & Skocpol, T. New politics of U.S. health policy. *J Health Pol Policy Law,* 1997; 22(2):315–336.

Institute of Medicine (IOM). *The Future of Public Health: Summary and Recommendations.* Washington DC: National Academy Press, 1988.

Johnson, H. & Broder, D.S. *The System: The American Way of Politics at the Breaking Point.* Boston: Little, Brown, 1996.

Kindig, D.A. *Purchasing Population Health: Paying for Results.* Ann Arbor: The University of Michigan Press, 1997; 11–23.

Lalonde, M. *A New Perspective on the Health of Canadians.* Ottawa: Government of Canada, 1974.

Lasker, R.D., & The Committee on Medicine and Public Health. *Medicine and Public Health: The Power of Collaboration.* Chicago: Health Administration Press, 1997; 11–22, 29–43, 47–53.

Lee, P.R. Prologue. In Lee, P.R., Brown, N. & Red, I. U.S.W. (Eds.). *The Nation's Health.* San Francisco: Boyd & Fraser, 1981; xix.

Longest, B.B. Jr. *Health Policymaking in the United States.* (2nd ed.). Chicago: Health Administration Press, 1998.

McKeown, T. *The Modern Rise of Populations.* New York: Academic Press, 1975.

McKeown, T. *The Role of Medicine.* London: Provincial Trust, 1976.

Navarro, V. A historical review (1965–1997) of studies of class health, quality of life: A personal account. *Internat J Health Serv,* 1998; (3):389–406.

Nestle, M. Food lobbies, the food pyramid and U.S. nutrition policy. *Internat J Health Serv,* 1993; 23:483–496.

Salmon, J.W. A perspective on the corporate transformation of health care. *Internat J Health Serv,* 1995; (1):11–42.

Skopcol, T. *Boomerang: Clinton's Health Security Effort and the Turn against Government in U.S. Politics.* New York: Norton, 1996.

Starr, P. *The Social Transformation of American Medicine: The Rise of a Sovereign Profession and the Making of a Vast Industry.* New York: Basic Books, 1982.

U.S. Department of Health and Human Services. *Surgeon General's Report on Health Promotion and Disease Prevention.* Washington D.C: Public Health Service, 1977.

U.S. Department of Health and Human Services. *Surgeon General's Report on Promoting Health/Preventing Disease: Objectives for the Nation in the U.S. Public Health Service.* Washington DC: Public Health Service, 1980.

U.S. Department of Health and Human Services. *Healthy People 2000: National Health Promotion and Disease Prevention Objectives.* Washington DC: Public Health Service, 1990.

U.S. Department of Health and Human Services. *Healthy People 2010: Objectives.* Washington DC: Public Health Service, 2000.

Department of Health and Social Security. Prevention and Health: Everybody's Business: A Reassessment of Public and Personal Health. London: Her Majesty's Stationary Office (HSMO), 1976.

Young, T.K. *Population Health: Concepts and Methods.* New York: Oxford University Press, 1998; 1–22.

ACKNOWLEDGMENTS

CHAPTER 1

William G. Rothstein. (1995). "Trends in Mortality in the Twentieth Century." In: Rothstein, W.G. *Readings in American Health Care.* Madison, Wisconsin: University of Wisconsin Press, pp. 71–86. Reprinted by permission of The University of Wisconsin Press.

Office of Public Health and Science, Department of Health and Human Services. (January 2000). *Healthy People 2010 Objectives, Goals.* Washington, D.C: Department of Health and Human Services, pp. Goals 1–15, Goals 19–23.

CHAPTER 2

Thomas McKeown. (1978). Determinants of Health. From *Human Nature Magazine,* April 1978 issue, Copyright by Human Nature, Inc. Reprinted by permission of the publisher.

Nancy Moss. (1999). Socioeconomic Disparities in Health in the U.S.: An Agenda for Action. *Social Science and Medicine.* Reprinted by permission of Elsevier Science and author.

Vicente Navarro. (November 19, 1990). Race or Class versus Race and Class: Mortality Differentials in the United States. *The Lancet* 336:1238–1240. Reprinted by permission of The Lancet Ltd.

CHAPTER 3

Donald A. Barr, Philip R. Lee, and A.E. Benjamin. (1999). "Health Care and Health Care Policy in a Changing World." In: Wallace, Helen et al. (eds.), *Health and Welfare for Families in the 21st Century,* Sudbury, Massachusetts: Jones and Bartlett Publishers, pp. 13–29. Reprinted with permission.

Beauford B. Longest, Jr. (1998). "The Process of Public Policymaking: A Conceptual Model." From *Health Policymaking in the United States* (2nd ed.). Chicago, Illinois: Health Administration Press, pp. 55–61. Reprinted and abridged with permission from the author.

Sherry Glied. (1997). *Chronic Condition: Why Health Reform Fails.* Cambridge, Massachusetts: Harvard University Press, pp. 1–16. Reprinted by permission of the Publishers from *Chronic Condition: Why Health Reform Fails* by Sherry Glied, Cambridge, Mass. Harvard University Press, Copyright 1997 by the President and Fellows of Harvard College.

Carroll L. Estes and Karen W. Linkins. (1991). "Decentralization, Devolution and the Deficit: The Changing Role of the State and the Community." In J.G. Ghoyna (ed.): *Resecuring Social Security and Medicare: Understanding Privatization and Risk.* Washington, D.C: The Gerontological Society, pp. 37–44. Reprinted with permission.

CHAPTER 4

Beauford B. Longest, Jr. (1998). "Ethics in the Political Market Place." In: *Health Policymaking in the United States.* (2nd ed.). Chicago, Illinois: Health Administration Press, pp. 52–54. Reprinted by permission of the author.

George J. Annas. (1998). A National Bill of Patients' Rights. *The New England Journal of Medicine* 338:697–699. Copyright 1998, Massachusetts Medical Society. All rights reserved. Reprinted with permission.

Richard A. Culbertson. (1999). Health Care as a Social Good: Trauma Care and the "Kindness of Strangers." *Journal of Health and Health Services Administration* (Winter) 21 (3):346–363. Reprinted by permission of the publisher and author.

CHAPTER 5

Jacob S. Hacker and Theda Skocpol. (Summer 1997). New Politics of U.S. Health Policy. Duke University Press, *Journal of Health Politics, Policy and Law* 22(2):315–336. Copyright 1997, Duke University Press. All rights reserved. Reprinted with permission.

Carroll L. Estes, Joshua M. Wiener, Sheryl C. Golberg, and Susan Goldenson. (1999). *The Politics of Long Term Care Reform under the Clinton Health Plan: Lessons for the Future.* Washington, D.C./San Francisco: Health Policy Center/Institute, The Urban Institute, Institute for Health and Aging, University of California, San Francisco, p. 1–18. Reprinted by permission of the authors.

CHAPTER 6

Centers for Disease Control and Prevention. (1999). Ten Great Public Health Achievements—United States, 1900–1999. *MMWR* 48:241–243. Reprinted with permission.

Centers for Disease Control and Prevention. (1999). Motor-Vehicle Safety: A 20th Century Public Health Achievement. *MMWR* 48:369–374. Reprinted with permission.

Centers for Disease Control and Prevention. (1999). Achievements in Public Health, 1900–1999: Control of Infectious Disease. *MMWR* 48(29):621–629. Reprinted with permission.

Centers for Disease Control and Prevention. (1999). Achievements in Public Health, 1900–1999: Decline in Deaths from Heart Disease and Stroke—United States, 1900–1999. *MMWR* 48(29):649–656. Reprinted with permission.

U.S. Preventive Services Task Force. (1996). *Guide to Clinical Preventive Services.* Alexandria, Virginia: International Medical Publishing Inc., pp. xxv–xxiv. Reprinted by permission of the publisher.

Roz D. Lasker and the Committee on Medicine and Public Health. (1997). *Medicine and Public Health: The Power of Collaboration.* pp. 11–22, 29–43, 47–53. Reprinted with permission from The New York Academy of Medicine. (Chicago: Health Administration Press.)

CHAPTER 7

Jennifer A. Campbell. (October 1999). Health Insurance Coverage: Consumer Income. *Current Population Reports,* U.S. Census Bureau/U.S. Department of Commerce, pp. 1–8. Reprinted with permission.

Robert Kuttner. (January 14, 1999). The American Health Care System: Health Insurance Coverage. *The New England Journal of Medicine* 340:163–168. Copyright 1999, Massachusetts Medical Society. All rights reserved. Reprinted with permission.

Robert Kuttner. (January 28, 1999). The American Health Care System: Employer-Sponsored Health Insurance. *The New England Journal of Medicine* 340:248–252. Copyright 1999, Massachusetts Medical Society. All rights reserved. Reprinted with permission.

CHAPTER 8

J.K. Iglehart. (January 28, 1999). The American Health Care System: Medicare. *The New England Journal of Medicine* 340:327–332. Copyright 1999, Massachusetts Medical Society. All rights reserved. Reprinted with permission.

Theodore Marmor and Jonathan Oberlander. (1998). Rethinking Medicare Reform. *Health Affairs* 17:52–67. Copyright © 1998, The People-to-People Health Foundation, Inc., All Rights Reserved. Reprinted with permission.

United States General Accounting Office. (June 23, 1999). Testimony Before the Committee on Finance, U.S. Senate. "Medicare: Considerations for Adding a Prescription Drug Benefit." Statement of Laura A. Dummit, Associate Director Health Financing and Public Health Issues: Health, Education, and Human Services Division, pp. 1–11. Reprinted with permission.

J.K. Iglehart. (February 4, 1999). The American Health Care System: Medicaid. *The New England Journal of Medicine* 340:403–408. Copyright 1999, Massachusetts Medical Society. All rights reserved. Reprinted with permission.

The Kaiser Commission on the Future of Medicaid. (May 1999). Medicare and Medicaid for the Elderly and Disabled Poor. Menlo Park, California: The Kaiser Family Foundation. This information was reprinted with permission of the Henry J. Kaiser Family Foundation of Menlo Park, California. The Kaiser Family Foundation is an independent health care philanthropy and is not associated with Kaiser Permanente or Kaiser Industries.

The Kaiser Commission on the Future of Medicaid. (November 1997). Medicaid Facts: Medicaid's Role for the Children. Menlo Park, California: The Kaiser Family Foundation. This information was reprinted with permission of the Henry J. Kaiser Family Foundation of Menlo Park, California. The Kaiser Family Foundation is an independent health care philanthropy and is not associated with Kaiser Permanente or Kaiser Industries.

CHAPTER 9

John Rother. (1996). Consumer Protection in Managed Care: A Third Generation Approach. *Generations* 20(2):42–46. Reprinted by permission of the author.

The Kaiser Commission on the Future of Medicaid. (October 1998). "Medicaid and Managed Care." Menlo Park, California: The Henry J. Kaiser Family Foundation. This information was reprinted with permission of the Henry J. Kaiser Family Foundation of Menlo Park, California. The Kaiser Family Foundation is an independent health care philanthropy and is not associated with Kaiser Permanente or Kaiser Industries.

CHAPTER 10

CHAPTER 11

PART 1

HEALTH OF THE NATION AND DETERMINANTS OF HEALTH

CHAPTER 1

THE HEALTH
OF THE NATION

This new chapter describes the changing health status of the population in the United States over the past 100 years. We begin with Rothstein's review of the dramatic improvements in the health status of the population of the United States during the 20th century. The sharp decline in deaths due to infectious disease, particularly among infants and children, led to a rapid increase in life expectancy at birth. Except for the 500,000 deaths in the United States due to the influenza pandemic of 1918–1919, the mortality rate for most infectious diseases declined until the HIV/AIDS epidemic in the 1980s. The resultant trend to increased mortality and a decreased life expectancy in the late 1980s has now been reversed with the new antiviral drugs and improved treatment of opportunistic infection in persons with AIDS.

The initial dramatic decline in mortality, particularly from infectious diseases, has been attributed primarily to improved socioeconomic conditions (e.g., nutrition, housing) and public health measures (safe water supplies, waste disposal, pasteurization of milk). Later, immunizations began to have an effect. The introduction of sulfonamides in the mid-1930s, penicillin in the early 1940s, and a host of antibiotics shortly thereafter resulted in a sharp drop in mortality from the mid-1930s to the late 1950s, when the rate of decline slowed. In addition to penicillin and the sulfonamides, the most important antimicrobial drug developed in the late 1940s was streptomycin, which proved to be the first drug to effectively treat tuberculosis.

Improvements in the health of the population actually began with the advent of the so-called sanitary revolution almost 150 years ago. Improvements in the health of the population of the United States during this period have been reviewed by Duffy (1990), Fee (1991), Breslow (1990), and Lee (1995). In the early years of the republic, before the sanitary revolution began in the 1850s, mortality rates from infectious diseases were high. Although the recurrent epidemics of cholera, yellow fever, and smallpox attracted the most public attention, mortality was also high for tuberculosis, pneumonia, and influenza. Infant mortality, due primarily to diarrheal diseases and respiratory infection, often in poorly nourished infants, was particularly important.

In the 1850s the sanitary revolution began with the first organized community efforts to deal with the unsanitary conditions in the environment, contamination of water supplies due to human and animal wastes and the primitive methods of waste disposal, and the miserable, overcrowded housing. The initial focus on environmental sanitation produced dramatic benefits for the health of the population, particularly with a reduction in mortality from diarrheal diseases and cholera epidemics. Although smallpox vaccination was begun by Jenner in England in the late 18th century, it did not become widespread until almost a century later. Tuberculosis began to decline even before the pioneering studies by Koch in the late 1800s, but it was still the nation's leading cause of death in 1900.

The application of Pasteur's and Koch's bacteriological research, Pasteur's germ theory of disease and Koch's postulates began to bear fruit after the turn of the 20th century. Specifically, the contributions of these two scientists were most noted in the development of bacteriological laboratories to identify specific bacterial causes of disease, and in practical public health applications such as the pasteurization of milk. The New York City Health Department led the nation in its development of milk stations to distribute safe milk to poor infants. These efforts, as well as the chlorination of water supplies and the development of sewer systems that included indoor plumbing and waste treatment facilities, were to dramatically reduce mortality from communicable diseases prior to the influenza pandemic of 1918–1919. The impact was most dramatic on infant mortality. These practical and scientific advances, and their resultant consequences, represented a transformation of both public health and medicine in the early 20th century.

Next, the introduction of the sulfonamides in the 1930s began the era of modern medical care with the development of a number of antimicrobial agents effective in treating a broad spectrum of infectious diseases, including tuberculosis. This resulted in a further fall in mortality from 1935 until the late 1950s.

From the late 1950s to the mid-1960s, little progress was made in reducing infant mortality or increasing life expectancy in the United States. Beginning in the mid-1960s, however, and continuing into the 1990s, America's health improved. Infant mortality began to decline again in the late 1960s. Following the implementation of Medicaid, which provided poor women and children on public assistance with state-administered health insurance; the expansion of the Department of Agriculture's Women, Infants, and Children (WIC) Program providing milk and other essential foods to poor women and children; and the rapid improvements in neonatal intensive care, infant deaths gradually dropped to about one-half the 1965 level. The life expectancy of those born in 1979 rose more than three years over that of 1965. By 1995, life expectancy was at its highest level ever.

Interestingly, although death from infectious disease has become much less significant, there has been a concomitant increase in what are known as the "diseases of Western civilization" such as cancer, coronary heart disease, diabetes mellitus, and emphysema. Known as the "epidemiological transformation," this shift is generally observed when a nation's life expectancy increases as mortality from infectious diseases decline and mortality from chronic and degenerative diseases predominate. Advances have been slow, and much remains to be understood, particularly with the gradual aging of society that will be discussed in Part V. For instance, only recently have mortality rates from cancers begun to decline. Particularly surprising was the decline in mortality from heart disease, particularly coronary artery disease in the past 30 years and stroke throughout the century. The causes of the dramatic decline in cardiovascular death rates is not well understood, but it is generally attributed to behavior change (reduced fat in the diet), public health efforts (e.g., smoking control), and improvements in medical care (e.g., treatment of hypertension). The mortality rate from stroke, however, had been declining from the turn of the century and could not be attributed to these interventions until after mid-century.

Our Recommended Reading list includes excerpts from The Commonwealth Fund's *Chartbook on Minority Health* (1999). By almost every measure (e.g., infant mortality, life expectancy, self-reported health status), the health of minorities is worse than that of the Non-Hispanic, white population. Within minority groups, such as Hispanics, there are differences, with Cubans usually in better health and living longer than Puerto Ricans or Mexican-Americans. Certain problems, such as low birth weight, particularly afflict African-Americans. While a number of the differences in the health status of minorities and the majority of the population (Caucasian) are related to socioeconomic status (SES), not all of the differences are due to socioeconomic factors.

In the late 1970s, a national focus began to be placed on achieving broader national health objectives. It began with Surgeon General Julius Richmond's *Report on Health Promotion and Disease Prevention* (1977). A process to establish national health objectives for 1990 was initiated that included state governments and many private sector organizations, including both commercial and voluntary organizations.

Based on the experience in the 1980s with the health objectives for 1990, the health objectives for the year 2000, *Healthy People 2000 National Health Promotion and Disease Prevention Objectives,* were launched in 1990. Healthy People 2000 had three goals: (1) to increase the span of healthy life for all Americans; (2) to reduce health disparities among Americans; and (3) to achieve access to preventive health care services for all Americans. To accomplish these goals, *Healthy People 2000* set forth 300 objectives in 22 priority areas. These goals were grouped into four categories: (1) health promotion, (2) health protection, (3) clinical preventive services, and (4) surveillance and data systems. The health promotion category addresses the social context, personal attitudes, and behaviors that affect health. The health protection priority emphasizes population-wide interventions that can confer protection for entire communities (e.g., safe water, food safety, and automobile safety). Clinical preventive services include counseling, screening, immunization, and chemoprophylaxis that are often provided through personal health services. Finally, surveillance and data systems include both public health data systems, such as vital statistics and surveys (Behavioral Risk Factor Survey, National Health Intervention Survey), as well as administrative data often collected for other purposes (e.g., medical care encounter, billing data).

We conclude Chapter 1 with excerpts from the *Healthy People 2010 Objectives* (January 2000), which provide an overview of the health status of the population and the goals for the next decade, particularly related to health disparities. Perhaps the most important shift between the goals of *Healthy People 2000 and Healthy People 2010* is the shift in goal number two from "narrowing" to "eliminating" the disparities in health status. To do this will require far greater emphasis on socioeconomic status and the gradient in health status than in the past. We deal with these issues in Chapter 2, in the papers by Moss and Navarro. The impact of SES is detailed not only in Chapter 2 but also in the data summarized in *Socioeconomic Status and Health Chartbook: Health, United States, 1998,* included in the Recommended Reading. Infant mortality and life expectancy are related to SES, which also correlates with education. Death rates for chronic diseases, communicable diseases, and injuries among persons age 25–64 years are inversely related to education for men and women. Less-educated men and women also have higher suicide rates. Cigarette smoking is more prevalent among those of lower socioeconomic status, and their death rates are higher for lung cancer and heart disease. The "Highlights" in this chartbook review some of the evidence related to SES and health status and give a clue as to why it will be a challenge to eliminate the health disparities by 2010.

In the *Healthy People 2010 Objectives* One and Two we include the goals, but not the hundreds of pages of detail about how the goals will be achieved. It is clear, however, that collaboration between medicine and public health, described in the monograph by Lasker and her associates (included in Chapter 6) will be a critical factor. As such, the first chapter furnishes a critical foundation for understanding not only where our nation has progressed from but also where it is headed.

In summary, the health status of the population in the United States has improved dramatically in this century. Initially, improvements in socioeconomic status and public health measures were most important in achieving the gains. In the past 30 years, improvements in medical care, particularly clinical preventive services, are also playing an important role.

REFERENCES

Adler NE, Boyce T, McChesney MA, Folkman S, Syme SL. Socioeconomic Inequalities in Health. No Easy Solutions. *JAMA.* 1993;239:3140–3145.

Breslow L. The future of public health: prospects in the United States for the 1990s. *Ann Rev Public Health.* 1990;11:1–28.

Duffy J. *The Sanitarians: A History of Public Health.* Chicago: University of Illinois Press, 1990.

Fee E. The origins and development of public health in the United States. In: Holland W, Detels R, Knox G. *Oxford Textbook of Public Health* (2nd ed.) New York: Oxford Medical Publications, 1991;657.

Lee PR. Keynote address: State of the nation's health. *Bull New York Acad Med* 1995;72(Winter suppl 2):552–569.

Collins KS, Hall A, Neuhaus C. *U.S. Minority Health: A Chartbook.* New York: The Commonwealth Fund, 1999, 2–5, 24, 25, 32–35, 50–51, 80–83, 86–89.

Lasker RD, and the Committee on Medicine and Public Health. *Medicine and Public Health: The Power of Collaboration.* Chicago: Health Administration Press, 1997;11–22, 29–45, 47–53.

Moss, N. Socioeconomic disparities in health in US: an agenda for action. *Soc Science Med* 1999;1–15.

Navarro V. Race or class versus race and class: Mortality differentials in the United States. *Lancet* 1990;336:1238–1240.

Pamuk E, Makuc D, Heck K, Reuben C, Lochnen K. *Socioeconomic Status and Health Chartbook. Health, United States.* Hyattsville, MD: National Center for Health Statistics, 1998;3–20. (Highlights).

Rothstein WG. Trends in mortality in the twentieth century. In: Rothstein WG. *Readings in American Health Care: Current Issues in Socio-historical Perspective.* Madison, WI: University of Wisconsin Press, 1995;71–86.

U.S. Department of Health and Human Services. *Surgeon General's Report on Health Promotion and Disease Prevention.* Washington, DC: Public Health Service, 1997.

U.S. Department of Health and Human Services. *Healthy People 2000: National Health Promotion and Disease Prevention Objectives.* Washington, DC: Public Health Service, 1990.

U.S. Department of Health and Human Services. (Jan. 2000). *Healthy People 2010: Objectives.* Washington, DC: Public Health Service, 2000.

TRENDS IN MORTALITY
IN THE TWENTIETH CENTURY

William G. Rothstein

This reading describes one of the most important developments in the modern history of the human race: the decline and changing causes of death in the twentieth century, often called an *epidemiological revolution.* This monumental change has affected every aspect of life in every advanced society in the world. Less developed nations have also experienced significant declines in their death rates, although to a much lesser extent than advanced nations.

Unfortunately, the large literature on this epidemiological revolution is technical. A useful non-technical historical account is Stephen J. Kunitz, "Explanations and Ideologies of Mortality Patterns," *Population and Development Review* 13 (1987): 379–408. Explanation of concepts at a level appropriate for undergraduate students are provided in Louis G. Pol and Richard K. Thomas, *The Demography of Health and Health Care* (New York: Plenum Press, 1992), and Judith Mausner and Shira Karmer, *Epidemiology—An Introductory Text* 2d ed. (Philadelphia: Saunders, 1985).

Descriptions of various diseases and their impact on modern societies include: Lois Verbrugge, "Recent, Present, and Future Health of American Adults," *Annual Review of Public Health* 10 (1989): 334; Robert W. Amler and H. Bruce Dull, *Closing the Gap: The Burden of Unnecessary Illness* (New York: Oxford University Press, 1987); and Walter H. Holland, Roger Detels, and George Knox, *Oxford Textbook of Public Health,* 2d ed. (Oxford: Oxford University Press, 1991). Historical trends are described in H. O. Lancaster, *Expectations of Life: A Study in the Demography, Statistics, and History of World Mortality* (New York: Springer-Verlag, 1990), and Kenneth F. Kiple, *The Cambridge World History of Human Diseases* (Cambridge, Eng.: Cambridge University Press, 1993). An account of the decline of infectious diseases is Harry Dowling, *Fighting Infection: Conquests of the Twentieth Century* (Cambridge: Harvard University Press, 1977).

Summaries of heart disease are provided in Millicent W. Higgens and Thomas Thom, "Trends in CHD in the United States," *International Journal of Epidemiology* 16 (1989), suppl. 1, pp. S58–S66; Millicent W. Higgens and Russell V. Luepker,

Trends in Coronary Heart Disease Mortality: The Influence of Medical Care (New York: Oxford University Press, 1988); and Lee Goldman and E. Francis Cook, "The Decline in Ischemic Heart Disease Mortality Rates," *Annals of Internal Medicine* 101 (1984): 825–36. An examination of sex differences in mortality rates is Ingrid Waldron, "Recent Trends in Sex Mortality Ratios for Adults in Developed Countries," *Social Science and Medicine* 36 (1993): 451–62.

This article examines one of the most remarkable transformations in the history of mankind. The twentieth century has witnessed the greatest and most rapid changes in both death rates and causes of death in recorded history. At the beginning of the century, infectious diseases were the paramount cause of death in all societies, killing millions of infants, children, and young adults. After 1900 death rates from these diseases declined rapidly in advanced countries, enabling many more people to live to old age. The increasing number of the elderly died from chronic and degenerative diseases, especially heart disease, cancer, and stroke. In recent decades, death rates from heart disease and stroke have declined, while those from cancer have not. The reasons for these trends have been the subject of continuing conjecture and debate.

DISEASES IN HUMAN HISTORY

Infectious diseases first became common thousands of years ago when human beings settled in villages to farm the land, tend domestic animals, and trade with residents of other villages. When those events occurred, enough people had contact with each other to enable the microorganisms that cause diseases to find a continuing reservoir of uninfected individuals and thereby survive indefinitely. In earlier hunting and gathering societies, the populations were so small that any pathogenic microorganisms soon ran out of uninfected individuals and died out. From the onset of village societies until early in the twentieth century, human beings fell victim to a growing number of infectious diseases, which became the major cause of death in all societies. Most of the victims of these diseases were children and young adults.[1]

The situation worsened when international and intercontinental travel dispersed diseases around the world, beginning in the late fifteenth century. The early European explorers spread tuberculosis, smallpox, measles, scarlet fever, and other infectious diseases to the Americas, the Pacific Islands, and other parts of the world that had never known them. They returned to Europe bringing yellow fever, cholera, and other infectious diseases from Africa and Asia. International travel also spread previously regional epidemics around the world as infected travelers unknowingly brought the diseases to different countries and continents.

Urbanization and industrialization in the eighteenth and nineteenth centuries forced the laboring classes of western nations to live in unsanitary housing, drink polluted water and milk, suffer diseases caused by unhygienic methods of sewage disposal, and eat a less nutritious diet than was available in many rural areas. Children suffered most from this unhealthy environment. In some American and European cities in the nineteenth century, one out of every four infants died before their first birthday.

Three fundamental changes were necessary to improve the health of the population. One was a higher standard of living to strengthen resistance to disease. This required better food, housing, and clothing, healthier home and work environments, lower birth rates, and a level of education that would enable people to understand and adopt the growing scientific knowledge about health care. The second change was improved public health measures by government to prevent diseases from infecting people. The third was effective clinical medicine, for the treatment of individual patients.

Perhaps the best available historical evidence concerning a society's standard of living is the height of its children and adults. A slow rate of growth during childhood and a short ultimate height that continues for decades in a society is clear evidence of a low standard of living. A study of the heights of British boys, adolescents, and military recruits found a slow but steady increase in the heights of those born from about 1750 to about 1840, a decline in their heights to the 1870s, a gradual return to early nineteenth-century heights by the end of the century, and a rapid increase in heights in the twentieth century. The study also found much taller heights among the children of the wealthy than other children before the twentieth century, indicating that heights throughout the period were strongly affected by the standard of living. Less comprehensive data showed that American men were one to two inches taller than the British (and other European) men throughout this period, but experienced the same growth trends as British men.[2]

These trends suggest that industrialization and urbanization had a deleterious effect on human health during the middle of the nineteenth century. Industrialization and world trade also lowered the standard of living of many rural people, whose cottage industry and small-scale farming could not compete with goods produced on a large scale elsewhere. A lower birth rate at the end of the nineteenth century and greater national wealth in the twentieth century increased the overall standard of living.[3]

Public health and clinical medicine advanced in the late nineteenth century due to better microscopes and related technologies that enabled scientists to explore the world invisible to the naked eye. During and after the 1870s, the disease-causing roles of many bacteria and other parasites were discovered. Government officials soon developed public health programs to keep bacteria from infecting human beings. Sewerage systems prevented sewage from contaminating water supplies and coming into contact with human beings, water supplies were chemically purified to destroy bacteria, milk and foods were made to conform to standards of bacteriological cleanliness, vectors of infectious diseases like mosquitoes and rodents were controlled, and housing standards were gradually raised.

The first effective clinical treatments for many diseases were developed about the same time. Surgery was revolutionized in the 1880s after it was discovered that antiseptic procedures and sterilization prevented the wounds from becoming infected. Diphtheria antitoxin, discovered in 1894, was the first effective treatment for a major infectious disease. In the ensuing decades, treatments were developed for diabetes, pellagra, and pernicious anemia. The most revolutionary improvements occurred in the late 1930s with the discovery of the sulfa drugs, the first general antibiotics. Penicillin, streptomycin, and other antibiotics followed in the 1940s.

Vaccines to immunize individuals against infectious diseases were also developed. Smallpox vaccination was developed in the late 1790s, but it remained unique until well into the twentieth century, when vaccines were developed for infectious diseases like diphtheria, tetanus, polio, rubella, and measles.

As fewer individuals died in childhood and early adulthood from infectious diseases, they lived to older ages and contracted diseases related to the aging process, such as heart disease, cancer, diseases of the blood vessels, and diseases of individual organs like diabetes, emphysema, or kidney disease. These chronic and degenerative diseases have become the major causes of death in advanced societies. The change in causes of death from infectious diseases to chronic and degenerative diseases, often called an "epidemiological revolution," has had a momentous effect on our society. The remainder of this article will examine the nature of these changes.

BASIC CONCEPTS

Two kinds of statistics are used to describe the state of health of a population. One concerns deaths or *mortality*. The other concerns illnesses or *morbidity*. Historical data on mortality are the most frequently used measures of trends in the health of the population because all deaths and their causes have been reported to local or state government agencies for many years. Reliable historical data on morbidity exist for only a small number of diseases, mostly communicable diseases, that must be reported to the government. Morbidity data also pose problems because illnesses vary in the degree and permanence of the disability they produce. The health impact of a common cold, a heart attack, and diabetes vary so greatly that it makes little sense to group them together in a single category.

In examining mortality trends in a population, we use death *rates* rather than numbers of deaths. The number of deaths are unsatisfactory because they increase or decrease with changes in the size of the population regardless of any change in its health status. Death rates enable us to compare populations of different sizes.

A mortality rate is a fraction in which the numerator consists of the number of persons who have had the experience in question (in this case, death) and the denominator includes all those who could have had that experience (the population). The formula for the *crude death rate* is the number of deaths in a population during a time period divided by the average population during the time period. The population in question may be the population of a nation, the population of a particular state or city, or the number of persons in a particular group, such as women aged 35–44. The time period is usually a specific year, but it can be a month or any other time period of interest.

Death rates always equal 1 or are less than 1, because the numerator (the number of people who died) can never be larger than the denominator (the population). This entangles us in decimal places. To eliminate this nuisance, we usually list death rates per 1,000 persons. For example, if 60 people in a community of 2,000 persons died in a given year, the crude death rate would be 60 divided by 2,000, which equals 0.03. This means that 3 of every 100 people in the community died in that year. We can change the statistic to the death rate per 1,000 population by multiplying .03 by 1,000, which equals 30. This says that 30 out of every 1,000 people in the community died in that year. The first number (0.03) gives us the death rate per person; the second (30) gives us the death rate per 1,000 persons.

Death rates per 1,000 persons are useful for examining total deaths, but most individual diseases produce so few deaths that we use death rates per 100,000 persons to eliminate the decimal point. For example, if 800 persons in a population of 20,000,000 died of a particular disease in a given year, the crude death rate equals 800 divided by 20,000,000, or .00004. If we multiply .00004 by 100,000, we get a death rate of 4 per 100,000.

Death rates can be very deceptive because of these arithmetic manipulations. It is easy to forget that the 4 in the above example represents 4 deaths from that disease per 100,000 persons in a given year. In a city of one million persons, only 40 would die from that disease in a year. Such statistics become even more misleading when people speak of changes like a doubling of the death rate. If the death rate just cited doubled in a year, which sounds quite alarming, the number of deaths from that disease would rise from 4 per 100,000 persons to 8 per 100,000 persons, or from 40 deaths per year in the city of one million to 80 deaths per year. Very few people would notice such a change.

One way to assess changes in the health status of the population is to compare death rates at different times. Because crude death rates disregard changes in the age distribution of the population, they can be misleading when used in this way. An increase in the crude death rate over time may indicate only that there were more old people and fewer young people in the population at the end of the period, not that the population was less healthy.

In order to deal with changes in the age distribution of a population, epidemiologists use age-specific and age-adjusted death rates. *Age-specific* death rates are death rates for specific age groups in the population, such as persons 1–4 years of age or 65–74 years of age. By examining death rates for specific age groups, we need not be concerned about changes in the age distribution. *Age-adjusted* death rates adjust the death rate in a population so that the age distribution in every year studied corresponds to the age distribution that existed in a base year chosen for convenience (1940 in most U.S. government statistics). The population for every year except the base year is mathematically adjusted so that the percentage of the population in each age group is the same as in the base year. Although the resulting data do not describe the actual death rates in the population in any year except the base year, they permit comparisons between death rates in different years while holding constant the age distribution of the population.

In addition to total death rates, we are also interested in death rates from specific causes, such as cancer, AIDS, or accidents. Death rates from specific causes are subject to several problems that do not occur with overall death rates.

Information about causes of deaths are obtained from death certificates filled out at the time of death by the patient's physician, or in some cases a medical examiner or a coroner. The death certificate requires the physician to list both the "immediate" and "underlying" causes of death, which might be pneumonia and a stroke, respectively. The physician selects the specific causes of death from the current revision of the *International Classification of Diseases.*

Several factors reduce the utility of time trends for causes of death for specific diseases. Many diseases, like heart attacks, cancer, stroke, and tuberculosis, are diagnosed differently now than they were early in the century, which makes it difficult to compare death rates at different periods. Physicians also tend to be more sensitive to diseases that are prevalent in the community. Early in the century, when heart disease was less prevalent than it is today, physicians often overlooked or misdiagnosed it. At the same time, they sometimes attributed deaths from other causes to tuberculosis, which was extremely common. Another problem, that has become more important in recent years, is that elderly people often have two or more serious diseases at the time of death, which makes it difficult to know the exact cause of death.

Nation-wide statistics on death rates were first gathered in the U.S. in 1900, but included only 10 states, the District of Columbia, and a number of cities in other states. This "Death Registration Area" was steadily expanded as more states gathered the necessary statistics until it covered the entire continental U.S. in 1933. Birth registration states (which are used to calculate infant mortality rates) were first listed in 1915 and did not include the entire continental U.S. until 1933 also. The original Death Registration Area consisted of the urbanized and older states, which had lower death rates than the nonreporting states, so that U.S. death rates before 1933 are very slightly lower than would have been the case had all states reported.[4]

THE DECLINE IN MORTALITY RATES

A remarkable decline in the crude death rate has occurred in the twentieth century. In 1900, there were 17.2 deaths for every 1,000 persons in the nation (for those states and cities in the Death Registration Area). In 1930, the rate dropped to 11.3 deaths per 1,000 persons, in 1960 to 9.5, and in 1991 to 8.6 deaths for every 1,000 persons. We may illustrate the significance of the decline in this way: In 1991, 2,169,000 persons died in the U.S.[5]; had the death rate of 1900 remained unchanged, 4,338,000 persons would have died in 1991. Thus, over 2 million lives were saved in 1991 compared to 1900 due to the decline in the death rate.

The decline was most rapid early in the century and has slowed in recent decades. Between 1900 and 1930 the death rate dropped by 5.9 deaths per 1000 persons, while between 1960 and 1991 the decline was only 0.9 deaths per 1000 persons.

Deaths throughout the century have been most likely to occur at the extremes of the life cycle—among the very young and the very old. This has been true from time immemorial. Death rates are high in the first year of life, but they drop very rapidly, so that the death rate over the entire life cycle reaches its nadir between the ages of 5 and 14. It rises slowly during early adulthood, and then ascends quite rapidly among the oldest age groups.

The greatest change in age-specific mortality rates in the twentieth century has been the decline in death rates among the young. In 1900, 162.4 of every 1,000 infants born alive died in the first year of life. This amounted to 1 out of every 6 infants, an appalling toll. The rate has declined steadily to 9.2 per 1,000 in 1991, or 1 out of every 109 infants. The significance of this change may be indicated thus: in 1991 there were 36,766 deaths in the first year of life.[6] Had the 1900 infant mortality rate remained unchanged, there would have been 649,000 deaths in the first year of life in 1991.

The death rate among children 1–4 years of age also plummeted from 19.8 per 1,000 in 1900 to only 0.5 per thousand in 1989. This age group, which had a higher than average death rate in 1900, now has the second lowest death rate among all age groups.

In 1900 only one age group had a death rate of less than 5.9 deaths per 1000: 5–14 years of age. In 1989, every age group from 1–4 years of age to 45–54 years of age bettered that statistic. Death has now become a rarity among children and young and middle-aged adults.

There have also been impressive declines in death rates among the elderly from 1900 to 1991, but they are less striking than the declines among the young. Among those age 65–74, the drop has been from 56.4 to 26.2 deaths per 1000 persons. Among those 75–84, the drop has been from 123.3 to 58.9 deaths per 1000 persons, and among those 85 and over, the drop has been from 260.9 to 151.1 deaths per 1000 persons.

Another important factor affecting mortality rates is sex. Throughout the century females have had lower death rates than males in all age groups. Among the very youngest, the sex difference has narrowed since 1900, so that female infants and young children now have only a slightly lower death rate than males. At the oldest ages, on the other hand, the sex difference has steadily widened, so that older women now have significantly lower death rates than older men.

Some may conclude that if fewer people are dying today, the American population should be growing at a faster rate than it did in 1900. Population growth depends on three factors: the number of deaths, the number of births, and the migration of people to and from America. Since 1900 both the birth and net migration rates have declined substantially, so that overall population growth has slowed substantially.[7]

INCREASES IN LIFE EXPECTANCY

Life expectancy tables show the average number of *remaining* years of life of a person of a given age. Life expectancy is not based on the actual experience of the people described, because that information will not be available until all of those persons have lived out their lives. Instead, it assumes that persons born now, for example, will have the same probability of being alive when they reach a given age that persons born that many years ago have of being alive now. Even though this is a poor assumption, it is the same throughout the table, so that the comparisons are useful even though the predictions will not be.

Average life expectancy at birth has increased by about 25 years for men and 30 years for women from 1900 to 1989. Life expectancy at birth has increased so greatly because death rates drop sharply after the first year of life. If an infant survives the first year of life, the chances are very good that he or she will live for another 60 years or more. Consequently every infant death that is prevented has a dramatic impact on total life expectancy.

The sex difference in life expectancy at birth has also grown. In 1900 the average female could expect to live 2 years more over her lifespan than the average male; by 1989 this difference had expanded to almost 7 years. Both social and biological factors contribute to this difference. With regard to social factors, men engage in many life-shortening behaviors to a greater extent than women: for example, they are more likely to smoke cigarettes (although the sex difference is narrowing), use beverage alcohol and drugs, commit suicide, and die of violence or injuries sustained at work or in other accidents. Biological factors are believed to have some involvement in women's lower rates of heart disease, stroke, and some other diseases.[8]

When we examine changes between 1900 and 1989 in the average number of years of life remaining at age 65, the increases are considerably smaller, especially for men. In 1900, a 65-year-old man could expect to live an average of 11.5 more years, to age 76.5, while a woman of the same age could expect to live an average of 12.2 more years, to age 77.2. In 1989, men 65 years of age lived an additional 3.7 years on the average (to age 80.2), while women 65 years of age lived an additional 6.6 years on the average (to age 83.8).

These data indicate clearly that a revolutionary decline has occurred in death rates, that this revolution has had its greatest impact on the young and least impact on the elderly, and that females have benefited more than males, especially among the elderly. We will now examine explanations for these remarkable changes.

THE DECLINE IN INFECTIOUS DISEASE DEATH RATES

In order to understand the reasons for the declining death rates of the U.S. population, and particularly the great reduction in death rates among the very young, we must examine the causes of death for the whole population and for individual age groups. These show clearly that a decrease in death rates from infectious diseases among the young has been responsible for most of the decline in mortality.

In 1900, nine categories accounted for 63 percent of all deaths. Five of them, mostly infectious diseases, had their greatest impact on the young. Influenza and pneumonia were major causes of death among infants and very young children, as were gastritis and enteritis, which were caused by bacteria-laden milk, water, and food. The communicable diseases of childhood included diphtheria, measles, scarlet fever, and whooping cough. Tuberculosis was primarily a killer of adolescents and young adults, but it prevented millions from living to old age. Accidents, too, were major killers of the young.

Deaths from these diseases declined markedly from 1900 to 1950. Mortality rates from the infectious diseases in the group—influenza, pneumonia, tuberculosis, diphtheria, measles, scarlet fever, and whooping cough—dropped from 472 deaths per 100,000 persons in 1900 to 55 deaths per 100,000 persons in 1950. Gastritis and enteritis also declined greatly. By 1991 tuberculosis had practically disappeared (although it reappeared in the 1990s in AIDS patients), pneumonia and influenza have become diseases of the elderly rather than diseases of the young, and the other diseases that affect the young have become insignificant as causes of death.

These declines were due more to improvements in the standard of living and public health measures than to better medical treatment of the sick. Gastritis and enteritis were eliminated by measures such as pasteurization of milk and purification of water supplies. Death rates from tuberculosis, pneumonia, and communicable diseases of childhood experienced most of their decline long before effective treatments existed for them. Although public health measures like better housing and quarantine of the infected played a role, most of the decrease appears to have been due to a higher standard of living that strengthened the resistance of people to the diseases and enabled them to survive the diseases if they became ill.[9]

Public education was also important in this revolution. Until well into the twentieth century, millions of Americans drank from metal drinking cups kept next to fountains for all to use, did not sterilize bottles or take other measures necessary for hygienic feeding of infants, let their children sleep in the same bed and play with siblings with contagious diseases like diphtheria and scarlet fever, purchased unrefrigerated and bacteria-laden milk and meat, used polluted wells and water supplies without boiling the water, and took baths in bathtubs after others had used the same water. These and many other similar behaviors have disappeared because the public has been educated about personal hygiene.

One type of medical care that has been related to the decline in infectious diseases is vaccination. It is widely agreed that smallpox vaccination played a role in the decline of that disease and some studies have found that diphtheria vaccine played a much greater role than diphtheria antitoxin in the decline of that disease. Vaccines for measles and polio are believed to have contributed to the decline in those diseases. Support for this view was shown by the rise in the measles case rate when federal support for measles immunization was reduced in the 1980s.

The decline in infectious diseases had important indirect health benefits as well. Nephritis and other kidney diseases are more likely to occur in adults who contracted scarlet fever or other streptococcal infections as children. As the incidence of streptococcal diseases has declined, so has the incidence of kidney diseases, which have dropped from a major cause of death in 1900 to a relatively minor one today.[10]

CHRONIC AND DEGENERATIVE DISEASES AS MAJOR CAUSES OF DEATH

As fewer young persons died from infectious and bacterial diseases, they survived to old age and succumbed to chronic and degenerative diseases like heart disease, cancer, and cerebrovascular disease (stroke). Crude death rates from these three diseases combined increased from 308 per 100,000 in 1900 to 546 per 100,000 in 1991.

In describing recent trends in mortality we can avoid the problems created by changes in the age distribution of the population by using age-specific or age-adjusted death rates. For this reason we will limit the analyses to the years since 1950.

The nine leading causes of death categories in 1991 together accounted for 80 percent of all deaths in 1991. Each category listed (except AIDS) includes a number of specific diseases. For example, within the heart disease category, the most common condition is ischemic (meaning deficient in blood) heart disease (often called coronary heart disease or heart attack), in which the blood supply to the heart muscle is interrupted, killing some heart muscle cells (called a myocardial infarction). Cancer encompasses hundreds of specific diseases involving different organs and types of cell abnormalities. The most common cerebrovascular (meaning the blood vessels of the brain) disease is stroke, which is an interruption of the blood supply to the brain. Chronic obstructive pulmonary (pertaining to the lungs) diseases include emphysema, bronchitis, and asthma, all disorders affecting the supply of air to the lungs. Diabetes encompasses a number of conditions involving excessive urination, the most important of which is diabetes mellitus, a malfunctioning of the cells that produce insulin. The trends shown are for all diseases in each category; trends for specific diseases within a category can vary.

Age-adjusted death rate trends from 1950 to 1991 differ substantially by category. The death rate for heart disease has declined substantially, although it remains the major cause of death. A drop has also occurred in the mortality rate for cerebrovascular diseases and, to a lesser extent, from diabetes. Pneumonia and influenza have continued to decline as causes of death. The death rate from cancer, the second largest cause of death, has increased slightly, and that from chronic pulmonary diseases has shown an ominous rise.

From 1900 to about 1950, overall heart disease death rates rose steadily for each age group (the rates for ischemic heart disease continued to rise until the late 1960s). The growing proportion of older persons could not be responsible for the increase in heart disease death rates, because a larger proportion of people *within* each age group died of heart disease in 1950 than in 1900. It is now recognized that an epidemic of heart disease occurred in the first two-thirds of this century, and that it occurred in all advanced societies, not only the United States.[11] Then, beginning about 1950 for non-ischemic heart disease and in the late 1960s for the more prevalent ischemic heart disease, mortality rates declined steadily for all age groups. Currently heart disease death rates for the 45–54-, 55–64-, and 65–74-year age groups are lower than they were in 1900, and those for the older age groups have declined significantly from their 1950 levels but remain higher than their 1900 levels. A similar trend has occurred in many other advanced nations, although the declines began a few years later in some of them.

Ischemic heart disease mortality rates for both sexes increased from 1950 to 1970 (they actually peaked in the late 1960s) and have declined subsequently. Men have much higher death rates from ischemic heart disease in each age group than do women. The decline in ischemic heart disease mortality rates has benefited women as much as men, even though it is much less prevalent among women.

Understanding these trends has been made more difficult by changes in the diagnosis of heart disease by physicians.[12] Heart disease has no ubiquitous signs or symptoms. Many people have heart attacks without realizing it. Physicians often have difficulty diagnosing heart disease, because routine and even sophisticated diagnostic tests can fail to reveal abnormalities. If physicians do not look carefully for heart disease, they can easily overlook it.

At the beginning of the century, when heart disease was uncommon, physicians overlooked it quite often. As it became more prevalent, physicians became sensitized to it and were more likely to recognize it as a cause of death. The development of the electrocardiograph also made more accurate diagnoses possible. Even after midcentury, however, physicians continued to misdiagnose heart disease. A study in one hospital found that deaths diagnosed as due to heart disease were understated (as measured by autopsy findings) in the 1960s and 1970s compared to the 1980s. These findings suggest that the increase in heart disease death rates between 1900 and midcentury was smaller than the official statistics indicate and that the current decline may be greater.[13]

Regardless of diagnostic improvements, the overall trends are indisputable— heart disease mortality rates rose substantially early in the century and have declined in recent years. The trends occurred in many advanced nations with different systems of training physicians and different ways of recording vital statistics. Careful and thorough studies of trends in heart disease death rates in specific regions and cities in the U.S. and other nations covering a decade or more have shown conclusively that heart disease rates have declined in recent years.[14]

What factors caused the great increase in heart disease death rates from 1900 to midcentury and their subsequent decline? Several possible explanations can be easily dismissed. Both the upward and downward trends occurred so rapidly that they must have been caused by social and environmental changes, not changes in human biology. Both the rise and fall occurred in many advanced nations about the same time, so that they cannot be due to changes unique to American society. The trends occurred for both men and women, so that factors that would benefit one sex more than the other cannot be responsible.

The most frequently advanced reasons for the increase in heart disease death rates early in the century are based on the greater wealth of industrialized societies. Research has shown that "a diet excessive in calories, fat, and salt, sedentary habits, unrestrained weight gain, and cigarette smoking predispose to coronary heart disease."[15] It is claimed that early in the twentieth century higher standards of living enabled people to eat more meat and other fatty foods that occluded their arteries and made them overweight. Changing work and home activities and the use of automobiles and mass transportation resulted in less physical exertion and exercise. Cigarette smoking became popular. These and other changes also increased heart disease death rates indirectly by producing higher rates of hypertension, diabetes, and other conditions that made people more susceptible to heart disease.

The major issue in explaining the recent decline in heart disease death rates is whether it was caused by (1) preventive measures that reduced the incidence of fatal heart disease, or (2) better treatment of heart disease.[16] Are fewer people getting fatal heart disease or are people with heart disease receiving better treatment and so are less likely to die? The prevention theory attributes the decline to the same factors that are considered to have caused the rise in heart disease death rates: changes in diet, more exercise, cessation of smoking, reduced blood cholesterol levels, and, possibly, treatment of high blood pressure. The treatment theory points to pre-hospital life support systems and better hospital and continuing care of cardiac patients as enabling more heart disease patients to survive.

Studies of heart disease deaths in several American cities connect much of the decline in the heart disease mortality rate in recent years to a decline in out-of-hospital deaths.[17] This may indicate that fewer people were having heart attacks or that they were having milder heart attacks, supporting the prevention theory. A less likely but possible interpretation is that heart disease patients were receiving better care and so were less likely to have a fatal recurrence after leaving the hospital, supporting the treatment theory.

None of the explanations for the rise in heart disease mortality rates is entirely persuasive. Changes in diet and lifestyles that are supposed to have caused the increase in heart disease early in the century often did not occur until decades later. Cigarette smoking did not become popular until the 1920s and would not have had a measurable impact on heart disease death rates until the late 1930s. No evidence exists that physical activity decreased at the beginning of the century. The automobile was not widely used as a mode of transportation until the 1920s. Perhaps most puzzling is the fact that the increase occurred in many nations about the same time, but it has not been shown that they all experienced appropriate changes in diet and lifestyles at the same time.

Explanations for the decline in heart disease mortality rates are equally problematic. The decline began before public health programs designed to discourage cigarette smoking and change lifestyles could have had an impact, and it also occurred in nations without such programs. The decline has taken place in nations that have taken little interest in pre-hospital resuscitation, intensive coronary care units, or other methods of care in widespread use in the United States. Even programs to lower mild or moderate hypertension, which reduce the risk of stroke, have not been clearly linked to a reduced risk of coronary heart disease. One review has concluded that "no one has yet established a convincing fit of trends for any risk factor with cardiovascular mortality trends."[18]

The trends for cerebrovascular disease are very similar to those for heart disease, as are the issues involving causes. For those reasons, they will not be discussed here.[19]

When we turn to cancer, we find a disheartening picture. Overall cancer death rates for men aged 45 and over rose steadily from 1940 to 1970, while they declined for women over those years. From 1970 to 1988, cancer death rates declined for both men and women aged 35–44 and 45–54 (attributed to a decline in lung cancer death rates), but they have risen for all older groups of both sexes. Similar patterns have been found in other advanced nations, indicating that these patterns are also international in scope.[20]

Trends in overall cancer mortality rates are difficult to interpret because they can change if the mix of types of cancers changes, even if the mortality rate of each type of cancer does not change. For example, if cancers with higher mortality rates become more prevalent relative to cancers with lower mortality rates, overall cancer mortality rates will increase, even though mortality rates from each individual type of cancer have not changed.

National data on the incidence of cancer (the number of new cases) are available for selected areas in the United States since 1973. They show a steady increase in the age-adjusted rates of new cases of cancer per 100,000 population from 319.8 in 1973 to 376.6 in 1989.[21] The increases have occurred for both men and women.

Significant sex differences exist in cancer mortality rates. In 1988, the overall cancer mortality rate per 100,000 was 215.5 for men and 180.0 per women. With the exception of breast cancer, men had higher mortality rates from every major cancer site. The most important of these sex differences was for lung cancer death rates.[22]

In terms of specific cancer sites, mortality rates from two major kinds of cancer have changed dramatically in most western countries in the last half-century. One is the increase in death rates from lung cancer. The age-adjusted mortality rate from cancer of the respiratory system per 100,000 population increased from 12.8 in 1950 to 28.4 in 1970 and 59.1 in 1991.[23] This is attributed to cigarette smoking, based on three kinds of evidence. One consists of studies showing a strong relationship between smoking and lung cancer in individuals: individuals who smoke more cigarettes or have smoked cigarettes for a longer period of time are more likely to contract lung cancer. The second is that lung cancer, which was a very rare form of cancer in the nineteenth century, became more prevalent about two decades after cigarette smoking became popular, which is about the time it takes for smoking to produce cancer.

The third type of evidence is based on the decline in the proportion of persons 18 years of age and over who smoke cigarettes, from 42 to 25 percent between 1965 and 1990. The reduction has occurred for both sexes and all age groups. Lung cancer mortality rates have declined recently among younger age groups, who would be the first to benefit because they have smoked for fewer years. The mortality rates per 100,000 population for cancers of the respiratory system for those 45 to 54 years of age increased from 22.9 in 1950 to 56.5 in 1980 and then declined to 46.9 in 1991.

The comparable rates for those aged 65 to 74 increased from 69.3 in 1950 to 243.1 in 1980 and 300.0 in 1991.[24]

The other dramatic change in cancer mortality rates has been the striking decline in death rates from stomach cancer.[25] Before 1940 stomach cancer was a major cause of cancer mortality for both sexes and all age groups; today it is relatively uncommon. The decline has occurred in most western nations and Japan, although it has been greater and occurred earlier in the United States than most other nations. The most frequently proposed causal factors involve changes in diet, particularly the decline in the consumption of salted, smoked, and fried foods. Before the canning and freezing of vegetables and refrigeration of foods, human diet in western countries included substantial amounts of salted vegetables, such as pickles and sauerkraut, and meats preserved with salts and nitrates, including sausages, ham, salami, and bologna. Canning, refrigeration, and freezing have reduced the need for these methods of preservation. However, no clear-cut evidence exists to support the diet theory, especially in terms of showing appropriate and timely changes in diet in all the nations that have experienced declines in stomach cancer rates.

As with heart disease, changing methods of diagnosis have affected cancer mortality rates. A British authority on lung cancer concluded that lung cancer death rates were understated early in the century because of the difficulty of diagnosing what was then a rare disease. He believes that lung cancer mortality rates for non-smokers today are probably the same as the overall population rates before smoking became widespread. Consequently he estimates that the rise in lung cancer death rates during the first quarter of the century in England and Wales was due almost entirely to more accurate diagnoses (primarily by the use of chest X-rays) rather than an actual increase in lung cancer mortality.[26]

Most cancer is considered to be environmental in origin. This is based on regional differences in specific types of cancers and on the evidence that people who move from one region to another contract different types of cancer than those who remain. As an example, Japanese women who emigrated to Hawaii have much lower rates of stomach cancer than their grandmothers but much higher rates of breast cancer.[27] The specific environmental factors involved are seldom well understood, however.

The inability to identify the causes of individual cancers and other chronic diseases is due to the complex nature of the diseases. These diseases take decades to develop, are produced by several factors operating simultaneously, and are retarded by still other factors. Researchers must therefore obtain data on many details of an individual's life over many years, which is rarely possible. Furthermore, mortality rates are low enough that is it necessary to study many thousands of people to obtain enough cases for a meaningful study. To avoid these problems, researchers usually study populations rather than individuals, by, for example, comparing the diet of a country or region with a low rate of stomach cancer to the diet of another country or region with a high rate. Because people within each country or region have different diets, the results are much less useful than if only individuals with specified diets were studied. This kind of research produces suggestive rather than definitive findings. Most knowledge about the environmental causes of cancer and heart disease is based on suggestive findings from a number of studies.

Because most cancers cannot be cured, research has focused on trends on the number of years that cancer patients live after diagnosis. The standard measure of cancer survival is the five-year survival rate, which is defined as the number of persons who are alive five years after they have been diagnosed as having cancer, divided by the number of persons diagnosed with the disease at the beginning of the period. Five-year survival rates for individual cancer sites vary widely, from about 10 percent for lung cancer and even less for a few other sites, to over 70 percent for bladder, breast, skin, and prostate cancers.[28]

A major concern is whether five-year survival rates have increased in recent years. A federal government study comparing five-year survival rates in 1950 with those in 1982 found real improvements in a few cancers, mostly rare ones, but only marginal improvement in the most frequent cancer sites. Five-year survival rates have a major methodological limitation. As physicians have become more aware of cancer and have better diagnostic devices, they look for it and diagnose it earlier than they did in the past. Thus patients are more likely to survive for five years because the disease was diagnosed in an earlier stage. For example, if a physician who is not alert to the possibility of cancer diagnoses a case of cancer in 1994, the patient will have survived for five years in 1999. If the physician had been more alert to the disease or had better diagnostic tools and diagnosed the same case a year earlier, in 1993, the patient would have reached the five-year mark a year earlier, in 1998, when the disease was less advanced. Earlier diagnoses will improve five-year survival rates regardless of changes in treatment. Earlier diagnosis is widely believed to be responsible for most of the modest improvements in five-year cancer survival rates.[29]

AIDS is the only major disease cause of death to claim most of its victims among the young. The first cases of human immunodeficiency virus infection were observed in the early 1980s, but no U.S. death rates existed until 1987, when an age-adjusted mortality rate of 5.5 per 100,000 population was recorded. In 1991, the age-adjusted mortality rate reached 11.3 per 100,000 population. AIDS deaths in 1991 were concentrated in the 25–44 year age group, with a mortality rate of 47.3 per 100,000 among men aged 25–44 and 6.4 per 100,000 among women aged 25–44. Deaths from AIDS constituted 18.6 percent of all deaths among men and 6.2 percent of all deaths among women in that age group.[30] The sex difference is expected to diminish in the future.

SOCIAL CLASS AND MORTALITY

For many centuries the rich have been known to have lower mortality rates than the poor. During most of recorded history, the differences have been attributed to the higher standard of living of the rich, their physical separation from the poor that protected them from contagious diseases, and their access to better public health measures, including sewage disposal and uncontaminated water. They received their medical care from better trained physicians, but until the twentieth century this was of little benefit because physicians could do little to prevent death or cure illness.

During the last years of the nineteenth century and the first decades of the twentieth century, improvements in medicine aroused the expectation that equalizing access to medical care would eliminate the differences in mortality rates between the rich and the poor. National governments improved access to health care for the poor, at first in Germany and later in other European nations. National health care programs did not develop in the United States because health care for the poor was a local and state government responsibility (as well as private charity). Local and state governments operated public hospitals and/or reimbursed physicians and voluntary hospitals for the care of charity patients. A few cities (most notably New York City) and states accepted their responsibilities conscientiously, but most were parsimonious in providing medical care to the poor. In 1965, with the enactment of Medicare and Medicaid, the federal government assumed substantial responsibility for the medical care of the poor. These programs improved the quality of health care provided to the poor but did not make it equal to the care given others.

As the poor obtained access to better health care in all countries, it was expected that mortality rates would become more equal among socio-economic status (SES) groups. One possibility was a general narrowing of the differences in mortality rates for all SES groups. Another was a threshold effect, in which the rates for those above a certain SES level would become more similar, but the rates for the lowest SES groups would remain higher.

Data from the United States and England have shown that neither trend has occurred. The mortality rates of all SES groups have declined substantially, but the differences among them have increased. One British study placed men under age 65 in five occupational groups from high to low social status and found that the differences in mortality rates among the groups increased significantly between 1931 and 1981. A study of Americans 25 to 64 years of age found a greater difference in mortality rates between the lowest and highest educational groups and the lowest and highest income groups in 1986 than in 1960. These patterns held for white men, white women, black men, and black women. The same trends have also been found for the major diseases considered individually. For example, studies in several countries have found that the greatest decline in heart disease mortality rates has occurred in the higher educational and occupational groups.[31]

Several aspects of this phenomenon should be emphasized: (1) overall mortality rates for all SES groups have declined steadily over time so that members of all SES groups are living longer today; (2) the differences in mortality rates among SES groups in the U.S. exist for both men and women and for whites and blacks; (3) the differences in mortality rates among SES groups exist for all age groups and are not limited to the elderly or to infants; (4) the differences in mortality rates among SES groups exist for many individual diseases, including heart disease, cancer, and stroke; and (5) many SES factors operate together to cause the differences in mortality, including education, income, occupation, parent's SES (used as a measure of SES during a person's childhood), as well as other unknown factors.

The fundamental issue in mortality differences among SES groups is not the higher mortality rates of the lowest SES groups, for which many plausible explanations have been offered. The issue is the inability to explain the growing differences among the highest SES groups. Surely the second highest SES group, for example, has more than an adequate standard of living, benefits from public health measures, has ready access to high quality medical care, and possesses sufficient education and income to live healthy lifestyles. The differences between their death rates and those of the highest SES group should, therefore, be narrowing, but for unknown reasons they are widening.

SES differences in mortality provide an appropriate context to discuss racial differences in mortality rates. In 1991 white males had an age-adjusted mortality rate of 6.3 deaths per 1000 population, while black males had a rate of 10.5 per 1000 population. The corresponding figures for white and black females were 3.7 per 1000 population and 5.8 per 1000 population. Lower mortality rates for whites existed for all major disease categories except suicides. Socio-economic factors must be responsible for these differences, because no known biological factors can explain them. One study found that these so-called "racial" differences in mortality rates were due to differences in age, sex, marital status, family size, and family income between the white and black populations (married persons have lower mortality rates than unmarried ones and members of smaller families have lower mortality rates than members of large families).[32] Black-white differentials in mortality rates are manifestations of the broader SES and demographic differences that exist in our society.

CONCLUSION

In reflecting on trends in mortality rates during the twentieth century, no conclusion is more remarkable than the astonishing number of unanticipated and unexplained changes that have occurred. Death rates from infectious diseases, the major cause of death in the nineteenth century, declined much more spectacularly than any physician in 1900 would have dared to predict, but no explanations for the decline have received universal acceptance. Death rates from stroke and heart disease rose to epidemic proportions in the first half of the twentieth century. This led observers in the 1950s and 1960s to pontificate that increasing death rates from heart disease and stroke were the inevitable fate of mankind in a post-infectious disease era. Despite these claims, mortality rates from both diseases declined dramatically in recent decades. None of the proposed explanations for these rises and declines are supported by convincing evidence.

Other mortality trends have been less gratifying. Overall cancer death rates have remained stable in recent decades. Two favorable developments stand out: the recent decline in lung cancer rates among younger age groups, almost surely due to a decline in smoking, and the continuing decline in stomach cancer death rates, which has no accepted explanation. The lack of decline in death rates from other types of cancer is especially disappointing when we consider the billions of dollars that have been spent on cancer research. Other discouraging and unexplained trends include the widening differences in mortality rates among SES groups and the growing death rates from chronic obstructive pulmonary diseases, which occur after years of painful disability.

The trends in mortality rates are made more baffling by their multinational nature. Most advanced nations have experienced similar trends in death rates, but they differ in many factors that have been offered as explanations, including their social structures, cultures, diets, housing, industries, sources of energy, modes of transportation, occupations, pollutants, and geographic and physical environments.

When physicians are confronted with such inexplicable trends, they tend to explain them according to their cultural predispositions.[33] American physicians like to attribute the positive trends to medical interventions—new drugs, new types of surgery, new medical and surgical specialties, new health care procedures like intensive care units and helicopter evacuation teams, and new public health initiatives. They like to believe that the problem areas, like cancer, await the expenditure of more money on specialists, more money on research, more money on equipment, more money on treatment. British physicians, on the other hand, note that nations that have spent only a fraction of the money that Americans spend on health care have experienced the same positive and negative trends. They believe that more general social changes—in broad public health measures, in the standard of living, in lifestyles—are responsible.

Useful explanations of mortality trends can never be achieved by studying individual diseases as disconnected entities. The human being is an organism, which means that changes in one part of the organism affect the whole organism. To understand changes in the incidence of any particular disease, we must understand factors that affected the organism in the past or are affecting it currently. These include biological factors, like other diseases that the person had contracted, and social factors, including the society and culture in which the person lives, as well as the interrelationships between the two.

ABOUT THE AUTHOR

William G. Rothstein is Professor of Sociology at the University of Maryland, Baltimore County. He is the author of *American Physicians in the Nineteenth Century: From Sects to Science* and *American Medical Schools and the Practice of Medicine.* He is editor of *Readings in American Health Care.*

REFERENCES

1. A. Cockburn, *The Evolution and Eradication of Infectious Diseases* (Baltimore: Johns Hopkins Press, 1963).

2. R. Floud, K. Wachter, and A. Gregory, *Height, Health and History: Nutritional Status in the United Kingdom, 1750–1980* (Cambridge, Eng.: Cambridge University Press, 1990); and R. W. Fogel, "The Conquest of High

Mortality and Hunger in Europe and America: Timing and Mechanisms," in *Favorites of Fortune: Technology, Growth, and Economic Development since the Industrial Revolution,* ed. P. Hoginnet, D. S. Landes, and H. Rosovsky (Cambridge: Harvard University Press, 1991), 52–54.

3. J. R. Gillis, L. A. Tilly, and D. Levine, eds., *The European Experience of Declining Fertility, 1850–1970: The Quiet Revolution* (Cambridge: Blackwell, 1992).

4. F. E. Linder and R. D. Grove, *Vital Statistics Rates in the United States, 1900–1940* (Washington, DC: GPO, 1943), 95–96 and passim.

5. "Advance Report of Final Mortality Statistics 1991," *Monthly Vital Statistics Report* 42 (31 August 1993), suppl. 2, p. 16.

6. Ibid., 16.

7. See R. Daniels, *Coming to America: A History of Immigration and Ethnicity in American Life* (New York: HarperCollins, 1990).

8. I. Waldron, "Recent Trends in Sex Mortality Ratios for Adults in Developed Countries," *Social Science and Medicine* 36 (1993): 451–62; and L. M. Verbrugge, "The Twain Meet: Empirical Explanations for Sex Differences in Health and Mortality," *Journal of Health and Social Behavior* 30 (1989): 282–304.

9. For a discussion of the causes of the decline, see S. J. Kunitz, "Explanations and Ideologies of Mortality Patterns," *Population and Development Review* 13 (1987): 379–408, and articles in *Milbank Memorial Fund Quarterly* 55 (summer 1977).

10. H. Hansen and M. Susser, "Historic Trends in Deaths from Chronic Kidney Disease in the United States and Britain," *American Journal of Epidemiology* 93 (1971): 413–24.

11. R. Doll, "Major Epidemics of the 20th Century: From Coronary Thrombosis to AIDS," *Journal of the Royal Statistical Society* A 150 (1987): 373–95; T. J. Thom, "International Mortality from Heart Disease: Rates and Trends," *International Journal of Epidemiology* 18 (1989), suppl. 1, pp. S20–S28.

12. L. H. Kuller, "Issues in Measuring Coronary Heart Disease Mortality and Morbidity," and R. B. Wallace, "How Do We Measure the Influence of Medical Care on the Decline of Coronary Heart Disease?" both in *Trends in Coronary Heart Disease Mortality: The Influence of Medical Care,* ed. M. W. Higgins and R. V. Luepker (New York: Oxford University Press, 1988), 44–53, 88–93.

13. W. E. Stehbens, "An Appraisal of the Epidemic Rise of Coronary Heart Disease and its Decline," *Lancet* 1 (1987): 606–11; and B. Burnand and A. R. Feinstein, "The Role of Diagnostic Inconsistency in Changing Rates of Occurrence for Coronary Heart Disease," *Journal of Clinical Epidemiology* 45 (1992): 929–40.

14. See R. Beaglehole, "International Trends in Coronary Heart Disease Mortality, Morbidity, and Risk Factors," *Epidemiologic Reviews* 12 (1990): 1–15.

15. W. B. Kannel and T. J. Thom, "Declining Cardiovascular Mortality," *Circulation* 70 (1984): 332.

16. See T. J. Thom and W. B. Kannel, "Downward Trend in Cardiovascular Mortality," *Annual Review of Medicine* 32 (1981): 427–34; R. I. Levy, "The

28   *The Health of the Nation*

Decline in Cardiovascular Disease Mortality," *Annual Review of Public Health* 2 (1981): 49–70; L. Goldman and E. F. Cook, "The Decline in Ischemic Heart Disease Mortality Rates," *Annals of Internal Medicine* 101 (1984): 825–36; and Beaglehole, "International Trends."

17. L. H. Kuller et al., "Sudden Death and the Decline in Coronary Heart Disease Mortality," *Journal of Chronic Diseases* 39 (1986): 1001–19; and Beaglehole, "International Trends," 5.

18. Kannel and Thom, "Declining Cardiovascular Mortality," 335.

19. See B. Modan and D. K. Wagener, "Some Epidemiological Aspects of Stroke: Mortality/Morbidity Trends, Age, Sex, Race, Socioeconomic Status," *Stroke* 23 (1992): 1230–36; and J. P. Whisnant, "The Decline of Stroke," *Stroke* 15 (1984): 160–68.

20. R. Doll, "Are We Winning the Fight Against Cancer? An Epidemiological Assessment," *European Journal of Cancer* 26 (1990): 500–508; D. L. Davis et al., "International Trends in Cancer Mortality in France, West Germany, Italy, Japan, England and Wales, and the United States," *Annals of the New York Academy of Sciences* 609 (1990): 5–48.

21. Barry Miller, et al., eds., *Cancer Statistics Review, 1973–1989* (Washington, DC: National Cancer Institute, 1992), part 2, p. 4.

22. U.S. Bureau of the Census, *Statistical Abstract of the United States: 1991* (Washington, DC: GPO, 1991), 84.

23. National Center for Health Statistics, *Health United States, 1991* (Hyattsville, MD: Public Health Service, 1992), 169; and "Advance Report of Final Mortality Statistics 1991," 18.

24. National Center for Health Statistics, *Health United States, 1991,* 203, 169; and "Advance Report of Final Mortality Statistics," 18.

25. See J. Higginson, C. S. Muir, and N. Munoz, *Human Cancer: Epidemiology and Environmental Causes* (Cambridge, Eng.: Cambridge University Press, 1992), 273–82; and C. P. Howson, T. Hiyama, and E. L. Wynder, "The Decline in Gastric Cancer: Epidemiology of an Unplanned Triumph," *Epidemiologic Reviews* 8 (1986): 1–27.

26. Doll, "Major Epidemics," 376–77.

27. Davis et al., "International Trends," 6.

28. National Center for Health Statistics, *Health United States, 1991,* 199.

29. U.S. General Accounting Office, *Cancer Patient Survival: What Progress Has Been Made?* (Washington, DC: GPO, 1987).

30. National Center for Health Statistics, *Health United States, 1991,* 156; and "Update: Mortality Attributable to HIV Infection/AIDS Among Persons Aged 25–44 Years—United States, 1990 and 1991," *Morbidity and Mortality Weekly Report* 42 (2 July 1993): 482.

31. R. G. Wilkinson, "Socio-economic Differences in Mortality," in *Class and Health: Research and Longitudinal Data,* ed. Wilkinson (London, Eng.: Tavistock, 1986), 2; G. Pappas et al., "The Increasing Disparity in Mortality Between Socioeconomic Groups in the United States, 1960 and 1986," *New*

England Journal of Medicine 329 (1993): 103–9; C. C. Seltzer and S. Jablon, "Army Rank and Subsequent Mortality by Cause: 23-Year Follow-up," *American Journal of Epidemiology* 105 (1977): 559–66; Beaglehole, "International Trends," 4; and J. P. Bunker, D. S. Gomby, and B. H. Kehrer, eds., *Pathways to Health: The Role of Social Factors* (Menlo Park, CA: Henry J. Kaiser Family Foundation, 1989).

32. "Advance Report of Final Mortality Statistics 1991," 15; and R. G. Rogers, "Living and Dying in the U.S.A.: Sociodemographic Determinants of Death among Blacks and Whites," *Demography* 29 (1992): 287–303.

33. Cf. Kunitz, "Explanations and Ideologies."

NB: Tables that were excluded from this article appear in W. G. Rothstein, *Readings in American Health Care: Current Issues in Socio-Historical Perspective* (The University of Wisconsin Press, 1995; 71–86).

ARTICLE 2

HEALTHY PEOPLE 2010 OBJECTIVES

Office of Public Health and Science, DHHS

INTRODUCTION

What Is Healthy People?

Healthy People is the national prevention initiative that identifies opportunities to improve the health of all Americans. For two decades, the U.S. Department of Health and Human Services (HHS) has used health promotion and disease prevention objectives to improve the health of the American people.

The first set of national health targets was published in 1979 in *Healthy People: The Surgeon General's Report on Health Promotion and Disease Prevention*. This set of five challenging goals, to reduce mortality among four different age groups—infants, children, adolescents and young adults, and adults—and increase independence among older adults, was supported by objectives with 1990 targets that were designed to drive action. Through the combined efforts of the Nation's public health agencies, the 1990 targets set for infants, children, and adults were achieved. Adolescent mortality did not decline sufficiently to reach the 1990 target, and data systems could not adequately track the older adults' target.

Healthy People 2000. Healthy People 2000 built upon the lessons of the first Surgeon General's report and is the product of unprecedented collaboration among government, voluntary and professional organizations, businesses, and individuals. Several themes distinguished Healthy People 2000 from past efforts, reflecting the progress and experience of 10 years, as well as an expanded science base for developing health promotion and disease prevention objectives. Many of the year 2000 objectives specify improving the health of groups of people bearing a disproportionate burden of poor health compared to the total population. The framework of Healthy People 2000 consists of three broad goals:

1. Increase the span of healthy life for Americans,
2. Reduce health disparities among Americans, and
3. Achieve access to preventive services for all Americans.

Organized under the broad approaches of health promotion, health protection, and preventive services, the more than 300 national objectives are organized into 22 priority areas. This framework provides direction for individuals to change personal behaviors and for organizations and communities to support good health through health promotion policies.

Year 2010 Objectives. The context in which Healthy People 2010 is being developed differs from that in which Healthy People 2000 was framed—and will continue to evolve throughout the decade. Advances in preventive therapies, vaccines and pharmaceuticals, assistive technologies, and computerized systems will all change the face of medicine and how it is practiced. New relationships will be defined between public health departments and health care delivery organizations. Meanwhile, demographic changes in the United States—reflecting an older and more racially diverse population—will create new demands on public health and the overall health care system. Global forces—including food supplies, emerging infectious diseases, and environmental interdependence—will present new public health challenges.

This next set of national objectives will be distinguished from Healthy People 2000 by the broadened prevention science base; improved surveillance and data systems; a heightened awareness and demand for preventive health services and quality health care; and changes in demographics, science, technology, and disease spread that will affect the public's health in the 21st century. The widespread use of the year 2000 objectives by States, localities, and the private sector also provides a base of experience upon which to build the 2010 objectives. While the Federal Government has taken the lead in developing the initial draft objectives for 2010, this process is designed to be very participatory.

GOAL #1: INCREASE QUALITY AND YEARS OF HEALTHY LIFE

The first goal of Healthy People 2010 is to increase the quality as well as the years of healthy life. Here the emphasis is on the health status and nature of life, not just longevity.

The life expectancy of Americans has steadily increased. In 1979, when the first *Healthy People: The Surgeon General's Report on Health Promotion and Disease Prevention*[1] was published, average life expectancy was 73.7 years. Based on current mortality experience, babies born in 1995 are expected to live 75.8 years. However, people have become increasingly interested in other health goals such as preventing disability, improving functioning, and relieving pain and the distress caused by physical and emotional symptoms. For the purposes of understanding broad trends in the public's health and comparing the value of health promotion strategies, it is helpful to have some overall measures of health and well-being in addition to information on specific aspects or dimensions of health that are the focus of the objectives in the specific focus areas of Healthy People 2010.

From an individual perspective, healthy life means a full range of functional capacity at each life stage, from infancy through old age, allowing one the ability to enter into satisfying relationships with others, to work, and to play. From a national perspective, healthy life means a vital, creative, and productive citizenry contributing to thriving communities and a thriving Nation. The proportion of the population who assess their current health status positively has not changed substantially during the past decade. In 1987, 90.5 percent of the population assessed their health status as good, very good or excellent.[2] In 1994, the percentage was 90.4 percent. During the same period, the percentage of the population reporting that they were limited in major activity due to chronic conditions actually increased from 18.9 percent in 1988 to 21.4 percent in 1995.

As the limitations of separately measuring mortality and morbidity have been recognized, many individuals and organizations have begun developing new measures that reflect both life duration *and* morbidity or health-related life quality.[3] The goal of increasing quality and years of healthy life will be tracked with a set of measures of population health that capture some of the aspects of this goal. Some measures focus on mortality, others focus on morbidity, and some measures incorporate aspects of both mortality and morbidity. The attributes of health (sometimes called domains or dimensions) that are captured by the different measures vary. Hence, a range of measures will be used to evaluate progress toward accomplishing this goal.

Measures of Mortality and Life Expectancy

Historically, measures of mortality have been important tools for assessing the health status of a population. Because information on every death occurring in the United States is available, mortality measures are especially important for population health surveillance at the State and local levels. Most prominent among measures of mortality are death rates, life expectancy, and years of potential life lost before age 75 (YPLL-75). These measures can be calculated for the total population and can also be broken out by demographic subgroups and cause-of-death.

Total Mortality

1. **Decrease the total death rate to no more than 454 per 100,000 by 2010.**
    (Baseline: 503.9 age-adjusted death rate per 100,000 in 1995)

Select Populations	1995
African American	765.7
American Indian/Alaska Native males	468.5
Asian/Pacific Islander males	298.9
Hispanic	386.8
White, non-Hispanic	475.2
Male	646.3
Female	385.2

Target Setting Method: 10 percent improvement.
Data Source: National Vital Statistics System (NVSS), CDC, NCHS.

2. **Reduce the death rate for adolescents and young adults (15–24 years) to no more than 81 per 100,000 by 2010.** (Baseline: 95.3 per 100,000 in 1995)

Select Populations	1995
African American	159.8
American Indian/Alaska Native	134.6
Asian/Pacific Islander	57.4
Hispanic	107.1
White	84.3
Male	140.5
Female	48.1

Target Setting Method: 10 percent improvement.
Data Source: National Vital Statistics System (NVSS), CDC, NCHS.

3. **Reduce the death rate for adults (25–64 years) to no more than 358 per 100,000 by 2010.** (Baseline: 397.3 per 100,000 in 1995)

Select Populations	1995
African American	691.1
American Indian/Alaska Native	416.8
Asian/Pacific Islander	175.8
Hispanic	288.4
White	365.4
Male	517.3
Female	280.9

Note: Within the Maternal, Infant, and Child Health focus area, objectives tracking infant mortality and child mortality are included.
Target Setting Method: 10 percent improvement.
Data Source: National Vital Statistics System (NVSS), CDC, NCHS.

Life Expectancy

4. **Increase life expectancy to 77.3 years by 2010.** (Baseline: 75.8 years in 1995)

Select Populations	1995
African American	69.6
American Indian/Alaska Native	Not available
Asian/Pacific Islander	Not available
Hispanic	Not available
White	76.5
Male	72.5
Female	78.9

Target Setting Method: Assumes a 10-year increase of 1.5 years.
Data Source: National Vital Statistics System (NVSS), CDC, NCHS.

Years of Potential Life Lost

5. **Decrease years of potential life lost before age 75 to no more than 7,315 per 100,000 by 2010.** (Baseline: 8,128.2 age-adjusted years of potential life lost before age 75 per 100,000 in 1995)

Select Populations	1995
Male	
African American	20,272.8
American Indian/Alaska Native	12,349.1
Asian/Pacific Islander	5,310.0
Hispanic	9,989.4
White, non-Hispanic	9,226.3

Select Populations	1995
Female	
African American	10,179.7
American Indian/Alaska Native	6,788.9
Asian/Pacific Islander	Not available
Hispanic	4,378.8
White, non-Hispanic	4,968.7

Target Setting Method: 10 percent improvement.
Data Source: National Vital Statistics System (NVSS), CDC, NCHS.

Measures of Health-Related Quality of Life

Overview

What Is Quality of Life?   *Quality of life (QOL)* is a popular expression that, in general, connotes an overall sense of well-being when applied to an *individual* and a pleasant and supportive environment when applied to a *community*. QOL is a global outcome that is highly valued by all populations.

Why Is QOL an Important Public Health Issue?   One result of our success in extending the normal span of human life is that attention is now shifting to apply scientific methods to improve the *quality* of our longer lives. As public health agencies evolve, their traditional roles are changing to reflect current community needs and issues, such as the *quality of life,* an issue with broad implications. The concept of health-related quality of life (HRQOL) provides the health community with a popularly supported and justifiable approach for expanding the recent morbidity and mortality-related definition of "health" to include aspects of *functional status, well-being,* and *participation.*

HRQOL Definition and Measurement.   *Health-Related Quality of Life (HRQOL)* is a broad concept of health that includes aspects of both physical and mental health and their determinants. Whereas general or *global QOL* includes all aspects of life—including beauty, culture, rights, values, beliefs, and aspirations—HRQOL is limited to those aspects that can be clearly shown to affect the physical or mental health of individuals or communities. It is based on technically sound measures that track the functional status and well-being of individuals, largely through surveys of health perceptions. On the community level, accumulated population HRQOL data help to assess health needs and guide efforts to provide services and environments conducive to better individual-level HRQOL.

On the *individual level,* HRQOL has a strong relationship to a person's health perceptions and ability to function. It integrates mental and physical health concepts and provides a reasonable way to expand the definition of "health" beyond simply being the opposite of the negative concepts of death and disease. On the *community level,* HRQOL includes all aspects of community life that have a direct and *quantifiable* influence on the physical or mental health of its members. The chart below shows key distinguishing aspects of "health," HRQOL, and QOL on both individual and community levels.

"HEALTH"	**vs. HRQOL**	**vs. QOL**
INDIVIDUAL LEVEL		
death	functional status	happiness
disease	well being	life satisfaction
COMMUNITY LEVEL		
life expectancy	environment	participation
	livability	sustainability

HRQOL Measures.   Several HRQOL survey measures and their associated summary scales and indexes have also been used with success during the 1990s to directly assess the HRQOL of large segments of the population. Among these are the Medical Outcomes Study Short Form 36 (SF-36) and its shorter versions and the "healthy days" measures. Short Form measures are being used by the Health Care Finance Administration and are included in the National Committee for Quality Assurance's Health Plan Employer Data and Information Set (HEDIS 3.0) recommended data set. Similarly, the Centers for Disease Control and Prevention (CDC) "healthy days" measures, developed by CDC, are being widely used by State and local health agencies and are recommended as community health profile indicators by the Institute of Medicine. Although no one HRQOL measurement approach presently meets all health policy needs, each measure and index included below is believed to be sufficiently valid and informative to warrant its use in monitoring the Nation's HRQOL.

Healthy Days Measures.   The "healthy days" measures are an integrated set of questions and a summary index designed to assess the physical and mental health perceptions of the population over time. Healthy days items on self-rated health, and recent physical health, mental health and activity limitations have been the first 4 questions asked by the State-based Behavior Risk Factor Survey since January, 1993, providing a continuous source of adult HRQOL surveillance data, that includes key behavioral risk factor and demographic data.[4–7] These measures have been used to derive three key indicators of population health: (1) *self-rated health* that tracks the percentage of adults with good or better health, (2) a summary *healthy days* index that estimates the recent person-days when both physical and mental health were felt to be at least good, and (3) an *activity days* indicator that estimates the recent reported capacity of persons to perform their usual activities due to good health. Other conceptually related measures including questions on recent pain, depression, anxiety, sleeplessness, and vitality, and on current activity limitation, disability, and broader quality-of-life concepts are also now in use by many BRFSS States.

Self-Rated Health

6. **Increase the percentage of persons reporting good, very good, or excellent general health* to at least 90 percent by 2010.** (Baseline: 86.2 percent of adults in 1993–96)

	1993–96			
	18–64 years		*≥65 years*	
Select Populations	*Men*	*Women*	*Men*	*Women*
African American	86.7	82.0	60.7	55.7
American Indian/Alaskan Native	85.3	80.1	64.9	55.1
Asian/Pacific Islander	92.7	91.6	74.4	81.6
Hispanic	84.8	80.5	67.0	60.2
White	91.5	91.0	73.1	72.1
Reported activity limitation	**	**	**	**
No reported limitation	**	**	**	**
Less than high school	74.9	69.7	58.3	56.1
High school graduate	90.5	89.7	74.3	74.1
College graduate	95.9	95.6	83.9	83.7
Less than $25,000	82.2	81.1	63.9	65.6
$25,000–$49,999	92.5	92.4	80.9	81.0
$50,000 or more	96.1	95.7	85.5	87.1
Employed	93.2	92.9	85.1	86.5
Unemployed/unable to work	63.8	62.5	34.3	33.0
Homemaker, student, other	86.5	87.5	71.1	69.9
Married	90.5	90.5	73.7	74.0
Widowed, divorced, separated	85.1	81.6	66.0	67.1
Never married	92.7	90.8	67.9	71.6
Insured	91.3	90.3	72.1	70.3
Uninsured	85.8	81.5	68.0	66.7

* Self-rated health is based on responses to a question in the BRFSS core questionnaire.
** Not available.

Target Setting Method: A target of 90 percent was selected based on an assumption that the 1993–96 level of 86.2 percent in the BRFSS could be raised to the nearest higher decile by 2010.
Data Source: Behavior Risk Factor Survey (BRFS). Based on overall 50-State data weighted to reflect the State age/race/sex population distribution. Not adjusted for institutionalized and other adults missed by survey methods.

Self-rated health (SRH) has potential policy value for community mobilization around health issues due to its simplicity and intuitive appeal. SRH is an independent predictor of important health outcomes, including mortality, functional status, and health services utilization. SRH has been found to be a good proxy index for chronic physical health conditions in populations; some studies have shown improvement in self-rated health following an intervention.[8]

SRH has been collected for many years on national NCHS surveys and since 1993 on the State-based BRFSS. SRH is also included in the Medical Outcomes Study Short Form (SF-36, SF-12), and Years of Healthy Life (YHL) index. The percentage of adults reporting good to excellent health is recommended by the Institute of Medicine as one of 25 Community Health Profile Indicators.[9]

Healthy Days

7. **Increase healthy days* to at least 26 days during the past 30 days by 2010.** (Baseline: 24.7 days in 1993–96)

| | 1993–96 | | | |
| | 18–64 years | | ≥65 years | |
Select Populations	*Men*	*Women*	*Men*	*Women*
African American	25.7	23.6	23.6	22.0
American Indian/Alaskan Native	23.8	21.3	24.2	24.5
Asian/Pacific Islander	26.8	25.4	25.4	25.2
Hispanic	25.3	23.5	22.8	21.9
White	25.8	24.0	24.7	23.5
Reported activity limitation	**	**	**	**
No reported limitation	**	**	**	**
Less than high school	23.7	21.4	22.7	21.4
High school graduate	25.6	23.8	24.9	23.8
College graduate	26.7	25.2	26.1	25.1
Less than $25,000	24.0	22.4	23.3	22.6
$25,000–$49,999	26.2	24.5	26.0	25.1
$50,000 or more	26.9	25.3	26.4	25.8
Employed	26.5	24.7	***	***
Unemployed/unable to work	17.8	17.1	***	***
Homemaker, student, other	25.2	24.0	***	***

Continued

	1993–96			
	18–64 years		≥65 years	
Select Populations	Men	Women	Men	Women
Married	26.2	24.6	24.9	24.0
Widowed, divorced, separated	23.9	21.9	23.2	22.7
Never married	25.5	23.6	24.3	24.2
Insured	26.0	24.2	24.6	23.4
Uninsured	24.5	22.5	23.0	21.1

* Healthy days are recent days when both physical and mental health are believed to be at least "good" and are based on responses to Q2 and Q3 in the BRFSS core questionnaire.[10–13]
** Not available.
*** Not applicable.

> **Target Setting Method:** A target of 26.0 mean healthy days was selected based on an assumption that the BRFSS overall population level of 24.7 days in 1993–96 could be raised by 5 percent by 2010.
> **Data Source:** Behavioral Risk Factor Surveillance System (BRFSS),[14,15] CDC, NCCDPHP. Based on overall 50-State data weighted to reflect the State age/race/sex population distribution. Not adjusted for institutionalized and other adults missed by survey methods.

The *healthy days index* provides a performance-based approach for tracking population health-related quality of life (HRQOL). With relative simplicity and good face validity, it is based on a broad definition of health that includes mental as well as physical health. Extensive population baseline data on adult healthy days, collected in the core BRFSS since January 1993, are available by State and many counties. The healthy days metric has also been found to have good construct validity[16–19] and has been acceptably cross-validated in a general population adult sample with the SF-36.[20]

An equivalent form of the healthy days index was recommended in 1997 by the Institute of Medicine as one of 25 Community Health Profile Indicators.[21] Related questions on recent days of pain, depression, anxiety, sleeplessness, and vitality are part of an expanded set of healthy days questions and provide more specific measures of HRQOL burden and needs.[22] In 1998 17 States are using the expanded set of HRQOL questions in their BRFSS, with most of these States also using several other activity limitation and quality-of-life questions developed by the CDC Office on Disability and Health.

Ability Days

8. **Increase recent days able to do usual activities due to good physical or mental health* to at least 28.7 days during the past 30 days by 2010.**
(Baseline: 28.3 days in 1993–96)

| | 1993–96 | | | |
| | 18–64 years | | ≥65 years | |
Select Populations	Men	Women	Men	Women
African American	28.3	27.9	26.3	26.4
American Indian/Alaskan Native	27.7	27.1	27.8	27.9
Asian/Pacific Islander	29.1	29.0	27.6	28.9
Hispanic	28.5	28.2	27.0	26.5
White	28.7	28.4	27.7	27.5
Reported activity limitation	**	**	**	**
No reported limitation	**	**	**	**
Less than high school	27.2	26.9	26.2	26.3
High school graduate	28.7	28.3	27.9	27.7
College graduate	29.2	28.9	28.4	28.3
Less than $25,000	27.6	27.6	26.9	27.0
$25,000–$49,999	29.0	28.7	28.4	28.3
$50,000 or more	29.3	28.9	28.6	28.5
Employed	29.2	28.9	***	***
Unemployed/unable to work	22.6	23.0	***	***
Homemaker, student, other	28.3	28.5	***	***
Married	28.8	28.6	27.7	27.8
Widowed, divorced, separated	27.8	27.3	27.0	27.0
Never married	28.8	28.4	27.5	27.4
Insured	28.7	28.4	27.6	27.4
Uninsured	28.3	27.9	25.6	25.9

* Recent ability days are the complement of activity limitation days (30 days minus the number of recent days when usual activities are not performed due to poor physical or mental health.) This measure is based on responses to Q2–Q4 in the BRFSS core questionnaire.[23–25]
** Not available.
*** Not applicable.

Target Setting Method: A target of 28.7 mean days without activity limitation was selected based on an assumption that the 1993–96 BRFSS level of 28.3 days could be raised by 0.4 days (about a 24% reduction in recent activity limitation days).
Data Source: Behavioral Risk Factor Surveillance System (BRFSS), CDC, NCCDPHP. Based on overall 50-State data weighted to reflect the State age/race/sex population distribution. Not adjusted for institutionalized and other adults missed by survey methods.

Extensive population baseline data on adult *"ability days,"* collected in the core BRFSS since January 1993, are also available by State and many counties. More than 500,000 adults have reported their recent ability days as of the end of 1997. This measure is one of the few examples of a global disability question in use in a surveillance system.[26] It is being used to help provide State and local intercensal estimates of work disability and other forms of disability. The metric has also been found to have good construct validity in relation to other health constructs measured in the BRFSS[27-29] and has been acceptably cross-validated in a general population adult sample with the Medical Outcomes Study Short-Form 36 (SF-36) widely used clinical HRQOL measure.[30] A measure of recent days of ability due to good health also offers promise for tracking population HRQOL good enough to provide persons with the capacity to perform their usual activities, such as work, self-care, and recreation. This measure is derived from a question on days of recent activity limitation due to poor physical or mental health asked of all respondents in the BRFSS.

Medical Outcomes Study Short Form Scales

The SF-36 and its subset, SF-12, are a widely used and clinically-validated set of HRQOL measures, subscales and summary scales designed to measure key aspects of physical and mental health. Both of the commonly used short forms include validated questions from each of eight HRQOL domains (i.e., physical functioning, social functioning, role limitation (physical), role limitation (emotional), mental health, energy/vitality, bodily pain, and general health perception), and both can be scored to produce summary scales for physical health and mental health.

The main strengths of the Short Form measures are that they are broadly accepted in many areas of health services and medical research (www.SF36.com) and are now being used to monitor the health of large populations—particularly patient populations (HEDIS 3.0) and groups with a high prevalence of chronic health conditions, such as older adults. In particular, the SF-36 has proven psychometric and empirical strength,[31,32] standardized data collection and scoring procedures, and documented population norms. For cross-cultural comparisons, there is also a vibrant and extensive body of research on the use of these measures in both developed and developing countries.

Summary Measures That Combine Mortality and Morbidity

Overview.   As defined by the Institute of Medicine (IOM),[33] *measures of population health* involve mortality data or morbidity data. However, *summary measures of population health* combine both mortality and morbidity data to represent overall population health in a single number.

Definition and Measurement.   Summary measures of population health are constructed by evaluating a measure of the health-related quality of life (HRQOL) and then linking this measure to life expectancy to produce a single measure of population health. For some measures, population health is evaluated as a decrement from full, healthy potential life. That is, the summary measure is the decrement from a hypothetical population in which all the people live healthy lives until a specified age. Therefore, as the longevity and quality of healthy years increases, these measures decrease in value. In other cases, the summary measure is an accumulation of years, in which each year is weighted by a HRQOL. That is, the summary measure increases as the longevity and quality of healthy years increases. A variety of methodologies have been developed during the previous decade to measure the HRQOL. The measures are used as numerical weights that adjust life expectancy. *Health-adjusted life expectancy* utilizes a numerical weight representing average health status at that age. *Quality-adjusted life expectancy* represents people's preferences for different health States. *Disability-adjusted life years* uses expert-derived weights for the value of additional years of life at each age and weights for more than 100 categories of health deficits resulting from different diseases and injuries.

The Years of Healthy Life measure was developed for the purpose of monitoring progress for Healthy People 2000. This measure will be continued for Healthy People 2010. Additional summary measures will be considered for inclusion in the set of measures used to monitor the goal of increasing years and quality of health life.

Years of Healthy Life (All Ages)

9. **Increase years of healthy life* to at least 66 years.** (Baseline: 63.9 years in 1995)

Select Populations	1995
African American	56.0
American Indian/Alaska Native	Not available
Asian/Pacific Islander	Not available
Hispanic	64.2 (1994)
White	65.0

*Years of healthy life was used to track the first goal of Healthy People 2000. The measure was calculated by combining self-rated data on limitation of activity and self-perceived health status from the National Health Interview Survey with life-expectancy data from life tables from the National Vital Statistics System.[34] The methodology has been adopted by 18 States using data from the Behavioral Risk Factor Surveillance System (Years of Healthy Life module) and State vital statistics.
Target Setting Method: Target is an increase of 2 years over the national average.
Data Sources: National Health Interview Survey (NHIS), CDC, NCHS; National Vital Statistics System (NVSS), CDC, NCHS.

Years of healthy life is a summary measure that combines mortality and health-related quality of life data into a single population measure. Its main strengths are its use of national population data dating back many years and its comprehensiveness in that it produces an estimate for the entire population—including young and old, whether residing in the community or an institution, and regardless of ability to respond to survey questions. Years of healthy life was developed for Healthy People 2000 in response to the need for a summary measure that could be assessed annually with existing data systems. Because it was a key guiding objective for Healthy People 2000, its continued use provides continuity with that effort—particularly as an overall national summary measure.

Years of Healthy Life (Older Adults)

10. **Increase years of healthy life* for persons 65 and older to 14 years.**
    (Baseline: 12.0 years in 1995)

Select Populations	1995
African American	9.7
American Indian/Alaska Native	Not available
Asian/Pacific Islander	Not available
Hispanic	13.8 (1994)
White	12.3

*Years of healthy life was used to track the first goal of Healthy People 2000. The measure was calculated by combining data on limitation of activity and self-perceived health status from the National Health Interview Survey with life-expectancy data from life tables from the National Vital Statistics System.[35] The methodology has been adopted by 18 States using data from the Behavioral Risk Factor Surveillance System and State vital statistics.

Target Setting Method: Target assumes an increase of 2 years from the national baseline.

Data Sources: National Health Interview Survey (NHIS), CDC, NCHS; National Vital Statistics System (NVSS), CDC, NCHS.

The proportion of the population that suffers from chronic disease and disability and requires assistance with activities of daily living increases with age. In 1994, the proportion of the population with limitation of activity was 10.1 percent among 15- to 44-year-olds, but increased to 38.2 percent among those 65 years and over, and to 44.1 percent for 75 years and older.[36] Therefore, the elderly segment of the population has a substantial influence on the overall Years of Healthy Life for the total population. Improving the longevity and quality of healthy life among these older adults will have an important impact on the overall health of the Nation.

GOAL #2: ELIMINATE HEALTH DISPARITIES

In the first round of public comments on the proposed framework for Healthy People 2010, "Eliminate Health Disparities" met with resounding support from a wide range of constituent groups. Many advocacy groups felt that accepting lower standards for racial and ethnic groups as compared to the total population was unjust. During the 1997 Healthy People progress reviews for Hispanics and Asian American and Pacific Islanders, a consensus emerged to do away with differential targets for racial and ethnic minority groups in Healthy People 2010. Subsequently, this recommendation was extended to people with low income, people with disabilities, women, and people in different age groups.

Eliminating disparities is a bold step forward from the goal of Healthy People 2000, which was to reduce disparities in health status, health risks and use of preventive interventions among population groups. Healthy People 2000 special population targets were established for racial and ethnic minority groups, women, people with low incomes, people with disabilities, and specific age groups (i.e., children, adolescents, and the elderly). Targets were set, challenging and calling for greater improvements for each of these groups than for the total population. However, with the exception of service interventions, these targets rarely aimed at achieving equity by 2000. Healthy People 2010, on the other hand, is setting the goal of eliminating these disparities during the next decade.

Eliminating disparities by the year 2010 will require new knowledge about the determinants of disease and effective interventions for prevention and treatment. It will also require improved access for all to the resources that influence health. Reaching this goal will necessitate improved collection and use of standardized data to correctly identify all high-risk populations and monitor the effectiveness of health interventions targeting these groups. Research dedicated to a better understanding of the relationships between health status and income, education, race and ethnicity, cultural influences, environment, and access to quality medical services will help us acquire new insights into eliminating the disparities and developing new ways to apply our existing knowledge toward this goal. Improving access to quality health care and the delivery of preventive and treatment services will require working more closely with communities to identify culturally sensitive implementation strategies.

In February 1998, President Clinton committed the Nation to eliminate health disparities between racial and ethnic minority groups by the year 2010 in six health issue areas. These areas are infant mortality, cancer screening and management, cardiovascular disease, diabetes, HIV/AIDS, and childhood and adult immunizations. This commitment is the foundation for the Department of Health and Human Services' Initiative to Eliminate Disparities in Health and reinforces the principle of equity that undergirds the change in Healthy People 2010 from a goal of reducing to one of eliminating disparities. While a separate initiative from Healthy People 2010, the HHS initiative to eliminate racial and ethnic disparities in health utilizes Healthy People objectives as outcome measures in each of the six health areas.

Compelling evidence that race and ethnicity correlate with persistent, and often increasing, health disparities among U.S. populations demands national attention. Indeed, despite notable progress in the overall health of the Nation, there are continuing disparities in the burden of illness and death experienced by African Americans, Hispanics, American Indians and Alaska Natives, and Pacific Islanders, compared to the U.S. population as a whole. These disparities are even greater if comparisons are made between each racial and ethnic group and the white population. Infant mortality rates are 2½ times higher for African Americans and 1½ times higher for Native Americans. African-American men under 65 suffer from prostate cancer at nearly twice the rate of whites. Vietnamese women suffer from cervical cancer at nearly five times the rate of whites. African-American men suffer from heart disease at nearly twice the rate of whites. Native Americans suffer from diabetes at nearly three times the average rate, while African Americans suffer 70 percent higher rates than whites and prevalence of diabetes in Hispanics is nearly double that of whites. Racial and ethnic minorities constitute approximately 25 percent of the total U.S. population, yet they account for nearly 54 percent of all AIDS cases. These disparities are not acceptable. We must do more than work toward reduction; we must work toward elimination.

The demographic changes that are anticipated over the next decade magnify the importance of addressing disparities in health status. Groups currently experiencing poorer health status are expected to grow as a proportion of the total U.S. population; therefore, the future health of America as a whole will be influenced substantially by our success in improving the health of racial and ethnic minorities. While disparities among racial and ethnic groups—especially between whites and African Americans—have received considerable attention over the last decade, differential access to social and health care resources most often reflect occupational, educational, and income and wealth differences among Americans. Differences in the life circumstances of those with less income and those with more income in the United States are substantial. Furthermore, education is a major determinant of earnings potential. These differences in access to economic and social resources appear to drive many of the health disparities found across Americans.

Growing inequalities in income and wealth over the last two decades should refocus attention on socioeconomic position as a key determinant of growing disparities in health in the coming decade. Evidence suggests that socioeconomic inequalities in health are increasing. Widening disparities in mortality by educational level and by income level have been observed despite the overall decline in mortality rates. The population-attributable death rate due to poverty increased between the early 1970s and early 1990s. Mortality rates for both children and adults are directly related to poverty as well as the degree of income inequality.

Socioeconomic disparities in health have been identified across time and place. Yet identifying and understanding the causes for these differences remain a challenge. Socioeconomic disparities in the United States are apparent in smoking, overweight, elevated blood lead, sedentary lifestyle, oral diseases, health insurance coverage, physician and dentist visits, ambulatory care sensitive hospitalizations, low birthweight, heart disease mortality, personal health perceptions, diabetes mortality, and activity limitations.

Income- and education-related differences in knowledge and time to pursue healthy behaviors, adequate housing, nutritious foods, safe communities to live in, and healthy environments to work in may influence the health and well-being of Americans in different socioeconomic positions. Certainly the stresses and strains of individuals with lower incomes imposes an emotional and psychological cost that is reflected in poorer health. Alternatively, individuals with higher education may have greater exposure to health related information that assists them in adopting health promoting behaviors.

Income is perhaps the most relevant indicator of socioeconomic position with regard to health policy formulation and social program implementation. Yet, income is not a simple variable to collect. Income tends to be poorly reported and nonresponse to questions about income is often high. Despite these limitations, income provides an assessment of the resources available to individuals or families to acquire the resources, such as food, housing, clothing, and health care, needed to maintain or improve their well-being. Income, however, may not adequately reflect the longer term accumulation of assets among the elder population who can use these resources to acquire needed services or other material goods.

As more HHS surveys incorporate additional measures of income, we can rely on various indicators of income, such as family income adjusted for family size (poverty index), or family income and education, as measures of socioeconomic position that reflect resource based assessments. Occupation or type of job can also serve as an indicator of socioeconomic position that reflects income and education as well as social prestige. Alternatively, linking census-based socioeconomic measures and health data may aid efforts to monitor health disparities.

Furthermore, examinations of the relationship of socioeconomic position or socioeconomic status and health have focused largely on the lowest end of income distribution. Comparisons often focus only on people below the Federal poverty line compared with people above that threshold. These comparisons imply a great homogeneity among people above the thresholds of poverty. This approach contributes to the stigma associated with the poor while obscuring the social gradient that puts lower and middle income people at increased risk of ill health. Evidence from many countries, including the United States, indicates that the relationship between socioeconomic status and health takes the form of a gradient. In general, poor people have worse health status than people of middle income who in turn have worse health status than people of higher income. Each increase in social position, measured by income or education, improves the chances of being in good health.

No single factor accounts for the relationship between socioeconomic position and health. Investigators have identified multiple interconnected pathways through which a person's health can be helped or harmed by his/her standard of living, working conditions, social interactions with others and the environment. Our society's commitment to ensuring healthy living and working conditions, as well as opportunities for individuals and communities to secure their well-being, serve as mediating factors along these pathways.

Progress toward the Healthy People 2000 objectives for the population as a whole appears primarily to reflect the achievement among the higher socioeconomic groups; lower socioeconomic groups continue to lag behind. For example, substantial progress has occurred in mortality from heart disease, lung cancer, infant mortality, low birthweight, dental caries prevalence, cigarette smoking, receipt of early prenatal care, and having regular mammograms. Further gains in these areas require further improvements among people in lower socioeconomic positions.

Although health statistics on race, ethnicity, socioeconomic status and disabilities are sparse, the data we do have demonstrate the volume of work needed to eliminate health disparities. The greatest opportunities for improvement and the greatest threats to the future health status of the Nation reside in the population groups that have historically been disadvantaged economically, educationally and politically. We must do a better job in identifying the disparities that exist, work toward elimination, and strive to create better health for all.

ABOUT THE AUTHOR

Office of Disease Prevention and Health Promotion/Public Health and Science, Office of the Assistant Secretary for Health, Department of Health and Human Services, Washington, DC.

REFERENCES

1. U.S. Department of Health, Education and Welfare. *Healthy People: Surgeon General's Report on Health Promotion and Disease Prevention.* Publication no. PHS 79-55071. Washington, DC: Government Printing Office, 1979.

2. National Center for Health Statistics (NCHS). *Health United States 1998 and Socioeconomic Chartbook.* Hyattsville, MD: NCHS, 1998.

3. Field, M.J. and Gold, M.R., eds. *Summarizing Population Health: Directions for the Development and Application of Population Metrics.* Washington, DC: Institute of Medicine, 1998.

4. Centers for Disease Control and Prevention (CDC). Health-related quality-of-life measures—United States, 1993. *MMWR* 44:195–200, 1995.

5. Field and Gold, op. cit.

6. Health Care Financing Administration (HCFA). Operational Policy Letter #47 (revised) Medicare Managed Care, April 14, 1997. World-Wide Web site http://www.hcfa.gov/medicare/op1047.htm. Accessed June 10, 1998.

7. Durch, J., Bailey, L.A., Stoto, M.A., eds. *Improving Health in the Community: A Role for Performance Monitoring.* Washington, DC: National Academy Press, 1997.

8. CDC, 1995, op. cit.

9. NCHS, op. cit.

10. U.S. Department of Health, Education and Welfare, op. cit.

11. CDC, 1995, op. cit.

12. Field and Gold, op. cit.

13. Durch, Bailey, and Stoto, op. cit.

14. Field and Gold, op. cit.

15. Durch, Bailey, and Stoto, op. cit.

16. U.S. Department of Health, Education and Welfare, op. cit.

17. CDC, 1995, op. cit.

18. Field and Gold, op. cit.

19. Durch, Bailey, and Stoto, op. cit.

20. CDC. *Workshop on Quality of Life/Health Status Surveillance for States and Communities. Report of a Meeting Held on December 2–4, 1991, Stone Mountain, Georgia.* Atlanta: Centers for Disease Control and Prevention, 1993.

21. NCHS, op. cit.

22. HCFA, op. cit.

23. U.S. Department of Health, Education and Welfare, op. cit.

24. CDC, 1995, op. cit.

25. Field and Gold, op. cit.

26. CDC. Quality of life as a new public health measure—Behavioral Risk Factor Surveillance System, 1993. *MMWR* 43:375–380, 1994.

27. U.S. Department of Health, Education and Welfare, op. cit.

28. CDC, 1995, op. cit.

29. Field and Gold, op. cit.

30. CDC, 1993, op. cit.

31. Ibid.

32. CDC, 1994, op. cit.

33. Field and Gold, op. cit.

34. NCHS, op. cit.

35. Field and Gold, op. cit.

36. NCHS, op. cit.

CHAPTER 2

DETERMINANTS OF HEALTH

As noted in Chapter 1, there has been a dramatic improvement in the health and life span of Americans during the past 150 years. This largely reflects a general improvement in the socioeconomic status of the population, improvements in nutrition, changes in reproductive behavior, advances in environmental sanitation (e.g., chlorination of water supplies, pasteurization of milk), and, more recently, improvements in medical care. Until the last 60 years, improvements in medical care had relatively little impact on the decline in mortality, which was mostly a product of the decline in mortality from tuberculosis, diarrheal diseases, (e.g., cholera), and other infections (e.g., smallpox). Particularly important were declines in infant and maternal mortality (McKeown, 1978; Rothstein, 1996; CDC, 1999).

In his pioneering studies, the late British physician Thomas McKeown analyzed trends in morbidity and mortality in England and Wales during the 19th and 20th centuries with a view toward understanding the impact of improvements in socioeconomic status, health care, and public health on the human life span and quality of life. These trends are of interest to policy makers and analysts as a means to understand the determinants of health and point the direction for future policy decisions. All analysts, however, do not draw the same conclusions from available data and thus the assessments and forecasts vary.

Using primary data on death rates (mortality), McKeown reviewed the reasons for the decline in the death rate since the eighteenth century in what became a seminal article for the field of determinants of health. He noted that much of the decline took place before the introduction of specific medical interventions, such as antibiotics. As such, McKeown argued that improved nutrition, a safer, cleaner environment, and a change in sexual behavior (smaller family size) were more significant determinants of health than were improvements in medical care before the mid-20th century. He also suggested that greater improvements in health would result from changing our ways of living and personal health habits than from over-reliance on personal health care. These ideas were more fully developed in his book *The Role of Medicine* (McKeown, 1979), included in our Recommended Readings.

Today the leading causes of death are diseases of the heart, malignant neoplasms, cerebrovascular disease, unintentional injuries, chronic obstructive pulmonary disease, pneumonia and influenza, diabetes mellitus, chronic liver disease and cirrhosis, atherosclerosis, and suicide. Among those ages 25–44 years, acquired immunodeficiency syndrome (AIDS) has become a leading cause of death. These modern killers result in part from socioeconomic conditions, the ways we choose to live, and the environments we create. Management of these problems requires different strategies than for the infectious diseases that were the leading killers during the early part of this century. We cannot rely solely on the cures of modern medicine but must combine these with broad public health measures. Today, ensuring good health and controlling disease requires a focus on (1) socioeconomic factors (e.g., income, education, work); (2) individual behavior and the factors that influence health-related behaviors; (3) physical and social environments; (4) human biology; and (5) access to health care. The Centers for Disease Control and Prevention (CDC) of the U.S. Public Health Service have analyzed the relative importance of four of these factors to the ten leading causes of premature mortality in the United States (U.S. Department of Health and Human Services, 1980). Although socioeconomic factors influence all other determinants of health, except human biology, the CDC did not explicitly include socioeconomic status as a determinant of health. The first analysis was done in 1977 and repeated in 1990 (U.S. Department of Health and Human Services). By examining the contribution of each of the four major determinants of health to premature mortality, personal behavior/lifestyle accounted for approximately 47 percent; human biology (inherited and genetic factors) 27 percent; environmental factors 16 percent; and, inadequacies in health care contributed 10 percent. These references are included in the Recommended Readings.

Taking a different approach that did not include an explicit treatment of socioeconomic status (SES), McGinnis and Foege (1993) found that approximately half of all deaths in 1990 could be attributed to the following nine factors: (1) tobacco (400,000 deaths); (2) diet and sedentary activity patterns (300,000 deaths); (3) alcohol abuse (100,000 deaths); (4) microbial agents (90,000 deaths); (5) toxic agents (60,000 deaths); (6) firearms (35,000 deaths); (7) sexual behavior (30,000 deaths); (8) motor vehicle accidents (20,000 deaths); and (9) illicit drug use (20,000 deaths). Here, again, we see the importance of personal behavior and environment. Socioeconomic status, although not specifically analyzed by McGinnis and Foege, is clearly a factor related to both behavior and the environment (see Chapter 1 Recommended Readings, particularly "Highlights" from *Socioeconomic Status and Health Chartbook: Health, United States, 1998*).

Although it is likely that the CDC analysis still holds in regard to the relative importance of each determinant, recent studies by Bunker and his associates (Bunker, 1995; Bunker, Frazier, & Mosteller, 1994) suggest that personal medical care, particularly clinical preventive services, play a larger role than in the past. They estimated that medical care contributed 6 of the 30 years of increased life expectancy

(20 percent) since the turn of the century and three of the seven years (43 percent) since 1950.

In addition, Newacheck, Jameson, and Halfon (1994), analyzing data from the National Health Interview Study, found that low-income, uninsured children are less likely than nonpoor insured children to receive timely physical and visual examinations and preventive dental care. Poor children with insurance use preventive services at about the same rate as nonpoor children. The authors conclude:

> "These findings suggest expanding the provision of insurance to all low income children could help to close the remaining gaps in the use of preventive services and, eventually to eliminate existing disparity in the preventable health problems described earlier." (p. 232)

Medical care not only contributes to reducing premature mortality and increasing life expectancy but also significant affects the quality of life. Several examples include cataract surgery, total hip replacement, and coronary artery bypass graft surgeries, as well as the treatment of hypertension, stroke, and many chronic illnesses. As such, these studies together clearly illustrate the importance of both population-based (public health) and individually directed (personal medical/health care) approaches to the reduction in premature mortality and morbidity.

In their article, "Producing Health, Consuming Health Care," (included in Recommended Readings) Evans and Stoddart (1990) present an analytic framework for understanding the determinants of health. They contend theirs is more comprehensive and flexible than the traditional framework, which essentially defines health as the absence of disease or injury and presents the health care system as a feedback mechanism to disease or injury. The authors' broad, complex framework encompasses meaningful categories that are responsive and sensitive to the ways in which a variety of factors interact to determine the health status of individuals and populations. The proposed framework includes a definition of health that reflects the individual's experience as well as the perspective of the health care system. It is therefore of particular relevance to the current policy debate because it encourages consideration of both behavior and biological factors and acknowledges the economic tradeoffs involved in the allocation of scarce resources. The principal weakness of their concept is the lack of emphasis on public health. These and other important ideas are discussed in depth in their book, *Why Are Some People Healthy and Others Not? The Determinants of Health of Populations* (Evans, Barer, & Marmor, 1994).

In "Health Inequalities and Social Class," also included in the Recommended Reading, M.G. Marmot and associates present evidence drawn from the 1985–1988 Whitehall II study, concerning the degree and causes of differences in mortality rates in a cohort of over 10,000 British civil servants. This was a follow-up to the original Whitehall study in 1967, which demonstrated an inverse relationship between employment grade and mortality. The importance of social class to health is evident at every level—from the lowest socioeconomic group to the highest. Those at the top of the social ladder show lower mortality than the next highest, and so on down the social hierarchy to where the lowest social classes show the highest mortality rates. Self-perceived health status and symptoms were also worse in workers in the lower-status jobs. This concept of a gradient, as opposed to a social class or socioeconomic status (SES) threshold below which health is impaired, was a very important advance. Moreover, the inferences that can be drawn from these studies are far-reaching, including factors such as early life environment, leisure-time activity, social networks, housing circumstances, education, and control over the work environment. One of the most important findings relates to the diminished level of healthy behaviors practiced by those in the lower socioeconomic groups, which was reflected in the fact that fewer of those in lower-status jobs believed that they could reduce their risk for a heart attack. This group also demonstrated a higher incidence of smoking, less vigorous exercise, more obesity, less healthy diet patterns, and more stressful life events. Overall, the study has many important policy implications, including the fact that people in lower socioeconomic groups are not benefiting from our vast knowledge about the close relationship between health status and behavioral factors. Moreover, it is important to recognize that these socioeconomic factors continue to have a strong influence in this population despite the availability of universal health care through the National Health Service in the United Kingdom.

The impact of SES on health, reviewed by Adler and her colleagues (1993) in our Recommended Reading, builds on the classic study by Marmot by documenting the wealth of research that demonstrates a mortality gradient at all socioeconomic levels with a variety of diseases. Navarro (1990) focuses on the importance of class and racial disparities in health status. These studies raise as many questions as they answer, including the impact of SES on morbidity.

While a growing number of studies support the view that the relationship between health and SES is best represented as a gradient and not a threshold phenomenon, the mechanisms underlying this relationship between SES and health are unclear. Many studies have focused on the behavioral characteristics of individuals of different occupations, educational levels, income, and social class. Where one lives also makes a difference. In a recent study of mortality rates in poverty and non-poverty areas Waitzman and Smith (1996) found in a younger group residing in the poverty area an all-cause mortality rate 1.5 times those in the nonpoverty area. Income inequality has also been recognized as a factor in life expectancy in industrialized countries. Wilkinson (1992) demonstrated that those industrialized countries with a greater equality income distribution had a proportionately greater increase in life expectancy. In the United States, Kaplan and colleagues (1996) demonstrated a correlation between household income and all-cause mortality, with the less fortunate demonstrating significantly higher mortality rates. Income inequality was associated with higher rates of low birth weights, homicide, violent crimes, work disability, smoking, and sedentary lifestyle. A number of studies demonstrate that access to health care alone (e.g., the National Health Services in the United Kingdom) does not overcome the profound effects of SES on health. Indeed, the gap between the higher and lower socioeconomic groups has grown, particularly in the

United States in the past 15 years, with potentially serious implications for the health of the general population.

The issues of race, class, and health status have been examined by Navarro (1990), Pappas (1994), Williams and Collins (1995), and Krieger, Williams, and Moss (1997). Although much of premature mortality in African Americans can be attributed to socioeconomic status, race is of great significance when considering problems such as low birth weight, homicide, diabetes mellitus, and access to medical care. Pappas also notes that the most important factor in the increasing difference in life expectancy between whites and African Americans is related to the slower decline in heart disease mortality in African Americans in recent decades. Navarro's (1990) analysis, included in this chapter, suggests the mortality differentials by social class are greater than mortality differentials due to race. Another understudied area is whether (and how) social differences in health vary by age groups across the life course. Such data are essential to formulating and targeting effective public health policies (Jefferys, 1996). Despite the importance of SES, there is little data to document and explain social inequities in health. In her paper, included in Chapter 2, Moss (1999) reviews current policies and proposes additional strategies for raising the level of awareness of SES, as well as improving the collection and use of relevant data.

An important paper, included in the Recommended Reading in Chapter 2 by Power and Hertzman (1997), examines the evidence for a pathway linking early life factors and adult disease. Their analysis, which is fairly technical, takes account of "the interrelationships between social and biological risks throughout the life course" (p. 210). They carefully examine the association between birth weight, placenta size, and weight gain in the first year of life with cardiovascular disease in the fifth decade. In addition to this "latency" model, they propose a "pathway" model that relates early life events to subsequent life trajectories. The complex relationships between "latency" and "pathway" effects is illustrated by examination of data from the 1958 birth cohort study in the United Kingdom, in which subjects have been tracked from birth to age 33 years as of the most recent follow-up. The data show a clear relationship between social class at birth and health status in early adulthood. Social class differences were least for males with back pain and greatest for obesity, respiratory symptoms, psychological distress, and poor/fair self-rated health status. This is a critically important study.

Recently, Kuh and Ben-Shlomo (1997) have reviewed the evidence supporting the importance of early life for adult chronic disease. They noted that the scientific literature includes a large number of scattered observations that associate a range of early life factors, particularly related to deprivation, that correlate with later adult risk factors or disease. Conditions included cardiovascular disease and its risk factors, chronic bronchitis, thyroid function, allergy, stomach cancer, and even suicide. We have included this very interesting paper in the Recommended Reading.

In summary, Chapter 2 deals with the growing body of knowledge related to the determinants of health of the population, particularly the importance of socioeconomic status. Although the knowledge of the determinants of health has grown dramatically in the past 30 years and is beginning to influence health policies at the national, state, and local levels, it has had relatively little impact on biomedical research policies or on the allocation of resources to achieve national health goals.

REFERENCES

Adler NE, Boyce T, Chesney MA, Folkman S, Syme L. Socioeconomic inequalities in health: No easy solution. *JAMA* 1993;269(24):3140–3145.

Bunker JP, Frazier HS, Mosteller F. Improving health: measuring effects of medical care. *Milbank Q* 1994;2:225–258.

Bunker JP. Medicine matters after all. *J Royal Coll Physic* (London) 1995;29:105–112.

Centers for Disease Control and Prevention. Ten Public Health Achievements—United States, 1900–1999. *MMWR* 1999;48:241–243.

Evans RG, Barer ML, Marmor TR. eds. *Why Are Some People Healthy and Others Not? The Determinants of Health of Populations.* New York: Aldine De Gruyter, 1994.

Kaplan GA, Pamuk ER, Lynch JW, Cohen RD, Balfour JL. Inequality in income and mortality in the United States: analysis of mortality and potential pathways. *BMJ* 1996;312:999–1003.

Krieger N, Williams DR, Moss NE. Measuring social class in U.S. public health research: Concepts, methodologies, and guidelines. *Annu Rev Public Health* 1997;18:341–378.

Kuh, D, Ben-Shlomo Y. Eds. *A Life Course Approach to Chronic Disease Epidemiology.* New York: Oxford University Press, 1997.

McGinnis JM, Foege WH. Actual causes of death in the United States. *JAMA* 1993;270:2207–2212.

McKeown T. *Determinants of health.* Abridged from *Human Nature,* April 1978. Copyright 1978 by Human Nature, Inc.

McKeown T. *The Role of Medicine: Dream, Mirage, or Nemesis?* Princeton, NJ: Princeton University Press, 1979.

Moss, N. Socioeconomic disparities in health in U.S.: An agenda for action. *Social Science and Medicine* 1999;1–15.

Navarro, V. Race or class versus race and class: Mortality differentials in the United States. *Lancet* 1990;336:1238–1240.

Newacheck P, Jameson WJ, Halfon N. Health status and income: The impact of poverty on child health. *J School Health* 1994;64:229–233.

Pamuk E, Makuc D, Heck K, Reuben C, Lochnen K. *Socioeconomic Status and Health Chartbook, Health, United States, 1998.* Hyattsville, MD: National Center for Health Statistics, 1998;3–20 (Highlights).

Pappas, G. Elucidating the relationship between race, socioeconomic status, and health. *American J Public Health* 1994;84(6):892–893.

Rothstein WG. Trends in Mortality in the Twentieth Century. In: Rothstein WG. *Readings in American Health Care: Current Issues in Socio-historical Perspective.* Madison, WI: University of Wisconsin Press, 1995;71–86.

U.S. Department of Health and Human Services. *Ten Leading Causes of Death in the United States in 1977.* Public Health Service. Atlanta, GA: Centers for Disease Control and Prevention, 1980.

U.S. Department of Health and Human Services. *Healthy People 2000: National Health Promotion and Disease Prevention Objectives.* Washington, DC: Public Health Service, 1990.

Waitzman, NJ, Smith KR. Phantom of the area: Poverty, residence and mortality in the U.S. Presented at the Forum on Social and Economic Disparities in Health and Health Care, Salt Lake City, UT, 1996.

Wilkinson, RG. Income distribution and life expectancy. *BMJ* 1992;304:165–168.

Williams, DR, Collins C. U.S. Socioeconomic and Racial Differences in Health: Patterns and Explanations. *Annu Rev Sociol* 1995;21:349–386.

ARTICLE 1

DETERMINANTS OF HEALTH

Thomas McKeown

Modern medicine is not nearly as effective as most people believe. It has not been effective because medical science and service are misdirected and society's investment in health is misused. At the base of this misdirection is a false assumption about human health. Physicians, biochemists, and the general public assume that the body is a machine that can be protected from disease primarily by physical and chemical intervention. This approach, rooted in 17th-century science, has led to widespread indifference to the influence of the primary determinants of human health—environment and personal behavior—and emphasizes the role of medical treatment, which is actually less important than either of the others. It has also resulted in the neglect of sick people whose ailments are not within the scope of the sort of therapy that interests the medical professions.

An appraisal of influences on health in the past suggests that the contribution of modern medicine to the increase of life expectancy has been much smaller than most people believe. Health improved, not because of steps when we are ill, but because we become ill less often. We remain well, less because of specific measures such as vaccination and immunization than because we enjoy a higher standard of nutrition, we live in a healthier environment, and we have fewer children.

The utmost in healing can be achieved when there is unity, when the internal spirit and the external physical shape perfect each other.
—The Yellow Emperor
   China, 1000 BC

For some 300 years, an engineering approach has been dominant in biology and medicine and has provided the basis for the treatment of the sick. A mechanistic concept of nature developed in the 17th century led to the idea that a living organism, like a machine, might be taken apart and reassembled if its structure and function were sufficiently understood. Applied to medicine, this concept meant that understanding the body's response to disease would allow physicians to intervene in the course of disease. The consequences of the engineering approach to medicine are more conspicuous today than they were in the 17th century, largely because the resources of the physical and chemical sciences are so much greater. Medical education begins with the study of the structure and function of the body, continues with examination of disease processes, and ends with clinical instruction on selected sick people. Medical service is dominated by the image of the hospital for the acutely ill, where technological resources are concentrated. Medical research also reflects the mechanistic approach, concerning itself with problems such as the chemical basis of inheritance and the immunological response to transplanted tissues.

No one disputes the predominance of the engineering approach in medicine, but we must now ask whether it is seriously deficient as a conceptualization of the problems of human health. To answer this question, we must examine the determinants of human health. We must first discover why health improved in the past and then go on to ascertain the important influences on health today in the light of the change in health problems that has resulted from the decline of infectious diseases.

It is no exaggeration to say that health, especially the health of infants and young children, has been transformed since the 18th century (Figure 1). For the first time in history, a mother knows it is likely that all her children will live to maturity. Before the 19th century, only about three out of every 10 newborn infants lived beyond the age of 25. Of the seven who died, two or three never reached their first birthday, and five or six died before they were six. Today, in developed countries fewer than one in 20 children die before they reach adulthood.

The increased life expectancy, most evident for young children, is due predominantly, to a reduction of deaths from infectious diseases (Figure 2). Records from England and Wales (the earliest national statistics available) show that this reduction was the reason for the improvement in health before 1900 and it remains the main influence to the present day.

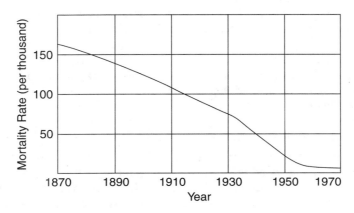

Figure 1   Infant mortality rate.

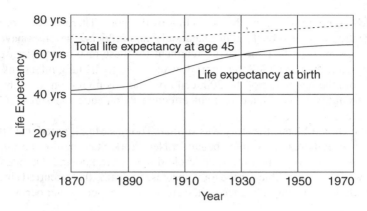

Figure 2   Life expectancy.

But when we try to account for the decline of infections, significant differences of opinion appear. The conventional view attributes the change to an increased understanding of the nature of infectious disease and to the application of that knowledge through better hygiene, immunization, and treatment. This interpretation places particular emphasis on immunization against diseases like smallpox and polio, and on the use of drugs for the treatment of other diseases, such as tuberculosis, meningitis, and pneumonia. These measures, in fact, contributed relatively little to the total reduction of mortality; the main explanation for the dramatic fall in the number of deaths lies not in medical intervention but elsewhere.

Deaths from the common infections were declining long before effective medical intervention was possible. By 1900, the total death rate had dropped substantially, and over 90 percent of the reduction was due to a decrease of deaths from infectious diseases. The relative importance of the major influences can be illustrated by reference to tuberculosis. Although respiratory tuberculosis was the single largest cause of death in the mid-19th century, mortality from the disease declined continuously after 1938, when it was first registered in England and Wales as a cause of death.

Robert Koch identified the tubercle bacillus in 1882, but none of the treatments used in the 19th or early 20th centuries significantly influenced the course of the disease. The many drugs that were tried were worthless; so, too, was the practice of surgically collapsing an infected lung, a treatment introduced about 1920. Streptomycin, developed in 1947, was the first effective treatment, but by this time mortality from the disease had fallen to a small fraction of its level during 1848 to 1854. Streptomycin lowered the death rate from tuberculosis in England and Wales by about 50 percent, but its contribution to the decrease in the death rate since the early 19th century was only about 3 percent.

Deaths from bronchitis, pneumonia, and influenza also began to decline before medical science provided an effective treatment for these illnesses. Although the death rate in England and Wales increased in the second half of the 19th century, it has fallen continuously since the beginning of the 20th. There is still no effective immunization against bronchitis or pneumonia, and influenza vaccines have had no effect on deaths. The first successful treatment for these respiratory diseases was a sulfa drug introduced in 1938, but mortality attributed to the lung infections was declining from the beginning of the 20th century. There is no reason to doubt that the decline would have continued without effective therapeutic measures, if at a far slower rate.

In the United States, the story was similar: Thomas Magill noted that "the rapid decline of pneumonia death rates began in New York State before the turn of the century and many years before the 'miracle drugs' were known." Obviously, drug therapy was not responsible for the total decrease in deaths that occurred since 1938, and it could have had no influence on the substantial reduction that occurred before then.

The histories of most other common infections, such as whooping cough, measles, and scarlet fever, are similar. In each of these diseases, mortality had fallen to a low level before effective immunization or therapy became available.

In some infections, medical intervention *was* valuable before sulfa drugs and antibiotics became available. Immunization protected people against smallpox and tetanus, antitoxin treatment limited deaths from diphtheria; appendicitis, peritonitis, and ear infections responded to surgery; Salvarsan was a long-sought "magic bullet" against syphilis; intravenous therapy saved people with severe diarrheas; and improved obstetric care prevented childbed fever.

But even if such medical measures had been responsible for the whole decline of mortality from these particular conditions after 1900 (and clearly they were not), they would account for only a small part of the decrease in deaths attributed to all infectious diseases before 1935. From that time, powerful drugs came into use and they were supplemented by improved vaccines. But mortality would have continued to fall even without the presence of these agents; and over the whole period since cause of death was first recorded, immunization and treatments have contributed much less than other influences.

The substantial fall in mortality was due in part to reduced contact with microorganisms. In developed countries, an individual no longer encounters the cholera bacillus, he is rarely exposed to the typhoid organism, and his contact with the tubercle bacillus is infrequent. The death rate from these infections fell continuously from the second half of the 19th century when basic hygienic measures were introduced: purification of water, efficient sewage disposal, and improved food hygiene—particularly the pasteurization of milk, the item in the diet most likely to spread disease.

Pasteurization was probably the main reason for the decrease in deaths from gastroenteritis and for the decline in infant mortality from about 1900.

In the 20th century, these essential hygienic measures were supported by improved conditions in the home, the work place, and the general environment. Over the entire period for which records exist, better hygiene accounts for approximately a fifth of the total reduction of mortality.

But the decline of mortality caused by infections began long before the intro-duction of sanitary measures. It had already begun in England and Wales by 1838, and statistics from Scandinavia suggest that the death rate had been decreasing there since the first half of the 18th century.

A review of English experience makes it unlikely that reduced exposure to mi-croorganisms contributed significantly to the falling death rate in this earlier period. In England and Wales that was the time of industrialization, characterized by rapid population growth and shifts of people from farms into towns, where living and working conditions were uncontrolled. The crowding and poor hygiene that resulted provided ideal conditions for the multiplication and spread of microorganisms, and the situation improved little before sanitary measures were introduced in the last third of the century.

A further explanation for the falling death rate is that an improvement in nutri-tion led to an increase in resistance to infectious diseases. This is, I believe, the most credible reason for the decline of the infections, at least until the late 19th century, and also explains why deaths from airborne diseases like scarlet fever and measles have decreased even when exposure to the organisms that cause them remains al-most unchanged. The evidence demonstrating the impact of improved nutrition is indirect, but it is still impressive.

Lack of food and the resulting malnutrition were largely responsible for the predominance of the infectious diseases, from the time when men first aggregated in large population groups about 10,000 years ago. In these conditions an improve-ment in nutrition was necessary for a substantial and prolonged decline in mortality.

Experience in developing countries today leaves no doubt that nutritional state is a critical factor in a person's response to infectious disease, particularly in young children. Malnourished people contract infections more often than those who are well fed and they suffer more when they become infected. According to a recent World Health Organization report on nutrition in developing countries, the best vac-cine against common infectious diseases is an adequate diet.

In the 18th and 19th centuries, food production increased greatly throughout the Western world. The number of people in England and Wales tripled between 1700 and 1850 and they were fed on home-grown food.

In summary: The death rate from infectious diseases fell because an increase in food supplies led to better nutrition. From the second half of the 19th century this advance was strongly supported by improved hygiene and safer food and water, which reduced exposure to infection. With the exception of the smallpox vaccina-tion, which played a small part in the total decline of mortality, medical procedures such as immunization and therapy had little impact on human health until the 20th century.

One other influence needs to be considered: a change in reproductive behavior, which caused the birth rate to decline. The significance of this change can hardly be exaggerated, for without it the other advances would soon have been overtaken by the increasing population. We can attribute the modern improvement in health to food, hygiene, and medical intervention in that order of time and importance—but we must recognize that it is to a modification of behavior that we owe the permanence of this improvement.

But it does not follow that these influences have the same relative importance today as in the past. In technologically advanced countries, the decline of infectious diseases was followed by a vast change in health problems, and even in developing countries advances in medical science and technology may have modified the effects of nutrition, sanitation, and contraception. In order to predict the factors likely to affect our health in the future, we need to examine the nature of the problems in health that exist today.

Because today's problems are mainly with noncommunicable diseases, physicians have shifted their approach. In the case of infections, interest centers on the organisms that cause them and on the conditions under which they spread. In noninfective conditions, the engineering approach established in the 17th century remains predominant and attention is focused on how a disease develops rather than on why it begins. Perhaps the most important question now confronting medicine is whether the commonest health problems—heart disease, cancer, rheumatoid arthritis, cerebrovascular disease—are essentially different from health problems of the past or whether, like infections, they can be prevented by modifying the conditions that lead to them.

A wise man should consider that health is the greatest of human blessings, and learn how, by his own thought, to derive benefit from his illness.
—Hippocrates
  460–400 BC

To answer this question, we must distinguish between genetic and chromosomal diseases determined at the moment of fertilization and all other diseases, which are attributable in greater or lesser degree to the influence of the environment. Most diseases, including the common noninfectious ones, appear to fall into the second category. Whether these diseases can be prevented is likely to be determined by the practicability of controlling the environmental influences that lead them.

The change in the character of health problems that followed the decline of infections in developed countries has not invalidated the conclusion that most diseases, both physical and mental, are associated with influences that might be controlled. Among such influences, those which the individual determines by his own behavior (smoking, eating, exercise, and the like) are now more important for his health than those that depend mainly on society's actions (provision of essential food and protection from hazards). And both behavioral and environmental influences are more significant than medical care.

The role of individual medical care in preventing sickness and premature death is secondary to that of other influences; yet society's investment in health care is based on the premise that it is the major determinant. It is assumed that we are ill and are made well, but it is nearer the truth to say that we are well and are made ill. Few people think of themselves as having the major responsibility for their own health, and the enormous resources that advanced countries assigned to the health field are used mainly to treat disease or, to a lesser extent, to prevent it by personal measures such as immunization.

The revised concept of human health cannot provide immediate solutions for the many complex problems facing society: limiting population growth and providing adequate food in developing countries, changing personal behavior, and striking a new balance between technology and care in developed nations. Instead, the enlarged understanding of health and disease should be regarded as a conceptual base with implications for services, education, and research that will take years to develop.

The most immediate requirements in the health services is to give sufficient attention to behavioral influences that are now the main determinants of health. The public believes that health depends primarily on intervention by the doctor and that the essential requirement for health is the early discovery of disease. This concept should be replaced by recognition that disease often cannot be treated effectively, and that health is determined predominantly by the way of life individuals choose to follow. Among the important influences on health are the use of tobacco, the misuse of alcohol and drugs, excessive or unbalanced diets, and lack of exercise. With research, the list of significant behavioral influences will undoubtedly increase, particularly in relation to the prevention of mental illness.

Although the influences of personal behavior are the main determinants of health in developed countries, public action can still accomplish a great deal in the environmental field. Internationally, malnutrition probably remains the most important cause of ill health, and even in affluent societies sections of the population are inadequately—as distinct from unwisely—fed. The malnourished vary in proportion and composition from one country to another, but in the developed world they are mainly the younger children of large families and elderly people who live alone. In light of the importance of food for good health, governments might use supplements and subsidies to put essential foods within the reach of everyone, and provide inducements for people to select beneficial in place of harmful foods. Of course, these aims cannot exclude other considerations such as international agreements and the solvency of farmers who have been encouraged to produce meat and dairy products rather than grains. Nevertheless, in future evaluations of agricultural and related economic policies, health implications deserve a primary place.

Perhaps the most sensitive area for consideration is the funding of health services. Although the contribution of medical intervention to prevention of sickness and premature death can be expected to remain small in relation to behavioral and environmental influences, surgery and drugs are widely regarded as the basis of health and the essence of medical care, and society invests the money it sets aside for health mainly in treatment for acute diseases and particularly in hospitals for the acutely ill. Does it follow from our appraisal that resources should be transferred from acute care to chronic care and to preventive measures?

Health signifies that one's life force is intact, and that one is sufficiently in harmony with the social, physical, and supernatural environment to enjoy what is positively valued in life, and to ward off misfortunes and evils.
—Bantu African Medical Theory

Restricting the discussion to personal medical care, I believe that neglected areas, such as mental illness, mental retardation, and geriatric care, need greatly increased attention. But to suggest that this can be achieved merely by direct transfer of resources is an oversimplification. The designation "acute care" comprises a wide range of activities that differ profoundly in their effectiveness and efficiency. Some, like surgery for accidents and the treatment of acute emergencies, are among the most important services that medicine can offer and any reduction of their support would be disastrous. Others, however, like coronary care units and iron treatment of some anemias are not shown to be effective, while still others—most tonsillectomies and routine check-ups—are quite useless and should be abandoned. A critical appraisal of medical services for acute illnesses would result in more efficient use of available resources and would free some of them for preventive measures.

What health services need in general is an adjustment in the distribution of interest and resources between prevention of disease, care of the sick who require investigation and treatment, and care of the sick who do not need active intervention. Such an adjustment must pay considerable attention to the major determinants of health: to food and the environment, which will be mainly in the hands of specialists, and to personal behavior, which should be the concern of every practicing doctor.

ABOUT THE AUTHOR

The late Thomas McKeown, MD, was Professor Emeritus, Department of Social Medicine, University of Birmingham, England, and author of *The Role of Medicine: Dream, Mirage, or Nemesis?*.

A R T I C L E   2

SOCIOECONOMIC DISPARITIES
IN HEALTH IN THE UNITED STATES:
AN AGENDA FOR ACTION

Nancy Moss

The ideal of equality has governed constitutional change and significant aspects of public policy-making for generations. Most recently, a wave of legislation culminated in the Johnson Administration's War on Poverty during the 1960s, when the issues of racial, gender, and economic equality of opportunity rose to the fore. (In the 18th century, equality was about political power rather than social norms and was extended neither to women nor to slaves.) The past decade has seen a resurgence of interest in inequality, motivated by concern with results attained rather than opportunity. This chapter addresses trends in economic inequality in the United States; the relationship of economic inequality to variations in health; recent actions in the United States to draw attention to health inequalities; the creation of health inequalities as a public policy issue in the United States and Europe; and, based upon these experiences, next steps that could be taken.

INEQUALITY OF INCOME AND WEALTH
IN THE UNITED STATES

The period of economic and social expansion that began in the post–World War II era ended in the early 1970s when income gains made by Americans during the 1950s and 1960s began to erode, leading to increasing income inequality between those at the top and those at the bottom of the nation's social hierarchy. During the 1980s, political and economic trends toward deregulation of financial markets, the globalization of capital, and social conservatism drove interest in socioeconomic equality and the consequences of poverty off of the public agenda. The demise of the Soviet Union as an external threat coincided with a reopening of internal debates about economic inequality within the United States, as issues that had been marginalized during the late 1970s and the 1980s moved back to center stage. Nonetheless, this change has occurred primarily among the media and academic elites, not in the public-at-large.

Despite the rhetoric of constitutional ideology and the recent rediscovery by the media of inequality of income and wealth, it is nothing new in the United States. The extent of inequality has risen and fallen periodically during the past 300 years. During the colonial and post-colonial periods inequality was relatively constrained but it increased during the 19th century with the erosion of the frontier, urbanization, and the technological development that made access to an educated workforce and financial capital more important and reinforced urban social hierarchies dominated by capitalist elites. After brief leveling during World War I, inequality of wealth and income rose during the 1920s to retreat during the years of the Depression and World War II.

During the post-World War II period, income inequality declined 7.4 percent until 1968 when it began to rise again. By 1982, income inequality equaled and then surpassed its post-war level, a trend that has continued, albeit somewhat less dramatically than during the 1980s. Since 1968 the share of total income received by the top 5 percent of households has grown from 16.6 percent to 21.2 percent in 1994, more than eight times as much as households at the 20th percentile or bottom of the income distribution. Accounting for non-cash income such as government transfers somewhat modifies but does not alter this picture. Only recently has there been some stabilization of the long-term growth in income inequality in the United States.

The recent rise in inequality of income and wealth in the United States is mirrored by trends in other industrialized countries; data from the Luxembourg Income Study show that by 1987 income inequality was greater in the United States than in comparable industrialized nations such as Canada, the United Kingdom, France, and Germany.

Explanations proposed to account for the recent rise in income inequality in the United States include the inflow of baby-boom age workers during the 1970s competing with lower-skilled, older workers; the decline of manufacturing and the erosion of good jobs for less-educated workers; globalization of labor and capital markets; the growth of the lower-wage service sector; changes in technology's demands on labor; and the decline of labor unions that could press for higher wages. Changes in social welfare programs eroded the cash value of benefits. Income inequality for white households during this period would probably be even worse were it not for increased contributions of women's earnings to the household, although there are signs that the moderating effect of women's wage work may be leveling off.

Inequalities in wealth, while less-often studied than inequalities in income, present a similarly dismal picture. The share of marketable net worth held by the top 1 percent of wealth holders declined (unevenly) from 1930 until the mid-1970s, when it began a steep and unabated rise back to pre–World War II levels. In the United States, nearly 40 percent of total household wealth belongs to 1 percent of the population.

Until recently, poverty rather than inequality was the focal point among U.S. policy makers and scholars trying to understand how social class differences affect people's well-being. While World War II had served as a leveler after the Great Depression, by the early 1960s the claims of poor whites and poor blacks left behind in the post-war economic expansion helped to make the War on Poverty the focus of social policy. The institutionalization of the "poverty line," an average subsistence income threshold adjusted by the annual Consumer Price Index and weighted by family size, made it possible to monitor health and social trends among the poor and nonpoor. The recent increasing concentration of income and wealth among a small percentage of Americans, and declines in wage growth for middle-class households, have stimulated renewed attention to inequality and its consequences for health and well-being.

Inequality and Health

Variations in educational attainment, wealth, income, and occupational position as markers of socioeconomic inequality have long been associated with variations in health and mortality risk. While the impact of socioeconomic inequality varies by gender, age, and ethnicity (and by choice of independent and dependent measures), the overall message is consistent: socioeconomic inequalities affect health.

Not all inequalities in health or in health care are due to socioeconomic antecedents. Given the same socioeconomic profile and the same environmental constraints, two individuals may differ in genetic heritage as well as behavioral choices, and the result may well be different sequelae of disease or disability. The pathways by which socioeconomic inequality affects health are complex. Macroeconomic events and policy—translated into investments—shape the occupations and industries of employment, which in turn determine labor-market opportunities and workplace conditions. In differing ways a number of the body's organs and systems are affected by expressions of inequality that influence the endpoints of disease, disability, and death. Inequality shapes health through intergenerational genetic and socioeconomic heritage; neighborhood and environmental quality; household patterns, including gender and economic equity; and personal behaviors. Access to goods and services, including health care, can be a consequence or modifier of inequality.

With an idea in mind of how inequality's effects shape health we return to our major question: are there steps that policy makers can take to reduce the impact of inequality on health? How can data be used to make policy action possible?

ATTENTION TO INEQUALITIES IN HEALTH IN THE POLICY SPHERE

The relationship of socioeconomic inequality and health is an old—not a new—area of concern for public health policy. The public health community in the United States has a longstanding interest in socioeconomic differences in health, with advocates promoting and performing much of the work of monitoring and investigating these relationships. Many public health researchers over the years have attempted to highlight health inequalities using a variety of socioeconomic measures. Even *Healthy People 2000,* which set decennial public health goals for the 1990s, contains a surprising number of references to income disparities, albeit under the heading "Special Populations." *Healthy People 2000* states:

> For the coming decade, perhaps no challenge is more compelling than that of equity. The disparities experienced by people who are born and live their lives at the lowest income levels define the dimensions of that challenge. The relationships between poverty and health are complex and cannot be reduced to a simple one-to-one relationship between dollars available and levels of health. Low income may, in fact, be a product of poor health, just as poor health may be caused by environmental exposures, material deficiencies, and lack of access to health services that adequate income might correct or improve. While, from a public health perspective, the leverage available to effect improvements is limited largely to the availability and quality of health services, improvements in education, job training, and other social services are necessary to erase the health effects of current income disparities. [pa. 31]

This excerpt from *Healthy People 2000* explicitly identifies equity as a public health objective. Subscribing to the goal of equity is an important rationale for the systematic collection and distribution of information, and for public health and social policy. But there are drawbacks to the approach of *Healthy People 2000*. By emphasizing the health of the poor vs. non-poor, it ignored research showing that social and occupational hierarchies have adverse consequences even at middle and upper socioeconomic levels. It emphasized programs to ameliorate the effects of socioeconomic disparities while taking their existence as a given. The text cited above highlights the "drift hypothesis" which views poverty as a product of poor health, although most evidence points to a far stronger effect of poverty, social class, and inequality on health. On the positive side, *Healthy People 2000* recognized that improvement in health disparities attributable to income differentials will not come solely from improving access to medical care and recognized the importance of cooperation with other sectors, such as education, job training, and social services. In an exciting step forward, the template for *Healthy People 2010* includes race ethnicity, gender, and either income or education, expressed as a modest gradient, for virtually all health goals.

Actions to Reduce Socioeconomic Disparities in Health

Individual behaviors are, to a large extent, shaped by social class position and the material environment. During the past 25 years, U.S. government intervention to improve health has come primarily through initiatives aimed at changing individual behavior and only secondarily through regulatory action; the public has been urged to eliminate cigarette smoking, eat more fruits and vegetables, reduce fat consumption, modify alcohol intake, and use seat belts. Only recently have there been a resurgence of attempts to limit the tobacco companies' marketing efforts and to improve food safety. The agencies charged with regulatory action, including the Food and Drug Administration, the Environmental Protection Agency, and the Occupational Safety and Health Administration, are sometimes successful in socially directed initiatives, although more often embattled.

Recognizing that increasing inequalities in wealth and income during the past 25 years have resulted in disparities in mortality and other health indicators. Cognizant of the power of the *Black Report* and *The Health Divide* in the United Kingdom to serve as rallying points for research and policy change, a number of scientists inside and outside the U.S. government have begun to search for ways to improve the monitoring of inequalities in health and to find new ways to report to the public on socioeconomic inequalities in health. Activities include:

1. The publication in recent years of widely cited papers drawing attention to the worsening consequences of socioeconomic inequalities for health
2. Revised National Institutes of Health (NIH) Guidelines on the Inclusion of Women and Minorities in Clinical Research explicitly encouraging researchers to take into consideration socioeconomic gradients among study populations
3. A multidisciplinary workshop conducted at the National Institute of Child Health and Human Development, NIH in October 1993 on data and measurement issues relating to social class and health, followed by a conference the following fall on the same topic, resulting in recommendations to add and/or improve socioeconomic measures in vital statistics, government and nongovernment health surveys, and disease registries to better monitor social inequalities in health and for research
4. Support by conference participants for what was to have been called the *Lee Report on Social Inequalities in Health in the US,* inspired by the United Kingdom's *Black Report*. The plan was for the *Lee Report* to be prepared at the National Center for Health Statistics (NCHS) under the auspices of Dr. Philip R. Lee, then Assistant Secretary for Health and head of the U.S. Public Health Service. The report became a highly contentious activity partly because of concerns raised by results of the 1994 congressional elections, which had resulted in a conservative Republican majority, and the imminent 1996 presidential election. Ultimately the *Lee Report* was replaced by a chartbook, *Health, United States, 1998* focusing on ethnic and socioeconomic differences in health
5. The 1995 hiring of Norman Anderson, a social psychologist, as the first Associate Director of the Office of Behavioral and Social Science Research, NIH. Anderson's major scientific work has been on the impact of race on hypertension; his conceptual model is explicitly focused on the broader dimension of social inequality.
6. The 1995 conference on "Socioeconomic Status and Cardiovascular Health and Disease," organized by the National Heart, Lung, and Blood Institute
7. Research initiatives of the Centers for Disease Control addressing social class and racial differences in health

8. A series of regional workshops in 1999 sponsored by the National Institute of Environmental Health Sciences on "Decreasing the Gap: Developing a Research Agenda on Socioeconomic Status, Environmental Exposures and Health Disparities"

At the same time, there has been a growing interest in the topic of health inequalities in the private sector. The John D. And Catherine T. MacArthur Foundation's support of a working group to explore how social inequality and specifically social hierarchies "get into the body" led to the creation of a research network. The 1999 meeting of the New York Academy of Sciences at the National Institutes of Health, "Socioeconomic Status and Health in Industrial Nations: Social, Psychological and Biological Pathways," was an important outgrowth of this network. Advocacy groups have joined forces with public health researchers to highlight health inequalities at meetings sponsored by organizations such as the American Public Health Association.

Despite the increase in economic productivity and full employment in the United States during the mid- and late 1990s, inequalities of income and wealth, if not their consequences for health, have enjoyed full play in the *New York Times* and the *Washington Post*. Much thinking and communication about the issue of inequality and its consequences for Americans' well-being has been directed at elite audiences, but more attention needs to be directed at the public-at-large.

How can socioeconomic inequality and its consequences for health become a compelling issue for policymakers and the public as it has in the United Kingdom, where *The Black Report and The Health Divide* received widespread attention? It also has been possible to put health inequalities on the health policy agendas of the Netherlands, Sweden, and Spain as well as the European Union. These efforts have partially counterbalanced the privatization of national insurance, dismantling of social safety nets, and widening income disparities in European nations.

CREATING A PUBLIC POLICY ISSUE: LESSONS FROM EUROPEAN COLLEAGUES

While member countries have varied in the attention given to health inequalities as a policy issue, the European Union has identified it as a priority research area. Public debate on inequality in Europe is part of a long tradition supported by powerful political parties. The United States has neither the collective support of a supranational body nor a major political party that is comfortable addressing inequality. The United States and Europe differ in two other important ways. The United States has lacked the visible social crises and political and economic deterioration experienced in some areas of western and eastern Europe and the former Yugoslavia. While inequalities in income and wealth as well as in health have increased in the United States during the past 25 years, the mid-to-late 1990s has been a time of prosperity with decreasing unemployment and real income gains for some, though not all, population groups. Also, while both North America and Europe are experiencing population aging, public concern in the United States centers not around the vulnerability of the elderly but around the impact of the costs of services for the aging baby boom cohort. On the other hand, the United States shares with Europe a widening gap in health status between those better and worse off socioeconomically.

Public action in European countries has depended on different country-specific strategies. The Dutch found, for example, that including a broad spectrum of governmental and non-governmental policy makers was as important as the language used to frame policy debate. In the Netherlands, politicians were more eager to act when debate centered "on the wasted potential attributable to the excess morbidity and mortality of the more disadvantaged social groups" than when the discussion concerned social justice or equity.

The atmosphere around health policy in the United Kingdom was contentious following the release of *The Black Report* and throughout the Thatcher period. Britain lacked the widespread agreement of a broad spectrum of advocacy organizations or politicians that health inequalities constituted a major public policy issue. Nonetheless, organizations like the King's Fund and civil servants in the Department of Health were able to reverse this dismal situation over time, working through European Union activities and within the United Kingdom by modifying their rhetoric, keeping up a steady stream of pressure in elite publications such as the *BMJ* and *Lancet,* and making sure that the effect of poverty on well-being was highlighted in the popular media. *The Black Report* and its successor, *The Black Report and The Health Divide,* have received widespread attention, and there have been a number of other reports on socioeconomic variations in health.

Success in putting health inequalities on the public agenda in Europe has depended upon some of the same strategies that have been successful in getting public health issues such as adolescent pregnancy and infant mortality on the policy agenda in the United States. These include:

1. *Bringing research evidence to the attention of decision-makers* by using elite publications including academic journals and national press; special reports that are visible and highly readable; and popular media that help to fan public attention
2. *Reframing the categories and attending to language* in ways that obtain and encourage consensus among divergent factions and agencies. Focusing on equity, disparities, and variations in health proved more palatable than talking about inequality
3. *Keeping action steps firmly in view* of policy makers and advocates. These include policy alternatives as well as recommendations on measuring and monitoring
4. *Communicating across a wide variety of settings and constituencies,* using different media
5. *Playing on public and political concern about international ranking*

6. *Linking common goals* and action targets across agencies
7. *Developing a research program* supported by elite foundations, scientific agencies, and other shapers of the policy agenda
8. Encouraging advocates, including authoritative medical and scientific organizations, to *design realistic policy alternatives*
9. *Creating networks* among public and private agencies and advocates to evaluate and disseminate policy options

What Should the United States Do to Take Action on Inequalities in Health?

The foregoing suggests that strategies can be grouped into three categories: those that raise the awareness level among the general public and policy makers as well as among scientists and advocates; those that address the policies at the federal, state, and local level that shape inequality; and the development of interventions that target the mediators and consequences of socioeconomic disparities in health. A first step in the United States is to create a climate of unacceptability for socioeconomic differentials in health. In order to do this, the European experience suggests that the U.S. public health community should undertake the following activities:

1. *Improve measures and data sources* at local, state and national levels, and in the public and private sectors. Local health and hospital systems can improve their socioeconomic data as, for example, a working group at Kaiser Permanente, the oldest and largest health maintenance organization in the United States, has attempted to implement in the 1990s in order to better monitor the health of its own patient populations. Core national health data sets should have the most succinct, best-validated socioeconomic measures.
2. *Use the data which are available.* Many socioeconomic measures are available in state and local health data systems but too often the will or the resources to analyze them are not available. State and local advocacy groups can draw renewed attention to the availability of these data and pressure for increased funds for analysis, reporting, and dissemination.
3. *Make sure that research findings are disseminated* to popular as well as to scholarly audiences. The growth of the Internet, the development of geographic information systems, and other new technologies are available to assist in this process.
4. *Build on already existing initiatives* that have some credibility, for example, through the World Health Organization, *Healthy People,* and the Healthy Cities program, and they should interweave attention to socioeconomic variations in health into behavior and disease-based initiatives.
5. *Create multi-sectoral alliances* that cut across political boundaries. A decade ago, public, professional, and congressional concern with infant mor-

tality led to the formation of the National Commission to Prevent Infant Mortality and to a governmental interagency committee to coordinate activities. Partnerships could be created between public health advocates and officials with colleagues and agencies in education, labor, and justice; these agencies have a stake in the consequences of increased socioeconomic disparities in the United States, and maintain their own research and policy staffs. Shared goals and moderate language facilitate intersectoral and cross-party alliances.

6. State, county and city health departments could *take the lead in forming task forces* to monitor, report on, and design interventions to tackle socioeconomic differences in health. Task forces have mobilized communities around adolescent pregnancy, infant mortality, and AIDS. While the health of the poor, vulnerable, and "special" populations is a natural focus at the community level, it will be important to educate the public about relationships that transcend all gradations in social hierarchies.

7. Move away from the concept of the dependent poor and *highlight the human potential presented by reducing socioeconomic disparities in health.* These include a more productive workforce; the lessening of social and interpersonal violence; diminished costs of health care; and other economic as well as equity rationales.

8. *Use media creatively.* In 1996 Channel 4 (ITV) in the United Kingdom broadcast a series on poverty created by a small commission that included Peter Townsend among its members. The series attracted significant media attention.

9. Groups concerned with equity in health should try to *attract new funders.* Foundation assets have grown significantly during the 1990s, and a number of foundations are experiencing changes in leadership that open up new opportunities for individuals concerned about socioeconomic disparities in health. Academics and advocates have a role to play in shaping funders' priorities, and foundations often help to form the vanguard of public opinion. Conservatives have learned this lesson well by successfully using institutions such as the Heritage Foundation and the Manhattan Institute to shape public discourse.

10. *Healthy People* should move from framing health goals for poor and nonpoor populations to *establish quantitative targets to reduce health disparities across the socioeconomic spectrum,* while still recognizing the disproportionate disadvantage borne by vulnerable populations including the poor.

CONCLUSION

The renewed interest in socioeconomic disparities in health, sparked by growing inequality in an era of unprecedented prosperity suggests that it is time to bring new thinking to this area. Although data from the United Kingdom and other Western European countries suggest that universal health care does not dissolve inequalities in outcomes, they provide instructive examples of how, with will, imagination, and energy, health inequalities can be tackled at local and national levels. Recent general prosperity in the United States and the beginning of a new century provide an opportune moment for conveying the discussion of socioeconomic inequalities in health from academic to popular and policy discourse and action.

ABOUT THE AUTHOR

Nancy Moss, PhD, a social demographer, served as Special Expert at the National Institutes of Health from 1989 through 1996, where she took the lead in initiatives on social class and Latino ethnicity in health. Much of her work has examined the consequences of social and economic policy, including WIC, Medicaid, and anti-immigrant legislation, and the health of women and infants. Dr. Moss is a consultant and an Associate of the Pacific Institute for Women's Health.

REFERENCES

Adler NE, Boyce T, Chesney MA, et al. Socioeconomic status and health: the challenge of the gradient. *American Psychol.* 1994;49:15–24.

Amick BC III, Levine S, Tarlov A, Walsh DC. eds. *Society and Health* New York: Oxford University Press, 1995;3–17.

Anderson, N. Psychosocial, behavioral and educational factors that affect population differences in health among women. Paper presented at "Beyond Hunt Valley: Research on Women's Health for the 21st Century." Office of Research on Women's Health, National Institutes of Health, Santa Fe, NM: July 22–23, 1997.

Antonovsky, A. Social class, life expectancy and overall mortality. *Milbank Q* 1967;45:31–73.

Atkinson A, Rainwater L, Smeeding T. Income distribution in advanced economies: evidence from the Luxembourg Income Study. Working Paper no. 120, Maxwell School of Citizenship and Public Affairs, Syracuse University, Syracuse, NY. 1995a.

Atkinson AB, Rainwater L, Smeeding TM. *Income Distribution in OECD Countries.* Paris: Organisation for Economic Cooperation and Development, 1995b.

Barker DJP. *Mothers, Babies and Health in Later Life.* Edinburgh: Churchill Livingstone, 1998.

Benzeval M, Judge K, Whitehead M. eds. *Tackling Inequalities in Health: an Agenda for Action.* London: King's Fund, 1995.

Berkman LF, Macintyre S. The measurement of social class in health studies: old measures and new formulations. In, Kogevinas M, Pearce N, Susser M, Boffeta P. eds. *Social Inequalities and Cancer.* IARC Scientific Publications No. 138. Lyon: International Agency for Research on Cancer, 1996.

Bradsher K. Gap in wealth in US called widest in West. *New York Times,* April 17, 1995, A1, D4.

Braveman P. *Equity in Health and Health Care: A WHO/SIDA Initiative.* Geneva: World Health Organization, 1996.

Cancian M, Danziger S, Gottschalk P. The changing contributions of men and women to the level and distribution of family income, 1968–88. In: Papadimitriou G, Wolff E. *Poverty and Prosperity in the Late Twentieth Century,* New York: Macmillan, 1993;317–353.

Citro CF, Michael RT. eds. *Measuring Poverty: A New Approach.* Washington, DC: National Academy Press, 1995.

Danziger S, Gottschalk P. *America Unequal.* Cambridge, MA: Harvard University Press, 1995.

Davey Smith G, Egger M. Socioeconomic differentials in wealth and health: Widening inequalities in health- the legacy of the Thatcher years. *BMJ.* 1993;307:1085–1086.

Duncan GJ, Smeeding TM, Rodgers W. W(h)ither the middle class? A dynamic view. In: Papadimitriou G, Wolff E. eds. *Poverty and Prosperity in the Late Twentieth Century.* New York: Macmillan, 1993;240–271.

Duncan GJ. Income dynamics and health. *Internat J Health Serv.* 1996;26:419–444.

Elo IT, Preston SN. Effects of early life conditions on adult mortality: A Review. *Population Index.* 1992;58:186–212.

Guest AM, Almgren G. The ecology of race and socioeconomic distress: infant and working-age mortality in Chicago. *Demography.* 1998;35:23–34.

Haines A, Smith R. Working together to reduce poverty's damage: Doctors fought nuclear weapons, now they can fight poverty (editorial). *BMJ.* 1997;314:529–530.

Hemingway H, Nicholson A, Stafford M, Roberts R, Marmot M. The impact of socioeconomic status on health functioning as assessed by the SF-36 questionnaire: the Whitehall II study. *Am J Pub Health.* 1997;87:1484–1490.

Kaplan GA, Lynch JW, Cohen RD, Balfour JL. Inequality in income and mortality in the United States: analysis of mortality and potential pathways. *BMJ.* 1996;312:999–1003.

Kaplan GA. People and places: contrasting perspectives on the association between social class and health. *Internat J Health Serv.* 1996;26:507–519.

Karasek R, Theorell T. *Healthy Work: Stress, Productivity and the Reconstruction of Working Life.* New York: Basic Books, 1990.

Kennedy BP, Kawachi I, Prothrow-Stith D. Income distribution and mortality: cross-sectional ecological study of the Robin Hood index in the United States. *BMJ.* 1996;312:1004–1007.

Krieger N, Chen JT, Ebel G. Can we monitor socioeconomic inequalities in health? A survey of US health departments' data collection and reporting practices. *Public Health Reports.* 1997;112:481–494.

Krieger N, Williams DR, Moss NE. Measuring social class in US public health research: concepts, methodologies, and guidelines. *Annu Rev Public Health.* 1997;18:341–378.

Krieger N, Fee E. Measuring social inequalities in health in the United States: a historical review, 1900–1950. *Internat J Health Serv.* 1996;26:391–418.

Krieger N, Moss N. Accounting for the public's health: an introduction to selected papers from a U.S. conference on "Measuring Social Inequalities in Health." *Internat J Health Serv.* 1996;26:383–390.

Kuh D, Ben-Shlomo Y eds. *A Lifecourse Approach to Chronic Disease Epidemiology: Tracing the Origins of Ill-Health from Early to Adult Life.* Oxford: Oxford University Press, 1997.

Larin, K, McNichol E. *Pulling Apart: A State-by-State Analysis of Income Trends.* Washington, DC: Center on Budget and Policy Priorities, 1997.

Luker K. *Dubious Conceptions: The Politics of Teenage Pregnancy.* Berkeley, CA: University of California Press, 1996.

Lynch J, Kaplan GA, Cohen RD, Kauhunen J, Wilson TW, Smith NL, Salonen JT. Childhood and adult socioeconomic status as predictors of mortality in Finland. *Lancet.* 1994;343:524–527.

Marmor TR, Barer ML, Evans RG. The determinants of a population's health. In: Evans RG, Barer ML, Marmor TR. eds. *Why are Some People Healthy and Others Not?* New York: Aldine de Gruyter, 1994;217–230.

Marmot M, Bobak M, Davey Smith G. Explanations for social inequalities in health. In: Amick III BC, Levine S, Tarlov AR, Chapman Walsh D. eds. *Society and Health,* New York: Oxford University Press, 1995;172–210.

Massey DS, Denton NA. *American Apartheid and the Making of the Underclass.* Cambridge, MA: Harvard University Press, 1993.

Miller SM. Thinking strategically about society and health. In: Amick III BC, Levine S, Tarlov AR, Chapman Walsh D. eds. *Society and Health.* New York: Oxford University Press, 1995;342–358.

Moss N, Krieger N. Measuring social inequalities in health. *Public Health Reports.* 1995;110:302–305.

Nathanson, C. *Dangerous Passage: The Social Control of Sexuality in Women's Adolescence.* Philadelphia: Temple University Press, 1991.

Pamuk E, Makuc D, Heck K, Reuben C, Lochner K. *Socioeconomic Status and Health Chartbook. Health, United States, 1998.* Hyattsville, MD: National Center for Health Statistics, 1998.

Pappas G, Queen S, Hadden W, Fisher G. The increasing disparity between socioeconomic groups in the United States, 1960 and 1986. *New Eng J Med.* 1993;329:103–109.

Pérez-Peña R. New York's income gap largest in nation. *New York Times,* December 17, 1997, A25.

Recommendations of the Conference: Measuring Social Inequalities in Health. *Internat J Health Serv.* 1996;26:521–527.

Rich, S. Study finds nest eggs vary greatly. *Washington Post,* July 25, 1995, A11.

Rowley D, Tosteson H. eds. Racial Differences in Preterm Delivery: Developing a New Research Paradigm. *Am J Prevent Med.* 1993;9(suppl.).

Smith JP, Kington RS. Demographic and economic correlates of health in old age. *Demography.* 1997a;34:159–170.

Smith JP, Kington RS. Race, socioeconomic status, and health in later life. In: Martin LG, Soldo BJ. eds. *Racial and Ethnic Differences in the Health of Older Americans.* Washington, DC: National Academy Press, 1997b.

The National Commission to Prevent Infant Mortality *Death before Life: The Tragedy of Infant Mortality.* Washington, DC: United States Congress, 1988.

The Report of the Channel 4 Commission on Poverty. *The Great, the Good, and the Dispossessed.* London: Channel Four Television, 1996.

Townsend P, Davidson N, Whitehead M. *Inequalities in Health: The Black Report and The Health Divide.* London: Penguin Books, 1992.

UK Department of Health. Variations Sub-Group of the Chief Medical Officer's Health of the Nation Working Group. *The Health of the Nation. Variations in Health. What Can the Department of Health and the NHS Do?* London: Department of Health, 1996.

US Department of Commerce, Bureau of the Census. Current Population Reports, Series P60–185, *Poverty in the United States, 1992.* Washington, DC: Government Printing Office, 1993.

US Department of Health and Human Services, Public Health Service. *Healthy People 2000: National Health Promotion and Disease Prevention Objectives.* DHHS Publication No. (PHS) 91–50213. Washington, DC: Government Printing Office, 1991.

Vagero D. Health inequalities as policy issues—reflections on ethics, policy and public health. *Sociol Health Illness* 1995;17:1–19.

Weinberg D. *A Brief Look at Postwar U.S. Income Inequality.* Current Population Reports, P60–191. Washington, DC: US Department of Commerce, Bureau of the Census, 1996.

Weinberg D. *Money Income in the United States: 1996.* Washington, DC: US Department of Commerce, Bureau of the Census, 1997.

Whitehead M. *Bridging the Gap: Working towards Equity in Health and Health Care.* Sundyberg, Sweden: Karolinska Institutet, 1997.

Whitehead M. Diffusion of ideas on social inequalities in health: a European perspective. *Milbank Q.* 1998;76:469–492.

Whitehead M, Dahlgren G. What can be done about inequalities in health? *Lancet.* 1991;338:1059–1063.

Whitehead M, Scott-Samuel A, Dahlgren G. Setting targets to address inequalities in health. *Lancet.* 1998;351:1279–1282.

Wilkinson RG. "Variations in health" the costs of government timidity (editorial). *BMJ.* 1995;311:1177–1178.

Wilkinson RG. *Unhealthy Societies: The Afflictions of Inequality.* London: Routledge, 1996.

Williams DR. Race and health: basic questions, emerging directions. *Ann. Epidemiol.* 1997a;7:322–333.

Williams DR. Missed opportunities in monitoring socioeconomic status. *Public Health Reports.* 1997b;112:492–494.

Williams DR, Collins C. US socioeconomic and racial differences in health:patterns and explanations. *Ann Rev Sociol* 1995;21:49–86.

Williamson G, Lindert PH. *American Inequality: A Macroeconomic History.* New York: Academic Press, 1980.

Wilson WJ. *The Truly Disadvantaged: The Inner City, the Underclass, and Public Policy.* Chicago: University of Chicago Press, 1987.

Wilson WJ. *When Work Disappears: The World of the New Urban Poor.* New York: Alfred A. Knopf, 1996.

Wolff EN. *Top Heavy: A Study of Increasing Inequality of Wealth in America.* New York: The Twentieth Century Fund Press, 1995.

ARTICLE 3

RACE OR CLASS VERSUS RACE AND CLASS: MORTALITY DIFFERENTIALS IN THE UNITED STATES

Vicente Navarro

The latest annual report of the US federal government about the health of the US population[1] has created enormous concern about the mortality differentials between whites and blacks. For example, in 1988 life expectancy at birth was 75.5 years for whites but only 69.5 years for blacks. For most causes of death, the death rate in blacks is higher than that in whites, and for many causes of death mortality differentials are increasing rather than decreasing. Alarming reports about these differences have appeared in both the lay press[2] and medical publications.[3] Consequently, it makes sense that the federal government has chosen the reduction of these differentials as one of its top objectives and has called for a "decrease [of the] disparity in life expectancy between white and minority populations to no more than four years."[4]

Although this emphasis on reducing race differentials is undoubtedly very important, another component of the nation's health that is highly relevant to race differentials in mortality has passed unnoticed. The stark fact is that these differentials cannot be explained merely by looking at race. After all, some blacks have better health indicators (including mortality rates) than some whites, and not all whites have similar mortality indicators. Thus we must look at class differentials in mortality in the US, which are also increasing rather than declining. Class is harder to define than race, but the most frequent indicators of social class used for morbidity and mortality statistics in the western industrialised world are occupation, education, and income.[5]

IMPORTANCE OF CLASS DIFFERENTIALS

The US is the only western developed nation whose government does not collect mortality statistics by class. The federal report[1] on health indicators in the US— *Health, United States, 1989*—tabulates mortality statistics by age, sex, and race but

79

not by class indicators such as income, education, or occupation. With the active encouragement of the European office of the World Health Organisation, most European countries have chosen as the top target in their health policies a reduction, by the year 2000, of the differentials in health status among classes.[6] By contrast, the US is alone among major industrialised nations is not aiming for this goal—in the US, race is used as a *substitute* for class. What the US government seems to ignore is that even if there were no race differentials in mortality, most blacks would still have higher mortality rates than the median or the mean rate in the US population. To understand this point, one has to appreciate that the US has classes as well as races.

How people live, die, and get sick depends not only on their race, gender, and age but also on the class to which they belong. There is empirical information to sustain this position. On one of the few occasions (in 1986) that the US government collected information on mortality rates (for heart and cerebrovascular disease) by class, the results showed that, by whatever indicators of class one might choose (level of education, income, or occupation), mortality rates are related to social class. People with less formal education, with lower income, and belonging to the working class (eg, labourers in the US Census categories of operator and services) are more likely to die of heart disease than are people with more formal education, with higher income, and belonging to the upper classes (eg, managerial and professional).[7]

Mortality Differentials

Managerial and professional groups had lower mortality rates for heart disease than did major components of the working class, such as operators and service workers.

Data from the same survey (1986 National Mortality Followback Survey) also show that most of those who died of cerebrovascular disease and all other causes had family incomes of less than $25,000 in 1985 and less than a high school education; the largest proportion of the deceased had worked in technical, sales, and operator occupations—the main occupational groups in the working class.[8] Similar class mortality differentials have been found for breast cancer and for all causes of death.[9,10]

For both causes of mortality—heart disease and cerebrovascular disease—the class differentials in mortality were larger than the race differentials. The mortality rate for heart disease in blue-collar workers (operators) was 2.3 times higher than the rate in managers and professionals.

For 1986, the heart disease mortality rate for black males was 1.2 times higher than for white males, and for black females was 1.5 times higher than for white females.[11]

Morbidity Differentials

Although there are no published data to show mortality rates by class and race, it is likely that the mortality rates for white service workers, for example, are closer to those of black service workers than to those of white professionals. Since there are no data to establish this point, we can look instead at data on morbidity. Morbidity differentials by class are much larger than differentials by race. In 1986, those making $10,000 or less per year reported 4.6 times more morbidity than those making over $35,000, while blacks reported 1.9 times more morbidity than whites.[12] The race differentials were less than half the class differentials. The same report shows that race differentials within each income group are less pronounced than those between income groups. Morbidity rates for blacks making less than $20,000 were much closer to those for whites in the same income group than to those for blacks in income groups greater than $20,000. Similarly, morbidity rates for whites with incomes below $20,000 were closer to those of blacks in the same income group than to those of whites in income groups over $20,000. Whites making under $20,000 had higher morbidity rates than blacks earning over $20,000.

A similar pattern is observed when occupation is used rather than income. Thus blue-collar workers (operators) reported a morbidity rate (9.5%) that was 2.9 times higher than that of professionals (3.2%), while blacks reported a morbidity rate 1.9 times higher than that of whites.[13]

Consideration of the annual percentage of persons with limited activity due to chronic conditions rather than self-reported morbidity provides further confirmation. Class differentials (measured by income differentials) are larger than race differentials.[14] Moreover, these class differentials have grown larger during the 1980s—even larger than race differentials.

DISPARITY OF WEALTH AND INCOME BY CLASS

Within each class (measured by education, income, or occupation), blacks often have worse health indicators than whites. These are the differentials that the US government is targeting for reduction, an important and much-needed task. But the overwhelming majority of blacks (and other minorities) are members of the low-paid, poorly educated working class that have higher morbidity and mortality rates than high-earning, better educated people. The growing mortality differentials between whites and blacks cannot be understood by looking only at race; they are part and parcel of larger mortality differentials—class differentials. In the 1980s, the US witnessed an increased class polarisation of the population, with a reduction of the middle class, and a rapid growth of the low-paid, unskilled working class. Members of the working class are increasingly nonunionised, poorly paid, and part-time, and with a preponderance of minorities and women. The low-earners comprise a heterogeneous group—blacks, Hispanics, whites, men, and women—whose standards of living are rapidly deteriorating because of the growing wealth and income differentials between the upper and lower classes. These social groups belong to the 40% of the population who received only 15.7% of the total income in 1984, the lowest figure since data collection was initiated in 1947. By contrast, the wealthiest 20% received 42.9% of total income, the highest ever.[15] This growing disparity of wealth and income by class mainly, but not exclusively, explains the race differentials in morbidity and mortality.

The growing class differential in mortality rates is not unique to the US. Other countries have noticed that these differentials are not only persistent but growing,[16] and a large national and international debate about the reasons for these class differentials has been initiated.[17] However, in the US there is a deafening silence on this topic. If a prerequisite for finding the right answer is to ask the right question, then it is unlikely that by concentrating solely on race differentials we will ever be able to understand why the health indicators of our minorities are getting worse.

ABOUT THE AUTHOR

Vicente Navarro, PhD, is Professor of Public Policy, Sociology and Policy Studies, Department of Health Policy and Management, School of Hygiene and Public Health at Johns Hopkins University in Baltimore, Maryland.

REFERENCES

1. Health, United States, 1989. Washington, DC: US Department of Health and Human Services, 1990.

2. US health gap is widening between whites and blacks. *New York Times,* March 23, 1990: A17.

3. Greenberg DS. Black health: grim statistics. *Lancet.* 1990;335:780–81.

4. Goals for the nation for the year 2000. Washington, DC: Public Health Service, US Department of Health and Human Services, 1989.

5. Liberatos P, Link GB, Kelsey LJ. The measurement of social class in epidemiology. *Epidemiol Rev.* 1988;10:87–121.

6. Targets for health for all: targets in support of the European regional strategy for health for all. Copenhagen: World Health Organisation, Regional Office for Europe, 1980:24–25.

7. Kapantais G, Powell-Griner E. Characteristics of persons dying of diseases of the heart. Preliminary data from the 1986 national mortality follow-back survey. Washington, DC: National Center for Health Statistics. Advance data from vital and health statistics. No. 172, Aug. 24, 1989: 7, 9, 12 (tables 3, 4, 5).

8. Powell-Griner E. Characteristics of persons dying from cerebrovascular diseases. Washington, DC: National Center for Health Statistics. Preliminary data from vital and health statistics, No. 180, Feb. 8, 1990: 2–3.

9. Krieger N. Social class and the black white crossover in the age-specific incidence of breast cancer: a study linking census derived data to population-based registry records. *Am J Epidemiol.* 1990;131:804–14.

10. Marmot MG, Kogevinas M, Elston MA. Social economic status and disease. *Annu Rev Publ Health.* 1987;8:111–13.

11. Age adjusted death rates for selected causes of death, according to sex and race: United States, selected years, 1950–87. Table 23 in Health, United States, 1989. Washington, DC: US Department of Health and Human Services, 1990:121–22.

12. Self assessment of health according to race and income. Table 45 in Health, United States, 1987. Washington, DC: US Department of Health and Human Services, 1988:91.

13. Percent of persons 18 years of age and over in the labor force with respondent-assessed health status of either fair or poor, by employment status and by occupation: US, 1983–85. Table D in Health Characteristics by Occupation and Industry: US, 1983–85. Washington, DC: US Department of Health and Human Services, 1989:11.

14. Average annual percent of persons with limitation of activity due to chronic conditions by race, age, and family income: US, 1985–87. Fig. 4 in Health of black and white Americans, 1985–87. Vital and health statistics. Washington, DC: National Center for Health Statistics, 1990; ser 10, no 171:12.

15. Harrison B, Bluestone B. The great U-turn: corporate restructuring and the polarization of America. New York: Basic Books, 1988:128.

16. Vagerö, D, Lundberg O. Health inequalities in Britain and Sweden. *Lancet.* 1989;ii:35–36,

17. Townsend P. Widening inequalities of health: a rejoinder to Rudolph Klein. *Int J Health Serv.* 1990;20:363–72.

PART 2

HEALTH POLICY AND THE POLITICS OF HEALTH

CHAPTER 3

HEALTH POLICY

In this chapter we use the term *policy,* as does Longest in his book, *Health Policymaking in the United States* (1998), to describe public policies. These are, he notes, "authoritative decisions that are made in the legislative, executive or judicial branches of government. These decisions are intended to direct or influence the actions, behaviors, or decisions of others" (p. 4). The same definition can be applied to long-term care policy, which focuses on areas such as skilled nursing home care, home health care, adult day care, and meals on wheels programs. Health policy and long-term care decisions are made at the federal, state, and local levels. The various forms of health policy described by Longest include laws, rules/regulations, and judicial decisions; and he adds macropolicies, such as Medicare and the regulation of pharmaceuticals, which are in fact a reflection of laws, regulations, and judicial decisions (e.g., a women's right to privacy in the 1973 Supreme Court decision in *Rowe v. Wade* related to a woman's choice of whether or not to have an abortion). Initially, the federal government had little engagement in health or long-term care policies, except with foreign quarantine and medical care for merchant seamen, soldiers, and sailors (U.S. Navy). With the advent of the sanitary revolution, states and local governments began to establish departments of health or public health to deal with communicable diseases. At the local level, medical care was mostly a private affair of little health benefit to the patients or the community. Gradually, local governments assumed responsibility for the care of the indigent sick, including the elderly, through municipal hospitals.

The Marine Hospital/Service, which was established in 1798, became the U.S. Public Health Service in 1912. However, it was almost 90 years before the first elements of the modern U.S. Public Health Service were established. It began with the creation of the Hygienic Laboratory in 1887, which became the National Institute of Health in 1930. Then, the Food and Drug Administration followed, tracing its origins to the Biologics Control Act of 1902 and the Pure Food and Drug Act of 1906.

The Programs of the Indian Health Service were first authorized in 1921. These were transferred to the U.S. Public Health Service in 1955. The multiple categorical grant-in-aid programs for public health that made provisions for maternal and child health had their origins in the Social Security Act of 1935. Soon tuberculosis control and venereal disease control programs were added in the late 1930s and early 1940s. These programs grew gradually after World War II, until a proliferation of categorical public health programs in the 1960s and 1970s. Programs to treat mental illness were first authorized by Congress in 1948, but it was not until the 1970s that major public health programs were launched to deal with substance abuse. In 1944, the Program for Malarial Control in War Zones became the Communicable Disease Control Program and later the Centers for Disease Control and Prevention. A number of environmental health programs, such as air and water pollution control, which began in the U.S. Public Health Service, were transferred to other agencies and departments in the 1960s and 1970s, including the Environmental Protection Agency. The Nation's Highway Safety Administration/Department of Transportation and the Occupational Safety and Health Administration/Department of Labor became the base for highway safety and occupational safety and health programs in the late 1960s and early 1970s. It was not until 1965, when Medicare and Medicaid joined the range of federal health programs, that substantial federal health spending was first directed toward medical care as opposed to public health programs. However, they were soon to consume the bulk of federal dollars devoted to the nation's health.

Today, policymakers and citizens continue to debate the relative efficacy of various methods to tackle the fragmentation in financing and provision of health care and long-term care. Because of its costs, the custodial nature of much long-term care, and the lack of effective treatments for many of the disabling illnesses of old age (e.g., Alzheimer's disease), it has never had the priority at the federal or state level accorded by health care. The formulation of health policy across several levels of government and hundreds of programs is complex. The health policy framework described by Longest in this chapter is widely accepted. Barr, Lee, and Benjamin (1999) identified four characteristics of the policy process in the United States: (1) the American character; (2) federalism and the role of government in health care; (3) pluralism and the role of special interest groups; (4) and incrementalism as the principal means of health policy. All of these characteristics enter into attempts to deal with current problems of crippling cost escalation, high expenditures for administration, the commercialization of medicine, the trend toward defensive medicine, the erosion of physician authority, the lack of access to health care for increasing numbers of U.S. citizens, and the deterioration of the public health infrastructure, particularly at the local level. Twenty years ago, in her book, *The Aging Enterprise* (1979), Estes described the equally fragmented state of politics related to long-term care. The article "Eighty Health Programs for the Elderly," which describes many of the programs that bear on the multiple issues related to long-term care policy today, illustrates the problem.

Crafting workable policy solutions is thus a very complex and dynamic endeavor. While we deal separately with health and long-term care politics, it is important to recognize their interconnection. In this edition of *The Nation's Health,* we have included "Health Care and Health Policy in a Changing World" in which Barr, Lee, and Benjamin update the previous work of Lee and Benjamin (1993) and identify and discuss the political influences on health policy formulation over the past 200 years. The authors' documentation of the evolution of U.S. health policy indicates that although consensus has emerged about the nature of the problems confronting the system, by no means is there agreement on the solutions. This conclusion was reflected in the health care reform debates of the early nineties. Even when the nation was engaged in a major debate on health systems reform in 1993 and 1994, disagreements about how such reform was to be accomplished and the influence of interest groups produced a deadlock in the policy process.

In their discussion of incrementalism as the principal means of health policy reform, they note the value of understanding the policy process first described by Kingdon (1995) and more recently by Longest (1998) through a conceptual framework or model. Because we have found the description of the process by Longest very useful, we include the description of the conceptual model from his book (pp. 55–63) and we include his last chapter in our Recommended Reading. Longest's book is devoted largely to a detailed development of the phases in health policy making: policy formulation and policy implementation phases, with both subsequently influenced by policy modification.

Included in the article by Barr, Lee, and Benjamin in addition to the factors influencing policy making, is a short history of the four distinct periods in the evolution of health policy:

1. A limited role for the federal government (1798–1862)
2. The emergence of a larger federal role (1862–1932)
3. The expansion of the federal role (1935–1969)
4. New Federalism (1969–Present)

While President Nixon first coined the phrase "New Federalism" to describe in broad terms his approach to domestic policy, he nonetheless had a very expansive view of the federal role in health. In his special message to Congress on health, "National Health Strategy—A Comprehensive Health Policy for the 1970s," he maintained that the federal government bears a special responsibility in three areas: (1) to help all citizens achieve equal access, removing racial, economic, social, and geographic barriers to health care; (2) to balance supply and demand; and, (3) not merely "to finance a more expansive system" but to organize "a more efficient one" (Cater, 1979). This was a time when access to adequate health care was considered a right, not a privilege, by many health policy makers and the public. How times have changed.

Nixon introduced legislation not only to provide national health insurance through an employer mandate but also to establish health maintenance organizations (HMOs) and fund a war on cancer. His health insurance proposal failed, but both the

HMO legislation and the war on cancer were enacted. He also championed the creation of the Environmental Protection Agency.

New federalism took a different direction under President Reagan with budget reductions in exchange for the transfer of the authority for many categorical programs to the States in the form of block grants (e.g., mental health and substance abuse, maternal and child health, and prevention). This trend was reemphasized by President Clinton and the Republican Congress when the 80-year-old Aid to Families with Dependent Children (AFDC) program was terminated in favor of creating Federal Grants to States for Welfare, which stress work instead of a continued welfare dependency.

After the failure of President Clinton's health care reform proposal and the Republicans' capture of Congress in 1994, as well as the government's shutdown stemming from the president's opposition to proposed Republican budget cuts in 1995, the approach has been one of confrontation (e.g., the battle over the federal budget of fiscal year 2000) and incremental reform. The major pieces of health care reform legislation have included the Health Insurance Portability and Accountability Act of 1996 (Kennedy–Kassebaum), the Food and Drug Amendments of 1997, and the Balanced Budget Act of 1997, which included the most significant reform in Medicare since its enactment in 1965. Disputes arose between the Republicans and the Democrats in 1999 regarding the allocation of current and projected budget surplus, which emerged as a result of rigorous efforts by the Clinton Administration and the Congress to balance the budget, beginning with legislation enacted (with only Democratic support) in the summer of 1993. High on President Clinton's agenda is assuring the continued soundness of the Medicare Program in the upcoming millennia. As such, much of the debate has centered on the possibility of endowing the Medicare trust fund (Part A) and the medical insurance component (Part B) with additional funds.

In light of these ever-pressing disagreements and failed policy attempts, however, we have included the introduction from Sherry Glied's book, *Chronic Condition: Why Health Reform Fails,* in Chapter 3. Glied provides an excellent description of what happened in health reform, and she addresses the fact that this issue of health care reform never goes away. She contrasts the views of the medicalists (favor single-payer models) and marketists (favor managed competition models) and discusses why neither approach can resolve the issues that must be addressed. She proposes a direct tax on health care spending that provides a fresh, creative approach that should be considered.

A key health policy issue, indeed one that affects much of domestic policy, is dealt with by Estes and Linkins in their article "Decentralization, Devolution, and the Deficit: The Changing Role of the States and the Community" from their 1998 text. They deal first with the issue of the very legitimacy of the state (government) in a range of public policy areas. Then, they deal with another critical issue, the definition of privatization and the emphasis placed in achieving national goals in the nonprofit sector (emphasized in the 1960s–1980s) and the for-profit sector (emphasized particularly by Presidents Reagan and Bush and, more recently, the Republican-controlled Congress).

Federal issues are as old as the republic, and the current debate on devolution began with President Nixon's "New Federalism" of the 1970s, with significant modifications by Presidents Reagan and Clinton. Hacker and Skocpol (see Chapter 5) also deal with this issue. In their chapter, they use both managed care and long-term care for the elderly to highlight the issues of decentralization and devolution.

In summary, health policy deals with authoritative decisions by government, including the legislative, executive, and judicial branches. The role of the federal government in health policy has changed dramatically, particularly since the enactment of Medicare and Medicaid in 1965. While there is often agreement on the issues (e.g., the HIV/AIDS epidemic, controlling the rising costs of health care), there is often strong disagreement among the political parties on the solutions.

REFERENCES

Barr DA, Lee PR, Benjamin AE. Health care and health care policy in a changing world. In Wallace H, Green G, Jaros KJ, Paine LL, Story M (eds.). *Health and Welfare for Families in the 21st Century. Boston, MA, Jones & Bartlett, 1999;13–29.*

Cater D, Lee PR (eds.). *Politics of Health.* Robert E. Krieger, Huntington, NY, 1979.

Estes CL. *The Aging Enterprise: A Critical Examination of Social Policies and Services for the Aged.* Jossey-Bass Publishers, San Francisco, 1979; 76–117.

Estes CL, Linkins KW. Decentralization, devolution, and the deficit: The changing role of the state and the community. In Gonyea JG (ed.). *Resecuring Social Security and Medicare: Understanding Privatization and Risk.* The Gerontological Society of America, Washington, DC, 1998; 37–43.

Glied S. *Chronic Condition: Why Health Reform Fails.* Harvard University Press, Cambridge, MA, 1997; 1–16.

Kingdon JW. *Agendas, Alternatives, and Public Policies* (2nd ed.). Harper Collins, New York, 1995.

Lee PR, Benjamin AE. Health policy and the politics of health care. In Williams SJ, Torrens PR (eds.). *Introduction to Health Services* (4th ed.). Baltimore, MD, Delmar Publishers, 1993.

Longest, BB. *Health Policymaking in the United States* (2nd ed.). Health Administration Press, Chicago, 1998; 4–27, 55–61.

Skocpol T. *Boomerang: Clinton's Health Security Effort and Turn Against Government in U.S. Politics.* New York, W.W. Norton, 1996; 1–19.

HEALTH CARE AND HEALTH CARE POLICY IN A CHANGING WORLD

Donald A. Barr, Philip R. Lee, and A. E. Benjamin

The organization of medicine is not a thing apart which can be subjected to study in isolation. It is an aspect of culture, whose arrangements are inseparable from the general organization of society.[1]
—Walter H. Hamilton

Understanding the structure of a health care system first requires understanding the society in which that system exists. The health care system that has evolved in the United States reflects not only the impact of science and technology but also the politics, cultural values, and priorities that have deep historical roots. In other texts, we have described five characteristics of American society and policy that have had powerful influences on the evolution of the health care system, including the American character (e.g., individualism), federalism, pluralism, and incrementalism.[2,3] We will briefly describe each of these and will then offer a historical perspective of how they have shaped health care policies over time and how each of them has contributed to the problems our health care system now faces.

THE AMERICAN CHARACTER

The concept of autonomy and the ethical principle of respect for autonomy has been one of the fundamental building blocks of public policy since the founding of the nation. The policies that established the nation were built on the strongly held view that the right of individuals to their own beliefs and values should be protected by government and protected from the government. To this day the principles of individual choice, confidentiality, and privacy are strongly held. In 1990, the Patient Self Determination Act (P.L. 101–508) translated the concept of autonomy into public health policy concerning the individual's right to make decisions with respect to his or her own medical care, to refuse treatment, and to prepare advanced directives regarding care.

Along with the concept of autonomy has been a deeply held distrust of government. Although the distrust of government waxes and wanes, it is ever present and is reflected in the limited role of government in dealing with such issues as the financing of health care. Distrust of government was one of the factors that resulted in the lack of action by the United States Congress on the health care reforms proposed by President Clinton in 1993. In 1993, the President raised the issue of health care reform to the top of the domestic policy agenda, but the United States Congress ended more than a year of deliberation without taking any action. In this case, it was in part the concentrated interests of those who opposed reform (insurance industry, small business) that tapped the broad distrust of government to sap public support and generate opposition to the proposed reforms. The creation of three branches of government by the founding fathers reflected in part the distrust of government and the need to create the necessary checks and balances to prevent the abuse of power by any branch of government or by the majority of the populace.

Throughout the history of the country there have been shifts toward a strong federal role, originally advocated by Alexander Hamilton, and away from such a role. During the 20th century, periods of public action (1900s, 1930s, and 1960s) were preceded and followed by periods of private action (1890s, 1920s, 1950s, and 1980s).

FEDERALISM AND THE ROLE OF GOVERNMENT IN HEALTH CARE

Government at all levels plays an important role in planning, financing, organization, and delivering health services in the United States. At the federal level, Medicare is the dominant program for financing health care for the elderly. The Departments of Veterans Affairs, Defense, and Health and Human Services all maintain large, complex health care delivery systems to meet the needs of veterans, the military and their dependents, and American Indians and Alaska Natives.

The federal government, particularly through the U.S. Public Health Service, funds a range of categorical public health and medical care programs, largely through grants in aid to states and local governments.

At the state level, Medicaid has become the largest medical care program, financed with federal, state, and, in some cases, local government matching funds. The states have historically had the major role in public health programs in the financing and provision of care for the chronically mentally ill and in substance abuse prevention and treatment.

Local governments, particularly in urban areas, have often been major providers of medical care for the indigent, largely through public hospitals and clinics.

Much of the modern infrastructure for health care has been funded or subsidized with public funds during the past 50 years, including the construction of public and most voluntary hospitals, the training of most of the health professions, and the bulk of basic biomedical research. Currently, approximately 40% of all health care expenditures are provided by the federal, state, and local governments.

Although government's role in financing health care is a major one, this role is not the result of a consistent or comprehensive plan for the organization of health care services, but an episodic response to market failures (e.g., Medicare). Over time, as the private sector has been unable or unwilling to meet the health care needs of specific segments of the population, government has stepped in to fill the gap. Initially, the needs were met largely by local government and voluntary efforts. Later, states stepped in to meet the needs of the mentally ill. The federal government played a limited role, except for specific beneficiary groups such as veterans and specific public health problems (e.g., venereal disease, tuberculosis), until the enactment of Medicare and Medicaid in 1965. The Balanced Budget Act of 1997 includes some of the most significant changes ever made in the Medicare and Medicaid programs, providing states with greater flexibility in the administration of Medicaid and individuals greater choice of competing plans in Medicare. The result of this piecemeal approach to the development of health policy has been a proliferation of federal categorical programs administered by more than a dozen government departments and agencies (e.g., Department of Health and Human Services, Transportation, Agriculture, Energy, and the Environmental Protection Agency).

The role of government, particularly the federal government, has been at the heart of this debate about the future of health care in the United States since President Truman proposed a program of federally financed national health insurance in 1947.

This evolving role of government in the financing organization and delivery of health care reflects the role of federalism in the United States. The concept of federalism, and the concomitant role of the federal government in social policy, has evolved in the 200 years since the American Revolution and the drafting of the U.S. Constitution. After the failure of the Articles of Confederation, the drafters of the Constitution saw a need for a central government with clear but delineated authority in areas of common concern such as national defense and foreign policy. Functions such as education, police protection, and health care were left under state and local authority. The lines between federal and state authority were clearly drawn. It was not until after the Civil War, however, that state governments began to play a significant role in health care and public health policy.

This arrangement worked well so long as two conditions were met:

1. There was consistency between the levels of administrative authority and financial accountability.
2. The various levels of government involved had the appropriate resources and other capacities to carry out their responsibilities.

In health care, it is clear that these conditions have not been consistently maintained. The result often has been an increase in federal responsibility for health care, particularly in the financing of care. In some areas, such as Medicare, the shift to federal responsibility has included both administrative authority and financial accountability. In others, such as Medicaid and family planning, the disjunction between authority (i.e., federal) and accountability (i.e., states) has led to dysfunctional outcomes, including funding cutbacks, eligibility restrictions, low levels of payment to providers of care, and programmatic restrictions. The success of the federalist system depends on maintaining this balance between administrative authority and financial responsibility and between federal, state, and local responsibility.

There have been a number of reasons why state and local governments were not able to maintain their historical authority over social policy, not the least of which has been the lack of political will to extend government authority into new or controversial areas (e.g., civil rights). In parallel with the variation among states in the political will to assume responsibility for social needs have been variations in the ability of states to generate sufficient revenue through taxation and in the capacity to plan and administer complex programs. An important pattern has emerged as to how states respond to health programs that are initiated by the federal government for vulnerable populations but left to states to establish local eligibility and funding criteria: states will vary widely around a median level of benefits. Any federal attempt to guarantee a basic level of benefits using this decentralized approach will succeed for only a certain segment of the intended population.

One final consequence of the approach to health policy that decentralizes responsibility over health care programs has been the vulnerability of local governments and agencies to state funding cutbacks. These local entities are important providers of many health services, particularly hospital, outpatient, and emergency services for the poor; mental health and substance abuse services; and a variety of public health services. When local governments are mandated to provide these services (either by regulation or court order) but are not provided the supplemental resources to do so, both the quality of the local programs and the fiscal health of the local agency can be compromised. Although this does not usually occur during periods of sustained economic growth and low unemployment, quality of programs can vary strikingly from one community to another during economic downturns.

PLURALISM AND THE ROLE OF SPECIAL INTERESTS

In addition to establishing a central government with delineated authority, the founders of this country established a legislative and regulatory system based on pluralism in order to protect the individual from the power of government. Decision-making power in a pluralistic society is spread among many groups so that no one group gains excessive power. Over time, pluralism has become not only a mechanism for making decisions but also an ideology that shapes our perceptions of the proper role of government. In order for their voices to be heard, individuals have increasingly organized into groups with interests as broad as the political parties and as narrow as single issues (e.g., abortion). These groups not only are allowed to influence the legislation process, they are encouraged to do so. During the first half of this century, the groups that dominated the health policy process were characterized as an iron triangle, including legislative committees, executive branch agencies, and private interest groups (e.g., the American Medical Association [AMA]). More recently, the process has become more complex and the iron triangles replaced by policy networks. Peterson has observed that the health policy community today "is heterogeneous and loosely structured, creating a network whose broad boundaries are defined by shared attentiveness of participants to the same issues in the policy domain."[4]

The influence of special interests as a manifestation of our pluralistic system is clearly seen throughout the health policy process. In this century, the American Medical Association has exerted a powerful influence on health policy, although its influence has diminished significantly since the enactment of Medicare. Other influential interests have been the hospitals, the insurance industry, and the pharmaceutical companies. Although groups representing patients (e.g., American Association of Retired Persons, organized labor) have exerted influence over specific programs, it has been these four general groups that have tended to shape health policy in the period after World War II. More recently, business interest groups (e.g., Business Group on Health) have begun to be more influential.

Since the late 1960s, as the cost of health care has become a predominant issue, power over health policy has shifted from the providers to the purchasers (e.g., large employers). Regardless of this realignment of power among interest groups, the power of special interests over the process of establishing and implementing health policy has remained intact. The effectiveness of many of these interest groups (e.g., small businesses, insurance) was very evident in President Clinton's ill-fated attempt at health care reform. It is extremely difficult to achieve broad consensus or to implement broad health policy—or even to convince Congress to make minor changes in policy—in the face of the power of special interests. This inhibition inherent in the pluralistic system in the United States has shaped and continues to shape the health policy process.

INCREMENTALISM AS THE PRINCIPAL MEANS OF HEALTH POLICY REFORM

Kingdon[5] and more recently Longest[6] have provided a model for understanding how policy decisions are made. In Longest's model, the process includes policy formulation and policy implementation phases, with both influenced by a policy modification phase. It is very clear that although President Clinton played the key role in placing national health insurance on the policy agenda in 1993, he did not control the process after that. When a policy issue rises to the top of the agenda, two other factors must then be present for successful reform to take place: a policy solution that is broadly seen as successfully addressing the issue, and political circumstances that allow for reform to take place. When all three (agenda, solution, political circumstances) are present simultaneously, a "window of opportunity" exists for significant policy reform. If any one of the three is absent, the potential for significant reform is diminished substantially. A number of analysts have suggested that such a window for major health care reform existed in the early Clinton years, but his policy solution proved unacceptable to a majority in Congress and later the success of the "Republican Revolution" in 1994 fundamentally altered the political circumstances, thus removing one of the factors and dooming any efforts at major health care reform.

Once a policy has been enacted, a second process of implementation takes place, usually involving the executive branch agency responsible for establishing the necessary guidelines and regulations. In the case of Medicare, this is the Health Care Financing Administration (HCFA), Department of Health and Human Services (HHS). The HCFA also has a major role in approving state Medicaid regulations. For many categorical public health programs, although the authority is ultimately vested in the Secretary of HHS, the implementation is provided by the agencies (e.g., National Institutes of Health, Food and Drug Administration, Centers for Disease Control and Prevention). In addition to having the potential to influence all phases of the policy formulating phase, special interest groups can also play an important role in guiding policy implementation. Through ongoing relationships with the implementing agencies, they are able to influence the rules by which policy programs will operate. The AMA, for example, works closely with HCFA to influence Medicare regulations.

A third phase of the policy process as it affects health care—policy modification—has also been described by Longest.[6] Part of the responsibility of the legislative process is in oversight of the implementation of programs in achieving their intended goals. Oversight will become increasingly important in the future in view of the strict limits set on discretionary spending and in Medicare and Medicaid spending during the next five years. Although oversight has always been important in ensuring implementation, it is now being pursued vigorously because the Congress is in Republican hands and the Executive branch is controlled by the Democrats.

When policies either do not have clear goals by which to measure them or have not been successful in attaining their stated goals, they often enter back into the legislative process for further modification. From this perspective, the policy process becomes cyclical: policy formation leads to implementation, which leads to modification, which feeds back into the formation phase. In fact, many key health policies have been modifications to previously existing policies. For example, Medicare and Medicaid were amendments to the Social Security Act and were actually extensions of earlier programs (the Old Age, Survivors' and Disability Insurance program and the Kerr-Mills program to provide medical care for the elderly poor). Medicare, in turn, was shaped by major amendments affecting hospital payments (1983) and physician payments (1989), largely because of the rising costs of health care. The Balanced Budget Act of 1997 represented yet another major shift in Medicare policy, following years of oversight hearings.

The complexity of the policy-setting process, the susceptibility of policy implementation to outside influence, and the cyclical nature of policy modification all have led to a phenomenon that is characteristic of the United States government: the incremental approach to decision-making. Whether for health care or any other social issue, policy is usually made in this country in small steps (increments). An exception was welfare reform, which did call for sweeping changes. One of the reasons for the failure of Clinton's health care reform plan was that it did not propose an incremental approach to change.

Incrementalism has come to be understood by most of the players as the way things are to be done. There is a general hesitance to take anything but a small bite out of a major policy issue, both because of a general comfort with the status quo and because of the risk of unforeseen and unintended consequences of major policy modifications. It appears that only at times of crisis, when there is broad consensus that the need for major action overshadows the risk of unintended outcomes, is our governmental system able to adopt major policy reform. (It should be pointed out that the failed Clinton health care reforms were followed by incremental health insurance reform in the Kennedy-Kassebaum bill and the incremental expansion of health insurance coverage to a portion of uninsured children.)

HISTORICAL DEVELOPMENT OF AMERICAN HEALTH POLICY

Throughout most of the nation's history, the federal government played a minor role in health policy; most of the policy interventions in public health were at the state and local levels, and most of medical care was left to the private sector. At times of crisis, such as the Civil War, the Great Depression, or, more recently, the Civil Rights Movement, quantum shifts in authority from the state level to the federal level or from the private sector to the public sector take place.

In a series of earlier books,[1,2,7] we have reviewed the historical development of health policy in the United States. Others, including Rosemary Stevens[8,9] and Paul Starr,[10] have dealt with the sweeping changes in Medicare and Medical care, and Mullen[11] has provided a history of the U.S. Public Health Service.

We have described four distinct periods in the evolution of health policy:

1. A limited role for the federal government (1798–1862)
2. The emergence of a larger federal role (1862–1932)
3. The expansion of the federal role (1935–1969)
4. New federalism (1969–present)

In the early years of the republic, the Elizabethan poor laws of England were the foundation of most policies for the poor, the aged, and the infirm. In 1798, Congress passed the Act for the Relief of Sick and Disabled Seamen, imposing a twenty cent per month tax on seamen's wages to pay for their medical care. This legislation represented the first step in establishing the U.S. Public Health Service.[11]

After the Civil War, the development of the germ theory of disease by Pasteur was the most powerful force affecting both public health and medical care. In public health, progress was more rapid than in medical care, with policies related to environmental sanitation, clean water, the pasteurization of milk, and expanded programs of quarantine grounded largely in the police power of state and local governments. The first federal law directly related to public health broadly was the Biologies Control Act of 1902 (P.L. 57–244), followed by the Pure Food and Drug Act (P.L. 59–384) in 1906.

In addition to the gradual increase in federal authority during this period, significant shifts were taking place in the private sector's role in health care.

During the latter half of the 19th century, there was a rapid growth in the number and in the role of hospitals. During this period, there was also the establishment of proprietary medical schools (replacing apprenticeship training) and the development of state and local public health agencies. The fragmentation of the hospitals' governance and management began with the growing number of voluntary, nonprofit, often religious hospitals in addition to local public hospitals and the proliferation of proprietary hospitals, usually owned by physicians. As medicine began to be rooted in science, and physicians gained more respect, physicians began to replace the hospital trustees in determining who was and who was not admitted to the hospital.

Late in the 19th century and early in the 20th century, hospitals gradually shifted from places for the poor to come to die to centers of medical, but particularly surgical, care for the general public. Two general types of hospitals emerged: public hospitals financed largely at the local level, and private, community-based, nonprofit hospitals, many of them operated by religious institutions. Both the proprietary, hospital-based medical schools and physician-owned proprietary hospitals gradually disappeared in the early decades of the 20th century, largely due to the efforts of the American Medical Association, stimulated by the Flexner Report in 1910.[12]

It was also during this time that state governments, at the urging of state medical societies, became involved in licensing practitioners and supporting medical education. Thus, while government was becoming increasingly involved in guiding health policy during this period, most of this activity was at the state and local rather than the federal level, and the public role in health policy was still quite limited compared with that of the private sector.

Substitution of Public Services and Financing for Private Efforts (1935–1969)

The crisis presented by the Great Depression brought action by the federal government in areas that previously had been left to state and local control. From banking regulation to support for small businesses, from public employment to old age security, there was a broadly held perception that the federal government should do what state governments had been unable or unwilling to do to respond to the crisis. Over the span of a few years, the role of the federal government vis-à-vis the states changed fundamentally. American federalism evolved from a pattern of limited federal responsibility for domestic policy to a cooperative relationship between federal and state governments with a strong, often leading role for the federal government.

This new relationship is seen nowhere more clearly than in the Social Security Act. Included within the Act was the new principle of federal aid to the states for public health and welfare assistance, including grants for maternal and child health and crippled children's services (Title V) and for general public health programs (Title VI). The Old Age, Survivors' and Disability Insurance (OASDI) program included in the original Act provided the philosophical and fiscal basis for the Medicare program enacted 30 years later.

During this period of transformation, the National Cancer Institute was established (1938); the authority of the Food and Drug Administration (FDA) was greatly strengthened, requiring approval of drugs for safety before marketing (1938); and the Nurse Training Act was passed (1941), providing schools of nursing with direct federal aid to permit them to increase their enrollments and improve their physical facilities.

After World War II, there was a growing federal role in the support of medical research, mental health research and treatment programs, and the construction of community hospitals (Hill-Burnham Act of 1946). The establishment of the Department of Health, Education, and Welfare in 1953 (now the Department of Health and Human Services), including the U.S. Public Health Service, the then separate FDA, and the Social Security Administration, firmly established the federal government's role in the nation's health care system. This new role was not, however, the result of any comprehensive or coordinated plan to develop a national health care policy. Rather, it was the amalgamation of a variety of incremental steps taken for a variety of reasons at a variety of times.

In the 1960s, there was further expansion of this new federal role in health policy. Through the "creative federalism" followed by the Kennedy and Johnson Administrations, the federal government became increasingly involved in a number of areas, including environmental health (e.g., air pollution control), community mental health centers, neighborhood health centers, health professions training, family planning, and other efforts to improve health care delivery to underserved communities. Many of these programs were financed through direct federal support for local governments and local nonprofit agencies. One of the most important laws enacted in the 1960s was the Civil Rights Act of 1964, later used as the means to desegregate the hospitals in the south. A further extension of the federal government's direct regulatory authority came with the 1962 amendments to the Food, Drug, and Cosmetics Act, which specified that manufacturers must demonstrate that a drug is both safe and effective before marketing it. Congress, between 1965 and 1967, enacted more new health legislation than all the previous congresses in the nation's 175 years.

The most dramatic expansion of federal authority in health policy was through the Social Security Amendments of 1965, establishing the Medicare and Medicaid programs to finance health care for all people older than 65 and all people receiving cash welfare assistance. These policies marked one of the first times that major health care programs were enacted over the objection of the American Medical Association, fundamentally altering the power relationship between physicians and the federal government. Never again was the medical profession able to exercise veto authority over federal health policy.

These programs of the Kennedy and Johnson years had a profound effect on intergovernmental relationships and on federal expenditures for domestic social programs. The combination of direct federal payments for Medicare and Medicaid and federal grants-in-aid helped lead to a ballooning of the federal budget, which, in the face of the strain on the domestic economy caused by the Vietnam War, created a new crisis and a dramatic shift in the role of the federal government.

The trend away from community involvement in health care was temporarily reversed with an effort in the Great Society era to base health care for vulnerable, underserved populations in community-controlled programs (e.g., neighborhood health centers, community mental health centers). Other efforts to strengthen the communities' role in the 1970s include health planning and the beginning of the "health cities" movement. Market forces, which began to play an increasingly important role in health care in the 1970s and 1980s, can have either a positive or negative impact on the role of the community, but their initial impact has been to shift control away from communities.

Entering the Era of Limited Resources: The "New Federalism" (1969–1997)

First coined by President Nixon, the term *New Federalism* described a movement to reverse the swing of government power to the federal government, transferring authority over policy and program to the states. The Nixon and Ford administrations favored block grants to the states for the support of local policy initiatives, with relatively little federal oversight. Congress resisted this move, favoring instead the continued use of categorical grants requiring detailed provisions regulating the type and level of services to be provided.

While Congress and the President argued over the issue of block versus categorical grants in the 1970s, the federal government confronted the problem of skyrocketing health care costs, largely a result of the Medicare and Medicaid programs. Federal and state governments had become third parties that underwrote the costs of a fee-for-service-based health care system that included few if any mechanisms to constrain costs. Coupled with a growing physician work force and increasing specialization, the explosion of new technology catalyzed by the enactment of the Medicare and Medicaid systems and the rapid expansion of biomedical research funded by the National Institutes of Health helped lead to a rapid upward spiral in health care costs and thus in federal expenditures.

The federal response to rapidly rising health care expenditures assumed a variety of forms, ranging from the elimination of federal subsidies for hospital construction and health professions education to price controls for a limited period and more permanent limits on hospital and physician payments by Medicare.

Additionally, in a step that was to have profound effects on the direction later market-based reforms would take, the federal government stimulated the development and expansion of health maintenance organizations (HMOs) through the Health Maintenance Organization Act of 1972. Historically an anathema to most physicians and especially to the American Medical Association, HMOs had grown very slowly.

The movement away from federal responsibility for domestic social policy accelerated when Ronald Reagan was elected President in 1980. The most prominent changes enacted by the Reagan administration that directly affected health care included (1) a sharp reduction in federal expenditures for social programs, including elimination of the revenue-sharing program initiated by President Nixon; (2) decentralization of regulatory and programmatic authority to the states, particularly through the use or block grants that came with few strings attached; (3) an increasing reliance on market forces and private institutions to stimulate needed reforms and control rising costs; and (4) through across-the-board federal tax reductions, a substantial decline in the ability of the federal government to fund new health programs. Contrary to the "deregulatory" philosophy of the administration, it established the means to regulate hospital costs, using prospective payment through the diagnosis-related group (DRG) system as an alternative to Medicare's cost-based reimbursement for hospital costs.

No longer was the federal government to be the unquestioning payer for health services. No longer did the federal government have the capacity, even if the political will were present, to fund new health care programs. The rising budget deficit, not health care, became foremost on the national agenda. The Bush Administration followed in 1989 with its support for a congressionally initiated Medicare fee schedule, to be set by the government, to control Medicare payments to physicians specified in the Omnibus Budget Reconciliation Act of 1989 (P.L. 101–239).

At the state level, increasing policy authority brought with it increasing financial burdens. As states became more responsible for establishing and implementing their own programs, they also became increasingly responsible for the costs of those programs. In the area of health care, the spiral of rising costs of Medicaid continued largely unabated, leading to increasing strain on state budgets. Once again a situation was created in which there was a mismatch between authority over a policy program and the capacity to finance that program.

A number of states turned to the private market and to market-based competition as a means of holding down costs, both the costs of publicly financed programs and the costs of health care overall. An initial change that was to have profound effects on our system of health care was an increasing reliance on for-profit corporations to operate within the health care system. Traditionally functioning as nonprofit, community-based institutions, many hospitals were taken over by for-profit chains financed through the sale of stock. A number of organizations involved in the direct provision of care, such as home health agencies and kidney dialysis centers, shifted from community control or nonprofit status to a for-profit basis. The requirement that HMOs operate on a nonprofit basis, included in the original HMO Act, was removed, opening the market to for-profit companies to become directly involved in the financing and provision of care. A number of states chose to rely on private HMOs to provide care to Medicaid beneficiaries, leaving it to the HMO to determine what constitutes "medically necessary" care.

The continued increase in health care costs seen in the late 1980s coupled with the growing role of private markets in providing access to health care services led to a new awareness of what is really an old problem: the rising number of uninsured individuals and families. Currently as many as 44 million Americans have no insurance to pay for needed health care. The number of uninsured is increasing about 1 million per year despite the growing economy with its low levels of unemployment.

The dilemma that confronted the Clinton Administration when it took office in 1992 was that Americans want to have their health care cake and eat it too. They want health care made more available to the uninsured, and they want the cost of health care to come under control, but only if these actions don't diminish the ability of the average American to get whatever treatment he or she perceives to be necessary or appropriate in a timely manner. This perhaps is the fundamental American health policy dilemma. President and the Congress in 1993 faced conflicting needs and expectations with neither a mechanism to establish a broad-based consensus on how to reconcile them nor a mechanism to enact that consensus if it was achieved. President Clinton had campaigned on the need for the federal government to reassert itself in the area of health policy. With the broad goals of expanding coverage to the uninsured while simultaneously controlling health care costs, the Clinton health reform plan would have given broad new authority to the federal government to regulate the market for health insurance, while maintaining a reliance on market-based competition. It sought a new balance between the market-based delivery of care and a broad umbrella of federal oversight. The idea was an attempt to redefine the role of federalism in health policy, but it was seriously out of synch with the continued movement in the evolution of federal authority. As pointed out by Theda Skocpol,[13] the ebbing tide of federal authority over social policy had not yet run its course. With an irony that has not yet been fully appreciated, the country was ready for one part of the Clinton proposal but not the other. Although Congress rejected an increased role for the federal government in regulating the market for health insurance, the deliberations surrounding the Clinton proposal nevertheless opened the door even more widely for market-based competition among health plans to become the principal paradigm for American health care at the end of the 20th century. Although it is happening in some areas of the country more rapidly than others, there has been a clear shift to the evolving concept of managed care for the financing, provision, and oversight of health care to most Americans. The shift comes, however, without any organized system of oversight or regulation and with an increasing role for for-profit companies. As a reaction, many states are now proposing a variety of "consumer protective" laws (more than 400 bills introduced in state legislatures in 1997) to begin to place some limits on private sector managed care plans, and the President has proposed a "Consumer Bill of Rights." At the same time, states are increasingly mandating the enrollment of Medicaid beneficiaries (e.g., mothers and children) in managed care plans, and Medicare is poised to significantly expand the role of managed care plans.

Reductions in care, financial incentives that pit physicians' needs against those of patients, and a disavowal of responsibility for caring for the uninsured all are characteristics of this new American system of health care. In the words of one of the more vigorous advocates of for-profit health care plans,

> Investor-owned health plans are a driving force behind this transformation [of the health care delivery system in America], and nonprofit health plans, in my view, are a byproduct of the past . . . There is an appropriate role for nonprofit plans, but it is not in the operation of competitive health plans.[14]

Was this the health care system that the American public intended to have? Did the United States get here as a result of a well-thought-out policy deliberation? As with much of the history of American health policy, the answer to both questions is "no." Once again the separation of the authority over health policy and the financial responsibility for it has led to an outcome that was unintended and, as many believe, is not in the best interest of the American people.

While the private sector was moving rapidly, without adequate federal or state ground rules to "level the playing field," there was paralysis of health policy making at the federal level after the failure of President Clinton's health care reform proposals in 1993–1994. The situation only grew worse after the Republicans captured both the Senate and the House of Representatives in 1994. What followed was 2 years of ideological debate with a standoff between the President and the Congress. After President Clinton's reelection in 1996 and the continued control of Congress by the Republicans, the Congress and the Clinton Administration began to work together to produce potentially constructive changes in the Medicare program. The result was the Balanced Budget Act of 1997, signed by President Clinton in August 1997.

The basic Medicare provisions, including a 5-year spending reduction of $115 billion below Congressional Budget Office (CBO) projections based on existing policies, were

- Coordinated care plans, including HMOs, preferred provider organizations (PPOs), plans offered by provider sponsored organizations (PSOs), and point-of-service plans (POSs)
- Private fee-for-service
- On a demonstration basis, high deductible plans with medical savings account

The Balanced Budget Act of 1997 reflected a political consensus that had arisen from the ashes of the rancorous stalemate of 1995–1996 that followed the Republican capture of the Congress. The Medicare reform process reversed almost every aspect of the failed partisan debates of the previous 2 years. The Medicare reform process in 1997 was similar to the successful Medicare hospital and physician payment reform of 1983 and 1989 and the expansion of Medicaid eligibility for children in poverty in the early 1990s.

The direction for health care in the 21st century, at least in its early years, may well have been set by the Balanced Budget Act of 1997, just as it was set in the past 30 years by the Social Security Amendment of 1965, which established Medicare and Medicaid as public programs that bought into and reinforced the then dominant fee-for-service system. Times have changed and health care will change as well.

ABOUT THE AUTHORS

Philip R. Lee, MD, is Professor of Social Medicine Emeritus, School of Medicine, University of California, San Francisco and Consulting Professor, Human Biology Program, Stanford University. From 1993 to 1997, he served as Assistant Secretary for Health, U.S. Department of Health and Human Services.

A. E. Benjamin, PhD, is Professor, School of Public Policy and Social Research, University of California, Los Angeles, California.

Donald A. Barr, MD, PhD, is Lecturer and Coordinator of the Curriculum in Health Policy, Program in Human Biology, Stanford University, Stanford, California.

REFERENCES

1. Hamilton, W.H. *Medical care for the American people: The final report of the Committee on the Cost of Medical Care.* Adopted October 31, 1932. Chicago: University of Chicago Press, 1932.

2. Lee, P.R., and Benjamin, A.E. Health policy and the politics of health care. In S.J. Williams and P.R. Torrens (eds). *Introduction to health services.* 4th ed. Albany: Delmar Publishers, 1993.

3. Lee, P.R., Benjamin, A.E., and Weber, M.A. Policies and strategies for health care in the United States. In *Oxford Textbook of Public Health.* 3rd ed. Oxford: Oxford University Press, 1996.

4. Peterson, M.A. Political influence in the 1990s: From iron triangle to policy network. *Journal of Health Politics, Policy and Law.* Summer, 1993;18:395–438.

5. Kingdon, J.W. *Agendas, alternatives, and public policies.* Boston: Little, Brown, 1993.

6. Longest, B. *Health policymaking in the United States.* Ann Arbor, MI: Health Administration Press, 1994.

7. Lee, P.R., and Silver, G.A. Health planning—A view from the top with specific reference to the U.S.A. In J. Fry and W.A.J. Farndale (eds). *International medical care.* Oxford: MTP Medical and Technical Publishing, 1972.

8. Stevens, R. *American medicine and the public interest.* New York: Basic Books, 1971.

9. Stevens, R. *In sickness and in wealth: American hospitals in the twentieth century.* New York: Basic Books, 1989.

10. Starr, P. *Social transformation of American medicine: The rise of the sovereign profession and the making of a vast industry.* New York: Basic Books, 1982.

11. Mullen, F. *Plague and politics.* New York: Basic Books, 1989.

12. Flexner, A. *Medical education in the United States and Canada.* New York: Carnegie Foundation for the Advancement of Teaching, 1910.

13. Skocpol, T. *Boomerang: Clinton's health security effort and the turn against government in U.S. politics.* New York: W.W. Norton, 1996.

14. Hassan, M. Let's end the nonprofit charade. *New England Journal of Medicine.* 1996;334:1055–1057.

THE PROCESS OF PUBLIC POLICYMAKING: A CONCEPTUAL MODEL

Beauford B. Longest, Jr.

The most useful way to conceptualize a process as complex and intricate as the one through which public policies are made is through a schematic model of the process. Although such models, like the one used here, tend to be oversimplifications of real processes, they nevertheless can accurately reflect the component parts of the process as well as their interrelationships. Figure 1 is a model of the public policymaking process in the United States. A brief overview of this model is presented in this section.

Several general features of the model should be noted. First, as the model clearly illustrates, the policymaking process is distinctly cyclical. The circular flow of the relationships among the various components of the model reflects one of the most important features of public policymaking. The process is a continuous cycle in which almost all decisions are subject to subsequent modification. Public policymaking, including that in the health domain, is a process within which numerous decisions are reached but then revisited as circumstances change. The circumstances that trigger reconsideration of earlier decisions include changes in the way problems are defined as well as in the menu of possible solutions to problems. The new circumstances that trigger modification in previous decisions also routinely include the relative importance attributed to issues by the various participants in the political marketplace where this process plays out over time. For example, a problem with a low priority among powerful participants in the policymaking process may elicit a limited or partial policy solution. Later, if these participants give the problem a higher priority, a policy developed in response to the problem is much more likely. The major changes in Medicare policy made in 1997, for example, reflect a much more widely and deeply shared concern about the implications of this program for the federal budget than was previously the case.

Another important feature of the public policymaking process shown in the model is that the entire process is influenced by factors external to the process itself. This makes the policymaking process an *open system*—one in which the process interacts with and is affected by events and circumstances in its external environment.

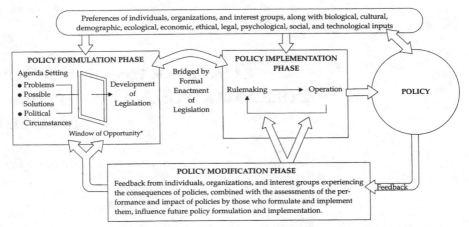

*The window of opportunity opens when there is a favorable confluence of problems, possible solutions, and political circumstances.

Figure 1   A Model of the Public Policymaking Process in the United States

This important phenomenon is shown in Figure 1 by the impact of the preferences of the individuals, organizations, and interest groups who are affected by policies, along with biological, cultural, demographic, ecological, economic, ethical, legal, psychological, social, and technological inputs, on the policymaking process. Legal inputs include decisions made in the courts that affect health and its pursuit. As was noted earlier, such decisions are themselves policies. In addition, decisions made within the legal system are important influences on the other decisions made within the policymaking process. Legal inputs help shape all other policy decisions, including reversing them on occasion when they are not consistent with the constitution.

A third important feature of the model is that it emphasizes the various distinct component parts or phases of the policymaking process, but also shows that they are highly interactive and interdependent. The conceptualization of the public policymaking process as a set of interrelated phases has been used by a number of authors, although there is considerable variation in what the phases of activities are called in these models as well as in their comprehensiveness. Brewer and de Leon (1983) provide a good generic example; Paul-Shaheen (1990) applies such a model specifically to health policymaking. The public policymaking process includes three interconnected phases:

- policy formulation, which incorporates activities associated with setting the policy agenda and, subsequently, with the development of legislation;
- policy implementation, which incorporates activities associated with rulemaking that help guide the implementation of policies and the actual operationalization of policies; and

- policy modification, which allows for all prior decisions made within the process to be revisited and perhaps changed.

The formulation phase (making the decisions that lead to public laws) and the implementation phase (taking actions and making additional decisions necessary to implement public laws) are bridged by the formal enactment of legislation, which shifts the cycle from its formulation to implementation phase. Once enacted as laws, policies remain to be implemented. Implementation responsibility rests mostly with the executive branch, which includes many departments that have significant health policy implementation responsibilities—for example, the Department of Health and Human Services (DHHS) (http://www.dhhs.gov) and the Department of Justice (DOJ) (http://www.usdoj.gov), and independent federal agencies, such as the Environmental Protection Agency (EPA) (http://www.epa.gov) and the Consumer Product Safety Commission (CPSC) (http://www.cpsc.gov). These and many other departments and agencies in the executive branch of government exist primarily to implement the policies formulated in the legislative branch.

It is important to remember that some of the decisions made within the implementing entities, as they implement policies, become policies themselves. For example, rules and regulations promulgated to implement a law and operational protocols and procedures developed to support a law's implementation are just as much policies as is the law itself. Similarly, judicial decisions regarding the applicability of laws to specific situations or regarding the appropriateness of the actions of implementing organizations are decisions that are themselves public policies. It is important to remember that policies are established within both the policy formulation and the policy implementation phases of the overall process.

The policy modification phase exists because perfection cannot be achieved in the other phases and because policies are established and exist in a dynamic world. Suitable policies made today may become inadequate with future biological, cultural, demographic, ecological, economic, ethical, legal, psychological, social, and technological changes. Pressure to change established policies may come from new priorities or perceived needs by the individuals, organizations, and interest groups that are affected by the policies.

Policy modification, which is shown as a feedback loop in Figure 1, may entail nothing more than minor adjustments made in the implementation phase or modest amendments to existing public laws. In some instances, however, the consequences of implementing certain policies can feed back all the way to the agenda-setting stage of the process. For example, formulating policies to contain the costs of providing health services—a key challenge facing policymakers today—is, to a large extent, an outgrowth of the success of previous policies that expanded access and subsidized an increased supply of human resources and advanced technologies to be used in providing health services.

One feature of the public policymaking process that the model presented in Figure 1 cannot adequately show—but one that is crucial to understanding the policymaking process—is the *political* nature of the process in operation. While there is a belief among many people—and a naive hope among still others—that policymaking is a predominantly rational decision-making process, this is not the case.

The process would no doubt be simpler and better if it were driven exclusively by fully informed consideration of the best ways for policy to support the nation's pursuit of health, by open and comprehensive debate about such policies, and by the rational selection from among policy choices strictly on the basis of ability to contribute to the pursuit of health. Those who are familiar with the policymaking process, however, know that it is not driven exclusively by these considerations. A wide range of other factors and considerations influence the process. The preferences and influence of interest groups, political bargaining and vote trading, and ideological biases are among the most important of these other factors. This is not to say that rationality plays no part in health policymaking. On a good day, it will gain a place among the flurry of political considerations, but "It must be a very good and rare day indeed when policymakers take their cues mainly from scientific knowledge about the state of the world they hope to change or protect" (Brown 1991, 20).

The highly political nature of the policymaking process in the United States accounts for very different and competing theories about how this process plays out. At the opposite ends of a continuum sit what can be characterized as strictly public-interest and strictly self-interest theories of the process. Policies made entirely in the public interest would be those that result when *all* participants act according to what they believe to be the public's interest. Alternatively, policies made entirely through a process driven by the self-interests of the diverse participants in the process would reflect an intricate calculus of the interplay of these various self-interests. Policies resulting from these two hypothetical extremes of the way people might behave in the policymaking process would indeed be very different.

In reality, however, health policies always reflect various mixes of public-interest and self-interest influences. The balance between the public and self-interests being served are quite important to the ultimate shape of health policies. For example, the present coexistence of the extremes of excess (e.g., exorbitant incomes of some physicians and health plan managers, esoteric technologies, and various overcapacities in the healthcare system) alongside true deprivation (e.g., lack of insurance for millions of people and inadequate access to basic health services for millions more) resulting from or permitted by some of the nation's existing health policies suggests that the balance has been tipped too often toward the service of self-interests.

This aside, public policymaking in the health domain in the United States is a remarkably complex and interesting process, although, as in all domains, clearly an imperfect process. The intricacies of the process are explored more thoroughly in the following chapters, where each of its interconnected phases is examined in more detail. One should keep in mind, as the separate components of the public policymaking process are examined individually and in greater detail, that policymaking, in general, is a highly political process; that it is continuous and cyclical in its operation; that it is heavily influenced by factors external to the process; and that the component phases and the activities within the phases of the process are highly interactive and interdependent.

SUMMARY

Health policies, like those in other domains, are made within the context of the political marketplace, where demanders for and suppliers of policies interact. The demanders of policies include all of those who view public policies as a mechanism through which to meet some of their health-related objectives or other objectives, such as economic advantage. Although individuals alone can demand public policies, the far more effective demand emanates from organizations and especially from organized interest groups. The suppliers of health policy include elected and appointed members of all three branches of government as well as the civil servants who staff the government.

The interests of the various and very diverse demanders and suppliers in this market cannot be completely coincident—often they are in open conflict—and the decisions and activities of any participants always affect and are affected by the activities of other participants. Thus, public policymaking in the health domain, as well as in other domains, is very much a human process, a fact with great significance for the outcomes and consequences of the process.

The policymaking process itself is a highly complex, interactive, and cyclical process that incorporates formulation, implementation, and modification phases.

ABOUT THE AUTHOR

Beauford B. Longest, Jr., PhD, is Professor of Health Services Administration in the Graduate School of Public Health, Professor of Business Administration in the Katz Graduate School of Business, and Founding Director of the Health Policy Institute, University of Pittsburgh, Pittsburgh, Pennsylvania.

REFERENCES

Alexander, J. A., and L. L. Morlock. 1997. "Power and Politics in Health Services Organizations." In *Essentials of Health Care Management,* edited by S. M. Shortell and A. D. Kaluzny, 256–85. Albany, NY: Delmar Publishers, Inc.

Anderson, G. F. 1992. "The Courts and Health Policy: Strengths and Limitations." *Health Affairs* 11:95–110.

Bauer, R. A., I. de S. Pool, and L. A. Dexter. 1963. *American Business and Public Policy.* New York: Atherton.

Beauchamp, T. L., and J. F. Childress. 1989. *Principles of Biomedical Ethics,* 3rd ed. New York: Oxford University Press.

Bibfeldt, F. 1958. *Paradoxes Observed.* Chicago: Perspective Press.

Brewer, G. D., and P. de Leon. 1983. *The Foundations of Policy Making.* Homewood, IL: Dorsey.

Brown, L. D. 1991. "Knowledge and Power: Health Services Research as a Political Resource." In *Health Services Research: Key to Health Policy,* edited by E. Ginzberg, 20–45. Cambridge, MA: Harvard University Press.

Buchholz, R. A. 1989. *Business Environment and Public Policy: Implications for Management and Strategy Formulation,* 3rd ed. Englewood Cliffs, NJ: Prentice Hall.

Christoffel, T. 1991. "The Role of Law in Health Policy." In *Health Politics and Policy,* 2nd ed., edited by T. J. Litman and L. S. Robins, 135–47. Albany, NY: Delmar Publishers, Inc.

Dye, T. R. 1978. *Understanding Public Policy,* 3rd ed. Englewood Cliffs, NJ: Prentice-Hall.

―――. 1990. *Who's Running America? The Bush Era,* 5th ed. Englewood Cliffs, NJ: Prentice-Hall.

Dye, T. R., and H. Zeigler. 1975. *The Irony of Democracy,* 3rd ed. New York: Wadsworth Publishing Company, Inc.

Encyclopedia of Associations. 1993. Detroit, MI: Gale.

Feldstein, P. J. 1996. *The Politics of Health Legislation: An Economic Perspective,* 2nd ed. Chicago: Health Administration Press.

French, J. R. P., and B. H. Raven. 1959. "The Basis of Social Power." In *Studies of Social Power,* edited by D. Cartwright, 150–67. Ann Arbor, MI: Institute for Social Research.

Green, J. 1995. "High-Court Ruling Protects Hospital-bill Surcharges." *AHA News* 31 (18): 1.

Greenberger, D., S. Strasser, R. J. Lewicki, and T. S. Bateman. 1988. "Perception, Motivation, and Negotiation." In *Health Care Management: A Text in Organization Theory and Behavior,* 2nd ed., edited by S. M. Shortell and A. D. Kaluzny, 81–141. New York: John Wiley & Sons.

Keys, B., and T. Case. 1990. "How to Become an Influential Manager." *The Executive* 4 (4): 38–51.

Lineberry, R. L., G. C. Edwards, III, and M. P. Wattenberg. 1995. *Government in America,* 2nd ed. New York: HarperCollins College Publishers.

Lowi, T. J. 1979. *The End of Liberalism,* 2nd ed. New York: Norton.

Marmor, T. R., and J. B. Christianson. 1982. *Health Care Policy: A Political Economy Approach.* Beverly Hills, CA: Sage Publications.

Mintzberg, H. 1983. *Power In and Around Organizations.* Englewood Cliffs, NJ: Prentice-Hall.

Moe, T. 1980. *The Organization of Interests.* Chicago: University of Chicago Press.

Morone, J. A. 1990. *The Democratic Wish: Popular Participation and the Limits of American Government.* New York: Basic Books.

Olson, M. 1965. *The Logic of Collective Action.* Cambridge, MA: Harvard University Press.

Ornstein, N. J., and S. Elder. 1978. *Interest Groups, Lobbying and Policymaking.* Washington, DC: Congressional Quarterly Press.

Paul-Shaheen, P. A. 1990. "Overlooked Connections: Policy Development and Implementation in State-Local Relations." *Journal of Health Policy, Politics and Law* 15 (4): 133–56.

Pear, R. 1993. "Clinton's Health-Care Plan: It's Still Big, But It's Farther Away." *The New York Times.* (June 13): E4.

Peters, B. G. 1986. *American Public Policy: Promise and Performance,* 2nd ed. Chatham, NJ: Chatham House.

Peterson, M. A. 1993. "Political Influence in the 1990s: From Iron Triangles to Policy Networks." *Journal of Health Politics, Policy and Law* 18 (2): 395–438.

Potter, M. A., and B. B. Longest, Jr. 1994. "The Divergence of Federal and State Policies on the Charitable Tax Exemption of Nonprofit Hospitals." *Journal of Health Politics, Policy and Law* 19: 393–419.

Rawls, J. 1971. *A Theory of Justice.* Cambridge, MA: The Belknap Press of Harvard University Press.

Starr, P. 1982. *The Social Transformation of American Medicine.* New York: Basic Books, Inc.

Truman, D. 1971. *The Governmental Process,* 2nd ed. New York: Knopf.

Wilsford, D. 1991. *Doctors and the State: The Politics of Health in France and the United States.* Durham, NC: Duke University Press.

Wilson, J. Q. 1973. *Political Organizations.* New York: Basic Books, Inc.

CHRONIC CONDITION:
WHY HEALTH REFORM FAILS

Sherry Glied

In the spring of 1993, comprehensive reform of the U.S. health care system seemed inevitable. In an April opinion poll, a majority of Americans asserted that even fundamental changes would not be enough to mend health care, and they called instead for a complete overhaul of the system. More than two-thirds of those polled favored a tax-financed national health insurance program (Jacobs, Shapiro, and Schulman 1993).

Republicans and Democrats, Congress and the White House–all seemed ready for significant action. Back in November of 1991, Pennsylvanian Harris Wofford, a political unknown campaigning on a platform of national health insurance, had climbed from forty points behind in the polls to beat former U.S. attorney general Richard Thornburgh in their race for a seat in the Senate. The stunning upset led to the introduction of more than seventy health reform bills in the following congressional session. While politicians disagreed about the best road to health reform, the primary goals of the effort–expanding coverage and reducing costs–were almost universally endorsed by members of Congress.

In February 1992, responding to the popular clamor for reform, President George Bush released a white paper proposing improvements in the health insurance system, changes in malpractice rules, and tax credits to enable poor Americans to buy insurance coverage. By the summer of 1992, Bill Clinton, campaigning for president, made health reform one of the centerpieces of his platform, calling for universal coverage financed through savings from a comprehensive cost-containment program. Three quarters of voters ranked health care as a very important issue in the presidential campaign. On this issue the electorate favored Clinton over Bush almost three to one—an important difference in light of Clinton's narrow margin of victory. Finally, in September 1993, when President Clinton made his long-awaited health care speech to a joint session of Congress, it seemed as though universal health care coverage, a goal of reformers for more than five decades, was just around the corner. Clinton's speech was greeted by tumultuous applause, a conciliatory response from Senate Republican leader Bob Dole, and enthusiastic support from ordinary Americans.[1]

But now, in Clinton's second term, national health reform aimed at guaranteeing coverage to all Americans is a dead issue. Rather than expanding the government's role in the system, Congress is chipping away at existing federal programs, subordinating health care spending to the overarching goal of deficit reduction. Where members of Congress once confidently boasted of extending Medicare-like health coverage to all Americans, today they whisper about cutting benefits to those who already have public coverage. Rather than giving President Clinton and the Democratic party a boost in popular support, some pundits argued, the attempt to reform health care in fact contributed to the party's defeat in the 1994 midterm elections (Balz 1994). Even Harris Wofford, the man who brought health reform into the political limelight, lost his seat that November.

The spectacular failure of the Clinton administration's attempt at health reform cannot be blamed on the missteps of this particular administration. None of the alternative plans put forward by the right, the left, or the center ever garnered much support either. Nor did the demise of health reform occur because the system somehow cured itself. None of the things that bothered Americans about their health care system in 1993 disappeared of its own accord. Nor is it likely that health reform has fallen off the public agenda forever. While renewed skepticism about the ability of government to address health care concerns may undermine popular support for reform, the continuing pressures of rising Medicare and Medicaid program costs ensure that Congress cannot simply avoid the issue.

Unfortunately, as I argue in the remainder of this book, the health care reform proposals most often considered cannot solve the problems of the health care system. They may lead to short-term improvements and even to some budget savings, but over time they will undoubtedly fail. In this context, the downfall of the Clinton plan is not only a matter of historical interest. The failure of the plan stems from problems that plague all health reform plans. Indeed, some of the same obstacles stymied congressional efforts to reform the Medicare program.

WHY DID AMERICANS WANT HEALTH REFORM?

Four issues drove health reform in the early 1990s: health security for the middle class, coverage for the uninsured, the mushrooming national cost of health care, and the effects of health spending on the federal budget.

Health Security

President Clinton called his plan for health care reform the Health Security Act. That title both alluded to the Social Security Act—President Franklin D. Roosevelt's popular legacy—and addressed a concern specific to health care. Even well-insured middle-class people fear that if they become ill or develop a marker for future illness, they will not be able to purchase health insurance coverage at affordable rates. Insurers today price policies according to the health condition of those who purchase them, and they often exclude preexisting health conditions from coverage.[2] For employees with good coverage through their current job, the risk of losing coverage is a disincentive to switching to a better job. Responding to these concerns, a central theme of the Health Security Act was to guarantee Americans benefits that could "never be taken away" (*Health Security Act* 1993).

To the president, and to many other policymakers, health security meant more than reform of the insurance market to constrain the extent of pricing according to health risk. Limiting risk-based pricing would lower the premiums of people with existing illnesses, but without further steps it would raise the premiums of Americans who were not ill. Such reforms might actually lead many young, healthy Americans to stop purchasing insurance coverage altogether. Furthermore, reform of the insurance market alone would not deliver coverage to most already uninsured Americans, and it would not erase the fear that losing a job might lead to a loss of health insurance coverage. Health security for the middle class would require more than simply improved coverage for the middle class. It would require universal coverage.

Coverage for the Uninsured

In the spring of 1993, more than 40 million Americans—15 percent of the population—lacked health insurance. The number of uninsured Americans had risen continuously every year since 1988.[3]

Being uninsured means getting less medical care. Although the uninsured do receive care, they receive substantially more limited care than do those with coverage; and the uninsured often receive medical attention later in the course of an illness, when doctors can do less to help them. Those who lack insurance may put off routine care. When they become seriously ill, most cannot, and do not, pay the cost of the expensive care they receive. Instead, most of these costs are absorbed by government programs and the hospitals and doctors who provide care, who then attempt to pass the costs along to paying patients.

When asked, Americans express concern for the plight of the uninsured. Most believe the uninsured should be able to obtain appropriate health care, and many are willing to pay at least some additional taxes to finance the costs of this care.[4] An overwhelming majority believe that the poor should be entitled to health care as good as the rich receive. Americans recognize that in today's high-cost health care system, "poor people [cannot] receive needed care" (Jacobs, Shapiro, and Schulman 1993, p. 404).

Cost Containment

Health care in the United States today is very costly. Americans on average spend more than $3,300 a year per person on health care, 14 percent of the nation's income

(Levit et al. 1994). Twice as much is spent on health care as on education, and about three times as much as on national defense. The United States spends about one-and-a-half times as much on care per capita as does Canada, the second-most-costly country. Health care costs are projected to continue rising well into the future, consuming ever more of the nation's gross domestic product (GDP).

Americans, even those who can readily afford their own insurance and direct medical care costs, want to control those costs. In the spring of 1993, 84 percent favored directly limiting health spending and constraining costs to the growth of the national economy (Jacobs, Shapiro, and Schulman 1993). In the speech presenting his health plan to Congress, President Clinton argued that "our competitiveness, our whole economy, the integrity of the way our government works, and, ultimately, our living standards depend upon our ability to achieve savings without harming the quality of health care" (quoted in Drew 1994, p. 302).

Federal Budget Deficit

Even without universal coverage, existing federal health care programs have a sizable impact on the nation's budget—and on the budget deficit. Medicare and Medicaid, the largest federal health programs, cost $275 billion in fiscal year 1995 and have been growing at a rate of 10 to 13 percent a year (CBO 1994a). Growing federal health care spending has subverted efforts to control the deficit. In President Clinton's first budget, delivered to Congress before the health plan had been formulated, almost 60 percent of new spending went to health programs. Projections show this problem getting worse. By 2000 over one-quarter of the federal budget will be devoted to health care. State and local governments also chafe under the increased burden of health spending. By the turn of the century states may be spending as much of their budgets on health care as they do on elementary and secondary education today.

The four problems of security, coverage of the uninsured, cost, and the budget are interrelated. If coverage were universal, security wouldn't be a problem. If health care didn't cost so much, it wouldn't be so hard to cover the uninsured. If existing federal programs didn't cost so much, it would be easier for the government to subsidize more people. Piecemeal reform can exacerbate one problem while curing another. The advantage of comprehensive reform is that it provides an opportunity to solve the whole health care puzzle at once.

PRESIDENT CLINTON'S PROPOSAL

Before taking office in January 1993, President Clinton promised the American people that he would bring them a plan for reform of the health system within 100 days of the inauguration. He missed the deadline by about 100 days, but in September and October 1993 he presented first a speech and then a plan for reform to Congress.

President Clinton's plan combined elements from two well-known policy proposals: single payer and managed competition. Under the single-payer concept, the government would assure health coverage to all. The government would pay all health bills, compensating doctors, hospitals, and other health providers according to centrally established fee schedules. By adjusting fee schedules (and taking other regulatory actions), the government would control the total amount the country spent on health care.

The second plan, managed competition, envisions a system of competing private insurers operating in a government-regulated marketplace. The managed-competition proposal emphasizes the importance of giving both consumers, who buy health care, and health care professionals, who provide care, incentives to use resources in the most cost-effective ways.

Academic researchers, interest groups, and policymakers have spent the past two decades refining these reform designs into coherent proposals. At the beginning of the decade, though, neither plan had the support of a majority of policymakers. In response to perceived failings in each of these plans, a small group of health policy analysts forged a new, compromise plan that they called managed competition under a budget.[5] This compromise plan, which combined the government-established limits on spending characteristic of the single-payer plan with the incentive-oriented competition among health plans that marked the managed-competition plan, became the basis for President Clinton's reform effort.

President Clinton's proposal, the Health Security Act, blended elements from existing plans and directly addressed each of the concerns that motivated the interest in health reform. Insurers would not be permitted to charge more to those with health problems and could not limit coverage for preexisting conditions, so under the plan, those in ill health would no longer pay higher insurance premiums. Consumers, rather than their employers, would choose their own health plans so that the fears of losing or being forced to change insurance as a consequence of a job change would be eliminated.

The plan would provide universal coverage. An employer mandate would ensure that all working Americans could participate in the system. Those not working would also be required to participate, and a system of government subsidies would help them afford coverage. All insurers would cover the same benefits and meet the same quality standards. Regulations would ensure that the quality of care received by poor Americans would not fall substantially below that received by those with higher incomes.

Both the regulatory and incentive-oriented elements of the plan would work to rein in costs. Consumers would have substantial incentives to seek lower-cost plans. In case these incentives did not keep costs in check, the plan included a cap on premium increases to ensure that costs did not increase faster than national income.

Finally, the plan would help the government balance the federal budget. Most of the financing would come through the employer mandate and flow directly to health insurers without ever passing through Washington. The cap on premiums, translated into limits on the growth of existing health programs, would reduce the rate of growth in federal health costs. Federal subsidies for low-wage employers and low-income Americans would not be allowed to grow any faster than the premium cap.

WHY DID THE PLAN FAIL?

On the surface, the Health Security Act seemed to solve every major problem propelling the interest in national health reform. It addressed the concerns of the uninsured and those who worried about becoming uninsured, and it guaranteed cost containment for the nation as a whole and for the government. It creatively combined elements from two of the most popular reform plans. Why then did it fail?

Supporters of health reform contend that politics doomed the Health Security Act. While political factors were extremely important, they alone cannot account for the failure of the effort. Rather, the failure of the plan stemmed from three problems. First, the beliefs that shape the proposals of the two main groups of reformers—those who support single-payer reform and those who support a more market-oriented, managed-competition approach—are so different that compromise is impossible. Second, both groups base their policy prescriptions on false assumptions about health care spending and the health sector, so their proposals are undermined as the weakness of their assumptions comes to light. Third, neither group successfully addresses the financing of health care reform. In today's antitax climate, both groups do whatever they can to avoid mentioning the fact that health reform must either cost money or reduce health care use.

Political Failures

There is no doubt that a variety of political factors severely handicapped the Clinton administration's efforts at health reform. But before analyzing the failure of current health policy initiatives, I want to make the case that the alternative hypotheses for why the Clinton plan failed—the strength of health care lobbies, the strategic ineptness of the administration, the complexity of the plan itself, the employer-mandate financing system, partisan politics—are not sufficient to explain the collapse of reform.

The death of past health reform efforts has been ascribed to opposition from health care interest groups.[6] The American Medical Association (AMA), the leading representative of doctors, almost scotched Medicare by railing about the dangers of socialized medicine. Health care lobbyists certainly participated actively in the 1993 debate and made substantial contributions to the political campaigns of both Democrats and Republicans. The health insurance industry, mounting a direct attack on the plan, ran a series of ads highly critical of the Clinton proposal.

Health lobbyists made it harder to pass the Clinton plan, but it is important not to overstate their role. Both the American Medical Association and the Health Insurance Association of America supported universal coverage and the requirement that employers pay part of health care bills (Starr 1995). In the wake of years of declining health insurance coverage, both groups had self-interested reasons for wanting some kind of health reform to pass. Most of the health care interest groups lobbied not against the passage of any legislation but for modifications of legislation to serve their own interests. Lobbying efforts did jeopardize particular features of the Clinton plan, but they did not turn the political climate against reform altogether.

Some observers of the political process have blamed the failure of the Health Security Act on political bungling by the Clinton administration. A number complain that Clinton's reform plan was designed in secrecy by a shadowy health care task force rather than in an open, public process. Others argue that the administration was too open to the complaints of outside interest groups and too quick to compromise. Some assert that the president seemed too ready to negotiate with Congress; others believe that he should have allowed the legislators to develop a plan themselves.[7] While more savvy political tactics would have helped the president, they do not explain the failure of the congressional efforts to develop a plan. By the fall of 1994, the president's plan was dead—but so were plans developed by representatives and senators well versed in political strategy.

The complexity of the Clinton plan, critics say, provides ample illustration of the political naiveté of its designers. The managed-competition structure depended on the creation of a hierarchy of new institutions—ready ammunition for analysts on the left and right who decided the construction of a brand-new bureaucracy. Combining these elements with the enforcement and monitoring structures needed to ensure compliance with the premium cap yielded a plan so mazelike that only a few hardy analysts could hope to negotiate it.[8]

The administration could and probably should have made the plan simpler by excluding peripheral elements, such as legislation to improve the Indian Health Service, reform medical education, improve Medicare's long-term-care coverage, and tie the health insurance system to the workers' compensation system. The elaborate structure of the plan, though, was largely a necessary consequence of its attempt to combine the managed-competition and single-payer proposals. The administration needed to guarantee that it could produce savings while providing universal and equitable coverage and retaining a market-based health insurance system. The difficulties of balancing all three objectives became evident as alternative "centrist" plans advanced in the House and Senate. Plans that relied on private insurance inevitably faltered when they had to guarantee to budget hawks that savings could be achieved.

Finally, the administration faced furious opposition from small-business interests angered by the employer-mandate financing system. In fact, the subsidy structure in the administration's plan provided substantial advantages to small businesses.[9] The smallest, lowest-wage businesses would pay only 3.5 percent of payroll for health insurance coverage, the equivalent of a 15-cent increase in the minimum wage. In polls most Americans supported requiring employers to purchase coverage for their employees. Nonetheless, the administration never effectively countered the small-business attack. Here, too, though, the peculiarities of the administration's plan cannot be blamed for the failure of the entire health reform effort. The administration and congressional reformers considered a panoply of alternative financing sources for health reform, from broad-based taxes to individual mandates. These plans, too, were swept away as the tide turned against health reform.

By the end of the process, congressional Republicans, some of whom had originally supported reform and even proposed reform bills of their own, recognized the partisan advantages of thwarting the president's initiative altogether. Senate minority leader Dole, who had originally applauded the president's efforts, now moved away from even his own earlier, moderate reform plan. Partisan politics was the proximate cause of the downfall of the Clinton reform proposal. But the nature of partisan politicking around the plan was itself a consequence of the general lack of enthusiasm for the plan. Republicans swung away from the plan only when it failed to garner widespread support.

Failure to Compromise

For those in the administration who designed the reform plans, the most disheartening aspect of the health reform debate was the tepid support offered by longtime partisans of health reform—the liberal lobbying groups, big businesses, unions, and assorted academics who had insisted that reform was essential. The Clinton plan was, after all, intended as a compromise between the two major camps of health reformers: those who favored a single-payer system and those who favored managed competition. Although no one expects a compromise to garner enormous enthusiasm, administration officials did expect that their proposal would form the basis for negotiation. That did not happen. Instead, the only thing both camps agreed to do was to dismantle the health alliances, the structural linchpin of the Clinton plan.

Differences among groups pressing for reform were a key factor in the deadlock on structural change. These differences stem from the distinct and conflicting views of health care held by the two main groups of reformers. Supporters of the single-payer plan do not just believe that their plan provides the best technical solution to the problems of the health care system. They also believe that medical care is quite different from other goods and services; that doctors, not consumers, should and do make health care decisions; that markets are an inappropriate instrument for allocating health care; and that health care should be distributed in an egalitarian fashion. Managed-competition supporters, by contrast, view health care as a good much like other goods. They grant preeminence to consumer choices, favor markets over bureaucracy, and would accept a less equal distribution of health care.

The proposals advanced by the two groups share goals and themes. Advocates of both styles of reform complain of massive inefficiency and waste in the current system. Each group maintains that its reform proposal could save enough money to expand coverage substantially without rationing care or raising taxes. Yet despite the rhetorical similarities between proponents of the two views and despite their agreement on the need for and goals of reform, their fundamental philosophies concerning the nature of health care and the role of markets are profoundly anti-thetical and deeply resistant to compromise.

Any significant reform of the health care system would entrench the views of one or the other group. As each side fought hard to avoid losing the battle over the future of health policy, it rejected proposals that would make any structural changes to the existing system that did not incorporate its basic assumptions. The only politically viable reforms that remain are modest adjustments to the existing institutional structure. The failure of structural health reform can be blamed as much on those who favored reform as on those who opposed it.

WHAT NEXT?

For a policymaker, whether a medicalist or a marketist, health care certainly *is* different from other policy-relevant goods and services. Other policy problems can be addressed once every twenty or thirty years; health reform never seems to go away. Health care changes constantly and rapidly. Consumers, who experience the pain and misery of illness and disability, quite sensibly demand more and more of this ever improving product. Costs, equally inexorably, rise. Policymakers must refinance or revamp their existing programs and address the concerns of those who now can no longer afford insurance coverage. By the time they finish acting, health care has changed again, setting off another cycle of policy action.

There is nothing new about this problem. Health care spending has been rising quite steadily since 1935. Per capita health costs in the United States have grown at an average annual inflation-adjusted rate of 4 to 5 percent since 1935. This simple reality has two profound implications. First, the potential money savings from any commonly cited reform of the system—such as administrative simplification, malpractice reform, or higher consumer out-of-pocket payments—pale in comparison with the differences in health spending from one year to the next. At best, reducing waste and inefficiencies today could free up resources for covering today's costs of caring for the poor and uninsured. But it would fail to cover the uninsured tomorrow, as costs continue to rise. Second—and more important, given the dynamic nature of health care—health reform proposals should be judged according to how well they respond to the problems of the future, not those of today. As I explain, neither of the two camps of health reformers proposes policy prescriptions that contend with the future of health care.

Medicalists support a government-run system that is centrally organized and financed. Such a system could produce egalitarian universal coverage along with health security for all, forever—but at a considerable price. A government-run, centrally organized system would retard organizational innovation. It would respond more slowly and less flexibly to inevitable, desirable changes in health care technology and consumer preferences. Such a system is at odds with the evolving nature of health care. Moreover, financing health care centrally means balancing the benefits of improved health technologies against the political and economic cost of higher taxes. The experiences of the Canadian health system and of the Medicare program show that this balancing act imposes an enormous strain on public finances. In time it leads to cutbacks in health spending that impose costs in terms of discomfort, inconvenience, and uncertainty that at least some citizens would gladly pay to avoid. By making life—and medical treatment—more comfortable and less inconvenient, rising health care spending has almost certainly improved, rather than harmed, America's national well-being. Constraining health spending to some predetermined fraction of national income would make some people worse off.

Rising health expenditures in aggregate make life better, but in the current U.S. health care system, some groups bear much more of the burden of rising expenditures than do others. Let us examine the problems of redistributing health care resources. Medicalists would limit increases in expenditures by slowing organizational and technological change in health care. While these restraints can reduce the quality of care, they also simplify the problems associated with distributing resources. Once a redistribution scheme is in place, technological and organizational change will occur slowly, allowing the process for financing health care to operate indefinitely.[10]

The competitive system supported by marketists avoids many of the problems of regulatory intervention and limits the fiscal vulnerability of the national treasury that plagues medicalist solutions. But the market solution has difficulty addressing the distributional concerns of health reformers. Market-based reform cannot promise adequate universal coverage and health security as health care changes. Marketists would permit rapid technological and organizational innovation, but would offer financing only for some predetermined and static "adequate" level of care. Americans' view of adequate care for others changes along with their view of adequate care for themselves. The marketist model, though, provides no way of judging how much should be spent to meet the changing costs of health care for those who cannot pay their own medical bills and have no way of financing these ever increasing costs.

Medicalists and marketists turn their particular views of health care into plans for reform by developing particular institutional models, such as the single-payer model and the managed-competition model. To be successful these institutional structures must accommodate changes in health care that improve people's well-being. The plans advanced by both medicalists and marketists fail this test in important ways. Medicalists rely heavily on a regulatory process that is likely to react slowly to change and to favor the interests of well-organized advocacy groups over the routine demands of ordinary Americans. Marketists criticize the regulatory process but fail to devote much attention to the less pervasive, yet nonetheless important, institutional structures of their own reform plans.

The weaknesses of both medicalist and marketist approaches suggest that reform along either line is unlikely to work in the long term. The appeal of a compromise solution, embraced by the Clinton administration, was to move away from these ideologically polarized visions of health care to a technical solution that drew on the strengths of the institutional structures developed by both models. But the fundamental logical conflict between the two plans means that true compromise is impossible.

Instead, the plan the administration finally developed was not so much a synthesis of the two plans as a concatenation of a marketist and a medicalist model: not managed competition under a budget, but managed competition that would turn into a budget. If costs did not rise, markets, albeit heavily regulated ones, would be used to finance and distribute health care. If costs did rise, an alternative, heavily regulatory institutional structure would manage the system. The decision to adopt this two-part plan arose as a way of mediating between the two models, but its final form was dictated by the strictures of the federal budget deficit. The federal budget deficit also undermined Congress's effort to legislate a purely marketist reform of the federal Medicare program in 1995.

The future of health care in America cannot be resolved by either the medicalist or the marketist policies that have been advanced so far. The egalitarian structure of medicalist models will erode as governments cut back services in the face of rising costs and stagnant revenues. The competitive processes on which marketists rely will be undermined as politicians strive to keep down the cost of care funded through government programs. I propose a direct tax on health care spending. This method of financing reform is consistent with either a marketist or a medicalist approach and would move the United States in the direction of a more sustainable system. In the context of marketist reform, this proposal would allow individual health care choices to yield an appropriate level of national health spending. At the same time, my proposal would provide a means of funding and redistributing health resources that would maintain a constantly changing "adequate" standard of care for all Americans.

ABOUT THE AUTHOR

Sherry Glied, PhD, is Associate Professor of Health Economics and Chair, Department of Health Policy and Management, Joseph L. Mailman School of Public Health, Columbia University, New York, New York. She is also the author of *Chronic Condition: Why Health Reform Fails.*

NOTES

1. Immediately after Clinton's speech, two-thirds of those polled approved of the plan (Brownstein 1993). Senate minority leader Dole recommended that Republicans work with President Clinton to produce a health care bill (Nelson 1993).

2. Insurance companies price policies to individuals based on individual health risks and to small groups based on average risk in the group. Most large group policies do not have an insurance-risk component. Insurance companies simply

administer the health care package. In such cases the "price" of insurance is the average cost incurred by the members of the group.

3. Insurance coverage may have been falling well before 1988. Changes in the way that data sources count the uninsured (especially a change in the definition in 1987) make it difficult to say with certainty.

4. Unfortunately, the amounts Americans say they would be willing to pay for universal coverage do not come close to the sums needed. In 1993, 41 percent said they would be willing to pay $480 more in taxes per year for national health insurance that would cover everyone and eliminate all other payments (Jacobs and Shapiro 1993). By my calculations the actual per capita cost of health care for this benefit is about five times that high.

5. The group was led by Paul Starr and Walter Zelman. Their article "A Bridge to Compromise: Competition under a Budget" (Starr and Zelman 1993) provides a description of the plan they devised.

6. Starr 1982 and Rothman 1993 discuss the role of health care lobbies in defeating earlier reform efforts.

7. For a discussion of these criticisms, see Fallows 1995.

8. Those who did read the plan uncovered enforcement and regulatory mechanisms that rarely figured in public discussions, and this prompted a sense that the plan was riddled with hidden dangers and booby traps. See Elizabeth McCaughey's very effective if, in many respects, inaccurate critique in *The New Republic* (McCaughey 1994).

9. Small, low-wage-businesses would pay a much smaller share of payroll for health insurance than would larger businesses. Small, low-wage business payments would be capped, while the largest employers would receive no subsidies at all. This subsidy structure was roundly criticized by economists for generating substantial distortions of the labor market. Over time this system could have been expected to lead to a concentration of low-wage workers in the smallest firms.

10. The rising private share of health care spending in Great Britain and the increasing interest in privatizing part of the system in Canada suggest that reform of financing mechanisms will be needed even in centrally constrained health care systems.

REFERENCES

Balz D. Health plan was albatross for Democrats. *Washington Post,* November 18, 1994; final edition, sec. A, p. 1, col. 1.

Congressional Budget Office (CBO). *Economic and Budget Outlook: Fiscal Years 1995–1999.* Washington, DC: Government Printing Office, 1994a.

Drew E. *On the Edge: The Clinton Presidency.* New York: Simon and Schuster, 1994.

Health Security Act. Washington, DC: Government Printing Office, 1993.

Jacobs LR, Shapiro RY, Schulman EC. Medical care in the United States—an update. *Public Opinion Quarterly* 1993;57(3):394–427.

Levit KR, Cowan CA, Lazenby HC, McDonnel PA, Sensenig AL, Stiller JM, Won DK. National health spending trends, 1960–1993. *Health Affairs* 1994;13:14–32.

Starr P. What happened to health care reform? *American Prospect* 20:20–31.

DECENTRALIZATION, DEVOLUTION, AND THE DEFICIT: THE CHANGING ROLE OF THE STATE AND THE COMMUNITY

Carroll L. Estes and Karen W. Linkins

During the past two decades, decentralization, devolution, and other reductions in the federal role in domestic health and human service policy have been fundamental processes shaping the structure and delivery of community services in the United States (Estes, 1986; Estes & Gerard, 1983; Estes & Linkins, 1997a). The 1996 Welfare Reform legislation signed by President Clinton is the latest evidence of this trend toward devolution of responsibility for policymaking from the federal to state level. This new law accords states much greater control in determining eligibility and benefit levels for welfare while it decouples the program from automatic Medicaid eligibility. As it signals the end of federal entitlement to cash assistance for qualified poor persons, the welfare reform legislation is accompanied by a cultural and political context favoring the use of state discretion to further rationalize and privatize the delivery of health and social services. For example, Governors are choosing to move Medicaid-eligible beneficiaries into for-profit managed care systems in ways that raise concerns regarding the viability of independent providers of nonprofit community social services (Estes & Linkins, 1997a). As states move to contract directly with managed care entities for all Medicaid patients, previous sources of state funding available to independent nonprofit service providers are being rolled into these state contracts. Managed care entities, rather than the state, are assuming decision-making power over whether many nonprofit health and social service providers are awarded contracts, or whether they themselves will offer these services, or even whether these services are necessary at all.

There continues to be no substantive national debate about privatization outside of the circles of academia, health care experts and policymakers, and there does not appear to be substantial public opposition to the movement toward greater privatization in America. This is indicative of: (1) the power of the privatization ideology in American thought (Drucker, 1984); (2) the weakness of the American welfare state (Quadagno, 1988); (3) the strength of business that is promoting the expansion of capital into new markets including those subsidized by the State (Estes & Alford,

1990); and (4) the reigning paradigm of economics in public policy in its concern for cost efficiency and deficit reduction. Until recently, the role and strength of support for the nonprofit sector and the legitimacy of its advocates (Smith & Stone, 1985) contributed to the positive attitude toward the private provision of services based on the theory that the private nonprofit sector would permit the expansion of welfare-state benefits without the commensurate growth in the state bureaucracy occurring in European welfare states (Kramer, 1981). Salamon (1983) has termed this use of the nonprofit sector as "third party government."

In this paper, we examine the devolving role of the state in health and social policy arenas and explore the varying definitions and processes of privatization. We then discuss the implications of the devolution revolution, and the possible ensuing "race to the bottom," for community-based long-term care and vulnerable populations. Finally, we discuss the role of managed care in the devolution process.

THE ROLE OF THE STATE (GOVERNMENT)

A primary feature of modern capitalist societies is that there are multiple sources of legitimacy for the state and private businesses, depending on socio-historical conditions (Estes & Alford, 1990). Legitimacy is crucial to the continued functioning of all organizations and institutions including the State. Two stunning accomplishments of the Reagan administration are its successful ideological assault on the legitimacy of government itself and its redefinition of government as the problem instead of the solution. An important consequence is that the State has confronted serious legitimacy problems in the face of its own politically defined economic crisis (Estes, 1991; Estes & Alford, 1990). The bold attempt of the 1994 Contract for America reflects these difficulties facing the State and the struggles surrounding them. Federal funding cuts, attacks on entitlements, and devolution of federal policy are all explicable as part of the State's response to its legitimacy problems. The transfer of State-funded medical care dollars from nonprofits to for-profits, and from small entities to large corporate conglomerates, has the dual advantage of addressing one aspect of socially constructed economic crisis—the need for new investment opportunities and profit potential—and simultaneously bolstering the legitimacy of State decisions to the extent that they are perceived as rationalizing and potentially lowering the cost of care. Most hospitable to the privatization of the State, the Reagan legacy is:

> the pronounced shift in state actions toward market norms and market solutions. For the elderly major issues have become the continued availability of legitimacy beliefs supporting the two cornerstones of aging policy. Social Security and the notion of universal health care for the elderly (Medicare's assurance of access to health care without respect for ability to pay) (Estes, 1994, p. 62).

The State performs several significant roles in relation to the community that are inextricably linked to (and vehicles of) the privatization of the welfare state (Estes & Alford, 1990; Offe, 1984). State policies create investment opportunities for private capital by rendering health and social service provision primarily through policies that promote and finance private rather than public provision of services. In addition, the State limits its own activities in health and social services to those that complement the market and encourage the rapid development and expansion of new proprietary forms of organization in the human services (e.g., managed care). The State also engages in "market replacing" actions as it subsidizes the cost of an increasingly inaccessible and private business by securing a system of civil law and regulation protecting the market, which, in turn, raises problems of accountability.

An example of the accountability questions that may be raised is contained in a recent lawsuit against the Health Care Financing Administration (HCFA) in which the plaintiffs charged that the Secretary of HHS abdicated her responsibility to monitor HMOs and to ensure that HMOs provide Medicare-covered benefits. HCFA argued unsuccessfully that HMOs are privately owned entities and their actions cannot be imputed to the federal government. Attorneys for HHS Secretary Shalala wrote, "This case involves the decisions of private HMOs and their health care professionals about what medical treatment is necessary. Such decisions are not made by government and the government has neither a role nor an interest in the decisions made by any HMO" (Grijalva v. Shalala, 1996, p. 26). Ruling against the Secretary of HHS, the federal court found that instead, the government has responsibility for assuring the Medicare patients are protected even in the case of HMO contracting.

The intensity of the current debate about the appropriate role of the government and of the private sector underscores the fundamental question of national purpose and goals, and the means by which these goals will be achieved. There is a continuing dispute about whether devolution reform can in fact achieve national goals other than those related to a reduced federal role in domestic health and social policy. Reagan and Sanzone (1981, p. 148) argue that the "belief that national goals can be achieved by decentralization subnational choice and policy priorities within broad federal parameters" is the "myth of decentralization."

Decentralization of program and fiscal responsibility through privatization is an ongoing political theme in the United States promoted through policies to reduce the federal role and responsibilities for social needs. The notion of federalism that underlies the decentralization and devolution debate dates back to the country's beginning and controversy about its form and function is heard among officials and citizens at all levels of government. Five consistent and important themes have emerged concerning the role of the State: (1) the delineation of government versus private responsibilities; (2) the capacity and structural incentives of government, and of different governmental levels versus those of private corporations; (3) questions of equity; (4) accountability; and (5) democratic participation and the distribution of power (Estes & Gerard, 1983).

DEFINITIONS OF PRIVATIZATION

The 1960s and 1970s forwarded a form of privatization built on the voluntary sector (Estes & Alford, 1990; Estes & Bergthold, 1989). President Reagan shifted the weight of ideological and fiscal resources to a new kind of privatization—one characterized by state subsidy of for-profit (in the place of nonprofit) enterprises in state-contracted and financed services (Estes, 1991) and privatization in the form of increased provision of services by the informal sector (e.g., increased post-acute work in the home following shortened lengths of hospital stays under Medicare prospective payment policies) (Binney, Estes, & Humphers, 1993).

Contrary to the classical economic theory of privatization, state-initiated privatization strategies do not necessarily reduce government involvement in terms of either public subsidy or regulation. Privatization may actually enhance the role of the state insofar as privatization policies of the state either maintain or increase public spending or the regulation of services. In such instances, it is more accurate to say that the state is being restructured than that there is a retrenchment by the state. An example is the successful recent reversal by Congress and the Reagan, Bush, and Clinton administrations of the direction of long-term trends toward expanding eligibility and benefits to the elderly under Medicare through policy changes without either reducing the share of GNP allocated to medical care programs or the total deficit (Estes, 1991).

Scarpaci (1989) observes that:

> Privatization takes many forms, so a simple interpretation is rarely sufficient. Nevertheless, there is strong consensus that privatization is effectively a political process (Barnes, 1985; Dunleavy, 1986; Heald, 1985; Mohan, 1986; Pirie, 1985). Because it includes both collective provision and more privatized systems, it can appear in several forms in the health care sector. Most health care privatization, however, tends to reduce state participation and increase private-sector activity. The state attempts to keep itself at arm's length while fewer public monies and personnel provide health services. The need for medical and health services has increasingly been met and satisfied in the marketplace. In many places these services are changing from an inalienable right of the citizenry to being treated as a commodity. This process . . . commodification of health services, is tied to technology that greatly enhanced the exchange value of such services (pp. 7–8).

Home care is a particularly important example of privatization, where high tech services and the more formal delivery system that are funded through reimbursements (e.g., Medicare and Medicaid) have made this a profitable, expansive market niche. A market has been created with so-called "tangible" services (Bergthold, Estes, & Villanueva, 1985; Estes & Linkins, 1994).

It is essential to view privatization as a multifaceted process that is not just a response to fiscal crises of the state. The role of the state changes in response to numerous pressures, challenges, and ideologies. As Scarpaci (1989) notes:

> the pressure for the state to become more economically efficient in social program delivery had been present, most centrally in the conceptual issues that are central to public-choice theory. Challenges for lower-cost private-sector delivery have perhaps

been most dramatically apparent in electoral politics among the advanced capitalist nations. There is strong electoral appeal in the state's abdication of services and production that are either perceived to be inapplicable to certain classes (job programs, relief, Medicaid for the "middle classes") or claim that services "can be provided at lower cost by the private sector . . . There is much debate about the rolling back of the welfare state and the deleterious effects such a process imposes on the poor. A more accurate appraisal is that privatization is neither a new process, nor a process that develops uniformity across space and time (p. 11).

THE DEVOLUTION REVOLUTION

Over the past several decades, three waves of federalism and devolution policies have been designed to reduce the federal role, commencing with President Nixon's introduction of revenue sharing and block grants in the early 1970s. While professing that this policy move was bringing government closer to the people, the community action program of President Johnson's War on Poverty was replaced by a significantly more distant (and weak) form of political participation—testimony of public hearings. The second wave of federalism commenced with the aforementioned ideological assault of the Reagan administration on government and the 1981 Omnibus Budget Reconciliation Act (OBRA) that implemented block grants for social services, mental health, substance and alcohol abuse, and community development, among others. Called by some, "Fend for yourself" federalism, devolution during this period was accompanied by declining federal revenues to the states and increased rationalization and privatization in the delivery of health and human services.

The present wave of decentralization, which Nathan (1996) has called "Newt Federalism," was a core element of the Contract for America accompanying the 1994 Republican Congressional and Gubernatorial sweep. Welfare reform and other current proposals for policy change are designed to transfer, and in some cases, abolish the federal role in redistributional outlays across entitlement programs as responsibility is devolved to the states.

The impact of the power shift from the nation's capital to statehouses through welfare reform is augmented by Medicaid cuts, managed care, and the massive restructuring of health care by the private market. The combination of these forces significantly raises the stakes in how the states will exercise their discretion and explains why the changes afoot may be appropriately called the "devolution revolution" (Nathan, 1996). A key question is: To what extent will this delegation of authority result in more or less responsive programs and expenditures? Absent national standards, federal requirements and oversight, devolution and myriad state level decisions are expected to promote politically based rather than need-based policies and allocations (Estes, 1979).

The long-term effects of the various forms of devolution for community-based long term care, the elderly and the disadvantaged are of concern. For one, decentralization assures that the dominant structural economic and political interest operating at the federal level (e.g., over economic and tax policy) will not be challenged by the fragmented, divergent, and weaker interests operating in support of welfare rights and equity for the disadvantaged that are able to mobilize to influence state and local policies. Second, the divestment of federal (and public sector) responsibility through deregulation and decentralization of policy goal-setting increases the influence of the private sector over the public interest in policy-making in the multiple and less visible state and local settings in which bartering over regulations and standards must be refought and renegotiated (and won or lost). Old age policies, especially long term care for the chronically ill and disadvantaged elderly, are mediated in largely unknown ways by business and provider interests. Third, highly discretionary programs limit the possibility of effective political action for all but the most organized and capitalized because such moves require having the capacity to mobilize across multiple and diverse geopolitical jurisdictions. Fourth, increased state and local fiscal and regulatory responsibility for services places human services demands on the most fiscally vulnerable and politically sensitive levels of decision-making (i.e., states and communities), given that the state and local jurisdictions have more variable and limited fiscal resources than the federal government. Hence, decisions about cash assistance and other services for many elderly, particularly the near poor and low income, are located precisely where pressures to control social expenses are greatest and necessarily the most conservative. Problems of access are likely to increase as well. Fifth, decentralization supplants national policy goals and commitments with the more autonomous and variable state and local policy choices, particularly with regard to essential programs for the aging, blunting the most progressive changes that may be effected at the national level. Sixth, decentralization raises important accountability issues as comparable data across multiple jurisdictions are more difficult to obtain, and assessments of the impacts of policies are difficult to make. (Estes, 1983, 1994).

COMMUNITY AND THE RACE TO THE BOTTOM

Two notions about community and community care are being debated by both progressive and conservative forces, and with distinctly different ideas about the goals of what is public versus private (Lloyd, 1991).

For conservatives, a revitalized concept of community and the promotion of community care may be seen as a mechanism to reduce the public costs of care and to restore the patriarchal family and women's proper role in it. Conservatives call for shrinking the welfare state and shifting care responsibility from the public to the private arena (Lloyd, 1991) based on assumptions that there is a potential caregiving population (informal sector of family, friends, neighbors) that can, and *should,* be expanded and exploited to provide even greater levels of support to elders (Lloyd, 1991). This call for increased family responsibility is interesting in view of the well-known fact that women and other informal caregivers already provide about 80 percent of long term care.

Progressives support the notion of community care to promote: (1) entitlement or a right to much needed long term care; (2) augmented public and inherently "social" responsibility; (3) a step toward gender, class, and ethnic justice; and (4) empowerment of both care recipient and caregiver. However, policies to promote care *by* the community rather than care *in* the community require an ever-widening circle of willing and largely unpaid members of the personal network or social world of the person needing help (Phillipson, 1982). In addition, the requirements and burdens of informal care are influenced by race, class, and gender.

The implications of privatization in its various forms are critical in the context of the intensifying process of devolution and decentralization. A key issue here is propensity for state to "race to the bottom" in welfare policy (Peterson & Rom, 1990; Peterson, Rom, & Scheve, 1995). Central issues are (Estes & Linkins, 1997b): (1) the extent to which state level discretionary policy options will alter (and potentially diminish or expand) priorities, services, and other policy outcomes for community-based long term care; (2) the existence of and extent to which a race to the bottom is occurring in long term care in the states; (3) whether long term care programs and populations are as vulnerable (or more or less vulnerable) to cuts and entitlement reforms as other health or welfare programs and populations; (4) the factors that influence the nature and direction of such changes; (5) the tradeoffs in and consequences of shifting policy and funding on long term care and recipients along generational, gender, racial and ethnic, and social class lines (Estes & Gerard, 1983; Estes, 1983; Polivka, Dunlop, & Rothman, 1996); (6) the role and effects of managed care on long term care including that on the "rest" of the nonprofit community-based services system (e.g., adult day care, nutrition, and personal assistance); (7) the effects of devolution on the health of communities (population health); and (8) the extent and effects of political mobilization of long term care and other advocates on state and local choices (Swan, Estes, & Wood, 1983).

DEVOLUTION AND MANAGED CARE

Given the newness and rapidity of the development of managed care and its use by an increasing number of states and localities to cut Medicaid and other public sector costs (e.g., mental health), there is a growing need for knowledge about the role and effects of managed care organizations on the health and human services that comprise the long term care continuum of services. Among the significant questions are their effects on the traditional nonprofit community-based social services and their potential to medicalize social services (Polivka et al., 1996).

Because of block granting social services may be reduced or lost altogether. Managed care entities, although organizationally configured differently than fee-for-service medicine, are culturally committed to the same acute care medical model. Managed care organizations will redefine the social support needs of older patients in medical terms (if they are defined as service eligible at all) in order for services to be provided under their plans. Services will have to be justified in terms of the bottom line—the acute care cost saved or profits. Social services are not likely

to "save" acute care dollars. Indeed, social services have historically been justified
as servicing other purposes, e.g., improving the quality of life or easing the burden
on the family members. Social services have not been the subject of much research
in general; thus, most such services have not been demonstrated as profitable or
beneficial in the rather narrow cost-benefit "metrics" or medical outcomes research.
Another result is likely to be the medicalization of social services in that their sole
justification for existence may be redefined in terms of their service to or function
for managed care or acute care objectives.

Managed Care and The Free Rider Problem

The free rider problem may be described as a situation in which people *"ride"* or
"mooch" on the system (Enthoven & Kronick, 1991; Reinhardt, 1996) without paying their way. Free riders are defined as those who are not willing to pay their costs.
At issue is the question: what new "uses" (or support) will managed care organizations extract from the home- and community-based long term care service system in
their drive to further reduce costly lengths of stay in hospitals and in their use of
outpatient procedures to do so? In the drive by managed care organizations to improve the bottom line, how will the meager resources of social supportive services
in the community be used; and whether they will be paid for by managed care entities; and what increases in the informal (family and friends) care work (burden)
will be generated by managed care? What will be the transfer (if any) of the profits
or "save" resources generated by managed care to compensate or pay for the increased home- and community-based long term care services that are (and will be)
drawn upon in order to maximize the cost savings of individual managed care corporations?

Research needs to document the public and private cost that managed care entities pass on to others via their decisions to reduce costs and increase profits, and
to institute practices such as "drive by" or "drive through" deliveries and mastecto-
mies—that some argue, "dump" patients out of the acute care system and who then
require considerable health and supportive care—that is, caring work that is ex-
tracted from the family and community and which is not paid for by the managed
care entities or by the public sector.

DEVOLUTION AND COMMUNITY-BASED
LONG TERM CARE FOR THE ELDERLY

Political, economic, and socio-cultural factors challenge the future of community-
based long term care particularly under policies of privatization. The resources
available for care in the community will be shaped by the outcomes of partisan
struggles in Congress and the White House concerning the fate of Medicare and
Medicaid and the decisions of the governors and state houses intent on tax and budget cuts in social programs to pay for them.

Political Factors

The power of corporations, particularly insurance and managed care corporations, has dramatically enhanced the ability of proprietary interest to shape (if not direct) the public policy agenda in ways that create change and uncertainty for the long term care industry. Resource and regulatory struggles between the nursing home and other long term care providers have intensified with increasing state power. Home- and community-based social supportive care are pitted against the highly influential nursing home and managed care interests. For nonprofit community care providers, these struggles are likely to be to protect themselves against drastic cuts; while for the more powerful managed care and nursing home interests, their lobbying will be not only to preserve, but also to expand state funding to increase their reimbursement rates and to obtain publicly granted waivers to include ever larger segments of the state patient populations. Similar struggles will be played out many times over in the different states between insurers, managed care companies, and the generally weaker social and supportive services in the long term care continuum.

Economic Factors

The vast and rising profits in medical care and the growing for-profit ownership and concentration in all aspects of the medical industrial complex (Estes, Harrington, & Davis, 1993) have vastly increased the stakes both for consumers and for private shareholders in the profitability of health and long term care. A contradiction is that the high and rising health costs produce and coincide with increased profits, while at the same time the escalating costs generate opposition forces from those in the public and private sector that pay them. Predictably, the state will be negatively impugned and the consumer of health care will be caught in a squeeze between these forces.

Socio-Cultural Factors

Ideological struggles and cultural shifts of note include: the pervasive and strong ideology of the market; with competition, efficiency, and rationalization as major mechanisms to achieve profits and cost containment. A problem is that, with the strong ideological commitment to the market that characterizes the 1990s, the "means" of competition efficiency, and rationalization have become "goal displaced" as "ends" in themselves. Accompanying these cultural factors is the pervasive ideology of individualism that tends to blame individuals rather than the system for their plight.

CONCLUSION

As community-based health and long term care services, welfare, and other entitlements are increasingly subject to threats and to new forms of privatization, it is

essential to ask whether or not "the business knowledge, more flexible organizational structures, and growing managerial and professional experience that have allowed corporations to generate high sales and sometimes substantial profits" will be
translated into the essential social provision that meets the standards of the public
good (Nelson, 1995, p. 138). The privatization of health and human services and entitlements in the present socio-historical context involves the crossing of what may
be called an "institutional divide" (Nelson, 1995) between business and public services. It highlights the tensions and contradictions between capitalism and democracy (Myles, 1993).

In the enthusiasm of privatization, it is well to remember the concept of "market failure" that has been employed to define and defend the admittedly marginal but
important role of the state. By 1996, the federally assured safety net of entitlement
to cash assistance known as welfare and that assurance of minimal access to health
care for those disqualified by the states (e.g., aliens) became "choices" that states
have the option of making. Privatization through decentralization supplants national
policy goals and commitments not only with the more autonomous and unstandard-
ized state and local policy choices, but also the less visible private decisions. Both
processes (privatization and decentralization) have particularly important consequences for the elderly and the disadvantaged, including long term care programs
historically located at the state and local levels. There is little assurance of consistency or uniformity of policy and little promise of equity for powerless groups
across different states. In the words of Katha Pollit, the behavior of the State is effectively "Turning the safety-net into a safety doily" (Pollitt, 1996).

ABOUT THE AUTHORS

Carroll L. Estes, PhD, is Professor of Sociology at the Institute for Health and Aging, where she was first and founding director, and in the Department of Social and
Behavioral Sciences, School of Nursing, at the University of California, San Francisco. Author of *The Aging Enterprise* and seven other books, she is former president of the Gerontological Society of America, the American Society of Aging, and
the Association for Gerontology in Higher Education.

Karen W. Linkins, PhD, is Senior Manager with The Lewin Group in Falls
Church, Virginia.

REFERENCES

Barnes, F. (1985). On the hill, raging representatives. *New Republic, 192,* 8–10.
Bergthold, L., Estes, C. L., & Villanueva, A. (1985). Public light and private
    dark: The privatization of home health services for the elderly in the U.S.
    Home Health Care Services Quarterly, 11, 7–33.
Binney, E. A., Estes, C. L., & Humphers, S. (1993). Informalization and

community care. In C. L. Estes, J. H. Swan, & Associates (Eds.), *The long term care crisis: Elders trapped in the no care zone* (pp. 155–170). Newbury Park, CA: Sage.

Drucker, P. (1984). Beyond the Bell breakup. *The Public Interest, 77,* 3–27.

Dunleavy, P. (1986). Explaining the privatization boom. *Public Administration, 64,* 13–34.

Enthoven, A. & Kronick, M. (1991). Universal health insurance through incentive reform. In P. R. Lee & C. L. Estes (Eds.), *The nation's health* (4th ed., pp. 284–291). Boston: Jones & Bartlett.

Estes, C. L. (1979). *The aging enterprise.* San Francisco: Jossey-Bass.

Estes, C. L. (1983). Austerity & aging in the United States: 1980 and beyond. In A. M. Guillernard (Ed.), *Old age and the welfare state* (pp. 169–185). Beverly Hills, CA: Sage.

Estes, C. L. (1986). The politics of ageing in America. *Ageing and Society, 6,* 121–134.

Estes, C. L. (1994). The Reagan-Bush legacy: Privatization, the welfare state and aging. In D. Challis, B. Davis, & K. Traske (Eds.), *Community care: New agendas and challenges from the UK and overseas* (pp. 211–248). PSSRU Studies Series and the British Society of Gerontology. Hants: Ashgate Publishing Ltd.

Estes, C. L. (1991). The new political economy of aging. In M. Minkler and C. L. Estes (Eds.), *Critical perspectives of aging.* Amityville, NY: Baywood Press.

Estes, C. L. & Alford, R. (1990). Systemic crisis and the nonprofit sector: Toward a political economy of the nonprofit health and social services sector. *Theory and Society, 19,* 173–198.

Estes, C. L. & Bergthold, L. (1989). The unraveling of the nonprofit sector in the U.S. *International Journal of Sociology and Social Policy, 9,* 18–33.

Estes, C. L. & Gerard, L. E. (1983). Governmental responsibility: Issues of reform and federalism. In C. L. Estes, R. J. Newcomer, & Associates (Eds.), *Fiscal austerity and aging* (pp. 41–58). Beverly Hills, CA: Sage.

Estes, C. L., Harrington, C., & Davies, S. (1992). Medical-industrial complex. In E. F. Borgatta & M. Borgatta (Eds.), *The encyclopedia of sociology, 3* (pp. 1243–1254). New York: Macmillan.

Estes, C. L. & Linkins, K. W. (1994). *Differences in access to home care: Certified and uncertified providers.* Paper presented at the American Public Health Association, Washington, DC.

Estes, C. L. & Linkins, K. W. (1997a). Long term care: Race to the bottom? In P. R. Lee & C. L. Estes (Eds.), *The nation's health* (5th ed., pp. 229–236). Boston, MA: Jones and Bartlett.

Estes, C. L. & Linkins, K. W. (1997b). Devolution and aging policy: Racing to the bottom in long term care? *International Journal of Health Services, 27,* 427–442.

Grijalvav, Shalala. (1996, October 17). Oppositional brief, CIV 93–711 TUCACM (D. Arizona).

Heald, D. (1985). Will the privatization of public enterprises solve the problem of control? *Public Administration, 63,* 7–22.

Kramer, R. M. (1981). *Voluntary agencies in the welfare state.* Berkeley: University of California Press.

Lloyd, P. C. (1991). The empowerment of elderly people. *Journal of Aging Studies, 5,* 125–135.

Mohan, B. (1986). *Toward comparative social welfare.* Cambridge, MA: Schenkman Books.

Myles, J. F. (1993). *Old age in the welfare state: The political economy of public pensions.* Lawrence, KS: University of Kansas.

Nathan, R. & Associates. (1996). The 'nonprofitization movement' as a form of devolution. In D. F. Burlingame, W. A. Diaz, W. F. Ilchman, & Associates (Eds.), *Capacity for change?: The nonprofit world in the age of devolution.* Indianapolis, IN: Indiana University Center on Philanthropy.

Nelson, J. I. (1995). Post industrial capitalism: *Exploring economic inequality in America.* Newbury Park: Sage.

Offe, C. (1984). *Contradictions of the welfare state.* Cambridge, MA: MIT Press.

Peterson, P. E. & Rom, M. L. (1990). *Welfare magnets: A case for a national standard.* Washington, D.C.: Brookings Institution.

Peterson, P. E., Rom, M. L., & Scheve, K. F. (1995). *The race among the states: Welfare benefits, 1976–1989.* Paper presented at the Annual Meeting of the American Political Science Association, San Francisco, CA.

Phillipson, C. (1982). *Capitalism and the construction of old age.* London: Macmillan.

Pirie, M. (1985). *Dismantling the state: The theory and practice of privatization.* Dallas, TX: National Center for Policy Analysis.

Pollitt, K. (1996). Subject to debate: No vote for Clinton? Readers bite back. *The Nation, 263* (16).

Polivka, L., Dunlop, D., & Rathman, M. B. (1996). *Long term care for the frail elderly in Florida: Expanding choices, containing costs.* Tampa, FL: Florida Policy Exchange Center in Aging. University of South Florida.

Quadagno, J. (1988). *The transformation of old age security, class and politics in the American welfare state.* Chicago: University of Chicago Press.

Reagan, M. & Sanzone, J. G. (1981). *The new federalism.* New York: Oxford University Press.

Reinhardt, U. (1996). The rise and fall of health care reform: A dialogue between Mark Pauly and Uwe Reinhardt. In *Looking back, looking forward: "Staying power" issues in health care reform.* The Richard and Hinda Rosenthal Lectures 1994–1995, Washington, DC: National Academy Press.

Salamon, L. M. (1983, May 3). *Nonprofit organizations and the rise of third-party government: The scope, character and consequences of government support of nonprofit organizations.* Paper presented at Independent Sector Research Forum, New York City.

Scarpaci, J. L. (1989). The theory and practice of health services privatization. In J. L. Scarpaci (Ed.), *Health services privatization in industrial societies* (pp. 1–23). New Brunswick, NJ: Rutgers University Press.

Smith, S. R. and Stone, D. A. (1985). *Privatization: Retrenchment or entrenchment of the welfare state?* Working paper for Conference on the Unravelling of the Welfare State, University of California, Santa Cruz.

Swan, J. H., Estes, C. L., and Wood, J. (1983). Fiscal crisis: Economic and fiscal problems of state and local governments. In C. L. Estes, R. J. Newcomer, & Associates (Eds.), *Fiscal austerity and aging* (pp. 113–132). Beverly Hills: Sage.

CHAPTER 4

ETHICS, VALUES, AND IDEOLOGY

I n previous editions, we have had articles on ethics scattered through various chapters (e.g., Jonsen and Lee's paper on the Right to Health Care in the 4th edition), and many papers have dealt with issues from a particular ideological point of view (articles that view medical care as a market good, like other goods and services, in a capitalistic society). In this edition, we have decided to group a few articles together and explicitly recognize the importance of ethics, values, and ideology in health policy.

Especially as we near the elections for the year 2000, the primacy of ideological concerns is brought to the fore. We noted in the introduction that former senator Bill Bradley, as a candidate for the nomination of the Democratic Party for president in the 2000 elections, re-ignited the debate on the issue of health care as a right. In stating "Health is a blessing, but health care in America should be a right," Bradley highlighted one of the most divisive issues fundamental to American health policy debate (September, 1999). The distinction Bradley makes addresses the central purpose of what health policy measures and reforms purport to accomplish. For example, an incremental approach to expanding health insurance coverage would be inappropriate if health care were indeed established as a right of all Americans. Sadly, the media has glossed over the essence of this debate by focusing on the *how,* rather than the *why* of the issue. The scope of most coverage has concentrated solely on the differences between Vice-President Gore's views for incremental reform and those of former senator Bradley for creating governmentally guaranteed health insurance for all Americans. Some additional attention has been paid to the dependence Bradley places on the federal budget surplus in financing the benefit. In doing so, opportunity is lost for a well-informed and truly meaningful public debate over the central issue of concern to our society: the difference in viewing health care as either a social good or as a market commodity.

When medical care is viewed as a market good, discussions of need are framed by the arguments of health economics. If a large number of people have health insurance (public or private), the argument is made that demand for medical care increases simply because the effective price to consumers (patients) is lower. Increased use of health care services then drives up the overall cost of health care to society, and may also drive up the prices of the services themselves. Continuing with this line of reasoning, a variety of direct charges to consumers, such as deductibles, copayments, or co-insurance, are necessary to successfully curb "excessive" demand. Physicians who share this view favor direct charges to patients, purportedly to inhibit "frivolous use" of services. While patients view these charges as "extra billing," physicians refer to them merely as "balance billing."

Although increased demand may indeed drive up costs as supply-and-demand theories predict, this argument involves an oversimplification. The critical factor in this view of medical care as a market good that is responsible for increasing costs is the behavioral response of the buyer, that is, the patient. In other words, only the patient, and the decisions they make to seek care, lead to an overuse of health care services and therefore overexpenditure and inflated prices. The suppliers of care (physicians and hospitals) thereby play a purely passive role in responding to the market.

There is some strong evidence, however, that the most important factor in increasing demand in a fee-for-service (FFS) system, such as the United States', is not the patient but the physician. Within the FFS mechanism, it is the physician who is rewarded financially for each service provided. For example, it has been shown that even when reimbursements to physicians are reduced for a particular service within Medicare and Medicaid, some providers compensate by rendering more services in order to achieve their "target" income. Accordingly, we find that in the United States the use of diagnostic and surgical procedures such as computed tomography (CT) scans, magnetic resonance imaging (MRI), and cataract surgery, which are better reimbursed than simple office visits for evaluation and management, is far higher than in many European countries that limit payments for procedural based services or limit access to such services, without a concomitant improvement in health status or medical outcomes.

The picture is not entirely one-sided, however. For certain prescription drugs that are advertised directly to consumers (e.g., allergy medicines, Viagra) patients do indeed play a role. Some may demand prescription of a brand-name product (usually that of the advertisement sponsor) rather than accepting a lower-priced generic drug. They may also demand a specific procedure (e.g., MRI of the knee), even when the physician advises against it.

Nevertheless, the view of medical care as a market good is not shared by all economists. They believe, as do we, that health care is not a commodity that can be bought or sold; and with illness, particularly one that is life-threatening, there is little room for choice in purchasing or not purchasing care. As such, market arguments, which equate *health care* with *health* in drawing comparisons to other commodities, are misleading. Moreover, theories, projections, and extrapolations are ill-founded, despite the fact that aspects of them (such as demand for brand-name prescriptions) may appear to hold true. The fundamental discrepancy between *health* and *health care* results in multiple "market failures." Moreover, beyond the arguments of health economics, ethical considerations are primary in the reasoning for the "social good" point of view, particularly those surrounding the ethical principle of justice.

However, this having been said, it should be noted that even the arguments about the right to health care, including those made by former senator Bradley, miss an important point. When health and principles of social justice are the bottom line, access to population-based health services is more important than access to medical care in protecting and promoting the health of the population. Failure to recognize this integral point goes back to the insufficient distinction between *health* and *health care* that pervades our society. While the public supports many public health programs for publicly funded services (e.g., immunization) or regulations (food safety), they are not widely appreciated as social goods.

As this brief discussion illustrates, in terms of the valuations we assign and the ideologies we as a society hold, nothing is ever straightforward, and rarely is a decision unequivocally right or wrong. Explicit consideration of these difficult subjects, however, is vital to goal setting and the health policymaking process. We begin Chapter 4 with a short excerpt from Longest's book *Health Policy Making in the United States* (1998) because it relates the ethical principles of autonomy, justice, beneficence, and nonmaleficence to health policy. Because justice plays such an important role in a well-ordered society, it is important to appreciate that "much of the impact on policies and on policy making hinges on defining justice as fairness" (Rawls, 1971). In health policy, many of the issues focus on distributive justice— how resources are allocated and the fairness in terms of the distribution of health-related burdens and benefit. As will be evident in Hacker and Skocpol's paper in Chapter 5, what is fair may be viewed very differently by different actors in the political process (e.g., the views of Republicans and Democrats on the matters of Medicare policy).

We follow Longest's short piece with Annas's very clear description of the movement to establish rights in health care that has gained forced since the early 1970s. Among the first was the right to informed consent, which was long-ago identified as among the most important of patient rights in the United States. Informed consent was quickly followed by other requirements intended to enhance patient autonomy. Some would define this largely in terms of the patient's right to choose. This principle was upheld in the U.S. Supreme Court decision in *Roe v. Wade* in 1973, establishing the women's constitutional right to privacy which included her right to continue or to terminate a pregnancy in the absence of a compelling state interest. The story moved forward, beginning in 1976, with the case of Karen Ann Quinlan, which affirmed the right of a patient to refuse any medical treatment. Another step came with the hospice movement for palliative care at the end of life, which also began in the 1970s, exemplifying a patient's right not only to refuse medical treatment but also to select the course of treatment or lack thereof. By recognizing the patient's right to refuse intensive therapy and choose comfort care, this expansion of patient autonomy ultimately implied conferral of a right to die. More recent decisions have tested interpretations of this in addressing the issue of physician-assisted suicide.

The most recent debate on patient's rights has been stirred by the managed care industry's attempt to convert patients into consumers. Although a series of court decisions in 1972 made it clear that "the law would treat the doctor-patient relationship as a fiduciary, or trust-based relationship, not as an arms length business relationship" (Annas, 1998), in the recent shift to managed care, particularly under for-profit schemes, medicine is big business. In for-profit managed care plans, hospitals and integrated delivery systems are viewed as investments and are intended not only as care centers, but also as businesses that will turn a profit for investors. A market-based response to rising costs, managed care (and particularly the for-profit plans) is firmly entrenched within the conception of health care as a market good. When medical care is considered a commodity; patients as ordinary consumers; and physicians as profit-maximizing producers, then it fundamentally alters the physician–patient relationship. No longer fiduciary, doctor–patient interactions are converted into a business transaction. Annas notes "the threat is real, frightening, and intolerable, which is why the new patient rights movement seeks to shift power not from physicians and hospitals, but from managed care companies, insurance companies, and health facilities to patients and their physicians" (1998). This issue is salient with respect to the Patients' Bill of Rights currently under consideration in Congress. Also, a recent decision of the U.S. Supreme Court to accept an appeal of the ruling by an appellate court in Illinois means that a patient has the right to sue their HMO based on a perceived breach of fiduciary relationship. Since HMOs are making decisions for insurance coverage of treatments, the appellate court ruled that they were in essence practicing medicine, potentially usurping the doctor–patient fiduciary relationship should they deem the prescribed treatment unnecessary. As such, they must be held accountable for denying coverage of care the doctor recommended. Should this decision hold, it would mark a significant turning point in the growing list of Patient's Rights.

In no small measure due to ethical issues such as this, in his article "Managed Care and the Morality of the Marketplace" (1995) in the Recommended Reading, Kassirer directly confronts the question of whether health care should be subject to the values of the marketplace. Given the heightened dimensions of the current managed care debate, as well as that of the role of profit status, this piece is even more timely in 2000 than it was when it was published in 1995. Kassirer's argument is not against managed care, which, as he noted, can have many benefits. Instead, it is against the abuses of managed care when coupled with the profit motive. Costs, not quality concerns, dominate the marketplace. Perverse financial incentives are put in place, and competition is limiting the patient's right to choose as market mechanisms for cost control translate into decisions made by economies of scale. Employers and other purchasers remove decision-making autonomy by simply choosing the least costly health plan. Kassirer makes the point very forcefully that "our leaders should reject market values as a framework for health care and the market driven mess into which our health system is evolving" (p. 127).

Correspondingly, Culbertson makes an eloquent case for trauma care as a public or social good and not a market commodity. Examining the impact of market forces on trauma centers and trauma care in Los Angeles County from the early 1980s to the late 1990s, his argument uses detailed case analysis of a specific delivery system (trauma) from which to derive more general conclusions about our health system. In addition to Culbertson's trauma case, two further examples of issues facing our current system illustrate this divisive difference between valuing medical care as a market good rather than a social good. First, the growing number of uninsured persons was likely one of the factors that prompted former senator Bradley to propose federal guaranteed health insurance for the uninsured. In 1998, there were 44.3 million Americans without health insurance. The number is now increasing by about one million per year, despite high levels of employment and the booming economy. As the tools of managed care and competition are used to control health costs, few employees, workers, and their dependents are fully insured by their employers, and more of the costs are shifted to the workers. Those most likely to be uninsured are youths aged 18 to 24, among whom 30 percent are uninsured, in contrast with 1 percent of the elderly; and Hispanics, 35 percent of whom are uninsured as compared with a mere 12 percent of non-Hispanic whites. Also among those at risk are children, who are particularly vulnerable because so many of them live in low-income families. It is also important to note that there are geographic differences among states in the numbers of uninsured persons. Residents of the state of the state of Texas (where 25 percent of the population are uninsured) are more likely to be uninsured than residents in most other states, particularly Hawaii (9 percent uninsured) (See Chapter 7). These discrepancies, particularly the regional variation, were the likely motivation for another component of former senator Bradley's plan calling for the assumption of full financial responsibility by the federal government for acute care services paid for by Medicaid. Currently, this responsibility is a shared federal/state program. As a trade-off, Bradley proposed transferring long-term care costs to the States.

Beyond the rising number of uninsured, our current system is also plagued with problems of under-insurance and inadequate resources available for providing care for certain vulnerable populations, such as the elderly, the chronically ill, and the disabled. In "Privatization, the Welfare States, and Aging: The Reagan-Bush Legacy" (1992), Carroll Estes contends that aging and health policy serve as a major battleground on which the nation's social struggles are being fought (Chapter 5 Recommended Reading). She outlines the various reasons given by policymakers for refusing to provide essential services, such as long-term care, and argues that their fundamental line of reasoning presumes that such care for older Americans should be provided by unpaid (female) caregivers. Estes also suggests that the chronic illness "burden" associated with elderly citizens is undeservedly blamed for crippling the national economy, raising the question of how the administration of President Bill Clinton would alter the course formerly set by Presidents Reagan and Bush. Dramatic improvements in the American economy, with deficit reduction, control of inflation, and the growth of the economy, presented an opportunity to move away from a "blame the victim" mentality, which Estes suggests predominated the Reagan–Bush eras. However, there has been a great deal of discussion about the impact of the aging baby boom generation, which will begin to reach age 65 years in 2007. While the budget surplus has assured the continued strength of the Social Security trust fund for a number of years, issues related to Medicare are more acute than ever and have stimulated a great deal of controversy (see Chapter 8).

Next, within our current system, not only the elderly but also children with chronic illnesses or disabilities are at particular risk, especially in the managed care environment. These children, with the high costs associated with their care, are least likely to be insured in a competitive environment when health insurance premiums are experience rated. To fill the gap, there are many publicly funded medical care and social services for children with chronic illnesses and/or disabilities (e.g., Medicaid). However, there are many problems with these programs, not the least of which are grossly inadequate levels of funding. These problems include fragmentation, poor coordination of services, lack of comprehensiveness, and inequities in access to care. The result is that to the parents of children, who must use the services, the programs often appear to be a jungle of complicated and sometimes contradictory approaches. The sheer complexity has led to the inability of many parents to secure available coverage for their children, especially among immigrant populations and others in resource-starved communities.

Clearly, values and the policy decisions that reflect these values are responsible for the current systems of financing and delivery of care. Some say the resources in the richest country in the world are too scarce to provide health insurance for the uninsured or comprehensive services for vulnerable groups, such as the elderly or disabled children. Moreover, other, more troubling values may also contribute to the current structure of the health care financing and delivery system in the United States. Among these are attitudes toward minorities and the stigmatization of the disabled, including the mentally retarded, as potentially unproductive and without hope of rehabilitation.

The problem, fundamentally, is the disparity between views of distributive justice versus views of "crisis rationing." Distributive justice calls for dealing with each individual according to his or her needs. As such, the high cost of caring for an individual, such as a chronically ill or disabled child, cannot be used as argument against the provision of comprehensive care that is appropriate to their needs. Alternately, crisis rationing would argue that we have limited resources that must be dedicated to those whom will reap the most benefit. Therefore, the relative cost versus the relative benefit of caring for a chronically ill or disabled person might be outweighed by the needs of those with a curable condition.

In summary, it is time to re-examine both our values and our policies. Although debates concerning ethical principles often become polarized and competitive, it is only by appreciating the full range of issues, along with the values underlying the arguments and their possible solutions, that we can evolve policy that is both worthwhile and realistic. Without consideration of the ethical implications, health policy cannot exist, let alone succeed. Yet concentrating exclusively on well-intentioned ideals neither lends itself to successful policy evolution (due to the range of competing perspectives) nor eventually to successful measures (due to the difficulty of implementation). The key in policy, as a population-based science, is to maintain a wide enough perspective to appreciate all the issues involved, and measure how the big picture can be most significantly benefited.

REFERENCES

Annas GT. A national bill of patient's rights. *NEJM* 1998; 338: 697–699.

Culbertson RA. Health care as a social good: Trauma care and the "kindness of strangers." *J Health Health Serv Admin* 1999; 21 (3): 346–363.

Estes CE. Privatization, the welfare state, and aging: The Reagan Bush legacy. Abridged From a paper presented at the 21st Annual Conference of the British Society of Gerontology, University of Kent at Canterbury, Sept. 19, 1992.

Hacker JS, Skocpol T. New politics of U.S. health policy. *J Health Polit Policy Law* 1997; 22 (2): 315–336.

Kassirer JE. Managed care and the morality of the marketplace. *NEJM* 1995; 333:50–52.

Longest BB. *Health Policymaking in the United States* (2nd ed.). Chicago, Health Administration Press, 1998; 4–27, 55–61.

Rawls, J. *A Theory of Justice.* Cambridge, MA, The Belknap Press of Harvard University Press, 1971.

San Jose Mercury News. "Bradley's Health Plan. It Would Widen Care Through Existing Insurers." San Jose, CA, September 29, 1999.

ARTICLE 1

ETHICS IN THE POLITICAL MARKETPLACE

Beauford B. Longest, Jr.

Political markets, as places where individuals, organizations, and groups seek to further their policy objectives, are controlled by humans. Thus, what takes place in political markets, including the public policymaking process, is influenced by various mixes of altruism and egoism. Human control of the public policymaking process means that its operation as well as its outcomes and consequences are directly affected by the ethics of those who participate in the process.

Ethics plays an important part in the operation of political markets and in the public policymaking processes that unfold within them. Ethical considerations help shape and guide the development of new policies by contributing to ways in which problems are defined and their policy solutions are structured. Ethical behavior, for any and all participants in the political markets where policymaking occurs, is guided by four philosophical principles: respect for the autonomy of other people, justice, beneficence, and nonmaleficence.

The ethical principle of *respect for autonomy* is based on the concept that individuals have the right to their own beliefs and values and to the decisions and choices that further these beliefs and values. This ethical principle undergirds much of the formal system of government the nation's founders envisioned. Beauchamp and Childress (1989) have pointed out that no fundamental inconsistency or incompatibility exists between the autonomy of individuals and the authority of government so long as government's authority does not exceed the limits set by those who are governed. In this context, autonomy pertains to the rights of citizenship in the United States. Specifically, autonomy relates to the rights of individuals to independent self-determination regarding how they live their lives and to their rights regarding the integrity of their bodies and minds. Respect for autonomy in health policymaking influences issues that pertain to privacy and individual choice, including behavioral or lifestyle choices.

Public policymaking that reflects a respect for the principle of autonomy can sometimes be better understood in contrast to its opposite—paternalism. Paternalism

151

implies that someone knows what is best for other people. Policies guided by a preference for autonomy limit paternalism. One of the most vivid examples of the influence of the principle of autonomy in health policymaking is the 1990 Patient Self-Determination Act (P. L. 101–508). This policy is designed to give individuals the right to make decisions concerning their medical care, including the right to accept or refuse treatment and the right to formulate advance directives regarding their care. These directives allow competent individuals to give instructions about their healthcare, to be implemented at some later date should they then lack the capacity to make medical decisions. In concept, this policy gives people the right to exercise their autonomy in advance of a time when they might no longer be able to exercise that right actively.

The principle of respect for autonomy includes several other elements that are especially important in guiding ethical behavior in policymaking. One of these is telling the truth. Respect for people as autonomous beings implies honesty in relationships with them. Closely related to honesty is the element of confidentiality. Confidences broken in the policymaking process can impair the process. A third element of the autonomy principle that is important to the policymaking process is fidelity. This means doing one's duty and keeping one's word. Fidelity is often equated with keeping promises. When participants in the policymaking process tell the truth, honor confidences, and keep promises, the process is more ethically sound than if these things are not done.

A second ethical principle of significant importance to public policymaking is the principle of *justice*. The degree of adherence to this principle directly affects the policymaking process and policies themselves. In Rawls' (1971, 5) words, "One may think of a public conception of justice as constituting the fundamental charter of a well-ordered human association." Much of its impact on policies and on policymaking hinges on defining justice as fairness (Rawls 1971). The principle of justice also includes the concept of just deserts, which holds that justice is done when a person receives that which he or she deserves (Beauchamp and Childress 1989).

The practical implications for health policymaking of the principle of justice are felt mostly in terms of distributive justice—that is, in terms of fairness in the distribution of health-related benefits and burdens in society. The key policy question deriving from the ethical principle of justice is, of course, "What is fair?" The various participants in political markets and in the health policymaking process hold varying opinions on the issue of what is a fair, or just, distribution of the benefits and burdens involved in the pursuit of health in American society. Useful insight into the range of possible views on fairness in this matter can be gained from considering the three most prominent perspectives on justice.

The *egalitarian* perspective of justice holds that everyone should have equal access to both the benefits and burdens arising from the pursuit of health and that fairness requires a recognition of different levels of need. The influence of the egalitarian view of justice can be seen in a number of health policies. Policies intended to remove discrimination in the provision of health services reflect the preference for equality. Policies intended to provide more resources to those thought to need them most (e.g., Medicare for the elderly or Medicaid for the poor) are also based on an egalitarian view of fairness.

The *libertarian* perspective of fairness holds that it requires a maximum of social and economic liberty for individuals. Policies that favor unfettered markets as the means of distributing the benefits and burdens associated with the pursuit of health reflect the libertarian theory of justice.

The third perspective, the *utilitarian* view of fairness, holds that it is best served when public utility is maximized. This is sometimes expressed as the greatest good for the greatest number. Many health policies, including those pertaining to restricting pollution, ensuring safe workplaces, and controlling the spread of communicable diseases, have been heavily influenced by a utilitarian view of what is just in the distribution of the benefits and burdens arising from the American pursuit of health.

The principle of justice provides much of the underpinning for all health policies, whether they are in the allocative or regulatory categories. Allocative policies that adhere closely to the principle of justice allocate benefits and burdens according to the provisions of a morally defensible system rather than through arbitrary or capricious decisions. Regulatory policies that are guided by the principle of justice have a fair and equitable impact on those to whom the regulations are targeted. The nation's legal system exists in part to help ensure that the principle of justice is respected in the formulation and implementation of public policies and to serve as an appeals mechanism for those who believe that the process has not adequately honored this principle.

Two other ethical principles have direct relevance to public policymaking— beneficence and nonmaleficence. *Beneficence* in policymaking means that participants in the process act with charity and kindness; that is, they overtly seek to do good. This principle is widely reflected in policies through which benefits in some tangible form are provided. Thus, application of the principle of beneficence characterizes such allocative policies as the Medicare and Medicaid programs. But beneficence includes the complex concept of balancing benefits and burdens. Participants in the political marketplace who seek policies that benefit them or their interests exclusively while burdening others, violate the principle of beneficence. Policymakers who are guided by the principle of beneficence make decisions that maximize the net benefits to society as a whole and balance the benefits and burdens of their decisions fairly.

Nonmaleficence, a principle with deep roots in medical ethics, is exemplified in the dictum *primum non nocere*—first, do no harm. Policymakers who are guided by the principle of nonmaleficence make decisions that minimize harm. The principles of beneficence (do good) and nonmaleficence (do no harm) are clearly reflected in health policies that seek to ensure the quality of health services and products. Such policies as those establishing Professional Review Organizations (PROs) to review the quality of care given to Medicare patients and the policies that the FDA uses to ensure the safety of pharmaceuticals are examples. Policies that support the conduct and use of outcome studies of clinical care, such as those that established and maintain the Agency for Health Care Policy and Research (AHCPR), are also examples of policies that reflect the principles of beneficence and nonmaleficence.

Having considered the context within which health policies are made, especially the structure and operations of the political markets for policies, and having identified the demanders and suppliers who interact in these markets as well as some of the important operational and ethical aspects of these interactions, it is now possible to consider the intricate process through which public policies are made.

ABOUT THE AUTHOR

Beauford B. Longest, Jr., PhD, is Professor of Health Services Administration in the Graduate School of Public Health, Professor of Business Administration in the Katz Graduate School of Business, and Founding Director of the Health Policy Institute, University of Pittsburgh, Pittsburgh, Pennsylvania.

REFERENCES

Alexander, J. A., and L. L. Morlock. 1997. "Power and Politics in Health Services Organizations." In *Essentials of Health Care Management,* edited by S. M. Shortell and A. D. Kaluzny, 256–85. Albany, NY: Delmar Publishers, Inc.

Anderson, G. F. 1992. "The Courts and Health Policy: Strengths and Limitations." *Health Affairs* 11: 95–110.

Bauer, R. A., I. de S. Pool, and L. A. Dexter. 1963. *American Business and Public Policy.* New York: Atherton.

Beauchamp, T. L., and J. F. Childress. 1989. *Principles of Biomedical Ethics,* 3rd ed. New York: Oxford University Press.

Bibfeldt, F. 1958. *Paradoxes Observed.* Chicago: Perspective Press.

Brewer, G. D., and P. de Leon. 1983. *The Foundations of Policy Making.* Homewood, IL: Dorsey.

Brown, L. D. 1991. "Knowledge and Power: Health Services Research as a Political Resource." In *Health Services Research: Key to Health Policy,* edited by E. Ginzberg, 20–45. Cambridge, MA: Harvard University Press.

Buchholz, R. A. 1989. *Business Environment and Public Policy: Implications for Management and Strategy Formulation,* 3rd ed. Englewood Cliffs, NJ: Prentice Hall.

Christoffel, T. 1991. "The Role of Law in Health Policy." In *Health Politics and Policy,* 2nd ed., edited by T. J. Litman and L. S. Robins, 135–47. Albany, NY: Delmar Publishers, Inc.

Dye, T. R. 1978. *Understanding Public Policy,* 3rd ed. Englewood Cliffs, NJ: Prentice-Hall.

———. 1990. *Who's Running America? The Bush Era,* 5th ed. Englewood Cliffs, NJ: Prentice-Hall.

Dye, T. R., and H. Zeigler. 1975. *The Irony of Democracy,* 3rd ed. New York: Wadsworth Publishing Company, Inc.

Encyclopedia of Associations. 1993. Detroit, MI: Gale.

Feldstein, P. J. 1996. *The Politics of Health Legislation: An Economic Perspective,* 2nd ed. Chicago: Health Administration Press.

French, J. R. P., and B. H. Raven. 1959. "The Basis of Social Power." In *Studies of Social Power,* edited by D. Cartwright, 150–67. Ann Arbor, MI: Institute for Social Research.

Green, J. 1995. "High-Court Ruling Protects Hospital-bill Surcharges." *AHA News* 31 (18): 1.

Greenberger, D., S. Strasser, R. J. Lewicki, and T. S. Bateman. 1988. "Perception, Motivation, and Negotiation." In *Health Care Management: A Text in Organization Theory and Behavior,* 2nd ed., edited by S. M. Shortell and A. D. Kaluzny, 81–141. New York: John Wiley & Sons.

Keys, B., and T. Case. 1990. "How to Become an Influential Manager." *The Executive* 4 (4): 38–51.

Lineberry, R. L., G. C. Edwards, III, and M. P. Wattenberg. 1995. *Government in America,* 2nd ed. New York: HarperCollins College Publishers.

Lowi, T. J. 1979. *The End of Liberalism,* 2nd ed. New York: Norton.

Marmor, T. R., and J. B. Christianson. 1982. *Health Care Policy: A Political Economy Approach.* Beverly Hills, CA: Sage Publications.

Mintzberg, H. 1983. *Power In and Around Organizations.* Englewood Cliffs, NJ: Prentice-Hall.

Moe, T. 1980. *The Organization of Interests.* Chicago: University of Chicago Press.

Morone, J. A. 1990. *The Democratic Wish: Popular Participation and the Limits of American Government.* New York: Basic Books.

Olson, M. 1965. *The Logic of Collective Action.* Cambridge, MA: Harvard University Press.

Ornstein, N. J., and S. Elder. 1978. *Interest Groups, Lobbying and Policymaking.* Washington, DC: Congressional Quarterly Press.

Paul-Shaheen, P. A. 1990. "Overlooked Connections: Policy Development and Implementation in State-Local Relations." *Journal of Health Policy, Politics and Law* 15 (4): 133–56.

Pear, R. 1993. "Clinton's Health-Care Plan: It's Still Big, But It's Farther Away." *The New York Times.* (June 13): E4.

Peters, B. G. 1986. *American Public Policy: Promise and Performance,* 2nd ed. Chatham, NJ: Chatham House.

Peterson, M. A. 1993. "Political Influence in the 1990s: From Iron Triangles to

Policy Networks." *Journal of Health Politics, Policy and Law* 18 (2): 395–438.

Potter, M. A., and B. B. Longest, Jr. 1994. "The Divergence of Federal and State Policies on the Charitable Tax Exemption of Nonprofit Hospitals." *Journal of Health Politics, Policy and Law* 19: 393–419.

Rawls, J. 1971. *A Theory of Justice.* Cambridge, MA: The Belknap Press of Harvard University Press.

Starr, P. 1982. *The Social Transformation of American Medicine.* New York: Basic Books, Inc.

Truman, D. 1971. *The Governmental Process,* 2nd ed. New York: Knopf.

Wilsford, D. 1991. *Doctors and the State: The Politics of Health in France and the United States.* Durham, NC: Duke University Press.

Wilson, J. Q. 1973. *Political Organizations.* New York: Basic Books, Inc.

ARTICLE 2

A NATIONAL BILL
OF PATIENTS' RIGHTS

George J. Annas

In one of the most enthusiastically received proposals in his January State of the Union address, President Bill Clinton called on Congress to enact a national bill of rights in health care. The President said, "You have the right to know all your medical options, not just the cheapest. You have the right to choose the doctor you want for the care you need. You have the right to emergency room care, wherever and whenever you need it. You have the right to keep your medical records confidential."[1]

The President's proposal is a follow-up to his November 1997 announcement that he would put the recommendations of his Advisory Commission on Consumer Protection and Quality in the Health Care Industry into federal law. This in turn follows proposals from almost every state legislature, the American Association of Health Plans (AAHP), and an ad hoc group of nonprofit health maintenance organizations to provide Americans enrolled in health plans with new protections. The last time patients' rights were at the center of national debate was in the early 1970s. In this article I summarize the short history of patients' rights in the United States and the attempt to transform patients' rights into consumers' rights, and I explain how a synthesis of patients' rights and consumers' rights, enacted in federal legislation, could move us toward a more responsive and responsible health care system.

PATIENTS' RIGHTS IN THE 1970s

As Starr has chronicled, in the early 1970s, the movement to establish a right to health care was joined (some would say eclipsed) by a movement to establish rights in health care.[2] The right to health care demanded federal legislation and financing, but rights in health care were almost always enunciated by the courts.[3]

The most important of all patients' rights, the right to informed consent, was firmly established in 1972 in a series of court opinions.[3] In these opinions the courts made it clear that the law would treat the doctor-patient relationship as a fiduciary, or trust-based relationship, not as an arm's-length business relationship. The nature of this relationship is that a sick person (a patient) seeks the help of a specially educated and experienced professional, who is licensed by the state to practice medicine and whose unequal status vis-à-vis the patient requires the physician to assume certain legal responsibilities for the patient. These responsibilities are inherent in the doctor-patient relationship and require that before obtaining the patient's consent to treatment, the physician provide the patient with basic information so that the patient (not the physician) can make the final decision about whether to proceed. This information includes a description of the proposed treatment, its anticipated risks and benefits, alternative treatments (including none) and their risks and benefits, the probability of success, and the chief anticipated problems of recuperation.[3,4]

All this seems fairly standard 25 years later, but it was radical at the time. Before the 1970s, informed consent was not promoted or embraced by physicians and had to be imposed on them by the courts. Nonetheless, the concept of informed consent quickly became an ethical precept and has served both patients and their physicians well.[5]

The requirement of informed consent was followed quickly by other requirements intended to enhance the autonomy of patients. Autonomy or liberty (sometimes reduced simply to the idea of choice) is, of course, the fundamental American value, and it is somewhat remarkable that medicine had been insulated from it until the 1970s. It is not surprising, then, that patients' rights based on autonomy quickly became the norm. In early 1973, for example, the U.S. Supreme Court issued what is still its most important medicine-related opinion, in *Roe v. Wade.*[6] The Court held that pregnant women have a constitutional right of privacy that includes their right to continue or terminate a pregnancy in the absence of the state's ability to demonstrate a countervailing and compelling state interest. The case has also come to stand for the proposition that the Constitution limits interference by the state in the doctor–patient relationship.[7]

Also in early 1973, the American Hospital Association issued a patients' bill of rights.[3] Although the 12-point bill was vague and general, it was the first such document and included many basic concepts of patients' rights, such as the rights to receive respectful care, to be given complete information about diagnosis and prognosis, to refuse treatment, to refuse to participate in experiments, to have privacy and confidentiality maintained, and to receive a reasonable response to a request for services.[3]

In an era when the use of medical technology was sometimes considered more important than its effectiveness in meeting patients' needs, the courts were again called on to enhance the power of patients. For example, in a series of cases, beginning in 1976 with the case of Karen Ann Quinlan and culminating in 1997 with cases concerning physician-assisted suicide, the courts affirmed that competent patients have the right to refuse any medical treatment, including life-sustaining treatment.[5] Moreover, a patient, while competent, is authorized by statute to designate another person to make treatment decisions for the patient, should he or she become incompetent (a health care agent or proxy), and the patient can make his or her wishes known in advance through a living will.[5,8]

Other important rights were recognized in the 1970s through federal regulations to protect research subjects and state laws and court decisions to protect medical privacy and confidentiality. Patients were also granted access to their medical records,[5] and the right to basic emergency care was protected.[5] Proposals for patients'-rights advocates or ombudspersons were not adopted, however, and patients were generally left on their own to exercise their rights. They had recourse to the courts only when their rights had been violated and they had been harmed.

PATIENTS' RIGHTS IN MANAGED CARE

The key to understanding patients' rights in managed care is to understand managed care's attempt to transform the patient into a consumer. Persons can be considered consumers of health plans if they can choose a plan on the basis of cost, coverage, and quality.[9] But the choice of a health plan is usually made by employers, and even when it is not, the choice is necessarily much more often based on cost than on coverage or quality. Nor is being a consumer of a health plan the same as being a consumer of health care. In virtually all settings, patients (not consumers) seek the help of physicians when they are sick and vulnerable because of illness or disability. The courts in the 1970s were correct: the doctor–patient relationship is not an arm's-length business transaction; it is a relationship in which trust is essential. Sick people, who are in no position to bargain and who know little about medicine, must be able to trust their physicians to be on their side in dealing with pain, suffering, disease, or disability.

Attempts to transform the physician–patient relationship into a business transaction fundamentally threaten not just physicians as professionals but people as patients. This threat is real, frightening, and intolerable, which is why the new patients'-rights movement aims not simply to preserve the physician–patient relationship in general but also to eliminate the financial conflicts of interest in managed care that are most threatening to the relationship.[10] Thus, the new patients'-rights movement seeks to shift power not from physicians and hospitals to patients but from managed-care companies, insurance companies, and health care facilities to patients and their physicians.

Some of the recent threats have been highlighted in the media and have already been the subject of federal legislation. Perhaps the most famous, dealt with in detail in a previous article, is "drive-through delivery."[11] Congress and a majority of states responded to limitations on hospital stays after childbirth by mandating coverage for a specific period of hospital care when a physician and a patient agree that it is needed.[11] The core response to the perception that health plans had gone too far was predictable: an attempt to put the power to make decisions back in the context of a consensual and informed doctor–patient relationship freed from financial conflicts of interest.[11]

In 1997, in response to subsequent proposals to limit "drive-through mastectomy" (modeled on the legislation on drive-through delivery), the AAHP offered "Putting Patients First," also known as the "Nine Commandments."[12] Kassirer has characterized this plan as "a thinly veiled attempt to ward off state and federal legislative actions to curb the abuses of managed care," and it may have been.[13] Nonetheless, the content of the plan is instructive. None of the nine provisions echo traditional patients' rights. Instead, they all concern areas in which health plans have been widely criticized for restricting care and areas in which medical decisions seem to be made by nonphysicians. For example, the AAHP's proposal would require members (not patients or consumers) to be informed about how the health plan works (e.g., how utilization review is performed, drug formularies are set up, doctors are paid, and treatments are designated as experimental), put decisions about hospitalization for mastectomy in the hands of physicians and their patients, remove any "gag rules" restricting physicians' conversations with their patients about treatment options, describe rights of appeal, and promise "physician involvement" in quality-improvement programs, practice guidelines, and the development of drug formularies.

The AAHP proposal is similar in spirit to the National Committee for Quality Assurance's document "Members' Rights and Responsibilities," which focuses on informing members of health plans about their contract with the plan, especially the rules the plan has adopted to make decisions about coverage and the procedures for addressing complaints and resolving disputes. These documents do not qualify as statements of patients' rights in any meaningful way, because they concentrate only on contractual provisions.

The 18 "Principles for Consumer Protection," promoted by Kaiser Permanente, Group Health of Puget Sound, the Health Insurance Plan (HIP), the American Association of Retired Persons, and Families USA in September 1997, seem to go one step further, but it is a small and pathetic step.[14] The main thrust of the provisions, other than those that duplicate provisions in the other two documents, is to require that all health plans provide certain benefits and services (such as coverage for out-of-area emergency care, availability of medical services at all times, and continuity of care through a primary care physician), to disclose specific information (such as the percentage of revenues actually spent on health care [the medical-loss ratio]), and to restrict financial incentives that create conflicts of interest for physicians (including financial incentives to limit care). As the authors concede, these 18 principles are meant not primarily to help patients or customers, but more as a marketing strategy to help health plans compete on an equal basis.[14]

The fact that these contract-centered proposals are almost irrelevant to the typical patient has made comprehensive federal legislation to enforce patients' rights seem both necessary and desirable. Enacting federal legislation is also the only way to protect all patients (not only those who are members of health plans) and to level the playing field for all health plans in the United States. What rights should be included in national legislation?

THE PRESIDENTIAL COMMISSION

In early 1997, President Clinton took the first step toward a national bill of rights for patients by appointing the Advisory Commission on Consumer Protection and Quality in the Health Care Industry. In November 1997, the commission issued its proposal. Although flawed and incomplete, it provides the basic outline of a national bill of rights for patients.[15,16] The proposal enumerates four categories of traditional patients' rights (the right to make medical decisions based on full information, the right to confidentiality, the right to emergency care, and the right to be treated with respect), as well as certain contract-based consumer protections (governing contract information, choice of a physician within a plan, and access to an independent appeals mechanism).[16]

The core of patients' rights is the right to receive care from an accountable physician who shares all relevant information with the patient and guarantees the patient the right to make the final decision about treatment. The patient must be able to trust the physician to act honestly and in the patient's best interests. Loyalty to the patient also requires that the physician act as an advocate for the patient when the treatment the physician believes is most appropriate is not covered by the patient's health plan or insurer. Only provisions that honor and reinforce a physician–patient relationship based on trust deserve to be designated patients' rights.

Consumer protection is also important but pales in comparison with the rights of sick people in dealing with physicians and other care givers. Thus, the commission is directly on target to stipulate that any bill of patients' rights include the following: the right to complete information about treatment, the right to emergency care based on what a prudent layperson would regard as an emergency, the right to confidentiality in the handling of medical information, and the right to respectful and nondiscriminatory treatment.[16] As for the rights of persons enrolled in managed-care plans, it is pretty thin gruel to guarantee access to the contracts they or their employers signed. Nonetheless, the call for an external, independent grievance mechanism to address denials of benefits is welcome. As I pointed out in a previous article, the grievance mechanisms available to patients are woefully inadequate in all health plans.[17] Much, much more is needed, and the commission is correct in noting that any appeals mechanism must be fair and independent of the health plan. The commission's proposal should have gone further. Patients need access to effective and independent advocates to help them exercise all the rights spelled out in a bill of patients' rights. Advocates can also help patients, together with their physicians, navigate the grievance and appeals procedures with the goal of resolving disputes at the lowest possible level and as quickly and fairly as possible.[3,18]

A BILL OF RIGHTS

The final shape of a national bill of patients' rights should be the subject of wide-ranging public and congressional debate in 1998. The model adopted, whether geared toward the consumer contract or the physician–patient relationship and whether implemented voluntarily or by federal legislation, will largely determine the ultimate content. And the ultimate content will itself determine whether federal preemption of this area is reasonable. We can call people who buy health insurance consumers and people who join health plans members, but we must recognize that sick people who seek medical care are patients with rights that should be protected. A national bill of patients' rights can and should protect consumers and members of managed-care plans. But its core purpose must be, as President Clinton properly noted, to provide all Americans with basic rights at the time when they mean the most to us—when we are sick and need medical care.[1]

Many of our rights as patients have already been articulated by the courts. Nonetheless, they often remain difficult for patients and providers alike to understand and are especially difficult for sick people to exercise.[5,18] Thus, enumerating all the essential rights in one document will facilitate an understanding of these rights and make it easier for patients to exercise them in their dealings with physicians, hospitals, and health plans. To this end, I believe a federal bill of patients' rights must include the five core provisions outlined below.

The Right to Treatment Information

The patient has a right to informed participation in all decisions involving his or her health care, including a clear, concise explanation, in lay terms, of all proposed treatments, the reasonable medical alternatives (whether or not they are covered by the plan), the risks of death and serious complications associated with each alternative (including no treatment), likely problems of recuperation, and the probability of a successful outcome (including the physician's experience with the treatment and its outcomes). The patient has a right to know the diagnosis and prognosis in as much detail as he or she desires, as well as the existence of any research protocols that are relevant to the patient's condition and their availability. A competent patient will not be subjected to any procedures or tests without first providing informed consent. For procedures that entail a risk of death or serious disability, all aspects of informed consent will be explained on a written form requiring the signature of the patient or the person with the authority to make treatment decisions for the patient, if the patient is incompetent.[4,5]

The patient has a right to know the identity, professional status, and clinical experience (including success rates) of all persons responsible for his or her care. The patient has a right to know about all financial arrangements and incentives that might affect his or her care. Any patient who does not speak English has a right to an interpreter.[5,10]

The Right to Privacy and Dignity

The patient has a right to privacy of both person and information with respect to all medical and nursing personnel, allied health care professionals, health plan and facility staff members, and other patients. All patients must be treated with dignity and without regard to race, religion, sex, sexual orientation, national origin, disability, age, socioeconomic status, or source of payment. The patient has a right to all the information contained in his or her medical record and has a right to examine the record on request, correct mistakes, and receive a copy of it. No one not directly involved in a patient's care or in quality assurance should have access to the patient's medical records without a written authorization by the patient that is dated and limited in time and that specifies the medical information to be disclosed. Further disclosure of medical information without authorization is prohibited.[5] The patient has a right not to be touched or treated by any particular physician or health care provider, including medical and nursing students.

The Right to Refuse Treatment

The patient has the right to refuse any drug, test, procedure, or treatment, whether the purpose is therapy, research, or education. A patient may not be discriminated against or denied any benefit by a health plan or health care professional because of the refusal to be touched or treated by a particular provider. A patient has the right to execute a health care proxy or a living will to direct treatment or nontreatment if the patient is no longer capable of making health care decisions, and health care professionals are obligated to honor these advance directives.[5,8,16]

The Right to Emergency Care

The patient has a right to prompt and competent attention in an emergency. The patient may not be transferred to another facility without his or her consent and, in any event, not before the patient's condition has been stabilized and it has been determined that the transfer is in the patient's best interests because of superior medical care. If the patient does not agree to the transfer, he or she may not be transferred.[5]

The Right to an Advocate

The patient has the right to the services of an independent patients'-rights advocate with the authority to help the patient assert all the rights specified in the bill of rights. In addition, a patient in a hospital or other health care facility has the right to reasonable visitation, parents have the right to stay with their child, and relatives have the right to stay with patients 24 hours a day. The patient has the right to have a friend or relative present during all consultations, examinations, and procedures, including the induction of anesthesia.[5,18]

Additional provisions of a national patients' bill of rights will involve contract-based consumer protection. How specifically such provisions are spelled out will depend on the extent to which Congress believes health-plan contracts must be regulated. In any event, the following obligations of health plans should be included. No health plan may interfere with or limit communication between the patient and his or her health care provider. Health plans must provide members with a reasonable choice of qualified primary care physicians and reasonable access to specialists. Health plans must disclose to members any and all financial arrangements that might encourage physicians to limit or restrict care, referrals to specialists, or recommendation of noncovered treatments. Health plans must provide payment for emergency services under circumstances that a prudent layperson would consider an emergency. Health plans must provide timely access to an independent appeals mechanism for denial or termination of benefits.[16]

The patient has a right to a copy of the entire contract for his or her insurance or health plan and to competent counseling in selecting a health plan. The patient has a right, regardless of the source of payment, to examine and receive an itemized and detailed explanation of all services rendered. The patient has a right to timely prior notice of termination of eligibility for coverage or denial of a health care benefit, with an opportunity to contest the termination or denial in a timely and fair manner before an independent, qualified, and neutral decision maker.[5,10,16]

CONCLUSIONS

A national bill of patients' rights must cover all Americans. On the other hand, health plans must be held accountable for providing the health care to their members that they hold themselves out as being able to provide. Thus, Congress should also pass legislation that permits members to sue their health plans directly for harm caused by wrongful acts on the part of the plans.[19,20] Once basic, uniform rights in health care are established, we can return to the equally important task of providing access to health care for all Americans. It seems correct to view universal access to adequate health care as our primary goal. But rights in health care are critical, since without them, citizens may wind up with access to a system that is indifferent to both their suffering and their rights.

ABOUT THE AUTHOR

George J. Annas, JD, MPH, is Edward R. Utley Professor Health Law, Chair of Health Law Department, School of Public Health, Boston University in Boston, Massachusetts, and author of twelve books.

REFERENCES

1. The prepared text of President Clinton's State of the Union message. New York Times. January 28, 1998:A19.

2. Starr P. The social transformation of American medicine. New York: Basic Books, 1982:388–93.

3. Annas GJ. The rights of hospital patients. New York: Avon, 1975.

4. Cobbs v. Grant, 8 Cal. 3d 229, 502 P.2d 1 (1972).

5. Annas GJ. The rights of patients. 2nd ed. Carbondale: Southern Illinois University Press, 1989.

6. Roe v. Wade, 410 U.S. 113 (1973).

7. Annas GJ, Glantz LH, Mariner WK. The right of privacy protects the doctor-patient relationship. JAMA 1990;263:858–61.

8. Annas GJ. The health care proxy and the living will. N Engl J Med 1991;324:1210–3.

9. Millenson ML. Demanding medical excellence: doctors and accountability in the information age. Chicago: University of Chicago Press, 1997.

10. Rodwin MA. Medicine, money, and morals: physicians' conflicts of interest. New York: Oxford University Press, 1993.

11. Annas GJ. Women and children first. N Engl J Med 1995;333:1647–51.

12. A new look: how managed care is trying to improve its battered image. Modern Healthcare. May 12, 1997:36–46.

13. Kassirer JP. Managing managed care's tarnished image. N Engl J Med 1997;337:338–9.

14. Pear R. Three big health plans urge national standards. New York Times. September 25, 1997:A1.

15. *Idem.* Panel of experts urges broadening of patient rights. New York Times. October 23, 1997:A1.

16. Advisory Commission on Consumer Protection and Quality in the Health Care Industry. Consumer Bill of Rights and Responsibilities: report to the President of the United States, November 1997.

17. Annas GJ. Patients' rights in managed care—exit, voice, and choice. N Engl J Med 1997;337:210–5.

18. Annas GJ, Healey J. The patient rights advocate: redefining the doctor-patient relationship in the hospital setting. Vanderbilt Law Rev 1974;27:243–69.

19. Furrow BR. Managed care organizations and patient injury: rethinking liability. Georgia Law Rev 1997;31:419–509.

20. Mariner WK. Liability for managed care decisions: the Employee Retirement Income Security Act (ERISA) and the uneven playing field. Am J Public Health 1996;86:863–9.

ARTICLE 3

HEALTH CARE AS A SOCIAL GOOD: TRAUMA CARE AND "THE KINDNESS OF STRANGERS"

Richard A. Culbertson

ABSTRACT

Urban trauma centers have been shown in the medical literature to be effective resources for dealing with traumatic injury in a manner which results in demonstrated increases in survival rates. Given that much debate exists over the relative efficacy of various technological medical interventions, the acceptance and diffusion of a "proven" technology such as trauma centers should be assured. Yet the significant investment of resources required to staff, equip, and maintain a trauma center coupled with a perceived fiscal deterioration of the provision of these services have resulted in a retreat from the concept through closure of the services. This is illustrated through the case of Los Angeles County, in which only 12 of the 23 centers which had competed for designation at the time of the network's creation in 1982 remain active. Reasons analyzed for these closures include changes in the perception of patients' financial resources from insured to uninsured and the deterioration in payment levels for multiple trauma which occurred under the diagnostic related group (DRG) program adopted in 1983. Trauma victims are increasingly stigmatized as accomplices in their own injuries rather than the earlier perception of accident victims (primarily auto) who are injured by chance. Yet the public policy issue to be resolved in the case of trauma services is truly one of community interest insofar as the risk of traumatic injury is present for all members of the community to a greater or lesser extent. Although youth might be inordinately impacted at present, it is suggested that incidence of trauma in the elderly will increase as a result of falls and other injuries. An "equitable" solution to the problem of trauma care requires community based solutions which transcend the interests of individual institutions and the marketplace. Only at this broader level can effective resource allocations be made to insure the establishment and maintenance of an effective system.

INTRODUCTION

This paper argues that trauma services, and emergency services in general, are the purest case supporting the position that health care is a social good. While the risk of injury may be greater among members of specific age categories and social groupings, all members of society are at some level of risk for injury. The fundamental operating premise of a trauma system and its component centers, is an "open door" policy, which assures all access, with economic questions secondary.

The author has two justifications for selecting a means for analysis of healthcare as a social or private economic good. From a methodological point of view, the renowned sociologist Max Weber (1980) argued that to understand a social phenomenon, one must analyze, in detail, a "pure" or "ideal" type of the subject at hand. It is the opinion of this author, based on his own experience as Chief Operating Officer of a Level I Trauma Center, that trauma care represents the extreme, or pure, case of health care as a social good. This can best be demonstrated through detailed case analysis of a specific system to derive general conclusions.

The second justification is the growing public awareness of trauma as a public health problem that threatens our very social order. Trauma care has gained significant public visibility through highly popular television series, such as "ER" and "Chicago Hope." Yet, prevention is an essential part of the problem, while at the same time, we recognize the need for resources devoted by the community for treatment and rehabilitation.

The public policy issue to be addressed in this case is truly one of community interest at the macro level insofar as the risk of traumatic injury is present for all members of the community to a greater or lesser extent. The problem is reminiscent of that of the commons identified by Hiatt in his classic article "Protecting the Medical Commons" (1975:235) At the time, Hiatt argued that society and physicians must recognize the need to balance needs of the individual patient with society's resources. The problem of trauma care is one that requires community based, system-wide solutions transcending the interest, however well intended, of individual institutions to maintain and conserve a resource that no single individual can afford. Only at this broader level can effective resource allocations be made to ensure the establishment and maintenance of an effective system.

In prior years, it could be argued that this exercise in "protecting the medical commons" was a purely intellectual one, as no individual as a purchaser of service could make decisions to enter or withdraw from the trauma system. With the widespread proliferation of managed care, however, the potential for group purchasing decisions on behalf of multiple patients became critical. It is this interplay that will determine the future viability of the trauma system as a social good as it has developed in the United States.

TRAUMA CARE DEFINED

A first step in addressing the problem of trauma care is to define the trauma center as an "organizational technology" representing the collection of a variety of skills and resources needed to cope successfully with multiple injuries in patients. The Committee on Trauma of the American College of Surgeons (ACS) has served a leadership role in this definition, and has identified detailed specifications for personnel and facilities required to maintain trauma centers at three increasingly sophisticated categories of operation (Flint and Flint, 1985:793). These distinctions occur around the mandatory on site presence of staff to care for patients on very short notice, notably surgery and surgical sub-specialists; anesthesiologists; and appropriately trained and specifically committed non-physician staff. Facility requirements apply to the emergency department; the immediate availability of a prepared operating theatre; and intensive care capability (Maull and Rhodes, 1996). The investment in capital resources and fixed personnel costs have limited entry of facilities to provision of this service.

One will note that the criteria are heavily surgically oriented, reflecting the interests of the ACS in this area. Trunkey and others have noted that the key element in the above description of personnel and facilities, which separates the trauma center from a mere list of ingredients, is team organization and medical direction (Trunkey, 1988). Here, too, the surgical model is apparent in definition of the organization.

THE COMMUNITY WIDE BASIS
OF THE TRAUMA SYSTEM

In addition, the internal hospital capability of the hospital based trauma center is invariably connected to a broader community scheme of regionalization. A Rand study describes elements of regionalization as including an explicit plan for a geographic area providing access to a total population to the full range of medical services defined in the plan. They contend that such systems feature a hierarchical division of duties and explicit assignment of responsibility by levels care and integration of the plan through coordination of the system using referral patterns, consultation, and education (Rand Corporation, 1984).

Public policy initiatives in the early 1970s reflected this perception of a community good in the passage of the Emergency Medical Systems Act of 1973. This act provided federal funds for planning and eventual implementation of regional trauma systems, but left details of specification of the system to states and private agencies. The work of the ACS Committee on Trauma was of particular importance in defining these standards (Flint, 1990).

While traumatologists might be content to see the diffusion of this form of organization to all communities and all hospitals, the necessity of coordination cited in the above definition, and the enormous capital and operating costs involved made creation of a formal system through a designation process a logical and even necessary step for communities (Pepler, 1980). With respect to necessary investment, Tuefel and Trunkey estimated, in 1977, that operating costs of a Level I trauma center at ACS standards would be $3,679,440 in direct cost of personnel and supplies, as well as revenue foregone from standby operations and other essential facilities (Boyd, 1980). Public policy directives to move in the direction of greater hierarchical organization and centralization of these services originating in the Emergency Medical Services Act of 1973, and the establishment of regional emergency medical system, were continued in PL93–641, enacted in 1975, which empowered local Health Systems Agencies (HSAs) to carry out such regional designations (Boyd, 1980).

THE EFFICACY OF TRAUMA CENTERS

Such considerations might appear merely political were there to be no demonstrable benefit from the establishment of trauma centers. The question to be answered at a basic level is the one posed by Tancredi (1982) of "medical efficacy." Can benefit be demonstrated for those who receive the services, setting aside for the moment the question of personal and societal efficacy? Trunkey has written extensively on this point, citing the development of trauma units for "definitive care" and the ensuing reduction in battlefield mortality in the Korean and Viet Nam conflicts (Pruitt and Fitzgerald, 1983:223). This model was then appropriated and applied to civilian settings with claimed comparable benefits.

West and his colleagues compared the results of non-central nervous system injured patients treated in Orange County in trauma centers vs. non-trauma centers. They observed that 9% of the trauma center deaths were preventable, based upon chart review, while 67% of the non-trauma center deaths were preventable—a difference statistically significant at the 0.01 level. Boyd cites studies in Illinois and Baltimore, Maryland, which identify comparable results to the Orange County study (Boyd, 1980). West and Trunkey undertook a comparison of injury-related deaths in Orange County vs. San Francisco, and judged that roughly two-thirds of the Orange County deaths were preventable (occurring in non-trauma centers), while only one such death occurred in San Francisco, with the presence of the organized trauma center at San Francisco General Hospital (Trunkey, 1980). In this conclusion, he writes that "We have concluded from this study that a trauma center does make a positive difference. The reasons include: Quicker access to definitive care; concentrated expertise available twenty-four hours a day; and a highly tuned facility constantly taking care of trauma victims." (Trunkey, 1980:86).

These results would be of little societal consequence were the epidemiology of trauma a limited one. Yet, trauma is the leading cause of death and disability among Americans between the ages of 1 and 44. (Jacobs and Jacobs, 1996.) Rice and MacKenzie (1989) report that 24 persons are injured per 100 U.S. residents annually. Among 15–24 year olds, injury accounts for 77% of all deaths in this age group.

Of special concern and public attention in recent years is the increase in murders as a particular manifestation of urban violence and resultant trauma, showing an increase from 8,464 in 1960 to 27,000 in 1987 (Trunkey, 1988).

A CASE STUDY IN MARKET FAILURE IN TRAUMA: LOS ANGELES

If one accepts the efficacy of these centers as presented in the studies cited here and the significance of the threat to health of trauma, the acceptance and diffusion of the "technology" of trauma centers should be assured. Such a facile conclusion has not proven to be true, however, and the adoption and subsequent retreat from the trauma center concept despite the continued demonstration of medical efficacy and public need pose significant public policy and ethical questions. There is no literature challenging these conclusions, although the number of studies supporting the assertion of center effectiveness is limited and the chart review method is open to scientific challenge. In order to address these questions in a focused manner, we will examine, as a case example, the development, disintegration and subsequent reintegration of the Los Angeles trauma system.

Los Angeles initiated its planning for trauma care on a community-wide basis consistent with the Emergency Medical Services statutes of the time. In a 1982 report on the development of the Los Angeles County plan, McElroy writes of the competition underway among hospitals for designation as trauma centers under an emerging regional system. He reported that 10 to 14 centers would be designated, with a future re-evaluation to take place as competition among facilities might impair the effectiveness of the young network. He writes that "The hospital council continues to support the concept that any hospital that meets certain criteria should be designated as a trauma center" (McElroy, 1983). Similar competition for designation occurred throughout the U.S., such as in Minneapolis–St. Paul under the aegis of the Metropolitan Health Board's categorization of trauma centers and trauma centers.

At the same time, McElroy finds this attitude a paradoxical one. He adds that "trauma has the reputation of disrupting orderly hospital administration precluding elective surgery, and potentially filling beds with undesirables who cannot or will not pay the cost of their care" (McElroy, 1983). His sentiments, in this instance, were to prove prophetic in the latter part of the decade, as perceptions shifted regarding the economic status of trauma victims and their social circumstances.

In fact, the network reached a total of 23 facilities at its high water mark (*Los Angeles Times,* 1990a). The *Times* Report noted that, at its establishment, the system was regarded as so prestigious that over 30 hospitals competed for inclusion in the network. It is noteworthy that the hospitals of the Kaiser Health Plan were not among them, nor were proprietary hospitals, with the exception of the Fountain Valley Hospital in Orange County (*Los Angeles Times,* 1989). Early signs of the weakening of the system (which one will recall only came about in 1983) were the withdrawal of two downtown Los Angeles hospitals, California Medical Center and Hospital of the Good Samaritan in 1986 and 1987, respectively. Hollywood Presbyterian Hospital, another facility adjoining the center city of Los Angeles, also left the system in 1987, in financial crisis blamed, in part, on the trauma center operation.

As a result of these withdrawals from the system, patients from the center of Los Angeles were transported greater distances to facilities, defeating, in large part, the advantages attributed to prompt definitive intervention. As pressure increased on remaining providers, others withdrew as well. St. Joseph's Hospital of Burbank left the system in 1989, followed by the withdrawal of Huntington Memorial Hospital of Pasadena on May 1, 1990. In a *Los Angeles Times* article of February 25, 1990 announcing the Huntington decision, staff writer Kenneth Garcia characterizes the decision as leaving "the San Gabriel Valley without a trauma center and opening another gaping hole in the trauma network, which was hailed as the nation's finest when it opened in 1983." (*Los Angeles Times,* 1990a) David Langness of the Hospital Council of Southern California (an early opponent of the network concept) is quoted as stating, "This kills it. The county's trauma network is now history. The demise of large trauma centers like Huntington's means that those remaining will be in severe and immediate jeopardy as well" (*Los Angeles Times,* 1990b:A–4). Later in the article, Dr. Allen Mathies, CEO of Huntington and former Dean of the USC School of Medicine, noted a commitment to the concept on the part of the hospital for provision of trauma care, but that the associated financial losses were no longer sustainable. He states in the article that "This means that there will be some (patients) who die. The question that the public has to answer is, are (those patients') deaths worse than raising taxes. . . ." (*Los Angeles Times,* 1990b:A–4).

The Los Angeles trauma system has restabilized with the decision of Huntington Memorial and several other major private providers not to leave the system. Nevertheless, the resultant upheaval in Los Angeles illustrates a profound case of the interrelationship of a community good and its economic moorings. Perhaps Flint has summarized the issue best when he writes:

"Economic concerns surface when hospitals and doctors are threatened with loss of income. Beginning in the early 1980s, hospitals interpreted the trauma system movement as a way to gain patients and market share, not only of trauma patients but of other patient groups as well. The commitment to funding by these hospitals was based on the assumption that trauma would at least pay for itself. The underestimation of the cost of the level of commitment necessary to participate in a regional trauma system, coupled with overestimation of the revenues to be realized, has caused major upheavals in trauma systems in Los Angeles County, California, and Dade County, Florida" (Flint, 1990:33). Now, a new challenge is posed by the rapid dominance of managed care as the form of health coverage for 85% of employed Americans and increasing numbers of Medicare and Medicaid participants, as will be discussed subsequently in this paper.

What has come into play in the Los Angeles situation is the interface of financial structures and ethical decisions which Engelhardt refers to as "macroallocative" and "microallocative" (Englehardt, 1986:344). In making this distinction, he refers to decisions made at the level of systems and resource allocations to those systems on the basis of "legitimate" public need versus allocations to individual patients. The hospital's decision to withdraw from the system rests at the macro level, while the continuation of treatment for individual conditions is a part of the micro sphere of the institution's own set of duties to fulfill its mission. At the most fundamental level, the problem evolves down to the direct encounter of the provider and the patient.

In this regard, the report of pressures from within the hospital staff itself are telling. Los Angeles emergency care officials (unidentified) are quoted as stating that the biggest reason for closure was lack of reimbursement for services rendered to an increasing number of indigent patients from South Los Angeles (reported at about 20% of 205 patients seen in the first two months of 1990). Dr. David Faddis is quoted as stating "You can't help but be unhappy . . . when you have a patient due for surgery and you have to postpone it to deal with a gunshot victim from South Central" (*Los Angeles Times*, 1990b:A–4). In a popular summary of the issue in *Time* (5-19-90) Robert Hockberger of Harbor-UCLA Medical Center states that "it's amazing to me that in 1983 all the hospitals didn't realize that most of the people who shoot and stab each other and wreck their cars at 3 a.m. don't have insurance" (*Time*, 1990).

FISCAL BARRIERS TO PARTICIPATION IN THE TRAUMA SYSTEM

At the macro level, then, it was initially thought that the financial support provided by the payment for services to individual patients who needed care would be adequate to offset losses to the under or uninsured. This assumption might have been questionable from the outset, but it also received three substantial blows over time.

The first of these, now a well accepted tenet of health policy in the US, is the development of a large group reported at 41.6 million individuals with no health insurance (U.S. Office of the Census, 1997). Many of these are young and unemployed or marginally employed—prime candidates on an epidemiological basis for trauma services. Sims and her colleagues (1989) have described trauma in an urban setting as a chronic disease strongly associated with unemployment, as well as environment and lifestyle.

The second problem was the institution, in 1983, of the Medicare DRG system and other subsequent fixed payment schemes, which pay a discrete and fixed amount for given diagnostic categories. This system is notorious in hospital financial circles for penalizing conditions, such as multisystem trauma (oncological diagnoses are another large category with the same problem), which present a variety of conditions simultaneously. A single diagnosis, usually the most severe, is paid at a primary rate with the secondary conditions factored down correspondingly. Thus, a multiple injured patient may be paid for as a craniotomy for neurological damage as primary;

but only secondarily and at lesser levels for procedures undertaken to arrest internal bleeding or repair a broken leg. Trunkey notes that a multiple injured patient in Utah's payment scheme with a severity score of 30 (severe injuries) would be paid at a rate $9000 below actual cost (Trunkey, 1988). Jacobs (1985) identified the problem of potential underpayment for trauma services in an early study, in which injury severity from multiple organ trauma did not correspond to hospital lengths of stay and cost.

Physician fees are similarly factored downward in these cases. With regard this, The Physician Payment Review Commission (PPRC) noted, in its *1992 Report to Congress,* inequities in payment of global surgical fees for trauma care. The Commission noted, with concern that trauma surgery may involve multiple surgeries by several different physicians. Further, critical care may well be required, even when the surgical procedures, when performed separately and on an elective basis in non-traumatic circumstances, would not require intensive care (PPRC, 1992).

This flaw in the physician payment system has been addressed by Health Care Financing Administration through use of special modifiers for multiple surgeries resulting from trauma. Nevertheless, the problem of the complexity of such billing is noted by the PPRC as a source of on-going physician resistance to organized trauma care (PPRC, 1992). As noted by Flint, "surgeons and other specialists resist implementation of trauma systems and trauma services because of fears that the system will place additional strains on already overburden personal and operating room schedules" (Flint, 1990:33).

In the early 1980s literature, the general focus is on the victim of automobile injuries. In Mattox's description of trauma needs, his argument focuses almost exclusively on auto accidents noting that more people have died (as of 1977) from auto crashes than all wars combined (Mattox, 1977). Investment in helicopters for the prompt transport of these victims is advocated on the assumption that they would be transferred rapidly from remote areas lacking definitive care where wrecks have occurred, or from congested urban freeways where surface transport is not sufficiently prompt. From a financial perspective, the critical element here is that the victim's auto insurance policy is the *primary* payer of medical expenses, superceding her/his health insurance coverage or lack thereof. In an ideal situation in which compulsory auto insurance laws theoretically mandate coverage for all vehicle operators, coverage and resultant payment are assured. Unfortunately, auto insurance coverage is widely variable across the states, despite laws to the contrary.

A fundamental societal problem which has affected public support for trauma care is the transformation of the image of the trauma "victim" to that of casualty of urban violence, usually associated in the popular mind with gang and drug related violence. Flint has stated this most powerfully when he writes that "the injured American typically is viewed by society as a 'loser' rather than a victim" (Flint, 1990:31). If so, this is a remarkable shift in public perception. The comments of the Huntington Memorial physicians reflect a perception that scheduled patients from "their" area are being displaced on operating room schedules by emergencies from inner city areas. The attitudes reflected here are reminiscent of those identified by

Roth in his study of "legitimate" and "illegitimate" demands in emergency room settings under the rubric of "moral evaluation and control" of emergency room patients. While Roth's study applies to a much lesser level of medical emergency than multiple trauma, the model seems appropriate in this much graver setting (Roth, 1986:332). In any event, the perception of institutions of the ability of these persons to pay for care is no doubt shaded by such perceptions, however real or anecdotal they may prove to be under objective scrutiny. Moving back to the framework of macro and micro allocations of resources, the hospital is now in the more comfortable position of justifying its decision to discontinue trauma services for its own self interest as well as that of its individual practitioners. There is less fear of community reproach when victims to be turned away are from other areas and involved in unsavory or illegal activities which may contribute, in the eyes of some, to their injuries.

ETHICAL CHALLENGES POSED BY
THE LOS ANGELES EXPERIENCE

Viewed from an ethical perspective, the Los Angeles trauma system case presents a troubling and difficult problem. Jonsen and his associates have argued that, in emergency cases, "physicians who work in institutions that receive emergency patients have an ethical obligation to assure that the traditional medical ethic of service to those in urgent need of care can be fulfilled in their institution" (Jonsen, Siegler, and Winsdale 1998:174). They continue that the transfer of a patient suffering from life threatening conditions [a microallocative problem in Englehardt's (1986) terms] or the refusal to accept transfer of that patient is indefensible medically, ethically, and legally. Yet in the instance of Los Angeles and other communities, the problem has been averted by the discontinuation of the service by the facility and the subsequent diversion of such individual difficult cases which might otherwise ethically tax individual practitioners. Now, the accepted solution becomes one of transfer of the patient to public institutions which remain in the system and provide an "open door" to trauma victims.

While leaving the system might solve the problem at the microallocative level of the institution, it is a troublesome challenge at the macro level to the well being of the entire community and the fulfillment of equality of opportunity for care as an obligation of a just system of health care. In addressing this issue, Jonsen suggests that hospitals "may determine the service mix' they offer, but should do so in a manner consistent with the hospital's resources and mission statement and the needs and resources of their community" (Jonsen, et al., 1998:174). He concludes by noting that, before discontinuing a service, hospitals should determine that comparable facilities exist elsewhere in the community. In the Los Angeles case, this admonition does not appear to have been followed, except in the most literal sense of the continuation of the publicly provided trauma center at Los Angeles County public hospitals—however stressed these facilities might be to handle the burden of such patients.

In a very real sense, trauma care and the Los Angeles experience expose the significant limitations of an economically driven competitive model of health care delivery to deal with broadly based community issues. The potential for blunt or penetrating traumatic injury exists regardless of social class or economic standing. The purchase of health services by the affluent might be possible in an economically directed system, but the urgency of time associated with trauma makes travel to another location or placement on a waiting list impossible for a victim. The existence of a market to deal preferentially with any member of society suffering traumatic injury is lost as the unique organization of personnel and facilities required to maintain the standby capability of the trauma center are disbanded or put to other uses. From the point of view of equity, it may be argued that no one is immune to this problem, although it may occur with greater statistical frequency among young adult males and minority populations. One can run from the problem but not hide; one may even flip one's Jaguar on the back roads of one's country estate. Public financing of this service is the only equitable method that serves the interests of all.

A special associated problem is that of prevention. It is an attractive suggestion to argue that funds expended on trauma care organization be redirected to support prevention measures which might alleviate the problem. Prominent examples here include more stringent gun control, auto air bags, and compulsory helmet use by motorcyclists. While these goals are laudable for education and public awareness, they may result in "victim blaming" strategies, which argue that the injury is the responsibility to some degree of the injured, and that the expenditure of funds for curative and rehabilitative purposes should be limited. This argument should be treated with concern—greater efforts at prevention are in order, but not at the expense of existing services.

MANAGED CARE AND TRAUMA SERVICES: THE FUTURE

In order to offset significant fixed costs of facilities and staffing, trauma centers have, historically, relied on subsidization of services by routine services delivered in the institutional setting. An urban setting may be expected to generate 1000 severely injured patients per 1,000,000 people annually, but such patients typically comprise no more than 10 to 15% of total emergency activity (Maull and Rhodes, 1996). Those costs were spread across patients accessing services of the emergency department of the facility through assessment of a facility of technical charge. Baker and Baker (1994) have reported charges for emergency service utilization that exceed, on average, charges for comparable services rendered in a physician's office by factor of 2.7. In addition, the rendering of physician fees associated with the visit is variable across facilities, and may result in multiple physician charges for a specified visit.

Given the perceived expense for each unit of service rendered, managed care plans have sought to curtail use of routine emergency services through a variety of administrative means. Kongstvedt (1997) has advocated a variety of strategies, including limitation on coverage, use of nurse authorization lines, and alternative settings for urgent care. These steps, he argues, are essential because the perception of emergent status is typically in the eyes of the member rather than a primary care provider or other professional. In addition, use of non-participating facilities which are not members of the managed care network by contract (often resulting in the exclusion of urban trauma centers) is discouraged or forbidden. Gray (1991) has identified the incidence of retrospective review of member utilization of emergency services and the denial of full or partial payment for care deemed unwarranted as a true emergency upon review.

The resulting acrimony from use of utilization review measures has caused managed care plans to impose co-pays and deductibles on members as a means of discouraging use of emergency services (Selby, Fireman, and Swain, 1996). It is suggested by these researchers that such measures can result in a decrease of 15% in emergency services for non-urgent conditions. In addition, prominent trauma centers such as Wishard Memorial in Indianapolis and Ramsey in St. Paul, Minnesota, have organized proximal urgent care centers to treat patients presenting with less-than-urgent symptoms while rendering a lower charge.

The net impact of this activity has been to focus costs on the actual trauma patients as opposed to spreading those costs across other users of service. Williams (1996) has identified the marginal costs of emergency services as relatively low in contrast to more typically cited average costs, resulting in much lower potential savings to the health system for care rendered instead in physicians' offices. However, for an individual health plan purchasing marginal units of service and paying average cost (or even full charges in the absence of contract), potential savings per visit are still substantial. As Kongstvedt (1997) has observed, managed care plans continue to view reduction in emergency department visits as an indicator of effective plan management. The net result, for the trauma center, is that costs are concentrated on fewer patients as less urgent patients are diverted elsewhere, resulting in increased charges to supplement lost revenue.

While managed care plans are loath to pay for less urgent patients in emergency settings, support for severely injured patients in trauma centers is not in dispute by plan executives. Culbertson (1997) observed support in four major U.S. markets for trauma services on the part of managed care executives, as these services are generally too costly and sophisticated to be provided in contracted hospitals. Further, he notes that managed care providers appeared content, at least for the time being, to pay for these services on a fee-for-service basis or with fee schedule arrangements, rather than attempt to move to more aggressive systems of payment for what might be episodic services. (Culbertson, 1997:1376). However, once the patient is appropriately stabilized and able to withstand the rigors of transfer, plan executives often insist that the patient be transferred to a contracting hospital for further recuperation and/or rehabilitation (Maull and Rhodes, 1996).

The general pattern, then, for managed care plans is to contract with community providers and around trauma centers as their services are seen as costly in general. Instead, plans will pay charges or case-by-case negotiated arrangements which are in the short term beneficial to the trauma center, but may, in the future, further isolate these providers from developing integrated systems of care.

THE FUTURE

The future configuration of trauma services, as with many aspects of health services, is a reflection of an aging society. This paper has concentrated in its case example and discussion, principally on trauma as an urban phenomenon. It is well to remember that a significant amount of trauma occurs in less dramatic fashion in rural settings and involves a differing mix of injuries, ranging from farm accidents to falls in the senior population (Rice and MacKenzie, 1989). As Medicare at risk arrangements for its beneficiaries become a major source of coverage, the influence of managed care plans on the trauma system of the future will increase.

Fischer and Miles (1987) projected demographics of trauma for 1995, which envisioned a decrease in penetrating trauma resulting from violence and blunt trauma from auto accidents as the at-risk population in the highly injury prone cohort (14/34 years) declines. However, this age group will again increase in numbers after the year 2000. In addition, social forces resulting in injury do not necessarily mirror epidemiological trends for other diseases. The result may be significant increases in certain social pathologies, such as homicide, which is projected to cause 50% of all deaths in black males aged 5 to 24 years and white males 5 to 29 years by the year 2000 (Jacobs and Jacobs, 1996).

The aging population will result in an increased need for trauma facilities attuned to health needs of seniors (Baker, O'Neill, Ginsburg and Li, 1992). This is a source of future concern for our health facilities. Fischer and Miles (1987:1235) have written that "our health system is virtually incapable of accommodating increased numbers of dependent elderly trauma victims." There is little on the horizon to change this projection and its potential strain on the trauma system.

CONCLUSION: TRAUMA CARE AS THE CONSUMMATE SOCIAL GOOD

Ethicists in all religious traditions have long acknowledged the obligation of the ethical person to sustain and support the injured and infirmed stranger. The parable of the Good Samaritan in the Christian tradition comes to mind, and the "Golden Rule" in a variety of forms is a staple of religious teaching (Darr, 1997). The plight of the victim has been eloquently stated in the literary tradition in Tennessee Williams' *A Streetcar Named Desire,* when Blanche DuBois says at its conclusion "I have always depended on the kindness of strangers" (Williams, 1947: 165).

The purpose of this paper has been to demonstrate the equalitarian nature of trauma, for which any of us is at risk. When the time comes, we cannot rely on the market; our best negotiating skills are to no avail. As with Blanche DuBois, it is our turn to "depend on the kindness of strangers," and we can only hope that a just society has made the necessary investments in system organization, capital facilities, and critical personnel to sustain us in our hour of untimely need. This can only be achieved by a community resource, which confers on us a beneficence no market can provide.

ABOUT THE AUTHOR

Richard A. Culbertson, PhD, is Professor, Chair, and Director of Doctoral Programs, Department of Health Systems Management, School of Public Health and Tropical Medicine, Tulane University in New Orleans, Louisiana.

REFERENCES

Baker, Laurence and Linda S. Baker (1994). "Excess Cost of Emergency Department Visits for Nonurgent Care" *Health Affairs.* 13(5):162–171.

Baker, Susan, B. O'Neill, M. Ginsburg, and G. Li. (1992). *The Injury Fact Book.* 2nd Ed. New York: Oxford University Press.

Boyd, David (1980). "Emergency Medical Services: Perspective of a National Initiative." *Emergency Medical Services: Measures to Improve Care.* Eds. J. Bowers, F. Purcell. New York: Josiah Macy Foundation, 1–24.

Culbertson, Richard A. (1997). Academic Faculty Practices: Issues for Viability in Competitive Managed Care Markets. *Journal of Health Politics, Policy and Law.* 22:6. (December). 1359–1383.

Darr, Kurt (1997). *Ethics in Health Services Management.* Baltimore Maryland: Health Professions Press.

Englehardt, H. Tristam (1986). *The Foundation of Bioethics.* New York: Oxford University Press.

Fischer, Ronald and David Miles (1987). "The Demographics of Trauma in 1995." *Journal of Trauma.* 27(11):1233–1235.

Flint, Lewis (1990). "Regionalization of Trauma Care." E. E. Moore, ed. *Early Care of the Injured Patient.* 4th Ed. Philadelphia: Decker, 27–35.

Flint, Lewis and Carolynne Flint (1985). "Evolution, Design, and Implementation of Trauma Systems." *The Management of Trauma* 4th Ed. Eds. G. Zuidema, R. Rusheford, W. Ballinger. Philadelphia: W. B. Saunders, pp. 1787–1801.

Gray, Bradford (1991). *The Profit Motive and Patient Care.* Cambridge, MA: Harvard University Press.

Hiatt, Howard (1975). "Protecting the Medical Commons: Who is Responsible?" *New England Journal of Medicine.* 293:5 (July 31, 1975) 235–240.

Jacobs, Barbara and L. Jacobs (1996). "Epidemiology of Trauma." In *Trauma.* 3rd Ed. Eds. D. V. Feliciano, E. E. Moore, and K. L. Mattox. pp. 15–30. Stanford, CT: Appleton and Lange.

Jacobs, L. M. (1985). The Effect of Prospective Reimbursement on Trauma Patients. *Bulletin of the American College of Surgeons.* 70(2); (February 1985) 17–22.

Jonsen, Albert, Mark Siegler, and William J. Winslade (1998). *Clinical Ethics.* 4th Ed. New York. McGraw-Hill.

Kongstvedt, Peter (1997). *Essentials of Managed Health Care.* 2nd Ed. Gaithersburg, MD: Aspen.

Los Angeles Times (1989). "A Model Expires." September 17, 1989. P. A-1.

Los Angeles Times (1990a). "Another Hospital to Ax Trauma Network; Blow is Called Fatal." February 25, 1990.

Los Angeles Times (1990b). "Trauma Care in State of Shock." Page M6, March 4, 1990.

Mattox, Kenneth (1977). "Trauma Centers and Emergency Medical Services." W. Portnay (Ed.). *Emergency Medical Care.* Lexington, MA: Lexington Press. pp. 1–18.

Maull, Kimball and M. Rhodes (1996). "Trauma Center Design, Trauma. 3rd ed. D. Feliciano, E. Moore, and K. Mattox (Eds). Stanford, CT: Appleton & Lange.

McElroy, Charles (1983). "Obstructions in the Road to Trauma Care." I. West (Ed). *Trauma Care Systems.* New York: Praeger, 23–33.

Pepler, Richard (1980). "Political and Economic Considerations of EMS." *Emergency Medical Services: Measures to Improve Care.* Eds. J. Bowers and E. Purcell, New York: Josiah Macy Foundation. 102–114.

Physician Payment Review Commission (1992). *Annual Report to Congress.* Washington, D.C., U.S. Government Printing Office.

Pruitt, Basil and Barry Fitzgerald (1980). "A Military Perspective." J. Bowers and E. Purcell (Eds.). *Emergency Medical Services: Measures to Improve Care.* Eds. Bowers and Purcell. New York: Josiah Macy Foundation. 223–245.

Rand Corporation (1984). *Effects of Efforts to Regionalize Emergency Medical Services.* Santa Monica, CA: Rand Corp.

Rice, Dorothy and Ellen MacKenzie (1989). *Cost of Injury.* Atlanta. Centers for Disease Control.

Roth, Julius (1986) "Some Contingencies of the Moral Evaluation and Control of Clientele: The Case of the Hospital Emergency Service." P. Conrad and R. Kern (Eds) *The Sociology of Health and Illness.* 2nd Ed. New York: St. Martin's Press. 322–333.

Selby, Joe, Bruce Fireman, and Bix Swain (1996). "Effect of Copayment on Use of the Emergency Department in a Health Maintenance Organization." *New England Journal of Medicine.* (March 7, 1996) 334:10.

Sims, Deborah (1989). B. Bivens; F. Obeid; H. Horst; V. Sorensen; and J. Fath "Urban Trauma: A Chronic Recurrent Disease." *The Journal of Trauma.* 29:7. (July) 940–946.

Tancredi, Laurence (1982). "Social and Ethical Implications in 'Technology

Assessment'." B. McNeil, E. Cravalho (Eds). *Critical Issues in Medical Technology.* Boston: Auburn House, Boston, 93–112.

Time (1990). "Do You Want to Die?" May 28, 1990. 58–65.

Trunkey, Donald (1988). "The Organization of Trauma Care." J. Binke, R. Boyd and C. McCabe (Eds). *Trauma Management.* Chicago: Year Book Publishers 1–10.

Trunkey, Donald (1980). "Problems in Trauma Care." J. Bowers and F. Purcell (Eds). *Emergency Medical Services.* New York: Josiah Macy Foundation, 80–88.

U.S. Office of the Census (1997). *Current Population Survey.* Washington, D.C.

Weber, Max (1980). *Basic Concepts in Sociology.* Ed. H. P. Secher. Secaucus, N.J.: Citadel Press.

Williams, Robert (1996). "The Costs of Visits to Emergency Departments." *New England Journal of Medicine.* 334:10. (March 7, 1996) 642–646.

Williams, Tennessee (1947). *A Street Car Named Desire.* New York: New Directions.

CHAPTER 5

THE POLITICS
OF HEALTH

Politics has often been described as the "art of the possible." It is politics and the political process that translate our ideas and values into public policy. In each edition of *The Nation's Health,* we have included articles or book chapters on the politics of health, beginning in the first edition with Douglass Cater's preface to Cater and Lee's book, *The Politics of Health* (1979). Cater's ideas grew out of his experience as a journalist in Washington, DC and as a senior staff member in President Lyndon Johnson's White House, during a period when more health legislation was passed by two Congresses than by all the previous Congresses put together. He coined the phrase "subgovernment of health" to describe the actors and the processes that influence federal health policy. Prior to the period of "Great Society" activism in the 1960s, political alignment on most health policy issues, except biomedical research, had been largely determined on a geographic (particular states) basis. The Hill–Burton Program for hospital planning and construction was the best postwar example of a major public health program that provided federal funds through the states to build a modern hospital system throughout the United States. The traditional grant-in-aid programs of the Public Health Service were virtually all granted to states for categorical health programs. The funding of biomedical research, through the National Institutes of Health, was the exception. While interest groups of one kind or another have characterized politics in the United States since the founding of the republic, they did not emerge as of importance in health policy, except for the American Medical Association (AMA), until World War II.

As in other areas of public policy, an "iron triangle" emerged. The "iron triangle" in health policy consisted of three elements. The first element comprised the private-sector interests, which included the medical profession, initially through the AMA and then involving multiple specialties and the medical schools. Along with the profession were the hospitals, the health insurance industry (especially after World War II) and the pharmaceutical industry, which focused most of its attention on drug regulation and the Food and Drug Administration. Second were legislative committees and their staffs. The third leg of the triangle comprised the executive branch agencies. Instead of an "iron triangle," this model now includes organizations of investigators; medical schools; academic health centers; the pharmaceutical, biotech, and medical device industries; voluntary health agencies (e.g., American Cancer Society); and many consumer groups (e.g., American Association of Retired Persons, or AARP). As health policy has become more complex, the subgovernment of health has become larger and more loosely structured. It is now referred to as a network rather than an iron triangle.

The role of pluralism and the role of special interests are described by Barr, Lee, and Benjamin (see Chapter 3). In the fourth edition, Lee and Benjamin's book chapter "Health Policy and the Politics of Health Care" (1993) described this process in more detail. While the advocates of the pluralist perspective find little problem with the proliferation of interest groups, it is clear that some, usually representing business, have a far more powerful voice than many nonprofit, voluntary agencies. Also, those who have a focused interest and greater stake in a particular policy (e.g., physicians in Medicare policies related to physician payment) will have more influence than those with a diffuse interest in the issue (e.g., taxpayers). Now representatives of special interests are among the greatest stakeholders and, as such, mobilize significant resources to influence the formulation of policy. Political action committees pour hundreds of millions of dollars to directly support candidates for office at all levels of government and additional millions of "soft" money to organizations where there is no public accountability.

The 1990s, and particularly the period since the demise of President Clinton's Health Security Act Proposal in 1994 and the election of Republican majority in both the U.S. Senate and House of Representatives in 1994, has witnessed major changes in the politics of health. In their paper, "The New Politics of U.S. Health Policy," Hacker and Skocpol (1997) focus on both an ideological shift and the overriding importance of the federal budget. The need to reduce the budget deficit, they argue is among the predominant concerns presently influencing the politics of health. Another factor—the strong antigovernment sentiment expressed by the Republicans—is the third factor influencing the politics of health. Altogether, Hacker and Skocpol describe the dramatic shift in the politics of health as a threefold strategy by the Republicans to (1) reduce spending on existing programs and preclude future spending increases by large tax cuts; (2) transfer authority to the states for programs that formerly were joint federal/state programs (e.g., welfare); and, (3) privatize public programs, which would permit beneficiaries of public services to purchase them from the private sector.

The importance of the federal budget, first because of the growing deficit from the early Reagan years and now as a result of the current and projected surpluses, are strongly influencing the politics of health. For years, the size of the deficit alone precluded major health policy initiatives, except those responding to the HIV/AIDS epidemic. Furthermore, it was the introduction of new budget procedures in 1990, making the budget process more restrictive, that made President Clinton's Health

Security Act almost impossible to enact without difficult tax increases. With the surplus, the political debate regarding health care is governed by the Republicans' push for a large tax cut, while the Democrats want to strengthen existing programs and add a prescription drug benefit for Medicare.

The changes are also dealt with by Glied (1997) and by Barr, Lee, and Benjamin (1999) in Chapter 3. In the past, Americans have placed great trust in the professionals who provide their health care, in the insurance companies that pay for much of their care, and in the government that regulates, oversees, and, to a great extent, finances the health care system. In the past 35 years, there has been a sharp decline in the public's trust in government to address key health issues, as well as other large policy issues. Only relatively recently has the American public begun to question the efficiency, effectiveness, and costs of their health care system. Only in response to constant media exposure and personal experience with a system rife with increasing costs, rationing, and decreasing access, has the magnitude of the problem become understood. Americans are now more critical of their health care system than are the citizens of Canada, the United Kingdom, Germany, or other industrialized countries. In the introduction to her book, *Chronic Condition: Why Health Reform Fails* (1997), Glied described the rapid shift in the public attitude toward health care reform between 1993 and 1994. Whereas health reform had been the key to election platforms in 1993, Glied noted that by "Clinton's second term, national health reform guaranteeing coverage to all Americans is a dead issue" (p. 2). One factor in the shift in the public's attitude was influenced by the huge investment by various interest groups (insurance industry, small business) in media campaigns and other activities designed to influence the public. Politics ultimately determines the struggle for financial resources and interest group control of various system components. Underneath the regulation and legislation are power struggles, the outcomes of which ultimately determine the availability, cost, and quality of health care services. They determine who will care for us when, where, and how; the methods by which we will pay for care; how much we will pay; and where hospitals will be located as well as their size and scope. The outcomes of these perpetual struggles also significantly influence the education of the health professions, Thereby determining the scope and direction of health-related research and the investment in public health programs. Whether the transformation in the politics of health will persist or whether a new balance will be struck will be greatly influenced by the elections in 2000. This is true not only of the President, one third of the Senate and the House of Representatives, but of elections at the State and local levels as well.

The politics of health has also been reflected in the politics of long-term care. The article by Estes, Weiner, Goldberg, and Goldenson (1999) updates the developments in long-term care policy and the politics of long-term care. Long-term care policy was a major issue discussed during the development of President Clinton's health care reform proposal, The Health Security Act. The discussions focused on both the elderly disabled and the disabled under age 65 years. The most important political development was the coming together of advocates representing both groups to agree on a common agenda. Politically, the initiatives in long-term care did not generate the groundswell of support that the Clinton Administration had hoped for. However, there were a number of lessons learned, including the return to incrementalism as the best means to advance the long-term care policy agenda. These lessons are detailed in the article included in this chapter.

We have included Marion Nestle's paper, "Food, Lobbies, The Food Pyramid, and U.S. Nutrition Policy" (1993), in our Recommended Reading because it illustrates yet another dimension of the politics of health. Her case study describes the potential conflict of interest when a government agency (in this case the Department of Agriculture) is simultaneously responsible both for advising the public on matters of nutrition and health and for regulating meat and poultry safety and promoting the sale of agricultural products. Dr. Nestle raises significant questions concerning the policy development process, when membership of both the authorizing and appropriations committees in congress emphasize agricultural rather than consumer interests and the Department of Agriculture must function despite a clear conflict of interest. Ultimately, the health of the U.S. population can be affected when nutrition, food safety, and health information for the public is impeded because of structural arrangements that limit information dissemination to protect the financial interests of agribusiness. To what extent will the new politics of health further tilt these public health functions in the direction of proprietary interests? This is a problem not only with respect to nutrition and food safety but also with prescription drugs, consumer products, occupational health and safety, and highway safety.

In summary, the politics of health and the health policy process, which it influences ultimately, allocate resources for the benefit of the population or special interests. Sometimes, both may benefit. The process is, in the long run, driven by our values, although at times what we say and what we do seem distant from one another.

REFERENCES

Cater D, Lee PR (Eds.). *Politics in Health.* Huntington, New York: Robert E. Krieger, 1979.

Glied S. *Chronic Condition: Why Health Reform Fails.* Cambridge, MA: Harvard University Press, 1997; 1–16.

Hacker JS, Skocpol T. New politics of U.S. health policy. *J Health Polit Policy Law.* 1997; 22(2):315–336.

Lee PR, Benjamin AE. Health policy and the politics of health care. From S. J. Williams SJ, Torrens PR (Eds.). *Introduction to Health Services* (4th ed.). Baltimore, MD: Delmar Publishers, 1993.

Lee PR, Benjamin AE, Barr DA. Health Care and Health Care Policy in a Changing World In Wallace H, Green G, Jaros KJ, Paine LL, Story, M. (Eds.). *Health and Welfare for Families in the 21st Century.* Boston, MA: Jones & Bartlett 1999; 13–29.

Nestle M. Food lobbies, the food pyramid, and U.S. nutrition policy. *Internat J Health Serv* 1993; 23(3): 483–496.

Weiner JM, Estes CL, Goldberg SC, Goldenson SM. *The Politics of Long Term Care Reform under the Clinton Health Plan: Lessons for the Future.* San Francisco: Health Policy Center and Institute for Health and Aging, 1999.

THE NEW POLITICS
OF U.S. HEALTH POLICY

Jacob S. Hacker and Theda Skocpol

ABSTRACT

Following the demise of comprehensive health care reform in 1994, some reformers are seeking comfort in the successful "incremental" strategy for enacting Medicare that emerged out of President Harry Truman's failed campaign for national health insurance in 1948–50. But despite similarities between the Truman and Clinton health security efforts, overall contexts of government and politics are much less hospitable to governmentally funded reforms today than they were after Truman's defeat. Back then, market transformations and political dynamics were both pushing toward expanded access to health services and insurance coverage. Today, by contrast, both push in the opposite direction. The private insurance market is fragmenting, federal budgetary constraints stymie new programs, and the deficit dominates debate over existing programs. Equally important, a stable proreform coalition like that of Truman's day has yet to emerge, while a new and fiercely conservative corps of Republicans is championing coherent programmatic alternatives based on anti-government premises. Although passage of the Kassebaum-Kennedy health insurance reform bill in 1996 unleashed a wave of enthusiasm about incremental health care reform, formidable political, fiscal, and technical obstacles continue to stand in the way of even relatively modest incremental solutions.

The rise and fall of health care reform is the oldest story in American health politics. Time and again in the twentieth century, reformers have unsuccessfully fought for expanded or universal health insurance. Then, in the aftermath of political defeats, private market actors have rapidly transformed patterns of health care financing and delivery. After World War II, this old story gained a new twist with the passage of federal legislation to augment the technological arsenal of American medicine. While proposals for national health insurance languished in Congress, the federal government pumped public funds into the medical industry, subsidizing private health insurance, hospital construction, and medical education and research, and generating new markets, profits, and political resources for major stakeholders in the one-seventh of the American economy now devoted to health care (Jacobs 1995).

Only in 1965, with the passage of Medicare and Medicaid, was the pattern of defeats followed by market transformations and incremental reforms momentarily broken. Yet that rare moment of victory for advocates of extended public financing of health care did not prove to be an entering wedge for universal health insurance through federal funding or mandates, as health reformers back then had hoped. By the 1970s, distrust of government, slow economic growth, and mounting fiscal constraints left reformers without much hope for achieving universal health insurance. Reformers found themselves struggling to protect existing public programs while advocating piecemeal regulations to control health care costs and narrow gaps in the private health insurance market.

The Health Security plan sponsored by President Bill Clinton during 1993 and 1994 aimed to break the political impasse facing post-1960s health reformers. With a "window of opportunity" for government-led reforms finally open (Kingdon 1995: 217–218; Hacker 1996), President Clinton sought to enact comprehensive federal rules that would, in theory, simultaneously control medical costs and ensure universal insurance coverage. The bold Health Security initiative was meant to give everyone what they wanted, delicately balancing competing ideas and claimants, deftly maneuvering between major factions in Congress, and helping to revive the political prospects of the Democratic Party in the process (Hacker 1997).

But, as everyone knows, the Health Security effort failed miserably (Skocpol 1996; Johnson and Broder 1996). And the electoral headway made by militant conservative Republicans in the wake of the Health Security debacle has threatened since 1994 to turn U.S. health politics entirely upside down. For more than a decade, congressional budget hawks and antigovernment conservatives have closed in on Medicare and Medicaid, two of the fastest growing items in the federal budget. During the 1980s, hard-core conservatives within the Republican Party gained influence and visibility while developing tough new strategies for achieving their goals. After the political reversals of 1994, the new Republican majority advanced proposals to rein in the growth of Medicare and Medicaid, fundamentally restructure Medicare, and devolve responsibility for determining Medicaid eligibility and benefits to the states. Those proposals ultimately provided the opening for countermaneuvers by President Clinton, who used his veto to bury the Republicans' balanced-budget initiative and thereby position himself for victory in the 1996 presidential election. During the budget battle, however, both President Clinton and congressional Democrats committed themselves to balancing the federal budget in the very near future, a move that could have serious consequences for Medicare and Medicaid.

The demise of the Health Security plan was not, therefore, a mere setback for advocates of publicly guaranteed health insurance. It was, rather, a potentially decisive turning point in U.S. health politics—one that could set the terms of the debate over U.S. health policy for years and even decades to come. The Clinton reform effort of 1993–94 reflected a widespread recognition of the limits of the private health insurance market and of the corresponding need for an inclusive public framework for pooling health risks, containing medical costs, and subsidizing low-income workers. Its defeat, however, has strengthened an alternative view of the government's role in the medical sector, a philosophy premised on the notions that health care should be treated as much as possible like other market goods and that large insurance pools should be split up to encourage individual cost awareness and personal responsibility (see, e.g., Tanner 1993; Armey 1995). This ideological transformation has been helped along by the fiscal constraints created by the federal budget deficit, by the need for budgetary adjustments in the Medicare program, and by dramatic changes in the private health insurance market that are moving more Americans than ever into managed care. Chastened by the implosion of the Health Security campaign in 1994, President Clinton and congressional Democrats have also backed away from the reform agenda of the early 1990s and moved to embrace minimal incremental changes in the private insurance market, such as those contained in the Kassebaum–Kennedy health insurance bill passed by Congress with overwhelming support in 1996.

The new agenda of antigovernmentalism underscores the historic turn that American health politics may be taking. In the past, failures to achieve comprehensive health care reform were followed by incremental but substantial government measures that simultaneously built up the private medical industry and used tax funds to extend health care to vulnerable groups of citizens not already covered by employer-sponsored health insurance. But in the aftermath of the Health Security debacle, reformers who favor a more active use of government face defeat without the confident expectation of future incremental victories. There may be no repeat of the detour toward Medicare and Medicaid that national health reformers took in the aftermath of President Harry Truman's failed effort to achieve national health insurance between 1948 and 1950.

DEFEAT AND ITS AFTERMATH, THEN AND NOW

Like President Clinton's ill-fated Health Security effort, President Truman's failed campaign for "compulsory health insurance" in the late 1940s is remembered more for what did not happen than for what did. But although Truman's struggle for national health insurance ended in failure, it gave birth to a new political strategy and proreform coalition that would eventually result in the greatest triumph yet won by U.S. health reformers: the passage of Medicare and Medicaid in 1965. A brief glimpse back at the Truman campaign and its aftermath suggests that despite the similarities between the Truman and Clinton reform efforts, the current prospects for future victories on the order of Medicare and Medicaid are much lower today than they were in the wake of Truman's defeat.

Harry Truman took office in 1949 accompanied by a newly Democratic Congress and intent on pushing an ambitious legislative agenda that included national health insurance. Truman's surprise 1948 victory at the polls and the return of Congress to Democratic control galvanized New Deal Democrats, who for years had seen their unfinished domestic agenda stymied by events abroad and conservatism at home. The seeming propitiousness of the moment led many left-leaning commentators to drop their early distrust of Truman and express unguarded optimism about the future of progressive reform. A liberal columnist writing in 1949 opined that "the President can get most of his program, and without too much compromise if he constantly calls upon the great public support manifest for him in the election . . . and uses his political skill to organize the progressive forces" (Thomas L. Stokes, quoted in Hamby 1973: 311). Another journalist of the day (Samuel Grafton, also cited in Hamby 1973: 312) went so far as to declare that national health insurance was as good as enacted. All this bears an uncanny resemblance to the brief consensus among media pundits in 1993 that the Clinton administration was "certain" to put through some sort of comprehensive health care reform proposal in 1994.

But, of course, it was not any easier to enact comprehensive health reform in 1949 than it was in 1994. Although Democrats nominally controlled Congress, the "conservative coalition" of southern Democrats and northern Republicans dominated Capitol Hill. Nearly all southern Democrats were against Truman's proposal. With Republicans also opposed, the Senate backers of the plan had no hope of bringing a national health insurance bill to the floor. Instead, the Senate passed the politically popular distributive elements of the Truman-supported health bill—measures funding medical research, public health programs, and the construction of scores of hospitals spread generously across congressional districts—while burying the proposal for national health insurance. In the House, only hospital construction survived (Poen 1979: chap. 6).

Although the health reformers of the Clinton administration did not face the conservative lineup of Truman's era, they did run into a surprisingly fierce counteroffensive against their proposed reforms—an offensive orchestrated nationally and in many congressional districts by small businesses, commercial insurance companies, and members of the Christian Coalition and other right-wing advocacy groups (Skocpol 1996: chap. 5; Johnson and Broder 1996). Back in 1949–50, the players were not exactly the same; but a similarly fierce attack unfolded. A massive public relations campaign launched by the American Medical Association (AMA)—then the key market actor with a stake in defeating national health insurance—linked Truman's proposal to growing public fears about socialism. Deploying more than $100 million on everything from national advertising to alarming pamphlets in doctors' waiting rooms, the AMA lobbying campaign was the most expensive and sophisticated in American political history (Poen 1979; Marmor 1973; Starr 1982).

The final blow to both Truman's and Clinton's health security campaigns was the midterm elections. Although Democrats in 1950 did not experience anything like the drubbing that befell Democrats after the failure of President Clinton's health plan, they did suffer substantial losses. The ranks of Truman's committed supporters in Congress were trimmed considerably, and among the electoral casualties were two cosponsors of the omnibus health bill that contained national health insurance (Poen 1979: 187). After 1950, Democratic proposals for universal government-guaranteed health insurance vanished from the political agenda for two decades. Today's Democrats appear similarly unwilling to revisit the ambitious reform proposals that opened the door for their defeat in the 1994 elections.

The two years since the demise of Clinton's Health Security effort have been marked by huge transformations in the private insurance and health care delivery systems—changes largely in the direction of cost cutting through managed care (Wines and Pear 1996). Despite the very different market arrangements of the late 1940s, the failure of the Truman reform effort also furthered major market changes. With the threat of national health insurance still vivid, private insurance companies teamed up with doctors and many large employers to expand employer-provided private health insurance. The big CIO unions made bargaining for worker health coverage a priority, and employers enjoyed tax advantages if they offered health benefits (Stevens 1988). For many full-time employed Americans, access to health insurance after 1950 came not through government-guaranteed health coverage, but through employer-provided private insurance, encouraged by subsidies in the federal tax code.

The political dynamics of the 1950s were also pushing toward expanded coverage and spending. Before the end of Truman's presidency in 1952, Congress passed important amendments to the Social Security Act funding state medical programs for recipients of public assistance. Truman's Republican successor, Dwight Eisenhower, oversaw the addition of disability insurance to Social Security, the extension of public medical provision to dependents of military personnel, the growth of government assistance for medical research, and the enactment of the 1960 Kerr–Mills program to help states pay for medical care for the elderly poor.

Meanwhile, a broader strategy was emerging among committed health reformers. Following the 1950 elections, Truman bowed to administration advisers who urged him to pursue a scaled-down reform proposal calling for federal hospital insurance for the elderly under Social Security (Poen 1979; Marmor 1973). Although Truman was not to see the fruits of this "incremental" strategy during his presidency, the proposal was kept alive into the 1960s by officials in the Social Security Administration (SSA) and by Democrats and their allies in organized labor. Year after year, Democratic advocates of public hospital insurance introduced bills in Congress and agitated quixotically on their behalf. This determined insurgent movement gained additional momentum in 1957 with the introduction of a revised old-age insurance bill strongly supported by the AFL-CIO. After the landslide Democratic victories of 1964, both federal hospital insurance and coverage for physician services were enacted as Medicare. At the same time, Congress replaced the Kerr–Mills program with a joint federal-state program for the poor known as Medicaid (Marmor 1973).

THE NEW POLITICS OF REFORM

Will contemporary proponents of universal health coverage be able to follow the path blazed by reform advocates in the 1950s and turn successfully toward major incrementalist steps to expanded coverage? Perhaps, but probably not. The surface similarities between the Truman and Clinton episodes should not obscure the fundamental differences in government and politics between then and now. Harsh and bitter as the battle over Truman's proposal was, it ended in a fiscal and political climate that would be scarcely recognizable today. American medical care was expanding rapidly as government support increased and private health insurance spread. The feared postwar recession never materialized, and the American economy continued to grow at an unprecedented pace through the 1960s. The fiscal picture was also rosy: The huge deficits run up during the war were replaced with balanced and even surplus budgets in the following decades. Although Republicans and southern Democrats remained opposed to major new social insurance programs, they were quite willing to move partway toward reformers' positions and support scaled-down forms of government assistance, particularly when money was sprinkled widely across congressional districts. President Eisenhower and congressional conservatives tried to hold the line on New Deal programs. They did not try to roll them back.

Furthermore, the coalition in support of old-age insurance that formed in the wake of Truman's defeat was stable, cohesive, and united behind President Truman and his aims (Marmor 1973; Derthick 1979). Advocates of publicly guaranteed health insurance almost universally agreed that federal hospital insurance for the aged was the appropriate first step toward their larger goals. They had a strong base of administrative support within the SSA, and enjoyed close ties with leading congressional liberals and organized labor. They also benefited from high levels of public trust and confidence in government—and in the popular Social Security program in particular. Throughout the 1950s, and well into the 1970s, Social Security steadily expanded under bipartisan pressure, with sizable benefit increases in election years (Derthick 1979).

By the mid-1970s, however, this stable expansionary pattern of politics had been eclipsed by rising medical costs, growing budget deficits, and the worsening state of the American economy. Perhaps the most telling change was the reversal of the steady postwar increase in the prevalence of health insurance. From the 1940s on, the share of Americans with private or public health insurance moved constantly upward, leveling off in the 1970s at approximately 85 percent. Since at least 1980, the proportion has dropped steadily, and the free fall shows no sign of stopping. Indeed, the decline in insurance coverage during the 1980s would have been even greater were it not for the significant Medicaid expansions enacted late in the decade (Levit, Olin, and Letsch 1992).

Yet the postwar expansion of private insurance was not the only trend that came to an end in the 1970s. In the troubled economic climate of the 1970s, government health programs collided with the costly medical sector they had helped construct, creating a volatile political mix. As federal health care spending exploded in the years after Medicare's passage, as the motive force of American health policy shifted from expansion to rationalization. Federal policy makers sought (with consistently limited success) to restrain the costs of the scattered set of public programs passed in the 1950s and 1960s (Brown 1983), while paying less and less heed to the lonely voices on the left still calling for expansionary reforms. The 1980s brought calls for full-scale retrenchment in the face of a burgeoning budget deficit and growing attacks on "out-of-control" entitlement programs like Medicare. Aided by the budget reconciliation process, Congress in 1982 and again in 1989 passed legislation to clamp down on Medicare payments to medical providers. These measures represented a sharp break with the open-ended spending and deference to professional authority that had characterized U.S. health policy in the past.

The shift from programmatic expansion to budgetary control may be the most important change in American health politics in the last two decades. Although budgetary constraints have certainly not halted the growth of public health insurance programs (which is in any case largely driven by general medical inflation), they have made such programs a central target of deficit-reduction efforts and strengthened the cause of those who wish to scale them back. Nearly every budget deal since 1981 has included sizable changes in the Medicare program designed to slow the program's growth. Medicaid has been the target of fewer retrenchment efforts, in part because the program's benefits eroded in the 1970s and were cut substantially in 1981 (Pierson 1994: 136–139). Indeed, notable expansions of Medicaid were enacted in every year between 1984 and 1990, though even with these expansions the ranks of the uninsured continued to grow. Still, Medicare and Medicaid now pay providers at rates below prevailing market levels, and the degree of financial protection offered by Medicare has declined markedly.

But if the budget deficit has not precipitated the dismantling of existing programs, it has placed a daunting barrier in the path of new programs, particularly since the introduction of new budget procedures in 1990. Under current budget rules, special procedural restrictions apply to legislative initiatives that the Congressional Budget Office (CBO) estimates will increase the deficit in any year subsequent to passage. President Clinton ran headlong into this harsh new fiscal reality when he began his reform effort in 1993 (White 1995).

More critical, perhaps, than the deficit itself have been the changes it has spurred in the strategies of conservative opponents of publicly funded health insurance. From the 1940s through the 1970s, opponents of government-led reforms could be counted on to offer private sector alternatives to national insurance proposals, and to work around the margins of existing public programs. By the end of the Truman administration, in fact, something of a reform consensus had emerged, not behind universal health insurance, of course, but behind incremental spending measures to expand the medical system and fill its most glaring gaps. Despite enduring differences, both reformers and their opponents agreed that medical care was not like other market goods, and that government had a responsibility to subsidize—and, when necessary, supplement—voluntary health insurance (Anderson 1968: 124–129).

This postwar consensus eroded in two stages. In the first, opponents of government-funded health insurance began to attack public programs indirectly as unrestrained budget busters that were spiraling out of fiscal control and imposing ever-larger tax burdens on the American public. Although President Ronald Reagan tiptoed around Medicare and Social Security in 1981, Medicaid was hit hard (Starr 1986). As the decade wore on and tax revenues failed to keep pace with rising spending on mandatory entitlement programs, the budget deficit emerged as the paramount domestic policy issue in American politics. In this austere fiscal climate, Medicare, Medicaid, and other nondiscretionary programs came under increasing attack as spendthrift entitlements that endangered America's productive capacity and threatened to bankrupt future generations. These complaints were voiced not just by conservatives opposed in principle to the welfare state, but also by moderate Democrats and Republicans who saw the deficit as a sign of political failure. And these sentiments were echoed by elites in the media, academia, and private think tanks who insistently asked why politicians did not take the "responsible" course of curbing runaway programs (White and Wildavsky 1989: 426–428).

The emergence of the deficit as a focal point for attacks on existing programs was only the prelude, however, to a far more portentous transformation of conservative strategy and rhetoric. In the years leading up to the Republican victories of 1994, critics of the welfare state moved beyond indirect attacks on government programs as unrestrained entitlements to frontal assaults on the programs themselves. Deficit reduction was no longer an end in itself, but a means to creating a smaller, less intrusive, less costly government. As Paul Pierson emphasizes, the Republican budget of 1995 aimed less at fiscal redistribution than at structural reform of government's role and purpose. Republican leaders "sought nothing less than a radical reduction in the political capacities of the federal government" (Pierson in press).

The budget battle of 1995 also demonstrated that conservatives were no longer willing to accept the rationale and structure of existing government programs, cutting here and there but leaving basic principles intact. Far from trimming around the edges of the current social policy thicket, the 1995 Republican budget presented coherent, integrated alternatives to existing programs that rejected wholesale previous philosophical and programmatic foundations. First, and most straightforwardly, Republicans sought to reduce spending on existing programs and put in place policy changes—such as large reductions in future tax revenues—that would prevent spending from rising again. Central to this strategy was the enactment of a balanced budget amendment to the Constitution, which failed by a single vote in the Senate in 1995 and failed again in early 1997.

Second, where programs were jointly run by the federal government and the states, Republicans sought to move key elements of fiscal and programmatic authority to the state level, while retaining sufficient federal control to mandate requirements for benefits and eligibility. Third, wherever possible, Republicans attempted to put in place programmatic mechanisms that allowed beneficiaries of programs to use public funds to purchase private alternatives to government-provided services. The primary goal of these privatization mechanisms was not budgetary savings, but the movement of most Americans out of social insurance programs and into private plans.

All three elements of the Republican budget strategy were on display in the congressional leadership's 1995 proposals to restructure Medicare and Medicaid. On Medicare, the Republican plan aimed to achieve $270 billion in savings by 2002, an amount that significantly exceeded the funds needed to place Medicare's hospital insurance trust fund on firmer long-term footing (and that bore a politically crippling resemblance to the $245 billion in tax cuts contained in the Republican seven-year budget plan). Yet the most important aspect of the Republican Medicare proposal was not the budget savings it proposed, but rather the profound structural changes in Medicare it envisioned. These changes included the broadening of the Medicare HMO option to include a range of managed care plans, the replacement of a guaranteed level of coverage with a fixed federal contribution to public and private policies, and the creation of tax-protected medical savings accounts (MSAs)—IRA-style accounts for the purchase of medical care (or, with a penalty, other goods), which are generally coupled with high-deductible insurance policies.

Although these features of the Republican proposal accounted for only a small share of the plan's $270 billion in total budgetary savings (the MSAs would in fact have *cost* $2 billion over seven years, according to the CBO), they posed a much more serious threat to the stability of the Medicare program than the proposal's reductions in payments to providers, which provided the bulk of the total savings. This is because spending on Medicare beneficiaries is extremely skewed: 10 percent of beneficiaries account for approximately 70 percent of program expenditures. Because MSAs and other private options are most attractive to the healthiest of older Americans, the Republican proposal threatened to set off a vicious cycle of adverse selection, saddling Medicare's traditional fee-for-service component with the sickest and most expensive of Medicare beneficiaries while siphoning Medicare spending into private plans whose healthy subscribers currently cost Medicare close to nothing. If this scenario had come to pass, it would no doubt have strengthened Republican claims about the unsustainability of Medicare's fee-for-service program.

On Medicaid, the Republican goals were in many ways even more ambitious. Not only did Republican leaders seek to eliminate the federal entitlement to Medicaid, they also proposed converting the program into various "block grants" and devolving most of the authority to determine eligibility and program structure to the states. The Republican sweep of 1994 had installed a large new coterie of Republican state governors who were eager to exchange reduced federal funding for greater control over their Medicaid programs. Throwing Medicaid to the states promised, moreover, to spare Republicans from some of the political fallout major programmatic retrenchment might otherwise entail. Most important, Republicans expected that the states would relentlessly contain future program growth, lopping people off the Medicaid rolls and speedily moving program beneficiaries into private managed care plans. In fierce competition with one another for capital and skilled labor, states would be sharply constrained in their ability to finance programs for the needy and disadvantaged (Peterson 1995).

A NEW BREED OF REPUBLICANS

Behind these ambitious proposals lies a historic transformation of Republican leadership and strategy. From the ashes of the 1992 defeat of George Bush, the conservative elements of the Republican Party forged a new and much more aggressive party agenda (Balz and Brownstein 1996). The political battles between congressional Republicans and President Clinton in 1993–94, particularly over the president's Health Security plan, vividly demonstrated to Republicans the power of denouncing taxation and government as the source of public anxiety and discontent. More than that, it provided the opening for activists within the party who ridiculed the mealy-mouthed Republican opposition of the past, symbolized among conservative Republicans by Bush's decision to abandon his no-new-taxes pledge during the 1990 budget summit. For more than a decade, the conservative wing of the Republican Party, led by House Republican Newt Gingrich, had been reaching out to like-minded lobbies and think tanks and setting up its own private organizations to disseminate ideas and recruit conservative congressional candidates. With the party in disarray after 1992, these allied forces became the backbone of a crusading movement within the party to capture the organs of national political power and inaugurate a new era of activist conservative governance.

The ascendance of Gingrich Republicanism was in equal parts a generational, regional, and ideological transformation. During the Truman administration, the South was still solidly Democratic, and the largest Republican contingents came from northern states like Pennsylvania, Illinois, and Ohio. Today, almost the opposite is true. After the 1994 elections, Republicans controlled the majority of southern seats in Congress, and the Republican Party itself was dominated by fiercely conservative southern Republicans (Elving 1996; Lind 1995). Although Republicans lost congressional seats nationwide in 1996, they continued to make strides in the South. Looking just at the House results, Republicans picked up a net total of thirty seats between the 1992 elections and the present: two in special elections, sixteen in the 1994 elections, four through conversions, and eight more in the 1996 elections. Over this same period, Democrats gained no southern House seats, although they did lose and then regain four.

Gone also are most of the moderate midwestern and northeastern stalwarts of the Republican Party who had been content to work around the edges of the New Deal and Great Society. In the House after 1992, the Republican leadership was composed almost entirely of southern Gingrich acolytes, the only exception being minority leader Bob Michel, who announced he would retire at the end of 1994. House Republicans removed moderate Californian Jerry Lewis from the chairmanship of the Republican House Conference and replaced him with the brash and fiercely ideological Texan Dick Armey, a former college economics professor with an almost religious antigovernment fervor. Armey ascended to the majority leadership in 1994 and was joined by minority whip Tom DeLay, another Texan and an equally tough-minded conservative. In the Senate, Kansas Republican Bob Dole's continued presence as majority leader prevented a southern capture of the leadership in 1995. But Dole's departure from the Senate permitted the elevation of Mississippian Trent Lott to the majority leadership and of Oklahoman Don Nickles to the number-two spot. This solid southern lineup was "without precedent," displaying not only the South's "extraordinary domination of the top jobs in both chambers" (Elving 1996: 1730), but also the emergence of a new generation of conservative southern politicians with national perspectives and ambitions.

Ideologically, too, the current crop of Republicans is a very different breed from their counterparts of even a decade ago. In the 1960s and 1970s, and even through much of the 1980s, Republicans were satisfied to let Democrats set the social policy agenda, to slow rather than halt the expansion of the welfare state, and to strike compromise deals inside Washington with their Democratic colleagues. Today's Republicans are much more conservative and much more hostile to inside-the-Beltway bargains. They are also much more skilled in the tools of modern mass media politics: polls, focus groups, political advertising, talk radio, and targeted media appeals. And they are able to link such tactics to grassroots mobilization through the Christian Coalition, the National Federation of Independent Business, the National Rifle Association, and other conservative advocacy groups with a strong presence in congressional jurisdictions. Republicans fought the health care reform debate of 1994 and the budget battle of 1995 using all the weapons of contemporary political warfare, taking their message to the public with rhetoric carefully crafted through public opinion research, and mobilizing local pressures on Congress throughout the South and West (Balz and Brownstein 1996).

Despite the tenacity with which Republican leaders have formulated their public pronouncements and the willingness they have shown to take on their opponents in the battle for public support, the contours of American public opinion may be the greatest barrier to the kinds of changes in public policy that the new Republican leadership envisions. A decade of experience with retrenchment initiatives both here and abroad suggests one unassailable truth about the politics of such reforms: The most popular proposals for deficit reduction are those that are never implemented. Americans may support a balanced budget in principle. They may see government as bloated, wasteful, and ineffective. But like citizens in all advanced industrial democracies, they express strong support for the universal social programs that make up the programmatic and fiscal core of the American welfare state. As a policy goal, budget balance has a weak and diffuse public constituency, whereas cuts in social programs impose direct and immediate losses to which service recipients and providers can easily respond. Every previous attempt at serious deficit reduction in the United States—in 1985, 1990, and 1993—has resulted in political losses for budget cutters (Pierson in press).

This was the dilemma Republican leaders faced in 1995. To unite deficit hawks and enthusiasts of tax cutting within the Republican Party, Republican leaders advanced a budget package with large tax cuts and correspondingly large reductions in future government spending. Some of these reductions could be obscured by phasing them in over a period of years, "backloading" them in the later years of the

Republicans' seven-year plan, or focusing them on service providers like doctors and hospitals. The bulk of them, however, had to come directly from popular social programs, most notably Medicare. Although Republicans tried to concentrate these remaining cutbacks on core Democratic constituencies, particularly the poor, their proposals were inevitably quite threatening to the working poor and lower-middle-class Americans who had defected to the Republicans in droves in 1994 (Teixeira and Rogers 1995). President Clinton and congressional Democrats seized on these cuts in their politically devastating portrayal of Republicans as heartless plutocrats robbing from average Americans and senior citizens to give tax breaks to the rich (Drew 1996). After scores of Clinton vetoes and two government shutdowns, the Republican budget package was fatally wounded by early 1996, and Republicans were frantically trying to pass measures that would improve their dismal public standing. A telling sign of the effectiveness of Democratic attacks was the decision by flagging Republican presidential candidate Bob Dole to embrace a supply-side tax reduction plan and pick Reaganite true believer Jack Kemp as his vice presidential running mate, thus effectively jettisoning his emphasis on a balanced budget during the home stretch of the 1996 presidential campaign.

The new terrain of U.S. health politics does not, therefore, guarantee conservative ascendance. Given the difficulties of moving bold new initiatives through the American legislative gauntlet and the fragility of public support for such proposals, proponents as well as opponents of comprehensive reform remain poised to block policy changes they dislike. Yet the tables are now far more tilted against reformers than they were in the wake of Truman's defeat. Whether today's health reformers can build the programmatic rationales and political coalitions necessary to return from the defeats of 1994 is the perhaps the most pressing question of the moment.

THE ROAD AHEAD

Five times in this century—during the Progressive Era, the New Deal, the 1940s, the 1970s, and the early 1990s—health reformers saw government-funded health insurance for working- and middle-class Americans slip from their grasp. Legislative campaigns that began with optimistic predictions about the inevitable enactment of national health insurance ended in despair. The reasons for special optimism in the early 1990s were numerous: a deteriorating health insurance market that increasingly hurt middle-income Americans, interest group dissatisfaction with the status quo, long-term institutional changes in Congress that decreased the power of conservative committee chairs, and, not least, the election of a unified Democratic government after twelve years of Republican presidential ascendancy (Peterson 1994). But these favorable conditions were not enough to overcome America's fragmented constitutional structure or the budgetary constraints and antigovernment sentiments that have come to characterize contemporary U.S. politics. Once again, reformers convinced that the United States would embark on the rational international path ran headlong into ideologically charged attacks, interest group opposition, and public skepticism about the capacities of government.

In the aftermath of defeat, it is tempting to conclude that the conditions for an incremental reform strategy are actually more propitious than they were when the Truman administration turned to the elderly in the wake of the 1950 elections. After all, the negative trends in U.S. medical care that first prompted political concern are still with us, and the public continues to believe that health care reform should be a top policy priority (Wines and Pear 1996). President Clinton and congressional Democrats have rebounded from the depths of 1994, largely because of their impassioned defense of Medicare and other government programs. They have also been able to secure real, if modest, victories on traditional Democratic policy issues like the minimum wage, and they seem determined to continue moving incrementally forward on these fronts. In addition, the ongoing transformation of the private insurance market toward highly restrictive forms of managed care seems poised eventually to spark public demands for a reinvigorated government role in health care financing. Such a backlash has already emerged at the state level, and recently surfaced in national politics with the passage of federal legislation requiring insurers to provide at least two days of hospital coverage to women who have just given birth. President Clinton's recently christened advisory commission on the quality of health care, comically denounced by Republican leaders as a reincarnation of Clinton's vilified 1993 task force, is just one sign of the gathering political response to middle-class fears about managed care.

Yet consider the contrasts between Truman's day and the present. Then, health insurance was just beginning its long postwar expansion, American medical care was comparatively inexpensive, and the economy was growing at a rate far in excess of the anemic growth of the past two decades. Although there was a large wartime debt to retire, the budget deficit was hardly a concern, and politicians eagerly larded up bills with "particularized benefits" for their constituents back home (Mayhew 1974). President Truman faced stiff resistance from Republicans and southern Democrats, but by the end of the 1940s, neither camp was willing to challenge the programmatic legacy of the New Deal (Hamby 1973). Now, however, politicians with reformist intentions must confront an enormously costly medical system and the easily ignited fears of the more than eight in ten Americans with some form of health insurance. And they must do this in a fiscal and economic climate characterized by slow economic growth and persistent budgetary strain.

The political opposition to reform is also more formidable than ever. Today's leading Republicans advance initiatives to scale back government that, as Dick Armey proudly notes in his book *The Freedom Revolution,* "would have been dismissed as impractical" (Armey 1995: 285) even during the Reagan years. In the two years since 1994, conservatives have shifted the terms of national political debate much farther to the right than their record of legislative accomplishment would suggest. Even if Democrats control Congress, the White House, or both in coming years, conservative Republicans will remain a formidable force in national politics by virtue of their strong southern base, their ties to grassroots conservative groups, and their willingness to use the Senate filibuster. Although forces of the left may make a comeback, American politics is likely to be driven by the Republican agenda of the last few years for some time to come.

Back in Truman's day, moreover, reformers occupied stable positions within the executive branch and worked in tandem with a labor movement at the zenith of its power. They largely agreed on the goals they were pursuing and the strategic means to achieve them. None of this is true today. President Clinton's discredited White House task force symbolized the long-term decline of administrative agencies as a source of policy initiatives (although, to be sure, executive branch officials did participate extensively in the Clinton working groups). Administrators of federal social programs have ceased to be the zealous program advocates that the SSA's heads were in the 1950s, when program executives allied with outside advocates to push for the expansion of Social Security and the creation of Medicare (Derthick 1979). Organized labor's share of the workforce has dropped precipitously since the 1940s and 1950s, especially within the private sector, and today's labor leaders face an uphill battle to rebuild the movement and protect the gains of the past, while formulating broader alliances on behalf of progressive economic and social programs.

Nor is there much agreement among the fragmented array of foundations, think tanks, and citizen groups that might make up an updated proreform coalition. As President Clinton's failed efforts at alliance formation in 1993 and 1994 painfully suggest, many of the groups that might be enlisted to support progressive reform proposals are mass-mailing organizations with limited grassroots presence and limited inclination to commit themselves fully to particular legislative initiatives (Skocpol 1996: chap. 3). These groups can be expected to coalesce in opposition to cutbacks in existing programs and to flex their muscles in Washington politics when their policy priorities are threatened. But they find it much more difficult to display the kind of unified front in support of positive goals that characterized the reform alliance of the 1950s and 1960s, much less to work at the local level to build stable majority coalitions from the ground up.

Perhaps the closest analogue to the Medicare strategy that exists today is represented by so-called kiddie-care proposals for covering all children. These proposals briefly appeared during the final hours of the Health Security plan's messy death in Congress, when they were endorsed by the *New York Times* and Senate liberals like Tom Harkin as a down payment toward the broader aims of reform. In the 105th Congress, Democratic leaders in both the House and the Senate have placed a high priority on the passage of some kind of kiddie-care scheme. President Clinton has also declared his support for expanded health insurance coverage for children, but his proposal to extend coverage to half of the ten million children who lack insurance falls short of what some Democratic congressional leaders would like to enact.

The kiddie-care approach quite consciously follows the Medicare strategy, focusing on a target population for which sympathy and concern can easily be raised. Today, nearly a quarter of the uninsured are children, a proportion that would be higher were it not for recent Medicaid expansions. Twenty percent of children are already insured by Medicaid, and the number is rising as private employers drop dependent coverage (U.S. General Accounting Office 1995). Children are also relatively inexpensive to insure, making them an ideal target group in today's straitened fiscal circumstances.

To hold down budgetary costs, however, most kiddie-care proposals attempt to target only uninsured children without affecting those who are currently insured by Medicaid or employment-based insurance arrangements. But fitting in a new federal initiative without modifying existing programs or employment-based insurance would be no small task. Moreover, the low medical expense of children notwithstanding, covering even a fraction of them would still require new federal budgetary commitments that have little chance of passage in the present antitax, antideficit climate on Capitol Hill. In the 1996 campaign, Democrats touted what they called a "families first" agenda, which included a proposal to require private insurers to offer kids-only policies that could not be discontinued when families moved or children became sick. Yet this initiative, like the rest of the families first agenda, was a modest mix of exhortations and regulatory gestures that steered well clear of promising new governmental resources for expanded insurance coverage.

A second incremental strategy—perhaps the most popular among those who still harbor hopes for comprehensive health care reform—turns away from the federal government and toward the states (Mashaw 1993–94). Although only Hawaii has come close to universal coverage, state-level insurance regulations and coverage expansions could allow some movement toward reform while national efforts remain stalled. Even if state efforts were modest, they would help many Americans who cannot currently obtain or afford health insurance, and they might even prod national employers and insurance conglomerates to demand encompassing federal standards.

But the political upheavals that brought Republicans into the congressional majority in 1994 also decisively moved the states into the Republican fold. Republicans now control nearly twice as many governorships as Democrats do—the highest ratio in the postwar era. At the state legislative level, Republicans made "striking" gains (Fiorina 1996: 139) in 1994 and suffered only minor losses in 1996 (Verhovek 1997). The states also face special barriers that the federal government does not, including limited resources, Employee Retirement Income Security Act (ERISA) restrictions, and fears of business outmigration. Finally, the experience at the state level so far has not been encouraging: Incremental movement toward coverage of the uninsured by states like Minnesota and Tennessee has been matched by dramatic backtracking by previous reform leaders like Washington State (Sparer 1996).

Health reformers at the federal level seem to have been left with one residual strategy: supporting modest insurance market reforms such as those contained in the Kassebaum–Kennedy bill, which was introduced in 1995 by Senators Nancy Kassebaum and Ted Kennedy. The original bill aimed to remove some of the barriers to insurance portability and continuity by limiting the use of preexisting medical condition exclusions and requiring insurers to continue covering workers even when they lose or change jobs. House Republicans, however, added several provisions that were more controversial—most notably tax-free MSAs, which could have the effect of undermining large private or public insurance pools, should they begin to spread in the U.S. health economy. The bill that was ultimately signed into law by President Clinton in 1996 included MSAs, but on an experimental basis and on a much smaller initial scale than Republicans had hoped.

It is easy to see why reform advocates would latch onto these minimal insurance regulations. After the stunning debacle of 1994, the only thing that advocates of reform appear to be able to agree on is that Democrats made a major mistake in not pushing for incremental steps toward universal coverage. Politicians find it irresistible to use regulations when tax revenues are unavailable, and the Kassebaum–Kennedy rules are deliberately designed to step ever so lightly on the toes of powerful stakeholders in the medical economy. Modest as these new regulations are, they have considerable public appeal and could ease the fears of millions of Americans who already have private insurance (Nadel 1995).

More hopes may be raised than met, however. Whatever the merits of insurance reforms, they will not do much for the uninsured, nor will they contain rising health care costs. Indeed, by forcing insurers to cover more people or more services, they could actually raise rates and cause low-income and young people to drop out of the insurance market altogether. Contrary to the claims of its supporters, the Kassebaum–Kennedy bill does not guarantee that workers will be able to retain health insurance when they lose or change jobs, for it does nothing to ensure that the jobless can afford coverage. Recognizing this, President Clinton has proposed a modest new initiative to fund state efforts to finance continuing coverage for the unemployed and their children. Attacked by Republicans as a risky new entitlement the costs of which could skyrocket during a recession, Clinton's proposal has also provoked worries among Democratic leaders in Congress, some of whom fear that health insurance for the unemployed could displace coverage for children on the increasingly crowded incremental reform agenda.

As a policy prescription, incrementalism has received little critical scrutiny. In policy discussions today, the term is used so loosely that it has come to encompass everything from minimal insurance market reforms to major steps toward universal coverage. If incrementalism is understood in the latter sense, as a steady step-by-step movement toward universal health insurance, perhaps there were crucial interim initiatives that President Clinton and his allies could have sponsored in 1993–94 instead of their unwieldy 1,342–page bill. But if incrementalism is understood, as it usually is, as marginal regulatory adjustments, then the argument that President Clinton should have embraced incremental reforms when he entered office in 1993 is both historically myopic and politically naive. The Clinton reform effort was launched with broad public support for universal coverage and a widespread perception among political insiders and the public that a major policy breakthrough was finally possible and desirable. President Clinton simply would not have been able to gain Democratic support in 1993 for small fixes in the insurance market to make life better mainly for already covered, middle-class employees. Even if he had received such support, he risked squandering a historic opportunity to do something substantial for millions of low-wage working Americans without health coverage. In

1993, there was a real possibility, however slim, that middle-class concerns and the needs of many low-wage workers could be addressed simultaneously. This was an opportunity that Clinton and congressional Democrats were understandably reluctant to let pass.

Perhaps enlarged opportunities for comprehensive reform will emerge again. Popular commentators have proclaimed the coming of a new wave of progressivism in American political life, as the public reacts against a Republican policy agenda that many Americans see as divisive, mean-spirited, and tilted toward the well-off (Dionne 1996; Lind 1996). Although the economy is by most measures fairly healthy, Americans remain worried about their economic future and the continuing replacement of stable, full-time jobs with part-time and contingent positions that offer few fringe benefits. By most measures, Americans are as concerned about the availability of affordable health insurance today as they were before President Clinton launched his reform effort (Wines and Pear 1996). They also have new concerns about the practices and procedures of managed care plans. It is very possible that over the next couple of decades there will be repeated waves of public calls for regulatory reforms, fueled by middle-class anger about insurance company practices and managed care.

But these trends will not by themselves revive the extension of coverage to the growing ranks of the uninsured as a compelling political issue. Real movement toward universal coverage and systemic cost containment will require not only the recognition of problems and the support of a receptive public, but also the ascendance of reform-minded political majorities with the strategic acumen and organizational infrastructure to build public support for a particular policy remedy. In this regard, the results of the 1996 elections augur poorly for reformers. Despite delivering a chastening blow to conservative House Republicans (a blow that has been magnified by Speaker Gingrich's well-publicized ethical troubles), the elections do not suggest that the deep political dissensus on health care reform will disappear soon. If anything, the distance between the two parties has grown in the past four years, as old-style congressional moderates have retired or been defeated (Binder 1996). Although Republicans only narrowly retained their majority in the House, they enlarged their seat share to fifty-five in the Senate and are virtually assured of augmenting their House and Senate majorities in the 1998 midterm elections. Bipartisan celebration of incrementalism notwithstanding, there is little guarantee that the vast differences between the two parties on health care will be bridged in this context. If a health policy breakthrough does occur in the coming decades, it will occur because advocates of reform have rebuilt the case for government action more generally, confronting head-on the negative policy and political legacies reformers in 1993–94 were forced to surmount.

The immediate challenge for American health reformers is more straightforward: to safeguard and maintain existing public efforts in health care. In the 1950s and 1960s, reformers had little to lose. Few health policy programs existed, none with the reach and scope of Medicare and Medicaid. Today, popular and successful programs exist, but they are under increasing challenge. If reformers are to rebuild momentum toward universal coverage, they will need to invest political energy and capital in the reconstruction and improvement of such programs. Equally important, they will have to work with like-minded organizations and movements to construct an institutional infrastructure and public philosophy of government on which a renewed campaign for insurance reform could rest. Without this broader effort, sentiments in favor of comprehensive reform might resurface. But there would be little reason to expect movement in the direction of universal health insurance.

ACKNOWLEDGMENTS

The authors thank Paul Pierson, Mark Peterson, David Mayhew, and Oona Hathaway for their helpful comments on earlier versions of this article. Support was provided by the Robert Wood Johnson Foundation.

ABOUT THE AUTHORS

Jacob S. Hacker is Fellow of the New American Foundation and Junior Fellow of the Harvard University Society of Fellows. He is also author of *The Road to Nowhere: The Genesis of President Clinton's Plan for Health Security* (Princeton University Press, 1997).

Theda Skocpol, PhD, is Professor of Government and Sociology, Harvard University in Cambridge, Massachusetts. She is the author of six books, including *Boomerang: Clinton's Health Security Effort and The Turn Against Government in U.S. Politics.*

REFERENCES

Anderson, Odin W. 1968. *The Uneasy Equilibrium: Private and Public Financing of Health Services in the United States, 1875–1965*. New Haven, CT: College and University Press.

Armey, Richard K. 1995. *The Freedom Revolution*. Washington, DC: Regnery Publishing.

Balz, Dan, and Ronald Brownstein. 1996. *Storming the Gates: Protest Politics and the Republican Revival*. Boston: Little, Brown.

Binder, Sarah A. 1996. Congress and the Incredible Shrinking Middle. *Brookings Review* (fall):36–39.

Brown, Lawrence D. 1983. *Politics and Health Care Organization: HMOs as Federal Policy*. Washington, DC: Brookings Institution.

Derthick, Martha. 1979. *Policymaking for Social Security*. Washington, DC: Brookings Institution.

Dionne, E.J. 1996. *They Only Look Dead: Why Progressives Will Dominate the Next Political Era*. New York: Simon and Schuster.

Drew, Elizabeth. 1996. *Showdown: The Struggle between the Gingrich Congress and the Clinton White House.* New York: Simon and Schuster.

Elving, Ronald D. 1996. Southern Republicans: A National Outlook. *Congressional Quarterly Weekly Report,* 15 June 1996, p. 1730.

Fiorina, Morris. 1996. *Divided Government.* 2d ed. Needham Heights, MA: Allyn and Bacon.

Hacker, Jacob S. 1996. National Health Care Reform: An Idea Whose Time Came and Went. *Journal of Health Politics, Policy and Law* 21:647–696.

———. 1997. *The Road to Nowhere: The Genesis of President Clinton's Plan for Health Security.* Princeton, NJ: Princeton University Press.

Hamby, Alonzo L. 1973. *Beyond the New Deal: Harry S. Truman and American Liberalism.* New York: Columbia University Press.

Jacobs, Lawrence R. 1995. Politics of America's Supply State: Health Reform and Technology. *Health Affairs* 14(2):143–157.

Johnson, Haynes, and David S. Broder. 1996. *The System: The American Way of Politics at the Breaking Point.* New York: Little, Brown.

Key, V. O., Jr. 1949. *Southern Politics in State and Nation.* New York: Alfred A. Knopf.

Kingdon, John W. 1995. *Agendas, Alternatives, and Public Policies.* 2d ed. New York: HarperCollins.

Levit, Katharine R., Gary L. Olin, and Suzanne W. Letsch. 1992. America's Health Insurance Coverage, 1980–91. *Health Care Financing Review* 14:31–57.

Lind, Michael. 1995. The Southern Coup. *New Republic,* 19 June, pp. 20–29.

———. 1996. *Up from Conservatism: Why the Right Is Wrong for America.* New York: Free Press.

Marmor, Theodore R. 1973. *The Politics of Medicare.* Chicago: Aldine.

Mashaw, Jerry L. 1993–94. The Case for State-Led Reform. *Domestic Affairs* 2 (winter):1–22.

Mayhew, David R. 1974. *Congress: The Electoral Connection.* New Haven, CT: Yale University Press.

Nadel, Mark V. 1995. Health Insurance Regulation: National Portability Standards Would Facilitate Changing Health Plans. Testimony before the U.S. Senate, Committee on Labor and Human Resources, Washington, DC, 18 July.

Neustadt, Richard E. 1974. Congress and the Fair Deal: A Legislative Balance Sheet. In *Harry S. Truman and the Fair Deal,* ed. Alonzo L. Hamby. Lexington, MA: D. C. Heath.

Peterson, Mark A. 1994. Congress in the 1990s: From Iron Triangles to Policy Networks. In *The Politics of Health Care Reform: Lessons from the Past, Prospects for the Future,* eds. James A. Morone and Gary S. Belkin. Durham, NC: Duke University Press.

Peterson, Paul E. 1995. *The Price of Federalism.* Washington, DC: Brookings Institution.

Pierson, Paul. 1994. *Dismantling the Welfare State? Reagan, Thatcher, and the Politics of Retrenchment.* New York: Cambridge University Press.

———. In press. The Deficit and the Politics of Domestic Reform. In *New Democrats and Anti-Federalists: Social Policymaking in the 1990s,* ed. Margaret Weir. Washington, DC: Brookings Institution.

Poen, Monte M. 1979. *Harry S. Truman versus the Medical Lobby: The Genesis of Medicare.* Columbia: University of Missouri Press.

Schear, Stuart. 1996. The Ultimate Self-Referral: Medicare Reform, AMA Style. *The American Prospect* 25 (March–April):68–72.

Skocpol, Theda. 1996. *Boomerang: Clinton's Health Security Effort and the Turn against Government in U.S. Politics.* New York: Norton.

Sparer, Michael S. 1996. Medicaid Managed Care and the Health Reform Debate: Lessons from New York and California. *Journal of Health Politics, Policy and Law* 21:433–460.

Starr, Paul. 1982. *The Social Transformation of American Medicine: The Rise of a Sovereign Profession and the Making of a Vast Industry.* New York: Basic Books.

———. 1986. Health Care for the Poor: The Past Twenty Years. In *Fighting Poverty: What Works and What Doesn't,* ed. Sheldon H. Danziger and Daniel H. Weinberg. Cambridge: Harvard University Press.

Stevens, Beth. 1988. Blurring the Boundaries: How the Federal Government Has Influenced Welfare Benefits in the Private Sector. In *The Politics of Social Policy in the United States,* ed. Margaret Weir, Ann Shola Orloff, and Theda Skocpol. Princeton, NJ: Princeton University Press.

Tanner, Michael. 1993. Returning Medicine to the Marketplace. In *Market Liberalism: A Paradigm for the Twenty-first Century,* ed. David Boaz and Edward H. Crane. Washington, DC: Cato Institute.

Teixeira, Ruy A., and Joel Rogers. 1995. Who Deserted the Democrats in 1994? *American Prospect* 23 (fall):73–76.

U.S. General Accounting Office. 1995. *Health Insurance for Children: Many Remain Uninsured Despite Medicaid Expansion.* Report to the Ranking Minority Member, U.S. Senate, Subcommittee on Children and Families, Committee on Labor and Human Resources, Washington, DC, 19 July.

Verhovek, Sam Howe. 1997. Legislators Meet, Surprised at Limit on Shift of Power. *New York Times,* 12 January, p. A22.

White, Joseph. 1995. Budgeting and Health Policymaking. In *Intensive Care: How Congress Shapes Health Policy,* ed. Thomas E. Mann and Norman J. Ornstein. Washington, DC: American Enterprise Institute and Brookings Institution.

White, Joseph, and Aaron Wildavsky. 1989. *The Deficit and the Public Interest: The Search for Responsible Budgeting in the 1990s.* Berkeley: University of California Press.

Wines, Michael, and Robert Pear. 1996. President Finds He Has Gained Even If He Lost on Health Care: Proposal Was Midwife to Swift Transformation. *New York Times,* 30 July, pp. A1, B8.

THE POLITICS OF LONG-TERM CARE REFORM UNDER THE CLINTON HEALTH PLAN: LESSONS FOR THE FUTURE

Carroll L. Estes, Joshua M. Wiener, Sheryl C. Goldberg, and Susan M. Goldenson

During 1993 and 1994, the United States debated but did not enact major health care reform. Although the primary focus of reform proposals was on providing health coverage for the uninsured and controlling acute care costs, many proposals included long-term care. President Clinton proposed a long-term care plan comprised of four key elements: 1) a large new home care program for the severely disabled of all ages and all income groups, to be administered with a lot of flexibility by the states, 2) a slight liberalization of the financial eligibility rules for the Medicaid nursing home benefit, 3) favorable tax clarification and tougher regulation of private long-term care insurance, and 4) tax credits for the long-term care expenses of the nonelderly disabled workers in order to permit the younger disabled to work without loss coverage. Significantly, the President's plan was a major departure from the current Medicaid-dominated financing system for long-term care in that it was not based on low income eligibility (i.e., means-tested), yet it was designed as a public program to be offered by the states. As proposed, the Clinton long term care plan was not an individual entitlement, but rather was described as an *entitlement to the states* to offer the program, and it was one that was "capped" in terms of federal funding.

While a lot has been written on what happened to health reform involving acute care during the early days of President Clinton's first term, the long-term care component of the debate has been largely ignored (Johnson and Broder; 1996; Skocpol, 1997; Aaron, 1996). The aim of this chapter is to describe some of the lessons learned from the long-term care component of the Clinton health reform debate.

This chapter is adapted and excerpted from Joshua M. Wiener, Carroll L. Estes, Susan M. Goldenson, and Sheryl C. Goldberg, *What Happened to Long Term Care in the Health Reform Debate of 1993–1994? Lessons for the Future.* Urban Institute, Washington D.C. and Institute for Health & Aging, University of California, San Francisco, 1999. Funded by the AARP/Andrus Foundation and The Commonwealth Fund. The authors acknowledge the assistance of reviewers at the Commonwealth Fund and AARP. The authors assume full responsibility for the interpretation of the data.

Long-term care was on the health policy agenda in 1993 and 1994 largely as a result of efforts of advocates for older people and the younger disabled and as part of the political calculus of the Clinton Administration to increase both the popularity and likely passage of the overall health reform package. The inclusion of long-term care in the larger health reform effort also was plausible because of the extremely comprehensive nature of the Clinton reform initiative and the personal backgrounds and experiences of President Clinton as a former state governor and those of his major health advisors.

As the Clinton Administration prepared its proposal, the high costs of a major long-term care initiative threatened, but in the end, did not thwart its inclusion. The long-term care plan contained a new home care proposal that represented a notable break from previous plans since it relied heavily on the states for the *design* as well as the administration of the program, it included younger people as well as older people with disabilities, and it allowed coverage of an extremely broad range rather than a limited number of specific services. Indeed, while designers started with a traditional notion of social insurance, the commitment to a very wide array of services within budget limits eventually forced the elimination of the concepts of a defined benefit and an individual entitlement. The long term care proposal was transformed from one linked to traditional notions of social insurance, to one linked to social insurance only by the nonmeans-tested eligibility criteria.

Politically, while the long-term care plan was generally supported by consumer advocacy groups, it did not generate the groundswell of enthusiasm for which the Clinton Administration had hoped. Support for health reform from the largest aging organization, the American Association of Retired Persons (AARP), was focused on many elements of the plan and the education of its membership in preparation for what it hoped would develop into a bipartisan proposal that the organization could fully endorse. AARP's strategy was interpreted by the media and politicians as granting only "tepid" support for both the President's larger health reform and the long-term care reform. Nevertheless, as health reform worked its way through Congress and efforts were made to reduce the costs of the package, long-term care succeeded in remaining a significant component of most of the Democratic plans, although generally on a smaller scale.

THEMES AND LESSONS FOR THE FUTURE

Participants in the long term care reform process were generally cautious in drawing lessons from the experience of 1993–1994 for future long-term care reform. According to a member of the Executive Branch, "long-term care was never seriously discussed. It was there, but it never was real." Others, however, contended that long-term care (LTC) was the most positive part of the Clinton reform package, as shown below. Nonetheless, there are at least seven major themes, lessons, or cautionary tales that can inform future action.

First, long-term care reform is a popular idea and did not cause the demise of health reform. In fact, long-term care was often described as one of the initiatives (although relatively neglected) that helped sustain commitment to health reform, although not a lot. One elderly advocacy organization representative contended that, "the fact that we got long-term care into the final package helped to obtain support for the final package." Among long-term care activists, there was a consistent belief that "there was always more public support for long-term care than for larger health reform." The fact that a public program for long-term care would not displace existing private sector insurance gave it a certain advantage over acute care.

Second, being part of a very large, comprehensive proposal for health reform does not necessarily aid long-term care reform. Although long-term care reform "tried to get on the big train," it got lost in the shuffle of the larger health care reform effort. Virtually all of the interest group representatives, including elderly and disability advocates, all agreed that "long-term care went down with the larger ship" and the "battle was not won or lost on long-term care." One elderly advocate put it this way, "You have to be careful what you hitch your wagon to. The big broad health reform approach is unlikely to happen." The lesson learned may be that the reform of long-term care needs to go its own way and not be part of health, Medicare, or Social Security reform.

Third, although inclusion of long-term care in the reform package had a clear political goal of increasing public enthusiasm for health reform, several key decisions in the design of the long-term care program and the inclusion of substantial Medicare cuts were thought to undercut its political support, although there was little unanimity on these points. The states were concerned about their potential financial liability in long-term care and did not receive fiscal relief for state nursing home care costs under Medicaid in the Clinton proposal. States were afraid of being "left holding the bag" for what some described as an "under-financed state level program that easily could be misunderstood as an individual entitlement." For elderly advocacy organizations, key problems were "the lack of a defined benefit and entitlement" for individuals, which made it difficult to explain to the public "what people were going to get." Also, support both for the president's long term care plan and larger health reform was diluted by the fact that there were substantial Medicare cuts on the table at the same time. According to the Clinton Administration, these cuts were needed to generate funds to pay for the proposed reforms for the elderly. Similarly, the proposed Medicare cuts in home health splintered the industry, leading some home care groups to actually oppose the president's Health Security Act.

Fourth, health reform generally, including long-term care, neglected certain political prerequisites. The expectation that major reform could be passed without significant bipartisan support in Congress was not realistic. An elderly advocate recounts that, "really we did not work with the Republicans at all; the sense was that we could do it without them. Hindsight is 20–20; it wasn't a very good idea." Further, for long-term care, there is the need for a spokesperson for whom this is *the* issue: "When our strongest Congressional advocate, Representative Claude Pepper, died we lost the voice. For years, we tried to find someone with the voice and commitment, but we never identified a true successor." In addition, stronger public education is needed to present the problem and policy solutions.

> We have to make people understand better the shortcomings of the current system. Ultimately, in the case of health insurance, most of us are covered. *In the case of long-term care, almost nobody is covered and they do not know it.* If we could get that point across, broaden the constituency, and sharpen the problem, long-term care would be much higher on the political agenda.

Fifth, long-term care policy is largely about money, i.e., how much are we willing to spend? While long-term care was in many ways politically popular, it was also expensive and added substantially to the costs of health reform, which some felt helped to drag down support for the reform package. Many participants in the process observed that the long-term care needs are so great and the current system so inadequate that, to do any significant reform requires spending billions of dollars. They pointed out that the first Clinton plan, which would only have covered home care for persons with severe disabilities was projected to cost an additional $36 billion a year when fully implemented (Office of the Assistant Secretary for Planning and Evaluation, DHHS, 1994).

Sixth, a major outcome of the failed health reform effort in 1994 is the begrudging acceptance of incremental rather than comprehensive change as the most feasible (if not the only) way to achieve policy reform in health and long term care. The recent trend towards incremental health care reforms has generated significant debate within the long-term care policy community. Advocates of long term care reform note ruefully, the difficulty, if not the impossibility of achieving success with any reforms that are seen as "big governmental programs." A Congressional staffer states bluntly, "We learned that a comprehensive proposal will not fly. You need to introduce incremental pieces to get anything accomplished." Another state official observes:

> We should never do such a big plan again. We should deal with health reform incrementally. You cannot fundamentally change 14 percent of the U.S. economy with a single piece of legislation . . . As a social movement emerges, there is piling on- with everyone trying to deal with everything at once. The problem is—especially if you are Democrats—is that you have so many constituencies who feel they need their piece of the pie to be dealt with. They think there is only one shot to get at something. You always live for another day. I strongly believe in incremental policy development.

The pervasive effect of this new incremental thinking has reached far and wide. Even the Long-Term Care Campaign, an intergenerational coalition of more than 100 organizations initially founded in 1988 to promote universal entitlement to social insurance for long-term care, has altered its approach to policy. A decade later (1998), the LTC Campaign endorsed something far short of its initial goals, as reflected in its *Policy Blueprint* (LTC Campaign, 1998). No longer promoting "a social insurance program like Social Security or Medicare, paid for by all ages" or using such explicit words as calling for "a comprehensive national solution" (LTC Campaign, 1994), the LTC Campaign now reaches for "appropriate, affordable solutions."

Five years after the defeat of health and long term care reform, President Clinton raised the political profile on long-term care by proposing a modest set of initiatives including a $1,000 tax credit for severely disabled individuals and their caregivers, unsubsidized private long-term care insurance to federal employees, limited funds for respite care, and an educational program for older people about the limits of Medicare and Medicaid long-term care coverage. These proposals sparked legislation to provide additional tax incentives for the purchase of private long-term care insurance, which were included in the 1999 tax bill passed by Congress and vetoed by President Clinton.[1]

Paradoxically, even the advocates of small scale improvements acknowledge the difficulty of doing anything meaningful incrementally in long-term care. One aging advocate notes, "long-term care is such a big issue in terms of what you have to deal with. In an era when incrementalism is how people think about health policy, it is hard to think what to do in long-term care without spending some big dollars." Even President Clinton's 1999 proposed tax credit for long term care, as limited as it was, would have cost $1 billion a year in lost revenue, not a trivial amount even in Washington, D.C. Nevertheless, others such as writer Robert Kuttner in *The Washington Post,* vehemently reject such incremental proposals as inadequate and cling to the hope of comprehensive reform (Kuttner, 1999). An Executive branch official scornfully confesses that "the incremental approaches in health reform of the last five years haven't gotten us much. The President's proposal for a tax credit for caregivers is less than one-half of a drop in the bucket."

The initiatives proposed by President Clinton and the Congress subsequent to the failed comprehensive health reform of 1994 illustrate the lesson that most participants enunciated: They are incremental in character and they use tax incentives rather than direct spending. For example, the President's 1999 longterm care plan would have cost a little more than $1 billion a year, a mere shadow of the $36 billion a year price tag that was envisioned in the 1993–1994 proposal. Demonstrating the case of dramatically reduced expectations, most elderly and disability groups supported the President's 1999 proposal, even though in the past they would have dismissed it as hopelessly inadequate. The advocacy groups' self-described explanation for currently supporting such small steps in long-term care policy is that the President's tax credit proposal "puts something on the agenda."

Seventh, there has been a profound shift in the framing of the options that is consistent with the recent acceptance of the "small steps, incremental approach." Traditional "social insurance" for long-term care in the mold of Medicare and So-

---

[1]The Republican tax bill would have allowed an "above the line" deduction for individual spending for private long-term care insurance, making its costs completely tax deductible within limits. However, note that even President Clinton's proposal would serve to promote private long-term care insurance.

cial Security is no longer actively debated as it was in the late 1980s. This is a result of at least two factors: a more conservative Congress, and the unintentional "de-construction" of the concept of social insurance through the design process of the long-term care component of the Clinton health plan, which replaced social insurance with a capped entitlement to the states for long term care. Under the Clinton plan, it was the states and not individuals that were to become entitled to having long term care programs.

Eighth, as incrementalism dominates current efforts to promote policy change in long term care and there is a dearth of major federal initiatives, there also has been the time and space for private sector interests and initiatives to develop. Members of the long-term care workgroup, advocates, provider groups, and Congressional members and staff concur that there are now increased interests working toward meeting long-term care needs through private insurance and other market mechanisms. One states that, "private long-term care insurance has become the primary policy where most of the work has been done."

Two additional lessons are that: 1) the President's long-term care proposal may have actually lost support because it was not a real social insurance program, which diluted the investment in it by the elderly and, perhaps, even by the states; and 2) the fact that there was no proposed dedicated revenue source for the long term care provisions, made it hard to give assurances of needed federal funding for the program proposed.

PROSPECTS FOR LONG-TERM CARE REFORM

So what are the prospects for long-term care reform in the near term and in the more distant future? For the more distant future, few observers doubt that when the baby boom generation needs long-term care, it will be a major domestic policy issue. If nursing home utilization rates remain constant on an age-specific basis, there will be nearly three times as many people in nursing homes as there were in 1990—5.7 million people in institutions in 2040 compared to 1.6 million in 1990 (U.S. Bureau of the Census, 1996). Whatever stage in life the baby boomers are, many argue that they tend to set the policy agenda.

For the near term, the political salience of long-term care is less certain. The changing demographic profile of the United States is expected to increase awareness of the long term care issue. While the baby boom generation is not yet using long-term care, many of their parents are. A Congressional staffer adds,

> Because the baby boomers are now caring for their parents, they are going to drive an interest in this issue in a way that hasn't been the focus before and they will also think about the need for long-term care for themselves. There will be a great demand for the government to address part of the problem.

Another provider commented, "The soccer moms are eight years older; now they are concerned with long-term care for their parents. Their needs are different." In contrast, there is also pessimism about the possibility for progress relating to long-term care due to its public or private cost, the desire for tax cuts, the funding and financing problems currently evident with Medicare and Social Security, and the lack of consensus in the policy community.

Finally, in what may be an important development for the future, a new Washington, DC, coalition was formed in 1999 to put long-term reform on the national agenda again. Chaired by former Senator David Durenberger (R–MN), Citizens for Long-Term Care (CLTC), is composed of organizations from all segments of the long-term care and political spectrum, including consumer groups, providers organizations, insurers, unions, women's groups, and business interests. Its goal is to educate the public by raising awareness of the issue of long-term care financing within the year 2000 presidential election. While this new coalition will function as a "clearinghouse of solutions," it will not endorse any particular proposal.

FINAL THOUGHTS

During long term care reform efforts in 1993–1994, an important alliance between the elderly and disability populations emerged and was solidified. The result is that, "aging groups in town are now better educated, especially about younger people with disability." The inter-generational solidarity and working relationships between the elder and disabled lobbies have endured throughout the 1990s. There is increased activism of the younger people with disabilities that continues to energize the now-ongoing coalition of the elderly and disability communities.

Another legacy of the long-term care reform of 1994 is significant change in the way long-term care is conceptualized. A major change has been the united commitment of the elderly and the younger disabled to the idea of intergenerational (cross-age) and cross-disability solutions to the long-term care problem. This new political alignment has been sustained in the post-reform period and aided in the successful defense against a proposed Medicaid block grant in the mid 1990s. Other significant changes are that the long-term care reform process and work between 1992 and 1994 contributed to a new paradigm that sought to counterbalance the bias and limits of 1) categorical thinking that previously allowed only specified medical and supportive services, and 2) institutional thinking in which the predominant public financing has been for nursing home care rather than for home and community care. Other elements of the strategy that also gained favor during the construction of the Clinton long term care plan sought to promote independent living and self-directed care models that challenge what has been described as the "over-professionalization" and the "over-medicalization" of long-term care.

The final approach contained in the 1993–1994 reform met the bottom-line requirement of many advocates that there be no means-testing in long-term care. In so doing, the design of President Clinton's long-term care reform plan finessed some of the most difficult stumbling blocks that could easily have set off unwanted opposition from the states and consumer groups to the proposed reform. For elder and disabled activists, the Clinton long-term care plan met the test of incorporating eligibility that was based solely on functional capacity and "looked like a social insurance program." For the states, the carrots were flexibility, no new individual entitlement, and sufficient "fiscal and political cover" for them to "buy in." The final plan strengthened and continued the state's primary role in long-term care, while—on the negative side—also ensuring the continuing unevenness and differences in long-term care benefits across the states.

The casualties of the health reform experience—almost all of which were previously non-negotiable by most elderly advocates at the outset of the Clinton Presidency—are the abandonment of the somewhat hallowed concepts of individual entitlement and a "defined benefit." Also lost under the long-term care plan was the idea that long-term care must be a uniform "universal national program," and, with it, the imperative of a traditional "social insurance" approach to the problem.

As we enter the next millennium, it appears that long-term care is coming back onto the national political agenda, albeit in a radically altered form.

ABOUT THE AUTHORS

Carroll L. Estes, PhD, is Professor of Sociology at the Institute for Health and Aging, where she was first and founding director, and in the Department of Social and Behavioral Sciences, School of Nursing, at the University of California, San Francisco. Author of *The Aging Enterprise* and seven other books, she is former president of the Gerontological Society of America, the American Society of Aging, and the Association for Gerontology in Higher Education.

Joshua M. Wiener, PhD, is Principal Research Associate of the Health Policy Center, Urban Institute, Washington, DC.

Sheryl C. Goldberg, PhD, MSW, is a Senior Research Associate at the Institute for Health and Aging, University of California, San Francisco and School of Social Work at University of California, Berkeley.

Susan M. Goldenson is a Research Associate at the Urban Institute's Health Policy Center. Her current research focuses on evaluating managed care in Medicaid and studying access to health care in rural areas. Previously, she served as a Policy Analyst at the Alzheimer's Association.

NOTE ON METHODS

Data for this article were collected primarily from interviews with 38 federal executive branch officials, health reform task force staff and members, representatives of nursing home, home care, elderly and disability organizations, state officials, legislators, Congressional staff, and researchers. Supplementary information was obtained from newspaper and other media accounts of health reform and government documents relating to the long-term care component of health reform. In addition, one of the authors was a member of the long-term care workgroup of the White House's Task Force on National Health Reform and provided his recollections of the process and lessons for the future.

REFERENCES

Aaron, Henry J. (editor). 1996. *The Problem That Won't Go Away: Reforming Health Care Financing.* Washington, D.C.: The Brookings Institution.

Johnson, Haynes and David S. Broder. 1996. *The System: The American Way of Politics at the Breaking Point.* Boston: Little, Brown & Co., 1996.

Kuttner, Robert. 1999. "Taking Exception" *Washington Post,* January 8, 1999.

LTC Campaign. 1998. *A Policy Blueprint.* Washington, D.C.: LTC Campaign.

LTC Campaign. 1994. *What is The Long Term Care Campaign?* Washington, D.C.: LTC Campaign.

Skocpol, Theda. 1997. *Boomerang: Health Care Reform and the Turn Against Government.* New York: W.W. Norton & Co., 1997.

PART 3

Public Health, Clinical Preventive Services, and the Emerging Collaboration of Medicine and Public Health

CHAPTER 6

PUBLIC HEALTH, CLINICAL PREVENTIVE SERVICES, AND THE EMERGING COLLABORATION OF MEDICINE AND PUBLIC HEALTH

Public health, clinical preventive services, and the collaboration of medicine and public health are included in Chapter 6 because they focus on the individual (clinical preventive services) and the population (public health) and the importance of collective efforts of medicine, public health, and community-based organizations in achieving health objectives. Working together, medicine and public health can better achieve both their individual targets and commonly held goals that cannot be achieved without collaboration.

In 1988, the Institute of Medicine (IOM) issued a critically important report, *The Future of Public Health* (see Recommended Reading), which reviewed the health problems facing the nation and proposed a conceptual framework for public health. They defined the term *public health* broadly:

> "Public health is what we, as a society, do collectively to assure the conditions in which people can be healthy. This requires that continuing and emerging threats to the health of the public be successfully countered. These threats include immediate crises, such as the AIDS epidemic; enduring problems, such as injuries and chronic illness; impending crises, foreshadowed by such developments as the toxic byproducts of a modern economy" (IOM, 1988, p. 7)

The IOM proposed that the three broad functions of public health include assessment, policy development, and assuring that policies are implemented and achieved. These functions are described more fully in the IOM Report and by Afifi and Breslow, who added to the IOM's description of public health (see Recommended Readings). They defined the core disciplines of public health as epidemiology and biostatistics (composing the "diagnostic tools"), followed by health behaviors, environmental health, and personal health services (the "treatment tools" of public health). They noted that public health practice "embraces all those activities that are directed to assessment of health and disease problems of the population; the formulation of policies for dealing with such problems; and the assurance of environmental, behavioral and medical services designed to accelerate favorable health trends and reduce the unfavorable" (Afifi and Breslow, 1994, p. 232).

After the 1988 IOM Report, further discussions such as these about the role and future of public health took place in many settings, and a great deal of action was generated, particularly in the public health community. The IOM established a public health roundtable funded by the U.S. Public Health Service and several major private foundations, in order to conduct major studies of prevalent public health problems. Local, state, and federal governments, as well as professional associations such as the American Public Health Association (APHA), State and Territorial Health Officers (ASJO), and the American Medical Association (AMA), moved to address the issues identified in the IOM report. In addition, the Robert Wood Johnson Foundation and the Kellogg Foundation launched a major public health initiative to strengthen state and local public health departments. In 1993, under the leadership of the Assistant Secretary for Health, the U.S. Public Health Service established a working group of federal, state, and local public health leaders to develop a clearer definition of the functions, organizations, and expenditures of public health agencies. The working group identified the following key functions of public health agencies: prevent epidemics and the spread of disease; protect against environmental threats; prevent injuries; promote and encourage healthy behaviors; respond to disasters and assist communities in recovery; and assure the quality and accessibility of health services. (See Lee & Paxman, Recommended Reading.)

President Clinton's Health Security Act of 1993 included a $6 billion public health initiative, but only one and a half billion dollars were earmarked for the support of core public health activities such as immunization, protection of the environment, housing, food and water safety, investigation and control of disease and injuries, and health-related data collection and outcomes monitoring. Although the Health Security Act was not enacted, a number of the public health components, such as food safety and immunization, has received significantly increased funding.

While the concept of core public health functions is useful at a very broad level, it does not translate easily into population-based services actually provided in the community. A study is currently underway that should help to better describe the core services at the local level and how these can be characterized after 60 years of federal categorical grants (e.g., tuberculosis, immunizations, STDs, HIV/AIDS, and maternal and child health). The proliferation of categorical grants, particularly since the 1960s, has made it increasingly difficult for states and local health departments to set priorities and allocate resources in relation to needs as identified at the local level. The public health system is, of necessity, large and complex because of the variety of problems to be addressed and the fact that responsibility for addressing these issues is split between public health and nonpublic health agencies. Some of these, such as STD control and immunizations, are in traditional health departments. Others, such as occupational health and safety, are in the federal Department of Labor and comparable state agencies. Air and water pollution are most often the domain of the environmental protection agency. Mental health and substance abuse prevention and treatment services may be in separate agencies at the state and local level, or may be included within a public health agency. In addition, medical care for indigent populations may be provided by local health departments or by separate counties or municipal public hospital systems. This issue is in the greatest state of flux given medical care cost crisis and a reduction in charity care by hospitals, physicians, and other providers, begging the question of who exactly is responsible for ensuring the availability of these basic services.

Furthermore, the organizational fragmentation makes it very difficult to determine how much of the $1.1 trillion in national health expenditures actually supports population health services (see Lee and Paxman). In 1993, only 2.8 percent ($24.7 billion) was for government public health activities, including $11.4 billion (1.4 percent of the total) for population-based health promotion, health protection, and disease prevention programs. Spending by state and local governments for essential public health functions in 1993 was estimated to be $6.4 billion, a little more than half of the total. By contrast, Medicaid expenditures (federal, state, and local) were $101 billion for acute and long-term care, and Medicare expenditures were $150 billion (Lee, Benjamin, and Weber, 1996). Expenditures for these two publicly funded medical care programs were ten times those for government public health programs and twenty-five times those for essential public health services. When considering the importance of public health to the health of the population, this discrepancy is difficult to justify.

Developments such as these in the decade since the IOM report are thoroughly addressed by four papers published in the *Annual Review of Public Health.* Breslow (1990) identified five major issues facing public health in the final decade of the 20th century: (1) the reconstitution of public health; (2) the setting of objectives for public health; (3) a shift in focus from disease control to health promotion; (4) an effort to redress continuing social inequities and their impacts on health; and (5) the health implications of accelerating developments in technology. These issues were further addressed by Afifi and Breslow in 1994, and by Lee and Paxman (1997) and Fielding (1999). In addition, Breslow revisited the issues in a 1999 *JAMA* article, "From Disease Prevention to Health Promotion." Additionally, two reports—"For a Healthy Nation: Returns on Investments in Public Health" (DHHS, 1995) and the "1992–1993 National Profile of Local Health Departments" (DHHS, 1995) give the most up-to-date picture of public health programs, among them polio immunization, fluoridation of water supplies, and elimination of lead in gasoline. These references are all included in the list of Recommended Reading.

In spite of the problems that have been described, great progress has been made in public health during this century. To review the progress in public health in the 20th century, we have selected the series from the Centers for Disease Control and Prevention, "Ten Great Achievements in Public Health 1900–1998." The CDC series was originally printed in the *MMWR* early 1999, and was later reprinted in *JAMA*. We have included several articles from this series in this chapter. Included among the discussions are achievements in motor vehicle safety, control of infectious disease, and the decline in deaths from coronary heart disease and stroke. Still to come are articles on safer and healthier foods, healthier mothers and babies, fluoridation of drinking water, and recognition of tobacco use as a health hazard. The accomplishments of public health to date are truly stunning, but much remains to be done as we enter a new millennium. What must be done constitutes not only much of this chapter but the rest of the book as well.

Despite aggressive measures, the current challenges to medicine and public health are many. As in 1988, at the time of the IOM report, the foremost challenges are tobacco use; HIV/AIDS and other newly emerging or re-emerging infections; current dietary patterns and sedentary lifestyles; alcohol and illicit drug abuse; injuries (including those due to violence); recurring adolescent health problems such as unintended pregnancies; and vaccine-preventable illnesses in children (e.g., pertussis, meningitis) and adults (e.g., pneumonia, influenza). Finally, chronic diseases, including heart disease, cancer, cerebrovascular disease, diabetes mellitus, and obesity, and a growing list of environmental hazards require prompt attention. Moreover, the public health and medical care response to terrorism, or the threat of terrorism, be it nuclear, chemical, biological, or conventional (e.g., bomb), must be added to the list of public health responsibilities in response to natural disasters in the modern day.

We include two examples of very different approaches to major public health problems: tobacco and HIV/AIDS. Few doubt, any longer, the role of tobacco as a major killer in the United States and the role of the tobacco industry in promoting the use of cigarettes, cigars, and chewing (spit) tobacco. In the fifth edition of *The Nation's Health*, we included papers by Kessler et al. (1996) and Glantz (1996) taking very different positions on the issue of how best to deal with these problems. In our Recommended Reading we include these papers as well as the Amicus Brief (No. 98–1152) submitted by the American Cancer Society to the U.S. Supreme Court in the case that will determine whether or not the FDA has the authority to regulate tobacco products. The decision in this case will likely be made during the 1999–2000 session of the Supreme Court. While critical with respect to the FDA's role in federal efforts to diminish the impact of tobacco on the health of the population, the verdict will not directly affect the actions of state and local governments in public education and tobacco control. Nor will it impact any settlements reached by the states with the tobacco industry. The second paper that we have included in Recommended Reading, by Coates and Collins (1999), is highly critical of the present federal, state, and local government efforts to slow the spread of HIV. They propose a program of prevention that is based on the best social and behavioral science research, as well as the practical approach of applying evidence-based public health at the local level.

Although there has been progress, the foundations of public health remain in a precarious state on the eve of the 21st century, as they were when the IOM report (1988) described them as in "disarray." Focusing national attention on the critical role of population-based public health functions may, or may not, result in a stabilization or even a strengthening of the public health infrastructure. Managed care, both in the private sector and in the Medicaid and Medicare programs, provides a worthwhile opportunity to achieve population-based public health objectives. However, there is equal possibility that it may also divert resources from public health, increase the number of uninsured persons, and increase the burden on local public health departments without commensurate increases in resources.

Clinical preventive services are of increasing importance in achieving both clinical and population-based health objectives. The context of clinical preventive services within the health care system has been described by Bodenheimer and Grumbach. In the Recommended Reading, we include a chapter on prevention from Bodenheimer and Grumbach's excellent book, *Understanding Health Policy: A Clinical Approach* (1995). They separate the traditional view of clinical prevention into three components:

Primary prevention—averting the occurrence of disease (e.g. immunization)
Secondary prevention—early detection (e.g. Pap smear) and intervention to reverse or retard progress (e.g., cervical cancer may be cured in early stages)
Tertiary prevention—includes efforts to minimize the effects of disease and disability (e.g., physical therapy to reduce disability in patients with arthritis)

In fact, as they note, secondary and tertiary prevention are not really prevention, but good medical care designed to reduce morbidity and mortality. Unfortunately, too few physicians practice primary or secondary prevention, as demonstrated by a recent Commonwealth Fund report on how few physicians advise their patients with respect to clinical preventive services. The Commonwealth Fund Survey of Preventive Care and Physician Counseling (1999) shows that an astoundingly low percentage of women receive counseling from their physicians on important issues such as violence at home, sexually transmitted diseases, alcohol, drugs, and smoking. Only for exercise do close to 50 percent of women receive advice or encouragement from their physicians.

Bodenheimer and Grumbach also summarize the three levels of interventions designed to prevent illness or injury at the community level. These include (1) societal measures to improve the standard of living; (2) public health interventions (e.g., pasteurization of milk); and, (3) clinical preventive services. Although this distinction is useful, when addressing the major health problems confronting the nation, it is often essential to coordinate interventions through all three levels and ensure effective collaboration of public health and medicine. The "Ten Great

Achievements in Public Health," which are included in this chapter actually illustrate the benefits of collaboration between medicine and public health (e.g., immunization, reduction of heart disease mortality).

We include in this chapter the "Overview" from the second edition of the *Guide to Clinical Preventive Services* (1996), prepared by the U.S. Preventive Services Task Force, because it emphasizes the importance of prevention, provides an historical perspective, and reviews the principal findings of the Task Force. The Task Force concluded that (1) interventions that address patients' personal health priorities are vitally important; (2) the clinician and the patient should share decision making; (3) clinicians should be selective in ordering tests and providing preventive services; (4) clinicians must take every opportunity to deliver preventive services, especially to persons with limited access to care; and, (5) for some health problems, community level interventions may be more effective than clinical preventive services. While clinical preventive services are of vital importance, they can often be carried out more effectively when medicine and public health work together.

A new approach by both medicine and public health—extending beyond that traditionally taken—is clearly called for. Accordingly, organized medicine (the AMA) and public health (the APHA) have formed an alliance to promote collaboration at the national level. Many states and communities are initiating similar collaborative approaches. In her monograph, *Medicine and Public Health—The Power of Collaboration* (1997), Lasker first describes the relationship between medicine and public health, then describes the forces that are propelling the growing interdependence of the two, and describes six models of collaboration, complete with four hundred examples (see Reading Reading). The conceptual model developed by Lasker and the examples of collaboration between medicine, managed-care, public health, and community-based organizations demonstrate that by collaboration much more can be accomplished, more effectively, than when the collaborators function alone. Moreover, commonly held objectives that would be impossible to accomplish without collective effort are made possible. The goals for both individual-level services and population-based efforts are achieved through collaboration. The implementation of this approach is equally important for medicine, including managed-care, as it is for public health.

It is very clear from the work of Lasker and her colleagues, as well as the experience of a growing number of communities, that the old ways of practicing public health and clinical medicine cannot deal with the range of health problems facing communities throughout the country. From asthma in children, to the HIV/AIDS epidemic, to obesity and diabetes in an aging population, all of these issues facing our modern society require modern solutions that are only beginning to be appreciated.

REFERENCES

Afifi AA, Breslow L. The maturing paradigm of public health. *Ann Rev Pub Health,* 15:223–235, 1994.

American Cancer Society. On Writ of Certiorari to the United States Court of Appeals for the Fourth Circuit in the Supreme Court of the United States, *Food and Drug Administration et al. Petitioners v. Brown and Williamson Tobacco Group Corporation et al.* Respondents. No. 98–1152, Milibank, Tweed Hadley and McCloy, LLP.

Breslow L. The future of public health: prospects in the United States for the 1990s. *Ann Rev Pub Health,* 11:1–28, 1990.

Breslow, L. From disease prevention to health promotion. *JAMA,* 1999; 281(11):1030–1033.

Center for Disease Control and Prevention. Ten great public health achievements—United States, 1900–1999. *MMWR,* 1999; 48:241–243.

Center for Disease Control and Prevention. Impact of vaccines universally recommended for children—United States. 1900–1998. *MMWR,* 1999; 48:243–248.

Center for Disease Control and Prevention. Motor-vehicle safety: A 20th century public health achievement. *MMWR,* 1999; 48:369–374.

Center for Disease Control and Prevention. Achievements in Public Health, 1900–1999: Improvements in Workplace Safety—United States, 1900–1999. *MMWR,* 1999; 48:461–469.

Center for Disease Control and Prevention. Achievements in public health, 1900–1999: Control of infectious disease. *MMWR,* 1999; 48(29):621–629.

Center for Disease Control and Prevention. Achievements in public health, 1900–1999: Decline in deaths from heart disease and stroke—United States, 1900–1999. *MMWR,* 1999; 48(29):649–656.

Coates TJ, Collins C. HIV prevention: A 10-point program to protect the next generation. San Francisco, CA: USCF AIDS Research Institute and Center for AIDS Prevention Studies (CAPS), Department of Medicine, University of California, San Francisco (to be published).

Fielding JE. Public health in the twentieth century: Advances and challenges. *Ann Rev Pub Health,* 1999; 20:xiii–xxix.

Glantz SA. Preventing tobacco use—the youth access trap. *Am J Pub Health,* 1996; 86:156–158.

Institute of Medicine (IOM). *The Future of Public Health: Summary and Recommendations.* Washington, D.C: National Academy Press, 1988.

Kessler DA, Witt AM, Barnett PS, et al. The Food and Drug Administration's regulation of tobacco products. *NEJM,* September 26, 1996; 335(13):988–994.

Lasker, RD, The Committee on Medicine and Public Health. *Medicine and Public Health: The Power of Collaboration.* Chicago: Health Administration Press, 1997; 11–22, 29–43, 47–53.

Lee PR, Paxman D. Reinventing public health. *Ann Rev Pub Health,* 1997; 18:1–35.

Lee PR, Benjamin AE, Weber MA. Policies and strategies for health in the United States. In Holland W, Detels R, Knox G. (Eds.). *Oxford Textbook of Public Health* (3rd ed.). Oxford: Oxford University Press, 1996.

Louis Harris and Associates, Inc. *Preventive Care and Physician Counseling.* New York: The Commonwealth Fund, 1999.

U.S. Department of Health and Human Services. For a healthy nation: returns on investment in public health. Washington, DC: Public Health Service, 1995.

U.S. Department of Health and Human Services. 1992–1993 National profile of local health departments. National association city county health office. Atlanta, GA: Centers for Disease Control and Prevention, 1995.

U.S. Preventive Services Task Force. *Guide to Clinical Preventive Services.* Alexandria, Virginia: International Medical Publishing, 1996; xxv–xxiv (Overview).

ARTICLE 1

TEN GREAT PUBLIC HEALTH ACHIEVEMENTS—UNITED STATES, 1900–1999

The Centers for Disease Control and Prevention

During the 20th century, the health and life expectancy of persons residing in the United States improved dramatically. Since 1900, the average lifespan of persons in the United States has lengthened by >30 years; 25 years of this gain are attributable to advances in public health.[1] To highlight these advances, *MMWR* will profile 10 public health achievements in a series of reports published through December 1999.

Many notable public health achievements have occurred during the 1900s, and other accomplishments could have been selected for the list. The choices for topics for this list were based on the opportunity for prevention and the impact on death, illness, and disability in the United States and are not ranked by order of importance.

The first report in this series focuses on **vaccination,** which has resulted in the eradication of smallpox; elimination of poliomyelitis in the Americas; and control of measles, rubella, tetanus, diphtheria, *Haemophilus influenzae* type b, and other infectious diseases in the United States and other parts of the world.

Future reports that will appear in *MMWR* throughout the remainder of 1999 will focus on nine other achievements.

Improvements in **motor-vehicle safety** have resulted from engineering efforts to make both vehicles and highways safer and from successful efforts to change personal behavior (e.g., increased use of safety belts, child safety seats, and motorcycle helmets and decreased drinking and driving). These efforts have contributed to large reductions in motor-vehicle-related deaths.[2]

Work-related health problems, such as coal workers' pneumoconiosis (black lung), and silicosis—common at the beginning of the century—have come under better control. Severe injuries and deaths related to mining, manufacturing, construction, and transportation also have decreased; since 1980, **safer workplaces** have resulted in a reduction of approximately 40% in the rate of fatal occupational injuries.[3]

Control of infectious diseases has resulted from clean water and improved sanitation. Infections such as typhoid and cholera transmitted by contaminated water, a major cause of illness and death early in the 20th century, have been reduced dramatically by improved sanitation. In addition, the discovery of antimicrobial therapy has been critical to successful public health efforts to control infections such as tuberculosis and sexually transmitted diseases (STDs).

Decline in deaths from coronary heart disease and stroke have resulted from risk-factor modification, such as smoking cessation and blood pressure control coupled with improved access to early detection and better treatment. Since 1972, death rates for coronary heart disease have decreased 51%.[4]

Since 1900, **safer and healthier foods** have resulted from decreases in microbial contamination and increases in nutritional content. Identifying essential micronutrients and establishing food-fortification programs have almost eliminated major nutritional deficiency diseases such as rickets, goiter, and pellagra in the United States.

Healthier mothers and babies have resulted from better hygiene and nutrition, availability of antibiotics, greater access to health care, and technologic advances in maternal and neonatal medicine. Since 1900, infant mortality has decreased 90%, and maternal mortality has decreased 99%.

Access to **family planning** and contraceptive services has altered social and economic roles of women. Family planning has provided health benefits such as smaller family size and longer interval between the birth of children; increased opportunities for preconceptional counseling and screening; fewer infant, child, and maternal deaths; and the use of barrier contraceptives to prevent pregnancy and transmission of human immunodeficiency virus and other STDs.

Fluoridation of drinking water began in 1945 and in 1999 reaches an estimated 144 million persons in the United States. Fluoridation safely and inexpensively benefits both children and adults by effectively preventing tooth decay, regardless of socioeconomic status or access to care. Fluoridation has played an important role in the reductions in tooth decay (40%–70% in children) and of tooth loss in adults (40%–60%).[5]

Recognition of tobacco use as a health hazard and subsequent public health anti-smoking campaigns have resulted in changes in social norms to prevent initiation of tobacco use, promote cessation of use, and reduce exposure to environmental tobacco smoke. Since the 1964 Surgeon General's report on the health risks of smoking, the prevalence of smoking among adults has decreased, and millions of smoking-related deaths have been prevented.[6] The list of achievements was developed to highlight the contributions of public health and to describe the impact of these contributions on the health and well being of persons in the United States. A final report in this series will review the national public health system, including local and state health departments and academic institutions whose activities on research, epidemiology, health education, and program implementation have made these achievements possible.

ABOUT THE AUTHOR

Centers for Disease Control and Prevention (CDC) in Atlanta, Georgia.

REFERENCES

Available from the CDC.

MOTOR-VEHICLE SAFETY: A 20TH CENTURY PUBLIC HEALTH ACHIEVEMENT

The Centers for Disease Control and Prevention

The reduction of the rate of death attributable to motor-vehicle crashes in the United States represents the successful public health response to a great technologic advance of the 20th century—the motorization of America. Six times as many people drive today as in 1925, and the number of motor vehicles in the country has increased 11-fold since then to approximately 215 million.[1] The number of miles traveled in motor vehicles is 10 times higher than in the mid-1920s. Despite this steep increase in motor-vehicle travel, the annual death rate has declined from 18 per 100 million vehicle miles traveled (VMT) in 1925 to 1.7 per 100 million VMT in 1997—a 90% decrease (Figure 1).[1]

Systematic motor-vehicle safety efforts began during the 1960s. In 1960, unintentional injuries caused 93,803 deaths[1]; 41% were associated with motor-vehicle crashes. In 1966, after 5 years of continuously increasing motor-vehicle-related fatality rates, the Highway Safety Act created the National Highway Safety Bureau (NHSB), which later became the National Highway Traffic Safety Administration (NHTSA). The systematic approach to motor-vehicle-related injury prevention began with NHSB's first director. Dr. William Haddon.[2] Haddon, a public health physician, recognized that standard public health methods and epidemiology could be applied to preventing motor-vehicle-related and other injuries. He defined interactions between host (human), agent (motor vehicle), and environmental (highway) factors before, during, and after crashes resulting in injuries. Tackling problems identified with each factor during each phase of the crash. NHSB initiated a campaign to prevent motor-vehicle-related injuries.

In 1966, passage of the Highway Safety Act and the National Traffic and Motor Vehicle Safety Act authorized the federal government to set and regulate standards for motor vehicles and highways, a mechanism necessary for effective prevention.[2,3] Many changes in both vehicle and highway design followed this mandate. Vehicles (agent of injury) were built with new safety features, including head rests, energy-absorbing steering wheels, shatter-resistant windshields, and safety belts.[3,4] Roads

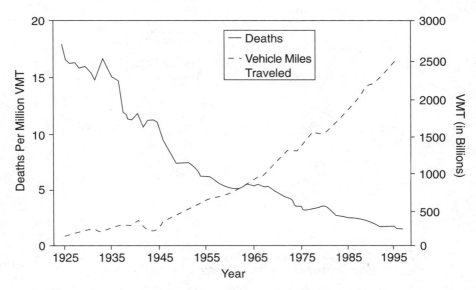

Figure 1 Motor-vehicle–related deaths per million vehicle miles traveled (VMT) and annual VMT, by year—United States, 1925–1997. (Source: US Department of Health and Human Services)

(environment) were improved by better delineation of curves (edge and center line stripes and reflectors), use of breakaway sign and utility poles, improved illumination, addition of barriers separating oncoming traffic lanes, and guardrails.[4,5] The results were rapid. By 1970, motor-vehicle-related death rates were decreasing by both the public health measure (deaths per 100,000 population) and the traffic safety indicator (deaths per VMT) (Figure 2).[1]

Changes in driver and passenger (host) behavior also have reduced motor-vehicle crashes and injuries. Enactment and enforcement of traffic safety laws, reinforced by public education, have led to safer behavior choices. Examples include enforcement of laws against driving while intoxicated (DWI) and underage drinking, and enforcement of safety-belt, child-safety seat, and motorcycle helmet use laws.[5,6]

Government and community recognition of the need for motor-vehicle safety prompted initiation of programs by federal and state governments, academic institutions, community-based organizations, and industry. NHTSA and the Federal Highway Administration within the U.S. Department of Transportation have provided national leadership for traffic and highway safety efforts since the 1960s.[2] The National Center for Injury Prevention and Control, established at CDC in 1992, has contributed public health direction.[7,8] State and local governments have enacted and enforced laws that affect motor-vehicle and highway safety, driver licensing and testing, vehicle inspections, and traffic regulations.[2] Preventing motor-vehicle-related injuries has required collaboration among many professional disciplines (e.g., biomechanics has been essential to vehicle design and highway safety

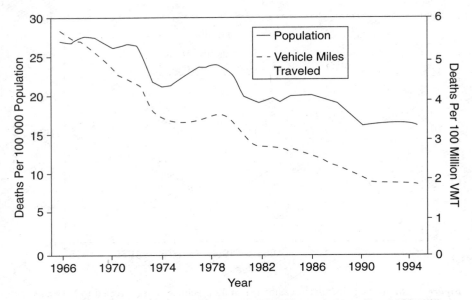

Figure 2   Motor-vehicle–related death rates per 100,000 population and per 100 million vehicle miles traveled (VMT), by year—United States, 1966–1997. (Source: US Department of Health and Human Services)

features). Citizen and community-based advocacy groups have played important prevention roles in areas such as drinking and driving and child-occupant protection.[6] Consistent with the public/private partnerships that characterize motor-vehicle safety efforts, NHTSA sponsors "Buckle Up America" week, which focuses on the need to always properly secure children in child-safety seats (additional information is available on the World-Wide Web at http://www.nhtsa.dot.gov).

SPECIFIC PUBLIC HEALTH CONCERNS

High-Risk Populations

Alcohol-Impaired Drivers.   Annual motor-vehicle crash-related fatalities involving alcohol has decreased 39% since 1982, to approximately 16,000; these deaths account for 38.6% of all traffic deaths.[9,10] Factors that may have contributed to this decline include increased public awareness of the dangers of drinking and driving; new and tougher state laws; stricter law enforcement; an increase in the minimum legal drinking age; prevention programs that offer alternatives such as safe rides (e.g., taxicabs and public transportation), designated drivers, and responsible alcohol-serving practices; and a decrease in per capita alcohol consumption.[5,6]

Young Drivers and Passengers.   Since 1975, motor-vehicle–related fatality rates have decreased 27% for young motor-vehicle occupants (ages 16–20 years). However, in 1997 the death rate was 28.3 per 100,000 population—more than twice that of the U.S. population (13.3 per 100,000 population).[9] Teenaged drivers are more likely than older drivers to speed, run red lights, make illegal turns, ride with an intoxicated driver, and drive after drinking alcohol or using drugs.[11] Strategies that have contributed to improved motor-vehicle safety among young drivers include laws restricting purchase of alcohol among underaged youths[6] and some aspects of graduated licensing systems (e.g., nighttime driving restrictions).[12]

Pedestrians.   From 1975 to 1997, pedestrian fatality rates decreased 41%, from 4 per 100,000 population in 1975 to 2.3 in 1997 but still account for 13% of motor-vehicle-related deaths.[9] Factors that may have reduced pedestrian fatalities include more and better sidewalks, pedestrian paths, playgrounds away from streets, one-way traffic flow, and restricted on-street parking.[6]

Occupant-Protection Systems

Safety Belts.   In response to legislation, highly visible law enforcement, and public education, rates of safety belt use nationwide have increased from approximately 11% in 1981 to 68% in 1997.[8] Safety belt use began to increase following enactment of the first state mandatory-use laws in 1984.[6] All states except New Hampshire now have safety-belt use laws. Primary laws (which allow police to stop vehicles simply because occupants are not wearing safety belts) are more effective than secondary laws (which require that a vehicle be stopped for some other traffic violation).[6,13] The prevalence of safety belt use after enactment of primary laws increases 1.5–4.3 times, and motor-vehicle–related fatality rates decrease 13%–46%.[13]

Child-Safety and Booster-Seats.   All states have passed child passenger protection laws, but these vary widely in age and size requirements and the penalties imposed for noncompliance. Child-restraint use in 1996 was 85% for children aged <1 year and 60% for children aged 1–4 years.[14] Since 1975, deaths among children aged <5 years have decreased 30% to 3.1 per 100,000 population, but rates for age groups 5–15 years have declined by only 11%–13%.[9] Child seats are misused by as many as 80% of users.[15–17] In addition, parents fail to recognize the need for booster seats for children who are too large for child seats but not large enough to be safely restrained in an adult lap-shoulder belt.[18]

21ST CENTURY CHALLENGES

Despite the great success in reducing motor-vehicle-related death rates motor-vehicle crashes remain the leading cause of injury-related deaths in the United States, accounting for 31% of all such deaths in 1996 (CDC, unpublished data, 1999). Furthermore, motor-vehicle-related injuries led all causes for deaths among persons aged 1–24 years. In 1997, motor-vehicle crashes resulted in 41,967 deaths (16 per 100,000 population), 3.4 million nonfatal injuries (1270 per 100,000 population),[9] and 23.9 million vehicles in crashes; cost estimates are $200 billion.[1]

The challenge for the 21st century is to sustain and improve motor-vehicle safety. Future success will require augmentation of the public health approach to (1) expand surveillance to better monitor nonfatal injuries, detect new problems, and set priorities; (2) direct research to emerging and priority problems; (3) implement the most effective programs and policies; and 4) strengthen inter-agency, multidisciplinary partnerships. Key public health activities will be to

- continue efforts shown to reduce alcohol-impaired driving and related fatalities and injuries.
- promote strategies such as graduated licensing that discourage teenage drinking and other risky driving behaviors such as speeding and encourage safety belt use.
- enhance pedestrian safety, especially for children and the elderly, through engineering solutions that reduce exposure to traffic and permit crossing streets safely and by encouraging safer pedestrian behaviors, such as crossing streets at intersections, and increasing visibility to drivers and driver awareness of pedestrians.
- accommodate the mobility needs of persons aged >65 years—a population that will almost double to 65 million by 2030—through a combination of alternative modes of transportation (e.g., walking and better public transportation) and development of strategies to reduce driving hazards.[6,19]
- encourage the 30% of the population who do not wear safety belts to use them routinely.
- encourage proper use of age-appropriate child-safety seats and booster seats, especially for older children who have outgrown their child seats but are too small for adult lap-shoulder belts.
- conduct biomechanics research to better understand the causes of nonfatal disabling injuries, in particular brain and spinal cord injuries, as a foundation for prevention strategies.
- develop a comprehensive public health surveillance system at the federal, state, and local levels that track fatal and nonfatal motor-vehicle-related injuries and other injuries and diseases (i.e., outpatient and emergency department visits, hospitalizations, disabilities, and deaths) as a basis for setting prevention and research priorities.

ABOUT THE AUTHOR

Centers for Disease Control and Prevention (CDC) in Atlanta, Georgia.

REFERENCES

Available from the CDC.

ARTICLE 3

ACHIEVEMENTS IN PUBLIC HEALTH, 1900–1999: CONTROL OF INFECTIOUS DISEASES

The Centers for Disease Control and Prevention

Deaths from infectious diseases have declined markedly in the United States during the 20th century (Figure 1). This decline contributed to a sharp drop in infant and child mortality (1,2) and to the 29.2-year increase in life expectancy (2). In 1900, 30.4% of all deaths occurred among children aged less than 5 years; in 1997, that percentage was only 1.4%. In 1900, the three leading causes of death were pneumonia, tuberculosis (TB), and diarrhea and enteritis, which (together with diphtheria) caused one third of all deaths. Of these deaths, 40% were among children aged less than 5 years (1). In 1997, heart disease and cancers accounted for 54.7% of all deaths, with 4.5% attributable to pneumonia, influenza, and human immunodeficiency virus (HIV) infection (2). Despite this overall progress, one of the most devastating epidemics in human history occurred during the 20th century: the 1918 influenza pandemic that resulted in 20 million deaths, including 500,000 in the United States, in less than 1 year—more than have died in as short a time during any war or famine in the world (3). HIV infection, first recognized in 1981, has caused a pandemic that is still in progress, affecting 33 million people and causing an estimated 13.9 million deaths (4). These episodes illustrate the volatility of infectious disease death rates and the unpredictability of disease emergence.

Public health action to control infectious diseases in the 20th century is based on the 19th century discovery of microorganisms as the cause of many serious diseases (e.g., cholera and TB). Disease control resulted from improvements in sanitation and hygiene, the discovery of antibiotics, and the implementation of universal childhood vaccination programs. Scientific and technologic advances played a major role in each of these areas and are the foundation for today's disease surveillance and control systems. Scientific findings also have contributed to a new understanding of the evolving relation between humans and microbes (5).

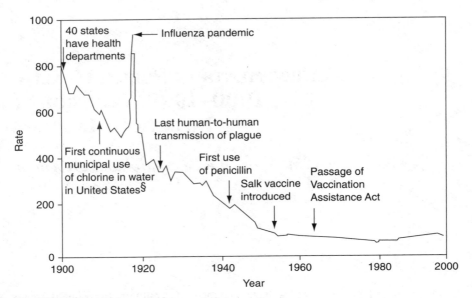

*Per 100,000 population per year.
†Adapted from Armstrong GL, Conn LA, Pinner RW. Trends in infectious disease mortality in the United States during the 20th century. JAMA 1999:281:61–6.
§American Water Works Association. Water chlorination principles and practices: AWWA manual M20. Denver, Colorado: American Water Works Association, 1973.

Figure 1   Crude death rate* for infectious diseases—United States, 1900–1996.†

CONTROL OF INFECTIOUS DISEASES

Sanitation and Hygiene

The 19th century shift in population from country to city that accompanied industrialization and immigration led to overcrowding in poor housing served by inadequate or nonexistent public water supplies and waste-disposal systems. These conditions resulted in repeated outbreaks of cholera, dysentery, TB, typhoid fever, influenza, yellow fever, and malaria.

By 1900, however, the incidence of many of these diseases had begun to decline because of public health improvements, implementation of which continued into the 20th century. Local, state, and federal efforts to improve sanitation and hygiene reinforced the concept of collective "public health" action (e.g., to prevent infection by providing clean drinking water). By 1900, 40 of the 45 states had established health departments. The first county health departments were established in 1908 (6). From the 1930s through the 1950s, state and local health departments made substantial progress in disease prevention activities, including sewage disposal, water treatment, food safety, organized solid waste disposal, and public education about hygienic practices (e.g., foodhandling and handwashing). Chlorination and other treatments of drinking water began in the early 1900s and became widespread public health practices, further decreasing the incidence of waterborne diseases. The incidence of TB also declined as improvements in housing reduced crowding and TB-control programs were initiated. In 1900, 194 of every 100,000 U.S. residents died from TB; most were residents of urban areas. In 1940 (before the introduction of antibiotic therapy), TB remained a leading cause of death, but the crude death rate had decreased to 46 per 100,000 persons (7).

Animal and pest control also contributed to disease reduction. Nationally sponsored, state-coordinated vaccination and animal-control programs eliminated dog-to-dog transmission of rabies. Malaria, once endemic throughout the southeastern United States, was reduced to negligible levels by the late 1940s; regional mosquito-control programs played an important role in these efforts. Plague also diminished; the U.S. Marine Hospital Service (which later became the Public Health Service) led quarantine and ship inspection activities and rodent and vector-control operations. The last major rat-associated outbreak of plague in the United States occurred during 1924–1925 in Los Angeles. This outbreak included the last identified instance of human-to-human transmission of plague (through inhalation of infectious respiratory droplets from coughing patients) in this country.

Vaccination

Strategic vaccination campaigns have virtually eliminated diseases that previously were common in the United States, including diphtheria, tetanus, poliomyelitis, smallpox, measles, mumps, rubella, and *Haemophilus influenzae* type b meningitis (8). With the licensure of the combined diphtheria and tetanus toxoids and pertussis vaccine in 1949, state and local health departments instituted vaccination programs, aimed primarily at poor children. In 1955, the introduction of the Salk poliovirus vaccine led to federal funding of state and local childhood vaccination programs. In 1962, a federally coordinated vaccination program was established through the passage of the Vaccination Assistance Act—landmark legislation that has been renewed continuously and now supports the purchase and administration of a full range of childhood vaccines.

The success of vaccination programs in the United States and Europe inspired the 20th-century concept of "disease eradication"—the idea that a selected disease could be eradicated from all human populations through global cooperation. In 1977, after a decade-long campaign involving 33 nations, smallpox was eradicated worldwide—approximately a decade after it had been eliminated from the United States and the rest of the Western Hemisphere. Polio and dracunculiasis may be eradicated by 2000.

Antibiotics and Other Antimicrobial Medicines

Penicillin was developed into a widely available medical product that provided quick and complete treatment of previously incurable bacterial illnesses, with a

wider range of targets and fewer side effects than sulfa drugs. Discovered fortu-
itously in 1928, penicillin was not developed for medical use until the 1940s, when
it was produced in substantial quantities and used by the U.S. military to treat sick
and wounded soldiers.

Antibiotics have been in civilian use for 57 years and have saved the lives of
persons with streptococcal and staphylococcal infections, gonorrhea, syphilis, and
other infections. Drugs also have been developed to treat viral diseases (e.g., herpes
and HIV infection); fungal diseases (e.g., candidiasis and histoplasmosis); and parasitic diseases (e.g., malaria). The microbiologist Selman Waksman led much of the
early research in discovering antibiotics. However, the emergence of drug resistance
in many organisms is reversing some of the therapeutic miracles of the last 50 years
and underscores the importance of disease prevention.

TECHNOLOGIC ADVANCES IN DETECTING
AND MONITORING INFECTIOUS DISEASES

Technologic changes that increased capacity for detecting, diagnosing, and monitoring infectious diseases included development early in the century of serologic testing and more recently the development of molecular assays based on nucleic acid
and antibody probes. The use of computers and electronic forms communication enhanced the ability to gather, analyze, and disseminate disease surveillance data.

Serologic Testing

Serologic testing came into use in the 1910s and has become a basic tool to diagnose and control many infectious diseases. Syphilis and gonorrhea, for example,
were widespread early in the century and were difficult to diagnose, especially during the latent stages. The advent of serologic testing for syphilis helped provide a
more accurate description of this public health problem and facilitated diagnosis of
infection. For example, in New York City, serologic testing in 1901 indicated that
5%–19% of all men had syphilitic infections (9).

Viral Isolation and Tissue Culture

The first virus isolation techniques came into use at the turn of the century. They involved straining infected material through successively smaller sieves and inoculat-
ing test animals or plants to show the purified substance retained disease-causing
activity. The first "filtered" viruses were tobacco mosaic virus (1882) and foot-and-
mouth disease virus of cattle (1898). The U.S. Army Command under Walter Reed
filtered yellow fever virus in 1900. The subsequent development of cell culture in
the 1930s paved the way for large-scale production of live or heat-killed viral vaccines. Negative staining techniques for visualizing viruses under the electron micro-
scope were available by the early 1960s.

Molecular Techniques

During the last quarter of the 20th century, molecular biology has provided powerful new tools to detect and characterize infectious pathogens. The use of nucleic acid hybridization and sequencing techniques has made it possible to characterize the causative agents of previously unknown diseases (e.g., hepatitis C, human ehrlichiosis, hantavirus pulmonary syndrome, acquired immunodeficiency syndrome [AIDS], and Nipah virus disease).

Molecular tools have enhanced capacity to track the transmission of new threats and find new ways to prevent and treat them. Had AIDS emerged 100 years ago, when laboratory-based diagnostic methods were in their infancy, the disease might have remained a mysterious syndrome for many decades. Moreover, the drugs used to treat HIV-infected persons and prevent perinatal transmission (e.g., replication analogs and protease inhibitors) were developed based on a modern understanding of retroviral replication at the molecular level.

CHALLENGES FOR THE 21ST CENTURY

Success in reducing morbidity and mortality from infectious diseases during the first three quarters of the 20th century led to complacency about the need for continued research into treatment and control of infectious microbes (10). However, the appearance of AIDS, the re-emergence of TB (including multidrug-resistant strains), and an overall increase in infectious disease mortality during the 1980s and early 1990s (Figure 1) provide additional evidence that as long as microbes can evolve, new diseases will appear. The emergence of new diseases underscores the importance of disease prevention through continual monitoring of underlying factors that may encourage the emergence or re-emergence of diseases.

Molecular genetics has provided a new appreciation of the remarkable ability of microbes to evolve, adapt, and develop drug resistance in an unpredictable and dynamic fashion. Resistance genes are transmitted from one bacterium to another on plasmids, and viruses evolve through replication errors and reassortment of gene segments and by jumping species barriers. Recent examples of microbial evolution include the emergence of a virulent strain of avian influenza in Hong Kong (1997–98); the multidrug-resistant W strain of *M. tuberculosis* in the United States in 1991 (11); and *Staphylococcus aureus* with reduced susceptibility to vancomycin in Japan in 1996 (12) and the United States in 1997 (13,14).

For continued success in controlling infectious diseases, the U.S. public health system must prepare to address diverse challenges, including the emergence of new infectious diseases, the re-emergence of old diseases (sometimes in drug-resistant forms), large foodborne outbreaks, and acts of bioterrorism. Ongoing research on the possible role of infectious agents in causing or intensifying certain chronic diseases (including diabetes mellitus type 1, some cancers [15–17], and heart conditions [18,19]) also is imperative. Continued protection of health requires improved capacity for disease surveillance and outbreak response at the local, state, federal, and global levels; the development and dissemination of new laboratory and epidemiologic methods; continued antimicrobial and vaccine development; and ongoing research into environmental factors that facilitate disease emergence (20).

ABOUT THE AUTHOR

Centers for Disease Control and Prevention (CDC) in Atlanta, Georgia.

REFERENCES

1. Department of Commerce and Labor, Bureau of the Census. Mortality Statistics, 1900 to 1904. Washington, DC: US Department of Commerce and Labor, 1906.
2. Hoyert DL, Kochanek KD, Murphy SL. Deaths: final data for 1997. Hyattsville, Maryland: US Department of Health and Human Services, Public Health Service, CDC, National Center for Health Statistics, 1999. (National vital statistics reports, vol 47, no. 19).
3. Crosby AW Jr. Epidemic and peace, 1918. Westport, Connecticut: Greenwood Press, 1976:311.
4. United Nations Program on HIV/AIDS and World Health Organization. AIDS epidemic update: December 1998. Geneva, Switzerland: World Health Organization, 1999. Available at http://www.unaids.org/highband/document/epidemio/wadr98e.pdf.
5. Lederberg J, Shope RE, Oaks SC Jr, eds. Microbial threats to health in the United States. Washington, DC: National Academy Press, 1992.
6. Hinman A. 1889 to 1989: a century of health and disease. Public Health Rep 1990;105:374–80.
7. National Office of Vital Statistics. Vital statistics—special reports, death rates by age, race, and sex, United States, 1900–1953: tuberculosis, all forms; vol 43, no. 2. Washington, DC: US Department of Health, Education, and Welfare, 1956.
8. CDC. Status report on the Childhood Immunization Initiative: reported cases of selected vaccine-preventable diseases—United States, 1996. MMWR 1997;46:665–71.
9. Morrow PA. Report of the committee of seven of the Medical Society of the County of New York on the prophylaxis of venereal disease in New York City. N York M J 1901;74:1146.
10. Institute of Medicine. Emerging infections: microbial threats to health in the United States. Washington, DC: National Academy Press, 1994:vi.
11. Plikaytis BB, Marden JL, Crawford JT, Woodley CL, Butler WR, Shinnick TM. Multiplex PCR assay specific for the multidrug-resistant strain W of *Mycobacterium tuberculosis*. J Clin Microbiol 1994;32:1542–6.

12. CDC. Reduced susceptibility of *Staphylococcus aureus* to vancomycin—Japan. 1996. MMWR 1997;46:624–6.
13. CDC. *Staphylococcus aureus* with reduced susceptibility to vancomycin—United States, 1997. MMWR 1997;46:765–6.
14. CDC. Update: *Staphylococcus aureus* with reduced susceptibility to vancomycin—United States, 1997. MMWR 1997;46:813–5.
15. Montesano R, Hainaut P, Wild CP. Hepatocellular carcinoma: from gene to public health. J Natl Cancer Inst 1997;89:1844–51.
16. Di Bisceglie AM. Hepatitis C and hepatocellular carcinoma. Hepatology 1997;26(3 suppl 1):34S–38S.
17. Muñoz N, Bosch FX. The causal link between HPV and cervical cancer and its implications for prevention of cervical cancer. Bull Pan Am Health Organ 1996;30:362–77.
18. Danesh J, Collins R, Peto R. Chronic infections and coronary heart disease: is there a link? Lancet 1997;350:430–6.
19. Mattila KJ, Valtonen VV, Nieminen MS, Asikainen S. Role of infection as a risk factor for atherosclerosis, myocardial infarction, and stroke. Clin Infect Dis 1998;26:719–34.
20. CDC. Preventing emerging infectious diseases: a strategy for the 21st century. Atlanta, Georgia: US Department of Health and Human Services, Public Health Service, 1998.

ACHIEVEMENTS IN PUBLIC HEALTH, 1900–1999: DECLINE IN DEATHS FROM HEART DISEASE AND STROKE— UNITED STATES, 1900–1999

The Centers for Disease Control and Prevention

Heart disease has been the leading cause of death in the United States since 1921, and stroke has been the third leading cause since 1938(1); together they account for approximately 40% of all deaths. Since 1950, age-adjusted death rates from cardiovascular disease (CVD) have declined 60%, representing one of the most important public health achievements of the 20th century. This report summarizes the temporal trends in CVD, advances in the understanding of risk factors for CVD, development of prevention interventions to reduce these risks, and improvements in therapy for persons who develop CVD.

DECLINE IN CVD DEATH RATES

Age-adjusted death rates per 100,000 persons (standardized to the 1940 U.S. population) for diseases of the heart (i.e., coronary heart disease, hypertensive heart disease, and rheumatic heart disease) have decreased from a peak of 307.4 in 1950 to 134.6 in 1996, an overall decline of 56% (1) (Figure 1). Age-adjusted death rates for coronary heart disease (the major form of CVD contributing to mortality) continued to increase into the 1960s, then declined. In 1996, 621,000 fewer deaths occurred from coronary heart disease than would have been expected had the rate remained at its 1963 peak (1).

Age-adjusted death rates for stroke have declined steadily since the beginning of the century. Since 1950, stroke rates have declined 70%, from 88.8 in 1950 to 26.5 in 1996. Total age-adjusted CVD death rates have declined 60% since 1950 and accounted for approximately 73% of the decline in all causes of deaths during the same period (1).

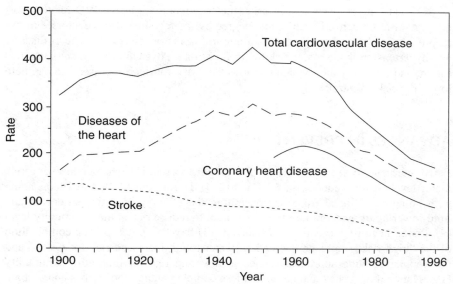

*Per 100,000 population, standardized to the 1940 U.S. population.
†Diseases are classified according to *International Classification of Diseases* (ICD) codes in use when the deaths were reported. ICD classification revisions occurred in 1910, 1921, 1930, 1939, 1949, 1958, 1968, and 1979. Death rates before 1933 do not include all states. Comparability ratios were applied to rates for 1970 and 1975.

Figure 1   Age-adjusted death rates* for total cardiovascular disease, diseases of the heart, coronary heart disease, and stroke,† by year—United States, 1900–1996. (Source: Adapted from reference 1; data provided by the National Heart, Lung and Blood Institute, National Institutes of Health)

DISEASE EPIDEMIOLOGY

Intensive investigation into the CVD epidemic largely began in the 1940s following World War II, although causal hypotheses about CVD and recognition of geographic differences in disease rates occurred earlier (2–4). Landmark epidemiologic investigations, including the cross-country comparisons of Ancel Keys (5) and the Framingham Heart Study (6), established the major risk factors of high blood cholesterol, high blood pressure, and smoking and dietary factors (particularly dietary cholesterol, fat, and sodium). The risk factor concept—that particular biologic, lifestyle, and social conditions were associated with increased risk for disease—developed out of CVD epidemiology (3,4). In addition to the major risk factors (i.e., high blood pressure, high blood cholesterol, and smoking), other important factors include socioeconomic status, obesity, and physical inactivity (7). Striking regional differences were noted particularly for stroke mortality, with the highest rates observed in the southeastern United States (1). Cross-national and cross-cultural studies highlighted the importance of social, cultural, and environmental factors in the development of CVD.

Coronary heart disease and stroke, the two major causes of CVD-related mortality, are not influenced to the same degree by the recognized risk factors. For example, elevated blood cholesterol is a major risk factor for coronary heart disease, and hypertension is the major risk factor for stroke. Physical activity, smoking cessation, and a healthy diet, which can lower the risk for heart disease, also can help lower the risk for stroke (8).

ADVANCES IN PREVENTION

Early intervention studies in the 1960s sought to establish whether lowering risk factor levels would reduce risk for CVD (2–4). During the 1970s and 1980s, along with numerous clinical trials demonstrating the efficacy of antihypertensive and lipid-lowering drugs, community trials sought to reduce risk at the community level (9). Public health interventions to reduce CVD have benefited from a combination of the "high risk" approach—aimed at persons with increased risk for CVD—and the population-wide approach—aimed at lowering risk for the entire community (10). National programs that combine these complementary approaches and that are aimed at health-care providers, patients, and the general public include the National High Blood Pressure Education Program (11), initiated in 1972, and the National Cholesterol Education Program, initiated in 1985 (12). Although earlier CDC community demonstration projects focused on cardiovascular health (9), CDC established its National Center for Chronic Disease Prevention and Health Promotion in 1989, with a high priority of promoting cardiovascular health.

FACTORS CONTRIBUTING TO THE DECLINE IN CVD DEATHS

Reasons for the declines in heart disease and stroke may vary by period and across region or socioeconomic groups (e.g., age, sex, and racial/ethnic groups). Prevention efforts and improvements in early detection, treatment, and care have resulted in a number of beneficial trends, which may have contributed to declines in heart disease and stroke. These trends include

- a decline in cigarette smoking among adults aged greater than or equal to 18 years from approximately 42% in 1965 to 25% in 1995 (13). Substantial public health efforts to reduce tobacco use began soon after recognition of the association between smoking and CVD and between smoking and cancer and the first Surgeon General's report on smoking and health published in 1964.
- a decrease in mean blood pressure levels in the U.S. population (11,13,14).
- an increase in the percentage of persons with hypertension who have the condition treated and controlled (11,13,14).

- a decrease in mean blood cholesterol levels (12–14).
- changes in the U.S. diet. Data based on surveys of food supply suggest that consumption of saturated fat and cholesterol has decreased since 1909 (15). Data from the National Health and Nutrition Examination surveys suggest that decreases in the percentage of calories from dietary fat and the levels of dietary cholesterol coincide with decreases in blood cholesterol levels (16).
- improvements in medical care, including advances in diagnosing and treating heart disease and stroke, development of effective medications for treatment of hypertension and hypercholesterolemia, greater numbers of specialists and health-care providers focusing on CVD, an increase in emergency medical services for heart attack and stroke, and an increase in coronary-care units (13,17). These developments have contributed to lower case-fatality rates, lengthened survival times, and shorter hospital stays for persons with CVD (1,17).

CHALLENGES FOR THE 21ST CENTURY

Despite remarkable progress, heart disease and stroke remain leading causes of disability and death. Estimated costs for morbidity and mortality from CVD, including health expenditures and lost productivity, are expected to be $286.5 billion in 1999 (18). In addition, the overall declines in heart disease and stroke mortality mask important differences in rates of decline by race/ethnicity, sex, socioeconomic status, and geographic region. During 1985–1996, for example, heart disease age-adjusted mortality declined 29% among white men, but only 10% among American Indian/ Alaskan Native women (13). Persons of lower socioeconomic status have higher mortality, morbidity, and risk factor levels for heart disease and stroke than persons of higher socioeconomic status (13,19). In addition, the social class gap in heart disease deaths may be increasing as the rates of heart disease decline faster among higher social classes (19). Geographically, declines in heart disease deaths did not occur at the same time for all communities. Areas with poorer socioeconomic profiles were more likely to experience a later onset of the decline of heart disease (19).

Public health programs at the state level for heart disease and stroke have been limited. In fiscal year 1999, through a new program, CDC funded 11 states with the highest CVD mortality rates to plan, develop, and implement state-based efforts for CVD prevention. In addition to activities such as surveillance, these programs will emphasize policy and environmental interventions, both social and physical, aimed at sustaining positive health behavior change.

Although many trends have been positive, trends for some important indicators have not improved substantially, have leveled off, or are reversing. For example, approximately 70% of persons with hypertension do not have the condition controlled at levels below 140/90 mm Hg, and death rates for stroke have not declined in recent years (1,11,13). Heart failure has emerged as a health concern for older adults (20), and adults who survive a myocardial infarction or other hypertension-related diseases remain at increased risk for heart failure. In addition, the prevalence of obesity has increased among both children and adults in the United States (13).

Major public health challenges for the 21st century include

- reducing risk factor levels and preventing the development of adverse risk factors. Continued research is needed to understand the determinants (social, psychological, environmental, physiologic, and genetic) of CVD risk factors.
- reducing the racial/ethnic disparities in heart disease and stroke mortality.
- increasing the ability to reach underserved groups with appropriate and effective public health messages.
- promoting policy and environmental strategies that enhance healthy behavior.
- determining the relation between genetics and disease. The associations of genetic variants with CVD, and especially the interplay between genetic and environmental factors, may play increasingly important roles in the nation's efforts to prevent CVD.
- identifying new or emerging risk factors and determining their potential for public health intervention. New or emerging risk factors that have been associated with CVD include elevated levels of total homocyst(e)ine, fibrinogen, and C-reactive protein, and infectious agents such as *Helicobacter pylori* and *Chlamydia pneumoniae*.
- focusing on secondary prevention and disability. An aging U.S. population and an increasing number of persons surviving life-threatening cardiovascular conditions requires public health programs to focus on issues such as disability and quality of life. Persons with existing cardiovascular conditions are at increased risk for future life-threatening events related to those conditions.
- addressing the needs of the global community. Although CVD death rates are higher in developed nations, most cases occur in developing nations (8). Developing countries may face a double burden of infectious and chronic diseases. International collaboration to improve cardiovascular health (9) will need to continue to reduce the burden of CVD worldwide.

ABOUT THE AUTHOR

Centers for Disease Control and Prevention (CDC) in Atlanta, Georgia.

REFERENCES

1. National Heart, Lung and Blood Institute. Morbidity & mortality: 1998 chartbook on cardiovascular, lung, and blood diseases. Rockville, Maryland: US Department of Health and Human Services, National Institutes of Health, 1998.
2. Epstein FH. Contribution of epidemiology to understanding coronary heart

disease. In: Marmot M, Elliott P, eds. Coronary heart disease epidemiology: from aetiology to public health. New York: Oxford University Press, 1992:20–32.

3. Epstein FH. Cardiovascular disease epidemiology: a journey from the past into the future. Circulation 1996;93:1755–64.

4. Stamler J. Established major coronary risk factors. In: Marmot M, Elliott P, eds. Coronary heart disease epidemiology: from aetiology to public health. New York: Oxford University Press, 1992:35–66.

5. Keys A. Seven countries—a multivariate analysis of death and coronary heart disease. Cambridge, Massachusetts: Harvard University Press, 1980.

6. Dawber TR. The Framingham study: the epidemiology of atherosclerotic disease. Cambridge, Massachusetts: Harvard University Press, 1980.

7. National Heart, Lung and Blood Institute. Report of the task force on research in epidemiology and prevention of cardiovascular diseases. Rockville, Maryland: National Institutes of Health, 1994.

8. Labarthe DR. Epidemiology and prevention of cardiovascular diseases: a global challenge. Gaithersburg, Maryland: Aspen, 1998.

9. CDC/Stanford University School of Medicine. Worldwide efforts to improve heart health: a follow-up of the Catalonia Declaration—selected program descriptions. Atlanta: US Department of Health and Human Services, CDC, 1997.

10. Rose G. The strategy of preventive medicine. New York: Oxford University Press, 1992.

11. National Institutes of Health. The sixth report of the Joint National Committee on Prevention, Detection, Evaluation, and Treatment of High Blood Pressure. Rockville, Maryland: US Department of Health and Human Services, National Institutes of Health, National Heart, Lung, and Blood Institute, November 1997. (NIH publication no. 98-4080).

12. National Cholesterol Education Program. Second report of the expert panel on detection, evaluation and treatment of high blood cholesterol in adults. Rockville, Maryland: US Department of Health and Human Services, National Institutes of Health, 1993. (NIH publication no. 93–3095).

13. National Center for Health Statistics. Health, United States, 1998 with socioeconomic status and health chartbook. Hyattsville, Maryland: US Department of Health and Human Services, CDC, 1998.

14. National Center for Health Statistics. Healthy people 2000 review, 1997. Hyattsville, Maryland: US Department of Health and Human Services, CDC, 1997.

15. Gerrior S, Bente L. Nutrient content of the U.S. food supply, 1909–94. Washington, DC: US Department of Agriculture, 1997. (Home economics research report no. 53).

16. Ernst ND, Sempos ST, Briefel RR, Clark MB. Consistency between US dietary fat intake and serum total cholesterol concentrations: the National Health and Nutrition Examination surveys. Am J Clin Nutr 1997;66:965S–972S.

17. Higgins M, Thom T. Trends in CHD in the United States. Int J Epidemiol 1989;18:S58–S66.
18. American Heart Association. 1999 Heart and stroke statistical update. Dallas, Texas: American Heart Association, 1998.
19. Kaplan GA, Keil JE. Socioeconomic factors and cardiovascular disease: a review of the literature. Circulation 1993;88:1973–98.
20. CDC. Changes in mortality from heart failure—United States, 1980–1995. MMWR 1998; 47:633–7.

ARTICLE 5

GUIDE TO CLINICAL PREVENTIVE SERVICES

U.S. Preventive Services Task Force

This report is intended for primary care clinicians: physicians, nurses, nurse practitioners, physician assistants, other allied health professionals, and students. It provides recommendations for clinical practice on preventive interventions—screening tests, counseling interventions, immunizations, and chemoprophylactic regimens—for the prevention of more than 80 target conditions. The patients for whom these services are recommended include asymptomatic individuals of all age groups and risk categories. Thus, the subject matter is relevant to all of the major primary care specialties: family practice, internal medicine, obstetrics-gynecology, and pediatrics. The recommendations reflect a standardized review of current scientific evidence and include a summary of published clinical research regarding the clinical effectiveness of each preventive service.

VALUE OF PREVENTION

Clinicians have always intuitively understood the value of prevention. Faced daily with the difficult and often unsuccessful task of treating advanced stages of disease, primary care providers have long sought the opportunity to intervene early in the course of disease or even before disease develops. The benefits of incorporating prevention into medical practice have become increasingly apparent over the past 30–40 years, as previously common and debilitating conditions have declined in incidence following the introduction of effective clinical preventive services. Infectious diseases such as poliomyelitis, which once occurred in regular epidemic waves (over 18,300 cases in 1954), have become rare in the U.S. as a result of childhood immunization.[1] Only three cases of paralytic poliomyelitis were reported in the U.S. in 1993, and none was due to endemic wild virus. Before rubella vaccine became available, rubella epidemics occurred regularly in the U.S. every 6–9 years; a 1964 pandemic resulted in over 12 million rubella infections, 11,000 fetal losses and

247

about 20,000 infants born with congenital rubella syndrome.[2,3] The incidence of rubella has decreased 99% since 1969, when the vaccine first became available.[4] Similar trends have occurred with diphtheria, pertussis, and other once-common childhood infectious diseases.[1]

Preventive services for the early detection of disease have also been associated with substantial reductions in morbidity and mortality. Age-adjusted mortality from stroke has decreased by more than 50% since 1972, a trend attributed in part to earlier detection and treatment of hypertension.[5–7] Dramatic reductions in the incidence of invasive cervical cancer and in cervical cancer mortality have occurred following the implementation of screening programs using Papanicolaou testing to detect cervical dysplasia.[8] Children with metabolic disorders such as phenylketonuria and congenital hypothyroidism, who once suffered severe irreversible mental retardation, now usually retain normal cognitive function as a result of routine newborn screening and treatment.[9–16]

Although immunizations and screening tests remain important preventive services, the most promising role for prevention in current medical practice may lie in changing the personal health behaviors of patients long before clinical disease develops. The importance of this aspect of clinical practice is evident from a growing literature linking some of the leading causes of death in the U.S., such as heart disease, cancer, cerebrovascular disease, chronic obstructive pulmonary disease, unintentional and intentional injuries, and human immunodeficiency virus infection,[17] to a handful of personal health behaviors. Smoking alone contributes to one out of every five deaths in the U.S., including 150,000 deaths annually from cancer, 100,000 from coronary artery disease, 23,000 from cerebrovascular disease, and 85,000 from pulmonary diseases such as chronic obstructive pulmonary disease and pneumonia.[18] Failing to use safety belts and driving while intoxicated are major contributors to motor vehicle injuries, which accounted for 41,000 deaths in 1992.[17] Physical inactivity and dietary factors contribute to coronary atherosclerosis, cancer, diabetes, osteoporosis, and other common diseases.[19–22] High-risk sexual practices increase the risk of unintended pregnancy, sexually transmitted diseases (STDs), and acquired immunodeficiency syndrome.[23,24] Approximately half of all deaths occurring in the U.S. in 1990 may be attributed to external factors such as tobacco, alcohol, and illicit drug use, diet and activity patterns, motor vehicles, and sexual behavior, and are therefore potentially preventable by changes in personal health practices.[25]

BARRIERS TO PREVENTIVE CARE DELIVERY

Although sound clinical reasons exist for emphasizing prevention in medicine, studies have shown that clinicians often fail to provide recommended clinical preventive services.[26–32] This is due to a variety of factors, including inadequate reimbursement for preventive services, fragmentation of health care delivery, and insufficient time with patients to deliver the range of preventive services that are recommended.[33–35]

Even when these barriers to implementation are accounted for, however, clinicians fail to perform preventive services as recommended,[28] suggesting that uncertainty among clinicians as to which services should be offered is a factor as well.

Part of the uncertainty among clinicians derives from the fact that recommendations come from multiple sources, and these recommendations often differ. Recommendations[a] relating to clinical preventive services are issued regularly by government health agencies and expert panels that they sponsor,[5,36-42] medical specialty organizations,[43-50] voluntary associations,[51-53] other professional and scientific organizations,[54,55] and individual experts.[56-59]

A second major reason clinicians might be reluctant to perform preventive services is skepticism about their effectiveness. Whether performance of certain preventive interventions can significantly reduce morbidity or mortality from the target condition is often unclear. The relative effectiveness of different preventive services is also unclear, making it difficult for busy clinicians to decide which interventions are most important during a brief patient visit. A broader concern is that some maneuvers can ultimately result in more harm than good. While this concern applies to all clinical practices, it is especially important in relation to preventive services because the individuals who receive these interventions are often healthy. Minor complications or rare adverse effects that would be tolerated in the treatment of a severe illness take on greater importance in the asymptomatic population and require careful evaluation to determine whether benefits exceed risks. This is particularly relevant for screening tests, which benefit only the few individuals who have the disorder but expose all the individuals screened to the risk of adverse effects from the test. Moreover, because recommendations for preventive services such as routine screening often include a large proportion of the population, there are potentially important economic implications.

HISTORICAL PERSPECTIVE

Uncertainties about the effectiveness of clinical preventive services raise questions about the value of the routine health examination of asymptomatic persons, in which a predetermined battery of tests and physical examination procedures are performed as part of a routine checkup. The annual physical examination of healthy persons was first proposed by the American Medical Association in 1922.[60] For many years after, it was common practice among health professionals to recommend routine physicals and comprehensive laboratory testing as effective preventive medicine. While routine visits with the primary care clinician are important, performing the same interventions on all patients and performing them annually are not the most clinically effective approaches to disease prevention. Rather, both the frequency and

---

[a]The recommendations cited here are illustrative only. Listings of recommendations made by other groups for each condition considered are cited in the relevant chapter.

the content of the periodic health examination should reflect the unique health risks of the individual patient and the quality of the evidence that specific preventive services are clinically effective. This new approach to the periodic visit was endorsed by the American Medical Association in 1983 in a policy statement that withdrew support for a standard annual physical examination.[61] The individualized periodic health visit should emphasize evidence of clinical effectiveness, and thus increased attention has turned to the collection of reliable data on the effectiveness of specific preventive services.

One of the first comprehensive efforts to examine these issues was undertaken by the Canadian government, which in 1976 convened the Canadian Task Force on the Periodic Health Examination (CTFPHE). This expert panel developed explicit criteria to judge the quality of evidence from published clinical research on clinical preventive services, and the panel used uniform decision rules to link the strength of recommendations for or against a given preventive service to the quality of the underlying evidence (see Appendix A). These ratings were intended to provide the clinician with a means of selecting those preventive services supported by the strongest evidence of effectiveness. Using this approach, the CTFPHE examined preventive services for 78 target conditions, releasing its recommendations in a monograph published in 1979.[62] In 1982, the CTFPHE reconvened and applied its methodology to new evidence as it became available, periodically publishing revised recommendations and evaluations of new topics. These were updated and compiled in 1994 in *The Canadian Guide to Clinical Preventive Health Care.*[63]

A similar effort began in the U.S. in 1984 when the Public Health Service commissioned the U.S. Preventive Services Task Force (USPSTF). Like the Canadian panel, this 20-member non-Federal panel was charged with developing recommendations for clinicians on the appropriate use of preventive interventions, based on a systematic review of evidence of clinical effectiveness.[64] A methodology similar to that of the CTFPHE was adopted at the outset of the project. This enabled the U.S. and Canadian panels to collaborate in a binational effort to review evidence and develop recommendations on preventive services. The first USPSTF met regularly between 1984 and 1988 to develop comprehensive recommendations addressing preventive services. The panel members and their scientific support staff reviewed evidence and developed recommendations on preventive services for 60 topic areas affecting patients from infancy to old age, published in 1989 as the *Guide to Clinical Preventive Services.*

THE SECOND U.S. PREVENTIVE SERVICES TASK FORCE

The USPSTF was reconstituted in 1990 to continue and update these scientific assessments.[65] Its charge has been to evaluate the effectiveness of clinical preventive services that were not previously examined; to reevaluate those that were examined and for which there is new scientific evidence, new technologies that merit consideration, or other reasons to revisit the published recommendations; and to produce this new edition of the *Guide,* with updated recommendations for the periodic health examination. In addition, a continuing mission of the USPSTF has been to define a research agenda by identifying significant gaps in the literature. The USPSTF has 10 members, comprising two family physicians, two internists, two pediatricians, two obstetrician-gynecologists, and two methodologists. Content experts from academic institutions and Federal agencies also joined the deliberations of the panel on an ad hoc basis. The USPSTF met quarterly between September 1990 and April 1994, with scientific support staff from the Office of Disease Prevention and Health Promotion, Public Health Service, U.S. Department of Health and Human Services, to analyze systematically scientific evidence pertaining to clinical preventive services that had been published since the first edition of the *Guide.*

The USPSTF greatly expanded its collaboration with medical specialty organizations and Federal agencies, and it has continued its close cooperation with the CTFPHE. Designated liaisons from primary care medical specialty societies (American Academy of Family Physicians, American Academy of Pediatrics, American College of Obstetricians and Gynecologists, and American College of Physicians), the agencies of the Public Health Service, and the CTFPHE attended all of the USPSTF meetings, and their respective organizations reviewed all draft recommendations. The USPSTF and the CTFPHE, which has also recently updated its analyses of the scientific evidence and recommendations,[63] shared background papers and draft chapters throughout their updating processes to avoid unnecessary duplication of effort. Seventeen chapters in *The Canadian Guide to Clinical Preventive Health Care*[63] were based in part on background papers prepared for the USPSTF, and 21 chapters in this edition of the *Guide* are based in part on papers prepared for the CTFPHE. The USPSTF also collaborated with the American College of Physicians' Clinical Efficacy Assessment Program (CEAP), which uses a similar evidence-based methodology. A liaison from the USPSTF regularly attended CEAP meetings, and several chapter updates were based on reviews prepared for CEAP.

PRINCIPAL FINDINGS OF THE U.S. PREVENTIVE SERVICES TASK FORCE

The review of evidence for the second edition of the *Guide to Clinical Preventive Services* has produced several important findings. These can be summarized as follows:

Interventions that address patients' personal health practices are vitally important. Effective interventions that address personal health practices are likely to lead to substantial reductions in the incidence and severity of the leading causes of disease and disability in the U.S. Primary prevention as it relates to such risk factors as smoking, physical inactivity, poor nutrition, alcohol and other drug abuse, and inadequate attention to safety precautions holds greater promise for improving overall health than many secondary preventive measures such as routine screening for early disease.[25] Therefore, clinician counseling that leads to improved personal health practices may be more valuable to patients than conventional clinical activities such as diagnostic testing. In the past, the responsibility of the clinician was primarily to treat illnesses; the asymptomatic healthy individual did not need to see the doctor. In addition, personal health behaviors were often not viewed as a legitimate clinical issue. A patient's use of safety belts would receive less attention from the clinician than the results of a complete blood count (CBC) or a routine chest radiograph. A careful review of the data, however, suggests that different priorities are in order. Motor vehicle injuries affect nearly 3.5 million persons each year in the U.S.;[66] they account for over 40,000 deaths each year.[67] Proper use of safety belts can prevent 40–60% of motor vehicle injuries and deaths.[68–70] In contrast, there is little evidence that performing routine CBCs or chest radiographs improves clinical outcome,[71,72] and these procedures are associated with increased health care expenditures.

An important corollary of this finding is that clinicians must assist patients to assume greater responsibility for their own health. In the traditional doctor-patient relationship, the patient adopts a passive role and expects the doctor to assume control of the treatment plan. Whereas the clinician is often the key figure in the treatment of acute illnesses and injuries, the patient is the principal agent in primary prevention that addresses personal health practices. Therefore, one of the initial tasks of the clinician practicing primary prevention is shifting control to the patient. To achieve competence in the task of helping to empower patients and in counseling them to change health-related behaviors, many clinicians will need to develop new skills.

The clinician and patient should share decision-making. Many preventive services involve important risks or costs that must be balanced against their possible benefits. Because not all patients weigh risks and benefits the same way, clinicians must fully inform patients about the potential consequences of proposed interventions, including the possibility of invasive follow-up procedures, tests, and treatments. Incorporating patient preferences is especially important when the balance of risks and benefits, and therefore the best decision for each patient, depends greatly on the values placed on possible outcomes (e.g., prolonged life vs. substantial morbidity from treatment, where evidence suggested that patient values were critical to the balance of risks and benefits (e.g., screening for Down syndrome or neural tube defects, hormone prophylaxis in postmenopausal women), the USPSTF specifically recommended patient education and consideration of patient preferences in decision-making rather than a uniform policy for all patients. Shared decision-making also requires explicitly acknowledging areas of uncertainty. Patients must understand not only what is known, but also what is not yet known about the risks and benefits from an intervention, in order to make an informed decision.

Clinicians should be selective in ordering tests and providing preventive services. Although certain screening tests, such as blood pressure measurement,[73-75] Papanicolaou smears,[8] and mammography,[76] can be highly effective in reducing morbidity and mortality, the USPSTF found that many others are of unproven effectiveness. Screening tests with inadequate specificity often produce large numbers of false-positive results, especially when performed routinely without regard to risk factors; these results might lead to unnecessary and potentially harmful diagnostic testing and treatment. Recognizing the cardinal importance of avoiding harm to asymptomatic patients ("primum non nocere"), the USPSTF recommended against a number of screening tests (e.g., serum tumor markers for the early detection of pancreatic or ovarian cancer) that had unproven benefit but likely downstream harms. Many tests that lack evidence that they improve clinical outcome, such as home uterine activity monitoring, have the additional disadvantage of being expensive, especially when performed on large numbers of persons in the population. In a few instances, the USPSTF found evidence that certain screening tests that have been widely used in the past (e.g., routine chest x-ray to screen for lung cancer, dipstick urinalysis for asymptomatic bacteriuria) are ineffective. Although the USPSTF did not base its recommendations on evidence of cost-effectiveness, judging health benefit based on scientific evidence provides a rational basis for directing resources toward effective services and away from ineffective services and from interventions for which the balance of benefits and risks is uncertain.[65]

In addition to weighing evidence for effectiveness, selecting appropriate screening tests requires considering age, gender, and other individual risk factors of the patient in order to minimize adverse effects and unnecessary expenditures. An appreciation of the risk profile of the patient is also necessary to set priorities for preventive interventions. The need for assessing individual risk underscores a time-honored principle of medical practice: the importance of a complete medical history and detailed discussion with patients regarding their personal health practices, focused on identifying risk factors for developing disease.

Clinicians must take every opportunity to deliver preventive services, especially to persons with limited access to care. Those individual's at highest risk for many preventable causes of premature disease and disability, such as cervical cancer, tuberculosis, human immunodeficiency virus infection, and poor nutrition, are the same individuals least likely to receive adequate preventive services. Devising strategies to increase access to preventive services for such individuals is more likely to reduce morbidity and mortality from these conditions than performing preventive services more frequently on those who are already regular recipients of preventive care and who are often in better health. One important solution is to deliver preventive services at every visit, rather than exclusively during visits devoted entirely to prevention. While preventive checkups often provide more time for counseling and other preventive services, and although healthy individuals might be more receptive to such interventions than those who are sick, any visit provides an opportunity to practice prevention. In fact, some individuals may see clinicians only when they are ill or injured. The illness visit provides the only opportunity to reach individuals who, due to limited access to care, would be otherwise unlikely to receive preventive services.

For some health problems, community-level interventions may be more effective than clinical preventive services. Important health problems that are likely to require broader-based interventions than can be offered in the clinical setting alone include youth and family violence, initiation of tobacco use, unintended pregnancy in adolescents, and certain unintentional injuries. Other types of interventions, such as school-based curricula,[77-81] community programs,[82-84] and regulatory and legislative initiatives,[85-87] might prove more effective for preventing morbidity and mortality from these conditions than will preventive services delivered in the clinical setting. There may, nevertheless, be an important role for clinicians as participants in community systems that address these types of health problems. Such a role might include becoming aware of existing community programs and encouraging patient participation and involvement; acting as a consultant for communities implementing programs or introducing legislation; and serving as an advocate to initiate and maintain effective community interventions.

A RESEARCH AGENDA IN PREVENTIVE MEDICINE

By reviewing comprehensively and critically the scientific evidence regarding clinical preventive services, the USPSTF identified important gaps in the literature and helped define targets for future clinical prevention research. Among the most important of these targets is more and better quality research evaluating the effectiveness of brief, directed counseling that can be delivered in the busy primary care practice setting. Given the importance of personal health practices, the scarcity of adequate evidence evaluating the effectiveness of brief counseling in the primary care setting is striking. The effectiveness of such counseling in reducing smoking and problem drinking is clear.[88-90] For many other behaviors, however, counseling has been tested and proven effective only in highly specialized settings (e.g., STD clinics[91-94]) or when delivered through multiple, lengthy visits with specially trained counselors (e.g., certain cholesterol-lowering interventions[95,96]). Whether the effects of these interventions can be reproduced by brief advice during the typical clinical encounter with a primary care provider is uncertain. Counseling to change some personal health practices (e.g., unsafe pedestrian behavior, drinking and driving) has received insufficient attention by researchers. Some personal health practices may not respond to brief clinician counseling in the context of routine health care. Therefore, research should also evaluate the effectiveness (and cost-effectiveness) of referring patients to allied health professionals with special counseling skills in their areas of expertise (e.g., dietitians, substance abuse counselors) and of using other modalities to educate patients in the primary care setting (e.g., videos, interactive software).

For screening interventions, randomized controlled trials are powerful in resolving controversy about the benefits and risks. Many important questions will be answered by major ongoing screening trials such as the Prostate, Lung, Colorectal,

Ovarian Cancer (PLCO) Screening Trial of the National Cancer Institute,[97] and by ongoing trials evaluating the clinical efficacy of treating common asymptomatic conditions detectable by screening, such as high cholesterol levels in the elderly and moderately elevated blood lead levels in children. For unproven screening interventions, finding ways to streamline randomized controlled trials so that they can be performed efficiently and cost-effectively is essential.

IMPROVING THE DELIVERY OF CLINICAL PREVENTIVE SERVICES

This report will help resolve some of the uncertainties among primary care clinicians about the effectiveness of preventive services, thus removing one barrier to the appropriate delivery of preventive care. The USPSTF did not, however, address other barriers to implementing clinical preventive services, such as insufficient reimbursement for counseling or other preventive interventions, provider uncertainty about how to deliver recommended services, lack of patient or provider interest in preventive services, and lack of organizational/system support to facilitate the delivery of clinical preventive services. Many of these barriers are addressed by "Put Prevention into Practice," the Public Health Service prevention implementation program.[98] Programs such as "Put Prevention into Practice" can help ensure that prevention is delivered at every opportunity that patients are seen. Other publications also provide useful information on the effective delivery of clinical preventive services.[99] The increasing formation of integrated health care systems (e.g., managed care organizations) may also create new opportunities for crafting better preventive practices.

The USPSTF explored issues of prevention for a wide range of disease categories and for patients of all ages. The comprehensive and systematic approach to the review of evidence for each topic should provide clinicians with the means to compare the relative effectiveness of different preventive services and to determine, on the basis of scientific evidence, what is most likely to benefit their patients. Organizations using evidence-based methodologies to develop guidelines on clinical preventive services are finding broad agreement on a core set of preventive services of proven effectiveness that can be recommended to primary care providers and their patients.[63,100] Basing preventive health care decisions on the evidence of their effectiveness is an important step in the progress of disease prevention and health promotion in the U.S.

ABOUT THE AUTHOR

Carolyn DiGuiseppi, MD, MPH, is Editor, Science Writer, and Project Director for the U.S. Task Force on Clinical Preventive Services.

U.S. Preventive Services Task Force

REFERENCES

1. Centers for Disease Control and Prevention. Summary of notifiable diseases, United States, 1993. MMWR 1994;42:1–74.

2. Witte JJ, Karchmer AW, Case G, et al. Epidemiology of rubella. Am J Dis Child 1969;118:107–111.

3. Orenstein WA, Bart KJ, Hinman AR, et al. The opportunity and obligation to eliminate rubella from the United States. JAMA 1984;251:1988–1994.

4. Centers for Disease Control and Prevention. Rubella and congenital rubella syndrome—United States, January 1, 1991–May 7, 1994. MMWR 1994;43:391, 397–401.

5. Joint National Committee on Detection, Evaluation, and Treatment of High Blood Pressure. The fifth report of the Joint National Committee on Detection, Evaluation, and Treatment of High Blood Pressure. Bethesda: National Institutes of Health, 1993. (Publication no. 93–1088.)

6. Garraway WM, Whisnant JP. The changing pattern of hypertension and the declining incidence of stroke. JAMA 1987;258:214–217.

7. Casper M, Wing S, Strogatz D, et al. Antihypertensive treatment and U.S. trends in stroke mortality, 1962 to 1980. Am J Public Health 1992;82:1600–1606.

8. IARC Working Group. Summary chapter. In: Hakama M, Miller AB, Day NE, eds. Screening for cancer of the uterine cervix. Lyon, France: International Agency for Research on Cancer, 1986:133–144. (IARC Scientific Publication no. 76.)

9. Berman PW, Waisman HA, Graham FK. Intelligence in treated phenylketonuric children: a developmental study. Child Dev 1966;37:731–747.

10. Hudson FP, Mordaunt VL, Leahy I. Evaluation of treatment begun in first three months of life in 184 cases of phenylketonuria. Arch Dis Child 1970;45:5–12.

11. Williamson ML, Koch R, Azen C, et al. Correlates of intelligence test results in treated phenylketonuric children. Pediatrics 1981;68:161–167.

12. Azen CG, Koch R, Friedman EG, et al. Intellectual development in 12-year-old children treated for phenylketonuria. Am J Dis Child 1991;145:35–39.

13. New England Congenital Hypothyroidism Collaborative. Elementary school performance of children with congenital hypothyroidism. J Pediatr 1990;116:27–32.

14. Rovet JF, Ehrlich RM, Sorbara DL. Neurodevelopment in infants and preschool children with congenital hypothyroidism: etiological and treatment factors affecting outcome. J Pediatr Psychol 1992;17:187–213.

15. Kooistra L, Laane C, Vulsma T, et al. Motor and cognitive development in children with congenital hypothyroidism: a long-term evaluation of the effects of neonatal treatment. J Pediatr 1994;124:903–909.

16. Fuggle PW, Grant DB, Smith I, et al. Intelligence, motor skills and

behaviour at 5 years in early-treated congenital hypothyroidism. Eur J Pediatr 1991;150:570–574.

17. Kochanek KD, Hudson BL. Advance report of final mortality statistics, 1992. Monthly vital statistics report; vol 43 no 6 (suppl). Hyattsville, MD: National Center for Health Statistics, 1995.

18. Centers for Disease Control. Cigarette smoking-attributable mortality and years of potential life lost—United States, 1990. MMWR 1993;42:645–649.

19. Centers for Disease Control and Prevention. Public health focus: physical activity and the prevention of coronary heart disease. MMWR 1993;42:669–672.

20. Bouchard C, Shepard RJ, Stephens T, eds. Physical activity, fitness, and health. Champaign, IL: Human Kinetics, 1994.

21. Department of Health and Human Services. The Surgeon General's report on nutrition and health. Washington, DC: Government Printing Office, 1988. (Publication no. DHHS (PHS) 88–50210.)

22. Food and Nutrition Board, National Research Council. Diet and health: implications for reducing chronic disease. Washington, DC: National Academy Press, 1989.

23. Hatcher RA, Trussell J, Stewart F, et al. Contraceptive technology. 16th ed. New York: Irvington Publishers, 1994.

24. Institute of Medicine. AIDS and behavior: an integrated approach. Washington, DC: National Academy Press, 1994.

25. McGinnis JM, Foege WH. Actual causes of death in the United States. JAMA 1993;270:2207–2212.

26. Lewis CE. Disease prevention and health promotion practices of primary care physicians in the United States. Am J Prev Med 1988;4(suppl):9–16.

27. National Center for Health Statistics. Healthy People 2000 review, 1993. Hyattsville, MD: Public Health Service, 1994. (DHHS Publication no. (PHS) 94–1232–1.)

28. Lurie N, Manning WG, Peterson C, et al. Preventive care: do we practice what we preach? Am J Public Health 1987;77:801–804.

29. Montano DE, Phillips WR. Cancer screening by primary care physicians: a comparison of rates obtained from physician self-report, patient survey, and chart audit. Am J Public Health 1995;85:795–800.

30. Dietrich AJ, Goldberg H. Preventive content of adult primary care: do generalists and subspecialists differ? Am J Public Health 1984;74:223–227.

31. Battista RN. Adult cancer prevention in primary care: patterns of practice in Quebec. Am J Public Health 1983;73:1036–1039.

32. Lemley KB, O'Grady ET, Rauckhorst L, et al. Baseline data on the delivery of clinical preventive services provided by nurse practitioners. Nurs Pract 1994;19:57–63.

33. Logsdon DN, Rosen MA. The cost of preventive health services in primary medical care and implications for health insurance coverage. J Ambul Care Man 1984;46–55.

34. Battista RN, Lawrence RS, eds. Implementing preventive services. Am J Prev Med 1988;4(4 Suppl):1–194.

35. Frame PS. Health maintenance in clinical practice: strategies and barriers. Am Fam Phys 1992;45:1192–1200.

36. Centers for Disease Control. Screening for tuberculosis and tuberculous infection in high-risk populations, and the use of preventive therapy for tuberculous infection in the United States: recommendations of the Advisory Committee for Elimination of Tuberculosis. MMWR 1990;39(RR-8):1–7.

37. Centers for Disease Control and Prevention. Injury control recommendations: bicycle helmets. MMWR 1995;44(RR-1):1–17.

38. Centers for Disease Control and Prevention. General recommendations on immunization: recommendations of the Advisory Committee on Immunization Practices (ACIP). MMWR 1994;43(RR-1):1–38.

39. National Institutes of Health. Early identification of hearing impairment in infants and young children. NIH consensus statement. Bethesda: National Institutes of Health, 1993;11:1–24.

40. National Cholesterol Education Program. Second report of the Expert Panel on Detection, Evaluation, and Treatment of High Blood Cholesterol in Adults. (Adult Treatment Panel II). Bethesda: National Heart, Lung, Blood Institute, National Institutes of Health, 1993.

41. Green M, ed. Bright Futures: guidelines for health supervision of infants, children and adolescents. Arlington, VA: National Center for Education in Maternal and Child Health, 1994.

42. National Cholesterol Education Program. Report of the Expert Panel on Blood Cholesterol Levels in Children and Adolescents. Bethesda: National Heart, Lung, Blood Institute, National Institutes of Health, 1991. (DHHS Publication no. (PHS)91–2732.)

43. American College of Physicians Task Force on Adult Immunization and Infectious Diseases Society of America. Guide for adult immunization. 3rd ed. Philadelphia: American College of Physicians, 1994.

44. Eddy DM, ed. Common screening tests. Philadelphia: American College of Physicians, 1991.

45. American College of Obstetricians and Gynecologists. Standards for obstetric-gynecologic services. 7th ed. Washington, DC: American College of Obstetricians and Gynecologists, 1989.

46. American Medical Association. AMA guidelines for adolescent preventive services (GAPS): recommendations and rationale. Chicago: American Medical Association, 1994.

47. American Academy of Family Physicians. Age charts for periodic health examination. Kansas City, MO: American Academy of Family Physicians, 1994. (Reprint no. 510.)

48. Peter G, ed. 1994 Red Book: report of the Committee on Infectious Diseases. 23rd ed. Elk Grove Village, IL: American Academy of Pediatrics, 1994.

49. Joint Committee on Infant Hearing. 1994 position statement. Pediatrics 1995;95:152–156.

50. American Academy of Ophthalmology. Policy statement. Frequency of ocular examinations. Washington, DC: American Academy of Ophthalmology, 1990.

51. American Cancer Society. Guidelines for the cancer-related checkup, an update. Atlanta: American Cancer Society, 1993.

52. American Diabetes Association. Screening for diabetes. Diabetes Care 1993;16:7–9.

53. American Heart Association. Statement on exercise: benefits and recommendations for physical activity programs for all Americans. Dallas, TX: American Heart Association, 1992.

54. American Optometric Association. Recommendations for regular optometric care. Alexandria, VA: American Optometric Association, 1994.

55. Consensus Development Conference: Diagnosis, prophylaxis, and treatment of osteoporosis. Am J Med 1993;94:646–650.

56. Frame PS. A critical review of adult health maintenance. Part 1. Prevention of atherosclerotic diseases. J Fam Pract 1986;22:341–346.

57. Frame PS. A critical review of adult health maintenance. Part 2. Prevention of infectious diseases. J Fam Pract 1986;22:417–422.

58. Frame PS. A critical review of adult health maintenance. Part 3. Prevention of cancer. J Fam Pract 1986;22:511–520.

59. Frame PS. A critical review of adult health maintenance. Part 4. Prevention of metabolic, behavioral, and miscellaneous conditions. J Fam Pract 1986;23:29–39.

60. American Medical Association. Periodic health examination: a manual for physicians. Chicago: American Medical Association, 1947.

61. American Medical Association. Medical evaluations of healthy persons. Council on Scientific Affairs. JAMA 1983;249:1626–1633.

62. Canadian Task Force on the Periodic Health Examination. The periodic health examination. Can Med Assoc J 1979;121:1194–1254.

63. Canadian Task Force on the Periodic Health Examination. Canadian guide to clinical preventive health care. Ottawa: Canada Communication Group, 1994.

64. Lawrence RS, Mickalide AD. Preventive services in clinical practice: designing the periodic health examination. JAMA 1987;257:2205–2207.

65. Sox HC Jr, Woolf SH. Evidence-based practice guidelines from the U.S. Preventive Services Task Force [editorial]. JAMA 1993;269:2678.

66. National Highway Traffic Safety Administration. Traffic safety facts 1992: a compilation of motor vehicle crash data from the Fatal Accident Reporting System and the General Estimates System. Washington, DC: Department of Transportation, 1994. (Publication no. DOT HS 808 022.)

67. National Highway Traffic Safety Administration. Traffic safety facts 1993. Washington, DC: Department of Transportation, 1994. (Publication no. DOT HS 808 169).

68. Campbell BJ. Safety belt injury reduction related to crash severity and front seated position. J Trauma 1987;27:733–739.

69. Cooper PJ. Estimating overinvolvement of seat belt nonwearers in crashes and the effect of lap/shoulder restraint use on different crash severity consequences. Accid Anal Prev 1994;26:263–275.

70. Department of Transportation. Final regulatory impact assessment on amendments to Federal Motor Vehicle Safety Standard 208, Front Seat Occupant Protection. Washington, DC: Department of Transportation, 1984. (Publication no. DOT HS 806 572.)

71. Tape TG, Mushlin AI. The utility of routine chest radiographs. Ann Intern Med 1986;104:663–670.

72. Shapiro MF, Greenfield S. The complete blood count and leukocyte differential count. Ann Intern Med 1987;106:65–74.

73. Collins R, Peto R, MacMahon S, et al. Blood pressure, stroke, and coronary heart disease. Part 2, short-term reductions in blood pressure: overview of randomised drug trials in their epidemiological context. Lancet 1990;335:827–838.

74. MacMahon SW, Cutler JA, Furberg CD, et al. The effects of drug treatment for hypertension on morbidity and mortality from cardiovascular disease: a review of randomized, controlled trials. Prog Cardiovasc Dis 1986;29(suppl):99–118.

75. Hebert PR, Moser M, Mayer J, et al. Recent evidence on drug therapy of mild to moderate hypertension and decreased risk of coronary heart disease. Arch Intern Med 1993;153:578–581.

76. Kerlikowske K, Grady D, Rubin SM, et al. Efficacy of screening mammography: a meta-analysis. JAMA 1995;:149–154.

77. Hansen WB, Johnson CA, Flay BR, et al. Affective and social influences approaches to the prevention of multiple substance abuse among seventh grade students: results from Project SMART. Prev Med 1988;17:135–154.

78. Abernathy TJ, Bertrand LD. Preventing cigarette smoking among children: results of a four-year evaluation of the PAL program. Can J Public Health 1992;83:226–229.

79. Elder JP, Wildey M, de Moor C, et al. The long-term prevention of tobacco use among junior high school students: classroom and telephone interventions. Am J Public Health 1993;83:1239–1244.

80. Schinke SP, Gilchrist LD, Snow WH. Skills intervention to prevent cigarette smoking among adolescents. Am J Public Health 1985;75:665–667.

81. Botvin GJ, Dusenbury L, Tortu S, et al. Preventing adolescent drug abuse through a multi-modal cognitive-behavioral approach: results of a three-year study. J Consult Clin Psychol 1990;58:437–446.

82. Rivara FP, Thompson DC, Thompson RS, et al. The Seattle children's bicycle helmet campaign: changes in helmet use and head injury admissions. Pediatrics 1994;93:567–569.

83. Schwarz DF, Grisso JA, Miles C, et al. An injury prevention program in an urban African-American community. Am J Public Health 1993;83:675–680.

84. Davidson LL, Durkin MS, Kuhn L, et al. The impact of the Safe Kids/Healthy Neighborhoods injury prevention program in Harlem, 1988 through 1991. Am J Public Health 1994;84:580–586.

85. Erdmann TC, Feldman KW, Rivara FP, et al. Tap water burn prevention: the effect of legislation. Pediatrics 1991;88:572–577.

86. Walton WW. An evaluation of the Poison Prevention Packaging Act. Pediatrics 1982;69:363–370.

87. Cote TR, Sacks JJ, Lambert-Huber DA, et al. Bicycle helmet use among Maryland children: effect of legislation and education. Pediatrics 1992;89:1216–1220.

88. Kottke TE, Battista RN, DeFriese GH, et al. Attributes of successful smoking cessation interventions in medical practice: a meta-analysis of 39 controlled trials. JAMA 1988;259:2882–2889.

89. Bien TH, Miller WR, Tonigan JS. Brief interventions for alcohol problems: a review. Addiction 1993;88:315–336.

90. Brief interventions and alcohol use. Bulletin 7. Leeds, UK: Effective Health Care, 1993.

91. Cohen DA, Dent C, MacKinnon D, Hahn G. Condoms for men, not women. Sex Transm Dis 1992;19:245–251.

92. Cohen DA, MacKinnon DP, Dent C, et al. Group counseling at STD clinics to promote use of condoms. Public Health Rep 1992;107:727–731.

93. Heaton CG, Messeri P. The effect of video interventions on improving knowledge and treatment compliance in the sexually transmitted disease setting. Sex Transm Dis 1993;20:70–76.

94. Rickert VI, Gottlieb AA, Jay MS. Is AIDS education related to condom acquisition? Clin Pediatr 1992;31:205–210.

95. Caggiula AW, Christakis G, Farrand M, et al. The Multiple Risk Factor Intervention Trial (MRFIT). IV. Intervention on blood lipids. Prev Med 1981;10:443–475.

96. The Writing Group for the DISC Collaborative Research Group. Efficacy and safety of lowering dietary intake of fat and cholesterol in children with elevated low-density lipoprotein cholesterol: the Dietary Intervention Study in Children (DISC). JAMA 1995;273:1429–1435.

97. Gohagan JK, Prorok PC, Kramer BS, et al. Prostate cancer screening in the Prostate, Lung, Colorectal, Ovarian Cancer Screening Trial of the National Cancer Institute. J Urol 1994;152:1905–1909.

98. Department of Health and Human Services, Public Health Service, Office of Disease Prevention and Health Promotion. Put Prevention into Practice education and action kit. Washington, DC: Government Printing Office, 1994.

99. Woolf SH, Jonas S, Lawrence RS, eds. Health promotion and disease prevention in clinical practice. Baltimore: Williams & Wilkins, 1995.

100. Hayward RSA, Steinberg EP, Ford DE, et al. Preventive care guidelines: 1991. Ann Intern Med 1991;114:758–783.

MEDICINE AND PUBLIC HEALTH: THE POWER OF COLLABORATION

Roz D. Lasker and the Committee on Medicine and Public Health

THE COLLABORATIVE IMPERATIVE

An Initial Paradox

When the committee began considering the relationship between medicine and public health, we sought to get a better understanding of the status quo—how professionals in medicine and public health view each other, and the extent and nature of their current interactions. Toward that end we conducted a series of focus groups with professionals and students in the two health sectors. These focus groups included professionals in a broad range of specialties and disciplines who work in diverse settings in the public and private sectors. They were held in five locations around the country—Seattle, WA; New York, NY; Houston, TX; Boston, MA; and Columbia, SC—providing us with urban, rural, and regional perspectives.

The common themes that emerged from these sessions confronted us with an interesting paradox. On the one hand, most of the participants in the focus groups talked about the two health sectors as though they were closely related. It was common for medical professionals to describe public health as a subspecialty of medicine, for example, and for public health professionals to refer to medicine as an arm of public health. Yet participants in both health sectors had quite a bit of difficulty articulating this relationship in practical terms. Most of them had little or no experience working with professionals or organizations in the other sector—in training or in practice. They did not feel that the other sector was particularly interested in their perspectives. They expressed considerable skepticism about each other's motivations. And very few could describe how the activities of the other sector were relevant to what they cared about or did.

These findings immediately raised several questions:

What is the basis for the two health sectors' sense of connection?
Why are they now functioning on separate tracks?

Should anyone be concerned about the current relationship?

Considering the dramatic changes that are occurring in the American health system, are there now compelling reasons for the medical and public health sectors to work more closely together?

The sections that follow attempt to answer these questions. We turn first to the historical relationship between medicine and public health, examining the scientific, political, and economic forces that first brought the two sectors together and that later contributed to their functional separation and cultural divergence. Over the years, leaders in medicine and public health have made a number of attempts to bridge that distance—in medical practice, in medical education, and in the orientation and allocation of health system resources. We review the strategies employed by these leaders and the reasons they failed to change the status quo.

Clearly, the way the medical and public health sectors evolved in this country reflects the response of health professionals and organizations to powerful external forces. In the current environment, however, these forces are changing substantially. We reassess the relationship between medicine and public health in the context of the crisis in health care costs, the marked response to that crisis, the "reinvention" of government, and the emergence of challenging health problems. Our analysis reveals striking shifts in the American health system that are making the two health sectors increasingly dependent on one another. It also identifies new incentives and organizational structures that are making it advantageous and feasible for professionals and organizations in medicine and public health to work more closely together. While the discussion that follows is generally chronological, that is not always the case. To facilitate the reader's orientation, a timeline encompassing the key events in the relationship between medicine and public health that are discussed in the text is presented in Figure 1.[30,107,153]

THE HISTORICAL RELATIONSHIP BETWEEN MEDICINE AND PUBLIC HEALTH

Historically, the relationship between medicine and public health in the United States can be characterized as having proceeded in three phases:

- an early supportive relationship prior to the early 20th century
- a period of professionalization and practice transformation spurred by the emergence of bacteriology
- an acceleration of functional separation in the post-World War II era

As the committee reviewed these phases, the perceptions of the focus group participants became easier to understand. Their tacit assumption of an interrelationship between medicine and public health is a vestige of a common framework the

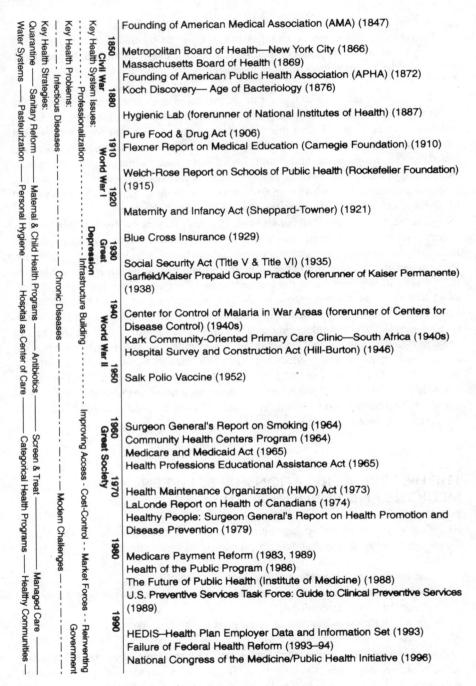

Founding of American Medical Association (AMA) (1847)

Metropolitan Board of Health—New York City (1866)
Massachusetts Board of Health (1869)
Founding of American Public Health Association (APHA) (1872)
Koch Discovery— Age of Bacteriology (1876)

Hygienic Lab (forerunner of National Institutes of Health) (1887)

Pure Food & Drug Act (1906)
Flexner Report on Medical Education (Carnegie Foundation) (1910)

Welch-Rose Report on Schools of Public Health (Rockefeller Foundation) (1915)

Maternity and Infancy Act (Sheppard-Towner) (1921)

Blue Cross Insurance (1929)

Social Security Act (Title V & Title VI) (1935)
Garfield/Kaiser Prepaid Group Practice (forerunner of Kaiser Permanente) (1938)

Center for Control of Malaria in War Areas (forerunner of Centers for Disease Control) (1940s)
Kark Community-Oriented Primary Care Clinic—South Africa (1940s)
Hospital Survey and Construction Act (Hill-Burton) (1946)

Salk Polio Vaccine (1952)

Surgeon General's Report on Smoking (1964)
Community Health Centers Program (1964)
Medicare and Medicaid Act (1965)
Health Professions Educational Assistance Act (1965)

Health Maintenance Organization (HMO) Act (1973)
LaLonde Report on Health of Canadians (1974)
Healthy People: Surgeon General's Report on Health Promotion and Disease Prevention (1979)

Medicare Payment Reform (1983, 1989)
Health of the Public Program (1986)
The Future of Public Health (Institute of Medicine) (1988)
U.S. Preventive Services Task Force: Guide to Clinical Preventive Services (1989)

HEDIS—Health Plan Employer Data and Information Set (1993)
Failure of Federal Health Reform (1993–94)
National Congress of the Medicine/Public Health Initiative (1996)

Figure 1   Medicine and public health timeline (1847–1997)

sectors once shared in addressing health and illness. Their inability to describe a cross-sectoral relationship in practical terms reflects the extent to which medicine and public health had become isolated—in training and in practice—by the time they embarked on their careers. While the factors accounting for this isolation are complex, the analysis that follows suggests that it has four underlying causes: (1) the progressive loss of any perceived need for the two sectors to work together; (2) the lack of adequate incentives or structural foundations to support cross-sectoral relationships; (3) recurring tensions deriving from overlapping interests; and (4) the development of striking cultural differences.

Although societies throughout the world have approached health problems from two distinct vantage points—public health and medicine—these perspectives have not been conceptualized independently. In Greek mythology, for example, the close relationship between healing and health was epitomized by two sisters: Panacea and Hygeia. In the fourth century B.C., Hippocrates espoused a framework that related medical and public health perspectives in practice. In approaching the individual patient, he urged physicians to pay attention to the environmental, social, and behavioral context in which illness occurs: the airs "peculiar to each particular region," the "properties of the waters" the inhabitants drink and use, and "the mode of life of the inhabitants, whether they are heavy drinkers, taking lunch, and inactive, or athletic, industrious, eating much and drinking little."[78]

In the United States, this type of comprehensive framework—encompassing prevention and treatment as well as a broad range of determinants of health—served as a common ground for leaders in medicine and public health from the mid-19th to the early 20th centuries. During this period, the nation's most pressing health problems were infectious diseases. Tuberculosis was "captain of the men of death." Influenza, pneumonia, streptococcal infectious and other airborne diseases struck the population with great force, mainly during the winter months. Infants died routinely as a result of acute communicable respiratory and diarrheal diseases. Measles and chickenpox were a "natural" part of childhood. It was not unusual for women giving birth to succumb to perinatal infections. Smallpox epidemics, with their considerable mortality, struck communities from time to time. Typhoid fever occurred on a small scale, spread within and between families, and occasionally erupted in outbreaks. Cholera epidemics created alarm and were a major cause of death in American ports.

With infectious diseases rampant, there was general agreement that an effective strategy required societal preventive action as well as medical care. Little could be done for patients once they were infected. Moreover, communicable diseases affected everyone—both the wealthy and the workforce—threatening not only people's health but also the economy. Although early public health workers lacked any knowledge of specific etiologic agents, they were able to relate infectious diseases to conditions associated with urbanization and industrialization. Citizen sanitary associations organized efforts to clean up squalid living conditions in the cities.[57] Health departments and boards of health were established to conduct and enforce sanitary measures, and to maintain birth and death records, which were needed to track disease. Together, these voluntary and governmental public health efforts were successful in addressing many of the important risk factors for transmission of communicable disease: overcrowding, poor nutrition, inadequate sewage systems, uncollected garbage, and contaminated water and food.

At this time, with the public health movement focused on sanitary engineering, environmental hygiene, and quarantine—activities unrelated to the direct care of patients—the strategies of public health and medicine were distinct. Nonetheless, leaders in the two sectors overlapped considerably, and many physicians were actively involved in public health efforts. For example:

> John H. Griscom, a physician at the New York Dispensary and the New York Hospital, served as City Inspector of New York. In 1842, he conducted one of the first surveys of conditions in tenement housing and basement schools. He also advocated the construction of better homes and appealed for the study of occupational health, arguing that improved health and longer life expectancy among the productive population made a sound public health investment.
>
> Nathan Smith Davis, one of the founders of the American Medical Association (AMA) in 1847, was instrumental in proposing and getting approval for the construction of a sewerage system and a general hospital in Chicago. He also spearheaded the formation of a local medical society and a society for the care of the poor.
>
> Stephen Smith, a surgeon in the Civil War, was a founding member of the American Public Health Association (APHA) in 1872. He was also a leading member of the New York Sanitary Association, the New York Citizens Association and the Special Council of Hygiene and Public Health, for which he directed a major sanitary survey of New York City, which led to the establishment of the Metropolitan Board of Health.
>
> Henry Bowditch, one of the founders of APHA, served as president of the AMA in 1877. He helped establish the Massachusetts Board of Health in 1869, and served on the National Board of Health in 1879. A paper he wrote in 1874, "Preventive Medicine and the Physician of the Future," condemned the "error and stupidity which does not believe in the duty of studying the physical causes of disease and at least in endeavoring to crush out these originators of pestilence and death."[23]

The key reason that leaders in medicine and public health had such a close relationship during this period was that neither sector could address the infectious disease problem alone; each was in need of something that only the other could provide. Physicians supported public health measures because they could do relatively little on their own. Clinicians could comfort patients and inform them about their prognosis, but medical interventions were relatively ineffective in curing or preventing infectious diseases. Caring about public health was also a status symbol for physicians. It marked the "distinguished practitioner who was above the commercial competition of merely dealing in drugs, bleeding, and purging."[57]

A close relationship with the medical sector also was of benefit to public health. The influence of physicians with policymakers and the public was of substantial value in efforts to institute sanitary reforms and establish health boards. Equally important, clinicians' contact with patients was a useful resource in targeting public health interventions. This was highlighted in an 1852 report of The New York Academy of Medicine, which stated that no one is as "well qualified for the examination and correction of public sources of diseases, in the cellars, the garrets, the courts and cul-de-sacs, and the hollows" as medical practitioners, "whose business it is now to treat, in these very localities, the diseases produced by them."[129]

The emergence of bacteriology in the late 19th century profoundly affected both medicine and public health. On the one hand, the identification of bacteria as the causative agents of infectious diseases contributed to the professionalization of both health sectors. By providing the medical sector with a sound intellectual base and a scientific body of knowledge, bacteriology contributed to its transformation into an organized profession with control over the substance and evaluation of its work. The new science of bacteriology meant that medical practitioners could be held to new standards of knowledge. Licensing regulations and medical practice acts created statewide standards for the practice of medicine. A professional code of ethics established the obligation of physicians to exercise their knowledge and skills in the patient's best interest. In 1910, Abraham Flexner's report for the Carnegie Foundation for the Advancement of Teaching led to a single standard of science-based medical education, expediting the death of proprietary medical schools.[58,109]

Although the public health movement already had a strong scientific foundation in biostatistics and epidemiology, bacteriology also catalyzed the professionalization of public health. The bacteriological laboratory became the symbol of scientific public health. Its operation justified the need for full-time, educated public health personnel, rather than part-time voluntary reformers. In 1913, state legislatures began passing laws requiring public health officers to have specialized training.[56]

In 1915, a Rockefeller Foundation report led to the establishment of science-based schools of public health that could provide this training.[55] These schools were designed to be distinct from schools of medicine for several reasons. A diverse spectrum of personnel—including but going well beyond physicians—are involved in public health. Independent schools of public health were needed to bring together the broad range of expertise and intellectual disciplines integral to their work, to give them a common professional identification and outlook, and to disentangle public health from competing loyalty to medical practice. The early schools of public health were closely tied to medical schools, however. It was commonly believed that public health professionals needed exposure to and understanding of medicine to deal with the prevention and management of disease. There also was a desire to imbue medical schools with the spirit of public health.

The rise of bacteriology as a science did more than professionalize the two health sectors; it also transformed the nature of medical and public health practice. In the medical sector, bacteriology established the biomedical paradigm for elucidating biological causes of disease and for developing therapies—such as antitoxins, and later, antibiotics—that could be directed at patients. By doing so, it dramatically increased the effectiveness of medical diagnosis and treatment.

In public health, the new science led to targeted strategies for controlling specific routes of disease transmission, replacing nonspecific sanitation efforts, which had frequently involved politically contentious social reforms.[56] Some of these new public health initiatives were directed at the environment, for example, the detection and control of bacteria in water systems, the pasteurization of milk, and the eradication of mosquitos to control yellow fever. But other activities were directed at people, previously the sole purview of medicine. Bacteriological laboratories developed tests to diagnose infectious diseases. The prevention of disease through the use of vaccines became a powerful public health and medical strategy.

NEW OPPORTUNITIES FOR INTERACTION

As the medical and public health sectors both began to target interventions at people, new opportunities arose for working together around health problems, which extended beyond the policy interactions that had led to health boards and sanitary reforms. In the area of communicable disease, complementary efforts of medical practitioners and public health professionals had the potential to assure that enough of the population was immunized to protect the health of the entire community. A close relationship between the two health sectors could provide medical practitioners caring for infected patients with valuable supports, such as laboratory testing, antitoxins, and vaccines. Effective avenues of cross-sectoral communication could link the diagnosis of infected individuals in private practices to the timely initiation of essential community-protection responses, such as isolation of the infected individual, disinfection of his or her home, and the identification and treatment of those who had been in contact with the patient.

The health benefits of working together were not limited to communicable diseases. In the early 20th century, the "New Public Health" increasingly focused its attention on health education, maternal and child health, and the detection of unrecognized but treatable impairments. Toward this end, well-baby clinics with home-visiting services were established that provided women with education about diet, child care, and living patterns. Public health nurses were posted in schools to test children for eye problems and other physical impairments that might interfere with learning. Public health campaigns were initiated urging everyone to get preventive health examinations.[160] In this context, a close working relationship between the medical and public health sectors had the capacity to assure that all women and children received appropriate health education; that all children diagnosed as having health problems were later treated by medical practitioners; and that all patients who were being urged to get preventive health examinations had a place to obtain them.

As the century reached its midpoint, and cardiovascular disease and cancer replaced communicable diseases as the major causes of death, further opportunities arose for the medical and public health sectors to combine their resources in addressing health problems. In part, chronic diseases emerged because people were no longer dying of infections in their early years. But these health problems also were a result of increasing economic opportunity, which allowed more people to avoid physical labor, eat fat-filled diets, smoke cigarettes, and consume alcohol. The medical sector tackled coronary artery disease, stroke, and cancer by attempting to elucidate the biological mechanisms of these diseases within the body and by developing effective procedures and drugs that could be used for diagnosis and treatment. The public health sector, on the other hand, worked to identify the environmental, social, and behavioral risk factors that caused such chronic diseases to emerge in susceptible individuals and to develop population-based interventions to reduce those risk factors.

One type of public health intervention centered on the promotion of screening, early diagnosis, and treatment. This approach was used for cancer for which there were effective screening tests (for example, breast and cervical cancer), and for asymptomatic but treatable diseases, such as hypertension and hypercholesterolemia, which increase the risk for stroke and coronary artery disease. Since most people in the country received personal health care services from medical practitioners in private practice, coordinated efforts by the medical and public health sectors had the potential to assure that all patients received appropriate clinical preventive services, and that all individuals identified as having abnormal results through population-based screening programs received follow-up medical services.

Another public health strategy for dealing with chronic diseases focused on modifying the behaviors that make susceptible people develop these problems in the first place. One aspect of this strategy involved counseling of high-risk individuals. Recognizing that lifestyle choices are not made in a vacuum however, the strategy also entailed community-wide campaigns to promote conditions that would make it easier for people to follow medical advice. (For example, to address tobacco use— a key risk factor in the development of both cardiovascular disease and cancer— cigarette taxes, restrictions on tobacco advertising, and smoke-free zones have been instituted to create an environment in which people were more likely to stop smoking—or not to start.)[25] By combining their authority and influence, the two health sectors had the ability not only to promote the adoption of healthful social policies, but also to encourage the provision of behavioral counseling in a broad range of practice environments.

EARLY BARRIERS TO CROSS-SECTORAL COLLABORATIONS

While opportunities for improving health by coordinating medical and public health activities expanded over the course of this century, few of these opportunities were realized in practice. One reason is that the heterogeneous and dispersed health system in this country has not provided a strong structural foundation to support cross-sectoral interactions. Until very recently, the loosely structured medical sector consisted of a vast number of autonomous professionals, most of whom were in solo or small group practices with no clear ties to defined populations. Its other main component, autonomous hospitals and medical centers, have had relationships with practitioners but no clear ties to public health. Although health departments originally were established to support community efforts aimed at the prevention of disease and the promotion of health, these agencies have varied substantially in their capacity to carry out this function. Moreover, they have had little or no jurisdiction over the medical sector.

Equally important, as public health activities increasingly focused on people—overlapping with what was considered to be the domain of the medical sector—thorny "turf" issues impeded the ability of the two health sectors to work cooperatively on health problems. To a large extent, tensions between the two sectors have been fueled by competition and concerns that public health—and government in general—was infringing on physician autonomy and interfering with the doctor-patient relationship. Problems of this sort were prominent in the early part of the century, when the medical sector had not yet solidified its stature in the public eye and when physicians were facing increasing competition from their own rapidly expanding numbers. For example, threatened by public health efforts that might provide free services to patients by whom they might otherwise be paid, some physicians actively resisted well-baby clinics, health centers, and mass immunization programs.[44,50] In the area of communicable disease control, the two sectors were at odds around compulsory reporting of tuberculosis and around the role of public health bacteriological laboratories in providing diagnostic testing for diphtheria and in producing diphtheria antitoxin.[50,57] While AMA and APHA have advocated the same policies in certain areas (for example, the short-lived National Board of Health in 1879, the Pure Food and Drug Act in 1906, and, more recently, the anti-tobacco campaign), they have tended to take opposite sides on issues involving patient care, such as the Sheppard-Towner Act of 1921, which provided federal funds for prenatal and child health clinics, and proposals for various forms of government-sponsored health insurance.[50,110]

Taken together, the lack of a structural foundation for coordinating overlapping activities and the tensions resulting from overlapping interests created significant barriers for medicine and public health collaboration. In 1924, William Henry Welch captured the situation well when he expressed his concern with "the lack of sufficient active participation of the general medical profession in public health activities, especially as developed in this country. The fault is on both sides. There has been encroachment upon the field of the private practitioner, and a lack of sympathy and cooperation with health officials and with health programs on the part of practitioners.[182]

These problems were serious, but they might have been overcome if further barriers to cross-sectoral collaboration had not emerged in the post-World War II era. During this period, rapid advances in scientific knowledge and the institution of new medical and public health programs made each health sector feel considerably more independent, dramatically reducing their perceived need to work together. As the American health system evolved, professionals and organizations had few, if any, incentives to interact with their counterparts in the other sector. With the proliferation of medical specialties, and the progressive categorization and fragmentation of public health, logistical impediments to collaboration became more of a problem. Finally, cultural differences and a growing imbalance in funding between the two health sectors compromised their capacity to trust, respect, and communicate with each other. As a result of these forces, the medical and public health sectors became increasingly isolated. Eventually, they functioned as separate, and virtually independent, parts of the larger health system.

THE IMPACT OF SCIENCE AND HEALTH POLICIES

A key factor in this separation was the success of the biomedical paradigm, which dramatically augmented the medical sector's ability to understand, diagnose, and treat disease. As an increasing array of pharmacological agents and diagnostic and therapeutic procedures became available in the post-World War II period, policies were adopted, which, through their funding streams and economic incentives, encouraged the medical sector to focus more and more exclusively on a "high-tech" curative approach.[57,68,105] Private health insurance—and, later, benefits through the Medicare program—primarily covered acute hospital care, laboratory tests, and procedures, providing generous reimbursement for these services through a fee-for-service payment system. The Hill-Burton Act of 1946 greatly increased the number of hospitals by providing states and localities with federal matching funds for hospital construction. Graduate medical education payments made through the Medicare program supported hospital-based training of large numbers of physicians, substantially increasing the proportion of procedurally oriented specialists. The country's impressive commitment to medical research, funded largely through the National Institutes of Health, centered on biological mechanisms and approaches to disease.

In this environment, careers in biomedical research and the provision of specialized, technologically sophisticated inpatient care were not only financially rewarding but also intellectually stimulating and prestigious. As a result, the medical sector expanded dramatically in the post-World War II period and became increasingly specialized. In 1942, 15 specialty boards were in existence.[161] By 1992, the American Board of Medical Specialties recognized 24 primary boards and 70 subspecialties.[74] For nurses, as well as for physicians, training focused on preparing professionals to perform in specialized, acute care hospital environments.[162] From the point of view of the general public and policymakers, this investment paid off. The pace of biomedical advances accelerated, generating more knowledge about how to diagnose and treat disease, as well as more specialists and hospitals to deliver "state-of-the-art" care. Medical achievements were hailed as "miracles" that provided patients with relief from conditions that would otherwise cause disability and suffering and shorten life. As public expectations grew, policies to encourage the development of biomedical advances and the provision of specialty care became even stronger, establishing a self-sustaining positive feedback loop.

From the point of view of the relationship between medicine and public health, the most important consequence of these developments was that the medical sector became less dependent on and less interested in public health. In contrast to the situation in the 19th and early 20th centuries, medical professionals now had a powerful and growing therapeutic armamentarium at their disposal—one that seemed applicable not only to medical problems but also to the domain of public health. As antibiotics that could cure infectious diseases became available, the importance of prevention seemed to diminish. Moreover, taking a curative approach to chronic diseases seemed to circumvent the need to promote difficult lifestyle changes. Increasingly capable of making great strides on their own, medical practitioners and researchers no longer perceived much need to work with their colleagues in public health. They also lacked any economic incentives to do so. Public and private health insurance provided much higher reimbursement for diagnostic and therapeutic procedures than for clinical preventive services, such as immunization, screening tests, and counseling. Funding streams of the National Institutes of Health set clear priorities for biologically oriented research; very few grant programs encouraged the study of the behavioral, socioeconomic, and environmental factors that influence health. In this context, it was difficult to sustain much interest among medical professionals or schools of medicine in the public health perspective.

While there was significant expansion of the public health sector in the post-World War II period, it was much less extensive than that of the medical sector. Reflecting public demand for biomedical advances, funding was considerably less generous for population-based public health programs than for medical care; for health departments than for hospitals; for epidemiologic and social science investigation than for clinical studies and basic science research; and for the education and training of public health professionals than for those in medicine. In 1990, for example, 2.7 percent of the nation's health dollars went for public health.[34]

To some extent, the growing imbalance between the two health sectors is related to the fact that public health is a public good rather than an individual good. Medical care does well in a free-market economy like the United States because it is closely tied to individuals; the benefits of seeing a medical practitioner are realized directly by the individual receiving care. In public health, on the other hand, the benefits of community-wide strategies to prevent disease and promote health are received by everyone, including people who do not seek out these benefits and those who do not pay for them directly. Moreover, the benefits of public health—the absence of disease—are largely unrecognized. Because the universality and invisibility of these benefits reduce every person's individual interest in paying for public health, funding necessarily depends on taxpayer and other broad-based support.

Ironically, the impressive successes of public health have led to increasing difficulty garnering support for these activities among the general public and policymakers. Historically, the need for a strong public health presence has been closely tied to people's fear of contracting infectious diseases. But with the successful control of polio in the 1950s, and the availability of a formidable array of antibiotics and vaccines, the communicable disease problem seemed to have been conquered. It was more difficult for the public to appreciate the role of public health in dealing with chronic illnesses. Since cardiovascular disease is not contagious—and, until recently, cancer was not seen as related to infectious agents[108]—these problems were not perceived as a public health threat. Moreover, both the public and policymakers favored medical treatments and cures over prevention efforts. Changing the social and environmental conditions that cause susceptible individuals to come down with chronic diseases is difficult and, at times, politically contentious. Curative strategies, by contrast, do not typically require behavioral change or engender opposition from businesses, such as tobacco companies, anxious to protect their economic interests.[147]

Responding to changes in public perceptions—as well as to available funding streams—the public health sector became increasingly fragmented and disease-oriented, and it devoted a greater proportion of its resources to providing safety-net services for people left out of the mainstream medical system. Prior to World War II, public health funding primarily had supported the development of health agencies at federal, state, and local levels (with limited resources for the training of public health personnel).[57,105] With the control of communicable diseases, however, it became more difficult to obtain support for "generic" public health. Beginning in the 1960s, legislators created new government agencies, apart from health departments, to deal with problems such as environmental protection, occupational safety, water quality, air pollution control, community-based mental health, and substance abuse.[25] They also created a plethora of categorical public health programs, each of which addressed a specific disease or targeted services to a particular population, and each of which was supported by a defined interest group.[57] With federal funding for community and migrant health centers and the introduction of the Medicaid program, a large part of the expansion of the public health sector centered on providing medical care for the poor. Over the last three decades, state and local health departments have become major providers, directly and indirectly, of personal health services to indigent populations.[117,119] Recent estimates suggest that these activities account for two-thirds of state budgets for public health.[36,117]

The nature of public health expansion further contributed to the separation of the two health sectors. Through its categorical programs and safety-net services, the public health sector reinforced prevailing policies by accepting responsibility for certain activities that the medical sector had the expertise and training to perform but had little incentive or interest to do. In addressing categorical problems such as immunization, lead toxicity, sexually transmitted diseases, and tuberculosis, the public health sector provided not only population-based services—such as surveillance, public education campaigns, screening, linkage with medical services, contact-tracing, and environmental detoxification—but clinical services as well. In addressing the medical needs of the poor, the public health sector provided not only outreach and enabling services (which help people gain access to a medical practitioner), but also primary care. While other approaches may not have been feasible, taking on these responsibilities effectively relieved the mainstream medical sector of any obligation to provide certain types of clinical services or to provide medical care for certain types of patients. Moreover, by providing essential linkages between medical and public health services within the context of its own programs and clinics, the public health sector also created the impression that there was little need for the two health sectors to interact.

Even if medical professionals had wanted to develop a closer working relationship with the public health sector, it was becoming increasingly difficult to know "whom to call." The progressive fragmentation of public health activities among numerous categorical programs and government agencies made it hard for virtually anyone to define or relate to public health. With its increasing safety-net activities, many people developed a distorted and narrow view of public health, equating it either with publicly financed medicine or with medical care for the poor.

SEPARATE AND INDEPENDENT HEALTH SECTORS

The divergence of the American health system during the post-World War II period led to the development of two distinct sectors—characterized more easily by their differences than by any common ground. The dominant, highly respected medical sector focused on individual patients, emphasizing technologically sophisticated diagnosis and treatment and biological mechanisms of disease. The considerably smaller, less well appreciated public health sector concentrated on populations, prevention, nonbiological determinants of health, and safety-net primary care. Medical investigation was based on biology, chemistry, and physics. Public health research was grounded in epidemiology and biostatistics, frequently making use of the social sciences as well. Medical practitioners were usually self-employed in the private sector, working autonomously in solo or small group practices. Virtually everyone in public health was employed by some type of organization, many by government agencies, which are closely linked to the political world. Payment in the medical sector tended to be on a fee-for-service or cost basis, which encouraged professionals to do everything possible for the patient at hand. Public health professionals typically worked from fixed budgets, juggling limited dollars to achieve the greatest benefit for the entire population.

Although these differences are striking, they need not have prevented constructive medicine and public health interactions in and of themselves. After all, the two sectors' professional perspectives and expertise were largely complementary, and professional relationships do not necessarily require that partners have the same views about financial matters and political strategies. For medicine and public health professionals, however, differences became stereotypical and, ultimately, a serious barrier because there was insufficient trust, understanding, and mutual respect to enable them to relate their activities and interests to each other or to accept differences in each other's points of view.[28] In part, this "cultural divide" stemmed from the striking imbalance between medicine and public health in terms of resources, income, value, and prestige, which created a virtual "class barrier" between the two sectors. It also was fueled by diminishing interactions. With little perceived need to work together—or meaningful incentives to do so—the two health sectors increasingly functioned as though they were separate and independent health systems, rather than reinforcing parts of a larger whole. By not working together—in training or in practice—they became more and more foreign to, and intolerant of, each other. As the cultural divide deepened, the capacity to trust, respect, and communicate with each other was weakened further, making collaborative relationships even more difficult than they had been before.

This environment, which shaped the training and practice experience of most health professionals working today, goes a long way toward explaining the results of our focus groups: the two sectors' lack of experience working together; their suspicions and skepticism about each others' motivations; their contention that the other sector is not particularly interested in their own perspectives; and their difficulty articulating what a meaningful collaborative relationship is or could be. It also helps to explain why so few cross-sectoral strategies—balancing prevention with treatment and addressing the full range of determinants of health—were implemented in the post-World War II period.

As medicine and public health became separate worlds, professionals in the two sectors lost the common framework they had shared in the 19th century, which had allowed them to appreciate the value and relevance of each other's perspectives. Without that mutually accepted framework, encompassing both prevention and treatment as well as the full range of determinants of health, it became very difficult for medical and public health professionals to understand each other's approaches to health problems or to see how the two sectors' unique skills and expertise could fit together in a coordinated strategy. As a result, approaches that were, in fact, complementary, were pursued independently by each sector, making them appear dichotomous and competitive.

In a health system increasingly dominated by the medical sector, it is not surprising that in the "contest" for resources, the biomedical approach usually "won." So, for example, preventive measures were difficult to sustain when drug treatment became available for tuberculosis. Strategies for addressing infant mortality focused far more on keeping low birthweight babies alive through neonatal intensive care units than on decreasing the incidence of low birthweight through the delivery of prenatal care or through community-wide strategies to reduce risk factors for low birthweight, such as smoking, drug abuse, and teenage pregnancy. For chronic diseases like noninsulin-dependent diabetes, far more attention was paid to developing pharmacologic interventions to control blood glucose levels than to addressing the social conditions and unhealthful lifestyles that triggered the development of diabetes in genetically susceptible individuals, for example, by increasing the availability of healthful food choices, by establishing incentives, opportunities, and safe environments for exercise, and by educating people at risk through individual counseling and media campaigns.

The point here is not to imply that either the medical or public health approach is better than the other—both clearly have important roles to play in any rational scheme to address these health problems. The real issue is that, in the diverging health system, the two sectors did not value each other's approaches or consider them together. Going off on separate tracks made it difficult to realize the full potential of the medical and public health perspectives or to allocate resources in the best interest of both individual and population health.

THE CURRENT PREDICAMENT

If the environment in which health professionals work had remained as it was in the late 1970s, it would be difficult to justify yet another attempt to bridge the gap between medicine and public health. The American health system, however, has undergone dramatic changes since that time. These changes have shattered any possibility of continuing the status quo, and they are making it not only desirable but also imperative for professionals in the two health sectors to re-evaluate their relationship. Today, in striking contrast to what had previously been the norm

- both sectors are concerned about the direction of the health system;
- both are under economic and performance pressure;
- neither can accomplish their mission alone.

Several forces are driving the destabilization and growing interdependence of medicine and public health. The crisis in health care costs, the market response to that crisis, and the movement to reinvent government are radically altering the environment in which medical and public health professionals work. At the same time, the changing spectrum of health problems in this country is having a profound impact on the work that health professionals need to do.

Between 1960 and 1990, spending for health care grew at almost 6 percent per year (adjusted for inflation)—more than double the growth rate of the rest of the economy.[63] Health expenditures in the United States are now approaching $1 trillion per year (or $4,000 for every person in the country).[105] In part, the cost crisis is a consequence of the two health sectors' success in preventing and treating acute disease, which has led to an expanding older population and an increasing burden of chronic disease. It also reflects the increasing availability of expensive drugs and medical technology in an environment in which economic incentives—such as fee-for-service and cost-based payment—actively encourage their use.

By the late 1970s, skyrocketing costs of Medicare, Medicaid, and employer-sponsored health insurance, coupled with a troubled economy, forced government and business to confront the expenditure issue. Various strategies were implemented to reduce health cost inflation, including wage and price controls, prospective hospital payment, physician fee schedules, selective contracting, and prepaid health plans.[19] In the early 1990s, with U.S. health expenditures higher than any other country in the world, with U.S. health indicators lagging behind those of many other developed countries, with a growing number of workers uninsured, and with mounting fears among the middle class about the loss of health insurance, the federal government considered comprehensive proposals for overhauling the health system.[105] When government-driven efforts at health reform failed in 1994, market forces took over the health care system, and a movement to reinvent government swept America.[69,131]

Currently, the market solution to escalating health care costs is managed care. The term "managed care" describes strategies that health care organizations use to control the cost and quality of medical services. In some more experienced organizations, it is defined as a style of practice. While all managed care organizations insure plan members and furnish the care they receive, they carry out these functions in diverse ways. Managed care organizations can be for-profit or not-for-profit, local or part of a national chain, tightly managed staff models or looser organizations that contract with independent providers, group practices, or networks. The growth of managed care has been accelerating in recent years—in both the private market and government-funded health programs. In 1995, 54 million Americans were enrolled in health maintenance organizations and as many as 130 million were insured in one or another form of managed care (including preferred provider organizations and point-of-service plans).[18] Nationally, more than 25 percent of Medicaid recipients and 10 percent of Medicare beneficiaries are currently enrolled in managed care organizations.[145] The most rapid rate of growth has been in for-profit managed care organizations.

Managed care uses market leverage to achieve what Americans have not allowed government to do: reduce the excess capacity in the medical sector that was stimulated by post-World War II policies and curtail the inflation of health care costs.[11,141] For the most part, managed care organizations do this by imposing large price discounts or financial risk on providers. The latter reverses fee-for-service incentives for ever-greater consumption of medical care. As a result of market forces, hospitals have been downsizing, merging, and closing. Physicians have been moving to employed positions, and some (particularly specialists) have been experiencing reductions in their incomes. Power has been shifting from specialists to generalists, from physicians to nonphysician practitioners, and from medical professionals to managers, corporate executives, and investors. Recently, the country has begun to experience a backlash to managed care. As a result, policymakers are focusing increasing attention on consumer protection and quality issues.

At the same time as the market is playing a greater role in the health system, government's role is being redefined. The government reform movement that the country is currently experiencing reflects the voters' lack of faith in government programs. While government is a key instrument of community action, it is increasingly being perceived as bureaucratic, regulatory, and inefficient. In this context, taxpayers appear unwilling to pay more money for publicly funded health programs. Along with market forces, this tightening of public funds is threatening support for the health system's public goods: research, health professions education, population-based public health programs, and care for the substantial number of un- and underinsured.

Government reform is being implemented through five key mechanisms: devolution, downsizing, privatization, integration, and "results budgeting." Consistent with the trend in the private sector to move away from top-down hierarchical systems, devolution is moving authority and fiscal responsibility from the federal government to the states, and from the states to counties and cities. Downsizing is being spurred by tax reductions as well as by concerns about future tax increases. Its main consequences for the health system have been reductions in personnel and funding for public health programs, and, in some cases, termination of programs. Downsizing coupled with the need for greater flexibility (for example, to implement a program rapidly or to overcome "red tape") is leading many state and local health departments to privatize certain public health services. Fueled by frustrations in addressing persistent health problems, government agencies are attempting to integrate related programs, and legislatures are beginning to link the appropriation of funds to documentation that desired results are being achieved (a process known as "results budgeting").

Compounding the anxiety that is being engendered by market forces and the redefined role of government, today's health professionals also are facing an extremely challenging and disconcerting set of health problems. They are witnessing the reemergence of diseases that many thought were "conquered," such as measles and tuberculosis. Drug resistance is becoming an increasingly common and worrisome phenomenon. New diseases are emerging, such as HIV/AIDS, that resist easy approaches to prevention or cure. "Old" diseases, such as cervical cancer and peptic ulcer, are being found to have new and unexpected causes. Chronic diseases are persistent, and, some, like noninsulin-dependent diabetes, seem to defy translating what is known about prevention and treatment into routine public health and medical practice. Problems with prominent social components, such as violence, substance abuse, and teenage pregnancy, which do not fit easily into the disease model, are being classified as health problems. And striking differences in health status—according to race, ethnicity, and socioeconomic status—are becoming a disturbing "norm" in America's increasingly diverse society. In this "brave new world," professionals and organizations in medicine and public health are under intense pressure. All are facing challenges to their stature and authority, all are concerned about their economic viability, and all are having difficulty carrying out their professional roles. At the same time certain aspects of the current environment are increasing the relevance of each sector's perspectives, resources, and skills to the other sector. Striking shifts in the health system are making the medical and public health sectors increasingly dependent on one another. New incentives are making it advantageous for professionals and organizations in the two sectors to work more closely together. And new organizational structures are making cross-sectoral interactions easier and more efficient to carry out. In this environment, continuing on separate tracks is not in the best interest of either medicine or public health. Today, professionals and institutions in the two sectors need each other and can help each other—not only in addressing their patients' and populations' health problems, but also in promoting their own professional and economic health.

Below, we discuss six factors that are contributing to these changes:

- shifts in patient populations
- shifts in clinical services
- shifts in perspectives
- shifts in financing streams
- economic and performance pressures
- consolidation and partnerships

SHIFTS IN PATIENT POPULATIONS

As states are moving to managed care contracts and "medical home" initiative to control costs in their Medicaid programs, increasing numbers of patients who previously had received care through public hospitals and public health clinics are being shifted to "mainstream" medical settings.[141] As a result, hospitals and physician groups that previously had little experience with Medicaid patients are now becoming involved in their care. As a group, Medicaid recipients differ in important ways from patients traditionally seen in the private sector. They tend to be poorer and less well educated. They also are more likely to have multiple risk factors for disease and to suffer from serious mental and physical health problems, such as cardiovascular disease, sexually transmitted diseases (STDs), lead toxicity, multidrug-resistant tuberculosis (MDR-TB), substance abuse, and HIV/AIDS.[32]

Because of these differences, it is more difficult to deliver medical care successfully to Medicaid recipients than to the healthier, more affluent enrollees traditionally covered by managed care organizations. Rather than simply waiting for patients to come into the office, effective care for many Medicaid recipients depends on the ability to overcome physical, cultural, and social barriers to care, to get into the home environment and provide follow-up services, and to link patients with other relevant services and programs in the community.[45]

In governmental and community-based public health clinics, medical care for Medicaid recipients traditionally has been linked to special "wraparound" services designed to meet these needs. Some of these services, such as transportation, translation, and child care, help patients gain access to and communicate with their practitioner. Others, such as home visits, reinforce and extend what takes place during an office or clinic visit. Home visits often are invaluable in providing follow-up care—for high-risk mothers, for instance—and in helping patients and their families deal with complex medical regimens, such as those used to manage asthma, diabetes, or HIV/AIDS. They also are of benefit in promoting compliance with treatment programs. For example, visits to a patient's home can reinforce the need for treatment in asymptomatic conditions, such as hypertension, and they can be used to verify that medications actually are taken by patients with problems like MDR-TB.

In addition to providing wraparound services, public health clinics also frequently have provided their medical practitioners with ways to link patient care to population-based public health services and to social support services in the community. Easy access to public health services is important in dealing with certain health problems that are prevalent in the Medicaid population, such as lead poisoning. To prevent the recurrence of lead toxicity in a child with that condition—and to protect other children from being exposed to lead from the same source—appropriate follow-up is needed to identify the source of the contamination, to educate the child's family, and to remove the lead hazard from the child's school or home. The availability of effective links to social support services also is valuable to clinicians caring for Medicaid recipients. These services can help assure that patients retain their health insurance coverage, obtain access to available nutritional support, and are referred to needed ancillary services, such as substance-abuse treatment programs.

With the shift to Medicaid managed care, many of these same wraparound, public health, and social services are now needed in mainstream medical settings. Without this support, it is virtually impossible for medical practitioners to provide effective medical care to many Medicaid recipients. But few managed care organizations, and even fewer medical practices, have the experience, expertise, or structures to provide such services themselves. Moreover, no states include in their contracts with managed care organizations all of the care and services they have been covering under their Medicaid programs.[32] To assure the provision of effective care to Medicaid recipients in mainstream medical environments, new relationships need to be established between professionals and organizations in medicine and public health.

SHIFTS IN CLINICAL SERVICES

The new health care environment is characterized not only by a shift of Medicaid recipients from public health settings to the mainstream medical sector but by a shift of clinical services as well. This shift in services goes beyond the medical care required by Medicaid patients themselves. It also encompasses clinical services that public health professionals previously had provided to some privately insured patients and Medicare beneficiaries: preventive services that the medical sector had few incentives to provide, and certain diagnostic and treatment services that are critical to protecting the entire community's health.

Two important changes in the health system are driving this shift in services. One impetus is the expanded coverage for clinical preventive services—such as immunizations, mammograms, Pap tests, and counseling—in private and publicly sponsored health insurance programs. Until recently, clinical preventive services were not commonly included in private health insurance, and were not part of the benefits package in the Medicare program. Consequently, most people either paid their regular medical practitioner for these services "out-of-pocket," obtained them in public health settings (such as clinics, health fairs, or other public health-sponsored events), or did not receive them at all.

In the current environment, however, public and private purchasers are increasingly requiring the inclusion of clinical preventive services by the plans with which they contract. These plans, in turn, are either reimbursing medical practitioners for the delivery of these services or including them as part of the capitation payments made to primary care practitioners. Through report cards such as the Health Plan Employer Data and Information Set (HEDIS), developed by the National Committee for Quality Assurance (NCQA), managed care organizations are reporting to purchasers the rate at which certain clinical preventive services are actually being delivered.[126] In part, expanded coverage for clinical preventive services reflects the increasing emphasis on primary care in the health system, the development of evidence-based guidelines for these services by the U.S. Preventive Services Task Force,[180] and the growing interest in wellness on the part of the public. It also has been fueled by the savings that can be achieved through the delivery of certain preventive services, such as childhood immunization, prenatal care, intensive ophthalmic screening in patients with insulin-dependent diabetes, and influenza immunization in the elderly.[166]

The other driving force behind the shift in clinical services is that managed care organizations are giving their enrollees fewer options to go "out-of-network" for care. Under unrestricted indemnity insurance, which is rapidly becoming extinct, all qualified providers—including public health clinics—were eligible to receive payment for covered services. Consequently, individuals who had such insurance could selectively obtain certain services in public health settings. Often they chose this route for concerns or problems that they did not want their regular practitioner (or parent or spouse) to know about, such as family planning, STDs, and HIV/AIDS. Under most forms of managed care, however, clinical services related to these problems are usually part of "in-network" benefits. If a public health clinic is not part of a managed care organization network, services provided in that setting are either partially covered by the managed care organization or not covered at all. Equally important, if certain services are covered under public managed care contracts, taxpayers are less likely to be willing to subsidize such services for managed care enrollees in publicly funded clinics as well. In some areas, and for some services, the impact of these forces is substantial. In San Francisco, for example, two-thirds of all STD cases are now diagnosed and treated in managed care settings rather than in traditional STD clinics.[89]

These shifts in services have the potential to improve clinical practice by integrating prevention and health maintenance more fully with medical diagnosis and treatment. At the same time, however, they are disrupting critical linkages between clinical and population-based services that had been established through categorical public health programs. Even more important, they are making the medical sector a key player in public health strategies that are critical to the entire community's health.

As the medical sector is becoming a *de facto* arm of prevention, the two health sectors are becoming considerably more dependent on each other than they have been for much of the post–World War II period. In the area of immunization, for example, the public health sector needs to be sure that immunizations included as medical benefits are, in fact, delivered. Otherwise, not enough of the population will be immunized to protect the community at large. The medical sector, on the other hand, is increasingly under pressure to document that target immunization rates have been achieved—not only for the sake of public health, but also for report cards, such as HEDIS.

Numerous studies have shown that it is not possible to achieve either of these goals simply by making immunizations available. In managed care organizations, for example, rates were found to be low even among children with multiple encounters per year, and even when immunization was not associated with any copayment.[80] In 1989–91, a failure in preschool immunization resulted in over 55,000 cases of measles in the United States with 130 measles-associated deaths.[14] To achieve adequate childhood immunization levels in today's environment, the medical sector's increasing attention to this problem needs to be reinforced with strategies that can help clinicians identify and influence parents who are not seeking out indicated immunizations, and account for children in their practices who are getting their immunizations elsewhere. Managed care organizations and structured practices can offer clinicians valuable supports in this regard, including patient education and outreach; reminders; tracking and feedback of results; and various incentives and rewards.[169,170] These can be reinforced substantially by community-wide public health strategies. Public education and media campaigns, for example, can help "funnel" patients in need of immunizations to their practitioners' offices; wraparound services can help address logistical barriers that some patients face in accessing care; and community-wide immunization registries can keep track of the immunization status of individual patients, regardless of where they obtain their care or whether they are stable members of a practice or managed care organization population.

The shift in services is making the two health sectors interdependent not only around immunization, but in other areas as well. As health problems such as lead poisoning, MDR-TB, and STDs increasingly are being diagnosed and treated outside of categorical public health programs, new linkages are needed between mainstream medical practice and public health agencies to assure that an adequate community protection response occurs. The discussion around shifts in the Medicaid population highlighted the importance of linking the diagnosis and treatment of children with lead toxicity to environmental lead-abatement interventions. Without such linkages, lead toxicity is likely to recur in affected children, as well as in other children in the same environment who also are at risk of developing the problem. Effective linkages also are needed in the area of communicable diseases, such as STDs, TB, and HIV/AIDS. For example, to limit the spread and long-term sequelae of these diseases, the diagnosis and treatment of an individual patient needs to be linked to public health efforts to identify and test those with whom the patient has been in contact. To assure compliance and prevent the development of drug resistance, mainstream medical practices need ready access to wraparound services, such as home visits and transportation, that can help patients manage complex medical regimens, and to programs providing directly observed therapy.

SHIFTS IN PERSPECTIVES

Another important aspect of the new environment is that certain perspectives and tools of public health are becoming considerably more relevant to the medical sector. To a large extent, this is happening because of the financial risk associated with managed care. All managed care organizations, regardless of type, contract with purchasers to provide a predetermined set of benefits to a defined population of enrollees for a fixed annual price. The risk for delivering medical care within this budget can be assumed by a managed care organization or integrated system that employs or contracts with medical professionals. Alternatively, it can be borne by practitioners themselves through capitated physician networks and large group practices.[142] In either case, as medical organizations and physicians take on financial risk, they are under increasing pressure to anticipate health service demands accurately and to practice cost-effectively. In effect, their economic viability is becoming dependent on population-based data, epidemiologic analyses, and public health strategies.

Managing financial risk successfully requires up-to-date information from the scientific literature about what works, what doesn't, for whom, and at what cost. It also requires a solid understanding of one's own medical organization: the health needs of the patient population in a medical practice, integrated system, or managed care organization; the way medical care is provided to that population; and the outcomes of that care. Data about the health status and health risks of the patient population are relevant to this need, as are epidemiologic analyses that assess the effectiveness and costs of the organization's medical practices. In addition to organizational-level data, information about the community at large—the pool from which the enrolled or practice population is drawn—is often critical as well. This is particularly true for managed care organizations, integrated systems, and group practices that are considering taking on financial risk for a new population, or that seek to expand their presence in a geographic area. In the latter case, the health of the entire community becomes relevant, since the health and behavior of those not enrolled in the organization can affect the medical needs (and costs) of its members. Moreover, anyone not enrolled today has a good chance of becoming enrolled tomorrow.[1]

Clearly, these changes are making the public health perspective more pertinent to the medical sector. Indeed, a growing number of medical professionals are seeking training in biostatistics, clinical epidemiology, and cost-effectiveness analysis.[174] At the same time, the move to managed care and the bearing of financial risk is making the medical sector more dependent on public health, and vice versa. Increasingly, professionals in medicine and public health have a common need for population-based data about health and functional status, the prevalence and underlying causes of disease and disability, and the utilization, costs, and effectiveness of health services.[75] Yet, in the current environment, neither sector is able to amass this information alone. As a greater proportion of the population is moving into managed care, public health agencies are losing certain sources of information (for example, fee-for-service claims data, and information they had collected about clients in their own programs), making it more difficult to compile community-wide health statistics. The medical sector also is experiencing information problems. The instability of some enrolled populations (especially those in the Medicaid program) is creating a need among managed care organizations and group practices for information frameworks, such as immunization registries, that go beyond the data that they can collect themselves.

As the medical sector takes on financial risk, it also is becoming economically dependent on the public health sector, particularly on the capacity of public health agencies to prevent unnecessary disease from occurring in the community. Under capitation—in striking contrast to fee-for-service or cost-based payment—treating medical problems consumes the medical sector's resources instead of increasing its revenues. Consequently, in today's environment, managed care organizations and capitated medical practices bear the costs of treating patients who come down with diseases that occur when efforts to protect the community's food, water, housing, and environment fail.[134] These costs can be substantial. The 1993 cryptosporidium outbreak in Milwaukee, for example, a result of a failure to protect the water supply, affected 370,000 people at a cost of $15.5 million.[105] To avoid such expenses, the medical sector has an incentive to pay more attention than it has in the past to the effectiveness and funding of agencies carrying responsibility for community health protection. It also has an incentive to work more closely with the public health sector in a variety of other prevention activities, such as immunization, bicycle helmet use, and initiatives to discourage drunk driving.

SHIFTS IN FINANCING STREAMS

With the move to Medicaid managed care, managed care organizations are not only taking over Medicaid patients, they also are taking over these patients' Medicaid revenue. This shift in financing streams is making it extremely difficult for public health "safety-net" providers to subsidize care for the uninsured. Equally important, it may be compromising the capacity of some public health agencies to provide population-based services that are essential to protecting the community's health.

A particularly disturbing aspect of the current environment is that a large number of people in the United States have no health insurance or inadequate coverage. Estimates suggest that 39 to 42 million people are uninsured at any one time, and as many as 60 million people are uninsured at some time during the calendar year.[141] People without health insurance have less access to medical care, and are twice as likely to be hospitalized for avoidable conditions.[141]

For most of the post-World War II period, medical care for the un- and underinsured has been provided primarily by a safety net of public health agencies, not-for-profit public health clinics, public hospitals, and academic health centers. To a large extent, these safety-net providers have funded their services with tax dollars and cross-subsidies from Medicaid reimbursement.[89] Mainstream hospitals and medical practitioners also have played a role, subsidizing the care they have provided to the uninsured by raising the fees they charged to paying patients. In the current context of discount pricing and financial risk, private hospitals and medical practices are less able to cross-subsidize care for the indigent. Moreover, as safety-net providers are losing both their Medicaid patients and Medicaid revenue, they are finding it increasingly difficult to finance the care of a rising proportion of uninsured patients.[45] The economic impact of these changes is being felt by both health sectors. Obviously, it is threatening the survival of many safety-net providers. But it is also a problem for the mainstream medical sector. When uninsured people lack access to timely medical care, high emergency room costs are borne not only by public hospitals but also by private hospitals and integrated systems. If public health clinics and public hospitals do not remain viable, the financial burden on these private institutions is likely to increase.

The shift in the Medicaid financing stream also may be having a less anticipated effect—it may be undermining the capacity of governmental public health agencies to deliver population-based services, such as monitoring of health status, disease investigation, and protection against outbreaks of disease. Recent estimates suggest that approximately 1 percent of the nation's health expenditures are devoted to these types of activities.[36,117] The reemergence of "conquered" health problems like tuberculosis, as well as recent outbreaks of preventable childhood diseases and of food-borne and water-borne diseases, have raised concerns that this level of funding is not adequate to protect the public's health. Indeed, the 1988 IOM report, *The Future of Public Health,* described the American public health system as in "disarray" and a "threat to the health of the public."[86] Since the publication of that report, a number of public health agencies have been reevaluating their role, and many are attempting to strengthen their capacity to provide essential population-based services, in some cases by moving away from direct patient care.

The delivery of personal health care services can either support or detract from population-based public health activities. With limited funds for population-based services, some health departments have used home health visits to underwrite community-wide prevention functions. For others, fulfilling the safety-net role has claimed staffing and funding that otherwise might have supported essential population-based activities.[68] Regardless of the approach used, the loss of Medicaid revenue is likely to have a detrimental effect on the capacity of these health departments to fulfill their community-wide responsibilities. It either will result in a loss of funds that previously were used to subsidize essential population-based services, or it may redirect limited health department resources away from population-based activities to more "urgent" safety-net medical care.

Various aspects of the current environment are influencing the ability of health departments to obtain public funds for generic population-based services. As described earlier, funding for such activities has been very difficult to achieve in the post-World War II period. On one level, it is even more difficult in the current environment. With the new focus of managed care on patient populations and on clinical prevention, some people have the misperception that managed care organizations are taking over responsibility for the entire population and for community-wide prevention activities. In this context, public health agencies are under increasing pressure to justify the need for what they do. On the other hand, the assumption of financial risk is making the capacity of public health agencies to prevent or quickly address community health problems a real economic concern to the medical sector. Consequently, managed care organizations and capitated practices could become a vocal constituency for adequate health department funding and staffing.

ECONOMIC AND PERFORMANCE PRESSURES

The striking shifts in the American health system—in patients, services, perspectives, and financing streams—are revealing various ways that the medical and public health sectors are becoming dependent on each other and can reinforce each other in today's challenging environment. The strongest impetus for actually *establishing* cross-sectoral relationships, however, may come from the health system's growing emphasis on cost containment and on documenting results. As economic and performance pressures intensify, success is much more likely if professionals and institutions in the two health sectors work together than if they continue to work alone.

As health expenditures in this country approach $1 trillion per year, pressures to contain costs are mounting. Purchasers of medical and public health services—government, employers, and consumers—are resisting increases in health insurance premiums, in taxes, and in out-of-pocket expenses. Moreover, they want every dollar that they spend to count—to go toward results they care about. These expectations are having a profound impact on the environment in which the two health sectors work. Through market forces and government reform, professionals and organizations in medicine and public health are expected to carry out their roles with fewer personnel and for less money. Through report cards, which sometimes are used for accreditation and performance-based contracting, they are expected to show that meaningful results are being achieved for that money. Increasingly, the types of results that they are being asked to document are not institutional process measures, but rather indicators of health outcomes and quality, such as access to care, satisfaction with care, delivery of essential health services, reductions in morbidity and mortality, reductions in risk factors, and improvements in health status and functional status.

In the medical sector, a variety of datasets are being used to assess the quality and results of clinical care for defined patient populations. These datasets include HEDIS (the National Committee on Quality Assurance report card referred to earlier), New York's Quality Assurance Reporting Requirements (QARR), and sets of performance indicators developed by the Joint Commission on Accreditation and Healthcare Organizations (JCAHO) and the Foundation for Accountability.[60,92,93,126] JACHO also requires community health status measures from hospitals.[92,93] In the public health sector, where health assessment focuses on the community at large, performance measurement has centered around *Healthy People* objectives. Beginning in 1980 with *Promoting Health/Preventing Disease: Objectives for the Nation,* these measures have been updated every ten years (the latest version is *Healthy People 2000*), and are reported nationally on a regular basis.[177-179] Faced with limited resources and a range of difficult health problems, state and local governments are prioritizing health objectives to address in their own communities. While these "health priorities," usually are selected from the measures included in *Healthy People,* they sometimes go beyond them.

Economic and performance pressures are providing compelling reasons for professionals and organizations in medicine and public health to work more closely together. In this type of environment, both sectors are looking for ways to achieve economies of scale, to provide services more efficiently, to reduce duplication of effort, and to increase productivity. When neither sector has the time or resources to do everything itself, collaborative relationships begin to make sense, particularly if each sector focuses on areas in which it has special expertise or which would be inefficient for the other sector to perform. In the medical sector, the shift from fee-for-service and cost-based payment to capitation and financial risk is reinforcing this incentive to partner. Under the old payment structure, medical practitioners and institutions were rewarded financially for doing more themselves. In the current environment, by contrast, they have an economic incentive to focus on what they do best and to work with others whose skills and resources complement their own.

Another compelling reason to collaborate is that the health outcomes that are being measured—whether they relate to improvements in health status for the community at large or to the delivery and quality of clinical services for defined patient populations—often depend on factors beyond any one sector's direct control. In today's environment, the medical sector's performance in HEDIS and JCAHO measures frequently is dependent on public health strategies. Similarly, the public health sector's capacity to achieve health priorities and *Healthy People 2000* objectives often is dependent on the involvement of a broad range of partners in the community, including the medical sector. Considering economic and performance pressures together, the two health sectors are likely to experience particularly strong incentives for working together around health outcomes that are being monitored in both sectors (for example, by HEDIS or JCAHO and by *Healthy People* or locally set health priorities) and in areas where collaborative relationships allow each sector to achieve its goals more efficiently as well as more effectively.

While the move to managed care has made performance measurement in the medical sector possible (by establishing clear denominator populations of sufficient size to be measured reliably), medical professionals, on their own, face serious challenges in meeting performance goals. For one thing, performance measurement dramatically changes the expectations of practice. Previously, a clinician's responsibility was to do everything possible for patients who took the initiative to visit the office. But achieving specific health outcomes means paying attention to patients who do not actively seek out care, and to factors, such as compliance and health-seeking behaviors, that depend on more than what medical practitioners can do in their offices. Linking some of the public health strategies described in this chapter to medical practice could be useful in addressing these challenges. Wraparound and outreach services, for example, can help patients overcome logistical barriers to accessing care and help them manage and comply with treatment regimens. Community-wide screening programs and public education campaigns can help funnel patients in need of care to their practitioner's offices. Community-wide information systems, such as immunization registries, can keep track of whether individuals have received particular clinical services, regardless of where these services are provided.

While the public health sector always has had a clear geopolitical population for measuring performance, making headway on the types of health problems that the public and policymakers care about requires considerably more than what public health professionals and agencies can do on their own. On the one hand, today's most pressing health problems have multiple, intertwined medical, social, and economic causes.[89] Equally important, the shifts in patient populations, clinical services, and financing streams that characterize the current environment are making it essential for the public health sector to work with and through the mainstream medical sector in achieving many of its *Healthy People 2000* goals. A number of medicine and public health linkages described earlier in this chapter could be useful in this regard. For example, public health goals that depend on the delivery of covered clinical services, such as up-to-date childhood immunizations, can be furthered by the institution of organizational supports—reminder systems, practitioner feedback, incentives and rewards—by managed care organizations and medical practices. Goals that depend on "screen and treat" strategies, such as the control of hypertension, are easier to achieve if mechanisms are in place to assure that individuals with abnormal results actually see a medical practitioner for follow-up diagnostic testing and treatment. The large number of health promotion goals that depend on influencing behavior are more likely to be achieved if medical practices and managed care organizations put in place incentive systems and organizational supports that promote the delivery of counseling to their patient populations—in such areas as smoking cessation, diet, physical activity, seat-belt use, and alcohol abuse—and if a broad range of groups within the community, including the medical sector, become involved in community-wide efforts to make the social environment more conducive to following counseling advice.

CONSOLIDATION AND PARTNERSHIPS

Even with compelling reasons for medicine and public health to develop a closer working relationship—and real incentives for doing so—it is difficult to put collaboration into practice without organizational structures that can bring together the perspectives, resources, and skills of diverse health professionals and organizations. As noted earlier, the loose structure of the American health system, and its increasing fragmentation, has served as one barrier to the coordination of medical and public health services. Moreover, little public support accrued to various attempts to rationalize the organization of the health system through the comprehensive health planning proposals in the 1960s and 1970s.[3,84,105] While some of the changes that are occurring in the health system are disrupting linkages of medical and public health services that had been established in the context of public health clinics and categorical programs, new organizational structures are beginning to emerge that may be better suited for supporting cross-sectoral interactions.

In some cases, partnerships between the two health sectors are occurring in response to mandates. Kentucky's 1115 waiver, for example, calls for the formation of cross-sectoral partnerships in Medicaid managed care. These partnerships are required to undertake community needs assessments and wellness-promotion programs, and to develop health education materials on topics such as nutrition, well-child care, childhood screening, injury prevention, and smoking cessation.[45] In Minnesota, managed care organizations are required to produce action and collaboration plans that demonstrate how they intend to work with local public health agencies to improve community health.[1]

Other relationships and organizational structures are being driven by market forces and the redefined role of government. As managed care becomes more widespread and as government funding declines, professionals and institutions in both sectors are perceiving the need to become part of larger systems in order to enhance their negotiating leverage, to achieve economies of scale, to manage risk more successfully, to maintain or expand their patient base, to enhance opportunities and venues for research, and to provide meaningful training experiences for students and residents. This trend toward consolidation has been associated with a plethora of mergers and joint ventures among and between hospitals, academic institutions, and medical practices.

It also is producing a remarkable transition in the practice organization of patient-care physicians. Between 1983 and 1994, the proportion of patient-care physicians practicing as employees increased from 24 to 42 percent, while the proportion in solo practices fell from 41 to 29 percent.[100] While much of the change is being driven by competitive pressure, it also is a response to the growing complexity of medical management and care. In the past, physicians had everything they needed between their ears and in their black bags.[18] Now, in order to do their jobs, they need an organizational structure that provides them not only with access to human resources—such as specialists, support staff, home care, and nursing home care—but also with information and computer systems that can help them keep up-to-date with the latest advances and apply that knowledge in their practices.

On the one hand, the forces that are driving consolidation are establishing an incentive for professionals and institutions within each health sector—and sometimes across health sectors—to come together. At the same time, the organizational structures that are emerging have the potential to facilitate new relationships between medicine and public health, and to reduce the costs of collaboration. At the least, the dramatic shift of physicians from solo practices to larger group practices and networks is reducing the number of independent medical practitioners with whom a public health agency needs to interact.[145] At best, highly integrated systems have the infrastructure to support the coordination of services among a broad range of organizations and personnel.

A NEW DILEMMA

Reviewing the historical relationship between medicine and public health in the United States, it is clear that two sectors have worked together around health problems in the past, and have continued to have ample opportunities to do so. For much of this century they have taken little advantage of these opportunities, however, because critical conditions for collaboration have not been met. Without a compelling need to work together, and without supportive incentives and organizational structures, the medical and public health sectors evolved along separate, and virtually independent, tracks. By not working together, their cultural differences became increasingly pronounced, making the possibility of future interactions less and less likely.

In the current environment, some of these conditions have changed dramatically. Today, professionals and organizations in medicine and public health clearly need each other—to achieve their missions, and to respond to the economic and performance pressures that they face. Moreover, with the emergence of new incentives and organizational structures, it should be more feasible for them to establish cross-sectoral relationships than it has been in the past. The changes in the health system have not influenced the cultural divergence between medicine and public health, however. Consequently, we now face a new dilemma. Will professionals and organizations in sectors that have become very foreign to each other be able to identify their mutual interests? Will they be able to overcome enough of their suspicions and skepticism to initiate a working relationship? Having had so little interaction over the last 50 years, will they be able to identify potential partners? Will they have a clear idea of how partners can combine their resources and skills in a collaborative endeavor?

The focus groups that we conducted around the country suggest that many health professionals in both sectors would not know where to begin. Overwhelmed by the changes that are occurring, and with little experience working with the other health sector, they do not look to collaboration as an obvious strategy for dealing with current challenges. In spite of these barriers, however, a substantial foundation for collaboration has been laid. Greater attention is being paid to primary care and to its relationship with public health.[159] Through the Health of the Public and other programs, some academic medical centers are increasing their focus on population-based medicine.[73,150,154] The public health sector is reexamining its role, emphasizing the need for broad-based community partnerships.[6,86,89,90] Numerous activities are underway examining the relationship between managed care and public health.[35,137,149,184] New community alliances are being established through Community Care Networks and the Healthy Cities and Healthy Communities movements.[4,39–41,59,76] And in many parts of the country, the medical and public health sectors have found it essential to work together to address emerging health threats such as the measles outbreak, MDR-TB, and HIV/AIDS.

In this context, it is not surprising that we collected 414 examples of medicine and public health collaboration. These cases suggest that for many health professionals around the country, current circumstances are providing compelling reasons to work more closely with the other health sector, and that it is possible to overcome the "cultural divide." In the next part of this monograph, we turn our attention to these collaborations, examining *what* the two health sectors can accomplish by working together and *how* collaborative work gets done.

MODELS OF MEDICINE AND PUBLIC HEALTH COLLABORATION

The Case Study

As soon as several of the inhabitants of the United States have taken up an opinion or a feeling that they wish to promote in the world, they look out for mutual assistance, and as soon as they have found each other out, they combine. From that moment, they are no longer isolated men, but a power seen from afar whose actions serve for an example and whose language is listened to.
—Alexis de Tocqueville, 1848[171]

Gentlemen, the world has found that there are tasks which one man cannot do alone; the day of isolated individual labor is forever gone. There are also tasks in our world of medicine which no man can accomplish alone . . . Cooperation! What a word! Each working with all, and all working with each. Can anyone doubt that we shall win our battle against low standards, indifferent laws and deadly disease if all work as one?
—Edward C. Register, 1915[110]

None of us is as smart as all of us . . . We all know that cooperation and collaboration grow more important every day. A shrinking world in which technological and political complexity increase at an accelerating rate offers fewer and fewer arenas in which individual action suffices.
—Warren Bennis, 1996[10]

Collaboration is damn tough.
—Focus Group Participant, 1997

The power of combining resources to achieve a shared objective has been appreciated for a long time. As the quotations above illustrate, collaboration has been discussed in general terms, medical terms, business terms—and even in what would now be considered sexist terms—over the course of the last 150 years. At an abstract level, few would oppose the application of this concept to medicine and public health. In the focus groups we conducted around the country, students and practitioners in both health sectors were open to the idea of collaboration. Moreover, the current environment provides compelling reasons for professionals and organizations in medicine and public health to give serious consideration to establishing closer working relationships. Yet, a concrete, practical framework for moving forward with cross-sectoral collaboration seems to be lacking. Very few professionals in the focus groups have had experience working with the other sector. Consequently, they had difficulty describing exactly what cross-sectoral collaboration means or how it could be beneficial to them or to the people they serve. Since working with other people and organizations is not easy, it is unrealistic to encourage the two health sectors to establish a closer relationship without a clear understanding of whether cross-sectoral collaborations can work—and, if so, how they work—in the real world.

To develop such an understanding, we solicited examples of medicine and public health collaboration from a wide range of sources. Beginning in August 1996, cases were requested by mail and through electronic postings to members of major medicine and public health associations, to officials in government health agencies, and to participants in potentially relevant foundation-sponsored initiatives. Using a self-administered written or Internet questionnaire, respondents were asked to provide some basic demographic information about themselves and to answer five open-ended questions: What made the collaboration happen? Who was involved? What was the collaboration trying to achieve? What actually happened? What do you think were the critical elements that determined the project's success or failure?

The response to the solicitation was far greater than any of us expected. Ultimately, over 500 cases were identified, of which 414 involved professionals and/or organizations in both medicine and public health. These collaborations, which also frequently involved other community partners as well, were entered in the database. Over 150 hours of telephone interviews were conducted with a subset of respondents to clarify and extend the information provided in their case reports.

The database of medicine and public health collaborations provides a rich and valuable resource for analysis. The cases are well-dispersed geographically, encompassing not only diverse regions of the country but also urban and rural communities. They were submitted by a broad array of professionals working in virtually every type of venue relevant to medicine and public health. They encompass all of the domains of medicine and public health: practice, policy, education and training, and research. In addition, they reflect activities at local, state, and federal levels. Because of this diversity, the database is likely to include most of the common types of medicine and public health interactions occurring in this country. Nonetheless, because the cases in the database are not a random sample, we cannot generalize from the frequencies observed.

A "grounded theory" approach was used to analyze this case material.[67,192] Starting with an open mind—without any preconceptions about what medicine and public health collaboration is or should be—we searched for commonalities and concepts that would elucidate the nature of these collaborative activities. In particular, we sought to answer three questions:

- How do professionals and organizations in medicine and public health combine their resources and skills?
- What is the structural foundation for interactions among the two health sectors?
- Considering the "cultural divide" that characterizes medicine and public health, how are relationships between the two health sectors established? What makes people and organizations willing to engage in collaborative enterprises, and what makes these partnerships work?

The sections that follow summarize the results of our findings. First, we describe six powerful ways that the medical and public health sectors can combine their resources and skills. The case database shows partners from the two health sectors—and often other sectors of the community as well—contributing the following array of assets to collaborative endeavors:

- technical, scientific, and pedagogic expertise
- methodologic tools
- individual-level services and population-based strategies
- administration and management skills
- legal and regulatory authority
- convening power
- influence with peers, policymakers, and the public
- data and information systems
- buildings and space
- financial support

These assets are valuable in and of themselves. But by combining them in certain ways, the individual partners in a collaboration are able to transcend their own limitations and achieve additional benefits that are important to their patients, their populations, and themselves.

We refer to reinforcing combinations of resources and skills as "synergies." In sections describing six distinct types of synergies, we discuss the particular building blocks involved, the value to different partners of combining them, and the models that people use to put the combination into action (Figure 2). Each model is "brought to life" with an illustrative example of a case from the database. Taken as a whole, the synergies clearly document the relevance of each health sector's activities to the other. Moreover, they show that the medical and public health sectors can reinforce each other in virtually everything they do: efforts related to individuals (Synergies

Synergy	Models
I Improving health care by coordinating services for individuals	A. Bring new personnel and services to existing practice sites B. Establish "one-stop" centers C. Coordinate services provided at different sites
II Improving access to care by establishing frameworks to provide care for the uninsured	A. Establish free clinics B. Establish referral networks C. Enhance clinical staffing at public health facilities D. Shift indigent patients to mainstream medical settings
III Improving the quality and cost-effectiveness of care by applying a population perspective to medical practice	A. Use population-based information to enhance clinical decision-making B. Use population-based strategies to "funnel" patients to medical care C. Use population-based analytic tools to enhance practice management
IV Using clinical practice to identify and address community health problems	A. Use clinical encounters to build community-wide databases B. Use clinical opportunities to identify and address underlying causes of health problems C. Collaborate to achieve clinically oriented community health objectives
V Strengthening health promotion and health protection by mobilizing community campaigns	A. Conduct community health assessments B. Mount health education campaigns C. Advocate health-related laws and regulations D. Engage in community-wide campaigns to achieve health promotion objectives E. Launch "Healthy Communities" initiatives
VI Shaping the future direction of the health system by collaborating around policy, training, and research	A. Influence health system policy B. Engage in cross-sectoral education and training C. Conduct cross-sectoral research

Figure 2   Models of medicine and public health collaboration

I and II), to populations (Synergies V and VI), and to combinations of the two (Synergies III and IV). In all of these interactions, both sectors benefit. Although the various synergies are described separately in the text, it should be pointed out that they are not mutually exclusive in practice. Cases in the database can, and often do, involve more than one synergy.

We turn next to the structural foundations for combining the two health sectors' resources and skills. While some medicine and public health collaborations take place within the confines of a single organization, the vast majority of cases in the database bring together health professionals from diverse disciplines who work in or represent an array of organizations, including:

- medical practices and community-based clinics
- laboratories and pharmacies
- hospitals and health systems
- managed care organizations
- health departments and other government agencies
- academic institutions
- professional associations
- voluntary health organizations
- community groups, such as businesses, labor organizations, schools, and religious organizations
- the media
- foundations

In each of these collaborations, professionals continue to work within their own organization while, at the same time, transcending the boundaries of that organization to link up with professionals and organizations in other sectors. Much has been written about inter-organizational arrangements within a particular sector (business or medical care, for example), and some investigators have begun to examine arrangements between health departments and managed care organizations.[2,75,95] Prior research, however, has not focused on cross-sectoral arrangements involving the range of partners seen in the database cases. In the section on structural foundations, we discuss the attributes of five types of arrangements used in the cases:

- coalitions
- contractual agreements
- administration/management systems
- advisory bodies
- intra-organizational platforms

Finally, we turn to partnership issues, which are a key determinant of success in the cases in the database. For collaborations to proceed smoothly, working relationships need to be established that allow a broad range of professionals and organizations to work together in a common endeavor. This is not an easy task in an environment in which all of the potential partners are under siege, few have any history of working together, and many are separated by suspicions, preconceptions, and deep cultural differences. Examining cases in the database that succeeded as well as those that did not, we discuss eight strategies that collaborations use to make the enterprise a high priority for all participants and to build and sustain confidence and trust:

- build on self-interests as well as health interests
- involve a "boundary spanner" in the project
- seek out influential backing and endorsements
- don't expect other partners to be like you
- be realistic
- pay attention to the process
- ensure adequate infrastructure support
- be "up-front" about competition and control issues

ABOUT THE AUTHOR

Roz D. Lasker, MD, is Director of the Public Health Division and the Center for the Advancement of Collaborative Strategies in Health at The New York Academy of Medicine in New York, New York. She is also the principal author of *Medicine and Public Health: The Power of Collaboration* (Health Administration Press, 1997).
    Committee on Medicine and Public Health

REFERENCES*

1. Alpha Center. 1996. Public health and managed care organizations—a new era of collaboration? *State Initiatives* (May/June 1996):2–4, 10.
    2. Alter, C., and Hage, J. 1993. *Organizations working together.* Newbury Park, CA: Sage Publications, Inc.
    3. Altman, D. 1995. The market and regulation: where community forces fit. *Frontiers of Health Services Management* 11 (4):49–50.
    4. American Hospital Association. 1994. Healthy Communities in action. Chicago: Hospital Research and Educational Trust of the American Hospital Association.
    6. Baker, E. L., Melton, R. J., Stange, P. V., Fields, M. L., et al. 1994. Health reform and the health of the public: forging community health partnerships. *Journal of the American Medical Association* 272 (16):1276–1282.
    10. Bennis, W., and Biederman, P. W. 1997. *Organizing genius: the secrets of creative collaboration.* Reading, MA: Addison-Wesley Publishing Company.

*Some references have been omitted to reflect abridgment of article.

11. Berenson, R. A. 1996. New market relationships and their effects on patient care. Paper read at a Robert Wood Johnson Foundation Invitational Meeting—A Market in Turmoil: Evolving Relationships, September 11, at Washington, DC.

14. Bernier, R. H. 1994. Toward a more population–based approach to immunization: fostering private- and public-sector collaboration. *American Journal of Public Health* 84 (10):1567–1568.

18. Blumenthal, D., and Thier, S. O. 1996. Managed care and medical education: the new fundamentals. *Journal of the American Medical Association* 276 (9):725–727.

23. Bowditch, H. 1874. Preventive medicine and the physician of the future. In *Fifth Annual Report of the State Board of Health of Massachusetts.* Boston: Wright and Potter (State Printers).

25. Breslow, L. 1990. The future of public health: prospects in the United States for the 1990's. *Annual Review of Public Health* 11:1–28.

28. Bulger, R. J. 1990. Reductionist biology and population medicine—strange bedfellows or a marriage made in heaven? *Journal of the American Medical Association* 264 (4):508–509.

30. Bullough, B., and Rosen, G. 1992. *Preventive medicine in the United States, 1900–1990: trends and interpretations.* Canton, MA: Science History Publications.

32. Bureau of National Affairs. 1997. Surveys and studies. *BNA's Health Care Policy Report* 5 (2/17/97):288–292.

34. Center for Studying Health System Change. 1996. Tracking changes in the public health system: what researchers need to know to monitor and evaluate these changes. *Issue Brief* (No. 2):1–4.

35. Centers for Disease Control. 1995. Prevention and managed care: opportunities for managed care organizations, purchasers of health care, and public health agencies. *Morbidity and Mortality Weekly Review* 44 (No. RR-14).

36. Centers for Disease Control. 1997. Estimated expenditures for essential public health services-selected states, fiscal year 1995. *Morbidity and Mortality Weekly Report* 46 (7):150–152.

39. Community Care Network Demonstration Program. 1996. The demonstration & finalist partnerships. Chicago: Hospital Research and Educational Trust.

40. Community Care Network Demonstration Program. 1996. Examples of emerging rural community networks. Chicago: Hospital Research and Educational Trust.

41. Community Care Network Demonstration Program. 1997. The 25 Community Care Network Demonstration partnerships: profiles in progress. Chicago: Hospital Research and Educational Trust.

44. Council on Scientific Affairs. 1990. The IOM report and public health. *Journal of the American Medical Association* 264 (4):508–509.

45. Cunningham, R. 1996. Renegotiating the social contract in public health. *Medicine & Health Perspectives* (August 5, 1996):1–4.

50. Duffy, J. 1979. The American medical profession and public health: from support to ambivalence. *Bulletin of the History of Medicine* 53 (1):1–22.

55. Fee, E. 1991. Designing schools of public health for the United States. In *A history of education in public health: health that mocks the doctors' rules,* edited by E. Fee and R. M. Acheson. New York: Oxford University Press.

56. Fee, E., and Rosenkrantz, B. 1991. Professional education for public health in the United States. In *A history of education in public health: health that mocks the doctors' rules,* edited by E. Fee and R. M. Acheson. New York: Oxford University Press.

57. Fee, E. 1997. The origins and development of public health in the United States. In *Oxford Textbook of Public Health,* edited by R. Detels, W. W. Holland, J. McEwen, and G. S. Omenn. New York: Oxford University Press.

58. Flexner, A. 1910. Medical education in the United States and Canada, Bulletin no. 4. New York: Carnegie Foundation for the Advancement of Teaching.

59. Flynn, B. C. 1996. Healthy cities: toward worldwide health promotion. *Annual Review of Public Health* 17:299–309.

60. Foundation for Accountability. 1995. Guidebook for performance measurement: prototype. Portland, OR: Foundation for Accountability.

63. Fuchs, V. R. 1997. Managed care and merger mania. *Journal of the American Medical Association* 277 (11):920–921.

67. Glaser, B. G., and Strauss, A. L. 1967. *The discovery of grounded theory: strategies for qualitative research.* Chicago: Aldine Publishing.

68. Gordon, R. L., Baker, E. L., Roper, W. L., and Omenn, G. S. 1996. Prevention and the reforming U.S. health care system: changing roles and responsibilities for public health. *Annual Review of Public Health* 17:489–509.

69. Gore, A. 1995. Reinventing government: national performance review. Washington, DC: Office of the Vice President of the United States.

73. Greenlick, M. R. 1995. Educating physicians for the twenty-first century. *Academic Medicine* 70 (3):179–185.

74. Hafferty, F., and Salloway, J. C. 1993. The evolution of medicine as a profession: a 75-year perspective. *Minnesota Medicine* 76 (January):26–35.

75. Halverson, P. K., Mays, G. P., Kaluzny, A. D., and Richards, T. B. 1997. Not-so-strange bedfellows: models of interaction between managed care plans and public health agencies. *Milbank Quarterly* 75 (1):113–139.

76. Hancock, T. 1993. The evolution, impact and significance of the healthy cities/healthy communities movement. *Journal of Public Health Policy* 14:5–18.

78. Hippocrates; Jones WHS. 1923. Airs, waters, places. In *Hippocrates.* Cambridge, MA: Harvard University Press.

80. Hughart, N., Guyer, B., Stanton, B., Strobino, D., et al. 1994. Do provider practices conform to the new pediatric immunization standards? *Archives of Pediatric Adolescent Medicine* 148 (9):930–935.

84. Institute of Medicine. 1982. *Health services integration: lessons for the 1980s.* Washington, DC: National Academy Press.

86. Institute of Medicine. 1988. *The future of public health.* Washington, DC: National Academy Press.

89. Institute of Medicine. 1996. *Healthy communities: new partnerships for the future of public health.* Edited by M. A. Stoto, C. Abel, and A. Dievler, *A report of the first year of the committee on public health.* Washington, DC: National Academy Press.

90. Institute of Medicine. 1997. *Improving health in the community: a role for performance monitoring.* Edited by J. Durch, L. A. Bailey, and M. A. Stoto. Washington, DC: National Academy Press.

92. Joint Commission on Accreditation of Healthcare Organizations. 1996. *Joint commission standards:* URL http://www.jcaho.org.

93. Joint Commission on Accreditation of Healthcare Organizations. 1996. Joint commission to create National Library of Healthcare Indicators. *Joint Commission Perspectives* 16 (2):1, 4.

95. Kanter, R. M. 1994. Collaborative advantage: the art of alliances. *Harvard Review* 72:96–108.

100. Kletke, P. R., Emmons, D. W., and Gillis, K. D. 1996. Current trends in physicians' practice arrangements. *Journal of the American Medical Association* 276 (7):555–560.

105. Lee, P. R., Benjamin, A. E., and Weber, M. A. 1997. Policies and strategies for health in the United States. In *Oxford Textbook of Public Health,* edited by R. Detels, W. W. Holland, J. McEwen, and G. S. Omenn. New York: Oxford University Press.

107. Litman, T. J. 1984. Appendix: chronology and capsule highlights of the major historical and political milestones in the evolutionary involvement of government in health and health care in the United States. In *Health politics and policy,* edited by T. J. Litman and L. S. Robins. New York: John Wiley & Sons.

108. Lorber, B. 1996. Are all diseases infectious? *Annals of Internal Medicine* 125 (10):844–851.

109. Ludmerer, K. M. 1985. *Learning to heal: the development of American medical education.* New York: Basic Books, Inc.

110. Madison, D. L. 1996. Preserving individualism in the organizational society: "cooperation" and American medical practice, 1900–1920. *Bulletin of the History of Medicine* 70:442–483.

117. McGinnis, J. M. 1997. What do we pay for good health? *Journal of Public Health Management and Practice* 3 (3):vii–ix.

119. Miller, C. A., Moore, K. S., Richards, T. B., Kotelchuck, M., et al. 1993. Longitudinal observations on a select group of local health departments: a preliminary report. *Journal of Public Health Policy* Spring:34–50.

126. National Committee for Quality Assurance. 1997. *Health plan employer data and information set, version 3.0 (HEDIS 3.0).* Washington, DC: National Committee for Quality Assurance.

129. New York Academy of Medicine Standing Committee on Public Health and

Legal Medicine. 1852. Medical aid to the indigent-sanitary police. New York: The New York Academy of Medicine.

131. Osborne, D. E., and Gaebler, T. 1992. *Reinventing government: how the entrepreneural spirit is transforming the public sector.* Reading, MA: Addison-Wesley Publishing Company.

134. Pearson, T. A., Spencer, M., and Jenkins, P. 1995. Who will provide preventive services? The changing relationships between medical care systems and public health agencies in health care reform. *Journal of Public Health Management and Practice* 1 (1):16–27.

137. Public Health/Managed Care Advisory Panel to the Pew Charitable Trusts. 1996. Academic public health and managed care: strategies for collaboration. New York: Columbia School of Public Health.

141. Robert Wood Johnson Foundation. 1996. Annual Report. Princeton, NJ: The Robert Wood Johnson Foundation.

142. Robinson, J. C., and Casalino, L. P. 1995. The growth of medical groups paid through capitation in California. *New England Journal of Medicine* 333 (25):1684–1687.

145. Rosenbaum, S., and Richards, T. B. 1996. Medicaid managed care and public health policy. *Journal of Public Health Management and Practice* 2 (3):76–82.

147. Rundall, T. G. 1994. The integration of public health and medicine. *Frontiers of Health Services Management* 10 (4):3–24.

149. Schauffler, H. H., Hennessey, M., and Neiger, B. 1997. Health promotion and managed care: an assessment of collaboration by state directors of health promotion. Berkeley, CA: Association of State and Territorial Directors of Health Promotion and Public Education.

150. Schroeder, S. A., Zones, J. S., and Showstack, J. A. 1989. Academic medicine as a public trust. *Journal of the American Medical Association* 262 (6):803–812.

153. Shonick, W. 1995. *Government and health services: government's role in the development of U.S. health services, 1930–1980.* New York: Oxford University Press.

154. Showstack, J., Fein, O., Ford, D., Kaufman, A., et al. 1992. Health of the public: the academic response. *Journal of the American Medical Association* 267 (18):2497–2502.

159. Starfield, B. 1996. Public health and primary care: a framework for proposed linkages. *American Journal of Public Health* 86 (10):1365–1369.

160. Starr, P. 1982. *The social transformation of medicine.* New York: Basic Books.

161. Stevens, R. 1971. *American medicine and the public interest.* New Haven, CT: Yale University Press.

162. Stevens, R. 1989. *In sickness and in wealth: American hospitals in the twentieth century.* New York: Basic Books.

166. Tengs, T. O., Adams, M. E., Pliskin, J. S., Safran, D. G., et al. 1995.

Five-hundred life-saving interventions and their cost-effectiveness. *Risk Analysis* 15 (3):369–390.

169. Thompson, R. S., Taplin, S. H., McAfee, T. A., Andelson, M. T., et al. 1995. Primary and secondary prevention services in clinical practice: twenty years' experience in development, implementation, and evaluation. *Journal of the American Medical Association* 273 (14):1130–1135.

170. Thompson, R. S. 1996. What have HMO's learned about clinical services? An examination of the experience at Group Health Cooperative of Puget Sound. *Milbank Quarterly* 74 (4):469–509.

171. Tocqueville, A. de. 1996. *Democracy in America.* New York: Harper & Row.

174. U.S. Department of Health and Human Services. 1991. *HHS Secretary's Report to Congress on the Status of Health Personnel in the United States.* Washington, DC.

177. U.S. Department of Health and Human Services. 1996. *Healthy People 2000 review 1995–96.* Washington, DC: DHHS Pub. No. (PHS) 96-1256.

178. U.S. Department of Health and Human Services—Public Health Service. 1980. *Promoting health/preventing disease: objectives for the nation.* Atlanta, GA.

179. U.S. Department of Health and Human Services—Public Health Service. 1991. *Healthy People 2000: national health promotion and disease prevention objectives.* Washington, DC: DHHS Pub. No. (PHS) 91-50212.

180. U.S. Preventive Services Task Force. 1996. *Guide to clinical preventive services: report of the U.S. Preventive Services Task Force, 2nd edition.* Washington, DC: Williams & Wilkins.

182. Welch, S. W. 1924. Cooperative relations between official and unofficial health agencies. *Public Health Report* 39:3243–3251.

184. Wendy Knight & Associates. 1996. Improving the public's health: collaborations between public health departments and managed care organizations. Vergennes, VT: Joint Council of Governmental Public Health Agencies.

192. Yin, R. K. 1984. *Case study research: design and methods.* Thousand Oaks, CA: Sage Publications.

PART 4

HEALTH INSURANCE AND HEALTH CARE SYSTEMS

THE HEALTH INSURANCE SYSTEM

I t is impossible to describe the health care system in a few pages or a few selected articles from the literature. Because of the complexity of the issues, we have chosen to divide the subject into four chapters: The Health Insurance System, Medicare and Medicaid, Managed Care, and Quality of Health Care. In Chapter 7, we deal with the health insurance system, giving particular emphasis to employer-sponsored health insurance coverage, the extent of health insurance coverage, particularly the large number of uninsured children, the high percentage of Hispanics who are not insured, and the failure of employer-sponsored health insurance to cover low-wage workers.

It is difficult to use the term *system* when describing the organization, financing, or delivery of health care in the United States. The system of financing includes public payers and providers at federal, state, and local levels, as well as a variety of other forms of subsidy through taxation and public programs. At the federal level, these include payers and providers in the Departments of Defense, Veteran Affairs, and Health and Human Services, including the Health Care Financing Administration (HCFA), which administers Medicare and Medicaid, and the U.S. Public Health Service, which furnishes, medical care to the U.S. Coast Guard, the Bureau of Prisons, and, through the Indian Health Service, both medical and public health services, such as environmental sanitation and immunization, for Native Americans and Alaska Natives. Similar complexity exists at the state level, with medical care in state prisons and state mental hospitals, and at the local level with public health clinics and county or municipal hospitals providing care for the indigent (together often called safety net providers). Next are public subsidy programs for public employees (e.g., Federal Employees Health Benefits Program), for dependents of military personnel (CHAMPUS) and for state and local government employees as well as federal tax subsidy of private health insurance provided by employers. These subsidies cost the taxpayers over $100 billion annually. Finally, for some who are uninsured by any of the above or through private coverage, costs may be waived by providers, or they may have to be paid by providers by cost-shifting to insured patients. Furthermore, even those patients provided for under these public and private programs contribute to the financing of care. For Medicare beneficiaries, for example, the Medicare program only covers about 50 percent of the total costs of medical care and long-term care. The remainder is paid by the patient, either by the payment of premiums for Medigap insurance or out-of-pocket spending directly for care, or by Medicaid (e.g., nursing home care). Out-of-pocket payments are also significant for many patients with private insurance who must pay a deductible before their coverage begins and/or a copayment at the time of service.

Health care in the United States has been transformed in the past 30 years. First by the growing impact of technology on the range of services provided (e.g., imaging technologies) and the costs of health care, and also by the growth of the for-profit sector of health care and the coming of managed care. These changes have been described by Starr (1982), Salmon (1995), Lasker (1997), and the article by Estes, Harrington, and Pellow (2000) included in the Recommended Reading.

The concept of the Medical-Industrial Complex was introduced in 1971 in the book, *The American Health Empire.* The growth of the Medical-Industrial Complex (sometimes referred to as the health care industry) is detailed in the article by Estes, Harrington, and Pellow. They note five important changes in the structure of the health care industry since 1970: (1) rapid growth and consolidation; (2) horizontal integration (e.g., the creation of hospital systems); (3) vertical integration (e.g., mergers of physicians, surgicenters, urgent care centers, and hospitals); (4) change in ownership from government to private, both nonprofit and for-profit organizations; and (5) diversification and corporate restructuring. After reviewing these developments, the authors shift focus to the financial and profit-making status of various components (e.g., multihospital systems, managed care plans) of the Medical-Industrial Complex and discuss the reasons behind growth in the for-profit sector. In their final section, Estes, Harrington, and Pellow identify four key issues raised by the medical industrial complex: commodification, commercialization, proprietarization, and monetarization.

The rising costs of health care continues to dominate the debate on health care, despite the slowing of cost increases in the 1990s by managed care in the private sector and government regulation of Medicare and Medicaid. The rapid restructuring of health care in the 1980s and its acceleration in the 1990s may be attributed to the increasing pressures for cost containment from both industry and government. At the same time, there is growing awareness of fundamental issues surrounding the large number of uninsured Americans (now exceeding 16 percent of the population) as more and more middle-class workers who change jobs are unable to purchase health insurance, the growing coverage problems for consumers with pre-existing conditions, the transfer of more and more costs to consumers, and the absence of national health insurance, among others. The failure of the Clinton health reform plan in 1994 accelerated reforms by the private insurance market. Managed care has revolutionized the financing, structure, and delivery of medical care. Accompanying the growth of managed care have been waves of mergers, consolidation, and concentration in the health insurance market as the for-profit industry continues to gain a larger market share of power and wealth.

With the slowing of cost increases, in 1997 national health expenditures reached $1.1 trillion, or almost $4,000 per capita. Health spending as a share of gross domestic product (GDP) stabilized in the 1990s and even fell slightly to 13.5 percent of GDP in 1997, the lowest level in 5 years (see Levit, et al in the Recommended Reading). This was the combined result of continued growth in the GDP and slower increases in health spending. Similarly, the decline in per capita spending on health care illustrates a decline in the growth of spending overall in the 1990s. From 1960 to 1970, the annual per capita growth of expenditures was 8.7 percent; from 1970 to 1980 it was 11.3 percent; from 1980 to 1990, 9.4 percent; from 1990 to 1995, 6.2 percent; and from 1995 to 1997 it was 3.9 percent. The reductions in the rate of increase in health care costs in the 1990s appear to be the result of the massive shift to managed care, particularly with reduced rates of hospitalization and costs. Now, little more can be gained from that shift, and costs are likely to return to increases largely driven by the growing use of technology.

The rise in personal health care expenditures can be broken down into four components: general inflation, medical price inflation above general inflation; population growth; and a group of other factors, including increases in the volume and intensity of services. Population growth accounted for the least (about 9 percent) and general inflation accounted for most (about 30 percent) of the increase in the past 20 years. Medical care price above general inflation accounted for 17 percent of the increase, and growth in the volume and intensity of services for approximately 28 percent. These components have been affected by an array of factors, including increased complexity of the patient's problems; a tendency in the delivery system toward specialization rather than primary care; concentration of physicians and hospitals in certain urban areas that leads to excess capacity, low productivity, and overutilization of services; including unnecessary and inappropriate care, which some analysts estimate may be as high as 25 percent of health care services; the practice of defensive medicine to avoid the threat of malpractice suits; and, finally, excessive administrative costs.

In the past, rising costs were exacerbated by the fact that the U.S. system insulated both providers and consumers through the cushion of third-party payers, and payments were largely on a fee-for-service or cost basis, thus avoiding incentives to seek or provide care in a cost-effective manner. A number of failures in the health care market have vastly influenced the way insurance companies try to cope with the rising cost of health care services. In order to contain their costs, employers often limit employee choice through the selection of managed care plans, shift costs to employees, and reduce or eliminate benefits.

While some economists and policymakers characterize the past decade as a period of increased competition and deregulation, during the same period, public programs were subject to growing regulation. This was particularly important in the Medicare and Medicaid programs, which pay for approximately 33 percent of all acute health care expenditures. In order to control costs, the federal government devised ingenious schemes to limit spending, most notably through the Medicare prospective payment system for hospitals, which was introduced in 1983, and the Medicare fee schedule for physicians with limits on extra billing by physicians and volume performance standards (expenditure targets) that went into effect between 1992 and 1996. These effects have slowed the rate of increase in Medicare costs in recent years. Another factor in the past few years has been the vigorous effort by the Department of Health and Human Services to curb fraud and abuse in the Medicare program. In addition, the Balanced Budget Act of 1997 reduced provider payments further and provided greater incentives for Medicare beneficiaries to enroll in managed care plans. With the efforts in the private sector to stimulate competition and require more and more patients to fit into managed care plans, cost increases have slowed dramatically since 1994. The trends in health care costs for the future is unknown, but HCFA has projected that expenditures will rise by 6 percent in 2001 and 7.5 percent in 2007. Health care costs in the United States are the highest of any nation in the world and have consistently risen well above the rate of growth of the gross domestic product for 50 years.

We have not included several articles from the fifth edition, but do include them in the Recommended Reading. Uwe Reinhart's paper "Providing Access to Health Care and Controlling Costs" (1994) compares the U.S. health care system with those of 23 other Western nations, with particular emphasis on costs of care and access to services. The greatest contrast is that the vast majority of these nations provide comprehensive, universal, first-dollar coverage for most major services. Another sharp contrast is that most consumers in these countries are much more satisfied with their health care systems than are consumers in the United States despite the larger American per capita expenditure on health care. That is to say Americans spend more on the health system than most countries, but are less satisfied with what their money buys them overall. Included in this article are a number of suppositions about how the European, Canadian, and U.S. systems might be influenced in the coming years by economic events and public attitudes such that our system might begin to look more like European systems, while Europe begins to adopt certain characteristics of our market approach.

We have included Karen Davis' article (1996) in our Recommended Reading list. Davis urges particular attention to finding practical mechanisms by which we can address the health care insurance coverage and access needs of the at-risk population, especially in light of the rapidly evolving market system that threatens to completely exclude certain sectors of society from any access to needed care.

Compounding the problem of rising costs, and with the move to increasing managed care, there has been a deterioration in access to care. Increasing numbers of people across all socioeconomic levels have found it difficult or impossible to obtain health insurance coverage, thus expanding the ranks of the uninsured to over 44 million (up from 37 million when the fourth edition of *The Nation's Health* was published in 1994 and 41 million when the fifth edition was published in 1997). More than 60 million Americans have been found to lack health insurance at one point in time during the year.

The growing number of uninsured has recently been highlighted by a report from the Bureau of the Census, which states that the number of uninsured persons has risen to 44.3 million. Prior to the enactment of Medicare and Medicaid the number of uninsured persons was 63 million. By 1970, the number had declined to 49 million. With the expansion of private health insurance, Medicaid, and Medicare, the number dropped to 23 million by 1976. Since then, the number of uninsured has risen steadily. In 1980, it was 30 million, in 1990, 36 million, and in 1993, 41 million. Those most likely to be uninsured are poor and young and belong to a minority group (e.g., Hispanic). Since 1995, there has been a significant decline in Medicaid enrollment, in part related to welfare reform and lower levels of unemployment. (See Chapter segment from Bureau of Census Report.)

There are many consequences of the lack of health care insurance, most related to the access to care, particularly clinical preventive services and delayed access to necessary care. In addition, many people go without any medical care (37 percent of uninsured and 10 percent of insured) and many, especially those with incomes below $20,000 per year, have difficulties paying their medical bills.

There is a growing interest in this issue of the uninsured. On June 14, 1999, the six major medical organizations (American Medical Association, American College of Physicians, American College of Surgeons, American Academy of Pediatrics, American College of Obstetricians and Gynecologists, and American Academy of Family Practice) issued a joint statement advocating universal coverage. Former Senator Bradley, a candidate for the Democratic Party's nomination for President, proposed a plan to provide health insurance for at least 95 percent of the population, guaranteed by the federal government. The Institute of Medicine held a conference on the uninsured and plans a series of studies to help illuminate the issues.

We have also included in the Recommended Reading the paper by Karen Donaldson and Associates "Whatever Happened to the Health Insurance Crisis in the United States?" (1996). National data indicate that the ranks of the uninsured continue to swell; yet there is a conspicuous absence of public debate or political attention to this now apparently invisible problem. The authors explore the results of nearly 4,000 focused interviews to answer difficult questions about issues plaguing our current system. The authors address complex topics surrounding the uninsured and why they do not have insurance, as well as the insured and what difficulty they face in obtaining care. Their results clearly indicate that there are millions in precarious situations regarding even their basic health care needs. Whether or not this crisis situation among a segment of Americans indicates a crisis in the U.S. health care system at large is a question that cannot be answered by quantitative data. As shocking as the numbers may be, the loss experienced by individuals in the quality of life and productivity is the only true measure of the cost to some of the failures addressing this issue.

At one time, Americans believed that theirs was the best health care system in the world. However, a 1989 Louis Harris and Associates survey reported that Americans were more dissatisfied with their health care system than either Canadians or Britons, despite the higher levels of health care spending by Americans. Polls repeated over the years have shown varying degrees of dissatisfaction with the health care system, particularly the high costs of care. Many surveys found that most Americans favored major reforms in the health care system. Other polls indicated that the majority favored some type of national health plan, although no single model stood out as the preferred plan. Despite the findings of the polls in the late 1980s and early 1990s, they did not translate into broad public support for the Clinton health care reform proposals.

Some say this is but another expression of the basic American wish to "have our cake and eat it, too." We want miracle cures, but we do not want prices to go up. Although the system is meeting the personal needs of many people, collectively, there are significant failures. These failures reflect the tradeoffs that are necessary under the current payment system. Those who have health insurance do not want their choices restricted, but they do want costs, particularly costs that they bear directly, controlled. Now, there seems to be less willingness than in the past to support universal health insurance. These views of the public are updated in the recent article by Blendon, et al, "Voters and Health Care in the 1998 Election" (1999) (in the Recommended Reading list). Among the three broad policy areas they explored in Medicare, the uninsured, and managed care, there was strong support for (1) expanding Medicare to include prescription drugs (68 percent) and long-term care (69 percent), even though it might mean higher taxes or Part B premiums; (2) helping the uninsured get health insurance (61 percent); and, (3) legislation that would require HMOs to provide people with information about their health plan, allow independent review, and make it easier to see specialists (78 percent).

In a recent investigation that illustrates the comprehensive nature of health care services, Berk, Schur, and Cantor (1995) (in the Recommended Reading list) construct estimates of American's self-reported ability to access appropriate and needed health care services. Although their findings support previous results that indicate approximately six percent of Americans believe they were unable to access needed medical and surgical services, these investigators include a more comprehensive list of services, including prescription drugs, eyeglasses, dental services, and mental health care or counseling. This research clearly documents the need to broaden our view of access to appropriate care to include the often neglected non–medically focused services that have quality-of-life implications and that may, indeed, affect the outcomes of other more routinely accessible medical and surgical services.

Among the 44.3 million uninsured, over 11 million are children. In order to try to ameliorate this problem the Congress enacted the Child Health Insurance Program (CHIP) as part of the Balanced Budget Act of 1997. The new program allocates $20.3 billion in federal matching funds over 5 years to states to expand health insurance to children. States can use the federal funds to expand coverage either through a separate state program or by broadening their Medicaid program, or both. The program is being implemented slowly in many states and quite effectively in only a few. (See paper on State Children's Health Insurance Program in Recommended Reading.)

Those who hold the purse-strings—third-party payers—have come to dictate treatment plans and hospital stays, as coverage has become increasingly limited. In many cases, people with chronic health problems cannot obtain health insurance benefits at all. This circumstance is called a *pre-existing condition,* and in recent years it has become common for insurance companies to exclude coverage for illnesses for which people are undergoing treatment at the time they apply for coverage. It has also been difficult for people to carry their coverage from job to job, referred to as *portability*. As a result of these problems, Congress, in late 1996, enacted the Health Insurance Portability and Accountability Act (Kennedy–Kassenbaum) to provide for portability of health insurance and limit exclusions because of preexisting conditions. Ironically, at the same time, as Medicaid eligibility shrank in relation to a growing need and other charity care began to decline, the political system effectively turned its back on the working poor. In the past, cost shifting by hospitals from the insured to pay for the care of the uninsured was common, but this has become increasingly difficult in the era of managed care. Welfare reform enacted and signed into law in 1996 denied medical care to millions of legal and illegal immigrants and increased state discretion over eligibility for and benefits of welfare programs. The impact on the Medicaid population is unclear, but in many states enrollment is declining.

One of the important stories in health care is told by Kuttner in his two articles on "Health Insurance Coverage" and "Employer Sponsored Health Coverage," which appeared in *The New England Journal of Medicine* in January 1999 as part of a series on the American health care system. Unlike Canada and European countries, the United States has relied heavily on tax-subsidized, employer-provided private health insurance for the great bulk of the working population since the 1950s. As Kuttner noted at the beginning of his first article: "The most prominent feature of American health insurance is its slow erosion, even as government seeks to plug the gaps in coverage through such new programs as Medicare + Choice, the Health Insurance Portability and Accountability Act (HIPAA), expansion of State Medicaid Programs and the $24 billion Children's Health Insurance Program of 1997" (p. 163). The number of uninsured persons continues to grow. In addition, the number of underinsured persons is growing even faster.

Kuttner summarized the current state of affairs in his second article, regarding the alternatives or lack of them available to workers. The current pattern of shifting costs to employees and paring the benefits, which subsequently result in increasing numbers of uninsured and underinsured workers, is likely to persist or worsen as long as the basic system of employer-provided health insurance continues.

A critical perspective not evident in Kuttner's articles on health insurance (1999) is provided by Salmon's article (1995), "A Perspective on the Corporate Transformation of Health Care" (in the Recommended Reading list). He describes the ever-increasing ownership of health service providers, suppliers, and insurers by investor-owned enterprises. He links the corporate transformation to the growth of managed care, fostered by competitive health policies. He describes the potential impact of the growth of large-scale nationwide managed care systems that integrate finance, administration, and delivery of care. The current state of turmoil makes it very difficult to describe the present or predict the future. We agree with Salmon's conclusion that "In sum, the economic megacorporate interests cannot be allowed to reign in a new reformed health care system. They will never bear a positive relation to promoting or sustaining health in the whole population where their sole objective is a bottom line return" (p. 35).

We include in the Recommended Reading list "The Status of Local Health Care Safety Nets" (1997) as a reminder of the critical role that so-called "safety net providers" at the local level play in the care of millions of Americans. Access to the freely rendered, uncompensated care these clinics provide is the only outlet to care for many Americans. Because financial and competitive reforms are increasing, thus limiting the flexibility of physicians to provide uncompensated care, it is likely that the importance of the safety net will only increase.

REFERENCES

Baxter, R., Mechanic, R. Status of local health care safety net. *Health Affairs,* 1997;16:7–22.

Berk ML, Schur, C. L., & Cantor, J. C. Ability to obtain health care: Recent estimates of the Robert Wood Johnson Foundation National Access to Care Survey. *Health Affairs,* 1995;14:138–146.

Blendon, R., Benson, J., Brodie, M., Altman, D., James M., & Hugick, L. Voters and health care in the 1998 election. *JAMA,* July 14, 1999; 282:189–194.

Donalen, K., Blendon, R.J., Hill, C.A., Hoffman, C., Rowland, D., Frankel, M., & Altman, D. Whatever happened to the health insurance crisis in the United States? *JAMA,* 1996;276(16):1346–1350.

Estes, C.L., Harrington, C., & Pellow, D. Medical industrial complex. *Encycloped Sociology,* 2000 (to be published).

Harris, L, and Associates, Inc. *Trade-offs & choices: Health Policy Options for the 1990s: A Survey.* Conducted for Metropolitan Life Insurance Company. New York: Metropolitan Life Insurance Company, 1990.

Kuttner, R. The American health system insurance coverage. *NEJM,* Jan. 14, 1999; 340:163–168.

Kuttner, A. The American health system employer-sponsored health insurance. *NEJM,* Jan 28, 1999; 340:248–252.

Lasker, R.D. & The Committee on Medicine and Public Health. *Medicine and Public Health: The Power of Collaboration.* New York: The New York Academy of Medicine, 1997; 11–22, 29–45, 47–53.

Levit, K., Cowan, C., Braden, B., Stiller, J., Sensening, A., & Lazenby, H. National health expenditures in 1997: more slow growth. *Health Affairs (Millwood)* 1998;17(6):99–110.

Salmon, J.W. A perspective on the corporate transformation of health care. *Internat J Health Serv,* 1995;25(1):11–42.

Starr, P. *The Social Transformation of American Medicine.* New York: Basic Books, 1982.

The Kaiser Commission on the Future of Medicaid. # *Legislative Summary: State Children's Health Insurance Program.* Menlo Park, CA: The Henry J. Kaiser Family Foundation, December 1997.

Article 1

Health Insurance Coverage: Consumer Income

Jennifer A. Campbell

An estimated 44.3 million people in the United States, or 16.3 percent of the population, were without health insurance coverage during the entire 1998 calendar year. This number was up about 1 million from the previous year; statistically, the proportion was not different than the 1997 value.

The estimates in this report are based on interviewing a sample of the population. (The uncertainty in the estimates should be taken into consideration when using these estimates.) Respondents provided answers to the survey questions to the best of their ability. As with all surveys, the estimates differed from the actual values.

HIGHLIGHTS

- The number of uninsured children (under 18 years of age) was 11.1 million in 1998, or 15.4 percent of all children. The status of children's health care coverage did not change significantly from 1997 to 1998.
- The Medicaid program insured 14.0 million poor people, but 11.2 million poor people still had no health insurance in 1998, representing about one-third of all poor people (32.3 percent).
- The uninsured rate among Hispanics was higher than that of non-Hispanic Whites—35.3 percent compared with 11.9 percent.[1]
- Among the general population 18–64 years old, workers (both full- and part-time) were more likely to be insured than nonworkers, but among the poor, workers were less likely to be insured than nonworkers. About one-half, or 47.5 percent, of poor, full-time workers were uninsured in 1998.
- The foreign-born population was more likely to be without health insurance than natives—34.1 percent compared with 14.4 percent in 1998. Poor immigrants were even worse off—53.3 percent were without health insurance.

---

[1]Hispanics may be of any race.

- People 18 to 24 years old were more likely than other age groups to lack coverage—30.0 percent were without coverage in 1998. Because of Medicare, the elderly were at the other extreme—only 1.1 percent lacked coverage.

EMPLOYMENT REMAINS THE LEADING SOURCE OF HEALTH INSURANCE COVERAGE

Most people (70.2 percent) were covered by a private insurance plan for some or all of 1998 (a private plan is one that is offered through employment—either one's own or a relative's—or privately purchased). Most private insurance was obtained through a current or former employer or union (see Figure 1).

The government also provided health care coverage (24.3 percent of people had government insurance), including Medicare (13.2 percent), Medicaid (10.3 percent), and military health care (3.2 percent). Many people carried coverage from more than one plan during the year; for example, 7.6 percent of people were covered by both private insurance and Medicare.

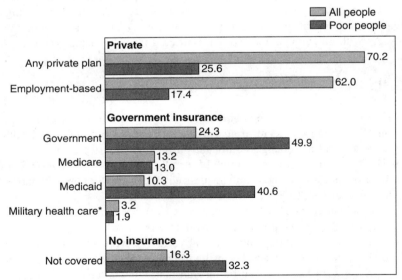

*Military health care includes CHAMPUS (Comprehensive Health and Medical Plan for Uniformed Services)/Tricare, CHAMPVA (Civilian Health and Medical Program of the Department of Veteran's Affairs), Veteran's, and military health care.
Note: The estimates by type of coverage are not mutually exclusive; people can be covered by more than one type of health insurance during the year.

Figure 1   Type of health insurance and coverage status—1998 (in percent) (Source: U.S. Census Bureau, Current Population Survey, March 1999)

THE POOR AND NEAR POOR ARE MORE LIKELY TO LACK COVERAGE

Despite the Medicaid program, 32.3 percent of the poor (11.2 million people) had no health insurance of any kind during 1998. This percentage—which was about double the rate for all people—was statistically unchanged from the previous year. The uninsured poor comprised 25.2 percent of all uninsured people.

Medicaid was the most widespread type of coverage among the poor, with 40.6 percent (14.0 million) of all poor people covered by Medicaid at some time during the year. This percentage is down significantly from the previous year, however, when 43.3 percent of poor people were covered by Medicaid.[2]

Among the near poor (those with a family income greater than the poverty level but less than 125 percent of the poverty level), 29.9 percent (3.5 million people) were without health insurance.

KEY FACTORS INFLUENCING THE CHANCES OF NOT HAVING HEALTH INSURANCE COVERAGE

Age—People 18 to 24 years old were more likely than other age groups to lack coverage during all of 1998 (30.0 percent). Because of Medicare, the elderly were at the other extreme (only 1.1 percent lacked coverage). Among the poor, adults age 18 to 64 had much higher noncoverage rates than either children or the elderly.

Race and Hispanic origin—Among these groups, Hispanics had the highest chance of not having health insurance coverage in 1998. The uninsured rate for Hispanics was 35.3 percent, compared with 11.9 percent for non-Hispanic Whites. Among the poor, Hispanics also had the highest noncoverage rates, with 44.0 percent of that population uninsured in 1998.[3]

Educational attainment—Among all adults, the likelihood of being uninsured declined as the level of education rose. Among those who were poor in 1998, there were no differences across the education groups.

Work experience—Of those 18–64 years old who were employed, part-time workers had a higher noncoverage rate (23.2 percent) than full-time workers (16.9 percent).[4] Among the general population of 18–64 year olds, workers (both full- and part-time) were more likely to be insured than nonworkers. However, among the poor, workers were less likely to be insured than nonworkers. About one-half of poor, full-time workers were uninsured in 1998 (47.5 percent).

---

[2]Changes in year-to-year Medicaid estimates should be viewed with caution. For more information, see the Technical Note.

[3]The uninsured rates for poor Asian and Pacific Islanders, poor Blacks, and poor non-Hispanic Whites were not statistically different from one another.

[4]Workers were classified as part time if they worked less than 35 hours per week in the majority of the weeks they worked in 1998.

Nativity—In 1998, a higher proportion of the foreign-born population was without health insurance (34.1 percent) compared with natives (14.4 percent).[5] Of the foreign-born, noncitizens were more than twice as likely as naturalized citizens to lack coverage—42.9 percent compared with 19.2 percent. Poor immigrants were even worse off—53.3 percent were without health insurance.

INCOME AND FIRM SIZE PLAY IMPORTANT ROLES

Noncoverage rates fall as household income rises. In 1998, the percent of people without health insurance ranged from 8.3 percent among those in households with incomes of $75,000 or more to 25.2 percent among those in households with incomes less than $25,000 (see Figure 2).

Of the 146.3 million total workers in the United States (15 years and older), 53.3 percent had employment-based health insurance policies in their own name. The proportion varied widely by size of employing firm, with workers employed by firms with fewer than 25 employees being the least likely to be covered (see Figure 3). These estimates do not reflect the fact that some workers are covered by another family member's employment-based policy.

CHILDREN'S HEALTH CARE COVERAGE STATUS WAS UNCHANGED IN 1998

The number of uninsured children (people less than 18 years of age) was 11.1 million (15.4 percent) in 1998; neither the number nor the percentage was significantly different from the previous year.

---

[5]"Natives" are people born in the United States, Puerto Rico, or an outlying area of the United States, such as Guam or the U.S. Virgin Islands, and people who were born in a foreign country but who had at least one parent who was a U.S. citizen. All other people born outside the United States are "foreign-born."

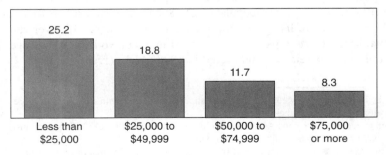

Figure 2   People without health insurance coverage by household income—1998 (in percent) (Source: U.S. Census Bureau, Current Population Survey, March 1999)

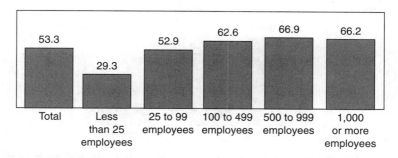

Figure 3 Workers (15 years old and over) covered by their own employment-based health insurance by firm size—1998 (in percent) (Source: U.S. Census Bureau, Current Population Survey, March 1999)

Among poor children, 3.4 million (25.2 percent) were uninsured in 1998, also statistically unchanged from the previous year. Poor children made up 30.6 percent of all uninsured children in 1998.

OTHER FINDINGS CONCERNING CHILDREN

- Children 12 to 17 years of age were slightly less likely to have health care coverage than those under age 12—16.0 percent were uninsured compared with 15.1 percent.
- Hispanic children were far more likely to be uninsured (30.0 percent) than children in other racial or ethnic groups. The rates were 19.7 percent for Black children, 16.8 percent for Asian and Pacific Islander children, and 10.6 percent for non-Hispanic, White children.
- While most children (48.6 million) were covered by an employment-based or privately purchased plan in 1998, about one-fifth (14.3 million) were covered by Medicaid (see Figure 4).
- In 1998, Black children were more likely to be covered by Medicaid than children of any other race or ethnic group. Medicaid provided health insurance for 38.8 percent of Black children, 29.8 percent of Hispanic children, 12.5 percent of non-Hispanic White children, and 19.2 percent of Asian and Pacific Islander children.

SOME STATES HAVE HIGHER NONCOVERAGE RATES THAN OTHERS

Uninsured rates ranged from 8.7 percent in Hawaii to 24.4 percent in Texas, based on 3-year averages for 1996, 1997, and 1998. We advise against using these estimates to rank the states, however. For example, the high noncoverage rate for Texas was not statistically different from that in Arizona (24.3 percent), while the rate for

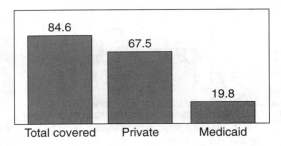

Figure 4   Children (under 18 years old) by type of health insurance and coverage status—1998 (in percent) (Source: U.S. Census Bureau, Current Population Survey, March 1999)

Hawaii was not statistically different from Wisconsin (9.4 percent) or Minnesota (9.6 percent), as shown in Figure 5.

Comparisons of 2-year averages (1997–1998 versus 1996–1997) show that noncoverage rates fell in eight states: Arkansas, Florida, Iowa, Massachusetts, Missouri, Nebraska, Ohio, and Tennessee. Meanwhile, noncoverage rates rose in 16 states: Alabama, Alaska, California, Illinois, Indiana, Maryland, Michigan, Montana, Nevada, North Dakota, Pennsylvania, South Dakota, Utah, West Virginia, Wisconsin, and Wyoming.

TECHNICAL NOTE

This report presents data on the health insurance coverage of people in the United States during the 1998 calendar year. The data, which are shown by selected demographic and socioeconomic characteristics, as well as by state, were collected in the March 1999 Supplement to the Current Population Survey (CPS).

In the Current Population Survey (CPS), Medicare and Medicaid coverage are underreported compared with enrollment and participation data from the Health Care Financing Administration (HCFA).[6] A major reason for the lower CPS estimates is that the CPS is not designed primarily to collect health insurance data; instead, it is largely a labor force survey, with relatively little training of interviewers on health insurance concepts. Data from HCFA represent the actual number of people who were enrolled or participated in these programs and are a more accurate source of data on levels of coverage. Also, many people may not be aware that they or their children are covered by a health insurance program and, therefore, do not report coverage.

Changes in Medicaid coverage estimates from one year to the next should be viewed with caution. Because many people who are covered by Medicaid do not report that coverage, the Census Bureau assigns coverage to those who are generally regarded as "categorically eligible" (those who received some other benefits, usually

---

[6]HCFA is the federal agency primarily responsible for administering the Medicare and Medicaid programs at the national level.

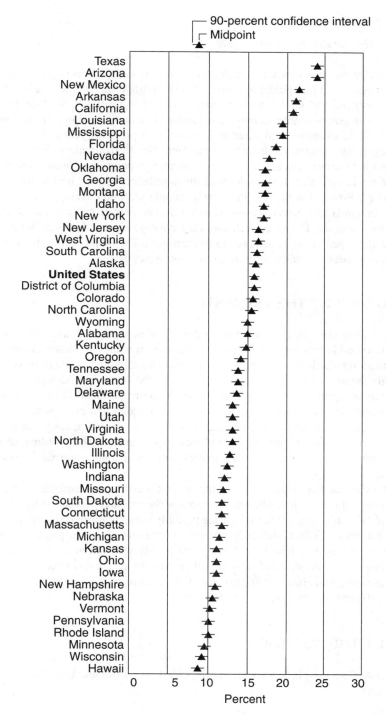

Figure 5 Percent of people without health insurance by state (3-year average)—1996–1998 (Source: U.S. Census Bureau, Current Population Surveys, March 1997, 1998, and 1999)

public assistance payments, that make them eligible for Medicaid). Since the number of people receiving public assistance has been dropping and the relationship between Medicaid and public assistance has changed significantly over the past few years, this imputation process may have resulted in a downward bias in the most recent Medicaid estimates compared with those from previous years.

Beginning with the publication of the 1997 Health Insurance Coverage report, as a result of consultation with health insurance experts, the Census Bureau has made a modification in the definition of the population without health insurance in the Current Population Survey. Previously, people with no coverage other than access to Indian Health Service were considered to be part of the insured population. Beginning with the 1997 Health Insurance Coverage report, that is no longer true; instead, these people are considered to be uninsured. The effect of this change on the overall estimates of health insurance coverage is negligible.

ACCURACY OF THE ESTIMATES

Statistics from surveys are subject to sampling and nonsampling error. All comparisons presented in this report have taken sampling error into account and meet Census Bureau standards for statistical significance. Nonsampling errors in surveys may be attributed to a variety of sources, such as how the survey was designed, how respondents interpret questions, how able and willing respondents are to provide correct answers, and how accurately the answers are coded and classified.

The Census Bureau employs quality control procedures throughout the production process—including the overall design of surveys, the wording of questions, review of the work of interviewers and coders, and statistical review of reports.

The Current Population Survey employs ratio estimation, whereby sample estimates are adjusted to independent estimates of the national population by age, race, sex, and Hispanic origin. This weighting partially corrects for bias due to undercoverage, but how it affects different variables in the survey is not precisely known. Moreover, biases may also be present when people who are missed in the survey differ from those interviewed in ways other than the categories used in weighting (age, race, sex, and Hispanic origin). All of these considerations affect comparisons across different surveys or data sources.

ABOUT THE AUTHOR

Jennifer A. Campbell is Statistician for the U.S. Census Bureau, U.S. Department of Commerce.

ARTICLE 2

THE AMERICAN HEALTH CARE SYSTEM: HEALTH INSURANCE COVERAGE

Robert Kuttner

The most prominent feature of American health insurance coverage is its slow erosion, even as the government seeks to plug the gaps in coverage through such new programs as Medicare+Choice, the Health Insurance Portability and Accountability Act (HIPAA), expansions of state Medicaid programs, and the $24 billion Children's Health Insurance Program of 1997. Despite these efforts, the proportion of Americans without insurance increased from 14.2 percent in 1995 to 15.3 percent in 1996 and to 16.1 percent in 1997, when 43.4 million people were uninsured. Not as well appreciated is the fact that the number of people who are underinsured, and thus must either pay out of pocket or forgo medical care, is growing even faster.

This report addresses several trends that account for the erosion of health insurance coverage. The most important trend is the deterioration of employer-provided coverage, the source of health insurance for nearly two in three Americans.[1] I will discuss this cause in detail in the next article in this series. To summarize briefly for now, a few employers have eliminated coverage entirely because of the escalating costs of premiums. Most employers have narrowed the choice of plans and shifted costs to employees by capping the employer's contribution, choosing plans with higher out-of-pocket payments, or both. These changes, in turn, have caused some employees to forgo coverage for themselves and their families and have also led to underinsurance, since many employees, especially those who receive low wages, cannot afford the out-of-pocket charges.

The following trends are also eroding insurance coverage of all types.

Rising premium costs, both for persons who have access to insurance through their employers and for those who buy insurance individually. Costs will rise in 1999 for both groups, but more sharply for persons with individual coverage.[2,3]

The trend toward temporary and part-time work, which seldom includes health care coverage. In 1997, about 29 percent of working Americans held "nonstandard" jobs, a category that includes temporary, part-time, contract, and day-labor positions.[4]

A reduction in explicit coverage, most notably pharmaceutical benefits. Most plans cap outpatient pharmaceutical benefits. Prescription drugs now constitute the largest category of out-of-pocket payments for the elderly, and the costs are rapidly rising.

Greater de facto limitations on covered care, especially by health maintenance organizations (HMOs). More stringent utilization reviews and economic disincentives for physicians and hospitals are resulting in denial of care and shifting of costs to patients.

A broad shift from traditional HMOs requiring very low out-of-pocket payments to point-of-service plans and preferred-provider organizations (PPOs) requiring higher payments by patients. Ostensibly, the rationale for this shift is to provide greater choice for consumers, but consumers often enroll in a PPO or a point-of-service plan not because HMOs restrict choice but because they are perceived as restricting care. By 1997, there were more than twice as many Americans enrolled in point-of-service plans or PPOs as there were in HMOs.[1]

Loss of Medicaid coverage due to welfare reform. The 1996 welfare-reform law separates Medicaid eligibility from eligibility for public assistance, but it also pushes many former welfare recipients into low-wage employment that does not provide health insurance. Although the termination of welfare benefits does not necessarily entail loss of Medicaid coverage, preliminary reports suggest that in practice the added administrative complexity is leading to reduced enrollment in Medicaid.[5]

The rising cost of "Medigap" coverage for the elderly, which leads to substantial underinsurance. In some states, such as Massachusetts, comprehensive Medigap policies are now in a death spiral: only a small number of persons with high medical expenses find it cost effective to buy such policies, and low enrollment, in turn, leads to even higher premiums and lower enrollment.

The crackdown on illegal immigrants and the reduction in services to legal immigrants. These policies are forcing many immigrants to forgo Medicaid and other forms of health coverage that are legally available to their children who are citizens.

The trend away from community rating of individual insurance premiums, which results in rising costs and, hence, reduced rates of coverage for middle-aged persons. For the 8.7 million Americans who buy insurance individually, premiums are partly adjusted for age and are also adjusted for prior medical conditions.

As a result of these trends, lack of insurance and underinsurance are becoming more widespread problems. Not surprisingly, it is lower-income Americans who bear the disproportionate costs, since as compared with higher-income Americans, they are more likely to work for employers who do not provide health care coverage or who require employees to make sizable contributions to insurance premiums, they are more likely to have part-time or temporary jobs with no health care coverage, and they are less able to afford individual insurance or high out-of-pocket payments.

Surprisingly, unemployment is scarcely implicated in these trends. Indeed, all of them have occurred while unemployment rates have been declining. Other things being equal, a decline in the unemployment rate should bring an increase in health insurance coverage, given the prevalence of employer-provided coverage. But the low unemployment rates of the late 1990s have not been sufficient to offset the above-mentioned trends. Today, the vast majority of uninsured persons are employed.

THE UNINSURED

The number of uninsured persons rose from 41.7 million (15.6 percent) in 1996 to 43.4 million (16.1 percent) in 1997, according to a September 1998 Census Bureau report.[6] This widely publicized increase tends to understate the extent of the problem, however. The Census Bureau also calculated that a much larger number of Americans, about 71.5 million, lacked insurance for at least part of the year. The latter figure was based on a study conducted from 1993 through 1995.[7] Poor and low-income persons, as well as members of minority groups, were most likely to have periods without coverage. Twenty-five percent of non-Hispanic whites had at least one month without coverage, as compared with 37 percent of blacks and 50 percent of Hispanics.

Lack of insurance is very closely correlated with low income. Whereas 8 percent of Americans with incomes over $75,000 and 16.1 percent of all Americans lacked health insurance in 1997, 24 percent of those with incomes of less than $25,000 had no coverage. Fifty percent of persons with incomes below the poverty line had at least one month without insurance, as compared with 27 percent of those with higher incomes. Despite Medicaid, 11.2 million persons with incomes below the poverty line, or 31.6 percent of all the poor, had no health insurance at all in 1997.[6]

The high cost of health insurance relative to income is the main reason for high rates of uninsurance among poor and low-income persons. A study conducted by KMPG Peat Marwick for The Commonwealth Fund found that a person with an annual income at the poverty threshold would need to pay 26 percent of that income to purchase health insurance. In more expensive markets, this cost rises to 40 percent of income for a family of four.[8] Since such families are barely able to pay for food and shelter, these figures suggest that for poor and low-income persons, health insurance is effectively unaffordable unless it is provided by employers or the government.

Lack of insurance is also correlated with loss of employment. According to the Census Bureau during the period from 1993 to 1995, 44 percent of persons who lost their jobs also reported loss of insurance coverage. At the same time, however, almost half (49 percent) of fully employed people with incomes below the poverty line had no insurance.[7] The figure was even higher in 1996, when 52 percent of poor full-time workers had no insurance. This study was conducted before the enactment in 1996 of the HIPAA, which makes it easier for persons who have lost employer-provided insurance to qualify for other coverage.

However, to the extent that loss of insurance coverage is the result of lost purchasing power due to job loss, HIPAA is of no help, because it provides no subsidy and does not regulate price. The 1985 Consolidated Omnibus Budget Reconciliation Act (COBRA), which allows people leaving employment to pay insurance premiums out of pocket for up to 18 months in order to retain their coverage, likewise fails to address economic barriers to coverage. Moreover, although HIPAA prohibits outright denial of insurance because of previous medical conditions, it allows insurers to charge people with previous conditions substantially higher premiums, thus sharply limiting effective coverage.[9] Although in principle HIPAA protects as many as 25 million people from loss of insurance, in practice it benefits only a few hundred thousand.[10]

A 1997 national survey of health insurance conducted by Louis Harris Associates for the Henry J. Kaiser Family Foundation and The Commonwealth Fund confirms these trends. According to the survey, one in three adults between the ages of 18 and 64 years had been without insurance at some point in the previous two years. The survey confirmed that persons with low incomes were most likely to lack coverage: 59 percent of adults with incomes below $20,000 had been without coverage, as compared with 8 percent of adults with incomes above $60,000. [11] The survey also confirmed that lack of insurance was more often due to the high cost of coverage (reported by 51 percent of respondents) than to job loss or the employer's failure to provide access to coverage (reported by 25 percent). Fifty-seven percent of respondents without insurance were employed full time.[12] The survey also showed considerable discontinuity of coverage, with one third of insured adults reporting that they had been enrolled in their current health plan for less than two years.[13]

CHILDREN WITHOUT INSURANCE

Several reports have documented high and rising rates of uninsurance among children. According to a March 1997 Families USA report based on Census data, approximately one child in three had no insurance coverage for one or more months during 1995 and 1996.[14] Almost half these children (47 percent) were uninsured for a year or more. Unemployment of the family breadwinner was not the main reason, since 91 percent of the children who lacked health coverage for the entire two years lived in households where the breadwinners were employed all or part of the 24-month period. Lack of insurance was more closely correlated with low income. Fifty percent of children with family incomes between $15,000 and $25,000 had no health care coverage. For the very poor, Medicaid in principle provides coverage. According to the General Accounting Office, however, nearly 3 million children who are eligible for Medicaid are not enrolled in the program[15] because of inadequate outreach, fears on the part of immigrants that enrollment will lead to problems with the authorities, and other barriers.

On the basis of a survey of health care coverage for children, the Census Bureau reported that the proportion of children lacking insurance rose from 12 percent in 1989 to 15 percent in 1996,[16] a period of increasing prosperity in general, decreasing unemployment, and nominal expansion of eligibility for Medicaid. Noting that the number of poor children covered by Medicaid fell from 16.5 million to 15.5 million between 1995 and 1996, the Census Bureau observed, "The growth in the number of children lacking health insurance is largely attributable to the fall-off in Medicaid coverage."[16] Some 34 percent of the survey respondents whose children did not receive regular medical care reported that the reason was that they had no insurance and could not afford visits to doctors.[17] Approximately 800,000 children were taken to emergency rooms for all their care.[18]

In 10 jurisdictions, at least 37 percent of children went without insurance for some portion of the period from 1995 through 1996: Texas (46 percent), New Mexico (43 percent), Louisiana (43 percent), Arkansas (42 percent), Mississippi (41 percent), the District of Columbia (39 percent), Alabama (38 percent), Arizona (38 percent), Nevada (37 percent), and California (37 percent).[19]

Not surprisingly, several studies confirm that children without health insurance receive less care in the form of diagnostic, screening, and immunization services than children with coverage. Uninsured children have fewer checkups, are less likely to be treated for chronic conditions such as asthma and recurrent ear infections, are less likely to be treated by doctors for injuries, and are more likely to go without eyeglasses or prescribed drugs.[20]

THE UNDERINSURED

The increasing prevalence of underinsurance may well be the more serious trend. Underinsurance here refers to medical needs that either are not covered by health plans at all or are covered but with high copayments that force beneficiaries to forgo treatment. Stringent "management" of care that results in denial of medically necessary treatment may also be considered a form of underinsurance.

Studies by the Employee Benefit Research Institute, several private consultants, and Consumers Union all document substantial cost shifting and rising rates of underinsurance. A January 1998 study conducted by the Lewin Group for Consumers Union found that 11 million families without elderly members (1 in 8 families) spend on average more than 10 percent of their income on out-of-pocket health care costs and health insurance premiums not paid for by employers.[21] This figure rises to 20 percent for families with members who are 55 to 64 years old, and to 50 percent for families with members who are 65 or older. Among all age groups, the 10 percent of people with the most serious health problems spend an average of $21,000 a year in premium and out-of-pocket payments.[21]

In addition, recent trends in both employment and health insurance have made ties between patients and doctors less stable. The Kaiser–Commonwealth survey found that 34 percent of insured adults under the age of 65 had been enrolled in their current health plan for less than two years.[22] Only 36 percent had had the same primary care doctor for five years or more.[23] Respondents with conventional Medicare or Medicaid coverage actually had more stable relationships with providers than those in managed-care plans, a finding that is largely due to the fragmentation and turbulence of the managed-care industry.

PHARMACEUTICAL COVERAGE

The costs of prescription drugs continue to rise faster than the costs of other components of health care, and they are increasingly less likely to be covered by insurance. Total expenditures for prescription drugs increased by 85 percent between 1993 and 1998, with an estimated 17 percent increase from 1997 to 1998 alone, or more than four times the rate of increase for all health care expenditures in that period.[24] In 1995, more than half of all pharmaceutical costs were paid out of pocket,[25] and the proportion is almost certainly higher now.

The elderly are most dependent on prescription drugs, which Medicare does not cover. More than 19 million elderly persons, or about half of all Medicare enrollees, have no drug coverage. Press reports indicate that countless prescriptions go unfilled because elderly patients cannot afford to pay for them.[26] Expenditures for prescription drugs account for 34 percent of medical expenditures by the elderly, representing a larger proportion of expenditures than that for either hospital charges or physicians' services, according to the American Association of Retired Persons.

In 1995, elderly people with some pharmaceutical benefits received them through HMOs (12 percent), Medicaid (6 percent), employer-provided supplemental policies for retirees (26 percent), or privately purchased Medigap policies (9 percent).[27] Each of these sources, however, is being cut back, either in diminished coverage or in diminished enrollment. In 1998, some Medicare HMOs quit the business and others capped or dropped drug coverage. In the case of Medigap plans, only 3 of the 10 standard plans mandated by the 1990 federal Medigap legislation provided any prescription-drug coverage, and only a small minority of people who bought Medigap coverage purchased these plans. According to the Lewin Group, the proportion of employer-provided supplemental plans for retirees that included prescription-drug coverage declined from 90 percent in 1989 to 81 percent in 1995.[28] And the proportion of employers offering retirees supplemental health coverage declined from over 60 percent in the 1980s to less than 40 percent today, according to the General Accounting Office.[29]

Virtually all supplemental plans for the elderly require copayments for prescription drugs. In 1998, only 9 percent of Medicare beneficiaries who were enrolled in HMO plans had unlimited prescription-drug benefits; 43 percent were in plans that had no annual dollar cap but that limited coverage to generic drugs or drugs on an approved formulary. In the case of plans that provided coverage for brand-name drugs, more than half of enrollees had an annual cap of $1,000 or less.[30]

McCormack et al.[31] reported in 1996 that 84 percent of Medigap policies in six states provided drug coverage at all, and only 7 percent provided "high-option" coverage (Plan J), with an annual benefit cap of $3,000. Such plans cost over $200 per month, which few elderly people can afford. The lower-option policies (Plans H and I) required a $250 annual deductible for drug costs, a 50 percent copayment, and a $1,250 annual cap. The Lewin Group, using a different method, found that 28 percent of persons with Medigap policies had some pharmaceutical benefits but confirmed that most did not have the high-option plan. Medigap policies paid for only 3 percent of all prescription-drug costs for the elderly. The largest source of insurance coverage, accounting for 21 percent of the costs, was employer-provided supplemental plans; 52 percent of drug costs were paid out of pocket.[32] Obviously, as drug prices keep rising, the relative value of the covered benefit declines. The drug industry continues to resist efforts by Representative Pete Stark (D-Calif.) and others to add drug coverage to Medicare by using federal purchasing power to buy discounted drugs, and such measures currently have little chance of enactment.

THE OUTLOOK

Few of these trends toward increasing numbers of uninsured and underinsured Americans show signs of abatement or reversal. Although managed care dramatically reduced the inflation in health insurance costs for employers in the mid-1990s, this seems to have been a one-time savings. The underlying demographic and technological trends are unchanged, and employers and benefit consultants report sharply rising premium costs in 1999.[3] Employers, facing little resistance from unions or public policy, are continuing both to reduce the options for coverage and to shift costs to employees, leading to both lack of insurance and under-insurance.

Likewise, despite the early promise of Medicare HMOs, the gaps in Medicare coverage are growing larger. Even before the implementation of Medicare+Choice (which allows the insurance industry to market a wider variety of point-of-service plans and PPOs), private insurers had already begun to reduce benefits or withdraw from selected markets. In October 1998, insurers announced they were dropping coverage for some 400,000 of the approximately 6 million enrollees in Medicare HMOs.[33,34]

With premium costs continuing to rise, more employers are dropping or reducing coverage than are expanding it. Health care coverage is seen as a particular burden by smaller businesses, which represent the fastest-growing sector of American employers.[35] And as the shift from full-time to part-time and temporary jobs continues, more employees are likely to find themselves with no benefits.

Congress, in several budget resolutions beginning 1989, has extended Medicaid eligibility, especially to children who are living in poverty but are not on welfare. Some states, such as Oregon and Tennessee, have sought to turn Medicaid into a nearly universal health insurance program for the working poor as well as the indigent. However, these programs entail a degree of rationing, which is either explicit, as in the Oregon program, or implicit, as in Tennessee's stringent approach to managed care. Rationing, in turn, gives people the "choice" of paying for uncovered services out of pocket or doing without them. The shift to Medicaid managed care suggests that although more people will be nominally covered, many will in effect have less coverage.

The expansions in Medicaid are also offset by the 1996 welfare-reform law, Temporary Assistance to Needy Families, which limits the duration of welfare benefits. As the welfare limits gradually become effective in most states during 1999, millions of people will lose their eligibility for Medicaid along with their welfare benefits. Many heads of households will take relatively low-paid jobs, most of which do not offer health insurance; even those that do tend to require high premium payments by employees.

One small bright spot is the likelihood that the number of uninsured children will decline, thanks to the new Children's Health Insurance Program. Enacted as part of the 1997 Balanced Budget Act, the program provides the states with $24 billion over a period of five years. Some states are using these funds to expand Medicaid, and others are setting up new, parallel children's programs.

However, the interactions among Medicaid, the welfare-reform law, and the Children's Health Insurance Program are highly complex and confusing. For example, most children whose mothers will lose Medicaid coverage under welfare reform may retain their eligibility for Medicaid, but coverage is not automatic. Moreover, press reports indicate that immigrants, both legal and illegal, are reluctant to obtain coverage for their children for fear that enrollment will bring investigations by the immigration authorities. As of November 1998, California, which has a complex 28-page application for coverage that includes several questions about immigration status, had enrolled only 4 percent of 580,000 eligible children,[36] despite a payment of $25 to $50 to insurance vendors for every child they enroll. The Congressional Budget Office estimates that the net effect of the welfare-reform law, the Children's Health Insurance Program, and Medicaid expansions will be to extend coverage to some 2 million of the 10.6 million children who were uninsured as of 1997.[37]

With unemployment rates approaching a 30-year low, the overall trend in declining health insurance coverage is, if anything, understated. In the next recession, when the unemployment rate increases, loss of coverage is likely to increase apace. Because all sources of coverage are eroding, the long-term trend is toward a continued decline in both nominal and effective rates of coverage, unless there is a dramatic change in national policy.

ABOUT THE AUTHOR

Robert Kuttner is Coeditor of the *American National Prospect* and National Policy Correspondent of *The New England Journal of Medicine*. He is the author of *Everything for Sale: The Returns and Limits of Markets*.

REFERENCES

1. Fronstin P. Features of employment based health plans. Washington, D.C.: Employee Benefit Research Institute, 1998.

2. Kilborn P. Premiums rising for individuals. *New York Times.* December 5, 1998:A7.

3. Freudenheim M. Employees facing steep increases in health care. *New York Times.* November 27, 1998:A1.

4. Mishel L, Bernstein J, Schmitt J. The state of working America, 1998–99. Washington, D.C.: Economic Policy Institute, 1998:243.

5. Greenberg M. Participation in welfare and Medicaid enrollment. Menlo Park, Calif.: Kaiser Family Foundation, September 1998.

6. Bureau of the Census. Health insurance coverage, 1997. Washington, D.C.: Government Printing Office, September 1998 (P60–202).

7. *Idem.* Dynamics of economic well-being: health insurance, 1993–1995. Washington, D.C.: Government Printing Office, September 1998 (P70–64).

8. Gabel J, Hunt K, Kim J. The financial burden of self-paid health insurance on the poor and near-poor. New York: Commonwealth Fund, 1998.

9. Kuttner R. The Kassebaum–Kennedy bill—the limits of incrementalism. *N Engl J Med* 1997;337:64–7.

10. Department of Health and Human Services, Department of Labor, Department of the Treasury. Rulemaking package implementing HIPAA. Washington, D.C.: Government Printing Office, April 1, 1997:72.

11. Schoen C, Hoffman C, Rowland D, Davis K, Altman D. Working families at risk: coverage, access, cost and worries. New York: Commonwealth Fund, 1998.

12. *Idem.* Working families at risk: coverage, access, cost and worries. New York: Commonwealth Fund, 1998:12.

13. *Idem.* Working families at risk: coverage, access, cost and worries. New York: Commonwealth Fund, 1998:6.

14. One out of three: kids without health insurance, 1995–1996. Washington, D.C.: Families USA, 1997.

15. General Accounting Office. Health insurance for children: private insurance coverage continues to deteriorate. Washington, D.C.: Government Printing Office, 1996. (GAO/HEHS 96-129.)

16. Bureau of the Census. Census brief: children without health insurance. Washington, D.C.: Government Printing Office, 1998.

17. *Idem.* Census brief: children without health insurance. Washington, D.C.: Government Printing Office, 1998:5.

18. *Idem.* Census brief: children without health insurance. Washington, D.C.: Government Printing Office, 1998:6.

19. One out of three: kids without health insurance. Washington, D.C.: Families USA, 1997:5.

20. One out of three: kids without health insurance. Washington, D.C.: Families USA, 1997:9.

21. Shearer G. Hidden from view: the growing burden of health care costs. Washington, D.C.: Consumers Union, 1998:3.

22. Schoen C, Hoffman C, Rowland D, Davis K, Altman D. Working families at risk: coverage, access, cost and worries. New York: Commonwealth Fund, 1998:25.

23. *Idem.* Working families at risk: coverage, access, cost and worries. New York: Commonwealth Fund, 1998:51.

24. Tanouye E. U.S. has developed an expensive drug habit; now, how to pay for it? *Wall Street Journal.* November 16, 1998:A1.

25. Current knowledge of third party outpatient drug coverage for Medicare beneficiaries. Fairfax, Va.: Lewin Group, 1998.

26. Lagnado L. Drug costs can leave elderly a grim choice: pills or other needs. *Wall Street Journal.* November 17, 1998:A1.

27. Current knowledge of third party outpatient drug coverage for Medicare beneficiaries. Fairfax, Va.: Lewin Group, November 9, 1998:4.

28. Current knowledge of third party outpatient drug coverage for Medicare beneficiaries. Fairfax, Va.: Lewin Group, 1998:7.

29. Closing the huge hole in Medicare's benefits package. Remarks by Congressman Pete Stark, U.S. House of Representatives, Washington, D.C., October 9, 1998.

30. Current knowledge of third party outpatient drug coverage for Medicare beneficiaries. Fairfax, Va.: Lewin Group, 1998:19.

31. McCormack LA, Fox PD, Rice T, Graham ML. Medigap reform legislation of 1990: have the objectives been met? *Health Care Financ Rev* 1996;18(1):157–74.

32. Current knowledge of third party outpatient drug coverage for Medicare beneficiaries. Fairfax, Va.: Lewin Group, 1998:13.

33. Pear R. HMOs are retreating from Medicare, citing high costs. *New York Times.* October 2, 1998:A17.

34. *Idem.* Clinton to announce help as HMOs leave Medicare. *New York Times.* October 8, 1998:A20.

35. National survey of small business executives on health care. Menlo Park, Calif.: Henry J. Kaiser Family Foundation, June 1988.

36. Healthy Families Program subscribers enrolled by county. Sacramento: California Managed Risk Medical Insurance Board, November 24, 1998.

37. Congressional Budget Office memorandum: budgetary implications of the Balanced Budget Act of 1997. Washington, D.C.: Congressional Budget Office, December 1997:54.

ARTICLE 3

THE AMERICAN HEALTH CARE SYSTEM: EMPLOYER-SPONSORED HEALTH COVERAGE

Robert Kuttner

Most Americans rely on their employers for health insurance. In 1997, of the 167.5 million nonelderly Americans with private health insurance, 151.7 million belonged to employer-provided health plans.[1] In response to the escalating cost of health insurance coverage in the 1980s, employers began devising new strategies of cost containment. These included contracting with health plans that practiced a stringent form of managed care, substituting cheaper forms of health coverage for more expensive ones, limiting employees' choice of health plans, and shifting costs to employees in a variety of ways. These measures have stabilized health insurance costs for employers. However, they have left many employees paying more out of pocket and often with inferior forms of health coverage, and they have contributed to an overall increase in the proportion of Americans who are uninsured.

The percentage of nonelderly employees who received their health insurance from their employers declined sharply from 69.2 percent in 1987 to a low point of 63.5 percent in 1993 and then increased slightly to 64.2 percent in 1997, according to the Census Bureau.[1] Slightly more employers are offering health insurance, but fewer workers are taking it, either because of economically onerous cost shifting to employees or because relatively more workers are part-time or temporary employees who do not qualify for insurance benefits. The percentage of workers whose employers offered health insurance increased from 72.4 percent in 1987 to 75.4 percent in 1996. But the "take-up" rate—that is, the proportion of workers who actually got the insurance—fell from 88.3 percent in 1987 to 80.1 percent in 1996.[2]

REDUCING EMPLOYERS' COSTS

Employers' new strategies began to have a dramatic effect in 1993. By 1996, they had virtually eliminated the seemingly chronic escalation of health insurance costs to businesses. Before the managed-care revolution, the annual costs of health coverage to employers regularly escalated at double-digit rates. Between 1980 and 1993, private health insurance costs per enrollee increased by 218 percent in inflation-adjusted dollars, while the inflation-adjusted gross domestic product per capita rose by just 17 percent.[3] The increased costs were simply passed along by insurance plans to employers, in annual premium increases. In one year alone, 1988–1989, employers' health insurance costs rose by 18 percent.[4] Between 1980 and 1993, spending by employers on health care as a percentage of total compensation to workers increased from 3.7 percent to 6.6 percent.[5]

Aggressive cost-containment and cost-shifting measures have stanched this escalation of employers' costs. Since 1993, inflation in health insurance costs to employers has slowed to roughly the overall rate of inflation, and in some years the inflation-adjusted cost has actually declined. Indeed, employers' health insurance costs as a percentage of total compensation to workers declined from a peak of 6.6 percent in 1993 to 5.9 percent by 1996.[5] A survey by KPMG Peat Marwick of 1000 randomly selected large and small employers found that their annual increases in health insurance premiums gradually declined from 11.5 percent in 1990 to 8.0 percent in 1992, 4.8 percent in 1994, and 0.5 percent in 1996.[4]

Since the underlying sources of inflation in medical costs have, if anything, intensified during this period—most notably, new technology and an aging population—it is evident that this impressive cost containment has come less from a shift to more efficient uses of health dollars than from limiting the care actually provided or shifting costs to employees. Moreover, since 1997 there have been preliminary signs that the relatively easy gains due to managed care and cost shifting have now been realized, and employers' costs have begun rising again. The *Wall Street Journal* recently cited a survey of Fortune 500 benefits managers, who anticipate premium increases averaging 10.3 percent for 1999, as compared with 5.9 percent for 1998.[6] Small businesses' costs are expected to rise even faster.

MANAGED CARE AND DIMINISHED CHOICE

Employers have achieved the cost containment that marked the mid-1990s in several ways. The most powerful method has been a shift from traditional unmanaged indemnity insurance to tightly managed plans, both health maintenance organizations (HMOs) and point-of-service or network plans. These plans have in common, of course, strict controls on the use of medical services, as well as financial incentives to physicians and hospitals aimed at cutting both services and costs.

Between 1984 and 1993, the proportion of employees enrolled in HMOs increased from 5 percent to 50 percent.[4] By 1998, 85 percent of employees with health insurance coverage were in some form of managed-care plan, whereas 15 percent were in fee-for-service indemnity plans (employees were typically charged more for such plans).[7] Meanwhile, the percentage of employers who even offered indemnity plans gradually declined from 89 percent as recently as 1989 to 57 percent by 1996.[4]

The shift to stringently managed care has stabilized costs to employers, though not to employees. After steadily increasing during the 1980s and early 1990s, the average premium charged to employer-sponsored plans began declining in the mid-1990s. The monthly cost of an employee-only HMO benefit declined from $166 a month in 1994 to $157 a month in 1996. The average monthly cost of HMO family benefits fluctuated narrowly between $453 in 1994 and $448 in 1996.[4] Even the costs of indemnity plans declined by approximately the same percentage, reflecting the fact that many of the same cost-containment strategies (utilization review and physician profiling, steeply discounted fee-for-service schedules, and shifts from in-patient to outpatient settings) have been incorporated into relatively unmanaged indemnity policies as well.

Historically, most large employers offered workers broad medical choices through indemnity insurance. As recently as 1990, according to Hewitt Associates, 69 percent of the 681 large employers in their survey offered both HMO and indemnity plans. By 1995, that percentage had dropped to 22 percent.[8] Instead, by the mid-1990s, firms were offering coverage through traditional HMOs, point-of-service HMOs, and preferred-provider organizations (PPOs). Today, the main group of employees who still enjoy broad choices are those in the public sector, through such programs as the California Public Employees' Retirement System and the Federal Employees Health Benefits Program. A small number of groups of private-sector employers are attempting to offer the same kind of choice that is available to most federal and state employees, but they still make up only a tiny minority of employers.

Often, employers contract with a single health plan but offer their employees more choices within that plan. For example, an employee may choose a point-of-service option that allows a patient to pay extra for the privilege of going out of the network of providers of a basic HMO plan. This trend is important, because the market model of health care, like all markets, relies on consumer choice to discipline suppliers. With the absence of such choice, the consumers' option of changing providers is precluded.

COST SHIFTING TO EMPLOYEES

Large employers, who began providing health insurance benefits to their employees in the 1940s, typically extended such benefits to workers' families as well. Today, according to several benefits consultants cited by the General Accounting Office,[4] employers increasingly give financial inducements to employees to choose employee-only, as opposed to family, coverage. The widespread shift to "cafeteria" benefits packages essentially gives each employee a fixed dollar amount that the company will contribute for benefits. Since family coverage costs about three times as much as individual coverage, employees with families generally exhaust the cash value of their employer-provided benefits and must either tap their salary income to pay the additional costs of family coverage or do without. Most employees with capped benefits finance much of the coverage for their families out of their own pockets.[4] Some 5 percent of firms do not offer family benefits at all, even if the employee pays the full cost.[4]

As recently as the mid-1980s, large corporations that provided comprehensive health insurance usually paid the full cost. But in the past decade, cost sharing with employees became widespread. Indeed, reductions in health insurance coverage were the single largest cause of labor disputes in that decade. By 1990, the percentage of employers paying the full cost of employees' health care coverage declined to 27 percent in the case of indemnity coverage and 30 percent in the case of PPOs. By 1995, that share had declined further to just 7 percent and 11 percent, respectively. For workers who also obtained coverage for their families, the employee was required to share costs in nearly all cases.[8]

Cost shifting takes a variety of forms. It includes capping the employer's total benefit contribution and thus requiring the employee to trade off health insurance against pension and other fringe benefits; requiring employees to bear some of the cost of premiums; covering employees but not their family members; offering only health plans that stringently cap some services such as prescription drugs and nonemergency outpatient psychiatric benefits; and increasing the amounts of deductibles or copayments for indemnity and PPO plans. According to Hewitt Associates, 16 percent of employers offering indemnity plans in 1990 had individual annual deductibles of $250 or more. By 1995, that percentage had increased to 43 percent. For PPO plans, the percentage with such deductibles rose from 15 percent in 1990 to 32 percent in 1995.[8]

Moreover, the amount of the average employee's contribution to the cost of health insurance premiums also increased dramatically during this period, from $60 per month for family coverage in 1988 to $107 per month in 1993. According to Department of Labor statistics cited by the General Accounting Office, 16 percent of employees with coverage classified as "employer-provided" actually pay $150 or more monthly out of their own pockets.[4] Hewitt Associates, surveying 681 large U.S. employers, found that the median contribution of employees to the costs of family coverage rose 64 percent in the case of indemnity plans and 63 percent for PPO coverage between 1990 and 1995.[8] This was, of course, a far faster increase than that in employers' costs, suggesting substantial cost shifting.

A Kaiser Family Foundation study, citing data from KPMG Peat Marwick, put the average contribution by employees at $1,615 per year in 1996, or about 30 percent of the total premium.[9] The General Accounting Office found that escalating cost shifting resulted in many lower-income and part-time employees' deciding not to take the health coverage, either for themselves or for their families, because they could not afford it.[4] For a low-income worker, defined as one earning less than $7 per hour, this average premium cost would represent about 12 percent of pretax income.

In addition to the employees' rising share of premiums, deductibles, copayments, and other out-of-pocket costs have lately risen at a faster rate than health expenditures generally. In 1997, out-of-pocket payments increased by 5.3 percent, whereas total health care costs rose only 4.8 percent.[10]

SQUEEZING OUT LOWER-INCOME EMPLOYEES

The General Accounting Office attributes much of the recent decline in health coverage to changing practices by employers—either dropping health coverage or shifting costs to employees:

> As employers dropped coverage or raised the cost of coverage for employees and families, the percentage of people with private health insurance declined. In 1989, 75 percent of people under 65 years of age had private health insurance; by 1995, this number had dropped to just under 71 percent. Most of this decline was among dependents.[4]

Not surprisingly, the loss of health coverage was more dramatic among lower-income workers, for whom cost shifting represents a larger economic burden. Between 1989 and 1995, according to the General Accounting Office, the rate of private insurance coverage declined from 89 percent to 87 percent of the population under 65 years of age with incomes in excess of 200 percent of the federal poverty level, but it declined from 45 percent to 40 percent for people with incomes at or below that income threshold.[4] A September 1998 Kaiser Family Foundation study found that the proportion of low-wage workers (those paid less than $7 per hour) who had access to employer-provided insurance declined by 5 percentage points between 1987 and 1996, but the proportion who actually accepted such coverage declined by 13 percentage points.[9]

In other words, the proportion of employees who could not afford to pay their rising share of the cost of nominally available coverage, and thus declined it, rose more sharply than the proportion whose employers did not provide coverage at all. By cost shifting, employers effectively price many lower-income workers out of economically meaningful access to health insurance. This, in turn, saves employers what would otherwise be their share of coverage for such workers, reducing employers' costs even further—and displacing those costs onto the portion of the system that bears the expense of uncompensated care or forcing these employees and their families to go without care altogether.

Employer-provided coverage for higher-wage workers has also involved shifted costs and constrained choices, but more affluent workers have been able to absorb these costs. In 1996, the proportion of high-wage workers (those paid $15 per hour or more) who had employer-provided coverage was 90 percent, a decline of 3 percentage points since 1987.[9]

Health insurance coverage provided by employers also varies according to the size of the company. Every Fortune 500 firm offers health insurance coverage.

However, only 49 percent of employers with fewer than 200 workers provide health insurance, and smaller companies are more likely to offer less comprehensive plans. Among very small companies, with fewer than six employees, only 30 percent provide any form of health benefits.[6]

Over a longer period, from 1979 to 1993, the percentage of all workers with employer-provided health insurance declined from 71 percent to 64 percent, a drop of 7 percentage points, whereas coverage for those in the lowest income quintile dropped by 13 percentage points, from 40 percent to 27 percent.[11] Although expansions in Medicaid eligibility and new federal and state programs aimed at providing coverage for uninsured children have made up some of this lost coverage, they have not filled the gap. One study attributed 83 percent of the decline in private health insurance coverage to changes in employers' behavior and 17 percent to expansions of Medicaid, mainly directed to pregnant women and children.[12] The vast majority of employees who have lost private coverage provided by their employers neither purchase individual insurance nor qualify for Medicaid.

Nor is the loss of employer-provided coverage substantially related to unemployment (which has declined in the 1990s). The vast majority of people who lack health insurance—79 percent—are in families with at least one full-time worker.[9] But either these workers are employed by companies that do not provide insurance or the cost-sharing provisions make such insurance prohibitively expensive for low-wage employees.

In sum, the primary reason for the lack of health insurance among millions of people and their families is that their employers either fail to provide it or burden employees with onerous costs. The recent increase in the number of uninsured people reflects cost shifting more than it reflects termination of coverage by employers. The percentage of high-income workers who have access to employer-provided plans has actually increased slightly, from 92 percent in 1987 to 96 percent in 1996, whereas the percentage of low-income workers with access to employer-provided plans fell from 60 percent to 55 percent. The Kaiser Family Foundation calculated that even if the rate of acceptance of insurance offered by employers were identical for low-income and high-income employees, the percentage of low-income employees with insurance would rise only from 42 percent to 51 percent—still far below the 90 percent rate of coverage among high-income workers.[9] Low-income employees tend to be concentrated in companies that either do not offer insurance or offer it in a form that is effectively too expensive for the employee.

The Kaiser Family Foundation study found that the most dramatic erosion in the provision of health insurance by employers occurred between 1988 and 1993 and that the rate has been essentially stable since 1993.[9] However, the intensification of managed-care cost-containment strategies and shifting of costs to employees have both continued.

Interestingly, although the price of comprehensive basic health coverage is out of the reach of some employees, employers are adding relatively low cost features, such as vision care and dental care, to their health plans. The fraction of employers offering these additional benefits increased between 1990 and 1995, according to Hewitt Associates.[8]

REDUCING BENEFITS TO RETIREES

Although the federal Medicare program provides basic health care coverage to the elderly, large corporations have long supplemented Medicare in programs for their retirees. For corporations with static or diminishing work forces in an era of downsizing, the ratio of workers to retirees declines and the burden of supporting retired workers increases.

Since the early 1990s, health benefits for retired employees have followed the same downward trajectory as coverage for current employees. The percentage of employers that bear the full cost of retirement coverage declined from 27 percent in 1990 to 8 percent in 1995.[8] In addition, more employers provide coverage to retirees only until the age of 65. In 1990, 85 percent of the companies in the Hewitt Associates sample extended retirement coverage to people over the age of 65. By 1995, that percentage had declined to 76 percent.

CONCLUSIONS

The cost savings realized by employers since 1993 has been greater than can be attributed to the overall slowing of health cost inflation. Much of the savings is simply the result of shifting costs to employees and their families. In addition, the kind of insurance made available to employees is much more likely to be some form of managed care, which often includes more subtle cost shifting in the form of restrictions on covered benefits. Although HMO coverage is nominally comprehensive, with fewer deductibles and copayments as well as more preventive services and pharmaceutical coverage, it nonetheless tends to shift costs to consumers by displacing onto patients and their families the burden of recuperative care, psychiatric care, and care for other conditions that managed-care organizations do not deem eligible for coverage.

A generation ago, when there was more of a long-term social compact between corporations and their employees, it was reasonable that companies would function more or less as proxies for their employees in purchasing health insurance on their behalf. In the 1990s, although concern about quality is regularly invoked by corporate benefits managers, corporations today are more likely to pursue cost containment as their paramount objective in negotiating with health plans and in structuring benefit packages with employees. Moreover, despite the shorter job tenure that is characteristic of the 1990s and the greater proportion of workers with temporary or part-time jobs, workers are still highly reliant on their employers for their health coverage, because high-quality affordable individual insurance is even harder to obtain.

Regulatory measures such as the Health Insurance Portability and Accountability Act (the Kassebaum–Kennedy act), which allows employees who have lost or changed jobs to purchase other health insurance without being excluded on medical grounds, do not address the problems discussed here: the decision by some employers to drop medical coverage, to limit employees' choices, and to shift costs to employees. The trends discussed in this article have no current regulatory remedy.

The spread of employer-provided health insurance resulted from the conjunction of three developments during World War II. The war gave rise to wage and price controls, worker shortages, and strong unions. Under the regulations of the War Labor Board, companies that were short of employees could not recruit workers by offering higher pay, but they were permitted to lure them with fringe benefits, such as pension and health plans. Unions welcomed such benefits, which quickly became customary among major corporations. By the 1950s, large employers generally had high-quality health plans for their (typically unionized) workers. Nonunion employers matched and even exceeded the terms of such health plans, partly as a way of avoiding unionization.

In the 1990s, this logic has been thrown into reverse. Unions are far weaker, and despite low unemployment, employees have relatively less bargaining power and less connection to the firm than in the past. Although employers are no longer reliable sources of health coverage for employees and their families, few consumers have other attractive alternatives. The current pattern—shifting of costs to employees, paring of benefits, and resulting increases in the number of the uninsured and underinsured—is likely to persist as long as the basic system of employer-provided health insurance continues.

ABOUT THE AUTHOR

Robert Kuttner is Coeditor of the *American National Prospect* and National Policy Correspondent of *The New England Journal of Medicine*. He is the author of *Everything for Sale: The Returns and Limits of Markets*.

REFERENCES

1. Fronstin P. Sources of health insurance and characteristics of the uninsured: analysis of the March 1998 Current Population Survey. Washington, D.C.: Employee Benefit Research Institute, December 1998. (Issue brief no. 204.)

2. Cooper PF, Schone BS. More offers, fewer takers for employment-based health insurance: 1987 and 1997. *Health Aff (Millwood)* 1997; 16(6):144.

3. Annual report to Congress, 1996. Washington, D.C.: Physician Payment Review Commission, 1996:figure 1–2.

4. General Accounting Office. Employment-based health insurance: costs increase and family coverage decreases. Washington, D.C.: Government Printing Office, February 1997:2. (GAO/HEHS-97-35.)

5. Fronstin P. Features of employment-based health plans. Washington, D.C.: Employee Benefit Research Institute, 1998:1.

6. Buss DD. Businesses' health premiums are rising. *Wall Street Journal.* November 17, 1998:A2.

7. Facts on job-based health care benefits and self-funded care plans. *EBRI News.* September 25, 1998.

8. Salaried employee benefits provided by major U.S. employers in 1990 and 1995. Lincolnshire, Ill.: Hewitt Associates, 1996.

9. O'Brien E, Feder J. Medicaid and the uninsured. Washington, D.C.: Henry J. Kaiser Family Foundation, September 1998:2.

10. Levit K, Cowan C, Braden B, Stiller J, Sensenig A, Lazenby H. National health expenditures in 1997: more slow growth. *Health Aff (Millwood)* 1998;17(6):108.

11. Mishel L, Bernstein J. The state of working America: 1997–1998. Washington, D.C.: Economic Policy Institute, 1997.

12. Cutler DM, Gruber J. Does public insurance crowd out private insurance? NBER working paper no. 5082. Cambridge, Mass., 1995.

CHAPTER 8

MEDICARE AND MEDICAID

Medicare is one of the largest and most popular social programs administered by the U.S. federal government. It now provides medical benefits to nearly 40 million Americans. Created in 1965, Medicare was intended to reduce the economic burden of illness on the elderly and their families and to ensure access to acute medical care for the elderly who were Social Security beneficiaries. While Medicare aimed to alleviate the special situation of the elderly, who incurred higher medical expenses, earned less income than workers under age 65 years, and were less well-insured (only about half had any health insurance), the economic protection of the program and its institutional design were also meant to appeal to younger people who would be contributing to the program during their working years.

The principal architects of the program were thus not merely focused on health care for the elderly; Medicare was the vessel in which to commence the passage toward universal health insurance for all Americans. Medicare's benefits were quite limited and not tailored to the chronic medical care needs of the elderly. This reflected the view of its founders that Medicare was merely to serve as the foundation for a more comprehensive and universal system of national health insurance in this country.

Notable changes in the basic characteristics of the Medicare program have occurred during the past 35 years since its enactment, and some overarching trends in the political development of the program have occurred.

CHANGES IN BASIC CHARACTERISTICS OF THE MEDICARE PROGRAM

- The size of the population eligible for Medicare has doubled from 19 million in 1966 to 38 million in 1997. The program covered 9.4 percent of the total

341

U.S. population in 1967 and 13.6 percent in 1994. Medicare processed 19 million claims in 1967 and 784 million claims in 1995.

- The original program extended eligibility to individuals over age 65. Legislation in 1972 made Medicare coverage available to the permanently disabled who had received Social Security benefits for two years and to individuals with end-stage renal disease.
- The program originally guaranteed limited coverage of inpatient hospital care, nursing home care, and home health visits to cover acute episodes of illness through the Hospital Insurance program (Part A), all financed by a Social Security payroll tax. It provided voluntary coverage for physician services through the Supplementary Medicare Insurance program (Part B), financed by general revenues and premiums paid by beneficiaries. Over time, Medicare has provided limited additional coverage of home health care, preventive services, rural health clinics, and hospice care. Catastrophic insurance coverage and limited benefits for prescription drugs and other services were adopted in 1988 but most were repealed in 1989.
- Federal spending for Medicare more than doubled every five years in the first two decades of the program, rising from $3.7 billion in 1967 to $14.9 billion in 1975 to $69.1 billion in 1985. This growth has moderated somewhat in the past decade. In 1999, payments for all Medicare services are projected to be $212 billion. Medicare accounted for 3 percent of the federal budget in 1970 and is expected to account for 12 percent in fiscal year (FY) 1999.
- The vast majority of Medicare beneficiaries are enrolled in the fee-for-service portions of the program. In fiscal year 1999, 17 percent were enrolled in managed care plans paid through capitation contracts or in cost-reimbursed HMOs. Enrollment in managed care is growing rapidly, and the Congressional Budget Office projects that the number of beneficiaries electing to join a Medicare risk (capitated) HMO will reach 34 percent by 2005.

Today, Medicare is seen by many Americans and policy makers in a very different light than it was 35 years ago. In the last two sessions of Congress, the usual concerns about slowing Medicare spending within Medicare were joined with an unprecedented battle over the size and role of government (see Hacker and Skocpol, Chapter 5). As the largest available source of budget "savings" (Social Security was technically and politically put off limits by both parties), Medicare became a main focus in a partisan showdown between President Clinton and the new Republican majorities in Congress. Spending per se was not the only issue—however; the fundamental nature of the entitlement to senior citizens was being challenged, as was the division of responsibilities between public and private sectors (See Estes and Linkins, Chapter 3). Two experienced Washington reporters wrote: "It was not consensus politics being practiced in Washington, or even conservative politics as previously defined. This was ideological warfare, a battle to destroy the remnants of the liberal, progressive brand of politics that had governed America throughout most of the twentieth century" (Johnson and Broder 1996, p. 569). Medicare had entered into the realm of electoral and ideological politics for the first time since 1964, and the simplistic and polarizing policy debate and political deadlock that ensued was regarded as a symptom of a broader breakdown in "The System" of American politics (Johnson and Broder, 1996).

The Medicare debate since 1995 has reflected the bitter debate that was ignited by President Clinton's health care financing and reform proposal in 1993–1994. That debate, as Glied (1997) (see Chapter 5) has pointed out, was fundamentally between those who believe that medical care is a public good (primarily advocates of single-payer plans, including traditional Medicare) and those who believe that medical care should be treated like any other market good (including those who favor competition among health plans and a voucher or guaranteed contribution rather than a guaranteed benefit in Medicare). In addition, in the end, the debate surrounding the Clinton health plan became a polarized struggle that the Republicans pursued for partisan political gain, which contributed to their capture of the House of Representatives and the Senate in the 1994 election. The stage was thus set for a showdown in 1995 on the budget and also on reductions in future Medicare increases (often called "cuts") that would be acceptable to the public. This strategy of the Republican Party, which has prevailed since the 1994 elections, is detailed in the Hacker and Skopcol article (included in Chapter 5). Historical shifts such as these are a reminder that the state of the Medicare program cannot be understood apart from developments in American politics.

Beyond the politics of entitlements and privatization, there are many issues concerning the substantive design of the Medicare program. Is Medicare serving the economic and health needs of beneficiaries, and is it doing so in an efficient manner? In much of the country, the health care system has been undergoing turbulent changes and, in some cases, has been completely transformed in recent years, with implications for senior citizens as well as the general population (e.g., Robinson, 1996; Enthoven and Singer, 1996). In some areas fragmented systems of care are giving way to integrated, coordinated systems. Yet, as fast as these are emerging in some areas, they are collapsing in others (e.g., Southern California). Some argue that Medicare has not kept pace with these developments in health care organization and financing. While the private sector has emphasized competition and managed care to control the rising costs of health care, Medicare has emphasized regulation with prospective payments for hospitals based on a standard known as diagnosis, related groups (DRGs) and a fee schedule for physicians. Does Medicare cover an appropriate range of services and institutional settings for care of the elderly and chronically ill? Should Medicare attempt to move more rapidly into various forms of prepayment and managed care? A variety of analysts have suggested that it may also be necessary or appropriate to shift government's responsibility from covering defined benefits (whatever the cost) to a fixed monetary contribution toward each senior citizen's health insurance coverage (e.g., Aaron and Reischauer, 1995; Fox, Etheredge, and Jones, 1996).

To rectify the uncertainty of Medicare's role for the future, we need to better understand and explain the evolution of Medicare in the years since its inception.

The original idea underlying the program was simple, but efforts to convert that purpose into a stable and effective program have led to a set of complex relations with the nation's health care and political systems.

Prior to the Balanced Budget Act of 1997, the biggest changes in Medicare were related to payment for Hospitals (1983) and payment for physician services (1984–1996). In 1983, Congress mandated the establishment of a system of prospective payment for hospitals based on diagnosis-related groups (DRGs). This system dramatically restructured the financial incentives for hospitals by defining specific groupings of conditions for which Medicare patients were hospitalized and setting specific payment amounts for each of these DRGs. This policy overturned the previous method of paying hospitals on the basis of costs incurred in treating patients (cost based reimbursement), similar in many ways to fee-for-service reimbursement of physicians.

Beginning in 1984, Congress began to regulate direct Medicare payments to physicians as well as the ability of physicians to "balance bill" Medicare beneficiaries. Balance billing refers to the practice of charging the beneficiary for any difference between the physician's charge and Medicare's reimbursement payment. This practice became much more limited in the wake of 1984 reforms. The following year they directed the Secretary of Health and Human Services to develop a resource-based relative value scale for physician payment and established the Physician Payment Review Commission to advise the Department of Health and Human Services (DHHS) on physician payment policies. In 1988, the Commission endorsed the concept of replacing the customary, prevailing, and reasonable (CPR) system of payment with a fee schedule. In the CPR system, the payment was based on the physician's customary charge, modified by the prevailing charge for the same service in the community. In 1989, a resource-based fee schedule with limits on balance billing and an annual expenditure target to restrain rising costs were recommended by the Commission. These recommendations were basically adopted by Congress in 1989, with the fee schedule implemented in 1992.

While Medicare was adopting a regulatory approach to both hospital and physician payments, the private sector, driven by employers' desires to slow the rising costs of health care, turned to managed care. The most significant changes have been the shifts from indemnity insurance, with fee-for-service payments to physicians and cost-based payments to hospitals, to capitated payment and managed care, with the integration of the financing and delivery of medical care.

Prior to the Balanced Budget Act of 1997, Medicare was gradually expanding its Medicare Managed Care options. At the beginning of the program, Medicare allowed certain prepaid organizations to receive a cost reimbursement, instead of a fee-for-service payment for Medicare enrollees. After a risk-sharing demonstration project was initiated in the 1980s, Congress authorized managed care payments based on a prospective payment methodology in 1982.

Medicare HMO enrollment has increased steadily since risk contracting began in 1985. One million new beneficiaries enrolled in HMOs from 1987 to 1991 and by 1993, 3 million beneficiaries had enrolled. While the enrollment of Medicare beneficiaries in risk contracting plans continues to grow, the number of beneficiaries in cost reimbursement plans has been relatively steady for the past decade. In 1996, nearly 9 percent of Medicare beneficiaries were enrolled in risk contracting HMOs. In recent years, Medicare risk contracting has grown rapidly, particularly in California, Oregon, Arizona, and Hawaii. The HMO option is attractive to many elderly because it often includes a prescription drug benefit and limited out-of-pocket expenses.

The Balanced Budget Act of 1997 established the Medicare+Choice program (Part C) to expand options for enrollment in managed care, altered the financing of home health services and graduate medical education, and made available medical savings accounts. These were the most significant reforms in the Medicare program since its enactment and reduced projected Medicare expenditures by $115 billion by 5 years. In 1999, Congress reversed some of these decisions to ease the financial impact on providers.

The Bipartisan Commission on the Future of Medicare developed proposals to change the nature of the Medicare entitlement, while adding prescription drug coverage. The Commission failed to achieve support necessary to send formal recommendations to Congress. (See Vladeck's paper, "Plenty of Nothing—A Report From the Medicare Commission" in the Recommended Reading list.)

We have sought to identify in this chapter the predominant forces underlying the major episodes of Medicare reform and to determine the impact those forces have on the structure and operation of the program. We have also sought to identify how Medicare has affected many aspects of the American health care system. Even before it was fully implemented on July 1, 1966, Medicare was used to enforce the 1964 Civil Rights Act in 1965 and 1966 and almost instantly ended racial segregation in the great majority of hospitals in the South. It has substantially underwritten the costs of graduate medical education (e.g., physicians trained in hospitals), affecting the number and degree of specialization of U.S. physicians. Its prospective hospital payment system accelerated the movement toward greater use of ambulatory care settings (e.g., surgicenters, outpatient clinics, and physician offices), resulting in shorter hospital stays, and dramatically changed the economic incentives for hospital care. Physician payment reforms enacted in 1989 and implemented from 1992 through 1996 had a less dramatic effect, although they did narrow the gap in payments to physicians for procedural and evaluation and management services. The payment methods for hospitals and physicians have been used to bolster health services in rural areas. Finally, the failure of Medicare to promote managed care has in many ways left it far behind the private insurance sector in organizational innovation.

In the Winter 1995 issue of *Health Affairs,* there was a comprehensive review of Medicare and its future from a variety of perspectives. We included the article by Marilyn Moon and Karen Davis, "Preserving and Strengthening Medicare," in the Recommended Reading list because it argues for preserving the integrity of the program as reform is considered. In their article, Moon and Davis describe the strengths of Medicare (universal for all those age 65 years and older, risk is shared across a large population group, strong cost containment policies), and its problems (the high cost of health care and the increasing growth of Medicare outlays). Then, they analyze the Medicare managed care option and argue it could be expanded incrementally while still protecting beneficiaries.

In 1999, *Health Affairs* devoted three issues (January/February), (March/April), and (July/August) largely to Medicare issues. We include "Health Care for the Elderly: How Much? Who Will Pay For It?" (Victor Fuchs), "Purchasing Medicare Prescription Benefits: A New Proposal" (Lynn Etheredge), and Vladeck's paper on the National Bipartisan Commission on the Future of Medicare in our Recommended Reading. We have also included some basics on Medicare: *The New England Journal of Medicine* article on Medicare by John Iglehart, as well as a more controversial article that represents the strongly held views by some of Medicare's most astute observers, Marmor and Oberlander. Also included is testimony before the Committee on Finance, U.S. Senate (1999), on the issue of adding a prescription drug benefit to the Medicare program.

Medicaid is included in this chapter because of its origins with Medicare in 1965 and its growing importance as a source of health care financing for the poor. We begin with Iglehart's basic description of Medicaid (1999) and end with a series of articles from the Kaiser Medicaid Commission, a major source of recent information on Medicaid for policy makers and the public.

Medicaid has been the principle source of payment for medical care for those eligible through public assistance (AFDC, SSI) for the past 30 years. Because of expanded enrollments in recent years, which were mandated by Congress in the late 1980s, costs have continued to rise and have increased strain on states' discretionary budgets. In recent years, the Henry J. Kaiser Family Foundation has provided a wealth of information about the programs. We include several of the Commission Policy Briefs to illustrate the type of material produced.

The pressures to curtail costs in the Medicaid program have lead states to turn increasingly to managed care, described in the articles by Roland and Hanson (*Health Affairs,* 1996). Several states, including Oregon and Tennessee, used Section 1115 waivers, allowing innovative approaches to bypass federal restrictions to both broaden access for low income populations and slow the increase in costs. In Tennessee, the emphasis was on managed care. In Oregon, limits were placed on benefits, particularly those that were not considered cost effective. In his article, included in the fifth edition, Bruce Vladeck reviewed the developments in the 1115 Waiver Program in 1995. The pace of state applications continued, but will now be unnecessary because of the Balanced Budget Act of 1997.

There have been a number of potential problems with the rapid shift to managed care. Many of the traditional safety net providers, particularly urban public hospitals, may lose a disproportionate share of funding to cover the costs of serving the uninsured populations (see Baxter and Mechanic, Chapter 7 Recommended Reading). There have been concerns expressed about access to care for the chronically ill, the disabled, those with a history of substance abuse and alcoholism, the homeless, and children with chronic illness. If public hospital systems lose Medicaid patients to competing private health plans, their capacity to meet community-wide needs for trauma care and neonatal intensive care services may be compromised, as noted by Culbertson in Chapter 4.

The jury is still out on Medicaid managed care. Although there are opportunities to improve the quality of care and contain rising costs, these concerns pertaining to access and other issues must be addressed.

REFERENCES

Aaron, H.J., Reischauer, R.D. The Medicare reform debate: What is the next step? *Health Affairs,* 1995; Winter.

David D., Hanson, K. Medicaid: Moving to managed care. *Health Affairs,* 1996; 15(3):150–181

Enthoven, A.C., Singer, S.J. Market-based reform: What to regulate and by whom. *Health Affairs,* 1995; Spring:105–119.

Etheredge, L. Purchasing medicare prescription drug benefits. *Health Affairs,* 1999; 18:7–19.

Fox. P.D., Etheredge, L., Jones, S.B. Addressing the Needs of Chronically Ill Persons Under Medicare. *Health Affairs,* 1996; March/April:144–150.

Fuchs, V.R. Health care for the elderly: How much? Who will pay for it? *Health Affairs,* 1999; January/February:18(1):11–20.

Glied, S. *Chronic Condition: Why Health Reform Fails.* Cambridge, MA: Harvard University Press, 1997; 1–16.

Himelfarb, R. *Catastrophic Politics: The Rise and Fall of the Medicare Catastrophic Coverage Act of 1988.* University Park, PA: Pennsylvania State University Press; 1995.

Iglehart, J.K. The American Health System: Medicare. *NEJM,* 1996; 340:327–332.

Iglehart, J.K. The American health care system: Medicaid. *NEJM,* 1999; 340:403–408.

Johnson, H., Broder, D.S. *The system: The American Way of Politics at the Breaking Point.* Boston: Little, Brown, 1996.

Marmor, T., Oberlander, J. Rethinking medicare reform. *Health Affairs,* 1998; 17:52–67.

Moon, M., Davis, K. Preserving and strengthening medicare. *Health Affairs,* 1995; 14(4):31–46.

Robinson, J.C. Decline in hospital utilization and cost inflation under managed care in California. *JAMA,* 276(13):1060–1064.

The Kaiser Family Foundation. *Summary of Traditional Medicare,* Menlo Park, CA: Kaiser Family Foundation, 1999.

The Kaiser Commission on the Future of Medicaid. *Medicaid and Long Term Care.* Menlo Park, CA: Kaiser Family Foundation, February 1996.

The Kaiser Commission on the Future of Medicaid. *The Medicaid Program at a Glance.* Menlo Park, CA: Kaiser Family Foundation, November 1997.

The Kaiser Commission on the Future of Medicaid. *Medicaid for the Children.* Menlo Park, CA: Kaiser Family Foundation, November 1997.

The Kaiser Commission on the Future of Medicaid. *The Medicaid Program at a Glance.* Menlo Park, CA: Kaiser Family Foundation, November 1997.

The Kaiser Commission on the Future of Medicaid. *Medicaid and Managed Care.* Menlo Park, CA: Kaiser Family Foundation, October 1998.

The Kaiser Commission on the Future of Medicaid. *Medicare and Medicaid for the Elderly and Disabled Poor.* Menlo Park, CA: Kaiser Family Foundation, May 1999.

The Kaiser Medicare Policy Project. *Medicare+Choice.* Menlo Park, CA: Kaiser Family Foundation, July 1998.

United States General Accounting Office. Testimony Before the Committee on Finance, U.S. Senate. Medicare: Considerations for Adding a Prescription Drug Benefit. Statement of Laura A. Dummit, Associate Director Health Financing and Public Health Issues. Health, Education, and Human Services Division. GAO, 1999.

Vladeck, B.C. Medicaid 1115 demonstrations: Progress through partnership. *Health Affairs,* 1995; 14:217–220.

Vladeck, B.C., King, K.K. Medicare at 30: Preparing for the future. *JAMA,* 1996; 274:260–263.

Vladeck, B.C. Plenty of nothing—a report from the Medicare Commission. *NEJM,* 1999; 340:1503–1506.

ARTICLE 1

THE AMERICAN HEALTH CARE
SYSTEM: MEDICARE

John K. Iglehart

Six times in the 20th century, America has flirted unsuccessfully with national health insurance legislation—the provision of medical care to all citizens. Instead, policy makers have allowed subsidies to finance part of private health insurance by exempting employer-paid premiums from taxation. The government has also provided or funded services for groups deemed particularly vulnerable or entitled to them— Native Americans, migratory workers, other categorically defined poor people, veterans of military service, the permanently disabled, people with end-stage renal disease, and all elderly people. Medicare, which provides the nation's elderly with ready access to short-term medical services, represents the most ambitious dimension of this strategy of incrementalism. The program is the single largest payer in the U.S. medical care system, purchasing about 20 percent of all personal health services in 1991, and its expenditures are expected to more than double by the year 2000 (Table 1). From an international perspective, it is a peculiar institution; no other nation has compulsory health insurance for its elderly citizens alone.

Medicare is the subject of this report, my fourth on the American health care system.[1-4] Enacted in 1965 after a debate that spanned decades, the Medicare law symbolized the continuing struggle over defining the government's role in America's predominantly private system of health care. At the time of its enactment, only 56 percent of the elderly had hospital insurance.[5] But not until the landslide 1964 presidential victory of Lyndon B. Johnson, who campaigned on a promise of establishing Medicare if elected, did the creation of the program become likely. The American Medical Association (AMA) bitterly opposed the measure because of its probable intrusion into clinical practice. To appease the AMA, the law's preamble expressly prohibited any federal "supervision or control over the practice of medicine or the manner in which medical services are provided." Although these words remain in the law, they have long been ignored.

Once the Medicare law was enacted, its implementation was regarded as a masterful managerial achievement because of its vast scope. Shortly before the

TABLE 1

ℰ PROJECTED ANNUAL GROWTH IN MEDICARE EXPENDITURES, 1992 TO 1997*						
	1992	*1993*	*1994*	*1995*	*1996*	*1997*
Hospital insurance (Part A)						
Expenditures (billions)	$ 78.4	$ 86.7	$ 96.2	$106.2	$117.8	$129.5
Growth rate (%)	—	10.6	10.9	10.4	10.9	10.0
Supplementary medical insurance (Part B)						
Expenditures (billions)	$ 52.2	$ 59.4	$ 67.5	$ 76.6	$ 87.1	$ 98.6
Growth rate (%)	—	13.9	13.6	13.6	13.7	13.2
Total Medicare outlay						
Expenditures (billions)	$130.6	$146.1	$163.6	$182.8	$204.9	$228.1
Growth rate (%)	—	11.9	12.0	11.7	12.1	11.4

*Data are from the Health Care Financing Administration. Because of rounding, not all values sum to the totals shown and not all percentages can be calculated from the values shown.

program's launch in 1966, President Johnson said: "Preparation for the program constitutes the largest managerial effort the nation has undertaken since the Normandy invasion." The providers of service generally entered into the program in a cooperative, albeit wary, fashion, after legislators accommodated organized medicine on many of the issues of concern; threatened rebellions and withholding of services did not materialize. After periods of quiet and turmoil, the attitude of many physicians toward Medicare has turned to anger and frustration over what they regard as the program's frequent policy changes dictated by Congress, its often inconsistent payment policies, other undue intrusions, and ongoing efforts to constrain the growth of expenditures. Yet an increasing number of doctors have been willing to care for Medicare patients in recent years.

Like America's social security program, Medicare's hospital-financing scheme is grounded in the principle of social insurance. That is, employees make mandatory contributions as defined in law to dedicated trust funds during their working years, with the promise of receiving benefits (income or services) after they retire. This concept was popularized in the late 1800s by German Chancellor Otto von Bismarck, who constructed Germany's national health insurance plan around it.[6] The principle applies only to Medicare's hospital trust fund. Medicare's other major component, supplemental medical insurance, was modeled after traditional indemnity coverage and was created to win the support of doubting Republicans. The money contributed by the nation's work force today for hospital insurance is not set aside to meet future health expenses. Rather, it is used to cover the medical bills of the people who are currently eligible. Overall, 88.8 percent of Medicare's annual revenue now comes from people who are under 65 years old (in payroll taxes, income taxes, and trust-fund interest), and 11.2 percent comes from people who are elderly (in premiums).

As an enterprise, Medicare's scope is daunting, although the Health Care Financing Administration (HCFA), which oversees the program, is remarkably small, given the expenditures it manages and the increasing number of tasks Congress assigns to it. Its full-time-equivalent staff dropped from 4857 people in 1981 to 3962 in 1991, a period during which the Reagan administration waged its assault on the federal work force. Medicare's estimated outlay of $130.6 billion in 1992 overshadowed the budgets of all of America's private corporations and most of the world's nations. The program has virtually created whole new medical enterprises (kidney-dialysis centers, home health companies, and the suppliers of medical equipment for home use) that flourish as the result of a congressional decision to add a benefit. In 1991 the private insurers with whom Medicare contracts to administer the program paid 518 million claims to some 600,000 physicians and medical suppliers and 92 million claims to 6487 hospitals, 9674 skilled-nursing facilities, and 5730 home health agencies. Medicare also does business with 4926 independent clinical laboratories, 1355 ambulatory surgical centers, 2130 kidney-dialysis centers, 1057 hospices, 1317 outpatient physical-therapy units, and 692 rural health clinics.

Medicare has evolved during an era in which the health status of the elderly has improved appreciably. The improvements in life expectancy and reduced morbidity are attributable in part to a decrease in the risk of death from heart disease and cerebrovascular disorders. Changes in lifestyle have also played a part. In 1990, 12.6 percent of the U.S. population was 65 years old or older, and the elderly accounted for more than one third of total personal health expenditures. People over 85 consume the most medical care per capita and are the fastest growing population group (Manton K, Duke University: personal communication).[7]

Currently, 35.6 million people are eligible to receive medical benefits financed by Medicare: 31.8 million who are over the age of 65, 3.6 million who are permanently disabled, and some 165,000 who have endstage renal disease. Medicare's end-stage renal disease program is unique; it is the only instance in which a diagnosis provides the basis for Medicare benefits for persons of all ages. It is also the classic example of how government operates as the virtual single payer for a private medical service.

BENEFITS

Medicare's covered benefits apply mostly to the treatment of patients with acute illnesses. Although chronic conditions are addressed, the supportive long-term care often needed by patients with such conditions is not generally covered despite a perceived need. Medicare also does not pay for outpatient prescription drugs or routine foot, hearing, vision, and dental care. As a consequence of the original compromise that stitched together several disparate bills, Medicare is divided into two parts: Part A is hospital insurance, and all eligible elderly beneficiaries are automatically enrolled. Part B is supplemental medical insurance, and enrollment is voluntary, although the vast majority of elderly beneficiaries sign on. The compulsory nature of Part A is a key feature of social insurance. This part of Medicare finances inpatient hospital services, care in a skilled-nursing facility for continued treatment or rehabilitation after hospitalization, home health care services, and hospice care for the terminally ill. Under Part A, Medicare pays for all reasonable expenses, minus a deductible amount ($652 in 1992), for the first 60 days in each benefit period. For days 61 to 90 a daily coinsurance payment ($163 in 1992) is also charged. Since the repeal of the Medicare Catastrophic Coverage Act of 1988, there has been no cap on beneficiaries' out-of-pocket liability.

Part B pays for physicians' services and outpatient hospital services, including emergency room visits, ambulatory surgery, diagnostic tests, laboratory services, outpatient physical therapy, occupational-therapy and speech-pathology services, and durable medical equipment. Generally, Part B does not pay for routine physical examinations, preventive care, or services not related to the treatment of illness or injury. Under Part B, Medicare pays 80 percent of the approved amount (according to a fee schedule, reasonable charges, or reasonable costs) for covered services in excess of an annual deductible of $100.

Expenditures for personal health care services for the elderly nearly quadrupled between 1977 and 1987, rising from $43 billion to an estimated $162 billion. About two thirds of these expenditures were covered by Medicare and Medicaid in 1987.[8,9] Medicare pays for about half the average elderly person's medical bill, a proportion that has remained reasonably constant over the years. However, enrollees are spending an increasing share of their incomes for medical care. In 1975 about 4.2 percent of enrollees' per capita income went to cover their share of Medicare costs; by 1990 that figure had increased to 5.7 percent. Total health care spending as a percentage of after-tax income increased substantially for the elderly between 1972 and 1988. In 1972 out-of-pocket health care spending represented 7.8 percent of after-tax household income among the elderly, but by 1988 out-of-pocket spending had increased to 12.5 percent of after-tax income.[10]

To protect beneficiaries against larger increases in their out-of-pocket costs, the HCFA has encouraged doctors to become participating physicians and thereby accept assignment (defined as 80 percent of the fee-schedule amount, less any unmet deductible) as payment in full. The encouragement takes three forms: fee-schedule amounts are 5 percent higher for participating physicians, claims are paid more expeditiously, and Medicare carriers publish directories of participating physicians for free distribution. No additional charges, known as balance-billing charges, may be levied by participating physicians directly on beneficiaries. In 1992 participating physicians represent 52.2 percent of doctors who treat Medicare patients; this is the first year that a majority of practitioners have accepted this status. By comparison, the rate of participation of medical suppliers, such as those providing ambulance services or durable medical equipment, was only 23.7 percent in 1992. Assigned Medicare claims—those in which physicians do not bill patients directly—represented 87.6 percent of Part B's covered charges for medical services in 1991. Because Medicare does not provide complete insurance coverage for its eligible population, about 75 percent of its elderly beneficiaries obtain supplementary packages from private insurers or through their previous employers.

Because Medicare's Part A is compulsory, eligibility for it is determined primarily by age, and there is only one standard benefit package; the program has no sales, marketing, risk-assessment, or insurance-commission costs. In addition, because a higher proportion of its submitted claims are transmitted electronically, Medicare's administrative costs are lower than the comparable costs of private insurers (Table 2).[11] Medicare claims payments are administered by private health insurers that operate under contract to the HCFA. These agents, called intermediaries if they remunerate institutions and carriers if they pay physicians' claims, were designated at the outset to serve as buffers between the government and providers.[12] They operate with a substantial degree of flexibility in deciding what is a covered benefit and how much to pay for it, a freedom that often leads to conflicts with

TABLE 2

 TYPE OF HEALTH INSURANCE AND ESTIMATED ADMINISTRATIVE EXPENSES IN THE UNITED STATES IN 1990*

Type of Coverage	Millions of Persons	Administrative Costs as % of Spending
Private		Average, 14.2
Employment based	150	5.5–40
Individual	15	40
Self-insured	NA	5–12
Prepaid, HMO	35	2.5–7
Public		
Medicare		
Total	34	2.1
Part A	34	1.2
Part B	33	3.5
Medicaid	23	3.2–11.8; average, 5.1
Uninsured	34	NA
Total†	256	5.8

*Data are from Thorpe.[11] HMO denotes health maintenance organization, and NA not available.
†Some people have more than one type of coverage.

physicians. Now, in an effort to unify the 14 different systems used by Medicare's 82 contractors, the HCFA is seeking proposals from organizations that specialize in information processing, as well as from health insurance companies, to assume this task in the future.

FINANCING

Medicare is financed from four different sources: mandatory contributions by employers and employees, general tax revenue, beneficiaries' premiums, and deductible and copayment amounts. Part A is financed by a payroll tax of 2.9 percent of the gross income of some 137 million workers; employers and employees each pay 1.45 percent. Until 1990 this payroll tax was imposed on a person's annual salary up to the level of $51,300, but in its continuing search for additional revenue, Congress then raised the maximal salary to which the tax applied; it is $130,200 in 1992. All the proceeds of the payroll tax ($77.9 billion in 1991) are placed in a trust fund dedicated to the payment of Part A benefits. Part B is financed by general tax revenues (72 percent), premiums paid by beneficiaries (25 percent), and interest on trustfund assets (3 percent). The current monthly premium is $31.80, and by law it will increase to $46.10 by 1995.

Every year, the majority of Medicare's expenditures go to a relatively small proportion of its beneficiaries, a feature common to all insurance schemes. In 1990, 27.1 million beneficiaries (80 percent of all enrollees) received covered services under Medicare. The total program payments for that year were $101.4 billion, an average payment of $4,011 per user. But 18.8 percent (5.1 million) of all eligible persons who received treatment accounted for 80 percent ($81.1 billion) of the total program payments (Figure 1). Most of those who require medical care receive far more from Medicare than they contributed in payroll taxes. For example, a couple retiring in 1991, with one wage earner who had paid average Medicare taxes since 1966, would have contributed $8,480, not including the employer's equal contribution. The present value of future Part A benefits for such a couple is estimated to be $86,320, more than 10 times the amount they paid into the trust fund. For Part B, retirees receive benefits that average four times their premiums. Put another way, if retirees were required to pay a monthly premium that was equivalent to the actuarial value of their Part B benefit, it would be $125.40, rather than the current amount of $31.80.

PAYMENT

When Medicare was enacted, the program embraced the methods of payment advocated at the time by hospitals and physicians, in an effort to win their support. Thus, Medicare agreed to pay hospitals the reasonable costs they incurred in providing services to eligible beneficiaries and agreed to reimburse physicians on a fee-for-

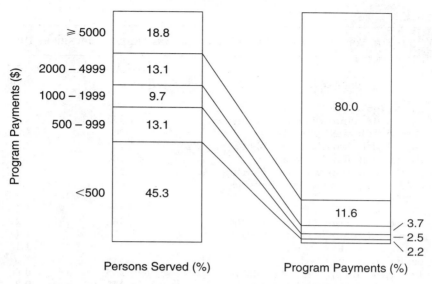

Figure 1 Allocation of Medicare program payments in 1990. (Source: Data are from the HCFA)

service basis, using the "customary, prevailing, and reasonable" method. In 1990 the bulk of the program's payments remunerated hospitals (62.7 percent of the total) and physicians (27.2 percent) for services to patients; a decade earlier, the hospitals' share was 67.5 percent and the physicians' share 22.9 percent. During the 1980s, outlays for long-term care benefits—skilled-nursing facilities and home health services—more than doubled, from 2.9 to 6.1 percent of total payments. In 1990, Part B services provided by surgical specialists accounted for 34.3 percent of allowed amounts, by generalist physicians for 30.6 percent, and by nonsurgical specialists for 19.6 percent. During the period from 1986 to 1990, surgical charges submitted by ophthalmologists, gastroenterologists, and cardiologists more than doubled as a proportion of the total. Cardiologists had the highest average compound rates of spending growth as a consequence of the high incidence of cardiac disease among beneficiaries, the availability of new forms of technology to treat it,[13] and the increasing number of doctors. The top 20 services, out of more than 7000, accounted for 36 percent of all spending for physicians' services in 1990 (Table 3).

As medical costs continued to soar well beyond the rate of inflation in the 1980s, Congress acted twice to reduce the discretion previously enjoyed by hospitals and physicians to establish their own prices, subject to various constraining factors imposed by government. In 1983, Congress authorized the creation of Medicare's prospective payment system for hospitals.[14] The policy required Medicare to fix prices in advance on a cost-per-case basis, using as a measure 467 diagnosis-

TABLE 3

THE TOP 20 SERVICES BILLED BY PHYSICIANS UNDER MEDICARE IN 1990*		

Description and Service Code	Allowed Amounts (Millions of $)†	Percent of Total‡
Cataract (66984)	1,938	6.2
Office visit, intermediate (90060)	1,452	4.6
Office visit, limited (90050)	1,242	4.0
Hospital visit, intermediate (90260)	1,001	3.2
Hospital visit, limited (90250)	806	2.6
Consultation, comprehensive (90620)	635	2.0
Initial hospital visit, comprehensive (90220)	487	1.6
Office visit, extended (90070)	388	1.2
Electrocardiography (12 leads) (93000)	362	1.2
Electrocardiography (12 leads) (93307)	357	1.1
Lasering, secondary cataract (66821)	340	1.1
Hospital visit, extended (90270)	315	1.0
Office visit, comprehensive (90080)	265	0.8
Eye examination, established patient (92014)	255	0.8
Electrocardiography, interpretation and report only (93010)	250	0.8
Office visit, brief (90040)	246	0.8
Total knee replacement (27447)	244	0.8
Transurethral resection of prostate (52601)	241	0.8
Office visit, comprehensive, new patient (90020)	237	0.8
Diagnostic colonoscopy (45378)	216	0.7
Total	11,277	35.9

*Data are from the HCFA.
†Amounts for surgical procedures include fees for primary and assistant surgeons, but not for anesthesiologists.
‡Values do not sum to the total shown because of rounding.

related groups. Through the 1983 law, Congress changed what was paid for, who determined the price, and how that price would be calculated and thereby reduced the growth rate of the program's expenditures for inpatient hospital care.[15] There has been a cyclical trend in total hospital margins (the net amount by which a hospital's revenues exceed its expenses, expressed as a percentage) over the past 15 years. The Prospective Payment Assessment Commission, which monitors Medicare Part A for Congress, reported that in the early years of the prospective payment system, when most hospitals had large Medicare surpluses, total margins were healthy, peaking at 6 percent in 1985. In subsequent years, as Medicare tightened its control of increases in payment rates for inpatients, the total margin began to fall, dropping to 3.3 percent in 1988.[16] Some hospitals were able to recoup lost Medicare revenue by increasing their charges to private insurers, a practice called cost shifting. The prospective payment system has recognized the higher costs associated with teaching hospitals, and payments can be adjusted for these purposes. At the direction of Congress, the HCFA is now developing a method to pay for hospital outpatient services on a prospective basis.

An extensive literature has examined whether the prospective payment system has led to a deterioration in the quality of inpatient care.[17,18] No study has uncovered a systematic pattern of diminished quality as a consequence of the prospective payment system or determined that access to life-sustaining treatments has been systematically limited by this approach to payment.[19] What have changed demonstrably are hospital stays (1.8 days [18 percent] shorter in 1991 than in 1981), nursing home admissions (252,000 in 1982 and 765,000 in 1991, although the Catastrophic Coverage Act, since repealed, pushed the 1991 figure up), and clinical instability, which has increased among patients discharged to their homes.[20] Early on, politicians registered their concern that beneficiaries were being released from hospitals "quicker and sicker" because of the economic incentives that underlie the prospective payment system. They provoked an unintended but important response from the HCFA administrator at the time, Dr. William L. Roper, who launched an ambitious effort to improve the quality and effectiveness of medical care.[21–23]

More recently (in 1989), Congress directed the HCFA to pay physicians according to a fee schedule based on a resource-based relative-value scale, an activity that will inevitably require the agency to dissect more minutely the cost and consequences of the doctor-patient encounter.[24,25] The new system was also designed to increase the financial protection afforded beneficiaries by placing stricter limits on the amount in excess of the fee schedule that physicians can charge patients directly. Congress authorized the creation of a uniform fee schedule for some 7000 medical procedures on the assumption that fee-for-service medicine will remain a dominant mode of payment and in the belief that the disparity between fees for diagnostic and surgical procedures and fees for evaluation and management should be reduced. The Physician Payment Review Commission estimated that by 1996 fees paid to generalist physicians would be 39 percent higher than they would have been under the previous payment method, whereas those paid to thoracic surgeons and ophthalmologists would be 35 and 25 percent lower, respectively.

As the Medicare fee schedule has been implemented, organizations that represent primary care physicians have increasingly questioned whether it will achieve its intended goal. As a consequence, physician support for the program has suffered. The immediate issue provoking the controversy was a recommendation issued on May 21 of this year by Health and Human Services Secretary Louis W. Sullivan that Congress mandate separate but unequal relative-value-scale conversion factors for surgical and nonsurgical services when it updates Medicare rates for 1993. The present conversion factor ($31) is the number used by the HCFA to convert the relative values for physicians' services into Medicare payment amounts.

Sullivan, following the legal requirement that separate conversion factors be established for 1993, recommended that fees for surgical services be increased by 2.6 percent, and fees for nonsurgical services by just 0.3 percent. The recommendation, Sullivan said, reflects the degree to which the 1991 growth rates in Medicare payments to physicians were above or below those projected by the "volume performance standards" established by Congress. According to Sullivan, Medicare's spending for surgical services increased by 2.9 percent, 0.4 percent below the 1991 growth target of 3.3 percent, whereas spending for nonsurgical services increased by 10.5 percent, or more than the growth target of 8.6 percent. The American College of Physicians, the American Society of Internal Medicine, and the American Academy of Family Physicians took strong exception to Sullivan's recommendation, saying that it would subvert physician payment reform before it was a year old. Economist William C. Hsiao, the key architect of the resource-based relative-value scale, agreed, declaring in an interview: "If this is allowed to go on, it will undermine the reform." Dr. James S. Todd, the AMA's executive vice-president, expressed a similar view.[26] Congress, the final authority on fee updates, did not alter Sullivan's recommendation. In the future, however, Congress may settle on one uniform conversion factor, an approach the Physician Payment Review Commission favors.

QUALITY

Medicare's network of peer review organizations, created by Congress to protect its beneficiaries against the provision of unnecessary or low-quality care, has reviewed millions of inpatient hospital records over the past decade. The HCFA recently acknowledged that physician review of hospital medical records to determine the quality of care has been only moderately reliable, that such actions by peer review organizations tended to "lead to acrimonious disagreements" with doctors, and that "measuring the impact of actions based on case-by-case review is almost impossible."[27]

The peer review program is being modified to focus on "patterns of care" rather than case-by-case review, a change that is expected to reduce conflict with physicians.[28] Using more nationally uniform criteria, the HCFA plans to implement a new "Health Care Quality Improvement Initiative" that will seek to educate physicians whose practice patterns deviate from the norm rather than take more punitive actions as an initial step. A key element of the new effort will be the cooperative cardiovascular project, a collaborative effort by the HCFA, peer review organizations, the American College of Cardiology, and other medical and hospital organizations to improve the care of patients hospitalized for acute myocardial infarction, coronary-artery bypass grafting, or percutaneous coronary angioplasty.

THE FUTURE

Medicare achieves its highest marks from the millions of elderly beneficiaries who depend on the program to pay for a substantial portion of their medical care, but surveys of public opinion also show widespread support for it among people under 65. The support of physicians has waned substantially, but there is no documented evidence that beneficiaries' access to medical services is eroding, despite physicians' concern that Medicare's fees are lower than those of private payers for similar services. A new national survey of practicing physicians underwritten by the Physician Payment Review Commission and conducted by Louis Harris and Associates found that of doctors who are accepting new patients (946 of the 1000 practitioners queried), 93 percent said they were accepting new Medicare patients.

There is every likelihood that Medicare, given its rapid rate of growth, will remain at the center of government efforts to trim the massive budget deficit. In the 1980s, budget-cutting exercises exacted most of their toll from providers, and they remain a prime target now. But providers are scarcely prepared to be the sole stakeholders who accept sacrifice. The only other real options are raising taxes on the general population, reducing Medicare benefits, or asking the elderly to pay more on some income-related basis. However, elected politicians of almost every stripe have shown no disposition to embrace any of these unpopular approaches, suggesting by their inaction that we can somehow have it all. That is indeed a fanciful formula for the future.

ABOUT THE AUTHOR

John K. Iglehart is Editor of *Health Affairs,* Project HOPE in Bethesda, Maryland.

REFERENCES

1. Kassirer JP. A look at ourselves—an overview of the American health care system. *N Engl J Med* 1992;326:945–6.
2. Iglehart JK. The American health care system—introduction. *N Engl J Med* 1992;326:962–7.
3. *Idem.* The American health care system—private insurance. *N Engl J Med* 1992;326:1715–20.
4. *Idem.* The American health care system—managed care. *N Engl J Med* 1992;327:742–7.
5. Gornick M, Greenberg JN, Eggers PW, Dobson A. Twenty years of Medicare and Medicaid: covered populations, use of benefits, and program expenditures. *Health Care Financ Rev* 1985;Suppl:13–59.
6. Iglehart JK. Germany's health care system. *N Engl J Med* 1991;324:503–8, 1750–6.

7. Senate Special Committee on Aging, American Association of Retired Persons, Federal Council on Aging, Administration on Aging, Aging America: trends and projections. 1991. Washington, D.C.: Department of Health and Human Services, 1991. (DHHS publication no. [FCoA] 91-28001.)

8. Waldo DR, Lazenby HC. Demographic characteristics and health care use and expenditures by the aged in the United States: 1977–1984. *Health Care Financ Rev* 1984;6(1):1–29.

9. Waldo DR, Sonnefeld ST, McKusick DR, Arnett RH III. Health expenditures by age group, 1977 and 1987. *Health Care Financ Rev* 1989; 10(4):111–20.

10. Committee on Ways and Means. House of Representatives. Overview of entitlement programs. 1992 Green book. Ways and Means Committee Print:102–44. Washington, D.C.: Government Printing Office, 1992.

11. Thorpe KE. Inside the black box of administrative costs. *Health Aff (Millwood)* 1992;11(2):41–55.

12. Coben WJ. Reflections on the enactment of Medicare and Medicaid. *Health Care Financ Rev* 1985;Suppl:3–11.

13. Berenson R, Holahan J. Sources of the growth in Medicare physician expenditures. *JAMA* 1992;267:687–91.

14. Iglehart JK. Medicare begins prospective payment of hospitals. *N Engl J Med* 1983;308:1428–32.

15. Smith DG. Paying for Medicare: the politics of reform. New York: Aldine de Gruyter, 1992.

16. Prospective Payment Assessment Commission. Medicare and the American health care system: report to the Congress. Washington, D.C.: Prospective Payment Assessment Commission, 1992.

17. Coulam RF, Gammer GL. Medicare's prospective payment system: a critical appraisal. *Health Care Financ Rev* 1991;Suppl:45–77.

18. Kahn KL, Rubenstein LV, Draper D, et al. The effects of the DRG-based prospective payment system on quality of care for hospitalized Medicare patients: an introduction to the series. *JAMA* 1990;264:1953–5.

19. Office of Technology Assessment Task Force. Life-sustaining technologies and the elderly. Washington, D.C.: Government Printing Office, 1987. (OTA-BA-306.)

20. Kosecoff J, Kahn KL, Rogers WH, et al. Prospective payment system and impairment at discharge: the 'quicker-and-sicker' story revisited. *JAMA* 1990;264:1980–3.

21. Roper WL, Winkenwerder W, Hackbarth GM, Krakamer H. Effectiveness in health care: an initiative to evaluate and improve medical practice. *N Engl J Med* 1988;319:1197–202.

22. Gornick M, Lubitz J, Riley G. U.S. initiatives and approaches for outcomes and effectiveness research. *Health Policy* 1991;17:209–25.

23. Relman AS. Assessment and accountability—the third revolution in medical care. *N Engl J Med* 1988;319:1220–2.

24. Hsiao WC, Braun P. Yotema D. Becker ER. Estimating physicians' work for a resource-based relative-value scale. *N Engl J Med* 1988;319:835–41.

25. Iglehart JK. The new law on Medicare's payments to physicians. *N Engl J Med* 1990;322:1247–52.

26. Knox RA. Surgeons' Medicare fee hike runs counter to reform plan. *Boston Globe,* May 25, 1992.

27. Jencks SF, Wilensky GR. The health care quality improvement initiative: a new approach to quality assurance in Medicare. *JAMA* 1992;268:900–3.

28. McIlrath S. Slowly but surely, PROs starting to change focus. *American Medical News.* September 7, 1992:P1.

ARTICLE 2

RETHINKING MEDICARE REFORM

Theodore Marmor and Jonathan Oberlander

PROLOGUE

Medicare, the nation's insurance program for elderly and disabled persons, has been the subject of intense debate and periodic reform since its passage thirty-three years ago. Current versions of the Medicare reform debate reflect a split of opinion that, surprisingly, does not always fall along classically political lines. The issue at hand is financing. Evidence is mounting that the program is in financial trouble, despite short-term solutions crafted as part of the Balanced Budget Act of 1997. Lawmakers still disagree on how to address the dwindling levels of the program's two trust funds. One approach would make managed competition the key strategy: Beneficiaries would receive vouchers for a defined amount and seek care in the private health care marketplace. An opposing view, espoused by Ted Marmor and Jonathan Oberlander in this paper, is an attack on conventional wisdom in 1998 America, in that it looks abroad to Canada and western Europe for models of health care cost control. Their internationally inspired approach involves budgetary caps and public regulation of payments to providers.

    Marmor is a longtime participant in the debate surrounding both medical care costs and Medicare policy. A professor of politics and public policy at Yale's School of Management and Department of Political Science, Marmor also directs Yale's Robert Wood Johnson postdoctoral program in health policy and social science. He holds a doctorate in politics and history from Harvard. The second edition of his *Politics of Medicare* will be published by Aldine de Gruyter in 1998. Oberlander is an assistant professor of social medicine at the University of North Carolina, Chapel Hill, School of Medicine and teaches in the political science department. He received his doctorate in political science from Yale. He is revising his dissertation on the administrative politics of Medicare for book publication.

ABSTRACT

Many health policy analysts argue that demographic pressures, the inflationary nature of fee-for-service payment, and the uncontrollable nature of defined-benefit insurance make Medicare unsustainable in its current form. They assert that Medicare can remain fiscally viable in the next century only by embracing a voucher system and exposing beneficiaries to the economic consequences of their medical care decisions. We argue here, however, that Medicare need not rely on vouchers or on placing financial incentives on individual beneficiaries to control costs. Instead, we contend that Medicare can control expenditures the way most other industrial democracies do: through budgetary caps and centralized regulation of provider payments.

An increasing number of health policymakers and analysts argue that Medicare is "unsustainable in its current form" and can remain viable into the next century only if a voucher system is adopted.[1] Under such a scheme, beneficiaries would receive a voucher (or a "defined contribution") to purchase private health insurance, replacing the government-organized insurance Medicare now provides. Transforming Medicare into a voucher system would create economic incentives for beneficiaries to enroll in low-cost health plans, since they would bear the costs of health insurance premiums that exceeded the value of the federal voucher. Voucher advocates warn that without this fundamental change in program philosophy and beneficiary incentives, Medicare will soon face an unappealing choice between draconian cuts in services for beneficiaries or staggering increases in taxes.[2]

The increasingly prominent notions that vouchers represent the only, or the best, solution for Medicare reform and that program costs can be controlled only through subjecting beneficiaries to economic incentives are, we contend, wrong. Medicare does face serious financial pressures. However, it is simply not the case that the character and scale of these problems require a voucher solution to "save" Medicare. We have two purposes here: to examine the assumptions underlying the argument for Medicare vouchers, and to propose an alternative path for program reform. In particular, we pay attention to the medical care and aging experiences of other industrialized countries. Inattention to these comparative data—"policy parochialism"—has restricted the scope of debate over the choices available to Medicare. Analysis of this international experience suggests two conclusions. First, the demographic "peril" that the baby-boom generation poses for health care costs in the United States has been exaggerated. And second, Medicare can control program expenditures through a global budget and centralized regulation without adopting a voucher system that makes beneficiaries the center of cost control.

To support our argument, we first critically review the standard assumptions of voucher advocates. Next we outline how a program budget would work in Medicare. Finally, we address likely objections to this approach to Medicare reform.

ASSUMPTIONS BEHIND THE VOUCHER ARGUMENT

Is Medicare Unsustainable?

Voucher advocates contend that the projected rate of growth in Medicare spending is, because of "budgetary and demographic developments," unsustainable.[3] In the short run, Medicare faces a projected deficit in its Hospital Insurance (HI) trust fund beginning in 2007 as well as powerful pressures from federal budget politics. Medicare expenditures have risen about three times as fast as inflation in the past few years, making the program one of the fastest-growing items in the federal budget. Most balanced-budget plans, including the current budget bargain agreed to by the congressional Republican leadership and the Clinton administration, assume significant reductions in the rate of growth in Medicare spending.

In the long run, Medicare must absorb the medical care costs of the baby-boom generation retiring after 2010. The number of Americans age sixty-five and older is projected to rise from thirty-two million in 1990 to sixty-eight million in 2040, with especially large growth among persons over age eighty-five.[4] Enrollment in Medicare is expected to increase from 14 percent of the population in 1995 to 22 percent by 2030.[5] Voucher advocates argue that the implications of this so-called fiscal tsunami are straightforward.[6] According to Stuart Butler and Robert Moffit, "Demographic projections indicate clearly that Medicare cannot deliver promised benefits to the next generation of retirees without fundamental changes in the program. The only way to avoid heavy increases in payroll taxes and other revenues, or a sharp cutback in services, is to change the economics of the system to achieve better value for money."[7]

In addition, demographers expect an accompanying decline in the present ratio of three workers for every retiree to two workers for every retiree in 2030. At Medicare's projected rate of future growth, the fear is that the working population will not be able or willing to support the increasing number of elderly retirees eligible for program benefits. Similar fears also have been raised about Social Security pension benefits. "The burden of providing retirement income and health care for the elderly," Victor Fuchs argues, "will become unsustainable when the baby boomers reach age 65. . . . Can Medicare be saved? In its present form and in the long run, the answer is clearly no."[8] Medicare thus poses, according to these analysts, an unaffordable burden on future generations.[9]

The implication is that there is a demographic imperative for radical restructuring of Medicare. But is the future burden of the medical care costs of the baby-boom generation really this perilous? International experience suggests that the relationship between aging populations and medical care costs is not as simple as is commonly assumed. American commentators may be surprised to learn that from 1960 to 1990 there was no correlation across Organization for Economic Cooperation and Development (OECD) nations between aging populations and growth in medical costs. As Thomas Getzen reports, "in those [OECD] countries where the fraction of population over age 65 has grown most rapidly, spending has not increased any more rapidly than in countries where the elderly population has grown most slowly."[10] His conclusion is underscored by the fact that four of the oldest industrial countries—Norway, Denmark, Sweden, and the United Kingdom—are now among the lowest spenders on health care in the OECD. Sweden, which in 1994 had 17.5 percent of its population over age sixty-five (an age structure that the United States will not reach until 2025), spent only 7.7 percent of its gross domestic product (GDP) on health care, 45 percent less than U.S. spending. In fact, Denmark and Sweden both lowered the proportion of GDP they spent on health care from 1980 to 1992, while their populations aged.[11]

The point is not that demographic changes exert no influence on health care costs; clearly, their pressure can be substantial. Rather, it is that international experience is too variable to assume that demography is destiny. The impact of aging on medical care costs is not driven by demographic numbers alone. The per capita costs of medical care (the rate of medical inflation and the intensity of services provided to the elderly) are crucial. If these costs are restrained, older populations can be absorbed into public health insurance programs without the radical restructuring that some analysts argue is necessary for Medicare. How much social costs rise because of aging populations, as OECD data indicate, is a question of policy choice and political will.[12]

This does not mean that we should be unconcerned about fiscal pressures from the retirement of the baby boomers. Demographic changes undoubtedly will increase Medicare costs, but this is neither surprising nor a sign of programmatic failure. It is striking that a number of European countries have already experienced the demographic pressure that the United States will confront in the next century without devastating effects on their health spending. Nor is there any evidence in these countries of draconian limits on medical care for elderly or nonelderly persons.

Moreover, the fiscal sustainability or affordability of Medicare ultimately depends on public willingness to finance program expenditures and our choice of social priorities. The brunt of the costs of a growing Medicare population will have to be financed through higher taxes. But the required tax increases, while substantial, are hardly unmanageable. The Congressional Budget Office estimates, for example, that raising the Medicare payroll tax from its present 1.45 percent to 2.05 percent would keep the HI trust fund (Part A) in balance through 2025.[13] Medicare has consistently ranked at or near the top in public support for welfare-state programs. Are we to believe that the public is unwilling to accept tax increases of this magnitude to support the growing numbers of their parents and grandparents who become eligible for Medicare? Put simply, the claim that Medicare is unaffordable and that a demographic imperative exists for radical restructuring of Medicare is exaggerated.

Is Defined-Benefit, Fee-for-Service Insurance Uncontrollable?

Although the demographic pressures described above require firm controls, voucher advocates claim that Medicare is financially uncontrollable. This is ostensibly because of the program's reliance on defined benefits and fee-for-service (FFS) payment. The case against FFS reimbursement is familiar: Physicians are paid for each service they provide, so they are financially rewarded for providing more—and more costly—medical care. FFS payment is consequently believed to encourage physicians to provide Medicare beneficiaries with too many services of low medical value and to distort program spending toward expensive specialty services.

In contrast to capitated payment, FFS payment does not necessarily establish any prospective limit on total reimbursement to physicians for the medical care of enrollees. Moreover, a defined-benefit insurance structure does not provide beneficiaries with economic incentives to enroll in a more efficient plan or seek out lower-cost treatments and providers. All beneficiaries are legally entitled to federal payment for any Medicare-covered services they receive. Thus, there is no limit on program expenditures for individual beneficiaries. Medicare's costs in any given year therefore depend on the volume of services provided to beneficiaries, and their prices. According to Henry Aaron and Robert Reischauer, since Medicare "cannot (and should not) control the quantity of services, it cannot control the total cost of care or total federal spending."[14] The implication of Medicare's supposed incapacity to restrain the volume of medical services is clear. Medicare cannot, it is presumed, control its costs through any type of regulatory framework as long as it relies on FFS payment and defined-benefit insurance.

Yet the majority of industrial democracies with lower medical care costs than those of the United States and universal coverage—including Canada, Germany, Australia, and France—rely on both FFS payment and defined benefits. If FFS payment and defined benefits are inherently uncontrollable, then how, one might ask, have these countries managed to contain spending on medical care? And if economic incentives for patients are, as voucher advocates argue, necessary for cost control, then how have these countries controlled costs without exposing individuals to such incentives?[15]

Although precise strategies differ from country to country, there is a clear "international standard" to cost containment outside the United States.[16] The fundamental element is that governments budget in advance roughly how much they are going to spend on medical care in the coming year. Hospitals receive fixed budgets to cover their operating expenses or are subject to annual sectoral caps limiting total spending on hospital services. Physicians receive payments according to uniform fee schedules and are subject to expenditure caps that penalize unexpected volume increases.[17] If physicians' billings exceed projected costs during a specified period, their payments during the next period will be reduced ("clawbacks") to compensate for unexpected outlays. Capital investments in medical technology are similarly limited through regulation. Cost control in these nations, then, is a collective endeavor. Budgetary limits and efficiency incentives for medical providers are the key elements.

Taken together, budgetary caps and fee schedules permit other industrial democracies to constrain both price and volume. From an international perspective, then, Aaron and Reischauer's contention that Medicare, as a defined-benefit FFS program, cannot control its total costs is empirically wrong. Other health care systems combine defined health benefits with restrained volume and limited spending. Similarly, OECD experience demonstrates that medical costs can be effectively controlled through collective mechanisms and without placing economic incentives for cost control on patients. There is no reason that Medicare, given the proper tools and the will, cannot do the same.

Are Vouchers the Only Feasible Solution for Medicare?

Many advocates argue that vouchers are the only feasible option to make Medicare financially sound. If one accepts that the retirement of the baby boomers makes the present course in Medicare unsustainable, and that a defined-benefit insurance program that relies on FFS payment cannot adequately control costs, it is a short step to the conclusion that a voucher system offers the only way out of the program's financing dilemma. "Only by eventually moving all seniors to privately managed systems operating under a defined federal contribution," Thomas Scully claims, "can the federal government truly restrain cost growth and drive efficiency into the system."[18] This assumption echoes Alain Enthoven's long-standing claim that managed competition is "the only practical solution" for the problems of U.S. medical care.[19]

Yet not one of the OECD nations—not even those with older populations than in the United States—has used a voucher system to control medical costs. Why then should one believe that vouchers are the "only" solution to paying the medical costs of the elderly in the United States? Clearly, the technical justification for this argument is unconvincing.

There is, however, a second dimension of policy feasibility: political acceptability. Even if analysts accepted that vouchers are not the only feasible technical option for Medicare, advocates might still claim that they represent the only politically viable option. Much of the argument for vouchers is, whether explicitly stated or not, a political calculation about what is possible and impossible in U.S. politics. The presumption behind the voucher argument is that the United States would never accept the type of regulatory and centralized budgeting strategies used in other OECD nations' health care systems because they run counter to our national culture and institutions. In other words, policy choices in Medicare are limited, regardless of the substantive merit of alternative approaches, by American exceptionalism.

This view of political feasibility in American health policy is not particularly compelling. If U.S. political culture is incompatible with central budgeting, it is difficult to explain why we budget other public programs. Nor is it, from this perspective, possible to explain the advent of a Medicare administered-pricing regime in the 1980s. In fact, with the adoption of the prospective payment system (PPS), the resource-based relative value scale (RBRVS) fee schedule, and volume performance standards (VPS), Medicare policy has been moving precisely in the direction of centralized budgeting. Notwithstanding claims of cultural exceptionalism, the methods Medicare has adopted for paying physicians and hospitals already resemble those used abroad in many respects. Over time, the trajectory of Medicare spending has been toward increasing the scope of the program that is subject to prospective payment and budgeting. In this context, introducing an aggregate cap on Medicare expenditures hardly seems an insurmountable step or a great leap beyond the limits of U.S. political culture and program philosophy. Rather, it is vouchers that would radically depart from Medicare's programmatic culture. Neither the transformation of a defined-benefit plan into a defined-contribution plan nor the move away from the program's social insurance roots are consistent with that culture.

PROBLEMS WITH VOUCHERS

The case for considering alternatives to vouchers for reforming Medicare is not simply that these alternatives are substantially more feasible than some analysts have allowed. It is also that introducing a voucher system in Medicare would create serious problems for both beneficiaries and the program. These problems, we argue, could be mitigated by instead adopting a program budget without defined contributions. Here we discuss four of these problems.

Cost Burden on Beneficiaries

First, vouchers would shift the burden of medical care inflation to program beneficiaries. If health care costs rose faster than the value of the federal voucher, beneficiaries would have to spend more of their incomes on insurance. Yet many elderly persons are in no position to supplement the voucher with their own funds. On average, the elderly already spend 20 percent of their income on medical care, and in 1992 fully 75 percent of the elderly had incomes below $25,000. [20] The notion that the financial impact of medical inflation should be placed on elderly and disabled beneficiaries, rather than on medical providers or broader contributors to federal revenues, is distributionally troubling.

Managed Care

Second, a voucher system presumes that Medicare beneficiaries should be moved into managed care plans.[21] Voucher advocates anticipate that managed care plans will thrive in a competitive Medicare market and that if program beneficiaries are forced to pay the extra cost of choosing an indemnity plan such as public Medicare, they will opt for a lower-cost option such as a health maintenance organization (HMO). Despite the rhetoric of choice, a central goal of voucher plans is for beneficiaries to leave the one type of health insurance plan—indemnity insurance—that guarantees free choice of physicians. This incentive is considered desirable because HMOs are believed to deliver medical care more efficiently than indemnity plans do, thereby holding out the promise of financial savings for the program and wider benefits for beneficiaries. However, evidence shows that chronically ill and poor elders do not fare well in HMOs and that capitated systems may affect their health status adversely.[22] Consequently, vouchers would create financial incentives for many Medicare beneficiaries to join health plans that might provide them with inadequate care.

Adverse Selection

Third, a voucher system would unfairly penalize beneficiaries who enrolled in high-cost health plans. A central tenet of voucher proposals is that beneficiaries should bear the costs of their health insurance choices. If they choose a health plan that costs more than the voucher, they should pay the extra cost out of their own pockets. The aim is to force beneficiaries to make more cost-conscious, efficient decisions in selecting medical insurance. In a competitive health care system, beneficiaries are expected to become, as Uwe Reinhardt has noted, "the agents of cost control."[21] Voucher advocates argue that this arrangement rightly rewards those who choose efficient, low-cost health plans while penalizing those who select more-expensive plans. The problem is that there is no way of knowing whether the price discrepancies between health plans are attributable to differences in efficiency or to risk selection (one plan may cost more than another because it enrolls a higher number of expensive patients). In a voucher system, an enrollee who selected such a plan would be penalized financially simply for being in the wrong risk pool. In theory, this problem could be corrected through risk adjustment; in practice, no working risk-adjustment system exists. Moreover, this punitive feature of vouchers would fall most heavily on the sickest Medicare beneficiaries, who are the most likely to choose to stay with their present physicians despite price incentives to switch plans.

Unraveling of Social Insurance

Fourth, a voucher system would help to further unravel Medicare's social insurance foundations. Medicare's philosophical commitment has always been to universalism: that regardless of beneficiaries' income before or after retirement, they would be entitled to equal medical care coverage, and that all elderly would participate in the same insurance program. This commitment, mainly because of benefit limitations and cost-sharing requirements, has not been fully realized in Medicare. Vouchers would only take the program much further away from this goal and repudiate the norm itself. Vouchers represent the triumph of individualism over universalism. Beneficiaries would segment into different insurance plans and obtain varying degrees of health care coverage on the basis of health status and ability to pay. The danger is not just that the poor and sick would fare badly in a segmented insurance market; it is that the embrace of individualism would erode programmatic ideals of social community and collective responsibility for financing medical care, weakening Medicare's political foundations.

OUR PROPOSAL: A PROGRAM BUDGET FOR MEDICARE

As international experience suggests, Medicare can avoid the problems associated with vouchers and still impose strict controls on program expenditures. The required policy is a program budget that limits aggregate Medicare spending without defined contributions for beneficiaries. In contrast to vouchers, program cost control would remain a collective, rather than an individual, responsibility.

How would a program budget operate in Medicare? The federal government would set an annual budget for all Medicare expenditures over the coming year. The rate of annual growth in Medicare could be restricted to the expected increase in gross national product (GNP), adjusted for enrollment increases, or to any other specified level of growth. Separate caps could be set for spending on physician, hospital, home health, and skilled nursing facility care. Separate caps would apply to payments for beneficiaries enrolled in HMOs and other private insurance plans contracting with Medicare. An annual limit on hospital expenditures could be imposed on top of the existing diagnosis-related group (DRG) reimbursement system, with the annual update in DRGs periodically reduced if costs exceeded predetermined targets. On the physician side, the existing RBRVS-based fee schedule and VPS could be retained. However, the volume standards should be revised from their present form (two-year delayed reductions in physician fees) to resemble the stronger clawback mechanisms in other countries.

While a prospective budget should be the starting point for controlling Medicare spending, other measures also should be taken to shore up the program's financing. As already noted, taxes should be increased to help meet the costs of Medicare's growing enrollment over the next three decades. Beneath a program budget, Medicare should use additional cost containment strategies, such as physician profiling to detect inappropriate high spenders and a prospective or bundled payment system for postacute services.

Our proposal is different from current arrangements in Medicare, as well as the incremental proposals put forward by some analysts, in its introduction of a budget encompassing aggregate (as opposed to specific-sector) Medicare expenditures.[24] By establishing an aggregate limit on top of volume and price regulations, a program budget would commit Medicare to a specific level of cost control for a given year and thereby would help to guard against the consequences of unexpected cost increases in any one area, as has happened with hospital payments and postacute care in recent years. The political commitment to a global constraint on Medicare spending clearly would impose stronger fiscal discipline than any form of cost containment used thus far. In contrast to vouchers, however, a program budget would not individualize cost containment. The burden of excess medical spending would fall most directly on medical providers, not on Medicare beneficiaries.

There is no magic to making a program budget work. The instruments—fee schedules, volume limits, and spending caps—are relatively simple and crude. What is needed is the political imagination to accept the idea of introducing global constraints to Medicare and the political will to make them work. We do not know if the United States will develop that political will or choose this path of reform. But we do know that this approach has worked in other countries; presuming the impossibility of its adoption in the United States, as some analysts have done, prevents us from considering a proven method for cost control.

We readily admit that, in some important respects, a program budget for Medicare alone has more limitations than would a global budget on all health expenditures in the context of a universal health insurance system. A budget for only one part of the population must address issues of cost shifting, provider exit, and cross-subsidization. Although Medicare can deal with these issues, they are less of a concern in universal insurance systems. These limitations, however, are not an indictment of a program budget, but of any Medicare-specific cost-control effort. And in the absence of a universal health care system, a program budget, with its emphasis on collective rather than individual cost control, remains a better alternative for Medicare reform than vouchers.

OBJECTIONS TO OUR PROPOSAL

Access

There are three likely objections to our proposal. The first is that setting a prospective budget for Medicare would erode access to medical services for elderly and disabled beneficiaries. Budgetary limits would inevitably result in reduced payments to medical providers, many of which, critics argue, would then refuse to accept Medicare patients. Beneficiaries in this scenario would lose access to mainstream health services. This fear is based in part on the experience of Medicaid recipients with access problems.[25]

Clearly, maintaining reasonable access for beneficiaries should be a critical goal of any Medicare reform plan. But would the imposition of a Medicare budget erode access? There are good reasons to believe such fears of "Medicaidization" are exaggerated. Many commentators equate reductions in Medicare expenditures with cuts in program benefits. This confuses the price of medical care with the benefits of medical services. The value of Medicare to beneficiaries, as Mark Pauly rightly notes, "does not depend on what [payments] providers get."[26] Medicare can, within a broad range, reduce the price it pays for services without necessarily reducing benefits or the quality of its coverage. As the largest payer in the United States, Medicare has concentrated purchasing power to negotiate fee reductions. The size of the program and the high utilization rates of the elderly mean that most providers cannot afford to reject Medicare patients, even at reduced fee levels. They are simply too dependent on Medicare for patients and income.

Medicare's leverage to secure provider payment reductions has already been demonstrated. During the past decade Medicare reduced the rate of growth in its payments to hospitals and physicians with no deterioration in beneficiaries' access to services. The percentage of physicians accepting Medicare assignment—that is, taking federal reimbursement as payment-in-full for services rendered—increased during this period. There is no reason why Medicare cannot use similar leverage over providers in the future.

Recent developments in the private sector clearly make it easier for Medicare to reduce provider payments even more than it has to date. In the past, the scope of Medicare expenditure reductions has been constrained by fears of shifting costs to private payers. This is no longer the case. Private insurers have been aggressively cutting back their own payments to hospitals and physicians. Medicare has already gone from being a low payer to being a high payer in some markets. In this context, Medicare has substantial leverage to restrain its own expenditures more tightly. It is far less likely than ever before that providers will shun Medicare enrollees for higher-paying private patients; changes in the private health care system mean that these more profitable patients are no longer readily available. These changing conditions were clearly recognized by the Prospective Payment Assessment Commission (ProPAC) in its 1997 recommendation that hospitals should receive no increase in Medicare payments for 1998.[27]

The growing market power of managed care plans also has helped to create an oversupply of specialty physicians and hospital beds in many areas. Hospital occupancy rates are continuing to plummet as managed care organizations attempt to reduce their patient days. Similar surpluses have now been generated among specialty physicians as these plans turn toward primary care and away from more costly forms of medical delivery.[28] In the immediate future, Medicare beneficiaries should have no trouble gaining access to care despite reduced payments.

However, there may not be as great an oversupply of primary care physicians as of specialists, because of past training practices in medical schools and the primary care needs of managed care organizations.[29] Beneficiaries' access to primary care, though, could be protected by dividing the program's budget for physician services into separate caps for primary and specialty care, similar to those now used in the Medicare VPS. This would allow Medicare to adjust rates to each group as market conditions permit.

In sum, the market conditions that confront Medicare are substantially different—and more amenable to payment constraints—than those that Medicaid traditionally has confronted. In addition, there are crucial political differences between the two programs that make access problems much less likely in Medicare. The political constituency for Medicare—nearly forty million elderly and disabled persons and their families—is much stronger and has more organizational resources than is true for the coalition for Medicaid. Moreover, the political costs of providers' boycotting Medicare would be much greater than those of avoiding Medicaid. In sum, differential market conditions and political dynamics mean that Medicare beneficiaries are unlikely to ever experience the access problems that have plagued Medicaid.

That there is ample room for Medicare to reduce fees does not, of course, mean that the program's capacity to cut costs without harming access is unlimited. A Medicare program budget would cover, in contrast to other OECD nations, only one part of the population. In this sense, Medicare does not have the monopsonists' advantages that, for example, Canadian provinces enjoy in negotiating prices. Neither does Medicare have the same clout with respect to capital decisions or technology more generally. If private-sector medical inflation spurs upward again, the amount that Medicare can ratchet down on provider fees will of course be constrained. But this is not an argument against a program budget per se as much as it is a restriction on how tightly such a budget could be set. Moreover, it is too often forgotten that the problems of access and market dependency apply equally well to vouchers. If private-sector health costs rose faster than expected, either the amount of the federal voucher would have to be raised—in which case voucher systems would not save as much money as advocates anticipate—or costs would be shifted to beneficiaries, whose ability to afford health insurance would erode.

Rationing

A second and related objection is that adoption of a program budget would lead to the rationing of medical care services. The claim is that Medicare's coverage would be driven down to a level common in OECD health care systems, a level that critics presume would be unacceptable in the United States. This fear is based in large part on the type of images U.S. analysts have associated with "the painful prescription" supposedly doled out by other national health insurance systems: long queues, systematic denial of medically useful services, and severe limits on technology. The problem is that these images and the accompanying fear that a budgeted health insurance system produces widespread rationing do not reflect reality. European and Canadian patients average more physician visits, more hospitalizations, and longer hospital stays than their American counterparts do.[30]

Budgeted medical care systems do, of course, result in lower fees to medical providers. But lower fees induce physicians to provide more, not fewer, services, and this would likely be the case in a health care market in which providers can no longer easily substitute higher-paying private patients for Medicare beneficiaries. Budgeting also means limits on technological diffusion and on some expensive hospital services. Yet these limits are already well under way in the private-sector HMOs that contract with Medicare, and in any case, there is considerable room to reduce prices and the volume of some procedures from the currently excessive U.S. norm without triggering widespread denial of medically necessary services. And for those services that were limited as a consequence of budgeting Medicare, access would be based on medical need. In a voucher system, that access would be based on ability to pay.

What is rationed strictly in international health care systems is providers' incomes. Controlling the growth in Medicare costs entails explicit decisions about limiting how much we pay for medical services and, ultimately, restraining the growth in medical care providers' incomes. This is obviously an implication that such providers find unsettling. There is no basis, though, for arguing that the American public would not accept stronger limits on payments to Medicare physicians and hospitals. On the contrary, when compared to the alternatives—higher taxes or increased costs for beneficiaries—rationing providers' incomes is likely to be quite attractive. Given the fiscal realities of American political life, the weakened political power of physicians, and changing conditions in the private medical care system, Medicare has never been in a more favorable position to adopt such limits.

Balanced Budget Act

A third and final objection is that a Medicare budget is not feasible because it represents a different direction than that embodied in the recently enacted Balanced Budget Act. The 1997 legislation has opened Medicare up (much too widely, in our view) to a host of new insurance options, ranging from managed care plans to private-sector indemnity insurance and medical savings accounts. To be sure, these changes make it more difficult to impose a program budget. The number of budget caps beneath the aggregate total will have to be expanded to incorporate the new insurance options. This will be a complicated, but not impossible, task. There are lessons to be learned here from the Dutch and German experiences with operating broad constraints on medical expenditures for systems of multiple insurance plans and sickness funds. Moreover, public Medicare is still the core of the program (now enrolling 87 percent of all beneficiaries) and will remain so for the immediate future. Finally, while pushing Medicare toward a market for private insurance, the 1997 Balanced Budget Act simultaneously pushes Medicare in the direction of a program budget. By mandating a prospective payment system for postacute care, the legislation places budgetary controls on one of the major areas of the program that had been relatively unconstrained. Even in the absence of an explicit aggregate budget, then, public Medicare will soon have a series of sectoral caps and prospective payment mechanisms that together will create an implicit budget.

"Whatever everyone knows," Morris Barer and his colleagues write, "is usually wrong, and common sense is either not common, or not sense."[31] The assumption that the only solution to Medicare's long-term financing problems is a voucher system, while increasingly common, makes little sense. Neither Medicare's current financial problems, the demographic bulge of the baby-boom generation, nor the allegedly uncontrollable nature of FFS payment and defined-benefit insurance requires anything like a voucher solution. It is reasonable to conclude that Medicare spending can be controlled the same way other health care systems control their costs: through budgetary and regulatory limits on the price and volume of medical services. The experiences of other industrialized nations with aging populations clearly suggest that Medicare can absorb the baby boomers without adopting a voucher scheme, without making individual beneficiaries the central agents of cost control, and without suffering the fundamental socioeconomic dislocations that have been forecast in some quarters. In the end, the argument for vouchers is largely a political judgment that has been presented—incorrectly—as a technical necessity.

The inattention to international experience in the Medicare debate reflects a broader pattern of parochialism in U.S. social policy discussions. Apparently convinced that the United States is too different to learn from other countries, U.S. observers regularly overlook how other welfare states have coped with demographic changes and medical care inflation. This disregard occurs despite the fact that some

European nations have already faced the pressures of aging populations and have controlled medical care costs more successfully than we have. The debate on baby boomers and Medicare would be far more enlightening if more U.S. policy analysts paid attention to developments outside our borders.

Ultimately, the most prudent way for the United States to deal with the health care costs of aging and the pressures on Medicare is to create, as other nations have, a universal health care system that includes the elderly. Partitioning the elderly into Medicare magnifies the actual size of demographic pressures by isolating a growing population on its own financing base. If Medicare were merged into a national health care system, the fiscal burden of demographic trends would appear less fearsome, and solutions would rightly come in the context of systemwide debates over the appropriate direction of medical care delivery and organization. However, in the absence of a comprehensive solution to the problems of American medical care, we must not fall into the trap of believing that Medicare reform is unattainable.

ACKNOWLEDGMENTS

The authors are grateful to the Robert Wood Johnson Foundation for research support. Special thanks to Mark Goldberg for his help. The authors also thank Joe White, John Ellwood, Mark Schlesinger, Robert Ball, Annette Thorn, and two anonymous reviewers for their comments on a preliminary draft. An earlier version of this paper was presented at the Health Consumer Summit on Medicare and Universal Coverage, Washington, D.C., 25–26 April 1997.

ABOUT THE AUTHORS

Theodore Marmor, PhD, is Professor of Public Policy and Management and Political Science at the Yale School of Management in New Haven, Connecticut.

Jonathan Oberlander, PhD, is Assistant Professor in the Departments of Social Medicine and Political Science at the University of North Carolina at Chapel Hill Chapel Hill, North Carolina.

REFERENCES

1. R.D. Reischauer, "Medicare: What to Do?" *Brookings Review* 13, no. 3 (1995): 50.
2. V. Fuchs, "Perspective on Medicare," *Los Angeles Times,* 1 July 1996, B5.
3. H.J. Aaron and R.D. Reischauer, "The Medicare Reform Debate: What Is the Next Step?" *Health Affairs* (Winter 1995): 27.
4. T.S. Bodenheimer and K. Grumbach, *Understanding Health Policy* (Norwalk, Conn.: Appleton and Lange, 1995), 123.

5. Congressional Budget Office, *Reducing the Deficit: Spending and Revenue Options* (Washington: U.S. Government Printing Office, 1996), 462.

6. Reischauer, "Medicare: What to Do?" 50.

7. S.M. Butler and R.E. Moffit, "The FEHBP as a Model for a New Medicare Program," *Health Affairs* (Winter 1995): 60.

8. Fuchs, "Perspective on Medicare."

9. This analysis overlooks children and thus overstates the overall burden of "dependents" on the future working population. See also D.M. Cutler et al., "An Aging Society: Opportunity or Challenge?" *Brookings Papers on Economic Activity,* vol. 1 (1990): 5–16.

10. T.E. Getzen, "Population Aging and the Growth of Health Expenditures," *Journal of Gerontology* 47, no. 3 (1994): S102.

11. *OECD Labor Force Statistics, 1973–1994;* United Nations, *World Population Prospects: The 1994 Revisions;* and *OECD Health Data 96* database.

12. M.L. Barer, R.G. Evans, and C. Hertzman, "Avalanche or Glacier? Health Care and the Demographic Rhetoric," *Canadian Journal on Aging* 14, no. 2 (1995): 193–224; M.L. Barer et al., "Aging and Health Care Utilization: New Evidence on Old Fallacies," *Social Science and Medicine* 24, no. 10 (1987): 851–862; and R.G. Evans, "Illusion of Necessity: Evading Responsibility for Choice in Health Care," *Journal of Health Politics, Policy and Law* 10 (1985): 439–467.

13. June O'Neill, testimony on the financial status of the Medicare program before the House Committee on Ways and Means, 2 May 1995.

14. Aaron and Reischauer, "The Medicare Reform Debate," 22.

15. See "Understanding the Choices in Health Care Reform: Report of the Health Care Study Group," *Journal of Health Politics, Policy and Law* 19 (1994): 499–541.

16. See J. White, *Competing Solutions: American Health Care Proposals and International Experience* (Washington: Brookings Institution, 1995); and W.A. Glaser, *Health Insurance in Practice* (San Francisco: Jossey-Bass, 1991).

17. W.A. Glaser, "How Expenditure Caps and Expenditure Targets Really Work," *Milbank Quarterly* 71, no. 1 (1993): 97–127.

18. Thomas Scully, president, Federation of American Health Systems, quoted in C. Fraley, "Using Vouchers for Medicare May Help GOP Cut Costs," *Congressional Quarterly* (22 July 1995): 2189.

19. A.C. Enthoven, *Health Plan: The Only Practical Solution to the Soaring Cost of Medical Care* (Menlo Park, Calif.: Addison-Wesley, 1980).

20. M. Moon, *Medicare Now and in the Future,* 2d ed. (Washington: Urban Institute Press, 1996), 10; and *Medicare Chart Book* (Menlo Park, Calif.: Kaiser Family Foundation, 1995).

21. See J.B. Oberlander, "Vouchers for Medicare: A Critical Reappraisal," In *Critical Gerontology,* ed M. Minkler and C. Estes (Boston: Baywood, forthcoming).

22. J.E. Ware et al., "Differences in 4-Year Health Outcomes for Elderly and Poor, Chronically Ill Patients Treated in HMO and Fee-for-Service Systems,"

Journal of the American Medical Association 276 (1995): 1039–1047; and P.W. Shaughnessy et al., "Home Health Outcomes under Capitated and Fee-for-Service Payment," *Health Care Financing Review* (Fall 1994): 187–221.

23. U.E. Reinhardt, "Reforming the Health Care System: The Universal Dilemma," in *The Social Medicine Reader,* ed. G. Henderson et al. (Durham, N.C.: Duke University Press, 1997).

24. The incremental approach favored for Medicare reform by some voucher critics is exemplified in M. Moon and K. Davis, "Preserving and Strengthening Medicare," *Health Affairs* (Winter 1995): 31–46.

25. Medicaid pays physicians around 47 percent of the amount private insurers pay. And in a 1993 survey, only about 65 percent of physicians who were accepting new patients said that they would take Medicaid patients. See S. Trude and D.C. Colby, "Monitoring the Impact of the Medicare Fee Schedule on Access to Care for Vulnerable Populations," *Journal of Health Politics, Policy and Law* (February 1997): 67.

26. M.V. Pauly, "Will Medicare Reforms Increase Managed Care Enrollment?" *Health Affairs* (Fall 1996): 186.

27. S. Rich, "Freeze on Medicare Hospital Fees Urged," *Washington Post,* 20 January 1997, A4.

28. J.P. Weiner, "The Demand for Physician Services in a Changing Health Care System: A Synthesis," *Medical Care Review* (Winter 1993): 411–449.

29. We are grateful to Mark Schlesinger for this point. On Medicaid access problems, see Trude and Colby, "Monitoring the Impact of the Medicare Fee Schedule," 67.

30. See White, *Competing Solutions,* 128–62.

31. Barer et al., "Aging and Health Care Utilization," 851.

ARTICLE 3

MEDICARE: CONSIDERATIONS FOR ADDING A PRESCRIPTION DRUG BENEFIT
UNITED STATES GENERAL ACCOUNTING OFFICE: TESTIMONY BEFORE THE COMMITTEE ON FINANCE, U.S. SENATE

Laura A. Dummit

Mr. Chairman and Members of the Committee:

I am pleased to be here today as you consider a prescription drug benefit for Medicare beneficiaries. Over the past several months, this Committee has held a series of hearings on Medicare reform issues to determine the nature and extent of changes needed to modernize the program and control its impact on the federal budget. These discussions come at an important juncture in the program's history—the Congress passed landmark legislation in the Balanced Budget Act of 1997 (BBA) that has the potential to improve the financial underpinnings of the program. Yet, more work remains to ensure Medicare's continued financial viability. Budget projections show health care consuming ever-larger shares of the federal dollar, thus threatening to crowd out funding for other valued government programs and activities. At the same time, many believe that Medicare's current benefit structure should be updated to include a prescription drug benefit.

Studies suggest that broadening Medicare coverage to include prescription drugs could add between 7.2 and 10 percent to Medicare costs. Such an expansion would occur at a time when Medicare's rolls are growing and are projected to increase rapidly with the aging of the baby boom generation and during a time of major technological advances in medicine and biotechnology. Currently, some Medicare beneficiaries face a significant financial burden for outpatient prescription drugs. The policy dilemma before you today is that, on the one hand, Medicare's lack of a prescription drug benefit may impede access to certain treatment advances, whereas on the other, the cost implications of including a prescription drug benefit will be substantial. These additional costs would serve to erode the projected financial condition of the Medicare program, which, according to the Medicare trustees, is already unsustainable in its present form.

My remarks today will focus on the factors contributing to the growth in prescription drug spending for both the general population and Medicare beneficiaries and efforts to control that growth. I will also discuss benefit design and

379

implementation issues to be considered in deliberations about adding a new prescription drug benefit. My comments are based on analyses of recent data and our body of completed work on prescription drugs.

In summary, proposals to add prescription drug coverage to Medicare's benefits come during a period of rapid growth in national spending for pharmaceuticals and transformations in the prescription drug market. Increased coverage of drugs by health plans and insurers, advances in drug treatments, and aggressive marketing have spurred the growth in the use of pharmaceuticals, while the use of formularies, pharmacy benefit managers, and generic substitutions as cost control approaches have dramatically changed the nature of the market in which prescription drugs are purchased.

What remains unchanged since 1965, however, is the absence of coverage for outpatient prescription drugs by traditional Medicare. A third of the Medicare population lacks the supplemental drug coverage provided to most beneficiaries through employer-sponsored plans, managed care organizations, Medicaid, or Medigap insurance. Moreover, high drug utilization among the Medicare population translates into a potentially daunting financial burden.

The implications of adding prescription drug coverage to Medicare's benefit package depend on the choices made regarding details such as its scope and financing. Its design and implementation will also shape the impact of this benefit on beneficiaries, Medicare spending, and the pharmaceutical market. Recent experience provides at least two approaches for implementing a drug benefit. One would involve the Medicare program obtaining price discounts from manufacturers. Such an arrangement could be modeled after Medicaid's drug rebate program. While the discounts in aggregate would likely be substantial, this approach lacks the flexibility to achieve the greatest control over spending. It cannot effectively influence or steer utilization because it does not include incentives that would encourage beneficiaries to make cost-conscious decisions. The second approach would draw from private sector experience in negotiating price discounts from manufacturers in exchange for shifting market share. Some plans and insurers employ pharmacy benefit managers (PBM) to manage their drug benefits, including claims processing, negotiating with manufacturers, establishing lists of drug products that are preferred because of price or efficacy, and developing beneficiary incentive approaches to control spending and use. Applying these techniques to the Medicare program, however, would be difficult due to its size, the need for transparency in its actions, and the imperative for equity for its beneficiaries.

MANY FACTORS HAVE SPURRED PRESCRIPTION DRUG SPENDING AND FOSTERED MARKET CHANGES

Extensive research and development over the past 10 years have led to the introduction of new prescription drug therapies and improvements over existing thera-

TABLE 1

NATIONAL EXPENDITURES ON PRESCRIPTION DRUGS, 1992–1997			
Year	Prescription Drug Expenditures (in Millions)	Annual Growth in Prescription Drug Expenditures (Percent)	Annual Growth in All Health Care Expenditures (Percent)
1997	$78,888	14	5
1996	69,111	13	5
1995	61,060	11	5
1994	55,189	9	5
1993	50,632	9	7
1992	46,598	11	9
Average annual growth, 1992–97		11	5

Source: Health Care Financing Administration (HCFA). Office of the Actuary.

pies that, in some instances, have replaced other health care interventions. The growing importance of prescription drugs as part of health care has made the inclusion of drug benefits an attractive policy feature to consumers with a choice among health insurance products. Most commercial private health insurance products, Medicare+Choice[1] plans, and all Medicaid programs provide their beneficiaries with an outpatient prescription drug benefit. Health plans have found that including prescription drugs as a covered benefit helps attract members and is valuable to their beneficiaries. Prescription drug expenditures have outpaced other components of health care spending in recent years due to several factors. At the same time, the use of new approaches to dampen these expenditures is reshaping the prescription drug market.

Rise in Prescription Drug Spending

Over the past 5 years, prescription drug expenditures have grown significantly, both in total and as a share of all health expenditures. Prescription drug spending grew, on average, from 1992 to 1997 by 11 percent a year compared with a 5 percent average growth rate for health expenditures overall. (See Table 1.) Drug spending during that same period also consumed a larger share of total health care spending—rising from 5.6 percent to 7.2 percent.

---

[1]As an alternative to traditional Medicare fee-for-service, beneficiaries in Medicare+Choice plans (formerly Medicare risk health maintenance organizations) obtain all their services through a managed care organization and Medicare makes a monthly capitation payment to the plan on their behalf.

While total drug expenditures depend both on the prices paid and the volume used, the recent spending increases appear to have more to do with stepped up volume than price. A precise determination of how much is due to volume versus price increases is not possible since only data on the retail pharmaceutical prices are widely available. The actual prices paid are often lower than retail levels, as insurers, PBMS, and other purchasers negotiate significant discounts from manufacturers and other suppliers. Market changes in recent years have likely altered the size of those discounts.

Several factors have contributed to increased prescription drug use and the resulting spending increases: namely, more individuals have third-party drug coverage, new drug therapies have been introduced into the market, and manufacturers have marketed drugs more aggressively through advertising directly to consumers.

The increase in private insurance coverage for prescription drugs is a likely factor accounting for the rise in utilization. In the decade between 1987 and 1997, the share of prescription drug expenditures paid by private health insurers rose from almost a third to more than half. (See Figure 1.) The development of new, more expensive drug therapies—including new drugs that replace old drugs and new drugs that treat disease more effectively—also contributed to the drug spending growth. The average number of new drugs entering the market each year has grown from 24 at the beginning of the 1990s to 33 now. Similarly, biotechnology advances and a growing knowledge of the human immune system are significantly shaping the discovery, design, and production of drugs. Advertising pitched to the lay consumer has also likely upped consumers' use of prescription drugs. Between

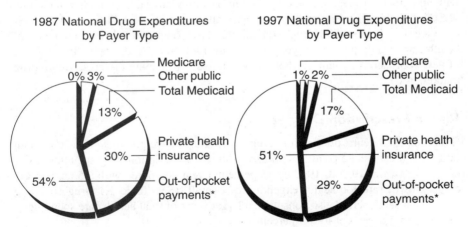

*Out-of-pocket expenditures include direct spending by consumers for all health care goods and services, such as coinsurance, deductibles, and any amounts not covered by insurance. Out-of-pocket premiums paid by individuals are not counted here.

Figure 1 Comparison of national drug expenditures, 1987 and 1997 (Source: Health Care Financing Administration, Office of the Actuary)

March 1998 and March 1999, industry spending on advertising grew 16 percent, to $1.5 billion.

Current Medicare Beneficiary Drug Coverage

Prescription drugs are an important component of medical care for the elderly because of the greater prevalence of chronic and other health conditions associated with aging. In 1995, Medicare beneficiaries had on average more than 18 prescriptions filled. This varies substantially across beneficiaries, however, reflecting the presence of chronic and other conditions that respond to drug treatment and also financial considerations such as third-party prescription drug coverage. In 1995, annual drug costs were $600 for the elderly, compared to just over $140 for the nonelderly population. For some, spending is considerably higher. In 1999, an estimated 20 percent of Medicare beneficiaries will have total drug costs of $1,500 or more—a substantial sum for those lacking some form of insurance to subsidize the purchase.

This financial burden is due, in part, to gaps in insurance coverage for prescription drugs. One third of the Medicare population lacks drug coverage altogether. Those with third-party protections often face deductibles, cost sharing, or limits on total benefit payments. The vast majority of the approximately 17 percent of Medicare beneficiaries enrolled in a Medicare+Choice plan have drug coverage, as do retirees who have employer-sponsored insurance. All beneficiaries who are enrolled in Medicaid receive drug coverage. Other beneficiaries may purchase Medigap policies that provide drug coverage, although Medigap policies involve significant cost sharing, impose annual limits, may contain significant exclusions, and can be expensive. A Medigap policy with drug coverage can cost $1,500 more per year than an otherwise comparable policy.

Medicare beneficiaries with drug coverage use more prescription drugs and have higher overall drug expenditures than those without drug coverage. This may be because beneficiaries with higher prescription drug needs may be more likely to obtain third-party protections. Alternatively, the lack of coverage for some may inhibit appropriate drug utilization.

Cost Control Approaches Reshaping Pharmaceutical Market

During this period of growth in the volume of prescription drugs used, third-party payers, which have been the primary purchasers, have pursued various approaches to controlling spending. These efforts have initiated a transformation of the pharmaceutical market. A world in which insured individuals purchase drugs at retail pharmacies at retail prices and then seek reimbursement is giving way to third-party payers influencing which drug is purchased, how much is paid for a drug, and where it is purchased.

A common technique to manage pharmacy care and control costs is to use a formulary. A formulary is a list of prescription drugs, grouped by therapeutic class, that a health plan or insurer prefers and may encourage to be prescribed for its enrollees. Decisions about which drugs to include on a formulary are based on their medical value and their price. Both inclusion of a drug on a formulary and its cost can affect how frequently it is prescribed and purchased and, therefore, can affect its market share.

Formularies can be open, incentive-based, or closed. Open formularies are often referred to as "voluntary" because enrollees are not penalized if their physicians prescribe nonformulary drugs. Incentive-based formularies generally offer enrollees lower copayments for the preferred formulary or generic drugs. Incentive-based or managed formularies are becoming more popular because they combine flexibility and greater cost-control features than open formularies. A closed formulary limits insurance coverage to formulary drugs only and requires enrollees to pay the full cost of nonformulary drugs prescribed by their physician.

Many health plans or insurers also contract with a PBM to administer and manage their prescription drug benefit. PBMs offer a range of services, including prescription claims processing, mail-service pharmacy, formulary development and management, pharmacy network development, generic substitution incentives, and drug utilization review. PBMs have successfully negotiated discounts and rebates on prescription drugs with manufacturers.

ISSUES TO CONSIDER IN BENEFIT DESIGN AND ADMINISTRATION

Policymakers considering proposals for including a prescription drug benefit in the Medicare program are facing a myriad of options. Assessing the merits of whether and how to implement these reforms will depend, in large measure, on whom the benefit covers and how it is financed. In such an assessment, it may be appropriate to recall the criteria that the Comptroller General enunciated before this Committee in testimony on March 10. These criteria could guide deliberations on expanding coverage to include prescription drugs: (1) affordability—a benefit should be evaluated in terms of its impact on the sustainability of program expenditures for the long term; (2) equity—a benefit should be fair across groups of beneficiaries and to providers; (3) adequacy—a benefit should foster cost-effective and clinically meaningful innovations, furthering Medicare's tradition of technology development; (4) feasibility—a benefit should incorporate such administrative essentials as implementation and monitoring techniques; and (5) acceptance—a benefit should account for the need to educate beneficiary and provider communities about its costs and the realities of trade-offs required when significant policy changes occur.

Although the Congress will likely examine a number of alternative benefit designs and administrative options, I would like to briefly discuss two approaches that may be considered. One would be similar to how drug benefits are provided in state Medicaid programs, which rely on federal authority to lower drug prices through rebates paid by drug manufacturers to control spending. The other would be modeled after approaches adopted by private sector health plans in which PBMs are typically used to administer various techniques to control pharmacy benefit costs. Each approach has some advantages and disadvantages.

Medicaid Programs Rely on Discounts, Limited Utilization Controls

Before the enactment of the Medicaid drug rebate program as part of the Omnibus Budget Reconciliation Act of 1990 (OBRA), state Medicaid programs paid close to retail prices for outpatient drugs. As the largest government payer for prescription drugs, Medicaid drug expenditures comprised about 13 percent of the domestic pharmaceutical market. Other purchasers, such as health maintenance organizations (HMO) and hospitals, negotiated discounts with manufacturers and paid considerably less.

The rebate program required drug manufacturers to give state Medicaid programs rebates for outpatient drugs. The rebates were based on the lowest or "best" prices they charged other purchasers. In return for the rebates, state Medicaid programs maintain open formularies that permit reimbursement for all drugs manufactured by pharmaceutical companies that entered into rebate agreements with the Health Care Financing Administration.

After the rebate program's enactment, a number of market changes occurred that affected other purchasers of prescription drugs and the amount of the rebates Medicaid programs received. For example, the prices many large private purchasers, such as HMOs, paid for outpatient drugs increased substantially. Moreover, the lowest prices in the market increased faster than the drugs' average prices as drug manufacturers significantly reduced the price discounts they offered private purchasers. As a result, within 2 years the rebates paid to state Medicaid programs fell to the minimum amount required by OBRA.

Although states have received billions of dollars in rebates from drug manufacturers since the enactment of OBRA 1990, state Medicaid directors have expressed concerns about the rebate program. The principal concern involves OBRA's requirement for open formularies, which limits the utilization controls Medicaid programs can use at a time when prescription drug expenditures are rapidly increasing. Although they can require recipients to obtain prior authorization for particular drugs and impose monthly limits on the number of covered prescriptions, other techniques to steer recipients to less expensive drugs are not available to them. These approaches can add to the administrative burden on state Medicaid programs, lead to purchasing more expensive drugs, and create access problems for certain individuals.

Other Payers Employ Various Techniques to Control Expenditures

Other payers, such as private employer health plans, Medicare+Choice plans, and insurance products for federal employees have taken a different approach to managing their prescription drug benefits. They use formularies and copayments to control drug utilization and obtain better prices by concentrating purchases on selected drugs. In many cases, these plans or insurers retain the services provided by a PBM to implement their pharmacy benefit.

Beneficiary cost sharing has had a central role in attempting to influence drug utilization. Copayments frequently are structured to both influence the choice of a drug and purchasing arrangements. While formulary restrictions can channel purchases to preferred drugs, closed formularies, which provide reimbursement only for preferred drugs, have generated significant consumer dissatisfaction. As a result, many plans link their cost sharing requirements and formulary lists. The fastest growing trend today is to maintain an open formulary in which all drugs receive some coverage, with beneficiaries paying different levels of cost sharing for different drugs—typically a smaller copayment for generic drugs, a larger one for preferred drugs, and an even larger one for all other drugs. Reducing the required copayments may also encourage enrollees using maintenance drugs for chronic conditions to use particular suppliers, like a mail-order pharmacy.

Plans and insurers have turned to PBMs for their expertise in establishing formulary lists, negotiating prices with manufacturers and suppliers, and processing beneficiary claims, as well as a variety of clinical services, such as drug utilization review. PBMs bring expertise and economies of scale to these tasks that individual plans or insurers may not have. In addition, they often may have more leverage than individual plans in negotiating prices as they combine the purchasing power of multiple purchasers.

Traditional fee-for-service Medicare has generally established administrative prices for services like physician or hospital care and then processed and paid claims with few utilization controls. Adopting some of the techniques used by private plans and insurers might have the potential for better control of costs. However, how to adopt those techniques to deal with the unique characteristics and enormity of the Medicare program raises many questions.

Negotiated or competitively determined prices would be superior to administered prices only if Medicare could employ some of the utilization controls that come from having a formulary and differential beneficiary cost sharing. In this manner, Medicare would be able to negotiate significantly discounted prices by promising to deliver a larger market share for a manufacturers' product. Manufacturers would have no incentive to offer a deep discount if all drugs in a therapeutic class were covered on the same terms. Without a promised share of the Medicare market, these manufacturers may reap greater returns from higher prices and concentrating marketing efforts on physicians and consumers to influence prescribing patterns.

Implementing a formulary and other utilization controls could prove difficult for Medicare. Developing a formulary involves determining which drugs are therapeutically equivalent so that several from each class can be selected as preferred. Plans and PBMS currently make those determinations privately—something that would not be tolerable for Medicare, which must have transparent policies that are determined openly. Given the stakes involved in being selected, one can imagine the intensive efforts to offer input to and scrutinize the selection process.

Medicare may also find it impossible to delegate this task to a PBM or multiple PBMS. A single PBM contractor would likely be subject to the same level of scrutiny as the program. Such scrutiny may compromise the flexibility PBMS have utilized to generate savings. An alternative would be to grant flexibility to multiple PBMS that are responsible only for a share of the market. Contracting with multiple PBMS, though, raises other issues. If each PBM had exclusive responsibility for a geographic area, beneficiaries who need certain drugs could be advantaged or disadvantaged merely because they live in a particular area. If multiple PBMS operated in each area, beneficiaries would choose one to administer their drug benefit. Then, how to inform beneficiaries of the differences in each PBM's policies and the possible need to risk adjust payments to PBMS for differences in health status of beneficiaries using them would become issues.

CONCLUDING OBSERVATIONS

Adding prescription drug coverage to the Medicare program would have a substantial impact on the costs of the program, in addition to the financial well being and health of many of its beneficiaries. The challenge will be in designing and implementing drug coverage to minimize the financial implications for Medicare while maximizing the positive effect of such coverage on Medicare beneficiaries. Most importantly, this substantial benefit reform must be consistent with efforts to ensure the sustainability of the program so that Medicare does not consume an unreasonable share of our productive resources and does not encroach on other public programs or private sector activities. Reconciling these needs will take the kind of leadership and creativity demonstrated by the Congress as it designed and implemented the BBA reforms that extended Medicare's financial viability.

It may also be instructive to return to lessons learned in implementing the BBA reforms. From those efforts, it is clear that major changes to the Medicare program need to be effective, flexible, and steadfast. Effectiveness must include the collection of necessary data to assess impact—separating the transitory from the permanent and the trivial from the important. Flexibility is critical to make changes and refinements when conditions warrant and when actual outcomes differ substantially from the expected ones. Steadfastness is needed when particular interests pit the primacy of their needs against the more global interests of preserving Medicare.

Mr. Chairman, this concludes my prepared statement. I will be happy to answer any questions you or other Members of the Committee may have.

ACKNOWLEDGMENT

Individuals who made key contributions to this testimony include Tricia Spellman, Kathryn Linehan, and Hannah Fein.

ABOUT THE AUTHOR

Laura A. Dummit is Associate Director of Health Financing and Public Health Issues for the Health, Education, and Human Services Division in the General Accounting Office of the U.S. Congress.

THE AMERICAN HEALTH CARE SYSTEM: MEDICAID

John K. Iglehart

Medicaid is the largest health insurer in the United States, in terms of eligible beneficiaries, covering medical services and long-term care for some 41.3 million people. In 1997, Medicaid expended $159.9 billion (12.4 percent of total national health care expenditures) to pay for covered services for low-income people who were elderly, blind, disabled, receiving public assistance, or among the working poor. The vast majority of such persons fall outside the employment-based insurance system, the mainstay of coverage for the working population. This fifth report in the series on the American health care system[1-4] examines the federal and state roles in Medicaid, program expenditures, eligibility for coverage, and Medicaid managed-care plans.

In recent years, Medicaid has changed in important ways. The change that has affected the greatest number of people is the expansion of the population eligible for Medicaid, from 28.3 million in 1993, when I last wrote about the program[5] in a series similar to this one, to 41.3 million today. The Republican-controlled Congress enacted legislation to shift most of the responsibility for Medicaid to state governments, but President Bill Clinton vetoed the measure in 1995. The growth in Medicaid expenditures, which almost tripled over the past decade, has slowed in recent years, with the smallest annual increase ever in 1997. An increasing number of eligible beneficiaries have enrolled in or are being required to join managed-care plans as a result of policies that no longer give them a choice of providers. However, none of these changes have made the program any more attractive to physicians, most of whom do not provide care for Medicaid beneficiaries because the payments to providers are low, and the associated administrative burden can be quite large.

Although Medicaid and Medicare were the key elements of historic legislation enacted in 1965 as part of President Lyndon Johnson's Great Society, Medicaid was essentially a creature of Congress. After Johnson's landslide victory in 1964, the enactment of Medicare seemed almost a foregone conclusion, although its final design reflected countless compromises. Medicaid, however, was largely a product of the

House Ways and Means Committee and its powerful chairman, Representative Wilbur Mills (D-Ark.), who favored the expansion of earlier federal efforts (embodied in the Kerr—Mills Act) to provide medical assistance to elderly and disabled people. During the congressional debate over the two programs, conservative legislators and the American Medical Association promoted a federal—state model for Medicare, but Mills instead chose this model for Medicaid.[6] Wilbur Cohen, who worked closely with Mills in crafting the Medicaid legislation and later became secretary of the Department of Health, Education, and Welfare, wrote: "Many people, since 1965, have called Medicaid the 'sleeper' in the legislation. Most people did not pay attention to that part of the bill. . . . [It] was not a secret, but neither the press nor the health policy community paid any attention to it."[7]

The structures of Medicare and Medicaid have little in common, except that both are now administered at the federal level by the same agency, the Health Care Financing Administration (HCFA). Congress made it clear in 1965 that providing health insurance to the elderly through Medicare was a federal responsibility. But the division of authority over Medicaid between the federal and state governments resulted in a persistent struggle over how to apportion payment of the bill. In 1997, of the total expenditures of $159.9 billion, the federal share was $95.4 billion, and the states' contribution (combined in some jurisdictions with local expenditures) was $64.5 billion. The federal share of expenditures is determined by a formula based on each state's per capita income, with a legislatively set minimum of 50 percent and a maximum of 83 percent. States with relatively low per capita incomes receive proportionately more federal funding. Medicaid expenditures represent about 40 percent of all federal funds received by the states.

STATE MEDICAID PROGRAMS

Following broad national guidelines established by Congress and monitored by HCFA, the states set their own standards of eligibility; determine the type, amount, duration, and scope of covered services; establish the rate of payment for services; and administer their own programs. At first, a guiding principle was to provide mainstream medical services to the poor. But Medicaid was grafted administratively onto state welfare programs, largely because the only social-service agency operating in every state at the time was the welfare authority, and its clients were recipients of public assistance.[8] Thus, the seeds of Medicaid as a welfare program were sown at the beginning, and ever since, it has been treated as a political stepchild by HCFA, the executive branch, and Congress.

Nevertheless, Medicaid is the main public insurance program for many people of limited means. Studies have found that poor persons enrolled in Medicaid are more likely to have a usual source of care, have a higher number of annual ambulatory care visits, and have a higher rate of hospitalization than poor persons with no public or private health care coverage.[9] Medicaid's eligible population comprises 21.3 million children, 9.2 million adults in families, 4.1 million elderly persons, and

6.7 million blind or disabled persons. Over the past decade, the national expansion in Medicaid's eligible population was driven by federal requirements to increase health care coverage for pregnant women and children, state efforts to cover more uninsured people of low income, and court-ordered expansions in coverage for the disabled. On average, Medicaid beneficiaries account for about 11 percent of a state's population, but some jurisdictions have substantially higher percentages, including Tennessee (21.7 percent), the District of Columbia (17.8 percent), Vermont (17.4 percent), New Mexico (16.1 percent), New York (15.1 percent), West Virginia (14.1 percent), California (13.6 percent), Michigan (13.6 percent), Washington (12.9 percent), Georgia (12.8 percent), Kentucky (12.8 percent), Mississippi (12.3 percent), and Hawaii (11.4 percent).[10]

Being poor does not automatically make a person eligible for Medicaid. Indeed, in 1997, Medicaid covered only 44.4 percent of nonelderly persons with an income of less than $13,330 for a family of three (Salganicoff A, Henry J. Kaiser Family Foundation: personal communication). Most people become eligible by meeting a federally defined criterion (i.e., advanced age, blindness, disability, or membership in a single-parent family with dependent children). Within the federal guidelines, the states set their own criteria for eligibility with respect to income and assets, resulting in large variations in coverage from state to state. Indeed, it is no exaggeration to say that there are actually more than 50 Medicaid programs—one in each state, plus the program in the District of Columbia and those in the U.S. territories—because the rules under which they operate vary so enormously.

THE CONCENTRATION OF MEDICAID SPENDING

Although adults and children in low-income families account for nearly three fourths of Medicaid beneficiaries, their medical care accounts for less than 30 percent of program expenditures (Figure 1). Elderly and blind or disabled persons account for most of the expenditures because of their greater use of acute and long-term care services. In 1997, Medicaid's costs per beneficiary were $9,539 for elderly persons, $8,832 for blind or disabled beneficiaries, $1,810 for adults in low-income families, and $1,027 for children (Hoffman D, HCFA: personal communication). The figures for elderly and blind or disabled persons do not include Medicare payments. Payments to physicians represented only 5.9 percent of Medicaid's total expenditures in 1996, less than the program paid out for home health services or prescription drugs (Table 1). By comparison, payments to physicians made up 25.4 percent of Medicare expenditures in 1996. According to the most recent study of Medicaid's payments to physicians, in 1993 average payments were about 73 percent of Medicare payments and about 47 percent of private fees.[11]

Medicaid covers a broad range of services with nominal cost-sharing requirements because of the limited financial resources of beneficiaries. The benefit package extends well beyond the services covered by Medicare and most employer-sponsored plans. By federal law, states must cover inpatient and outpatient hospital

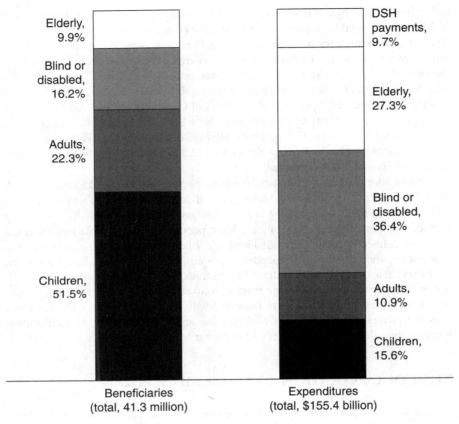

Figure 1   Medicaid beneficiaries and expenditures in 1996, according to enrollment group. Total expenditures exclude administrative expenses. DSH payments denotes disproportionate-share hospital payments. Percentages do not sum to 100, because of rounding. (Source: Data provided by the Kaiser Commission on Medicaid and the Uninsured)

services; care provided by physicians, midwives, and certified nurse practitioners; laboratory and radiographic services; nursing home care and home health care; early and periodic screening, diagnosis, and treatment for persons under 21 years of age; family planning; and care provided by rural health clinics and federally qualified community health centers. Medicaid also acts as a supplementary insurance program for elderly and disabled Medicare beneficiaries of low income, paying their Medicare premiums and cost-sharing requirements and covering additional services, most notably prescription drugs. The states have the option to cover additional services for Medicaid recipients and receive matching federal funds for them. Items commonly covered by the states include prescription drugs, clinic services, prosthetic devices, hearing aids, dental care, and services provided by intermediate-care facilities for the mentally retarded.

TABLE 1

MEDICAID PAYMENTS FOR SELECTED FISCAL YEARS, ACCORDING TO TYPE OF SERVICE*

Category	Payment†				Distribution in 1996 %
	1985	1994	1995	1996	
	Millions of Dollars				
Total	37,508	108,270	120,141	121,685	100.0
Inpatient services	10,645	28,237	28,842	27,216	22.4
General hospitals	9,453	26,180	26,331	25,176	20.7
Mental hospitals	1,192	2,057	2,511	2,040	1.7
Nursing facilities‡	5,071	27,095	29,052	29,630	24.3
Intermediate-care facilities‡	11,245	8,347	10,383	9,555	7.9
For mentally retarded persons	4,719	8,347	10,383	9,555	7.9
For all other persons	6,526	0	0	0	0
Physicians' services	2,346	7,189	7,360	7,238	5.9
Dental services	458	969	1,019	1,028	0.8
Other practitioners' services	251	1,040	986	1,094	0.9
Outpatient hospital services	1,789	6,342	6,627	6,504	5.3
Clinic services	714	3,747	4,280	4,222	3.5
Laboratory and radiologic services	337	1,176	1,180	1,208	1.0
Home health services	1,120	7,042	9,406	10,868	8.9
Prescription drugs	2,315	8,875	9,791	10,697	8.8
Family-planning services	195	516	514	474	0.4
Early and periodic screening	85	980	1,169	1,399	1.1
Rural health clinics	7	188	215	302	0.2
Other care	928	6,522	9,214	10,247	8.4

*Data are from the Health Care Financing Administration.
†Payments exclude premiums and capitation amounts. Total payments include payments for unknown services, which are not shown in this table. The percent distribution is based on rounded numbers.
‡Beginning in 1991, nursing facilities included skilled nursing facilities and intermediate-care facilities for all persons other than the mentally retarded.

THE DEVOLUTION OF FEDERAL AUTHORITY

When Republicans took control of the Congress in 1995, one of their overriding policy goals was to devolve federal authority and money to state governments, particularly in the realm of social welfare. A year later, Republicans were successful in reforming welfare policies, many of which had been enacted in 1935 as part of President Franklin D. Roosevelt's New Deal. The debate in Congress included "a massive reexamination of who 'deserves' public assistance."[12] The main decisions were that the states should decide who is needy, welfare should be linked to work,[13] cash assistance should be temporary, and immigrants who arrive in this country after the law's enactment should not receive full Medicaid benefits.[12] Congress scrapped the federal guarantee of cash assistance for the nation's poorest children and granted states the authority to operate their own welfare and work programs, largely with federal resources. These changes were incorporated into the Personal Responsibility and Work Opportunity Reconciliation Act of 1996, which President Clinton signed into law over the vigorous protest of the liberal wing of the Democratic Party.

Congress also enacted legislation in 1995 to recast Medicaid as it had welfare, converting the program from an open-ended entitlement program for eligible beneficiaries to essentially a state-operated program funded largely by a capped federal block grant. Clinton vetoed this measure and offered his own counterproposal, which the Republicans rejected. Two years later, in the Balanced Budget Act of 1997, Congress and the administration finally agreed on a new federal–state division of authority for Medicaid, although the debate on this subject continues.[14–16] Among various provisions, all of which granted the states more authority, the budget law repealed the Boren amendment (named after the Oklahoma senator who initially sponsored it),[17] which stipulated that the states must provide payments for services at levels that meet the costs incurred by "efficiently and economically operated" hospitals and nursing homes.

THE ELIGIBILITY MAZE

Medicaid's complex eligibility policy, which "both states and the federal government have relied on . . . as a tool for limiting their financial exposure for the cost of covered benefits,"[18] makes the program difficult for its beneficiaries to understand and for the states to administer. Before welfare reform was enacted, adults and children in low-income families that qualified for public assistance were automatically eligible for Medicaid. The new welfare law severed this link between Medicaid and public assistance, with the goal of preserving Medicaid coverage for poor families facing possible cutbacks in public assistance, but now one must apply to the program in order to be declared eligible for medical coverage. This policy has had an unintended consequence. As welfare caseloads have declined nationally, by about 42 percent since 1994, there have been unexpected reductions in the number of people seeking Medicaid coverage. In recent meetings involving administrators of state human-service agencies and specialists in Medicaid eligibility, sponsored by the Kaiser Commission on Medicaid and the Uninsured, the participants concluded that because many people now view public cash assistance as a temporary benefit, "even when Medicaid enrollment would be in the economic interest of the beneficiary, fewer potential recipients are likely to apply for coverage or to maintain Medicaid enrollment."[19] If the decline in Medicaid enrollment were explained by the transition from welfare assistance to jobs that offered health insurance, neither HCFA nor the states would be concerned, but most former welfare recipients who have found employment are in low-paying positions that do not provide health care coverage.

The number of people who are not taking advantage of Medicaid coverage is quite large, and the problem speaks to the obstacles that many poor people face in trying to navigate publicly run systems. State governments, in turn, have only limited success in persuading parents to enroll their children in the Medicaid program, almost regardless of the specific circumstance. One recent federal study estimated that 4.7 million children were uninsured despite their eligibility for Medicaid, representing about 2 of every 5 uninsured children in the United States.[20] A similar problem faces the new State Children's Health Insurance Program, which authorizes the expenditure of $24 billion over a period of five years to extend coverage to low-income children who are not already eligible for Medicaid.[21,22] Congress gave the states the option of using this money to expand their existing Medicaid programs, create new programs, or implement combined approaches. Recognizing the challenge of actually signing up children, federal and state governments and private foundations are investing hundreds of millions of dollars in outreach efforts to identify eligible children and enroll them in Medicaid or the State Children's Health Insurance Program.[23]

THE STATES' BOOMING ECONOMIES

Although the states are grappling with the multiple challenges of welfare reform, the State Children's Health Insurance Program, and Medicaid, they have more room to maneuver because the costs of Medicaid have been brought under strict control and the economies of most states are booming. Total Medicaid expenditures increased by only 3.8 percent in 1997, the slowest annual rate of growth since the program's inception. In its latest report on national health care expenditures, HCFA's Office of the Actuary stated:

> Average annual growth in Medicaid spending decelerated to 5.9 percent over the 1994–1997 period, compared with 12.7 percent for 1991–1994 and 19.5 percent for 1988–1991. The rapid growth over the 1988–1994 period is attributable to three basic factors: (1) an increase in the number of Medicaid enrollees, (2) an increase in nominal (not adjusted for inflation) spending per recipient, and (3) explosive growth in disproportionate-share hospital payments, a substantial portion of which states used to supplement their state treasuries in ways that Congress has now outlawed.[24]

(Disproportionate-share payments, which totaled $15 billion in 1996, are made to compensate hospitals for the higher operating costs they incur by treating disproportionately large numbers of low-income and Medicaid patients.[25])

At the start of 1999, despite five straight years of tax cuts and moderate increases in expenditures, all the states except Alaska and Hawaii had healthy budget surpluses that collectively are estimated to total $31 billion. As a percentage of the overall budget for all the states, this surplus is twice that of the federal budget, according to a report issued by the National Governors' Association.[26,27] Nevertheless, many governors have adopted social policies designed to slow, if not prevent, further expansion of publicly financed insurance programs. For example, California made an explicit decision under its former Republican governor, Pete Wilson, not to accept the full federal allotment of funds from the State Children's Health Insurance Program. Such policies reflect the concern that federal funding for Medicaid will eventually decline, forcing the states to make up the shortfall. In addition, Republicans see little political gain in creating new publicly financed programs in this era of limited government. Only Kentucky, Massachusetts, Nevada, and Vermont have said that they plan to spend their full allotment of funds from the State Children's Health Insurance Program this year. Many other states are in earlier stages of implementing the program and may not be able to spend all the available program funds in 1999.

MEDICAID MANAGED CARE

Since the 1980s, many states have experimented with managed care, largely as a means of limiting Medicaid expenditures, but they had no authority to require eligible beneficiaries to enroll in managed-care plans. Moreover, the beneficiaries had no incentive for enrollment, such as the extra benefits that elderly persons could obtain if they signed up with health maintenance organizations (HMOs) under Medicare. To make managed care mandatory, the states had to receive a waiver from HCFA. Under President Clinton, a former governor, HCFA adopted a liberal policy of issuing such waivers, which enabled some 40 states to make managed care mandatory in whole or in part for certain groups of beneficiaries. The Balanced Budget Act of 1997 eliminated the waiver requirement altogether, except for persons who are eligible for both Medicare and Medicaid (disabled and elderly poor people), children with special needs, and Native Americans. The budget law also eliminated the requirement that in HMOs with Medicaid beneficiaries, at least 25 percent of the members must receive coverage from third parties other than Medicaid. Congress had imposed this stricture as a proxy for ensuring that the plans would provide high-quality care.

Forty-nine states (all except Alaska) now rely on some form of managed care to serve their Medicaid populations. The proportion of Medicaid beneficiaries enrolled in managed-care plans increased from 9.5 percent (2.7 million people) in 1991 to 48 percent (15.3 million) in 1997. The states use one of three forms of

Medicaid managed care: arrangements with primary care physicians to act as gate-keepers, approving and monitoring the provision of services to individual beneficiaries in return for a fixed fee; enrollment of beneficiaries in HMOs that assume the full financial risk of providing a comprehensive package of services; and contracts with medical clinics or large group practices, which provide services but do not assume the full financial risk for them. In areas where HMOs are prepared to assume the full financial risk of enrolling Medicaid beneficiaries, the states are choosing this approach and turning away from the other two.

The most comprehensive examination of the effect of Medicaid's growing relationship with managed care is being conducted by researchers at the Urban Institute as part of an ambitious project called Assessing the New Federalism.[28] The project, funded by private foundations, is a major new effort to understand changes in health care and social programs at the state level.[29-37] Researchers have examined the effect of Medicaid managed care in 13 states (Alabama, California, Colorado, Florida, Massachusetts, Michigan, Minnesota, Mississippi, New Jersey, New York, Texas, Washington, and Wisconsin). Their preliminary conclusions, reached three years after the start of the study, which will continue for another three years or more, are as follows:

> The Medicaid managed care revolution has been more of a skirmish than a
> revolution. The goals of Medicaid managed care were to expand access to
> mainstream providers and to save money, but success on both fronts has been
> limited. Medicaid managed care is predominantly limited to children and younger
> adults; few states have extended enrollment to more expensive elderly and disabled
> enrollees, limiting potential savings. States are also finding that managed care savings
> are modest because traditionally low Medicaid fee-for-service payment rates make it
> difficult for states to substantially slash capitation levels or for HMOs to negotiate
> further discounts. In addition, safety net providers that need Medicaid revenues to
> survive have received special protections from states, which has both reduced
> potential savings and steered Medicaid beneficiaries to traditional providers of charity
> care. The combination of low capitation rates and protections for safety net providers
> have limited the willingness of commercial HMOs in several states to contract with
> states, thus restricting the expansion of access to maintain providers.[38]

A number of commercial HMOs that were enrolling Medicaid beneficiaries have withdrawn from the program in the past year, citing multiple reasons for their dissatisfaction.[39,40] In interviews conducted recently by Hurley and McCue at the Medical College of Virginia, state policy makers, health-plan executives, venture capitalists, and stock analysts expressed little optimism that commercial HMOs would continue to enroll Medicaid beneficiaries, particularly in states with very low per capita payment rates. Citing the views of stock analysts, Hurley and McCue note:

> The early promises of profitable market opportunities were overshadowed by
> unexpected rate rollbacks, contracting volatility, and administrative burdens which

soured analysts and investors on the Medicaid market. . . . Given this history, stock analysts see limited opportunities for success in Medicaid and view the exodus from the Medicaid market as evidence of management's desire to enhance stockholder wealth.[41]

CONCLUSIONS

Medicaid underscores the ambivalence of a society that continually struggles with the question of which citizens deserve access to publicly financed medical care and under what conditions. On a more positive note, Medicaid now provides health insurance to a larger population of poor persons than ever before, reflecting the strength of a bullish economy and expanded criteria for eligibility. Yet, nationally, the number of uninsured people grew to 16.1 percent of the population in 1997, the largest level in a decade, because employer-sponsored coverage has eroded.[2,3] This divergence prompts a question: What potential does Medicaid have for further expanding its eligible population so that poor families with incomes that minimally exceed the federal poverty level could be insured through this program? Some states (Massachusetts, Minnesota, Oregon, Tennessee, and Wisconsin are examples) have used public funds to broaden private coverage through managed care, and the welfare-reform law permits the states to raise the threshold for income and assets so that more beneficiaries will be eligible for Medicaid. But many states have shifted to managed care without expanding coverage for the working poor, a population that constitutes the bulk of the uninsured population, and rates of payment to providers remain woefully low.

Medicaid's architects envisioned a program that would provide poor people with mainstream medical care in a fashion similar to that of private insurance. As the decades have passed, that vision has largely faded, and several tiers of care have emerged. Mainstream medical care is provided to people covered by private insurance or Medicare. For the most part, poor people continue to rely on providers that make up the nation's medical safety net: public and some private not-for-profit hospitals and clinics and their medical staffs that, by virtue of their location or their social calling, provide a disproportionate amount of care to the poor. These providers are increasingly stressed as Medicaid diverts funds to managed-care plans. The United States remains the only industrialized nation that has never settled on a social policy that, however policy makers choose to accomplish it, offers a basic set of health care benefits to all residents regardless of their ability to pay—certainly a regrettable failure in a nation blessed with so many resources.

ABOUT THE AUTHOR

John Iglehart is Editor of *Health Affairs,* Project HOPE in Bethesda, Maryland.

REFERENCES

1. Iglehart JK. The American health care system—expenditures. *N Engl J Med* 1999;340:70–6.

2. Kuttner R. The American health care system—health insurance coverage. *N Engl J Med* 1999;340:163–8.

3. *Idem.* The American health care system—employer-sponsored health coverage. *N Engl J Med* 1999;340:248–52.

4. Iglehart JK. The American health care system—Medicare. *N Engl J Med* 1999;340:327–32.

5. *Idem.* The American health care system—Medicaid. *N Engl J Med* 1993;328:896–900.

6. Tallon JR, Brown LD. Who gets what? Devolution of eligibility and benefits in Medicaid. In: Thompson FJ, Dilulio JJ Jr, eds. Medicaid and devolution: a view from the states. Washington, D.C.: Brookings Institution Press, 1998.

7. Cohen W. Reflections on the enactment of Medicare and Medicaid. *Health Care Financ Rev* 1985;Suppl.

8. Friedman E. The little engine that could: Medicaid at the Millennium. *Front Health Serv Manage* 1998;14(4):3–24.

9. Berk ML, Schur CL. Access to care: how much difference does Medicaid make? *Health Aff (Millwood)* 1998;17(3):169–80.

10. Fronstin P. Sources of health insurance and characteristics of the uninsured: analysis of the March 1998 current population survey. EBRI issue brief no. 204. Washington, D.C.: Employee Benefit Research Institute, 1998.

11. Colby DC. Medicaid physician fees, 1993. *Health Aff (Millwood)* 1994;13(2):255–63.

12. Ellwood MR, Ku L. Welfare and immigration reforms: unintended side effects for Medicaid. *Health Aff (Millwood)* 1998;17(3):137–51.

13. Pear R. Most states meet work requirement of welfare law. *New York Times.* December 30, 1998:A1.

14. Spitz B. The elusive New Federalism. *Health Aff (Millwood)* 1998; 17(6):150–61.

15. Weil A, Wiener JM, Holahan J. 'Assessing the New Federalism' and state health policy. *Health Aff (Millwood)* 1998;17(6):162–4.

16. Bartels PL, Boroniec P. BadgerCare: a case study of the elusive New Federalism. *Health Aff (Millwood)* 1998;17(6):165–9.

17. Wiener JM, Stevenson DG. Repeal of the "Boren Amendment": implications for quality of care in nursing homes. Series A, no. A-30. Washington, D.C.: Urban Institute, 1998.

18. Schneider A, Fennel K, Long P. Medicaid eligibility for families and children. Washington, D.C.: Henry J. Kaiser Family Foundation, 1998.

19. Smith VK, Lovell RG, Peterson KA, O'Brien MJ. The dynamics of current Medicaid enrollment changes: insights from focus groups of state human service administrators, Medicaid eligibility specialists and welfare agency analysts. Washington, D.C.: Henry J. Kaiser Family Foundation, 1998.

20. Selden TM, Banthin JS, Cohen JW. Medicaid's problem children: eligible but not enrolled. *Health Aff (Millwood)* 1998;17(3):192–200.
21. Budetti PP. Health insurance for children—a model for incremental health reform? *N Engl J Med* 1998;338:541–2.
22. Newacheck PW, Stoddard JJ, Hughes DC, Pearl M. Health insurance and access to primary care for children. *N Engl J Med* 1998;338:513–9.
23. Kenesson MS. Medicaid managed care: outreach and enrollment for special populations. Princeton, N.J.: Center for Health Care Strategies, 1998.
24. Levit K, Cowan C, Braden B, Stiller J, Sensenig A, Lazenby H. National health expenditures in 1997: more slow growth. *Health Aff (Millwood)* 1998;17(6):66–110.
25. Coughlin TA. Changing state and federal payment policies for Medicaid disproportionate-share hospitals. *Health Aff (Millwood)* 1998;17(3):118–36.
26. Broder DS. States pass their fiscals: they're trimming taxes, beefing up 'rainy day' funds. *Washington Post.* December 31, 1998:A25.
27. Broder DS. Golden years for governors. Washington Post. January 3, 1999:C7.
28. Kondratas A, Weil A, Goldstein N. Assessing the new federalism: an introduction. *Health Aff (Millwood)* 1998;17(3):43–63.
29. Holahan J, Zuckerman S, Evans A, Rangarajan S. Medicaid managed care in thirteen states. *Health Aff (Millwood)* 1998;17(3):43–63.
30. Nichols LM, Blumberg JL. A different kind of 'new federalism'? The Health Insurance Portability and Accountability Act of 1996. *Health Aff (Millwood)* 1998;17(3):25–42.
31. Wall S. Transformations in public health systems. *Health Aff (Millwood)* 1998;17(3):64–80.
32. Wiener JM, Stevenson DG. State policy on long-term care for the elderly. *Health Aff (Millwood)* 1998;17(3):81–100.
33. Rajan S. Publicly subsidized health insurance: a typology of state approaches. *Health Aff (Millwood)* 1998;17(3):101–17.
34. Norton SA, Lipson DJ. Portraits of the safety net: the market, policy environment, and safety net response. Occasional paper no. 19. Washington, D.C.: Urban Institute, 1998.
35. Bovbjerg RR, Marsteller JA. Health care market competition in six states: implications for the poor. Occasional paper no. 17. Washington, D.C.: Urban Institute, 1998.
36. Wiener JM, Stevenson DG. Long-term care for the elderly: profiles of thirteen states. Occasional paper no. 12. Washington, D.C.: Urban Institute, 1998.
37. *Idem.* Controlling the supply of long-term care providers at the state level. Occasional paper no. 22. Washington, D.C.: Urban Institute, 1998.
38. Holahan J, Wiener J, Wallin S. Health policy for the low-income population: major findings from the Assessing the New Federalism case studies. Occasional paper no. 18. Washington, D.C.: Urban Institute, 1998.

39. Aston G. Widespread HMO defections starting to hit Medicaid, too. *American Medical News.* December 14, 1998:5.
40. McCue MJ, Hurley RE, Draper DA, Jurgensen M. Reversal of fortune: commercial HMOs in the Medicaid market. *Health Aff (Millwood)* 1999;18(1):223–30.
41. Hurley RE, McCue MA. Medicaid and commercial HMOs: an at-risk relationship. Princeton, N.J.: Center for Health Care Strategies, 1998.

ARTICLE 5

MEDICARE AND MEDICAID FOR THE ELDERLY AND DISABLED POOR

The Kaiser Commission on Medicaid and the Uninsured

Today 34 million elderly and 5 million disabled Americans depend on Medicare for help paying medical bills. The universal coverage of Medicare provides basic insurance coverage regardless of income, but gaps in the scope of Medicare benefits and financial obligations for coverage can often impose financial burdens. Low-income Medicare beneficiaries are particularly vulnerable because they are more likely to have health problems that require medical services than those who are economically better off, yet are less able to afford care because of their lower incomes.

LOW-INCOME MEDICARE BENEFICIARIES

Sixteen million Medicare beneficiaries (45%) are poor or low-income (Figure 1). Fourteen percent of Medicare beneficiaries (5 million people) have an income below the poverty level ($7,740 for a single adult and $10,360 for a couple in 1996). Nearly a third (11 million people) are near-poor (with incomes between 100 and 200% of poverty).

MEDICARE'S GAPS

Medicare provides basic health insurance, but the cost of uncovered services, coupled with substantial cost sharing and the Part B premium can impose a serious financial burden. Medicare pays only about 52% of the health costs of Medicare beneficiaries.

Low-income beneficiaries (with incomes below 200% of poverty) are especially vulnerable; they are nearly twice as likely as higher income beneficiaries (with incomes above 400% of poverty) to report their health status as fair or poor. Poor beneficiaries also bear a disproportionate burden in out-of-pocket health care costs,

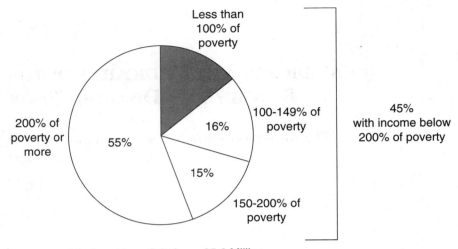

Medicare beneficiaries = 35.6 Million

Note: 1996 federal poverty was $7,740 for individuals, $10,360 for couples.

Figure 1   Medicare population by poverty level, 1996 (Source: Urban institute estimates based on the March 1997 Current Population Survey: non-institutionalized Medicare beneficiaries only)

spending more than a third of their income on health care, compared to 10% for higher income beneficiaries.

MEDICAID'S ROLE

Medicaid is a means-tested entitlement program funded by federal and state governments. Medicaid serves as an important complement to Medicare by assisting nearly 6 million low-income elderly and disabled Medicare beneficiaries with Medicare's financial requirements and providing coverage for prescription drugs and other services not available through Medicare. Medicaid is the primary payer for long-term care—a service too expensive for even better off elderly to finance on their own.

Medicaid reaches only half of all poor Medicare beneficiaries (Figure 2). The scope of coverage available from Medicaid varies with income. The poorest Medicare beneficiaries, and those who have exhausted their personal resources paying for health care, receive the full range of Medicaid benefits, including prescription drugs and long-term care. Other low-income Medicare beneficiaries may receive assistance primarily limited to Medicare premiums through four related programs (Table 1). Most (88%) of dual eligibles receive full Medicaid benefits.

Many Medicare beneficiaries who are eligible for the QMB and SLMB programs are not enrolled. Lack of significant outreach efforts, complex enrollment processes, and delays in activating eligibility for the buy-in contribute to limited en-

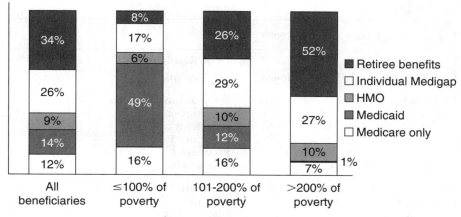

Note: Columns do not sum to 100%: other sources of public coverage not shown.

Figure 2 Health insurance coverage of Medicare beneficiaries, 1995 by income relative to poverty (Source: Urban Institute analysis of 1995 Medicare Current Beneficiary Survey, Cost and Use File)

rollment. Those not enrolled in the QMB/SLMB programs are more likely to be older and rely solely on Medicare.

HEALTH AND FUNCTIONAL STATUS OF DUAL ELIGIBLES

Medicare beneficiaries who participate in Medicaid (dual eligibles) are a vulnerable population. A quarter are in nursing homes, nearly half are in fair or poor health, about 30% have 2 or more limitations in activities of daily living, and over 40% have cognitive impairments.

Because of their extensive health care needs, dual eligibles account for a substantial share of spending under both Medicaid and Medicare ($106 billion combined). Dual eligibles account for 16% of all Medicare beneficiaries, but 30% of total Medicare spending. Similarly, they represent 17% of Medicaid beneficiaries, but 35% of Medicaid spending, most notably due to their use of expensive long-term care services.

MANAGED CARE

In 1996, about 4.5% of dual eligibles were enrolled in Medicare managed care (about a third the proportion for all beneficiaries, 12.7%). Enrollment of dual

TABLE 1

	MEDICAID'S PROTECTIONS		
Program	*Who's Eligible?*	*What Does Medicaid Pay?*	*Entitlement?*
Full Medicaid Benefits	73% of poverty* (SSI eligibility level)	Wrap around benefits: prescription drugs, long-term care, and Medicare Part B premium & cost-sharing	Yes
Qualified Medicare Beneficiary (QMB)	≤100% of poverty	Medicare Part B premium & cost-sharing**	Yes
Specified Low-Income Beneficiary (SLMB)	100–120% of poverty	Medicare Part B premium	Yes
Qualifying Individuals 1 (QI1)	120–135% of poverty***	Medicare Part B premium	No
Qualifying Individuals 2 (QI2)	135–175% of poverty***	A portion of the Medicare Part B premium	No

Note: Individuals must have limited assets (below $4,000 for an individual).
*Some states (209b) are permitted to set lower levels: states have the option to go to 100% of poverty.
**States are not required to pay Medicare cost-sharing if Medicaid payment rates are lower.
***The QI programs are block grants available on a first-come, first-served basis.

eligibles in Medicaid managed care is also limited but growing. Seventeen states require or allow dual eligibles to enroll in Medicaid managed care; nine states enroll some or all dual eligibles on a mandatory basis in Medicaid managed care through waivers. Managed care is attractive because of its potential to improve the delivery and coordination of services and reduce spending, but it is risky because people with chronic conditions may be underserved, not better served, in managed care. It is often suggested that fully integrating Medicare and Medicaid benefits and capitating payments for this vulnerable population will save money, but evidence is limited.

MEDICAID IMPROVES ACCESS AND REDUCES FINANCIAL BURDENS

Having Medicaid coverage substantially improves access to health care. Medicare beneficiaries with Medicaid are much less likely to have gone without a physician office visit during the year, and they are substantially less likely to have delayed seeking healthcare due to cost, compared to beneficiaries with only Medicare.

Medicaid provides important coverage of prescription drugs and long-term care. Because most dual Medicare/Medicaid beneficiaries receive assistance with the cost of prescription drugs, they pay 21% of the costs of prescription drugs out-of-pocket, compared to 80% for Medicare beneficiaries with individually-purchased Medigap and 100% for those relying solely on Medicare.

Medicaid covers nursing home care, covering nearly two-thirds of nursing home residents and financing 45% of nursing home costs. Dual eligibles also have substantially lower out-of-pocket spending than other beneficiaries. Poor dual eligibles with full-year Medicaid spend 8% of income on health care.

ISSUES AND CHALLENGES

Federal policy makers have historically relied on Medicaid to provide protections for low-income Medicare beneficiaries. More than 4 in 10 Medicare beneficiaries have low-incomes and already incur sizable financial burdens for health care. Proposed Medicare reforms have the potential to increase spending burdens for low-income beneficiaries and states may lack the capacity to absorb rising premiums and cost-sharing. To assure Medicare's adequacy for coverage of the elderly and disabled poor in future years, it is important to maintain the assistance with financial obligations and additional benefits that Medicaid provides today.

ABOUT THE AUTHOR

The Kaiser Commission on Medicaid and the Uninsured in Washington, DC, is headed by Diane Rowland, ScD, who is also Executive Director of The Kaiser Commission on the Future of Medicaid and Chair Senior Vice President of The Henry J. Kaiser Family Foundation.

ARTICLE 6

MEDICAID'S ROLE FOR CHILDREN

The Kaiser Commission on the Future of Medicaid

In 1995, 17.5 million children—one-quarter of all children under age 18—had Medicaid coverage for health care services. Medicaid, the federal/state health program for the poor, pays for a broad range of services for children including well-child care, immunizations, prescription drugs, doctor visits, and hospitalization, and a range of long-term care services for children with disabilities.

Medicaid plays a particularly strong role for low-income children, covering two-thirds (64%) of all poor children and a quarter (27%) of children with incomes between 100% and 199% of the federal poverty level (FPL). While employer-based insurance coverage of children declined from 1987 to 1995, expansions in Medicaid have resulted in greater coverage of children in low-income families. During this same period, Medicaid enrollment grew from about 10 million—15.5% of all children—to 17.5 million children (23.2%).

Despite the importance of Medicaid today, about 10 million children are uninsured. Lack of insurance is particularly high among low-income children. Seventy percent of uninsured children are in families with incomes below 200% of poverty. The new State Child Health Insurance Program, enacted as part of the Balanced Budget Act of 1997, is intended to provide coverage to this group.

ELIGIBILITY

Being poor does not automatically qualify a child for Medicaid. In the past 15 years, Medicaid eligibility for children has been broadened considerably through federal legislation and state optional expansions. Prior to 1986, Medicaid primarily served children who received AFDC cash assistance. Today, children qualify for Medicaid based on their age and income.

Medicaid coverage is especially prominent among young children, covering 33% of infants and 29% of children ages 1 to 5. Because recent expansions focused

408

on young children, older children are less likely to qualify for Medicaid. Medicaid covers 22% of children between the ages of 6 to 12 years and 17% of teens between the ages of 13 to 18 years.

Medicaid Coverage of Children

States are mandated to cover certain groups of children based on age and income criteria. By 2002, all states will be required to have phased-in coverage of children under age 19 with incomes below poverty. States can choose to expand Medicaid eligibility beyond federal minimum standards by raising age and income levels for children. They can also use Section 1115 research and demonstration waivers to broaden eligibility. In total, 41 states have expanded Medicaid coverage to children in one or more age or income levels. Federal coverage requirements for children are as follows:

- **Up to age 6 with family incomes up to 133% FPL.** For infants, 35 states have chosen to expand coverage beyond 133% FPL and 13 have expanded for children age one to six.
- **Age 6 to 14 with family incomes below 100% FPL.** Fifteen states have opted to expand eligibility beyond 100% FPL.
- **Age 15 to 19 if family income meets the AFDC criteria of August 1996** (state average is 41% of FPL) with coverage phased-in for poor children born before 9/30/83. 25 states have opted to accelerate this phase-in to cover older children up to age 18 with income below 100% FPL.
- **Children with disabilities** also qualify for Medicaid assistance on the basis of SSI eligibility. Medicaid covers about 1 million additional children with physical or mental disabilities.

Because states established varied Medicaid income eligibility levels for children, and because of state variations in per capita income there is considerable variation in Medicaid coverage, ranging from 13% of children in Colorado to 47% in West Virginia. Similarly, Medicaid pays for 39% of all births nationally, but coverage varies from 21% of births in Massachusetts to 61% in Georgia.

The Balanced Budget Act (BBA) of 1997 creates new options for states to strengthen and expand Medicaid coverage for children. The new State Children's Health Insurance Program (CHIP) was enacted as part of the Balanced Budget Act (BBA) of 1997. This new capped federal program allocates $20.3 billion over five years in the form of a matched grant to states to expand coverage to uninsured low-income children through either a separate state program or by broadening Medicaid—or both. The funds became available on October 1, 1997 and are targeted to uninsured children under 19 with income below 200% of poverty who are not eligible for Medicaid or not covered by private insurance.

Provisions of the Balance Budget Act also included some important changes to Medicaid. It clarifies the state Medicaid option to accelerate the phase-in for children born before September 30, 1983. In addition, the new law gives states the option to extend presumptive eligibility to children, meaning that services provided to low-income uninsured children will be covered by Medicaid before the Medicaid eligibility determination process is complete. States can also offer 12 month continuous eligibility to children, regardless of any changes in family income during that period.

SERVICES AND COSTS

Federal guidelines require that Medicaid cover a comprehensive set of services with nominal or no cost-sharing for children. Access to these services is important because poor children experience more health problems than more affluent children. Children with Medicaid are eligible to receive physician and outpatient services, prescription drugs, inpatient hospital care, and long-term care services.

Medicaid coverage also entitles children to early and periodic screening, diagnostic, and treatment (EPSDT) services including a comprehensive health and developmental history and physical exam, immunizations, laboratory tests including blood lead levels, and health education. Children found to have conditions requiring further attention are covered for needed treatment.

The importance of health insurance in securing access to health care services is well documented. Despite their complex health and social needs, children with Medicaid coverage have access to care that is similar to higher income privately insured children.

In 1995, Medicaid spent $25.4 billion on health care services for 17.5 million children in low-income families and about $7.1 billion for one million disabled children. The majority (93%) of the expenditures for non-disabled children are for acute care services, with one third for inpatient hospital care.

While low-income children represent half of the 35 million Medicaid beneficiaries, they account for only 16.7% of overall Medicaid spending. In 1995, Medicaid spent an average of $1,175 per low-income child enrolled in the program. On average, children cost less to care for than older Medicaid beneficiaries, but some disabled children have very costly health and long-term care needs. Medicaid spent an average of $6,421 per year per child qualifying on the basis of disability (Figure 1).

ISSUES AND CHALLENGES

Expanding Coverage. To broaden coverage of low-income uninsured children, Congress enacted the new State Child Health Insurance Program and included provisions to allow states to facilitate enrollment and continuity of coverage under Medicaid. Key issues facing state Medicaid agencies include how the new children's program will be structured, financed, and implemented, as well as how it will be integrated with or build on the state's existing Medicaid program.

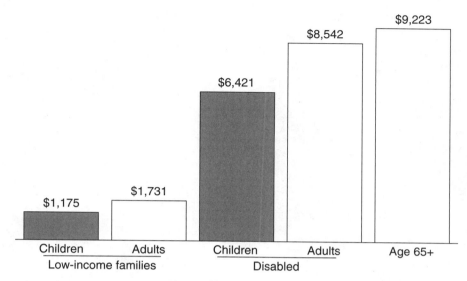

Figure 1   Medicaid spending per enrollee by age and eligibility group, 1995 (Source: The Kaiser Commission on the Future of Medicaid, 1997)

Participation. An estimated 3 million of the 9.8 million uninsured children are eligible for but not enrolled in Medicaid. This is largely due to enrollment barriers or lack of awareness of the program. States can streamline the eligibility process and facilitate enrollment. For example, 25 states allow mail-in eligibility applications and 29 states have dropped the asset test. Medicaid eligibility policy has also changed markedly as a result of the 1996 welfare law, which eliminated the automatic link between cash assistance and Medicaid. Ongoing and intensified outreach and educational efforts will be necessary to assure that all the children who are eligible for assistance under Medicaid are enrolled.

Managed Care. In 1996, 40% of beneficiaries were enrolled in managed care, mostly low-income children and their parents. The BBA of 1997 expands state flexibility by allowing states to mandate Medicaid managed care enrollment without requiring states to obtain a Section 1115 or 1915(b) waiver. States will still need a waiver to mandatorily enroll special needs children but will be able to enroll other non-disabled children. Managed care has the potential to improve access to preventive and primary care, but given the vulnerable nature of the Medicaid population, it requires careful implementation and monitoring to assure quality and access.

ABOUT THE AUTHOR

The Kaiser Commission on the Future of Medicaid, Washington, DC, is headed by Executive Director Diane Rowland, ScD, who is also Chair Senior Vice President of The Henry J. Kaiser Family Foundation.

CHAPTER 9

MANAGED CARE

At present, the American health care system is restructuring so rapidly that it is nearly impossible to keep abreast of the changes. However, general trends driving the overall reorganization are evident, particularly the growth of managed care. Several key factors are responsible for these changes. Of foremost importance are (1) the explosion of health-care costs in the 1970s and their continued increase in the 1980s; (2) the ability of large employers to self-insure due to the provisions of the 1974 Employee Retirement Income Security Act (ERISA); and, (3) the preference of big employers for a competitive, rather than regulatory, approach to health care cost containment that included managed care, limited employee choice (not consistent with a competitive model), and reduced employee benefits (particularly dependent coverage).

The evolution of the health care market in the United States has been described by Dr. J. S. Schwartz (1997). Schwartz documents the progression from an unstructured model with independent hospitals, independent physicians, and unsophisticated purchasers in a predominantly fee-for-service framework, to a competitive managed-care model with employer purchasing coalitions, integrated systems, and multiple types of managed care organizations.

Managed care means many things to many people. A widely accepted description, "any health care arrangement that integrates insurance coverage and health care service delivery," (Rosenbaum and Shin in Chapter 8, Recommended Reading) can include widely different health plans. Initially, the model for managed care was the health maintenance organization (HMO), which linked health insurance, hospitals, and physicians in what were capitated, prepaid group practice models. An example of such is Kaiser Permanente, where the employer contracts with the health insurance plan (Kaiser Health Plan) on a capitation basis and the plan, in turn, contracts with a multispecialty group practice (Permanente Medical Group) and its hospitals (Kaiser Hospitals). Another example of this initial category is the staff model, where the physicians are employed by the HMO (e.g., Group Health of Pudget Sound).

Other arrangements are similar. After legislation enacted in California in 1982 permitted Medicaid and private health insurance plans to contract selectively with hospitals, preferred provider organizations (PPOs) emerged. These were loose networks of hospitals and physicians that provided services on a discounted, fee-for-service basis. A third model, the individual practice association (IPA), emerged, which functioned as an intermediary between managed care organizations and physicians, creating a network of physicians where the IPA received a capitation payment and the physicians were paid by the IPA, often on a fee-for-service basis. Alternately, an IPA could also function as an HMO. Finally, many managed care plans permit enrollees to seek service outside the plan through "point of service" plans that are purchased for an additional premium or require additional out-of-pocket payments by the patient.

The evolution of managed care in the past 30 years has been the subject of numerous books, articles, issue papers, monographs, policy briefs, conferences, lectures, and congressional hearings. A number of recent articles by Ellwood and Enthoven (1995), Robinson and Casalino (1995), Luft (1996), Miller and Luft (1997), Remler, et al. (1997), Grumbach, et al. (1998), and Robinson (1999), as well as the monograph by Rosenbaum and Shin (1999) provide a picture of the evolution of managed care, its conceptual underpinnings, strengths and weakness, impact on costs, impact on physicians, levels of consumer satisfaction, and likely future developments.

Included in the Recommended Reading list is the paper from the fifth edition by Enthoven and Kronick, "Universal Health Insurance Through Incentives for Reform" (1991) because it provides a clear conceptual basis for managed competition. Enthoven and Kronick include a diagnosis of the paradox of excess (health care spending) and deprivation (lack of insurance coverage) and how the model of managed competition addresses the issue of economic incentives. It is important here to note that managed care and managed competition are not the same thing. Managed care involves health coverage, which is provided on a capitated basis. Managed competition, on the other hand, is a strategy for maximizing competition among various health plans (among which HMOs and other managed care options would be included) by guaranteeing universal coverage and leaving plans to compete for their share of the market.

Also in the Recommended Reading list is the 1995 paper by the two leading spokesmen for managed competition, Paul Ellwood and Alain Enthoven. The paper highlights their recommendations for Medicare; Medicaid; reforming the tax treatment of health insurance; health insurance reforms and expanding group purchasing opportunities; and improving the availability of comparative information on health benefits, quality of care accountability, costs and coverage data. Their ideas very much influenced the 1993–1994 debate on the Clinton plan and the 1997 debate that led to the broadened consumer choice in the Balanced Budget Act, federal and state debates on data requirements, and insurance reform. Other publications in the Recommended Reading list also deal with these issues, particularly the papers by Luft (1996), Robinson and Consalino (1995), and Grumbach, et al. (1999). In the list we also include Robinson's 1999 paper because it provides the best overall picture on the confusing changes that are rapidly taking place in managed care plans throughout the country. He notes at the beginning of his paper: "We are observing simultaneously the eclipse and expansion of managed care organizations. Health maintenance organizations (HMOs) and other insurers are hollowing out, yielding one function after another to purchasers and providers and thereby evoking questions about their future role and share of the premium dollar" (p. 8). He describes the organizational changes; the changing vertical arrangements, with downstream integration by purchasers and upstream integration by providers (e.g., capitation), and utilization management with a changing role for managed care plans. He describes the expanding scope of plans with increasing numbers of benefit options and the diversification of the channels of distribution. He also describes many of the problems encountered along the way. Since the publication of his paper in March/April, 1999, a number of the innovative physician practice management firms in California have encountered severe financial problems, including bankruptcy. A number of the integrated service delivery networks have collapsed and the turmoil he describes has only seemed to increase. One of the innovations that Robinson described, the "multiproduct health plan," where the health plan offers multiple plan options to employers, appears to be enduring.

In a paper reprinted for the sixth edition, John Rother (1996) explores consumer protection issues outlining three generations of approaches focused on (1) individual treatment decisions; (2) insurance-related practices of HMOs (e.g., marketing and risk selection); and (3) health plan performance aimed at the financial arrangements and incentives driving HMO behavior. The third-generation approach is essential, Rother suggests, including the examination of physician financial incentives, appropriate utilization, and regulation.

In one of our Recommended Readings, Boyle and Callahan (1996) address the ethical issues concerning managed care in mental health, contrasting them with those of the fee-for-service (FFS) system. Chief among the debatable issues are the roles of these two types of delivery systems in expanding or limiting access to mental health services and in addressing the use/misuse and rising costs of those services. Additional concerns are about quality and adverse effects on the provider-patient relationship in mental health service delivery.

Finally, we conclude the Chapter with Eli Ginzberg's perceptive analysis, "The Uncertain Future of Managed Care (1999)." While the recent literature, as reflected in this chapter, reflects the growing concerns about managed care, the limits it places on consumer choice, the high profits for proprietary health plans, growing provider dissatisfaction, and ethical issues, there is also a significant potential for managed care to place a greater emphasis on population health than is true in fee-for-service plans and to control costs while improving quality. These potential benefits are yet to be realized, but they must be carefully considered in the current spate of legislation, particularly at the state level, to turn back to indemnity insurance and fee-for-service medicine.

In many other chapters, especially the chapters on the politics of health, the health insurance system, and Medicare and Medicaid, we also deal with these issues.

REFERENCES

Ellwood, P.M., Enthoven, A. "Responsible choices": The Jackson Hole group plan for health reform. *Health Affairs,* 1995;Summer:24–39.

Enthoven, A., Kronick, R. Universal health insurance through incentives for reform. *JAMA,* 1991;265(19):2532–2536.

Ginzberg, E. The uncertain future of managed care. *NEJM,* 1999;340:488–492.

Grumbach, K. et al. Primary care physicians' experience of financial incentive in managed-care systems. *NEJM,* 1998;339:1516–1521.

Miller, R.H., Luft, H.S. Does managed care lead to better care or worse quality of care? *Health Affairs,* 1997;September/October:7–25.

Luft, H.S. Modifying managed competition to address cost and quality. *Health Affairs,* 1996;15(1):23–48.

Remler, D. et al. What do managed care plans do to affect care? Results from a survey of physicians. *Inquiry,* 1997;Fall:34:196–204.

Robinson, J.C. The future of managed care organization. *Health Affairs,* 1999;March/April:18:6–24.

Robinson, J.C., Casalino, L.P. The growth of medical groups paid through capitation in California. *NEJM,* 1995;333(25):1684–1687.

Rosenbaum, S., Shin, P. Medicaid managed care: Opportunities and challenges for minority Americans. Menlo Park, CA: Henry J. Kaiser Family Foundation, 1999.

Rother, J. Consumer protection in managed care: A third generation approach. *Generations,* 1996;20(2), 42–46.

Schwartz, J.S. *The Role of Cost Effectiveness in Defining Managed Care.* Philadelphia: Leonard Davis Institute, School of Medicine and the Wharton School, University of Pennsylvania, 1997; p. 6

ARTICLE 1

CONSUMER PROTECTION IN MANAGED CARE: A THIRD-GENERATION APPROACH

John Rother

The rapid expansion of managed care organizations has caught many consumer advocates trying to play catch-up in response to the sophisticated techniques that health maintenance organizations and other managed care plans use to lower their healthcare costs. The promise of prepaid healthcare seemed to be nonthreatening in such nonprofit, community-based movement is no longer growing. Instead, the rapid enrollment growth of for-profit plans, driven by the bottom line, has fueled the perception of many Americans that more aggressive consumer protection measures are necessary to safeguard the interests of the enrolled individual. Advocates have focused on three generations of consumer-protection issues.

FIRST GENERATION—INDIVIDUAL TREATMENT DECISIONS

Consumer advocates focused first on the more dramatic problems that HMOs have sometimes posed for the individual enrollee. The attention has been on the individual who wants treatment that the plan either does not cover or deems unnecessary. Because these issues often must be resolved quickly to avoid harm to the patient, and because the treating physician cannot be assumed to be the patient's advocate in these situations, there is a compelling need to establish appeals mechanisms that can resolve denial-of-treatment problems quickly and fairly.

Most HMOs today have internal mechanisms that, in effect, provide for a second medical opinion at the request of a member. Consumers have also advocated for external reviews by doctors not affiliated with the plan, to ensure objectivity. Medicare risk plans now have an established external appeals process, but the fact of life under capitation (payment of fixed amount per capita) is that some procedures and treatments of dubious or very marginal effectiveness will be discouraged or not covered, while others of untested efficacy will always be in the "gray zone" that may

417

be covered under some plans and not under others. This situation is a function of the dynamic nature of medical knowledge, and consumers will always have to test the boundaries of coverage when they or a loved one are seriously ill.

So the first generation of consumer protection issues in managed care has been a response to the anxiety caused by the possibility of undertreatment. Undertreatment is the most easily dramatized concern and has the greatest human-interest potential, even if it is relatively rare. The press usually uses undertreatment as an example when it wants to raise questions or challenge the growth of HMOs. Shortsighted and ill-advised plan practices like physician "gag rules" and a lack of standard definitions and applications of emergency care, urgent care, or experimental treatment classifications have fed concerns about undertreatment.

This individual, case-by-case perspective also characterizes the earlier consumer protection approach to concerns about overutilization that led to the establishment of the Medicare Peer Review Organization (PRO) program. The original impetus of that effort was to review medical charts in order to find and sanction "bad doctors" who were exploiting Medicare's fee-for-service payment system at the expense of their patients and the tax payers. Consumer advocates were supportive of the program's initial focus on overutilization and on the risks that inappropriate care posed to individual patients.

There are, however, very serious limitations to case-by-case approaches to consumer protection. Per case, they are expensive, they often catch only selected problems, and they ignore the functioning of the rest of the healthcare delivery system. They often do not lead to improved system performance even if the individual case is remedied. The PRO program was revised to respond to these shortcomings, and it no longer focuses on individual chart reviews. So, while the concern for the individual treatment decision is a necessary part of consumer protection efforts, it is clearly insufficient.

Medicaid managed care brings its own separate and urgent consumer protection issues. Separate because enrollment is not usually voluntary, and urgent because of the vulnerable nature of the Medicaid population, who have little financial or political clout to protect themselves. For this reason, I'll not try to address the special consumer protection needs of this population here, except to note that the rapid turnover of the Medicaid acute care population—turnover exceeds 40 percent per year—negates the usual incentives for managed care plans to perform with longer-term customer satisfaction or clinical outcomes in mind (Kaiser Commission on the Future of Medicaid, 1995).

SECOND GENERATION—INSURANCE PRACTICES AND RISK SELECTION

A second generation approach for some consumer advocates has been to examine the insurance-related practices of HMOs, primarily marketing and risk-selection

(Zelman, 1996). This approach reflects a focus not just on the treatment of the individual patient, but also on the impact that HMOs may have on the rest of the health insurance system—of particular interest to those who worry about the fate of the Medicare traditional indemnity program. Because it is widely assumed that Medicare HMOs are currently enrolling a healthier, younger segment of the Medicare population, and because risk-adjusted payments today are an inadequate correction for the favorable selection of enrollees, marketing and risk segmentation (marketing to and selecting for inclusion a lower-risk segment of the population) are important areas of concern. These concerns may be more pronounced in Medicare because of the individual, rather than employer-based, marketing and enrollment process.

Indeed, the 1995 debate in Washington about the structure of Medicare "reforms" was striking in how many of the policy differences were based on risk selection issues. Risk selection takes place when the risk pool is distributed unevenly, so some plans face much greater expense than others. Most consumer organizations quickly saw the dangers posed by Medical Savings Accounts and private fee-for-service options in Medicare. Even the Medicare negotiations among the president, the Speaker of the House, and the Senate majority leader stalled, not so much over the total level of budgetary savings as over the issues of risk selection and the related threat to the future integrity of the Medicare risk pool.

For consumers, the potential for plans to select members based on risk leads to an unstable and inadequate set of insurance choices over time. The "gaming" of enrollment by plans sets up a different kind of competition than the competition to promote access and quality that most consumers would prefer. Plans can profit much more easily by enrolling healthier individuals and groups than they can by better managing the delivery of healthcare, so there is a strong temptation to market themselves only to the healthy.

Today, there is evidence that within Medicare, HMOs enroll new members who, on average, have substantially lower than average health expenses. This phenomenon may be inevitable in the early stages of HMO enrollment growth, since younger and healthier Medicare beneficiaries are more likely to be open to joining an HMO. The more serious problem is indicated by "disenrollment" of higher-cost individuals. If those most in need of health services leave the HMO, that could indicate a failure of the plan to meet the needs of the enrollee. It could also mean that costs are being shifted back to other payers, and thus the claimed advantage of risk plans in saving costs would be nullified. We need much more scrutiny of those sicker disenrollees to see if plans themselves are encouraging higher cost enrollees to leave or are failing to meet the medical or service needs of those enrollees.

Benefit and network design is also a key element in this competitive environment. One way to attract better risks is for plans to develop benefits and provide affiliations that will appeal to low-cost individuals but not to potentially higher-cost ones. Many plans emphasize preventive programs, for example, but not the specialists, services, or facilities important to chronically ill or disabled individuals.

The competitive dynamic that these practices create is problematic in two ways. First, the lack of incentive to recruit and serve the most medically needy people means that the plans do not reach the population that could benefit the most from well-coordinated and integrated healthcare arrangements. Since most of the dollars spent in the healthcare system today are spent on seriously or chronically ill people, risk selection also means that the potential budgetary benefits of managed care to the overall health system may never be realized.

Another concern of consumers is that risk selection sets up a competitive dynamic that could lead to a "race to the bottom." If plans are, in effect, rewarded for avoiding risk, their benefit designs and provider networks may be deliberately skewed to avoid being too attractive to higher-risk individuals. In the long run, this dynamic could well lead to inadequate benefit plans that are not designed to serve the needs of the sicker enrollee. Plans doing a better job of serving the more difficult and expensive individuals will be financially penalized because a disproportionate number of high-risk, expensive individuals will be drawn to them, and they will be forced to adjust benefits downward to protect themselves. This situation penalizes precisely those plans that do the best job of serving the full range of consumer needs in healthcare.

It should therefore be no surprise that consumer advocates are moving to a second-generation focus on risk selection as the long-term consequences of inadequate safeguards become clearer. But given the inevitability of growing managed care choices and consequent risk segmentation, how can consumers best be protected from these adverse consequences?

The first step is to structure the enrollment process to minimize deliberate selection practices. Medicare itself should conduct the enrollment and regulate the marketing of risk plans, as the Office of Personnel Management does for federal employees. Certain marketing practices, such as the use of agents, should not be permitted because of the practices' inherent potential for abuse. Second, we can try to more accurately adjust Medicare payments to plans to reflect the risk profile of their enrollees. Health status should be included as a factor in the adjusted payments. The use of outlier payments (extra payments for very expensive cases) or carve-outs (benefits paid for separately as an exception to prepaid care, usually for well-defined, expensive conditions such as mental health, substance abuse) might reduce some of the risk to plans and therefore the incentive for the plan to underserve those truly high-cost, riskier patients. Finally, it is essential to prevent manipulation of benefit design to accomplish risk selection. The lack or limitation of a pharmaceutical benefit, for example, can discourage those in need of high-cost drugs from enrollment in a particular plan if they have the choice of better coverage elsewhere. Again, the plans that do offer more generous coverage are then faced with adverse selection—that is, they will be the choice of more high-risk, expensive enrollees—when competing with plans that offer more limited benefits. To protect themselves, the better plans will be forced to cut back benefits. For this reason, a more adequate standard benefits package must eventually be required.

Even with such protections in place, however, problems will remain. For example, the plans may well enroll a fair cross-section of the population only to provide inadequate service or poor quality care. So the insurance-related concerns that focus on marketing abuses or risk selection are, like concerns about individual treatment decisions, a necessary but insufficient agenda for consumer protection. I believe that consumer advocacy must therefore broaden its scope to encompass a third-generation approach to deal with the issues of health plan performance.

THIRD GENERATION—HEALTH PLAN PERFORMANCE

If consumer advocates truly want to maximize value in healthcare, protect quality, and promote accountable and responsible health plans, they will have to expand their focus to include the factors that actually guide and limit health plan performance. This calls for a sophisticated assessment of plan structure and performance that takes into account such factors as physician financial incentives, appropriate utilization, consumer satisfaction, outcomes information, and the need for strong public and private regulation and oversight.

It may not be much of an overstatement to say that money drives behavior in organizations, so the third-generation approach to consumer advocacy has to look at the financial arrangements and incentives that drive behavior within the HMO. Central to this inquiry is the way the health plan compensates its primary care physicians.

Financial compensation usually underlies the behavioral norms for delivering care within the health plan. Reimbursement incentives influence the culture of the organization and, thus, everyone who works for it. These incentives set up an ongoing set of rewards and penalties for clinical providers. Expecting occasional, individual appeals or sanctions to affect behavior within the plan is like expecting a beach sandcastle to hold back the tide.

It is increasingly common for HMOs to "dump" risk to the physician level rather than to pay salaries to the physicians while accepting risk at the plan level. The practice of putting physicians at full financial risk for the costs of their own treatment recommendations (physician capitation) raises the stakes for consumer protection and also raises some difficult ethical issues for the physicians (American Medical Association, 1995).[1] Under physician capitation, the primary care physician accepts a monthly payment per covered plan member, then pays for the cost of tests, specialist referrals, and hospitalizations out of that monthly payment. In comparison, salaried physicians are presumably able to practice with the least regard to financial incentives, but even they are often paid bonuses based on the attainment of budgetary targets (Relman, 1988).

Physicians may want to accept risk in order to gain more money and more autonomy for themselves in their practice of medicine. But from the patient's

---

[1]The most thorough overall examination of ethical issues in managed care is found in Rodwin, 1993.

perspective, the main question is. How strong is the financial pressure on the physician to underserve? If the physician group is relatively small and is at full risk, then the link between an individual treatment recommendation and the doctor's income may be direct and substantial enough to become a clear conflict of interest. If indicators of patient satisfaction and clinical quality are taken into account in determining a physician's compensation, then they may balance the other financial incentives satisfactorily. If the plan (or the physician's partners) simply use utilization data to identify outliers, then there is also less to worry about, so long as clinical decisions and practice styles conform to the latest guidelines.

Physicians paid on a fee-for-service basis are increasingly subject to a percentage "withhold" by preferred provider organizations or other forms of "managed care lite." The withhold has much the same impact on physician financial incentives as does capitation; it signals to the doctor that his or her expected income is possible only if certain utilization or budgetary targets are met. So, the healthcare consumer may soon face a medical delivery system in which, for better or worse, doctors are subject to a range of financial incentives that under some circumstances may not be in that individual's best interest. If program budgets are adequate, and the incentives light, then there may be little need for concern. But if the drive to cut costs becomes excessive, these tools are capable of creating serious conflicts of interest.

The most difficult and most worrisome situations involve high-cost treatments that are discretionary—that is, they are beyond the treatments indicated in practice guidelines for the patient's condition. Physicians who have accepted full risk for such a patient face a particularly direct ethical dilemma. How aggressive should their treatment recommendations be if high-cost aggressive treatment means a substantial negative effect on their income, and the net incomes of their partners? Disclosure of financial incentives in such situations is ethically required, but disclosure may not be sufficient by itself to protect the integrity of the physician-patient relationship.

Beyond these dramatic cases, however, lies the broader issue: What is it that we want to pay physicians, and plans, to do? What do we want them to be accountable for? What behavior do we want to reward? These are questions that consumer advocates must now address if they are to influence the direction our healthcare system will take.

For example, if we want plans to reach out to those segments of our population that are at greater risk and harder to serve, we will have to design and advocate for reimbursements that measure and reward such behavior. If we want to support "centers of excellence" that specialize in the treatment of a particular condition or disease, then we will need to become advocates for reimbursement arrangements that support access to such centers. If we want high clinical quality, then we have to measure and reward it through higher reimbursement and greater enrollment volume. If we want physicians to take the needs of the whole patient into account, and to be able to treat the whole person, then we must advocate for benefit designs and flexibility that permit and reward that kind of physician involvement.

Key to the attainment of goals for healthcare plans is the ability to measure performance (Epstein, 1995). Paul Ellwood has stated that organizations "are what they measure." Consumer advocates now need to pay close attention to what is being measured in managed care organizations. Is it what we most care about? Is it what we want plans to use as a basis for financial reward? If the only things that count in this new environment are what you can count, then consumers need to be clear about what counts with them. We need to know about how financial incentives and performance measures translate into quality patient care (Hillman, Pauly, and Kerstein, 1989).

These issues are difficult. Grappling with them requires a sophisticated knowledge of how capitated health plans function and how doctors and other providers within those plans behave. Also required is much more information and analysis than consumers may be used to, and it must be collected and presented on a provider, plan, and market-by-market basis, as well as nationally. For many individual consumers, this level of information will be overwhelming and functionally useless. Still, disclosure, while a necessary first step, is never going to be adequate by itself to assure good performance.

This analysis suggests the need both nationally and within specific healthcare "markets" to establish consumer protection organizations that can function as constructive participants in the necessary dialogue with plans and providers about how to improve healthcare coverage and services. Perhaps states can take the lead in making funding for these organizations available; perhaps the federal government could require that a small percentage of plan premiums be dedicated to such purposes. In any event, the need for an informed, sophisticated consumer advocacy network has never been greater.

Consumer advocates must now also focus on the need to establish an adequate regulatory and oversight infrastructure for managed care. Market-based purchasing decisions can promote good healthcare, but healthy competition can only work for the benefit of the consumer where there are clear, effectively enforced rules for competitive behavior (U.S. General Accounting Office, 1995). We are making a start on this structure already. The Health Care Financing Administration can exercise some oversight for Medicare enrollees, the National Committee on Quality Assurance can play a critically important role in both standardizing performance-related information and conducting accreditation reviews, and the PRO program is trying to monitor quality and resolve complaints within Medicare. But to date there is inadequate oversight in the states and local markets where the plans operate, especially for people under age 65. Where individual consumers need help is in making enrollment decisions and in dealing with problems once enrolled. National standards, combined with local oversight and enforcement, are necessary. Information alone, while necessary, will not be sufficient to protect most consumers.

Many large private employers have taken on the responsibility of assisting active employees in dealing with healthcare plans, but other large employers have reduced their employee assistance efforts. For employees of small and some large businesses, and for the self-employed and Medicaid and Medicare beneficiaries, accessible and effective remedies must be available to resolve problems. This is an urgent challenge for the consumer movement because of the speed and scope of the changes now occurring almost everywhere in healthcare insurance and delivery.

The dynamic character of the healthcare delivery system seems likely to continue for some years to come. Regional differences will continue to emerge, as will new organizational arrangements for financing care. If consumer advocates are to stay relevant to this process, they will need to expand their activities beyond concerns about individual treatment denials or risk selection. What is needed now is a third-generation approach to the behavior of these capitated healthcare organizations—an approach based on clearly stated systemwide goals for provider behavior and on the financial payments and incentives that support such behavior.

The promise of a new, more efficient, accountable, and more valuable healthcare system is incorporated in some of the managed care organizations that will soon provide healthcare coverage for most Americans. Without strong and informed consumer advocacy, that promise may never be realized. Consumer advocates must take up the challenge to engage health plans on their own terms—money and measurement—if the quest for a better healthcare system is to be fulfilled.[2]

ABOUT THE AUTHOR

John Rother is Director of Public Policy for the American Association of Retired Persons (AARP).

REFERENCES

American College of Physicians. 1996. *Medicare Managed Care: How to Ensure Quality.* Task Force on Aging Report. Philadelphia.

American Medical Association (Council on Ethical and Judicial Affairs). 1995. "Ethical Issues in Managed Care." *Journal of the American Medical Association* 23: 4.

Epstein, A. 1995. "Performance Reports on Quality—Prototypes, Problems, and Prospects." *New England Journal of Medicine* 333: 57–61.

Hillman, A. L., Pauly, M. V., and Kerstein, J. J. 1989. "How Do Financial Incentives Affect Physicians' Clinical Decisions and the Financial Performance of Health Maintenance Organizations?" *New England Journal of Medicine* 321:86–92.

Kaiser Commission on the Future of Medicaid. 1995. *Medicaid and Managed Care: Lessons from the Literature.* Washington, D.C.

---

[2]For good overviews of issues raised for consumers by managed care organizations, see also American College of Physicians, 1996.

Relman, A. S. 1988. "Salaried Physicians and Economic Incentives." *New England Journal of Medicine* 319:784.

Rodwin, M. 1993. *Medicine, Money and Morals.* New York: Oxford University Press.

U.S. General Accounting Office. 1995. *Medicare: Increased HMO Oversight Could Improve Quality and Access to Care.* Washington, D.C.

Zelman, W. 1996. *The Changing Health Care Marketplace: Private Ventures, Public Interests.* San Francisco: Jossey-Bass.

ARTICLE 2

MEDICAID AND MANAGED CARE

*The Kaiser Commission on Medicaid
and the Uninsured*

Medicaid provided health and long-term care coverage to 41.3 million low-income Americans in 1996. As a purchaser of health services for low-income families, Medicaid increasingly relies on managed care to deliver services. Almost half (48%) of Medicaid beneficiaries, predominately poor children and their parents, now receive health care services through a broad array of managed care arrangements.

MEDICAID MANAGED CARE ENROLLMENT

In 1997, 15.3 million Medicaid beneficiaries were enrolled in managed care, up from 2.7 million in 1991, more than a five-fold increase (Figure 1).

Today, all states (except AK and WY) are pursuing some managed care initiatives. As of June 1997, 40 states and D.C. had more than one-quarter of their Medicaid population enrolled in managed care. Of these, 12 states have more than 75% of their Medicaid beneficiaries enrolled in managed care.

MODELS OF MEDICAID MANAGED CARE

Managed care is designed to reduce costs by eliminating inappropriate and unnecessary services and relying more heavily on primary care and coordination of care. Managed care arrangements are characterized by formal enrollment of individuals in a managed care organization (MCO); contractual agreements between the provider and a payer; and some gatekeeping and utilization control.

The major Medicaid managed care models include:

- **Risk-Based Plans:** Under a fully capitated plan, a health plan is paid a fixed monthly fee per enrollee and assumes full-risk for the delivery of a compre-

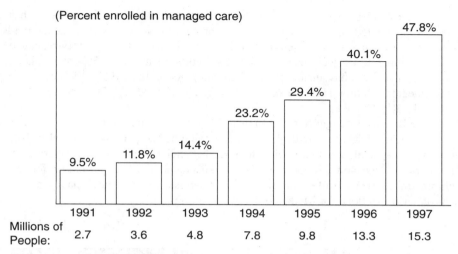

(Percent enrolled in managed care)

Note: Includes MCO and PCCM enrollment.

Figure 1 Growth in the share of Medicaid beneficiaries enrolled in managed care, 1991–1997 (Source: HCFA 1998)

hensive range of services. Some plans contract on a more limited basis (i.e., ambulatory care only).

- **Fee-for-Service Primary Care Case Management (PCCM):** In a PCCM plan, a provider, usually the patient's primary care physician, is responsible for acting as a "gatekeeper" to approve and monitor the provision of services to beneficiaries. These gatekeepers do not assume financial risk for the provision of services, and are paid a per-patient monthly case management fee.

As of June 1997, 568 Medicaid managed care plans, primarily full-risk HMOs, were in operation—double the number of plans in 1993. There has been significant growth in managed care plans that predominately or exclusively serve the Medicaid population. In 1996, nearly half of Medicaid enrollees in fully capitated arrangements were enrolled in "Medicaid-only" plans, comprised of safety net providers such as public hospitals and community health centers; commercial plan subsidiaries; provider-sponsored plans; and newly formed plans focusing on Medicaid.

STATE MANAGED CARE OPTIONS

States have long had the option to voluntarily enroll Medicaid beneficiaries in managed care plans. Legislative authority to require mandatory enrollment has evolved over time.

Under 1915(b) waivers, in place in 40 states, mandatory managed care has been implemented in part of the state or for certain categories of beneficiaries. Section 1115 waivers have been used to implement statewide mandatory managed care enrollment, as well as to waive the requirement that 25% of a plan's enrollment be privately insured (the 75/25 rule). As of June 1998, 14 states have implemented Section 1115 waivers (AZ, DE, HI, KY, MA, MD, MN, NY, OH, OK, OR, RI, TN, VT).

The Balanced Budget Act (BBA) of 1997 gives states new authority to mandate enrollment in MCOs for Medicaid beneficiaries without obtaining a federal waiver (except for special needs children, Medicare beneficiaries and Native Americans). Furthermore, the new law permits the establishment of Medicaid-only plans by eliminating the 75/25 rule. Finally, the law establishes certain new managed care consumer protections for Medicaid beneficiaries (Figure 2).

Enrollment/Marketing: States may mandate managed care enrollment, guarantee enrollment for 6 months for adults and 12 months for children, and "lock-in" beneficiaries for up to one year; door-to-door marketing is prohibited; and default enrollment systems must consider existing physician-patient relationships.

Plan Choice: Permits states to limit Medicaid beneficiaries to a choice of two MCOs in urban areas and one MCO in rural areas. Plans may serve Medicaid beneficiaries exclusively.

Access: Requires MCOs to comply with a "prudent layperson" emergency care standard and prohibits physician "gag rules."

Consumer Protections: States are required to provide comparative information on MCOs including a list of participating plans, the benefit package and cost-sharing, out-of-plan covered benefits, service area, and quality and performance indicators. Other information, available if requested, includes the identity and location of providers, enrollee rights and reponsibilities, and grievance and appeals procedures.

Plan Requirements: Requires plans to demonstrate adequate capacity, including an appropriate range of services and access to preventive and primary care services and a sufficient number, mix, and geographic distribution of providers.

Quality/Oversight: Increases the threshold for prior federal approval of managed care contracts to $1 million; requires states to develop and implement a quality assessment and improvement strategy by 1999; and establishes external independent review of MCO performance.

Figure 2   Medicaid managed care selected provisions in the Balanced Budget Act of 1997

ISSUES IN MEDICAID MANAGED CARE

Medicaid beneficiaries are economically disadvantaged, frequently reside in medically underserved areas, and often have more complex health and social needs than do higher-income Americans. Early evidence on the implementation of Medicaid managed care shows some improvement in access to a regular provider but more difficulties obtaining care and dissatisfaction with care compared to those in Medicaid fee for service.

Medicaid has operated under tight budget constraints. This has resulted in provider payment rates that are often substantially below market rates, contributing to access problems. Capitation rates need to be sufficient to assure that plans are able to adequately care for Medicaid enrollees. Medicaid-only MCOs, wholly dependent on Medicaid, do not have other payers to compensate for shortfalls.

Broadened use of managed care for low-income children and families is unlikely to accomplish large overall savings for Medicaid. Low-income children and adults account for 27% of program spending while 64% of spending is for the elderly and the disabled. Enrollment of elderly and disabled populations into managed care is increasing, but is complicated by difficulties in setting appropriate capitation rates, limited plan experience in providing specialized services, and lack of systems to coordinate Medicare and Medicaid benefits for "dual eligibles."

The future success of Medicaid managed care depends on the adequacy of the capitation rates and the ability of state and federal government to monitor access and quality. The BBA provides new standards to assure plan capacity and enforce consumer protections. However, the development of access and quality performance standards for Medicaid MCOs and the measurement of compliance with those standards is evolving. Assuring access and quality of care in a managed care environment will require fiscally solvent plans, established provider networks, education of provider and beneficiaries about managed care, and awareness of the unique needs of the Medicaid population.

ABOUT THE AUTHOR

The Kaiser Commission on Medicaid and the Uninsured in Washington, DC, is headed by Diane Rowland, ScD, who is also Executive Director of The Kaiser Commission on the Future of Medicaid and Chair Senior Vice President of The Henry J. Kaiser Family Foundation.

ARTICLE 3

THE UNCERTAIN FUTURE OF MANAGED CARE

Eli Ginzberg

The fortunes of managed care have taken a sudden downturn. Consider this: the oldest and largest and one of the most respected health maintenance organizations (HMOs), Kaiser Permanente, posted a loss of about $270 million in 1997, its first deficit in more than a half-century of operations. Informed sources predict even higher losses for 1998.

Oxford Health Plans, a Connecticut-based, for-profit managed-care company with many middle- and upper-income enrollees in the New York region, saw its stock-market price peak at close to $90 a share in early 1997, only to lose over 70 percent of that value by the year's end. The company still faces the challenge of borrowing several hundred million dollars in order to have the capital necessary to restructure itself. During the course of a recent annual ophthalmologic examination, my relatively young ophthalmologist mentioned in passing that Oxford owed him $40,000, a sum that he suspected would never be paid. It was, but at a collection cost of $20,000.

Despite the robust stock market, many for-profit managed-care organizations have lost their attractiveness to speculators, both professional and amateur. The reasons are not difficult to pinpoint. The early and middle 1990s saw rapid increases in the number of privately insured employees changing from fee-for-service coverage to HMOs, a shift that is associated with a one-time savings of between 10 to 15 percent of premiums. But now, with the majority of potential managed-care enrollees having already made the transition, the earlier, large-scale gains in enrollment, with their accompanying high profits, are over.

To make matters worse, groups of physicians have started to organize in order to improve their bargaining power with managed-care companies. At the same time, consumer groups are pressing their political representatives in Washington, D.C., and state capitals to pass consumer-protection legislation that will provide them with more choices, but such legislation will also reduce the profitability of managed-care plans.

What about the Balanced Budget Act of 1997 and the introduction of Medicare+Choice for Medicare recipients, which were designed to encourage Medicare recipients to enroll in managed-care organizations? In passing the Balanced Budget Act of 1997, Congress set a goal of reducing federal outlays for Medicare during the period from 1998 to 2002 by $115 billion, primarily by cutting back on payments to providers, hospitals, and physicians. The Medicare+Choice program reflects Congress's determination to increase the options available to Medicare beneficiaries beyond that of enrolling in an HMO. Medicare+Choice offers beneficiaries a wide range of additional options: if the beneficiary's employer joins the federal program, the beneficiary can choose to establish a medical savings account, enter into a private payment arrangement with his or her own physician, or receive coverage from a provider-sponsored organization.

Will there in fact be sizable increases in the number of Medicare beneficiaries who opt to join or remain in a managed-care organization because access to a broadened range of services will make it unnecessary for them to purchase a Medigap policy? Although the number of Medicare enrollees in managed-care plans is likely to continue to increase, until the Health Care Financing Administration issues its revised regulations and new payment schedules, we need to be cautious about such predictions. Recently, some managed-care plans have decided not to participate in the Medicare program, presumably because they do not believe it will be profitable.

The situation is also problematic for managed-care companies enrolling Medicaid recipients. A number of smaller states, such as Arizona, Oregon, and Tennessee, have had reasonable success in enrolling a large proportion of their low-income populations in managed-care plans. But similar efforts by the larger states, such as California, Illinois, and New York, have been delayed. There are no major barriers to enrolling mothers and children on Medicaid in managed-care plans. But although mothers and children account for about 70 percent of the population eligible for Medicaid, they account for no more than 30 percent of total Medicaid outlays. The much more difficult question is whether for-profit managed-care plans will be able and willing to enroll persons who are elderly, chronically ill, or disabled, who together account for about 70 percent of all Medicaid outlays.

A substantial number of for-profit managed-care organizations have decided not to bid, or not to continue to bid, on contracts to enroll these hard-to-serve populations, in part because several states have reduced their contract prices. Furthermore, many of these patients need a wide range of services, some of which fall outside the experience of managed-care plans. At this early stage of mandatory enrollment of the population eligible for Medicaid, one cannot predict how many severely handicapped patients will be forcibly enrolled in Medicaid managed-care plans, much less whether the plans will be able to make money while providing the quality and range of services that these patients received previously.

Most people who would be easy to enroll, and for whom the cost of care would on average be below that of people in the fee-for-service system, have already enrolled in managed-care plans. It is much more difficult for managed-care plans to enroll Medicare and Medicaid beneficiaries, realize profits from providing services to them, or both.

There is even more trouble ahead for managed care. Health insurance premiums are increasing again and may approach double-digit rates of increase in the near future. If that turns out to be the trend, one must anticipate that the number of employers who will continue to provide health insurance coverage for their workers will decline. Alternatively, employers will require their workers to pay a larger percentage of the premium, which will lead more workers to reject coverage. An even more worrisome problem is that a large number of managed-care organizations are heavily leveraged. Unless one believes that the stock market will continue its long-term upward climb, which seems improbable, a substantial correction will force many marginal managed-care companies into bankruptcy. This, in turn, will jeopardize the health insurance coverage of many millions of middle-class citizens. The federal and state governments may decide that they have to rescue many, if not all, of the bankrupt managed-care companies, but then again, they may not. If the stock market goes into a serious decline, greater numbers of people will lack coverage.

Some 43 million Americans are currently uninsured, and over 30 million are underinsured. With many Medicaid recipients being forced into managed-care plans whose ability to provide satisfactory care must still be proved and with additional millions of people perhaps no longer eligible for Medicaid because of the 1996 welfare-reform legislation, we could soon be facing a crisis in health insurance coverage affecting between one third and two fifths of Americans.

The expansion of managed care played a key part in moderating increases in health care costs during the early and middle 1990s, primarily by limiting the freedom of decision making that physicians and consumers had previously enjoyed. But these limitations led to serious backlashes in the legislatures, and the prospect that managed-care plans will continue to constrain health care costs is highly questionable. Moreover, both Congress and the President are committed to moderating, even reducing, the rate of increase in federal health care expenditures. So far, there is little evidence that the United States has taken any serious action to reduce the steep inflation in health care expenditures by effectively cutting back on the excess capacity of acute care hospitals, by reducing the numbers of physicians being trained, or by curbing the diffusion of new, expensive technology.

If Congress and the President continue to hold the line on moderating future federal expenditures for health care, the nation may be forced to bite several bullets. First and foremost, we will be forced to recognize that the critical issue is not to restrict total expenditures but, rather, to restrict federal expenditures, which will soon account for 40 percent of total health care outlays. In addition, the public will be forced to recognize that the U.S. health care system has always rationed care and will continue to do so in the future. With up to one in three Americans vulnerable to the loss of high-quality health care insurance, federal and state legislators may find it easier to provide universal coverage than to pursue any alternative policy.

According to the latest figures released by governmental statisticians, total government expenditures for health care amounted to $540 billion in 1998,[1] and according to a recent estimate,[2] the federal tax subsidy for private health insurance coverage amounts to an additional $100 billion. This means that there is over $600 billion potentially available in the federal and state payment pool to provide essential health care coverage for all citizens and permanent residents. This sum represents about 7 percent of our gross domestic product. In the United Kingdom, 7 percent of the gross domestic product provides total funding for the National Health Service. Of course, the United States is different from the United Kingdom, and we are used to a much more costly health care system, especially since the enactment of Medicare and Medicaid.

Admittedly, a federal–state plan providing essential health care coverage for all Americans would not be easy to legislate, but considering the alternatives, it might prove to be the least difficult response to a steep rise in the number of uninsured and underinsured persons, should many of the managed-care plans go into bankruptcy. Medicare+Choice may represent a template—an early stage in transforming Medicare from a defined benefit (specifying all authorized services) to a defined contribution approach (stipulating a monetary maximum of governmental outlays) that holds some additional promise of containing the rate of future federal spending.

Since managed-care plans will not be in a position to constrain rising health care costs in the face of consumers' demands for more choices and reduced interference in the patient–physician relationship, and since future health care costs must be controlled, at least as far as government expenditures are concerned, the best alternative is for government to provide essential coverage to the entire population and then let persons who want more and better care to cover the additional costs out of their own pockets, through privately purchased insurance, or through employer benefits.

The growing difficulties and uncertain future facing managed-care companies, particularly the for-profit companies, may offer an opportunity for the United States to provide basic coverage for the entire population, to control the rate of increase in future government expenditures for health care by linking it to the growth of the gross domestic product, and to allow marginal employers to free themselves in whole or in part from the burden of providing health insurance coverage for their employees. Some employers may decide to "cash out" the value of the health care benefit they have been providing by offering their employees an equivalent amount in increased wages or other benefits, and some may decide to offer a combination of increased wages and a supplementary health insurance benefit. Probably most employers and maybe most of their employees would welcome the decoupling of employment from health care. Under such circumstances, the future of managed care would become even more uncertain.

ABOUT THE AUTHOR

Eli Ginzberg, PhD, is Professor of Economics Emeritus at Columbia University, New York, New York.

REFERENCES

1. Smith S, Freeland M, Heffler S, McKusick D. The next ten years of health spending: what does the future hold? *Health Aff (Millwood)* 1998;17(5):128–40.
2. Reinhardt UE. Wanted: a clearly articulated social ethic for American health care. *JAMA* 1997;278:1446–7.

CHAPTER 10

QUALITY OF HEALTH CARE

I n the previous three chapters, we have addressed several critical access and cost issues emerging as the U.S. health care system undergoes unprecedented changes in the final decade of the century. We turn our attention now to specific concerns about the quality of health care services in the United States. Initial studies of quality focused on the process of care and the structure of services provided. In recent years, however, policymakers and researchers have turned their attention to whether the care provided is appropriate and effective, and to identifying the specific outcomes of the services provided. Without outcome measures for increasingly complex therapies and treatments, it is impossible to determine whether or not specific approaches are cost-effective and, importantly, beneficial to patients. Previous emphasis on the process (versus the outcome) of health care services has rendered clinicians, patients, payers, and policymakers woefully uninformed about the efficacy, desirability, and cost-effectiveness of many health care procedures and services that are routinely provided.

The emerging managed care environment insists, as a structural mandate, on measures that concretely indicate the cost-effectiveness of care. In combination with knowledge about the efficacy of interventions and the skills needed to deliver care, the movement to contain cost requires prudent use of outcomes data to inform the configuration of appropriate services. In the last two editions of *The Nation's Health,* we focused on the need to reduce uncertainty in medical care as much as possible while recognizing acceptable variations in professional practice and care. In this edition, we include papers from the fifth edition that represent recent attempts to better define, describe, and measure the quality, appropriateness, and effectiveness of health care services under the increasing specter of constrained resources.

The issues related to the quality of health care have been studied intensively in recent years. In the fall of 1998, a group assembled by the Institute of Medicine (IOM) of the National Academy of Sciences published the results of a multi-year study of health care quality in the United States. What they found was not encouraging. They concluded:

> Serious and widespread quality problems exist throughout American medicine. These problems, which may be classified as underuse, overuse, and misuse, occur in small and large communities alike, in all parts of the country, and with approximately equal frequency in managed care and fee-for-service systems of care. Very large numbers of Americans are harmed as a result. Quality of care is the problem, not managed care. (*JAMA,* Sept. 16, 1998, pp. 280.)

The range of problems related to underuse, overuse, and misuse, including mistakes in diagnosis, failure to apply effect of clinical preventive services (e.g., Pap smears, immunization), errors in medication use, failures of equipment and technologies, and unforeseen complications of treatment, have been documented repeatedly for decades. More recently, the Institute of Medicine issued an even more comprehensive report, *To Err Is Human: Building a Safer Health System.* The IOM estimated that 44,000 to 98,000 people die every year in U.S. hospitals as a result of medical error. The fundamental problem identified was not individual errors but basic flaws in the way the health system is organized. The committee that compiled the report recommended a four-part plan designed to create both regulatory and financial incentives that will lead to a safer health care system (IOM, 1999). President Clinton responded by ordering all the health plans serving federal employees to implement a system to ensure greater patient safety.

Whether one agrees with the IOM's estimates, there is no doubt that the problem of quality of health care is very serious and has not been adequately addressed by current strategies. Approaches to guaranteeing quality of care focused for too long on the "bad apples" (physicians who commit serious errors) rather than on preventing any adverse events in the first place. To do this would require a system-wide approach that includes both medicine and public health, as well as what a combination of clinical and population-based measures can accomplish. In its studies and reports (see Recommended Reading list) the Institute of Medicine has focused most of its attention on the health care system and not on the improvements that could follow extensive collaboration between medicine and public health (see Chapter 6).

In the first article included in this chapter, Bodenheimer (1999) reviews the magnitude of the problem. He documents the organizations concerned with quality assessment, reporting and maintenance, the difficulties in measuring quality, and attempts to maintain a standard of quality by pressuring institutions with policy measures from the outside, and by creating a culture of quality within institutions. Finally, he summarizes the evolution of federal policy on the issue quite succinctly:

> In 1972, Congress created Professional Standards Review Organizations, supplemented in 1982 by Peer Review Organizations (PROs), one in each state, which are authorized to monitor quality in the Medicare program. However, a 1990

study found that PROs used ineffective punitive methods such as retrospective case review with denials of payment and warnings to physicians. In 1992, HCFA transformed the PROs into organizations with staffs of medical professionals trained in quality improvement, who analyze patterns of care through the large Medicare database and feed these data back to physicians and hospitals in order to improve care for patients with common illnesses such as myocardial infarction, congestive heart failure, stroke and pneumonia. . . .

There are also a multiplicity of professionals and consumer-oriented organizations concerned with accreditation (e.g., National Committee for Quality Assurance), the development of standards (Foundation for Accountability), and consumer education and advocacy (AARP). Despite the efforts of these organizations and others, there is still the view among leaders in the field that "a fundamental change is needed within institutions to bring both a science and a culture of quality to U.S. medicine that are currently lacking in most hospitals and physicians' organizations" (Bodenheimer, p. 491). To date, there has been little fundamental change.

We include in this edition only one article by individuals who have been leaders in the field over the years (Brook et al.) Others were included in the fifth edition. We also include a few selected articles for the Recommended Reading list, all of which are reviewed in the Bodenheimer article.

Robert H. Brook, Karen J. Kamberg, and Elizabeth A. McGlynn (1996) identify eight issues related to the "cost-quality trade-off." While the issues of the trade-off between cost and quality were evident long before the current drive to managed care health services delivery systems, the authors raise the question of how intensifying efforts to curtail the growth rate in medical expenditures might affect the balance of this trade-off. Although these are critical questions within the context of medicine, the issues are also relevant to other health care disciplines. Inclusion of this paper is thus intended to stimulate readers' inquiry as to the important dilemmas facing health care professionals and policymakers on the eve of the 21st century. The authors have also included an insightful overview of the past 25 years of research on how health care system change affects quality of care and health status, and on evolving approaches to measuring quality of care. Finally, the authors address the very pertinent concern of the action required to keep the issue of quality at the forefront of future policy debates.

The essay in the Recommended Reading list by David L. Sackett and his colleagues discusses the concept of "evidence-based medicine" and again raises important issues relevant across health care disciplines. The overriding theme of this paper is the need to consider important and unique information about individual patients in light of research-based information about populations of similar patients, and to make clinical decisions that reflect these considerations. As defined by the authors, "Evidence based medicine is the conscientious, explicit, and judicious use of current best evidence in making decisions about the care of individual patients" (Sackett et al., 1996, p. 71). Their presentation and discussion encourages thought-provoking consideration of how health care professionals in general might balance internal (patient-centered) and external (population focused) evidence in formulating care decisions that are appropriate and effective, and that result in increasingly better quality at the individual and system levels.

John Wennberg (1993), building on nearly 20 years of research on measuring variations in the health care experiences of populations, provides us with a cogent history and update on this valuable approach to addressing questions of quality, appropriateness, and effectiveness of health care (see Recommended Reading). Wennberg's work and his presentation of future directions for similar study highlight the increasing importance of comprehensively documenting and describing the health care delivery system. His proposal to develop descriptive statistics of resource allocation and capacity is both timely and critical. Such information in conjunction with outcome measures will greatly enhance our abilities to accurately and adequately predict a reasonable balance to achieve optimum quality of services within specific fiscal constraints.

Although they have not been included in this book because of space limitations, several recent papers add important dimensions to the discussion concerning quality of, and access to, health care. These papers are timely and raise a broad spectrum of continuing issues in the policy arena. We have included these references in the Recommended Reading because of their importance. Friedman's (1995) informative paper describes the variety of issues in measuring and improving the quality of health care. In this comprehensive work, she provides an historical perspective on the evolution of the health care quality movement, addresses the conceptual issues that require attention in the definition and measurement of quality, and identifies several current measures of quality in diverse settings. She then reviews possibilities for use of existing Medicare data sets and development of new databases, and concludes with several suggestions for the future directions in the development and evaluation of quality measures. Other important articles on measuring and improving the quality of health care services are included in the issue of *Health Care Financing Review* (Summer 1995), in which this paper was originally published.

Appropriateness of care is also reflected in the study by Bindman and colleagues (1995) that investigated access to care for five chronic conditions and preventable hospitalizations in low income communities. This research supports increasing overall access to care as a strategy to reduce the [costly] and questionably efficacious hospital admission of patients with chronic conditions. He argues that hospitalization impedes chronic care patients from effectively receiving care that may have been more appropriately provided on an outpatient basis and thereby eliminated to the need for hospitalization altogether.

We conclude our Recommended Reading with a review of quality of care and managed care by Miller and Luft (1997). The picture remains mixed, but if anything, there is still substantial opportunity to improve the quality of care through managed care.

REFERENCES

Bindman, A. B., Grumbach, K., Osmond, D., Komary, M., Vranizan, K., Lurie, N., Billings, J., & Stewart, A. Preventable hospitalizations and access to health care. *JAMA,* 1995;274:305–311.

Bodenheimer, T. The American health care system: The movement for improved quality in health care. *NEJM,* 1999;340:488–492.

Brook, R.H., Kamberg, C.J., & McGlynn, E.A. Health system reform and quality. *JAMA,* 1996;276:476–480.

Friedman, M. A. Issues in measuring and improving health care quality. In *New Initiatives and Approaches in Health Care Quality. Health Care Financing Review,* 1995;16(4).

Kohn, L., Corrigan, J., Donaldson, M. (Eds., Committee on Quality of Health Care in America). *To Err Is Human: Building a Safer Health System.* New York: Institute of Medicine, 2000.

Institute of Medicine. Preventing death and injury from medical errors requires dramatic system-wide changes. New York: Institute of Medicine, Nov. 29, 1999. URL: http://www4.nationalacademies.org.

Lawrence, D.M. "Is Medical Care Obsolete?," National Press Club Speech, July 14, 1999.

Miller, R., & Luft, H. Does managed care lead to better or worse quality of care? *Health Affairs,* 1997;16:7–23.

Sackett, D.L., Rosenberg, W.M.C., Haynes, R.B., & Richardson, W.S. Evidence based medicine: What is it and what isn't it? *BMJ,* 1996;312(13):71–72.

Wennberg, J.E. Future directions for small area variations. *Medical Care,* 1993(Supplement);31:Y375–80.

ARTICLE 1

THE AMERICAN HEALTH CARE SYSTEM: THE MOVEMENT FOR IMPROVED QUALITY IN HEALTH CARE

Thomas Bodenheimer

A vibrant movement to improve the quality of health care has sprung up in the United States. Report cards on health plans, hospitals, medical groups, and even individual physicians have appeared on the front pages of newspapers, on television, and on the Internet. Projects to solve problems of quality within health care institutions dot the health care landscape. A small but determined cadre of physician leaders has developed a science of health care quality and is working to transform that science into a national movement.

Two main strategic threads intertwine to create the present and future agenda of the movement to improve quality in health care. First, activists are persuading the purchasers of health care—large employers and the government—to demand high-quality care from managed-care plans and health care providers. Second, leaders are attempting to inspire health professionals to create a "culture of quality" within their health care institutions. A description of these interrelated strategies is the subject of this Health Policy Report. The report is based on interviews with experts on the quality of health care in academic medicine, business, and government and with the leaders of organizations that focus on quality in health care. Before describing the two strategies of the movement, I will briefly review the nation's main problems with the quality of health care, how it is measured, and the most important organizations concerned with the quality of health care.

PROBLEMS WITH QUALITY

Problems with the quality of health care can be categorized as overuse, underuse, and misuse.[1] A number of studies have demonstrated overuse of health care services; for example, from 8 to 86 percent of operations—depending on the type—have been found to be unnecessary and have caused substantial avoidable death and disability.[2] Underuse is prevalent in the care of patients with chronic disease. For instance, many patients with diabetes do not have regular glycohemoglobin measurements and retinal examinations, and from 1993 through 1995, only 14 percent of patients with cardiovascular disease had achieved the serum lipid levels recommended in national guidelines.[3,4] Underuse also occurs in acute care. The failure to use effective therapies for acute myocardial infarction may lead to as many as 18,000 preventable deaths each year.[1]

Misuse is a pervasive problem. An estimated 180,000 people die each year partly as a result of injuries caused by physicians.[5] Fatal adverse drug reactions in hospitalized patients caused an estimated 106,000 deaths in 1994.[6] Fatal medication errors among outpatients doubled between 1983 and 1993.[7] The quality of care within hospitals has been found to be inferior for blacks and the uninsured.[8,9] To deal with the problem of misuse, the movement for quality has begun to target issues of patient safety.

MEASURING QUALITY

The Institute of Medicine has defined quality as "the degree to which health services for individuals and populations increase the likelihood of desired health outcomes and are consistent with current professional knowledge."[1] How does an individual physician, medical group, or health maintenance organization (HMO) know whether it is providing care of average, below average, or superior quality? The measurement of quality is an elusive but achievable goal.[10,11] Health care is not a single product, like a toaster or a lamp. It includes such diverse components as performing screening mammography in a healthy woman, optimally treating a patient with a myocardial infarction and cardiogenic shock, and counseling a depressed patient. Each intervention requires its own particular measurements of quality; some elucidate the processes of care, and some focus on outcomes. For patients with diabetes, the relevant measures might include the percentage of patients who undergo an annual retinal examination (a measure of process) and the percentage with normal glycohemoglobin levels (a measure of outcome). For patients with coronary heart disease, measures might include the percentage receiving aspirin and beta-blockers (process) and the percentage who have myocardial infarction or sudden death from cardiac causes (outcomes). Even when considering only one health care intervention—for example, coronary-artery bypass surgery—it is treacherous to compare the outcomes of one surgical team with those of another without adjusting for the age of the patients and the severity of their illness.

Different groups in the health care system have different issues of concern regarding the quality of health care and are interested in different measures of performance. Physicians view quality in health care as the application of evidence-based medical knowledge to the particular needs and wishes of individual patients. Patients may place more importance on how clinicians communicate with them, or how long they are kept waiting for appointments, than on the technical accuracy of the advice offered, though a new wave of health-conscious consumers is developing technical sophistication. HMOs may value patient satisfaction and the use of preventive services above clinical outcomes because satisfied patients are less likely to leave the health plan and because the application of preventive services is a measure on which HMOs are currently judged.

ORGANIZATIONS CONCERNED WITH QUALITY

The National Committee for Quality Assurance (NCQA) was formed in 1979 by managed-care trade associations hoping to fend off federal monitoring of health plans. In 1990, in order to reduce competition from newer, presumably lower-quality HMOs, a group of HMOs in coalition with some large employers engineered a restructuring of the NCQA's board, transforming the organization into something more than a mere advocate for the interests of HMOs.[12]

The NCQA has two main voluntary activities: the accreditation of HMOs and the publication of measures of performance in the Health Plan Employer Data and Information Set (HEDIS). As of October 1998, 48 percent of the nation's approximately 650 HMOs had requested accreditation surveys from the NCQA; 96 percent of those surveyed have received three-year, one-year, or provisional accreditation. Thirty large corporations, including Xerox, General Motors, and IBM, will not contract with health plans that are not accredited by the NCQA, but most employers do not make accreditation a requirement. Employers concerned with the quality of health care tend to be companies that have been forced by international competition to improve the quality of their own products. Forty percent of the NCQA's budget comes from fees paid by HMOs for accreditation surveys; the rest comes from foundation grants, contracts, educational programs, and publications.

The current data set from the NCQA, HEDIS 3.0/1998, includes more than 50 measures of performance, including patient satisfaction, rates of childhood immunization, percentages of enrollees of certain ages receiving screening for cervical and breast cancer, and percentages of patients with diabetes who undergo retinal examinations.[13] Ironically, although employers tend to associate higher quality with lower costs (achieved by reducing overuse and misuse of services), the NCQA's HEDIS measures focus mainly on the underuse of health care, the correction of which raises costs. The NCQA agrees that the HEDIS measures include few items related to chronic illness; the group hopes to add such items for the year 2000 data set.

A health plan can refuse to disclose its HEDIS profile to the public. A total of 329 HMOs (51 percent of all HMOs) allowed the 1996 data to be publicized, but only 292 plans (45 percent) permitted public reporting of the data for 1997. According to the NCQA, the plans that refuse to allow publication of HEDIS data have significantly lower scores than the plans that permit publication.

The Joint Commission on Accreditation of Healthcare Organizations (JCAHO), founded in 1952 under the aegis of the American Hospital Association and the American Medical Association (AMA), has the authority to terminate hospitals' participation in the Medicare program if the quality of care is found to be deficient.

Revenues for the commission come chiefly from fees paid by hospitals, home care agencies, and other facilities that it accredits. For years, the JCAHO attempted to launch outcomes-based accreditation standards that would allow the public to compare hospitals. Because of resistance from hospitals, this effort has been scaled down and converted to the ORYX program. ORYX allows a hospital to pick two measures of performance from a long list, including such items as mortality after coronary-artery surgery or the percentage of patients with diabetes who receive dietary counseling, as long as these measures are relevant to 20 percent of the hospital's patient population. Over time, hospitals must report more measures, but there is no requirement for the type of uniform reporting that would help the public compare one hospital with another.

The Health Care Financing Administration (HCFA) is responsible for ensuring that institutions providing services to Medicare and Medicaid beneficiaries meet certain standards of quality. In the past few years, HCFA has accelerated its quality-related activities and may soon be the nation's most influential organization working to monitor and improve the quality of health care. The Quality Improvement System for Managed Care (QISMC), established in 1996, sets quality standards for Medicare and Medicaid managed-care plans. In contrast to the NCQA, which reports HEDIS data only when health plans wish them to be released, HCFA has the authority to make public such data for all Medicare HMOs, but it has not yet done so. HCFA may eventually require hospitals that participate in Medicare to submit data on standardized measures of quality that consumers can use to compare hospitals, bypassing the more cautious approach of the JCAHO. HCFA is considering a similar approach for independent practice associations and group practices.

In 1972, Congress created professional standards review organizations, supplanted in 1982 by peer review organizations (PROs), one in each state, which are authorized to monitor quality in the Medicare program. A 1990 study found that PROs used ineffective punitive methods such as retrospective case review with denials of payment and warnings to physicians.[14] In 1992, HCFA transformed the PROs into organizations with staffs of medical professionals, trained in quality improvement, who analyze patterns of care through the large Medicare database and feed these data back to physicians and hospitals in order to improve care for patients with common illnesses such as myocardial infarction, congestive heart failure, stroke, and pneumonia.[15] PROs review individual cases in the event of complaints from patients and can deny payment for unnecessary services, but these constitute a small proportion of their work. Experts on quality inside and outside HCFA are concerned that Congress, intent on reducing fraud and abuse in the Medicare program, may require the PROs to return to their previous payment-denial practices and thereby compromise their quality-improvement activities.[16]

The Foundation for Accountability (FACCT) in Portland, Oregon, was created in 1995 on the initiative of Paul Ellwood. In contrast to the NCQA, an accrediting organization, FACCT is a think tank and educational vehicle whose purposes are to develop measures of performance that are relevant to consumers and to educate consumers about how to use this information. FACCT persuades the NCQA, JCAHO, HCFA, state governments, and employers to use its measures of performance.

For 10 years, the Institute for Healthcare Improvement (IHI) in Boston, founded by Donald Berwick, has organized an annual National Forum on Quality Improvement in Health Care; it has also developed a Breakthrough Series, bringing together leaders in health care organizations who are committed to solving problems of quality. The Breakthrough Series focuses on several collaborative efforts to improve care within institutions; the goals include reducing waiting times in emergency departments, preventing adverse events due to medications, and improving care for low back pain.

The National Patient Safety Foundation, located at offices of the AMA in Chicago, was established by the AMA in 1997 to change the attitudes of health professionals and the public regarding medical errors.[17] The foundation, with start-up funds from the AMA, sponsors research and educational efforts based on the assumption that errors are not personal failures deserving punishment but, rather, inadequacies of systems, which must be redesigned to help prevent errors. Leaders of the NCQA, JCAHO, FACCT, and IHI sit on the foundation's board of directors.

The National Roundtable on Health Care Quality, involving representatives from academic, business, consumer, provider, governmental, and publishing organizations, was convened by the Institute of Medicine in 1995 to heighten awareness of issues related to quality in health care. Funded by the federal government and private sources, the roundtable's 1998 report concluded that "serious and widespread quality problems exist throughout American medicine."[1] The Institute of Medicine is continuing the roundtable's work, looking at the dual strategies of changing health care institutions internally and fostering an external environment that encourages improvements in quality.

The Consumer Coalition for Quality Health Care in Washington, D.C.—formed in 1993 through the efforts of the American Association of Retired Persons and other consumer groups—represents labor, the elderly, and advocacy organizations and intends to bring the perspective of consumers to legislative and private initiatives to improve the quality of health care.

PRESSURING INSTITUTIONS FROM THE OUTSIDE

Accreditation, whether voluntary or compulsory, makes health care institutions satisfy a minimal standard of quality, thereby placing demands on these institutions to improve. The goal of the publication of performance measures, or report cards, is to put pressure on institutions in two ways. First, low scores on report cards may steer consumers or employers away from health plans, medical groups, or hospitals, and second, physicians within institutions that score poorly on report cards may be embarrassed into doing better.

Leaders in the movement for quality in health care, including those within the NCQA, view the commission's report cards as a first step toward improving quality, but they cite several limitations of the program:

Report cards may not channel most consumers to higher-quality health plans. Forty-seven percent of employees in large companies and 80 percent in small firms have no choice among health plans,[18] data on quality would therefore be of no use to them. Moreover, only 11 percent of 1500 employers recently surveyed relied on data on quality in selecting health plans; cost is the driving factor in most decisions by employers.[19]

Tens of millions of people receive health insurance through preferred-provider organizations, which are not included in the reporting on performance.

Patient satisfaction, an important component of HMO report cards for marketing purposes, is a questionable measure of the quality of care.[20] Patient satisfaction is an unreliable indicator because positive ratings from the great majority of enrollees—who are healthy and rarely use services—can dwarf the legitimate complaints of those who are sick.[21]

Gathering HEDIS data is costly to health plans and provider organizations, and the cost is ultimately shifted to purchasers and consumers. The movement for quality in health care brings profits to consultants as well as to the newest suppliers of health care products: computer and software companies.

If report cards truly channeled patients to higher-quality plans, those plans might attract a sicker, more expensive population of patients. The higher-quality plans would thus be punished rather than rewarded by the market, which does not adjust HMO premiums for severity of illness.

Although the impetus provided by report cards may boost quality within HMOs,[22] **only items measured by HEDIS are affected.** As pressure to reduce costs intensifies and the time patients spend with physicians decreases, overall quality could suffer even as HEDIS scores soar.[20]

What is the community of professionals concerned about the quality of health care doing about these shortcomings?

Some groups of employers, in particular the Pacific Business Group on Health (PBGH) and the Minnesota-based Buyers Health Care Action Group (BHCAG), are publishing report cards on medical groups and integrated care systems rather than focusing solely on health plans. A few purchasers are creating financial incentives aimed at improving the quality of care. PBGH pays health plans more money if they achieve negotiated preventive-services scores on HEDIS.[23] The huge Federal Employee Health Benefits Program is considering a similar move. General Motors reduces premiums for employees who choose high-quality plans.

A far more effective step is for employers to place clauses in contracts with health plans that require specific improvements in quality. This development comes from a leading-edge group called the Leapfrog Group. This is an informal think tank of several large employer organizations, including PBGH, BHCAG, and General Motors, whose goal is to make a direct assault on targeted issues related to patients' safety. The group, whose "epidemiology of opportunities for improving quality" is researched by PBGH medical director Dr. Arnold Milstein, has picked two issues as its initial focus on safety. The first is "evidence-based hospital referral"—that is, the channeling of patients to certain hospitals for conditions and procedures (including coronary angioplasty and bypass surgery, carotid endarterectomy, and repair of abdominal aortic aneurysm) for which clear evidence exists that a higher volume of procedures or teaching status is associated with better outcomes.[24–27] After learning that this program could save 500 to 1000 lives per year in California, PBGH (which is made up of employers that purchase care for a total of approximately 3 million employees and their dependents) is asking its California HMOs to use new performance standards for physician groups, hospital precertification, and enrollee education to advance evidence-based hospital referral for an initial subgroup of these interventions, beginning in urban areas. Although PBGH is beginning this effort with its HMOs, the intention of PBGH and the rest of the Leapfrog Group is to make these changes for all forms of health insurance.

The Leapfrog Group's second focus stems from research suggesting that medication errors at hospitals can be substantially reduced by installing computerized physician-order entry systems that display warnings in cases of drug interactions, known drug allergies, and incorrect dosages.[28] Employers could create contractual requirements, incentives, or consumer expectations for computerized physician-order entry systems.

The Leapfrog Group is intent on pushing the movement for quality forward in two ways: by bringing the safety of patients to the forefront of the consciousness of purchasers, and by going beyond the reporting of performance measures of health plans to make attention to quality improvement part of health plans' and providers' contractual obligations and market rewards.

CREATING A CULTURE OF QUALITY INSIDE INSTITUTIONS

External pressure from private purchasers and government regulators is necessary but not sufficient for improvement in quality.[29] Leaders in the field argue that a fundamental change is needed within institutions to bring both a science and a culture of quality to U.S. medicine that are currently lacking in most hospitals and physicians' organizations.

For years, experts on quality, most prominently Donald Berwick and Lucian Leape, have translated quality-enhancing techniques from other industries to health care.[5,30] Mark Chassin, cochair of the Institute of Medicine's National Roundtable on Health Care Quality, challenges the medical profession to strive toward "six sigma quality."[31] The six-sigma goal means tolerating fewer than 3.4 errors per 1 million events—a rate that lies outside six standard deviations of a normal distribution. Currently, the frequency of deaths during anesthesia has been reduced to 5.4

per million, close to the six-sigma goal. In contrast, 580,000 per million patients with depression (58 percent) are not given the correct diagnosis or treated adequately, and 790,000 eligible survivors of heart attacks per million (79 percent) do not receive beta-blockers; these rates are in the neighborhood of one sigma.[31]

Physicians, nurses, pharmacists, and other care givers cannot individually perform at a six-sigma level of reliability; meeting this goal requires building systems designed to prevent adverse consequences of unavoidable human errors.[5] For example, the use of information-and-reminder systems increases the proportion of patients with diabetes who regularly undergo glycohemoglobin tests and retinal and foot examinations.[32] The implication is that clinical care should be redesigned according to a team approach, so that goals for acute, long-term, and preventive care can all be met.

Some institutions are beginning to strive for six-sigma quality in specific areas. LDS Hospital in Salt Lake City designed computer programs to assist physicians in prescribing antibiotics and thus reduced mortality among patients treated with antibiotics by 27 percent.[33] A northern New England multihospital project used quality-improvement techniques to reduce mortality among patients undergoing cardiovascular surgery by 24 percent in three years.[34] The Community Medical Alliance in Boston has redesigned systems of care for patients with severe chronic disease by providing a wide range of services at home and greatly reducing the need for hospitals, specialists, and ambulances.[29] The IHI's National Forum and Breakthrough Series allow institutions across the country to learn from one another's quality-improvement projects. Given the tens of thousands of hospitals and medical practices in the nation, many of which do not have leaders capable of carrying through major quality-improvement projects, this strategy has had limited effects thus far.[1]

Leaders in the movement for quality in health care emphasize that health plans and providers will work toward six-sigma quality on a large scale only if they are rewarded in the market for doing so; currently, financial rewards favor low cost over high quality. Even with a fundamental change in the market, however, this level of quality is difficult to achieve. Physicians' offices, still the main site of clinical practice, are harder to redesign than larger multispecialty groups, which are more able to invest in information-and-reminder systems and to create team-based clinical care.

CONCLUSIONS

Why is the movement to improve the quality of health care active in the United States at a time when cost containment dominates the health care agenda? To some degree, improved quality can reduce costs, particularly costs due to overuse and misuse of services.[31] But substantial investment is needed to reduce misuse, and more funds are needed to address underuse. One cannot explain the existence of the movement simply as a cost-containment activity. A small number of people, mostly physicians, have brought the movement into being, to some extent against considerable odds. Overall, the movement for quality in health care expresses a human desire to do the right thing.

The movement has major barriers to overcome. Corporate purchasers and governments have reduced rates of reimbursement to providers, leading to reduced staffing in hospitals and less time with physicians for patients. Investor-owned health plans and provider organizations have exacerbated these trends by shifting dollars away from direct health services and toward profits and administration. Nonetheless, the goal of improving the quality of care has gained a prominent place on the nation's health care agenda.

ABOUT THE AUTHOR

Thomas Bodenheimer, MD, MPH, is Associate Clinical Professor in the Department of Family and Community Medicine at the University of California, San Francisco.

REFERENCES

1. Chassin MR, Galvin RW. The urgent need to improve health care quality. *JAMA* 1998;280:1000–5.
2. Leape LL. Unnecessary surgery. Annu Rev Public Health 1992;13:363–83.
3. Weiner JP, Parente ST, Garnick DW, Fowles J, Lawthers AG, Palmer RH. Variation in office-based quality. *JAMA* 1995;273:1503–8.
4. McBride P, Schrott HG, Plane MB, Underbakke G, Brown RL. Primary care practice adherence to National Cholesterol Education Program guidelines for patients with coronary heart disease. *Arch Intern Med* 1998;158:1238–44.
5. Leape LL. Error in medicine. *JAMA* 1994;272:1851–7.
6. Lazarou J, Pomeranz BH, Corey PN. Incidence of adverse drug reactions in hospitalized patients. *JAMA* 1998;279:1200–5.
7. Phillips DP, Christenfeld N, Glynn LM. Increase in US medication-error deaths between 1983 and 1993. *Lancet* 1998;351:643–4.
8. Kahn KL, Pearson ML, Harrison ER, et al. Health care for black and poor hospitalized Medicare patients. *JAMA* 1994;271:1169–74.
9. Burstin HR, Lipsitz SR, Brennan TA. Socioeconomic status and risk for substandard medical care. *JAMA* 1992;268:2383–7.
10. Brook RH, McGlynn EA, Cleary PD. Measuring quality of care. *N Engl J Med* 1996;335:966–70.
11. Eddy DM. Performance measurement: problems and solutions. *Health Aff (Millwood)* 1998;17(4):7–25.
12. Millenson ML. Demanding medical excellence. Chicago: University of Chicago Press, 1997.
13. Epstein AM. Rolling down the runway: the challenges ahead for quality report cards. *JAMA* 1998;279:1691–6.

14. Rubin HR, Rogers WH, Kahn KL, Rubenstein LV, Brook RH. Watching the doctor-watchers: how well do peer review organization methods detect hospital care quality problems? *JAMA* 1992;267:2349–54.

15. Jencks SF, Wilensky GR. The health care quality improvement initiative: a new approach to quality assurance in Medicare. *JAMA* 1992;268:900–3.

16. Prager LO. PROs aim to help curb payment errors. *American Medical News.* December 7, 1998:1, 38.

17. Leape LL, Woods DD, Hatlie MJ, Kizer KW, Schroeder SA, Lundberg GD. Promoting patient safety by preventing medical error. *JAMA* 1998;280:1444–7.

18. Gabel JR, Ginsburg PB, Hunt KA. Small employers and their health benefits, 1988–1996: an awkward adolescence. *Health Aff (Millwood)* 1997;16(5):103–10.

19. Prager LO. Top accreditor ties accountability to higher HMO quality. *American Medical News.* October 19, 1998:10, 13.

20. Brook RH, Kamberg CJ, McGlynn EA. Health system reform and quality. *JAMA* 1996;276:476–80.

21. Angell M, Kassirer JP. Quality and the medical marketplace—following elephants. *N Engl J Med* 1996;335:883–5.

22. Longo DR, Land G, Schramm W, Fraas J, Hoskins B, Howell V. Consumer reports in health care: do they make a difference in patient care? *JAMA* 1997;278:1579–84.

23. Schauffler HH, Rodriguez T. Exercising purchasing power for preventive care. *Health Aff (Millwood)* 1996;15(1):73–85.

24. Jollis JG, Peterson ED, DeLong ER, et al. The relation between the volume of coronary angioplasty procedures at hospitals treating Medicare beneficiaries and short-term mortality. *N Engl J Med* 1994;331:1625–9.

25. Grumbach K, Anderson GM, Luft HS, Roos LL, Brook R. Regionalization of cardiac surgery in the United States and Canada: geographic access, choice, and outcomes. *JAMA* 1995;274:1282–8.

26. Karp HR, Flanders WD, Shipp CC, Taylor B, Martin D. Carotid end-arterectomy among Medicare beneficiaries: a statewide evaluation of appropriateness and outcome. *Stroke* 1998;29:46–52.

27. Hannan EL, Kilburn H Jr, O'Donnell JF, et al. A longitudinal analysis of the relationship between in-hospital mortality in New York State and the volume of abdominal aortic aneurysm surgeries performed. *Health Serv Res* 1992;27:517–42.

28. Bates DW, Leape LL, Cullen DJ, et al. Effect of computerized physician order entry and a team intervention on prevention of serious medication errors. *JAMA* 1998;280:1311–6.

29. Berwick DM. Crossing the boundary: changing mental models in the service of improvement. *Int J Qual Health Care* 1998;10:435–41.

30. Berwick DM. Continuous improvement as an ideal in health care. *N Engl J Med* 1989;320:53–6.

31. Chassin MR. Is health care ready for six sigma quality? *Milbank Q* 1998;76:565–91.

32. McCulloch DK, Price MJ, Hindmarsh M, Wagner EH. A population-based approach to diabetes management in a primary care setting. *Effective Clin Pract* 1998;1(1):12–22.
33. Pestotnik SL, Classen DC, Evans RS, Burke JP. Implementing antibiotic practice guidelines through computer-assisted decision support: clinical and financial outcomes. *Ann Intern Med* 1996;124:884–90.
34. O'Connor GT, Plume SK, Olmstead EM, et al. A regional intervention to improve the hospital mortality associated with coronary bypass graft surgery. *JAMA* 1996;275:841–6.

Article 2

Health System Reform and Quality

Robert H. Brook, Caren J. Kamberg,
and Elizabeth A. McGlynn

The US health care delivery system is changing rapidly, dominated mainly by the shift from fee-for-service to managed care medicine. What are the implications for the practice of medicine as a result of the shift from patient-based to population-based medicine? As resources directed to health care are reduced, how will the trade-off between cost and quality be altered? Will quality even remain on the agenda as health system reform proceeds?

Health services research over the past 25 years has produced many findings relevant to these issues. For example, losing or acquiring health insurance affects people's health; but if economic incentives are used to alter the amount of care consumed, then the use of clinically based tools is required to avoid the approximately equal decline in necessary and less-than-necessary care. To keep quality of care on the agenda, physicians should be provided both information about the use of specific health services in their geographic catchment area, and the variability of quality as a function of plan, hospital, and, where appropriate, physician. Physicians should also use tools and guidelines both to coordinate care and to determine what care is to be provided in a population-based, multiprovider managed care system. Information must also be made available to the public about the level of quality provided. Finally, to help physicians resolve some of the tension between providing the best care to individual patients vs a group of patients, new ways to assess quality are required.

An article focusing on health system reform and quality of care may seem irrelevant in 1996, or at least too little, too late. Nevertheless, despite the failure to legislate health system reform at the federal level, the issues raised during the health care debate in 1993 and 1994 remain relevant and should continue to be addressed as the health system is "reformed" through market forces.

Even in the absence of national legislation, the health care delivery system in the United States is changing quickly and dramatically, dominated in particular by the shift from fee-for-service to managed care medicine and by the desire to contain the growth rate in medical expenditures. The emergence of managed care as the predominant force in the practice of medicine is virtually assured in the United States. Over 50 million people are currently enrolled in managed care organizations (approximately 20% of all Americans). Eleven managed care plans have more than 500,000 members, and one fourth of all managed care plans have at least 100,000 members. Predictions using reasonable rates of growth indicate that 40% to 65% of the US population will be enrolled in managed care plans in 5 years.[1]

The transition to managed care in the United States has been largely driven by a desire by employers, insurance companies, and the public to control soaring health care costs. Other countries have responded to similar economic pressure by cutting back on the supply of physicians or hospital beds. The curtailment of the growth of the health industry will continue to occur in the United States (and the rest of the world) even in the absence of national legislation.

Most of the literature related to health system reform has focused on macro-level issues such as the benefits of a single payer or whether a medical market can function efficiently. However, more fundamental issues occur at the micro level: As changes in health care payment and delivery systems occur, what are the clinical implications for the practice of medicine? More specifically, as the increase in health care resources is curtailed, how will the trade-off between cost and quality be affected?

Hopefully, this article provides new insights into the relationship between cost and quality, and the practice of medicine. We first present 8 critical questions that should be considered by everyone involved in the changing health care system. The questions are not meant to be exhaustive and critical questions are omitted. Our intent is not even to answer these questions. Rather, we use these questions to illustrate the importance of maintaining quality of care concerns on the policy agenda. The rest of this article provides information on what happens to quality when the system is changed, and how quality can be measured and maintained on the policy agenda. Finally, based on these questions and what we know about how quality can be measured, we suggest actions physicians as a group might pursue in order to ensure that quality remains a central value of the new American solution to the health care crisis of the 1990s.

EIGHT ISSUES RELATED TO THE COST QUALITY TRADE-OFF

(1) As the shift to managed care continues in response to cost pressures, will efforts focus solely on how to reduce expenditures, or will maintaining and even improving quality remain on the agenda? The principal concern at the employer and insurance company level has been the cost of health care. As health care delivery is transformed to a predominately managed care system, how can we ensure that quality of care remains part of the debate?

(2) How will the delivery of care change as a result of the shift from patient-based to population-based medicine? The emergence of managed care as the

predominant health care delivery mode has resulted in a fundamental change in the paradigm of medical care. Previously, a physician's primary responsibility was to do everything possible for the patient who visited his or her office. Today, some physicians are responsible for a population of patients and for a budget that needs to be spent wisely. In other words, the physician in a managed care setting is responsible for the health of an entire enrolled population, not just those patients who actively use the health care system. This raises a number of questions: How do physicians made trade-offs between patients competing for limited resources? How much physician time should be invested in dealing with people who do not return to see a physician, or who never see a physician, as opposed to those who use the medical care system voluntarily? What strategies should be undertaken by the physician to track the patient population in terms of mental, physical, and social functioning? Should patients be required to be active participants in evaluating both their health care system and the effectiveness of the services that they receive (eg, provide written information on their physical functioning after receiving a new pair of knees, or provide information that will be used to determine if their physician provided an appropriate physical examination)?

(3) How will a potential reduction in contact time affect the quality of the physician-patient encounter? Since the amount of time afforded these contacts is being reduced, improving the productivity of such encounters becomes even more important. However, several questions surround this issue of productivity. For example, how can the information needed by the physician to make clinical decisions be transmitted quickly and inexpensively? How will we produce outcomes consistent with patient expectations if reduced time with the patient means we do not have an opportunity to assess patient values, or explain the implications of different treatment options? Exactly what level and mix of clinical training is needed to provide the most efficient and effective care to patients?

(4) Will cost containment be a clinically rational process? Will we, like the Dutch[2] and Swedes,[3] set clinically based priorities defining which services should be provided (e.g., services for patients who cannot care for their basic needs due to physical or mental problems vs services to further life expectancy or control pain)? Or will care be cut without reference to its potential health benefits?

(5) Are we prepared as a society to take actions needed to improve the medical marketplace? Will we accept even minimal regulation of health plans? Will we require the public to provide or allow access to information necessary to assess both the quality and effectiveness of care?

(6) How much excess supply of health professionals is required to ensure that the level of quality of care is maintained? If we train only enough cardiac surgeons to meet specific demands, what happens if some fraction of them provide care below acceptable standards and the performance of these surgeons cannot be improved? Will the quest for efficiency eliminate a surplus of physicians, so that competition is reduced to a level that sacrifices quality? If all hospital beds are full, and it takes years to build a new hospital, is there any external motive for a hospital to improve its quality?

(7) What role does public information have in helping ensure that medical care provides the best value to all patients? Until recently, patients have not had access to data about the quality or cost of a particular type of care prior to receiving that care. This has changed somewhat with the public release of 2 forms of information. First, data about provider outcomes and cost have been released by several state and private agencies.[4-6] Second, procedure-specific guidelines are beginning to be published by government and private organizations.[7,8] Both of these forms of information are meant to help patients with their medical care decisions. However, several questions still remain.[9,10] Are the publicly available data on quality of care valid enough to be used by consumers in making health care choices? Are case-mix adjusters adequate to protect against gaming and misuse of data in ways that might actually reduce quality? What method of presenting information is most likely to facilitate consumer use? Indeed, will patients use this information to help them achieve the best value for their medical care dollars?

(8) What will be the effect on society as the currently disadvantaged populations learn, through the public release of information, that they are receiving inferior care? Both access to care and technical quality of care is inferior for disadvantaged populations.[11-16] For example, socioeconomically disadvantaged persons have a higher chance of dying than nondisadvantaged patients when they are hospitalized with a condition that responds positively to medical care (eg, myocardial infarction).[16] In this time of cost containment, is society prepared to make high-quality resources available to all persons?

LESSONS FROM RESEARCH

Health services research over the past 25 years has resulted in a dramatic increase in our knowledge about how changes in the health care system affect quality of care and health status, and about how quality of care and health status can be measured. We summarize the findings of some of this research below.

Changes in the Health System and Quality

First, radical changes in health policy, whether produced by the marketplace or government, will profoundly affect the health of people. For example, access to care is dramatically increased if one has health insurance, and this increased access has in turn been shown to improve outcomes, such as whether one lives or dies.[17-20] The most significant action within the health system that we can take to preserve health and improve longevity is to provide health insurance to everyone.

Second, research has shown that changes in economic policy or the organizational structure of the delivery system, short of eliminating health insurance, result in relatively equal reductions in both care that is necessary and care that is less than necessary to maintain health.[21,22] If we want to ensure that such reallocation decisions result in eliminating only less than necessary care, then new, clinically based tools must be provided to physicians and patients.

Third, the current practice of medicine is far from perfect. One fourth of hospital deaths may be preventable,[23] and one third of some hospital procedures may expose patients to risk without improving their health. One third of drugs may not be indicated, and one third of laboratory tests showing abnormal results may not be followed up by physicians.[24]

Fourth, we know that efficacy (the outcome of a procedure performed under ideal circumstances) may not predict effectiveness (the outcome of a procedure performed under usual circumstances), so that results from controlled clinical trials may mislead clinicians weighting the health risks and benefits of an intervention. Two examples illustrate this problem.

The first example is that of carotid endarterectomy. Methodologically sound randomized trials have established the efficacy of carotid endarterectomy in a number of clinical circumstances, including for people who have had a transient ischemic attack and who also have a 70% to 99% obstruction of the carotid artery that is responsible for the attack.[25,26] However, work in community-based practices has shown that the effectiveness of this procedure is much lower than its efficacy, i.e., that complication rates among community-based surgeons are not as low and outcomes are not as good as among those in sites participating in controlled clinical trials.[27] A primary care physician in a managed care organization, when faced with recommending either medical care or surgery to a patient for whom results from a controlled clinical trial would favor surgery, must have information about the complication rate and the experience of the surgeon to whom the patient is being referred. Without such information, making clinical decisions based solely on the results of the randomized controlled clinical trial may do more harm than good.

A second example concerns heart attack patients. Today it is believed that hospitalization in a modern coronary care unit results in better outcomes for patients with acute heart attacks than at home care. However, research has also demonstrated that, after controlling for patient severity at admission, hospital death rates for patients who suffer a myocardial infarction may vary by as much as 6 deaths per 100 patients admitted with this disease.[28] What are the implications for the physician who wants to optimize patient outcomes? First, the physician must have data about outcomes at hospitals to which the patient might be admitted. Second, he or she must know the risk of delay if the hospital with the best demonstrated outcomes is farther away than one with worse outcomes. Physicians must have a real-time system that enables them to assess the trade-off between better hospital care and the delay in obtaining it. Will such a system become available in the near future?

Measuring Quality of Care

Perhaps one of the greatest advances in health services research for facilitating the development of a clinically rational system for making resource allocation decisions has been what we have learned about measuring quality of care and health status.

First, we have learned that quality and health status can be measured.[29-34] Although instruments to measure quality of care and health status could, of course, be improved, they are as reliable and valid as the otoscope, the stethoscope, the x-ray, the medical history, and other tools currently used in medicine.[35,36]

Second, we know that the quality of both processes and outcomes of care can be evaluated. Process measures (what is done to a patient) are more sensitive measures of quality of care because poor outcomes (what happens to a patient) may not occur each time something is done incorrectly or something is omitted that should have been done. For example, a process criterion might state that all pregnant women should be screened for gonorrhea; however, omission of the test will result in a poor outcome only occasionally, because most pregnant women do not have the infection, and even if they do, it will not always result in harm. Similarly, failure to give appropriate myocardial infarction patients thrombolytic therapy will not result in the death of all of these patients.

Third, there are 5 different methods that can be used to evaluate quality.[37] The major differences between these methods are the aspect of care that is assessed (process, outcome, or overall) and whether criteria are established *a priori* to judge adherence to a standard (the explicit method) or if expert judgments are used (the implicit method). Although these 5 methods when applied will produce a different absolute value on a quality scale, the results from their application will correlate and an institution that is rated higher on one method will, in general, be rated higher on another.[38]

Fourth, we have determined that if one is to obtain a meaningful measure of quality of care, one usually cannot rely solely on administrative data. An exception to this general rule is the provision of many preventive services where administrative data are adequate to assess quality concerns. However, relevant clinical data to evaluate most aspects of acute and chronic care need to be collected, and this usually involves talking to the patient, observing the physician-patient encounter, or abstracting the medical record.[39-41]

Fifth, outcomes are multidimensional; a complete assessment of the outcome of care requires the measurement of general, physiologic, mental, physical, and social health and patient satisfaction. In addition, disease-specific outcome data must be collected to measure fully the outcome of care,[30,31] and patient preferences should be incorporated into these assessments. For example, in treating a patient for prostatic cancer one must ask questions about disease-specific outcomes, such as impotence or incontinence.[42]

Sixth, even though it is currently fashionable to measure outcomes other than mortality, such as functioning, we should not lose sight of the fact that mortality is a critical outcome when it comes to assessing quality of care. As stated above, perhaps one fourth of in-hospital deaths from some diseases could be prevented.

Seventh, data obtained by interviewing patients are not sufficient to assess technical quality. Treating a patient in a pleasant and respectful manner (i.e., having a high "art" of care) can mask poor technical care. The result is that poor technical quality of care and patient satisfaction can occur simultaneously. For example, a patient undergoing an unnecessary operation (and not realizing the operation is unnecessary) might be satisfied if the art of the care were to his or her liking. It is much easier for the patient to judge if the phone is answered promptly and if he or she can talk with the physician than to judge the clinical appropriateness of a medical procedure.

Finally, procedure-specific or disease-specific guidelines are valuable tools available to physicians when deciding how to treat or refer patients. In addition, clinically based guidelines, which combine science and judgment, help the physician improve patient outcomes.[43–45] Because physicians who perform a procedure are likely to be more enthusiastic about its use than can be justified by the existing science, these guidelines should be developed by multispecialty physician groups that explicitly use the input from all the types of physicians who care for patients with the given disease.[46,47]

WHY INFORMATION ON QUALITY IS ESSENTIAL FOR AN EFFECTIVE SYSTEM

Now that we have discussed some of the major issues facing the health system in a cost-containment era and some of the findings that can be reached from health services research, we turn to what physicians need to do, know, or lobby for to ensure that quality of care is kept on the agenda as the health care system changes.

First, physicians need to have access to information about the geographic distribution of health services. Where we reside determines to a large extent the procedures or services we receive, with use of many services varying more than 3-fold by geographic area.[48–51] There needs to be an interchange of information among physicians in different parts of the country and in different countries to address questions such as why a particular procedure is performed more in one place than in another. For example, the use of coronary artery bypass graft surgery in persons over 65 years of age is much lower in Canada than in the United States.[52] What is happening in Canada that enables this to occur? Based on clinical criteria and data, is there overuse of the procedure in the United States or underuse in Canada?[53] Is one's socioeconomic status a factor in the receipt of the procedure, regardless of where one lives? Practitioners need to know whether they practice in a low-use or high-use area, what policies or conditions motivate the level of use, and what the implications are for their patients.

Second, physicians (and their patients) need to know that where one receives care is the greatest determinant of the quality of care one receives. For example, quality of care for common medical conditions is worse in US rural hospitals than in urban hospitals.[38] Knowledge that quality varies as a function of hospitals and health systems needs to be disseminated among those who refer patients to hospitals as well as among the patients who receive that care.

Third, physicians need tools to coordinate their patients' care in a complex medical care system. As physicians increasingly practice in groups, the need to transfer information among providers will increase. Until electronic medical records become the standard, we must do better in making sure that patient information is transferred with the patient. For example, if a nursing home patient with a terminal illness arrives at the hospital emergency department, information should travel with that patient about his or her wishes for resuscitation. Similarly, hospital discharge summaries need to be available in the ambulatory setting in a timely fashion so that events and decisions made in the hospital can be incorporated into the patient's outpatient care.

Fourth, we need to recognize that practicing physicians need concise and immediate information about treating their patients. We need to recognize that although articles (such as this one) written for medical journals are useful to an interested audience, most physicians need real-time specific information in order to obtain the best value and quality of care for their patients. Guidelines, disease management strategies, and information on both the costs of different diagnostic strategies or different medications should all be accessible to physicians on a user-friendly computer. The development and implementation of this tool kit across the spectrum of medical care is certainly beyond the capability of individual physicians and most health care companies. It will require cooperation between the public and private sectors and between the producers and the users of clinical science. At a minimum, physicians should insist that the quality standards and criteria are in the public domain and the process by which the tools are produced uses a sufficient level of science to ensure the tools' validity. Evaluation of the adequacy of the science of the tool kit must include questions such as, "Was the scientific literature systematically collected and analyzed, and was expert judgment, when required, incorporated into the tool kit development process in a manner consistent with the best social science practices?"

Fifth, physicians must support the development of efficient, publicly accountable, quality-of-care reporting systems that incorporate the following:

- Results from quality-of-care systems should be consistent with economic incentives. Although physician or patient behavior can be changed by noneconomic means, this change is generally small and slow to occur.[54] Both physicians and patients respond strongly and quickly, however, to economic incentives. Patients assigned even a small coinsurance or deductible as part of the Health Insurance Experiment reduced their use of medical services to almost half that of patients with free care.[55] Changing the payment of hospitals from a cost-plus to a fixed-price system when prospective payment was introduced for Medicare resulted in lengths of stay being reduced by one fourth almost immediately.[56] Altering the amount of reimbursement to physicians in home care in Norway dramatically changed the number of home visits within a short period of time.[57] Providers (physicians and hospitals) need to be rewarded by an economic incentive, such as more money or higher market share, for producing better quality medical care.

- Quality-of-care reporting systems need to rely primarily on clinically valid process (vs outcome) measures. Outcomes often take too long to occur and can require very large samples to measure a statistically significant effect. For example, because the proportion of low-birth-weight babies delivered by women receiving poor prenatal care is very small, a large sample would be needed to observe differences in outcome (i.e., low-birth-weight babies) in one plan or another.[58] One could use process measures that have been shown to improve this outcome in comparing the adequacy of the process of prenatal care among plans.[59]
- The reporting system should be based on a model of medically preventable morbidity or mortality, with emphasis on technical quality of care and on preventing underuse of necessary care.
- The measures of quality should focus on cost-effective interventions, so that very small improvements in health are not produced at a price that is exorbitantly high.
- The measures should cover the scope of outcomes we are prepared to manage and pay for. For example, process measures to deal with helping the elderly to be less lonely should not be included in such a system unless we are prepared to consider relieving loneliness as part of the medical mission of managed care organizations and to reflect that mission in premium prices.
- The application of quality-of-care measures should allow us to determine if a managed care organization provides good quality across all diseases and patient subgroups, or if a particular organization is best in handling a specific disease or procedure.

FUTURE CHALLENGES

What does the future hold for managed care organizations? Unquestionably, their activities will be governed by a desire to be less expensive. But should they not also strive for high-quality care for their enrolled population?

One way that quality could be incorporated into the routine activities of a managed care organization would be to collect patient-level quality-of-care process data for use in a system designed to improve outcomes. For example, because managed care plans are responsible for enrolled populations, it would be possible for them to determine the proportion of patients who had died within the prior year. The organization could collect process data concerning each death from the plan's medical records and, by comparing those data to explicit models, or through the use of expert judgment, determine what fraction of deaths was preventable. Was a patient who died of lung cancer and who smoked given the opportunity to participate in a smoking cessation program? Was a heart attack patient who died and who was eligible for thrombolytic therapy given the drug in a timely manner in the emergency department? Disease-specific models could be developed and scores calculated that would indicate the proportion of deaths that could have been prevented by better primary, secondary, or tertiary care. A further analysis of what is needed to obtain better care could then be undertaken. Next, the cost of those actions could be calculated and the plan could decide whether or not to alter the care; and finally, the plan could evaluate its quality improvement strategies. A similar assessment of the potential for improving quality could be accomplished by having a sample of the enrolled population complete a functional status questionnaire. The plan could then determine, through record review or examination of the patient, which functional impairments might be preventable or correctable through the use of, for instance, hearing aids, treatment for depression, or walking aids. One could perform a cost-benefit analysis of proposed changes in process of care, implement changes, and then measure the extent to which those changes affected the population's functional status.

If quality stays on the agenda in a managed care environment, we will need to begin a dialogue about the reasonable limits of medicine. For example, how quickly must a nurse respond to the requests of a hospitalized patient? How often and how many at-home health services should be provided to discharged patients—many such services are labor-intensive, expensive, and may simply not be affordable. Is it the obligation of the physician to inform the patient of all potential options, or should the patient just be apprised of the options "most consistent" with available resources? If a physician does not offer a mammogram to a woman in her early 40s because the scientific evidence does not support the use of screening mammograms among her age group, must she be told of this deliberate decision? If a more expensive combination pill is available for the treatment of hypertension that allows the patient to take 1 pill a day instead of 3 at different times during the day, should that patient be offered the combination drug?

Finally, we need to address the tension between providing the best care to individual patients and providing the best care to a group of patients. How much in the way of resources should be invested in trying to provide quality care to patients who do not have regular recommended mammograms or flu shots, or who do not return to a physician for care for their chronic condition? Should we spend resources on assessing and improving the functional status of depressed patients who do not take their antidepressant medications? Or should resources be reserved for those who do participate in the medical system? As we move toward a combination of population- and patient-based medicine, we will need to address these issues.

These questions may provoke heated discussions between those who believe that quality should be optimized for the individual patient, and those who believe that resources should be allocated to maximize the health of a community. That is, in fact, our objective. No matter how one approaches the issues and no matter how (or if) the issues are resolved, it is very important that such discussions take place. If we do not experiment with new ways to address issues of quality, then it may be impossible to keep quality on the health system reform agenda and we will all be the worse off.

ABOUT THE AUTHORS

Robert H. Brook, MD, ScD, is Professor, Schools of Medicine and Public Health, University of California, Los Angeles, and is with the RAND Corporation, Santa Monica, California.

Caren J. Kamberg, MSPH, is with the RAND Corporation, Washington, DC.

Elizabeth A. McGlynn, PhD, is with the RAND Corporation, Santa Monica, California.

REFERENCES

1. *Managed Care Digest: HMO Edition.* Kansas City, Mo: Marion Merrell Dow; 1994.

2. Commission on Choices in Health Care. *Choices in Health Care.* Zoetermer, the Netherlands: Ministry of Welfare, Health, and Cultural Affairs; 1992.

3. Swedish Parliamentary Priorities Commission. *Priorities in Health Care: Ethics, Economy, Implementation.* Stockholm, Sweden: Swedish Parliamentary Priorities Commission; 1995:5.

4. Pennsylvania Health Care Cost Containment Council. *A Consumer Guide to Coronary Artery Bypass Graft Surgery: Pennsylvania's Declaration of Health Care Information.* Harrisburg: Pennsylvania Health Care Cost Containment Council; 1991.

5. Colorado Health Data Commission. *Colorado Hospital Outcomes: Mortality, Length of Stay and Charges for Cardiovascular and Other Diseases.* Denver: Colorado Health Data Commission; 1992. Clinical Data Project.

6. National Committee on Quality Assurance. *Report Card Pilot Project.* Washington, DC; National Committee on Quality Assurance; 1993. NCQA Technical Report.

7. Konstam M, Dracup K, Baker D, et al. *Heart Failure: Evaluation and Care of Patients With Left-Ventricular Systolic Dysfunction.* Clinical Practice Guideline No. 11. Rockville, Md: Agency for Health Care Policy and Research, Public Health Service, US Dept of Health and Human Services; 1994: AHCPR publication 94–0612.

8. Department of Practice Parameters, American Medical Association. *Directory of Practice Parameters: Titles, Sources and Updates.* Chicago, Ill: Department of Practice Parameters, American Medical Association; 1996.

9. US General Accounting Office. *Report Cards Are Useful but Significant Issues Need to Be Addressed: Report to the Chairman, Committee on Labor and Human Resources,* US Senate. Washington, DC: US General Accounting Office; 1994. Document GAO/HEHS–94–219.

10. US General Accounting Office. *Employers Urge Hospital to Battle Costs Using Performance Data Systems: Report to Congressional Requesters.*

Washington, DC: US General Accounting Office; 1994. Document GAO/HEHS–95–4.

11. Kasiske BL, Newlan JF, Riggio RR, et al. The effect of race on access and outcome in transplantation. *N Engl J Med.* 1991;324:302–307.

12. Yergan J, Flood AN, LoGerfo JP, Diehr P. Relationship between patient race and the intensity of hospital services. *Med Care.* 1987;25:592–603.

13. Burstin HR, Lipsitz SR, Brennan TA. Socioeconomic status and risk for substandard medical care. *JAMA.* 1992;268:2383–2387.

14. Wenneker MB, Epstein AM. Racial inequalities in the use of procedures for patients with ischemic heart disease in Massachusetts. *JAMA.* 1989;261:253–257.

15. Goldberg KC, Hartz AJ, Jacobsen SJ, et al. Racial and community factors influencing coronary artery bypass graft surgery rates for all 1986 Medicare patients. *JAMA.* 1992;267:1473–1477.

16. Kahn KL, Pearson ML, Harrison ER, et al. Health care for black and poor hospitalized Medicare patients. *JAMA.* 1994;271:1169–1174.

17. Lurie N, Ward NB, Shapiro MF, Brook RH. Termination from Medi-Cal: Does it affect health? *N Engl J Med.* 1984;311:480–484.

18. Lurie N, Ward NB, Shapiro MF, Gallego C, Vaghaiwalla R, Brook RH. Termination of medical benefits: A follow-up study one year later. *N Engl J Med.* 1986;314:1266–1268.

19. Weissman JS, Epstein AM. *Falling Through the Safety Net: The Impact of Insurance on Access to Care.* Baltimore, Md: Johns Hopkins University Press; 1994.

20. Franks P, Clancy CM, Gold MR. Health insurance and mortality: Evidence from a national cohort. *JAMA.* 1993;270:737–741.

21. Lohr K, Brook RH, Kamberg C. Use of medical care in the RAND Health Insurance Experiment: Diagnosis- and service-specific analyses in a randomized controlled trial. *Med Care.* 1986;24:S1–S87.

22. Soumerai SB, McLaughlin TJ, Ross-Degnan D, et al. Effects of limiting Medicaid drug-reimbursement benefits on the use of psychotropic agents and acute mental health services by patients with schizophrenia. *N Engl J Med.* 1994;331:650–655.

23. Dubois RW, Brook RH. Preventable deaths: Who, how often, and why? *Ann Intern Med.* 1988;109:582–589.

24. Brook RH, Kamberg CJ, Mayer-Oakes A, et al. Appropriateness of acute medical care for the elderly: An analysis of the literature. *Health Policy.* 1990;14:225–242.

25. North American Symptomatic Carotid Endarterectomy Trial Collaborators. Beneficial effect of carotid endarterectomy in symptomatic patients with high-grade carotid stenosis. *N Engl J Med.* 1991;325:445–453.

26. European Carotid Surgery Trialists Collaborative Group. MRC European Carotid Surgery Trial: Interim results for symptomatic patients with severe (70–99) or with mild (0–29) carotid stenosis. *Lancet.* 1991;337:1235–1243.

27. Winslow CM, Solomon DH, Chassin MR, et al. The appropriateness of carotid endarterectomy. *N Engl J Med.* 1988;318:721–727.

28. Kahn KL, Rogers WH, Rubenstein LV, et al. Measuring quality of care with explicit process criteria before and after implementation of the DRG-based prospective payment system. *JAMA.* 1990;264:1969–1973.

29. Berzon RA, Simeon GP, Simpson RL, Jr, Donnelly MA, Tilson HH. Quality of life bibliography and indexes: 1993 update. *Qual Life Res.* 1995;4:53–74.

30. Meenan RF, Mason JH, Anderson JJ, Guccione AA, Kazis LE. AIMS2: The content and properties of a revised and expanded Arthritis Impact Measurement Scales health status questionnaire. *Arthritis Rheum.* 1992;35:1–10.

31. Guyatt G, Mitchell A, Irvine EJ, et al. A new measure of health status for clinical trials in inflammatory bowel disease. *Gastroenterology.* 1989;96:804–810.

32. Donabedian A. *Explorations in Quality Assessment and Monitoring, Volume 1: The Definition of Quality and Approaches to its Assessment.* Ann Arbor, Mich: Health Administration Press; 1980.

33. Donabedian A. *Explorations in Quality Assessment and Monitoring Volume II: The Criteria and Standards of Quality.* Ann Arbor, Mich: Health Administration Press; 1982.

34. Donabedian A. *Explorations in Quality Assessment and Monitoring, Volume III: The Methods and Findings of Quality Assessment and Monitoring.* Ann Arbor, Mich: Health Administration Press; 1985.

35. Koran LM. The reliability of clinical methods, data and judgments, part 1. *N Engl J Med* 1975;293:642–646.

36. Koran LM. The reliability of clinical methods, data and judgments, part II. *N Engl J Med.* 1975;293:695–701.

37. Brook RH, Appel FA. Quality of care assessment: Choosing a method for peer review. *N Engl J Med.* 1973;288:1323–1329.

38. Keeler EB, Rubenstein LV, Kahn KL, et al. Hospital characteristics and quality of care. *JAMA.* 1992;268:1709–1714.

39. Iezzoni LI. Monitoring quality of care: What do we need to know? *Inquiry.* 1993;30:112–114.

40. Iezzoni LI, Foley SM, Daley J, Hughes J, Fisher ES, Heeren T. Comorbidities, complications, and coding bias: Does the number of diagnosis codes matter in predicting in-hospital mortality? *JAMA.* 1992;267:2197–2203.

41. Iezzoni LI, Restuccia JD, Shwartz M, et al. The utility of severity of illness information in assessing the quality of hospital care: The role of the clinical trajectory. *Med Care.* 1992;30:428–444.

42. Litwin MS, Hays RD, Fink A, et al. Quality-of-life outcomes in men treated for localized prostate cancer. *JAMA.* 1995;273:129–135.

43. Feder G, Griffiths C, Highton C, Eldridge S, Spence M, Southgate L. Do clinical guidelines introduced with practice based education improve care of asthmatic and diabetic patients? A randomised controlled trial in general practices in east London. *BMJ.* 1995;311:1473–1478.

44. Kravitz RL, Laouri M, Kahan JP, et al. Validity of criteria used for detecting underuse of coronary revascularization. *JAMA.* 1995;274:632–638.

45. Lennox EL, Stiller CA, Morris Jones PH, Kinnier Wilson LM. Nephroblastoma: Treatment during 1970–3 and the effect on survival of inclusion in the first MRC trial. *BMJ*. 1979;2:567–569.

46. Kahan JP, Park RE, Leape LL, et al. Variations by specialty in physician ratings of the appropriateness and necessity of indications for procedures. *Med Care*. 1996;34:512–523.

47. Scott EA, Black N. When does consensus exist in expert panels? *J Public Health Med*. 1991;13:35–39.

48. Chassin MR, Brook RH, Park RE, et al. Variations in the use of medical and surgical services by the Medicare population. *N Engl J Med*. 1986;314:285–290.

49. Wennberg J, Gittelsohn A. Variations in medical care among small areas. *Sci Am*. 1982;246:120–135.

50. McPherson K, Wennberg JE, Hovind OB, Clifford P. Small area variations in the use of common surgical procedures: An international comparison of New England, England, and Norway. *N Engl J Med*. 1982;307:1310–1314.

51. Bunker JP. Surgical manpower: A comparison of operations and surgeons in the United States and in England and Wales. *N Engl J Med*. 1970;282:135–144.

52. Anderson GM, Grumbach K, Luft HS, Roos LL, Mustard C, Brook RH. Use of coronary artery bypass surgery in the United States and Canada. *JAMA*. 1993;269:1661–1666.

53. McGlynn EA, Naylor CD, Anderson GM, et al. Comparison of the appropriateness of coronary angiography and coronary artery bypass graft surgery between Canada and New York State. *JAMA*. 1994;272:934–940.

54. Grimshaw JM, Russell IT. Effect of clinical guidelines on medical practice: A systematic review of rigorous evaluations. *Lancet*. 1993;342:1317–1322.

55. Newhouse JP, Manning WG, Morris CN, et al. Some interim results from a controlled trial of cost sharing in health insurance. *N Engl J Med*. 1981;305:1501–1507.

56. Brook RH, Kosecoff JB. Competition and quality. *Health Aff (Millwood)*. 1988;7:150–161.

57. Kristiansen IS, Holtedahl K. Effect of the remuneration system on the general practitioner's choice between surgery consultations and home visits. *J Epidemiol Common Health*. 1993;47:481–484.

58. Siu AL, McGlynn EA, Morgenstern H, Brook RH. A fair approach to comparing quality of care. *Health Aff (Millwood)*. 1991;10:63–75.

59. Chalmers I, Enkin M, Keirse MJN, eds. *Effective Care in Pregnancy and Childbirth*. Oxford, United Kingdom: Oxford University Press; 1989: vol I, *Pregnancy*, pt I–V and index; vol II, *Childbirth*, pt VI–X and index.

PART 5

WOMEN'S HEALTH AND AGING

CHAPTER 11

WOMEN'S HEALTH AND AGING

P rior chapters of this book have addressed issues of significant importance to the nation's health. As demonstrated in Chapters 1 and 2, improvements in health status have not been experienced evenly, and we now have a greater understanding of the influence of socioeconomic status and race/ethnicity on attainment of wellness. A new national agenda to eliminate racial and ethnic disparities in health has been adopted (DHHS, Healthy People 2010), and there is growing support for health care reforms to address current inequities. This chapter highlights the additional contribution that gender and age play in determining health. Initially we begin by examining the role of gender in health, followed by a look at health issues of aging, and we conclude by examining the intersection of gender and age. Throughout these articles the issues of race/ethnicity and socioeconomic status are again explored.

Recognizing the need to specifically address the health of women, the Institute of Medicine commissioned a report to document the ways in which the medical enterprise, both in scientific research and in clinical practice, has traditionally viewed women through a lens of male physiology and masculine experience and assumptions (Benderly, 1997a). In an effort to remove this distorting lens, the IOM report advances three themes: women have different biologies and physiologies, divergent life courses, and unequal social status (Benderly, 1997a).

"Women in the Health Care System," Chapter Eight of *Her Own Right: The Institute of Medicine's Guide to Women's Health Issues* (Benderly, 1997b), explores the experiences of women in their interface with the health care system. As Benderly explains, the American health care system is a mass of contradictions. We have the most sophisticated technologies, subspecialists, and research enterprise, yet rates of preventable diseases are among the highest in the industrial world. Within this structure, differences in health result from an organization of services that serve men's health care needs differently from those of women. Women have less money, lower rates of insurance coverage, and are more dependent on public health programs.

Benderly labels the current women's health care a "ghetto," in which women receive their care from a variety of specialists focused on body parts. She concludes by advocating for a model of health care across the life span that will benefit Americans of both genders (Benderly, 1997b).

The structure of health care is explored by David Oppenheimer and Marjorie Shultz in "Gender and Race Bias in Medical Treatment" (Oppenheimer & Schultz, 1999), which reflects on a groundbreaking study released in the February 1999 *New England Journal of Medicine* (Schulman et al, 1999). Finding that patients' race and gender influenced the type of care they received, the Schulman study stimulated attention on the role of provider behavior in perpetuating poorer health outcomes among women and minorities (Schulman et al, 1999). While this study generated controversy, even the most modest interpretation of the results supports the findings of disparate treatment of women of color. Oppenheimer and Shultz review the results of the Schulman study as well as provide historical support from other studies over the past 10 years, acknowledging the reluctance among researchers to conclude that gender and racial bias of physicians explain differential treatment. The implications of the Schulman study are discussed in terms of legal remedies, including the potential role of antidiscrimination law. Changing medical practice to ameliorate the problem of racially and sexually disparate treatment requires coming to terms with the compelling reality of the data and recognizing that many of the attitudes about race and gender are unconscious outgrowths of social history and accepted stereotyping (Oppenheimer & Schultz, 1999).

Dr. Susan Blumenthal's article is a more optimistic view of progress. In "Writing a New National Prescription for Women's Health," Blumenthal argues that as a result of government-sponsored public health interventions, the life span of women has increased by more than 30 years since the beginning of the century (Blumenthal, 1997). While acknowledging this progress, she expands the understanding of gender bias to include other key women's health issues: the failure to study women in clinical research trials, the lack of attention to gender differences in biomedical and behavioral research, the disparities in funding for research on women's health concerns, the lack of education of the public and health care professionals in women's health issues, and the dearth of women in senior scientific and health care leadership positions. She also reports on gender differences in health outcomes for conditions, including HIV/AIDS, reproductive health, breast cancer, mental illness, and domestic violence. Despite the existence of these gaps, Blumenthal argues that efforts have been undertaken to improve the health status of women, and consequently there is greater hope for solutions to many of the issues discussed. She concludes by stressing that in order to reap the benefits of recent medical advances, women must have available health care coverage (Blumenthal, 1997).

The importance of health care coverage is a critical issue addressed in the piece from the Commonwealth Fund 1998 Survey of Women's Health; a summary of the findings and selected portions of the survey results are presented (Collins et al, 1999). According to Collins et al, women's voices reveal a mixed story. Women are more knowledgeable about some health issues and are taking more steps to stay healthy. Unfortunately, progress towards promoting various health behaviors is uneven, and significant gaps remain in access to care. Despite a robust economy, more women are uninsured today than five years ago. Women experience high rates of violence and abuse as well as disproportionate rates of health problems (Collins et al, 1999). Consistent with many of the other works in this volume, low-income and less-educated women are less likely than higher-income, more-educated women to receive needed services. Collectively, these findings highlight ongoing deficiencies in the health care system.

Similar to the health status of women, the health status of older individuals is a mixed story. Improvements in overall public health (nutrition, water quality, hygiene) and technological advances in medicine have extended life expectancies. Unfortunately, these advances have been unevenly experienced, with low-income and minority, aging women experiencing poorer health outcomes, higher rates of poverty, and reduced access to care. The system's ability to respond to these and other health-related concerns is affected by the increasing numbers of older people, as well as their health and economic status.

Aging, however, is not gender neutral, as explored in Terrie Wetle's article "Aging Is a Women's Issue" (see the Recommended Reading). As Wetle notes, although more women live to older ages, some of the additional years are lived with multiple illnesses and disabilities. Wetle highlights progress made in delaying and reducing disabilities and reviews the results of four large studies of aging: the NIA Baltimore Longitudinal Study of Aging (BLSA); the Women's Health and Aging Study; the Frailty and Injuries: Cooperative Studies of Intervention Techniques (FICSIT); and the Study of Women's Health Across the Nation (SWAN). Despite the progress made in understanding potential prevention strategies to reduce disabilities in older women, Wetle reminds us that we still lack adequate knowledge to ensure long, healthy, and productive lives for all older women regardless of race/ethnicity and socioeconomic status (Wetle, 1997).

A woman's access to health care influences her ability to take advantage of the progress being made. For women, this access is interwoven with the future of Medicare, as discussed in the next article of this chapter, "Medicare: A Women's Issue" (Rice, 1999). Rice highlights women's greater dependency on Medicare, which results from increased longevity, higher rates of poverty, and poorer health status. Current gaps in Medicare, including lack of coverage for prescription drugs and insufficient long-term care, disproportionately affect older women, who consequently have higher out-of pocket costs despite lower incomes. However, as Rice notes, even within this critique of the limits of Medicare, women have benefited from its existence. As such efforts to reform Medicare that do not address current gaps or reduce access to current benefits, are potentially detrimental to the health of older women (Rice, 1999). As a function of greater longevity, women comprise a larger percentage of the Medicare beneficiaries than men and subsequently rely on Medicare for more years. Despite their increased longevity, women suffer from higher rates of chronic diseases and greater numbers of conditions per individual than men.

Consequently women report lower health status and higher utilization of health services. Unfortunately, health status is not the only characteristic that declines for women with age. Older women are twice as likely as older men to be poor, and poverty among older women increases with age. Much of this rise in poverty is explained by women's marital status and living arrangements, which change dramatically with age (Rice, 1999).

We conclude this chapter with an article from Estes and Weitz advocating a new paradigm that incorporates the contents of each of the articles composing this chapter. This new model recognizes the complex interaction of medical, social, and economic factors that affect women's wellness as they age and bridges the gap between those who are concerned about women and those concerned with aging. As Estes and Weitz explain, in order to meet the needs of this feminized aging population, the leadership of the aging movement and the women's health movement must work together to build a paradigm of health that promotes the wellness of older women. However, the hesitancy to look at aging issues from a gendered perspective, and the predominant focus of women's health on reproductive issues, have hindered this union and deferred to a medical disease-based health agenda for prevention. As such, the current women's health agenda is the result of independent and isolated efforts in the areas of aging, health, and women's issues. To "bridge the gap," old questions need to be examined in new ways, and new questions need to be asked about old assumptions. Estes and Weitz begin this endeavor by advancing four interrelated themes: (1) there is a gendered relationship between socioeconomic structures and health over time; (2) there are gender-specific implications of health care financing and policy; (3) there is a gender bias in the medical disease-based model of health; and (4) there are health consequences to the gendered nature of caregiving (Estes & Weitz, 1999).

REFERENCES

Benderly, B. L. *In Her Own Right: The Institute of Medicine's Guide to Women's Health Issues.* Washington, D.C.: National Academy Press, 1997a.

Benderly, B. L. Women in the health care system. *In Her Own Right: The Institute of Medicine's Guide to Women's Health Issues.* Washington, D.C.: National Academy Press, 1997b; 153–178.

Blumenthal, S. J. Healthy Women: 2000 and Beyond. *Writing a New National Prescription for Women's Health, Insights into the Future of Women's Health.* New York: Education Resources, 1997;2–9.

Collins, K. S., Schoen, C., Joseph, S., Duchon, L., Simantov, E., Yellowitz, M. *Health Concerns Across a Woman's Lifespan: The Commonwealth Fund 1998 Survey of Women's Health.* New York: The Commonwealth Fund, 1999.

Estes, C. L., Weitz, T. A. Bridging aging and gender: a new women's health agenda. Paper presented at the Older Women's Health and Wellness Summit, San Francisco, California, May 5, 1999.

Friedland, R. B., Summer, L. *Demography Is Not Destiny.* Washington, DC: National Academy on an Aging Society, 1999a.

Friedland, R. B., Summer, L. Introduction. *Demography Is Not Destiny.* Washington, DC: National Academy on an Aging Society, 1999b; 1–5.

Oppenheimer, D. B., Schultz, M. M. Gender and race bias in medical treatment. *J Gender-Specific Med* 1999;2(4):27–30.

Rice, D. P. (1999). Medicare: a women's issue. Paper presented at the "Women and Medicare: Agenda for Change," Jacobs Institute and Commonwealth Fund Meeting, Washington, DC, September 16, 1999.

Schulman, K. A., Berlin, J. A., Harless, W., Kerner, J. F., Sistrunk, S., Gersh, B. J., Dubae, R., Taleghani, C. K., Burke, J. E., Williams, S., Eisenberg, J. M., Escarce, J. J. The effect of race and sex on physicians' recommendations for cardiac catheterization. *NEJM,* 1999;340(8):618–626.

Wetle, T. Aging is a women's issue. *J Am Med Womens Assn,* 1997;52(3):98, 106.

WOMEN IN THE HEALTH CARE SYSTEM

Beryl Lieff Benderly

The American health care system is a mass of contradictions. Our great medical centers boast the most sophisticated technologies, the most expert subspecialists, the most massive research enterprise the world has ever seen. Yet our people meanwhile suffer some of the worst rates of infant mortality and cervical cancer, among other preventable tragedies, in the industrialized world. Our talented medical professionals perform at the peak of their art while many ordinary citizens go without routine care. To paraphrase a famous World War II military motto, the difficult we do immediately. The simple takes a lot longer.

In this increasingly complicated system, women's health needs present an especially confusing picture. Biochemical wizardry allows babies to be conceived in the laboratory in the same country—indeed, sometimes in the same hospital—where women who have gone their entire pregnancy without seeing a doctor arrive unannounced in advanced labor. Teams of specialists transplant bone marrow in hopes of saving women from late-stage breast cancer at the same time that many other women have no access to the routine exams and mammography that could detect tumors in the more easily curable early stages.

This tangle of paradoxes permits few sweeping generalizations about the American experience of health care, except perhaps for this: in a number of significant ways, the system treats the genders differently. Whether as patients or as health care providers, women function within it in a distinctively feminine fashion.

Differences show up most obviously, perhaps, in the health care professions. Large numbers of women now practice medicine, but men still predominate in such prestigious posts as those of professors and deans. Women throng the lesser-paying fields as nurses; allied health professionals like technicians, audiologists, and occupational therapists; and low-skilled workers like nurses aides and home health care aides. As patients seeking a doctor or trying to pay their bills, women also differ from men. They have specifically female patterns and needs, but the American health care system, like much else about the medical enterprise in the United States, still operates on a largely male model.

475

Most crucial from the patients' point of view, "men and women in the United States experience different access to health care," according to Nancy Anne Fugate Woods, Ph.D., professor of nursing and director of the Center for Women's Health Research at the University of Washington. Factors beyond most people's control decide who can get needed care and who cannot.[1] Do appropriate providers offer the right services at places and times the patient can get to? Do they have room for her in their schedules and practices? Will they accept her? Does she find the services acceptable? Can she pay for them? "Each of these factors is affected by gender," Woods notes.[2] Each plays out differently for males and females.

Women get sick more often than men, as we have already noted. Not surprisingly, they use health services more often and are more likely to seek them from a regular source of care; fully 84% of women, but only 75% of men, depend on a usual provider. And women's use of medical services follows a distinctive pattern. Until age 15 or so, girls and boys both see a pediatrician or family practitioner. For the next three decades, though, until the mid-forties, many women use an OB/GYN as their main medical advisor; men almost never get primary care from doctors who specialize in their reproductive system. Childbearing accounts for much of this difference, of course, and as women age their patterns again begin to more closely resemble men's. After menopause, they turn increasingly to family practitioners and internists.

Over their lifetime, women on average also spend more time in hospitals, including psychiatric ones, where they account for a larger portion of inpatient admissions than men. Both genders need and use more medical care as they grow older. Regardless of age, though, the poor visit doctors less often than other Americans.[3]

But the fact that women make greater use of medical facilities does not guarantee that they get all the care or the kind of care they need. Bureaucratic arrangements and intellectual assumptions, many totally unrelated to the real needs of real people, vastly complicate many women's quest for medical attention and deprive some of even rudimentary services. (Certain other aspects of the health care system, meanwhile, may have detrimental—though different—effects on certain men.) "Grounded in assumptions about men as normal and reproduction as a central aspect of women's health," Woods declares, "our current arrangements have created different access to health care for men and women and perpetuated an organization of health services that serves men's health care needs differently from those of women."[4]

GETTING WHAT ONE NEEDS

Central to any medical system is the basic question of whether people can get what they need when they need it. In this country, "money, time, and geography" determine the answer, according to Woods. Does a patient have a way of getting to a suitable facility at a time when it's offering service? Can she trust the quality of diagnosis and treatment? Can she afford to pay the bill? Women's experience differs from men's "in each of these dimensions," Woods notes, but finance "looms as the critical issue for the decade." As a group, women are far less able than men to pay for all the health care they need.[5]

One of the reasons is obvious: women simply earn less than men—72 cents for every male dollar in 1991, giving them less money to spend on both bills and insurance premiums.[6] More than three-quarters of all Americans—and a slightly higher percentage of women than men—nonetheless have some form of coverage. But women less often use private plans and more often depend on public assistance programs like Medicaid, which drastically curtail options because many providers refuse publicly funded patients.[7]

Of America's 37 million uninsured, whose choices are even more drastically limited, 17 million are female. Of the women who have insurance, the youngest and oldest are less likely than average to hold private policies; those under 24 are least likely of all. Nearly all women over 65—95% to be exact—have Medicare, and 77% carry additional private coverage.[8]

Indeed, "the elderly enjoy better access to care, in the form of insurance coverage, than any other age group in the nation," found IOM's Panel on the National Health Care Survey in 1992. "By contrast, individuals and families with low incomes"—a group that includes millions of mothers and children—"are not well covered by the federal-state Medicaid program."[9] Women in the childbearing years face the highest risk of inadequate coverage, at a time in their lives when need is often acute. Later, between menopause and Medicare—the decades from 45 to 65—they are likelier than men to have no insurance at all. These uninsured come disproportionately from the ranks of minorities, the unemployed, and singles, whether divorced, widowed, or never married.[10]

A woman's chance of getting medical care thus depends crucially on her employment and marital status; she may often find herself disadvantaged compared to a comparable man. Fewer female workers get insurance as a job benefit, with the disproportionately female holders of part-time and unskilled jobs least likely to enjoy this valuable "perk." Even among the overwhelmingly female health care workforce, many employees lack health coverage. Some 6% of those staffing doctors' offices, for instance, have no health insurance, and 52% get no employer contribution toward their premiums.[11] And even in this age of two-paycheck families, many mothers still cut back their work hours or leave the labor force altogether, at least temporarily. A full-time mom thus usually finds herself at the mercy of her husband's insurance, assuming that she has a husband and he has insurance. Today's high divorce rate, however, along with the fact that 15% of employed workers' dependents lack coverage, renders both assumptions tenuous for many.[12]

But even if a woman does have private insurance, she still may face special disadvantages because a policy as good as a man's still may not protect her adequately. Plans providing the same benefits for both genders often leave women uncovered during the two periods when they need it most, the childbearing years and old age. In the reproductive decades, most policies disallow pregnancies conceived before beginning a job and many exclude cancer screening, pregnancy, delivery, postpartum care, and abortion services. (However, the recent Kennedy–Kassebaum Health

Insurance Bill prohibits denying insurance coverage based on medical conditions.—ED.) More than 80% of family physicians offer family planning, but most private plans consider it unreimbursable preventive care, leaving patients to pay for office visits and birth control supplies out of their own pockets.

Poor women, of course, can resort to the nation's 5,000 family planning clinics, which together provide more than a third of total contraceptive services. But in public as well as private facilities, preventing a pregnancy and terminating it are two different stories. "In contrast to family planning services, abortion services are becoming less available to women," Woods notes, "even though the number of abortions performed remains relatively constant. Federal policy has left poor women without access to abortion care, and many private insurance carriers do not cover the service," which can cost between $300 and almost $2,000, depending on where and when it is performed. "The 1978 Pregnancy Discrimination Act permits abortion services to be excluded from coverage. To my knowledge, there is no other federal regulation that condones the exclusion of a health service to men."[13]

Then, in old age, Woods adds, women face the crushing costs of long-term care, whether in institutions or their own homes. Most policies, however, including Medicare, stress "acute care, such as hospitalization, emphasizing curative services more commonly needed by older men"—an oversight that pauperizes many old women. Overall, Woods concludes, omitting the services that women need most constitutes "unintended rationing of health care based on gender."[14]

Lack of child care during medical appointments and office or clinic hours that conflict with jobs and family responsibilities are among the more formidable non-financial obstacles. Indeed, women's very role as family nurturers, their "extra-market work as mothers, wives and informal caregivers paradoxically provides health care to others," Woods notes, but can prevent them from meeting their own needs. Although 82% provide an annual physical for their children, only 69% get one themselves.[15]

Further severe rationing occurs by race, income, and geography. "For poor patients, financial problems are exacerbated by the necessity of coping with lack of transportation, child care, and the ability to take time off from work," concurs a report by IOM's Committee on Monitoring Access to Personal Health Care Services.[16] In both city neighborhoods and rural counties across America, a severe shortage of doctors who accept Medicaid, or the total absence of any doctors at all, forces the ill and expectant to choose between long journeys and foregoing care altogether. More than 80% of America's counties, home to almost a third of reproductive-age women, lack any source of abortion services.[17]

Whether due to insufficient insurance or unmanageable logistics, inadequate access translates into needless suffering and death. People who cannot see a doctor, whatever the reason, miss the relatively cheap and simple preventive services and screenings that can forestall costly catastrophes like late-stage tumors and complicated births. Lack of prevention thus creates a deadly class discrepancy. Breast cancer strikes African American women less often than whites, for example—96.6 cases per 100,000 women as opposed to 112.9 per 100,000—but kills them more often—27 per 100,000 versus 23 per 100,000.[18] In poor areas, tumors are 20%

more likely to have reached the lethal late stages by the time they are found than in more affluent locales. Over a period of 15 years, incidence of late-stage cancers fell by more than 21% in high-income communities but by only 6% in poorer ones.[19] Simply having mammograms and breast examinations boosts by 20% a woman's chance of living 5 years.[20]

"Although we can detect tumors as small as 3 to 5 milligrams with mammography, we continue to see too many large, clinically obvious carcinomas that carry a poor prognosis," says Valerie P. Jackson, M.D., of the Indiana University School of Medicine. "Noncompliance is a problem for all groups of women, but it is particularly prevalent in our elderly and indigent populations," many of whom cannot afford even $50 for a potentially life-saving mammogram.[21] Since Medicare now pays for screening (as opposed to just diagnostic) mammograms, cost should no longer be a deterrent and compliance should improve.

Another deadly malignancy, vastly simpler than breast cancer to prevent, detect, and cure, reveals even more disturbing inequities of access. Cervical cancer, though easily found in its early, and even precancerous, stages by the cheap and reliable Pap smear, strikes African American women twice as often as whites and kills them three times as often. Many of these deaths, and particularly the "excess" ones, reflect plain neglect. A Pap test even once every five years slashes mortality by 84%, once every two years by 93%. In the early 1970s, African Americans had largely lethal late-stage diagnoses about as often as whites, but twice as often by the late 1980s.[22] So large a "relative difference in late-stage cancer among different groups is an important clue to the existence of problems with access and, potentially, with subsequent treatment," notes the IOM committee on access.[23]

Nor is cancer screening the only routine care whose lack disproportionately kills poor and nonwhite Americans. In the late 1980s, a deadly venereal disease supposedly vanquished decades before began an ominous rise. The syphilis rate among African American adults more than doubled in only four years, and the congenital form—fatal almost half the time—began showing up in African American infants. "Fully preventable by treating infected women with penicillin early in pregnancy," this killer "should be a disease of the past," declares a 1990 editorial in the *American Journal of Public Health* cited by the access committee. Instead, as a "sentinel health condition" it marks a serious public health failure.[24]

Such a lapse entails more than poor financial or physical access, however. Even getting herself to a clinic or doctor's office provides a poor person no assurance of good-quality care. Fully three-quarters of the women who missed a mammogram during a two-year period had seen a doctor during that time. Many of those physicians failed to convey the test's life-and-death importance. For the access committee, such failures raise "the question of why the test was not performed during the visit and whether the barrier to screening here is one of poor-quality care rather than access to care."[25]

Part of the answer lies in where a woman gets her care, a factor that can strongly influence its quality. Fully 85% of health maintenance organization members get a timely Pap smear, as opposed to 75% of private physicians' patients. Only 58% of those without a regular health care source had the test in the past three years, usually at a public health or community clinic. Doctors' attitudes also partially explain the Pap gap. Many feel awkward "pressing poor patients to pay for and undergo screening procedures," the access committee found, "particularly if the patients were having difficulty paying their rent. Similarly, when a diabetic patient can barely afford the cost of medication, her physician may be reluctant to urge her to have a mammogram that is expensive and often not covered by insurance."[26]

Then there is the "reluctance of some physicians" to do screening procedures like Paps and breast exams because they feel "discomfort" or think that "these tests are best left to gynecologists"—specialists whom poor women are exceedingly unlikely to visit. "Internists and family practitioners, however, are specifically trained in these procedures during residency," the committee notes. Altogether, these "structural deficiencies in the organization of care" add up to access problems reaching far "beyond the usual financial limits."[27]

Similar sorts of structural barriers, including physician attitudes, in fact reach well beyond preventive care. "Battering," the access committee stated, "is a major factor in injury and illness among women"—indeed, their commonest reason for visiting emergency rooms—"but it is often overlooked by medical professionals." Though violence may occasion up to a quarter of those trips, "emergency care providers typically identify less than 5 percent of the women with injuries or illnesses suggestive of abuse."[28] And if the abusing husband or boyfriend controls an abused woman's money, insurance, or car keys, she may never get to see a doctor about her injuries at all.

A similar kind of blind spot has kept many women from getting appropriate care for another "secret" disorder, alcohol and drug abuse. Based, as we have seen, on the model of the masculine alcoholic, treatment programs may not be meeting the true needs of women. "Although not substantiated by research, the myth prevails that women have a poorer treatment prognosis than men," observes IOM's Committee for the Study of Treatment and Rehabilitation Services for Alcoholism and Alcohol Abuse.[29] Indeed, even such basic questions as whether women would benefit from a somewhat different approach, from all-female groups, or from female counselors, remain unanswered. Because substance abuse accompanies depression or other affective disorders so much more often in men than in women, the committee believes that assessing general mental health and treating depression must play a prominent role in treatment from male-centered programs, include child care, support services for families, and help developing strategies for coping with stress.

"Structural barriers," in fact, seem to affect how doctors treat even so serious a condition as AIDS. When aerosolized pentamidine was the "therapy of choice," only half of all eligible patients received it. "Men were four times as likely as women" to get this optimal medication, even "after controlling for disease duration, drug use, and insurance status," noted the access committee.[30] Gay white men were likeliest of all. A similar inequity applied to use of AZT. Even "controlling for ability to pay and access to a regular source of care at a clinic," women got that cutting-edge treatment less often than gay white men. "Controlling for disease stage and past history of *Pneumocystis carinii*" as well as for "patients who received their medical care from public hospital clinics" also revealed significant bias against "minorities, women and intravenous drug users" as compared to gay white men.[31]

A FEMALE GHETTO?

"In the 70s, Barbara Seaman observed that women get into the health care system via their reproductive organs," Woods says. This remains the case today. "Indeed, some would argue that women's health has become a ghetto in which only obstetricians, gynecologists, midwives, obstetrical and gynecological nurse practitioners and physician's assistants assume responsibility. Outside the women's health care ghetto, women are relatively invisible and the male is taken as the norm." Because of this distorted focus, she sees "problems in diagnosing and treating women based on assumptions that limit clinicians' ability to understand health as it is experienced by people of both genders."[32]

Because women receive much of their care from a variety of specialists focused on parts of their bodies or lives—obstetricians concerned with pregnancy, geriatricians concerned with old age—"the segmented nature of women's health services has interfered with our ability to envision health care across the life span for women," Woods continues.

So how should we organize care? Some observers argue for a new specialty in women's health, "analogous to pediatrics or geriatrics . . . oriented to a specific population rather than an organ or body system."[33] Others advocate regrouping existing specialties so that internal and family medicine form women's main source of primary care, with obstetrics and gynecology providing mainly referral for special cases and surgical services. This would entail "interdisciplinary research to address the gaps in our knowledge of how women's reproductive and endocrine cycles affect health and disease," Woods believes. In addition, "medical students would learn how to identify themselves across gender lines, all specialties would become more user friendly to women, and the medical profession would rectify its past inequities in its conceptualization of women and the denial of leadership opportunities to women. That's a tall order."[34]

But navigating today's uncoordinated and costly care system is a tall order as well, and one that women must face throughout their lives, as they try to solve their own and their families' health problems. Spurred by their unique physiological needs and often complicated by their particular social and economic situation, that challenge will grow no easier until thoroughgoing reform puts adequate health care within the reach of all Americans of both genders.

ABOUT THE AUTHOR

Beryl Lieff Benderly is a health and medicine writer and is the Washington, DC, correspondent for *OnHealth's City Guides.* Her books include *Growth of the Mind* and *In Her Own Right: The Institute of Medicine's Guide to Women's Health Issues.*

REFERENCES

1. IOM 1992 Annual Meeting, p. 157.
2. Ibid.
3. Ibid., 157.
4. Ibid., 156.
5. Ibid., 159.
6. Ibid.
7. Ibid., 160.
8. Ibid., 160.
9. *Toward a National Health Care Survey: A Data System for the 21st Century,* 24.
10. IOM 1992 Annual Meeting, 160.
11. Ibid., 161.
12. Ibid.
13. Ibid., 163–4.
14. Ibid., 162.
15. Ibid., 165–6.
16. *Access to Health Care in America,* 134.
17. IOM 1992 Annual Meeting, 164.
18. *Access to Health Care,* 87.
19. Ibid., 88.
20. Ibid., 87.
21. *Effectiveness and Outcomes in Health Care,* 53–4.
22. *Access to Health Care,* 89.
23. Ibid., 86.
24. Quoted ibid., 66.
25. Ibid., 85.
26. Ibid., 85–6.
27. Ibid.
28. Ibid., 134.
29. *Broadening the Base of Treatment for Alcohol Problems,* 358.
30. *Access to Health Care,* 164.
31. Ibid., 165.
32. IOM 1992 Annual Meeting, 166–7.
33. Ibid., 167.
34. Ibid., 168.

ARTICLE 2

GENDER AND RACE BIAS
IN MEDICAL TREATMENT

David Benjamin Oppenheimer
and Marjorie M. Shultz

A recent medical publication by Schulman et al,[1] "The Effect of Race and Sex on Physicians' Recommendations for Cardiac Catheterization," garnered significant attention[2] and highlighted a significant problem. As a discipline rooted in science and practiced in a context of professional beneficence, medicine may have assumed that it stood above or outside the problems of race and gender that rend the fabric of American society. Recent evidence confirms that it does not.

GENDER AND THE TREATMENT
OF HEART DISEASE

The Schulman study examined the relationship of race and gender to physicians' recommendations for managing chest pain.[3] The study used professionally produced and recorded multimedia presentations of interviews of patients with chest pain. The patients were played by eight actors, reading scripted descriptions of their symptoms. The actors were dressed identically, presented as having identical insurance and occupations, and directed to act identically in their presentations, so that the only variables were the age, sex, and race of the patients to be evaluated. The presentation was shown to 720 physicians attending one of two national meetings of organizations of primary care physicians. The participating physicians knew that they were being surveyed on their diagnosis of chest pain, but did not know that the impact of the race and sex of the patients was being tested. The physicians were asked to evaluate the patient's chest pain and whether they wished to order further cardiac evaluations. They were then shown the result of a thallium stress test and were asked whether they wished to refer the patient for catheterization.

The study results revealed that when all variables but race and sex are controlled, men and whites were more likely than women and blacks to be referred for catheterization, and that black women were significantly less likely to be referred for catheterization than white men.[4] Heart disease is the number one killer in the United States,[5] for women as well as men,[6] blacks as well as whites.[7] Yet, as the Schulman study documents, recommended treatment for heart disease varies substantially based on race and sex.

Evidence of such disparities in treatment has repeatedly been shown over the past 10 years. Beginning in the 1980s, a number of studies have reported sex bias in the treatment of heart disease. In 1987, Tobin et al[8] reported that, in a study of 390 patients referred for nuclear exercise testing, 31% of the women and 64% of the men had abnormal results, yet only 4% of the women, compared with 40% of the men, were referred by cardiologists for catheterization. For more than 25% of the women with abnormal nuclear scans, symptoms were diagnosed by the examining cardiologist as somatic or psychiatric, an explanation given for only 12% of the men with abnormal results.[9]

In 1991, Ayanian and Epstein[10] reported the results of a retrospective examination by regression analysis of over 80,000 men and women treated for heart disease in Massachusetts and Maryland in 1987. Controlling for principal diagnosis, age, secondary diagnosis of congestive heart failure or diabetes, race, and insurance coverage, they found that women hospitalized for coronary heart disease underwent fewer major diagnostic and therapeutic procedures than men. In particular, they found that the odds of undergoing angiography were 15% to 28% higher for men than women, and the odds of undergoing revascularization were 27% to 45% higher for men than women.

A 1992 report by Heston and Lewis[11] revealed that among patients with acute nonpleuritic, nontraumatic chest pain, women were evaluated and managed less aggressively than men. This retrospective study tracked 445 patients over 35 years of age who presented at 10 St. Louis-area emergency departments over a two-week period in 1989. It was determined that men were seen more quickly and received an initial electrocardiogram more quickly than women. Among the subgroup diagnosed with acute myocardial ischemia, men were more likely to be admitted to an intensive care unit.[12]

A 1993 study by Dellborg and Swedberg[13] reported a sex difference in pharmacologic treatment of heart disease as well. They retrospectively examined the records of more than 1500 patients with acute myocardial infarctions admitted between 1989 and 1991 to the coronary care unit at a university hospital in Sweden. They found that women were less likely than men to receive infarct size—limiting drug therapy (as well as coronary angiography) during their hospital stay, after correcting for diabetes, age, symptoms, and prehospital delay.

RACE AND THE TREATMENT OF HEART DISEASE

The story is much the same regarding race and heart disease treatment. Numerous studies conducted in the 1980s and early 1990s reported that major procedures for diagnosing and treating coronary heart disease were used less frequently for blacks than whites.[14] Ayanian et al[15] disclosed further evidence of how widespread the differences are between heart disease care for whites and blacks. They retrospectively examined the treatment of more than 27,000 Medicare enrollees between the ages of 65 and 74 who were treated for coronary heart disease in 1987 at 1429 U.S. acute care hospitals that provided coronary angiography. Because these patients had Medicare A, were of the same age, and had already been examined by angiography by a heart specialist at an acute care hospital, many of the explanations suggested in prior studies to explain the difference in treatment were eliminated. Yet the study found that whites were far more likely to receive revascularization than were blacks, that men were far more likely to receive revascularization than were women, and that at the intersection of race and sex, white men were most likely, and black women were least likely, to receive revascularization. The likelihood of revascularization treatment following angiography was 57% for white men, 50% for white women, 40% for black men, and 34% for black women.

A second study published in 1993 added further evidence of race bias in treatment for heart disease. Whittle et al[16] examined the treatment between 1987 and 1991 of 822,930 coronary heart disease patients at U.S. Veterans Affairs (VA) hospitals. By using VA patients, the study eliminated any consideration of ability to pay—all VA patients receive free care. It also eliminated any incentive among the physicians to recommend unnecessary treatment—VA physicians are usually salaried. To avoid extraneous factors, it eliminated from consideration those patients diagnosed with cancer, renal failure, cirrhosis, drug or alcohol abuse, HIV-related disease, or diabetes.[17] In every diagnostic category, whites underwent the procedures more often than blacks. Overall, whites were 50% more likely than blacks to undergo angioplasty and 122% more likely to undergo coronary bypass surgery.[18]

A 1994 study by McBean and Gornick[19] examined the records of all Medicare hospital discharges for the years 1986 and 1992. The study found that black patients were far less likely than white patients to receive cardiac catheterization, coronary angioplasty, coronary artery bypass graft, and carotid endarterectomy.

SOURCES OF DISPARATE TREATMENT

Authors have been loath to conclude that gender and racial physician bias explained differential treatment. A number of these studies speculated that noted differences in treatment resulted from differences in insurance coverage, lack of access to specialists, communications barriers, differences in socioeconomic groupings, lack of access to health care, timing of patient visits, lack of patient cooperation, patient attitudes regarding invasive procedures, noncoronary patient health problems, or patient substance abuse.[20] Schulman et al[21] mention other possible explanations for their findings as well, but their results inescapably establish that race and gender attitudes of treating physicians significantly affect the treatment of heart disease.

Most attitudes about race and gender are unconscious outgrowths of social history and of familiar mental processes elucidated by cognitive psychology. In his path-breaking article, "The Id, the Ego, and Equal Protection: Reckoning with Unconscious Racism,"[22] Charles R. Lawrence III explored the multiple sources of unintentional racism and offered this observation: "[Racism] is part of our common historical experience and . . . culture. It arises from the assumptions we have learned to make about the world, ourselves, and others as well as from the patterns of our fundamental social activities."[23] The Schulman study provides evidence of race and gender stereotyping that is likely not intentional, but that does produce racially and sexually disparate treatment.

How do such disparities come about? The Schulman study not only requested treatment recommendations but also inquired about physicians' perceptions of the actor-patients' personal characteristics. The results showed that physicians regarded the black patients as more hostile, less self-controlled, less knowledgeable, less independent, and less likely to comply with treatment than the white patients. Doctors assessed the female patients as being less intelligent, less self-controlled, and more likely to overreport symptoms than the male patients. Physicians assessing white male patients as compared to black female patients saw white men as more friendly, more intelligent, more self-controlled, more communicative, more independent, and happier than the black women.[24]

These findings are consistent with surveys of white attitudes about blacks generally. A 1990 study by Smith[25] found that when whites were asked to compare whites and blacks generally, blacks were rated as less intelligent, less hard-working, less patriotic, and more violent than whites. The Schulman results strongly suggest a link between the stereotyping that permits physicians to view actors reading lines in terms of commonly attributed race and gender differences and the physicians' treatment recommendations, which favor white men while disfavoring blacks and women, and especially black women.

THE LAW AND DISCRIMINATION

Recent jurisprudence has emphasized proof of intentional discrimination as a predicate for corrective remedies.[26] It can be argued that, even absent specific intent, unreasonable carelessness with regard to disparate outcomes should be sufficiently blameworthy to be culpable.[27] American antidiscrimination law also addresses behavior that disparately impacts racial and sexual groups even though there is no provable racist or sexist motive. Both the Congress in the Civil Rights Acts of 1964 and 1991[28] and the Supreme Court in deciding cases under these statutes have expressed that, at least in the field of employment discrimination law, good faith is not a defense to discriminatory decision making; concern must be directed to the consequences of decisions, rather than simply to their intent.[29]

Which strand of antidiscrimination law should inform medical response to the Schulman study and its predecessors? If the goal were to identify and punish wrongdoers, or to impose legal remedies potentially burdening individuals deemed culpable, attention would focus on whether a given actor *intended* to treat racial and gender groups differently. However, in the context of medical practice, the issue is not so much finding someone to blame as it is rectifying unjustified differences in treatment. Race and gender attitudes of physicians can affect the treatment of heart disease in ways that may harm blacks and women.[30] That is the problem demanding attention.

NONMEDICAL ANALOGUES

Studies of other areas of American life have documented a race and gender hierarchy of treatment, with white men at the top and black women at the bottom. Ian Ayres,[31] an economist on the law faculty at Yale University, published a study in 1991 demonstrating that the price demanded for new cars in Chicago varied substantially according to the buyer's race and sex. In a test of 90 new car dealers using 180 trained testing teams, the study found that white men were offered new cars at an average price of $362 over dealer cost, while white women were offered the same cars at $504 over dealer cost, black men at $783 over dealer cost, and black women at $1237 over dealer cost.[32]

Ayres estimated the cost to black Americans of retail price discrimination in new car sales as $150,000,000 annually. The cost of the differentials in heart disease treatment would be harder to calculate, but the enormity is clear. The Schulman study showed that black women are harmed more than others. In part, this injury arises because black women suffer unfavorable disparities in treatment on the basis of both race and gender. But analysis based on one discrimination plus the other, considered separately, fails to capture the unique situation of those who are multiply burdened. Kim Crenshaw,[33] a critical race theorist at Columbia Law School, points out that discussion of sex discrimination often implicitly assumes that women are white, while appraisals of race discrimination often focus on black men. Such assumptions have the effect of "limiting the inquiry to the experiences of otherwise-privileged members of the group," thereby missing the reality that "the intersectional experience is greater than the sum of racism and sexism."

The findings of Schulman et al[1] stain the record of the medical profession. Changing medical practice to ameliorate the problem of racially and sexually disparate treatment will require special will, knowledge, and creativity. A vital first step is coming to terms with the compelling reality of the data. A second is to forge a determined commitment that where race and gender differences in treatment are rooted in stereotype rather than in symptom, they have no place in medical practice. Essential also is a recognition that precisely because the problem is not conscious, rectification necessarily involves developing new awareness that stereotypes do affect the judgments and perceptions of even the most well-intentioned people. Elimination of biases requires rigorous retraining of judgments and perpetual vigilance.

ABOUT THE AUTHORS

David Benjamin Oppenheimer, JD, is Professor of Law at Golden Gate University School of Law, San Francisco, California.

Marjorie M. Shultz, JD, is Professor of Law at the Boalt Hall School of Law at the University of California, Berkeley.

REFERENCES

1. Schulman K, Berlin J, Harless W, et al. The effect of race and sex on physicians' recommendations for cardiac catheterization. *N Engl J Med* 1999;340(8):618–626.

2. *See e.g.,* Abraham Verghese, *Showing Doctors Their Biases,* NY Times, March 1, 1999, at A2 1.

3. This article focuses on cardiac care. However, race and gender disparities in other aspects of medical care have also been documented. *See e.g.,* Kahn KL, et al. Health care for black and poor hospitalized Medicare patients. *JAMA* 1994;271(15): 1169–73; Hogue CJ, Hargraves, MA. Class, race, and infant mortality in the United States. *Am J Public Health* 1993;83(1):9–12; Amason WB. Directed donation: The relevance of race. *Hastings Cent Rep* 1991;23(6):13–19.

4. Schulman at 622–623.

5. Statistical Abstract of the United States 1998, Table 138 (Deaths and Death Rates, by Selected Causes: 1990 to 1996).

6. *Id.* at Table 145 (Death Rates From Heart Disease, by Sex and Age: 1980 to 1995).

7. *Id.* at Table 140 (Deaths, by Selected Causes and Selected Characteristics: 1995).

8. Tobin J, Wassertheil-Smoller S, Wexler J, et al. Sex bias in considering coronary bypass surgery. *Ann Intern Med* 1987;107:19–25.

9. *Id.* at 21–22 and Table 4.

10. Ayanian J, Epstein A. Differences in the use of procedures between women and men hospitalized for coronary heart disease. *N Engl J Med* 1991;325(4):221–225.

11. Heston T, Lewis L. Gender bias in the evaluation and management of acute nontraumatic chest pain. *Family Practice Research Journal* 1992;12(4):383–389.

12. *Id.* at 386–387.

13. Dellborg M, Swedberg K. Acute myocardial infarction: Difference in the treatment between men and women. *Quality Assurance in Health Care* 1993;5(3):261–265.

14. Eleven such studies are cited in Ayanian J, Udvarhelyi S, Gatsonis C, et al. Racial differences in the use of revascularization procedures after coronary angiography. *JAMA* 1993;269(20):2642–2646, at 2646 notes 1–11.

15. *Id.*
16. Whittle J, et al. Racial differences in the use of invasive cardiovascular procedures in the Department of Veterans Affairs medical system. *N Engl J Med* 1993;329(9):621–627. But see FN 13 in Schulman; Keil, Sutherland, et al. ("the black-white mortality rate ratios were not statistically significant, and the major risk factors for mortality from coronary disease were similar in blacks and whites").
17. *Id.* at 622.
18. *Id.* at 623, 625 Table 3.
19. McBean AM, Gornick M. Differences by race in the rates of procedures performed in hospitals for Medicare beneficiaries. *Health Care Financing Review* 1994;15(4):77–81.
20. *See, e.g.,* sources cited in Schulman at 618.
21. Schulman at 624.
22. 39 STAN. L. REV. 317 (1987). *See, generally,* Linda Krieger, The Content of Our Categories: A Cognitive Bias Approach to Discrimination and Equal Employment Opportunity, 47 STAN. L. REV. 1161.
23. Lawrence at 330.
24. Schulman at 623, Table 3.
25. Tom W. Smith. Ethnic Images, General Social Survey Topical Report No. 19, National Opinion Research Center 1990 at 9, Table 1.
26. *See, e.g.,* City of Richmond v. J.A. Croson Co., 488 U.S. 469 (1989).
27. *See* David Benjamin Oppenheimer, Negligent Discrimination, 141 U. PENN. L.REV. 899 (1993).
28. 42 U. S.C. Section 2000e-2(k).
29. Griggs v. Duke Power Co., 401 U.S. 424 (1971).
30. Logic suggests that analogous disparities may affect other races as well, but since the studies have focused on blacks, this article discussed the issue in terms of black and white.
31. Ian Ayres, Fair Driving: Gender and Race Discrimination in Retail Car Negotiations, 104 HARVARD LAW REVIEW 817 (1991).
32. *Id.* at 828, Table 1.
33. Kimberle Crenshaw, Demarginalizing the Intersection of Race and Sex: A Black Feminist Critique of Antidiscrimination Doctrine, Feminist Theory and Antiracist Politics, 1989 UNIV. OF CHICAGO LEGAL FORUM 139.

ARTICLE 3

WRITING A NEW NATIONAL PRESCRIPTION FOR WOMEN'S HEALTH IN THE 21ST CENTURY

Susan J. Blumenthal

Over the past century, American society has witnessed dramatic changes in women's lives. Since 1960, the proportion of women participating in the labor force has risen by more than 50 percent.[1] Today, women over the age of 18 make up 45 percent of the total labor force.[2] Women also have made remarkable advances in achieving a higher education. For the first time in history, there are more women than men pursuing either college or graduate degrees.[3] Women are also an important force in political decision making. They vote in greater proportion than men in federal, state, and local elections and in recent decades have made significant gains in elected offices and political appointments at the federal, state, and local levels.[3] Women are also living longer than ever before. Government-sponsored public health interventions have increased the life span of women by more than 30 years since the beginning of the 20th century.[4]

With women's changing status in the United States, increased national attention has been focused on the longstanding inequities they have faced in economic and occupational opportunities.[5] For example, women continue to earn an average of 76 cents for every dollar men earn,[6] and remain disproportionately clustered in low-wage, low-status occupations that offer no health care coverage or other benefits.[7] Women are more likely to be poor, especially if they are elderly or heads of single-parent households.[3,8]

There are also many disparities in the health status of men and women. Although women live longer than men, they face higher rates of chronic and disabling conditions.[9] Even discounting reproductive health problems, women report 25 percent more days in which their activities are limited by health problems than do men.[10] They are also bedridden 35 percent more days per year than men due to infectious or parasitic diseases, respiratory ailments, injuries, digestive system problems, and other acute conditions.[9] Women are more likely than men to suffer the negative health consequences of sexual harassment, discrimination in the workplace, and domestic violence.[11,12] In part because of biologic and environmental factors, women also face health problems associated with aging, like osteoporosis, depression, and Alzheimer's disease, in greater numbers than do men.[7]

Since 1990, increased public and scientific attention have finally focused on the medical and health care disparities that have placed women's health at risk: (1) the failure to include women in clinical research trials; (2) the lack of attention to gender differences in biomedical and behavioral research; (3) a lack of funding for research on women's health concerns; (4) the lack of public and health care professional education in women's health issues; and (5) the dearth of women in senior scientific and health care professional positions in our nation's federal, academic, and health care organizations.

In 1993, the Clinton Administration made women's health a top national priority and established the country's first Deputy Assistant Secretary for Women's Health to direct the U.S. Public Health Services' (PHS) Office on Women's Health in the Department of Health and Human Services and to coordinate research, health care services, and public and health professional education and training. A new national prescription is being written to advance women's health with new initiatives that address not only current trends, but also reflect the lessons of the past and incorporate a vision for the future.

Medical research, health care professional education, and treatment approaches have historically been based on a "male" model. In spite of well-documented differences in the bodies and experiences of men and women, there has been minimal funding for women's health issues in the past, and many research studies have been conducted on men only—but with the results generalized to guide the diagnosis, treatment, and prevention of disease in women.[13]

For example, many of the medications that are prescribed for women today were tested almost exclusively in men, despite the fact that women are prescribed more medications and have more side effects and fatal drug reactions than do men.[9] Little, if any, attention was paid to how sex differences in body weight, cerebral blood flow, gastric emptying time, diet, and use of hormones may affect drug metabolization differently in women and men. Studies—even recent ones—on the prevention of chronic illnesses, like some types of cancer and heart disease, were conducted mostly in men.[9] Until quite recently, the training of physicians in women's health focused almost exclusively on women's reproductive health. Public education efforts on the prevention of diseases such as AIDS, heart disease, and cancer did not specifically target women as a special population.[13]

The legacies of these past disparities are numerous and far-reaching. For example, heart disease, which has long been considered a "man's" disease, is in fact the leading killer of American women.[14] Recent studies on gender and heart disease show that women received fewer high-tech diagnostic and treatment interventions than do men.[15] Women are typically ten years older and sicker at diagnosis, and are less likely than men to be alive one year following a heart attack.[16] Similarly, lung cancer affected mainly men in the 1930s; its incidence was rare in women. Research and intervention programs targeted men with smoking prevention and cessation efforts.[17] As a result of this omission of women from prevention efforts, women around the world became targets for gender-specific tobacco advertising campaigns.[18] As women's smoking increased, so did mortality from lung cancer and chronic obstructive pulmonary disease. In fact, in 1987, lung cancer surpassed breast cancer as the leading cause of cancer deaths in women.[4] Recent studies also suggest that nicotine is more addictive in women than men and tobacco is more carcinogenic in females as compared to males.

Efforts to prevent the spread of AIDS were until very recently directed almost solely at men. One result of this has been the dramatic rise in HIV infection among women; 24 percent of cases are in women. In 1998, AIDS became the third leading cause of death for women of reproductive age in the United States.[19] Prior to 1992, numerous AIDS-related conditions exclusive to or more prevalent in women were not included in the Centers for Disease Control and Prevention (CDC) surveillance criteria for the disease, so that national figures underestimated this devastating epidemic's full impact on women.[20]

The one issue which has been historically associated with women—reproductive health—has been the subject of controversy. Consequently, our nation lags behind Europe in such areas as contraceptive research and development, and the United States has the highest teen pregnancy rate in the Western world.[21] The United States also has one of the highest infant and maternal mortality rates among industrialized nations. It is estimated that by age 21, one in five Americans will have a sexually transmitted disease, putting young women at increased risk of compromising both their fertility and health.[22] One couple in eight experiences fertility problems.[23] The average American woman spends more than a third of her life beyond menopause, yet research on older women's health issues, including osteoporosis, hormone replacement therapy, and Alzheimer's disease in women, has only recently received national attention.

It has also been in recent years that we have launched a serious war on breast cancer. Since 1960, the deaths among women from this disease have outnumbered the fatalities in World Wars I and II, and the Korean, Vietnam, and Persian Gulf Wars combined. Since 1950, the lifetime risk of breast cancer has risen from 1 in 2024 to 1 in 825 women. In 1997, over 176,000 women will be diagnosed with the disease, and more than 43,500 women will die of it.[24]

While men and women have similar rates of mental illness (affecting 1 in 5 Americans every year), women suffer from some mental illnesses at higher rates than do men. For example, women are twice as likely as men to experience clinical depression.[25] Yet powerful social stigma associated with mental illness has prevented many women from receiving effective treatment. Only 1 in 4 will be properly diagnosed, and only a fourth of these women will be properly treated for their disease—despite the fact that 80 percent to 90 percent of women with depression could be effectively treated.[26] Domestic violence is a major public health problem in the United States. It is estimated that 3 million assaults on women occur each year (two-thirds are committed by someone known to the woman), and it is estimated that 22 percent of women in the United States are victims of sexual and physical abuse in their lifetimes.[27] Although domestic violence is the leading cause of female injury in the nation,[28] only 5 percent of cases are detected by physicians.[29]

The serious lack of attention to women's health concerns in the past has put their health in jeopardy. Despite living longer than men by 7 years, women have poorer health outcomes and suffer from more chronic disability from disease than do men.[7] The reasons for these disparities in the health care of women are rooted in the history of women's roles in this country. Gender role stereotyping and gender bias have contributed to the minimization of women's health concerns,[30] even though women make the majority of the health care decisions and are the caretakers in their multiple roles as consumers, mothers, wives, and health care providers. Additionally, there has been a dearth of senior women scientists and leaders in U.S. medical schools and health organizations. While as many as 45 percent of medical students today are female, women remain grossly underrepresented in senior health and research positions in our medical and academic institutions.[9,30,30a] Additionally, medical school training has been very slow to abandon the "male" model of disease only recently paying greater attention to sex differences in the causes, treatment, and prevention of illness.

A VISION FOR THE FUTURE OF WOMEN'S HEALTH

In the 21st century, improving women's health means addressing the social, medical and environmental issues that will shape the landscape for women's health in the new millennium.

One of the most notable features of the health landscape in the 21st century will be the increasing numbers of women, minorities, and elders in America.[9a] By the year 2030, half the nation's children will be minorities, and by the year 2060, it is estimated that half of all Americans will be minorities. Yet, there are shameful disparities in the health of women of color, including lower life expectancy and higher death rates from heart disease, diabetes, AIDS, and breast cancer. Therefore, it is critical to focus not only on gender but also on racial/ethnic differences in the etiology, treatment, and prevention of disease to achieve health equality for all in the 21st century.

Because we, as a nation, are aging, the health of older women is of critical importance. It is estimated that by 2030, 20 percent of the female population in the United States will be over the age of 65.[9a] To ensure that the 30 extra years of life that women have gained in this century are truly healthier ones, priority must be given to increasing research and improving health practices for the care of older women.

Socioeconomic status is also a critical variable affecting women's health.[4] In fact, it is one of the most powerful predictors of health status. Poverty has been called a carcinogenic. Women are increasingly heading single-parent families and many of them live in poverty.[3] While two-thirds of all mothers are in the paid workforce (more than twice as many as 20 years ago),[7] fifteen percent of working women have no health care coverage, and many more do not access the health care they need due to financial and other constraints.[3] In 1999, there are 44 million uninsured Americans, and their ranks are growing. Developing strategies to provide health insurance to those now lacking it, and improving access to health care are critical issues that we must address if we are to safeguard the health of women in the 21st century.

Since 1950, thanks to an unprecedented explosion in advances from medical research, we have learned more about health and disease than in the entire history of medicine. Researchers have found treatments and vaccines for many of the world's major infectious diseases that killed Americans at the beginning of the 20th century. In fact, vaccinations are one of the major public health achievements of this past century. Today, new, sophisticated surgical techniques and powerful drugs are combating many illnesses, including heart disease, pneumonia, diabetes, depression, and epilepsy.

Additionally, it is estimated that with advances in molecular biology the entire human genome will be mapped within the next 2 years.[31] The promise of these findings is the hope for new treatment strategies and, ultimately, a way of repairing genes so that specific diseases, like breast and ovarian cancer, may never develop in some people. However, these exciting genetic discoveries also raise a plethora of complex and challenging legal and ethical issues, such as genetic testing, which are coming faster than society's ability to craft solutions. Health care reform legislation, passed by Congress and signed by President Clinton in August 1996, contains provisions to prevent discrimination by insurers against people who may have a genetic predisposition to various diseases or disabilities.[32]

Advances in both medical technology and telemedicine are dramatically changing the practice of medicine. New imaging technologies have significantly enhanced our ability to diagnose disease. Sophisticated lasers and microsurgical instrumentation have revolutionized cardiovascular, reproductive, and eye surgery. Telemedicine is bringing the advances of medicine to those who cannot access it because of geographic and financial barriers.

Again, as technological advances are developed, we must ensure that they work for women—including consideration of patient confidentiality, potential side effects, adjustability of the technology to women's unique needs, and the ethical and legal issues that may surround their use.

BEHAVIOR AND HEALTH

Government-sponsored public health interventions and advances from medical research have extended the lifespan of women by 30 years in this century.[33] However, longer is not necessarily better for women. Today, women's health is being comprised by chronic diseases, including heart disease, cancer, stroke, chronic lung disease, and diabetes. Behavioral and lifestyle factors—smoking, alcohol and substance abuse, poor diet, lack of physical activity, risky sexual practices, motor vehicle crashes, and failure to obtain preventive care—contribute as much as 50 percent of the cause of all ten of the leading killers of women in this country including heart disease.[34] Yet, in America, only 1 percent of a trillion dollar health care budget is spent on population-based prevention.

Developing community and individual-based strategies to reduce these behavioral risk factors could decrease as many as half of the 2 million deaths that occur annually in men and women in this country. Chronic disability could be significantly reduced and health care costs could be substantially lowered.[34,35] Prevention also means ensuring that every child has a healthy start: every child is a wanted child; pregnant mothers receive prenatal care; children receive education, immunizations, and health insurance; and that they are protected from tobacco, alcohol, substance abuse, and violence. Additionally, mental health must become a top priority.

THE CHANGING FACE OF MEDICAL PRACTICE

In the 21st century, the changing face of women's health and the delivery of health care demand a reexamination of both how physicians are trained and how they practice medicine. Given the changing demographics of the nation's population and of health care providers, it is critical that future physicians be trained in both gender differences in health and illness, and in cultural competence in the diagnosis, treatment, and prevention of disease in both women and men.

Changes in health care financing have changed the shape of the health care service delivery system and the role of the academic health center. To survive in these challenging economic times, academic health centers must become centers of excellence in community care and public health, as well as continuing their critical roles in medical education and research. Additionally, because of their multiple missions, strategies are needed to protect academic health centers from the impact of the managed care environment and budget cuts.

A NEW NATIONAL PRESCRIPTION FOR IMPROVING WOMEN'S HEALTH

The Clinton Administration has placed a new national focus on women's health, which is brightening the prospects for a healthier future for all American women. It has meant putting the financial muscle behind women's health programs. The 1998 budget for the U.S. Department of Health and Human Services alone included over $4 billion for programs directly targeting the health of women, a 30 percent increase from 4 years before. Legislation has been passed requiring that women and minorities be included when appropriate in all clinical research, supported by the National Institutes of Health (NIH); the Food and Drug Administration (FDA) now recommends that women should be included in testing of new drugs and medical devices. A senior health post, the Deputy Assistant Secretary for Women's Health was established in 1993 to coordinate and stimulate research, services delivery and education programs across the agencies of the Department of Health and Human Services and to work with other public and private sector organizations to advance women's health. Also, a women's health focus has been woven into the fabric of all federal health agencies.

Research is being supported on a broad spectrum of conditions and diseases affecting women over the life span. For example, one major study supported by the NIH, focuses on the behavioral determinants of adolescent health examining factors that may increase vulnerability for or protect against the development of disease later in life.[35] The NIH's Women's Health Initiative,[37] the largest clinical research study ever conducted in the United States is examining the major causes of death and disability in postmenopausal women, and is evaluating the effects of diet, exercise, hormone replacement therapy, and behavioral interventions on the prevention of disease in older women. The results of this intensified research should yield important answers for addressing the health needs of women in the 21st century.

THE BATTLE AGAINST BREAST CANCER

Eradicating breast cancer has become a top health priority. Funding for breast cancer research and programs across the federal government has grown dramatically from approximately $90 million in 1990 to over $600 million in 1997. The spectrum of research to find the causes and cure and to improve the treatment of breast cancer have both broadened and intensified. For example, new studies are focusing on the possible connections between environmental factors in homes, workplaces, and in the atmosphere and the elevated rates of breast cancer incidence observed in certain areas of the country. New medications are being designed to slow the growth of cancerous tumors. The FDA has put potential life-saving experimental cancer-fighting medications on a fast track for agency review and approval.[38] As a result, hopefully women with cancer will have more treatment options. A National Action Plan, a public-private sector partnership that is catalyzing new initiatives in the fight against the disease, has been established and implemented.

Until a cure or method of preventing breast cancer is discovered, early detection remains today's front-line defense against this killer of women. Mammography is a lifesaving technology, decreasing death rates by 30 percent.[39] To improve the early detection of breast cancer, the Health Care Financing Administration (HCFA) developed an educational initiative to encourage older women to use Medicare's mammography screening benefit. Additionally, the CDC's Early Breast and Cervical Cancer Screening Program provides mammography and Pap tests to low income women.[40] Over 1 million screening tests have been performed in women (many of whom otherwise would not have received either screening mammography or Pap tests) since the program began.[40]

To improve the quality and safety of mammography, the Mammography Quality Standards Act was passed by Congress in 1992. The FDA has implemented a national certification program that requires that every mammography facility in the country meet stringent standards for equipment safety, personnel training, and timely reporting of results to women. FDA certification is now required for the operation of every mammography facility in the country.

However, despite these improvements, mammography is still a 40-year-old technology. According to studies, 3 out of 4 lesions detected by mammography are benign.[41] Additionally, research suggests that mammography misses 15 percent of cancerous lesions.[41,42] Other research reveals variability in the interpretation of mammograms by radiologists.[42] To improve the accuracy and reliability of mammography, an initiative was developed that harnessed imaging technologies from the intelligence, defense, and space communities used for target and missile recognition to improve the early detection of breast cancer. Several of these technologies are currently being tested at major medical centers today.

VIOLENCE AGAINST WOMEN

The Clinton Administration has also undertaken a massive multifaceted program to address the epidemic of physical and sexual violence against women. The National Advisory Council on Violence Against Women—a joint program of the Department of Health and Human Services and the Department of Justice—unites leaders from the health, justice, entertainment, and sports industries to work together to develop innovative strategies to combat this public health problem.

The Department of Health and Human Services has established a national domestic violence hotline (1-800-799-SAFE). New funds have been committed to combat violence, to develop prevention programs, and to implement training programs for police and health care professionals.

EDUCATION CAMPAIGNS

Prevention is a major focus, ensuring that national programs, whether to stop smoking or to promote a healthy diet or physical activity, target women's unique needs. Several initiatives target the health of girls. The Department of Health and Human Services' *Safe Passages* promotes a healthy transition from childhood through adolescence to adulthood, with strategies coordinated across health care, social service, and education agencies. The *Girl Power!* Program focuses on enhancing the health of girls, including initiatives to reduce the incidence of smoking among girls and adolescent women, who record the highest rates of smoking for all populations, to prevent substance abuse, and to foster healthy self-esteem.

A Federal Coordinating Committee on the Environment and Women's Health has been established to develop strategies to eliminate environmental health hazards from women's lives. One major focus has been the examination of the role of environmental estrogens (found in some pesticides and some natural plant products in our diet) in the development of diseases such as breast cancer.

REPRODUCTIVE HEALTH

Reproductive health remains a critical issue throughout the course of a woman's life. The U.S. Department of Health and Human Services is actively engaged at the cutting edge of efforts here as well, with initiatives including: 1) reducing the alarmingly high teenage and unintended pregnancy rates; 2) developing new and more effective means of contraception; 3) examining the causes and designing interventions for infertility; 4) preventing HIV/AIDS and other STDs; 5) reducing the transmission of HIV from mother to fetus; and 6) evaluating the alternatives to hysterectomy for the treatment of non-cancerous uterine conditions.

NATIONAL WOMEN'S HEALTH INFORMATION CENTER

To improve public education about women's health, a National Women's Health Information Center (NWHIC) has been established. Accessible both on-line (www.4woman.org) and through a toll-free telephone line (1-800-994-WOMAN), the NWHIC provides consumers, health professionals and researchers with free, state-of-the-art information on women's health produced by the federal government, and links them to up-to-the-minute information in the private sector as well.

IMPROVING HEALTH CARE PROFESSIONAL EDUCATION

To ensure that physicians are trained to address women's health concerns, a model women's health curriculum for medical school education has been designed and disseminated and a directory of residency and fellowship programs in women's health has been produced.

HEALTH CARE REFORM

To reap the benefits of recent medical advances women must have available health care coverage. However, in 1994, nearly 17 percent of all American women under age 65 had no health insurance,[4] and many women who were insured were not covered for early detection, prevention, maternity, or mental health services.[44] In 1998, there were 44 million uninsured Americans and their ranks are growing.

To contain spiraling health care costs—costs that reached $1 trillion in 1998—a managed care revolution has swept across the country. Over 55 million Americans—25 percent of our citizens—receive health care through some type of managed care program, up from 5 percent in 1980.[44]

Managed care has some distinct advantages for women; for example, these plans often place emphasis "up front" by providing low-cost premiums, low cost-sharing, prevention, screening, and early intervention programs. They are also more likely to provide family planning services than other types of plans. Research has found that women are more satisfied with the range of preventive and primary care services in managed care systems than in fee-for-service plans.[45] However, there are also constraints for women in some managed care environments—less choice of physicians, barriers to specialist care, and shorter hospital stays, on average, than in fee-for-service plans. Additionally, a backlash has been brewing against managed care and the industrialization of medicine.

If we are truly going to safeguard women's health, then as a nation we must ensure that every woman, man and child in the United States has health insurance, without pre-existing condition exclusion clauses, lifetime caps, or restrictions on the treatment of mental illness or on the availability of preventive health services.

THE GLOBALIZATION OF HEALTH

And finally, as we enter the new millenium, we must adopt a global approach when it comes to women's health. After all, with telecommunications and international travel and trade, our world is shrinking. However, the spread of infectious diseases like AIDS and tuberculosis and environmental issues such as the safety of our food and water supply and the spread of toxins, like tobacco and guns and the threat of bioterrorism, don't recognize state or national boundaries.

INSIGHTS INTO THE FUTURE

In the coming decades, American society will continue to confront changing demographics and shifts in occupational opportunities, economic trends, and social roles for both women and men. We must continue to work together across the public and private sectors to improve research, services, and education about women's health issues. In the 21st century, the results of our efforts will hopefully be better health, not only for this country's women, but for all Americans.

ABOUT THE AUTHOR

Susan J. Blumenthal, MD, MPA, serves as U.S. Assistant Surgeon General, Rear Admiral, and Senior Science Advisor in the U.S. Department of Health and Human Services (DHHS) and as Clinical Professor of Psychiatry at Georgetown School of Medicine. She was the country's first Deputy Assistant Secretary for Women's Health in the DHHS.

REFERENCES

1. Costello C, Stone A. *The American Woman 1994–1995: Where We Stand.* New York: WW Norton & Co, Inc., 1994.

2. *Working Women: A Chartbook.* Washington, DC: US Department of Labor, 1991.

3. Costello C, Krimgold B. *The American Woman 1996–1997: Where We Stand.* New York: WW Norton & Co, Inc, 1996.

4. Centers for Disease Control and Prevention. *Health, United States, 1998 with Socioeconomic Status and Health Chartbook.* Hyattsville, MD: US Department of Health and Human Services, 1998. DHHS Publication (PHS) 98–1232.

5. Reich R, Asip P, Brown A, et al. A solid investment, making full use of the nation's human capital. Recommendations of the Glass Ceiling Commission. Washington, DC: US Department of Labor, 1995.

6. *Current Population Survey: 1918–1994 Annual Averages.* Washington, DC: Bureau of the Census, 1994.

7. Reich R. Press briefing by Secretary of Labor Robert Reach and the Director of the Women's Bureau, Karen Nussbaum, at the Department of Labor. Washington, DC: The White House Office of the Press Secretary, 1995.

8. *1993 Handbook on Women Workers Trends and Issues.* Washington, DC: US Department of Labor, 1994.

9. *Report of the National Institutes of Health: Opportunities for Research on Women's Health.* Hunt Valley, MD: US Department of Health and Human Services, 1992.

9a. Day JC. Population projections of the United States by age, sex, race and Hispanic origin: 1995–2050. Washington, DC: US Bureau of the Census, Current Population Reports, 1996; 25–1130.

10. Verbrugge L. Pathways of health and death. In: Apple R, ed. *Women, Health and Medicine in America: A Historical Handbook.* New York: Garland Publishing, 1990.

11. Bachman R, Saltzman L. *National Crime Victimization Survey. Violence Against Women: Estimates from the Redesigned Survey.* Washington, DC: Office of Justice Programs, 1995.

12. Lenhart S. Mental health aspects of gender discrimination. Presented at the First Annual Congress on Women's Health. Washington, DC, June 3, 1993.

13. Healy B. *A New Prescription for Women's Health: Getting the Best Medical Care in a Man's World.* New York: Penguin Group, 1995.

14. *Heart and Stroke Facts. 1996 Statistical Supplement.* Dallas: American Heart Association, 1995.

15. Steingart RM, Packer M, Hamm P, et al. Sex differences in the management of coronary artery disease. Survival and Ventricular Enlargement Investigators. *New England Journal of Medicine* 1991;325(4):226–30.

16. Kannel WB, Wilson PW. Risk factors that attenuate the female coronary disease advantage. *Archives of Internal Medicine* 1995;155(1):57–61.

17. Royce JM, Corbett K, Sorensen G, Ockene J. Gender, social pressure, and smoking cessations: the Community Intervention Trial for Smoking Cessation (COMMIT) at baseline. *Social Science and Medicine* 1997;44(3):359–70.
18. World Health Organization. *Women Who Smoke Like Men Face the Same Risks as Men.* Geneva, Switzerland: WHO, 1997.
19. Centers for Disease Control and Prevention. Update: mortality attributable to HIV infection among persons aged 25–44 years—United States, 1994. *MMWR* 1996;45:121–124.
20. Centers for Disease Control and Prevention. Revised classification system for HIV infection and expanded surveillance case definition for AIDS among adolescents and adults. *MMWR* 1993;41(RR-17):1–19.
21. Spitz AM, Velebil P, Koonin LM, et al. Pregnancy, abortion, and birth rates among US adolescents—1980, 1985, and 1990. *JAMA* 1996;275(13):989–94.
22. Mastroianni L, Donaldson P, Kane T. *Developing New Contraception Obstacles and Opportunities.* Institute of Medicine Report. Washington, DC: National Academy Press, 1990.
23. Eck Menning B, Colston Wentz A, Carner C. *Insight into Infertility.* Washington, DC: Georgetown University, 1987.
24. *Breast Cancer Network.* Atlanta, GA: American Cancer Society, 1997.
25. Regier DA, Boyd JH, Burke JD, Jr., et al. One-month prevalence of mental disorders in the United States. Based on five Epidemiologic Catechumen Area sites. *Archives of General Psychiatry* 1988;45(11):977–86.
26. Blumenthal SJ. Women and Depression. *J. of Women's Health,* 1994;3:467–479.
27. Wilt S, Olson S. Prevalence of domestic violence in the United States. *Journal of the American Medical Women's Association* 1996;51(3):77–82.
28. Plichta S. The effects of woman abuse on health care utilization and health status: a literature review. *Women's Health Issues* 1992;2(3):154–163.
29. Abbott J, Johnson R, Koziol-McLain J, Lowenstein SR. Domestic violence against women. Incidence and prevalence in an emergency department population. *JAMA* 1995;273(22):1763–7.
30. Blumenthal S (Ed.). Towards a women's health research agenda. Washington, DC: Society for the Advancement of Women's Health Research, 1991.
30a. Association of American Medical Colleges. Women in US Academic Medicine Statistics, 1998–1999. Washington, DC (website aamc.org/wim).
31. Dietrich WF, Miller J, Steen R, et al. A comprehensive genetic map of the mouse genome. *Nature* 1996;380(6570):149–52. (Erratum appears in *Nature* 1996;381(6578):172.)
32. HR. 3103 Health Insurance Policy Portability and Accountability Act of 1996, Public Law 104–191.
33. Blumenthal S. A new national focus on women's health. In: RP E, Stuart S, eds. *The Women's Complete Handbook.* New York: Delacorte Press, 1995.
34. McGinnis JM, Foege WH. Actual causes of death in the United States. *JAMA* 1993;270(18):2207–12.

35. Blumenthal S, Mathews K, Weiss S (Eds.). New research frontiers on behavioral medicine. Proceedings of the National Conference. National Institutes of Health. Washington, DC, 1994.
36. National Institutes of Health. NIH Adolescent Health Study.
37. National Institutes of Health Women's Health Initiative Research Study.
38. U.S. Food and Drug Administration Center for Drug Evaluation and Research.
39. Shapiro S. The status of breast cancer screening: a quarter of a century of research. *World Journal of Surgery* 1989;13(1):9–18.
40. National Institute of Health Consensus Development Statement. Breast cancer screening for women ages 40–49, Statement 1103, 1997.
41. Fletcher SW, Black W, Harris R, Rimer BK, Shapiro S. Report of the International Workshop on Screening for Breast Cancer. *Journal of the National Cancer Institute* 1993;85(20):1644–56.
42. Beam CA, Layde PM, Sullivan DC. Variability in the interpretation of screening mammograms by US radiologists. Findings from a national sample. *Archives of Internal Medicine* 1996;156(2):209–13.
43. Gold R, Richards C. Securing American women's reproductive health. In: Costello C, Stone A, eds. *The American Woman 1994–1995: Where We Stand.* New York: WW Norton & Co, Inc, 1994.
44. *HMO-PPO Digest.* Kansas City, MO: Hoechst-Marion Roussel Inc, 1995.
45. Wyn R, Collins KS, Brown ER. Women and managed care: satisfaction with provider choice, access to care, plan costs and coverage. *Journal of the American Medical Women's Association* 1997;52(2):60–4.

NB: This article was adapted from Blumenthal, SJ. Healthy Women 2000 and Beyond: Writing a New National Prescription for Women's Health in *Healthy Women 2000: Insights into the Future of Women's Health.* A continuing education monograph. Medical Educations Resources, New York City, NY, 1997, 2–9.

HEALTH CONCERNS ACROSS A WOMAN'S LIFESPAN: THE COMMONWEALTH FUND 1998 SURVEY OF WOMEN'S HEALTH

*Karen Scott Collins, Cathy Schoen, Susan Joseph,
Lisa Duchon, Elizabeth Simantov,
and Michele Yellowitz*

OVERVIEW OF SURVEY FINDINGS

Overall, *The Commonwealth Fund 1998 Survey of Women's Health* finds a mixed story with respect to progress in health care over the past five years. Women today are more knowledgeable about some health issues and are taking steps to stay healthy. Progress has been uneven across various aspects of health care, however, and significant gaps remain in access to essential care. Violence persists as a significant factor in the lives of women—lifetime rates of violent or abusive events are disturbingly high. Strikingly, more women are uninsured today than five years ago—despite an improved economy—creating access barriers to health care.

The survey findings are based on telephone interviews with 2,850 women and 1,500 men, including oversamples of African American, Hispanic, and Asian American women. Conducted by Louis Harris and Associates, Inc., from May through November 1998, the interviews provide a current look at access to care, health knowledge, health-related behaviors, violence, depression, use of hormone replacement therapy, and informal caregiving roles. The 1998 survey generated findings in several major areas, including:

Preventive Care.   Although breast and cervical cancer screening are central health care procedures, overall receipt of these clinical preventive services has changed little since 1993—despite the potential for increased emphasis on prevention through the growth of managed care. Notably, lower-income and less-educated women appear less likely than higher-income, more educated women to receive regular preventive services and counseling on choices of hormone replacement therapy. In addition, smoking rates among women have remained at 1993 levels, with rates notably higher among lower-income women.

The good news is that mammography rates are moving in the right direction: among women age 50 and older, they have increased from 55 to 61 percent.

Women's exercise rates are also up, and familiarity with osteoporosis and use of calcium supplements has increased since 1993. This progress, however, has been greatest among upper-income and college-educated women, and lower-income women lag far behind.

Violence and Abuse.   The 1998 survey found disturbingly high rates of violence and abuse rates among women, crossing income, ethnic, and geographic lines. Nearly two of five women (39%) report violence or abuse in their lifetime. Contrasts of health status among those with any experiences of violence and abuse reveal their corrosive effects, including significantly worse physical and mental health status across an array of indicators. Gaps in the extent of physician counseling on violence and abuse indicate that physicians are missing opportunities to discuss such sensitive topics. In general, the survey finds low rates of physician counseling across an array of topics related to women's health.

Caregiving.   Nine percent, or more than nine million women, are currently caring for a sick or disabled family member, often devoting 20 hours or more to provide supportive care. More needs to be done to support this important social role. Today, time burdens and lack of paid help weigh especially heavily on women with below-average family incomes.

Health and Economic Security.   The tie between overall health and economic security is telling. Good health and access to health care often depend on having a good job, while keeping a job depends on staying healthy. Poor health or family caregiving responsibilities can reduce opportunities to work, adding to economic stress. Half of all non-working women with incomes of $16,000 or less have a disability limiting their capacity to work or are caring for a sick or disabled child, spouse, parent, or other family member.

Insurance Status and Access to Care.   Despite a robust economy in 1998, more women are uninsured today than in 1993. Uninsured rates are up significantly among women with below-average incomes, perhaps reflecting welfare reform as well as continued erosion of employer-sponsored coverage. Although the vast majority of uninsured women were working full time or married to a full-time worker, half of women with family incomes of $16,000 or less— the bottom fourth of the income distribution of working age women—were uninsured when surveyed or had spent a time uninsured in 1998. Lack of insurance greatly increases the likelihood that lower-income and minority women will not obtain needed health care and will fail to receive regular preventive care.

The survey findings point to the challenge ahead in supporting women's efforts to lead healthy, productive lives while meeting family health concerns. Taking steps forward in women's health is likely to require the concerted efforts of health researchers, professionals, policymakers, and women as patients and advocates to ensure greater progress in the future.

SURVEY FINDINGS

No Major Improvements Made in Preventive Care

Although improving breast and cervical cancer screening rates have been central goals for women's health care over the past five years, overall receipt of clinical preventive services has changed little from 1993 to 1998. Mammography rates for women age 50 and older, however, did increase from 55 to 61 percent.

- **One-half to two-thirds of women received preventive care in the past year.** For example, 61 percent of women received a physical exam, 66 percent received a clinical breast exam, 64 percent received a Pap test, and 55 percent received a blood cholesterol test in the past year. These rates are virtually the same as those for 1993.
- **Receipt of preventive care was lowest among Asian American women.** Less than half of Asian American women had received the preventive services asked about in the survey. For Hispanic women, rates for physical exams, blood cholesterol tests, and clinical breast exams were below those for white and African American women: one of two Hispanic women had received these services in the past year. For women age 50 and older, mammography rates varied little among white, African American, or Hispanic women surveyed.
- **Higher use of preventive services was associated with increasing income and educational levels.**
- **African American and Hispanic women appear to have gained ground in breast cancer screening.** Among African American women age 50 and older, mammography rates increased from 37 percent in 1993 to 66 percent in 1998; for Hispanic women, they rose from 54 to 64 percent.[1]
- **Uninsured women remained at greatest risk for not receiving preventive care.** Nearly one of three women without health insurance (30%) did not receive preventive care in the past year, compared with one of seven insured women.

Managed Care is Widespread but Not Yet Delivering Fully on Improved Access to Primary and Preventive Care

As of 1998, three of four (76%) insured women under age 65 were in a health maintenance organization (HMO) or preferred provider organization (PPO), or in a health plan having some type of managed care feature, such as a primary care referral

---

[1]The trend for African American women is consistent with recent National Health Interview Survey analysis findings that the greatest increase in mammography screening from 1991 to 1994 occurred among low-income, African American women. D. Makuc et al., "Low Income, Race, and the Use of Mammography," *Health Services Research* 34 (April 1999):part II, pp. 229–239.

requirement for specialist services.[2] Enrollment in managed care is now high across all income groups and among women of all racial and ethnic backgrounds.

The survey finds that managed care has not yet yielded significant improvements in women's access to care or preventive care. Compared with women who had traditional fee-for-service (FFS) coverage, women in managed care were more likely to receive some but not all preventive care. They were more likely to report having a regular source of care. Comparisons of the care experiences of women ages 18 to 64 in managed care versus FFS indicated similar levels of access difficulties and low levels of physician counseling on a range of health topics.

- **Managed care rates are now high among all insured women under age 65.**
- **Reflecting the spread of managed care, women frequently needed the permission of their primary care physician before seeing a specialist or an obstetrician-gynecologist (OB-GYN).**
- **By some, but not all, measures, managed care plans have been more successful than FFS plans in making sure women receive regular preventive care.**
- **Women in managed care were more likely to identify a particular doctor as their regular source of care.**
- **Health plans have been making some outreach efforts to ensure preventive care services.**
- **Regardless of insurance type, insured women reported similar rates of health care access problems and ratings of physician care.**

Women Report Improvements in Knowledge About Selected Health Conditions and Behaviors

In the past five years, federal agencies and state and local groups concerned with women's health have mounted public campaigns to increase women's awareness of the benefits of behaviors likely to enhance long-term health. The survey finds evidence of pay-off for some—but not all—of these public health campaigns.

Contrasts of the 1993 and 1998 surveys find a sharp increase in the proportion of women who are aware of osteoporosis and that women are taking the steps to prevent health problems later in life, including taking calcium supplements. The percentage of women exercising three or more times per week has also risen since 1993, although this activity is concentrated among higher-income women. Smoking rates among women, however, have remained high and are virtually unchanged since 1993.

---

[2]Coverage was classified as managed care for insured women who answered yes to at least one of three questions: Is your health plan an HMO or a PPO? Does your health plan require you to get a referral from your primary care physician in order to receive specialty care? Does your plan require you to get a referral from your primary care physician in order to visit an OB-GYN (obstetrician-gynecologist)?

Missed Opportunities for Physician Counseling

The role of physicians and other health providers in influencing their patients' health behaviors through counseling is an important component of prevention. Physician counseling that could promote health in most areas is limited. Although one-half of women had received counseling on diet and exercise in the past year, other important health issues and behaviors were less frequently discussed.

Violence and Abuse Rates During Women's Lifetimes Remain High, with Negative Long-Term Health Effects

The survey finds that many American women experience violence or abuse in their lifetimes. Nearly two of five women (39%) had at some point been physically or sexually assaulted or abused, or had been a victim of domestic violence. While low-income women were at somewhat higher risk, violence cut across economic, racial, and other demographic characteristics. Comparisons of health status indicators for those who did and did not report violence or abuse strongly suggest that violence and abuse have lasting negative effects on women's physical and psychological well-being. Women with any type of violence or abuse in their history were significantly more likely to report they were in fair or poor health and nearly twice as likely to have depressive symptoms or to have been diagnosed with depression or anxiety.

- **Lifetime exposure to violence is high among women.** Two of five women reported having experienced at least one type of abuse or violence in their lifetime, including physical or sexual abuse as a child, rape or assault, or domestic violence.
- **Lifetime exposure to domestic abuse is disturbingly high, affecting nearly one-third of all women.**[3]
- **One of five women said she had been raped or assaulted in her lifetime.**
- **Childhood abuse affected one of six women.**
- **Women with a history of childhood abuse were at higher risk of experiencing domestic violence later in life.**
- **Abused women were at high risk for psychological problems.**
- **Abused women also had more physical health problems.**
- **One of three women with a history of violence or abuse faced problems with access to health care in the past year.**
- **While three-quarters of women exposed to domestic abuse had discussed these incidents with a friend or relative, only 29 percent had discussed them with a physician or health care professional.**

[3]Domestic violence is defined in the survey as having responded yes to any of the following items: spouse or boyfriend has ever thrown something at you; pushed, grabbed, shoved, or slapped you; kicked, bit, or hit you with a fist or some other object; beaten you up; choked you; forced you to have sex against your will.

- **The health care system may not be adequately responding to abused women's needs for referrals and support.**

Many Women at Risk for High Depressive Symptoms

Consistent with many studies, the survey finds that women are more likely than men to have problems with depression and anxiety. Two of five women reported having a high level of depressive symptoms in the past week.[4] Several types of circumstances put women at higher risk for depressive symptoms, including having low incomes and economic stress, caregiving responsibilities, lack of social support, and physical illness or disability. A history of violence or abuse also markedly diminished psychological well-being as measured by depressive symptoms or a diagnosis of depression. In addition, the survey finds that women may be receiving only limited help for their problems.

- **Women were more likely than men to report feeling depressed in the past week.**
- **Younger women were more likely to have depressive symptoms.**
- **African American women reported somewhat higher levels of depressive symptoms.**
- **More than one-half of women under economic stress had high levels of depressive symptoms.**
- **Single women with children experienced higher rates of depressive symptoms.**
- **Two-thirds of women without social support had high levels of depressive symptoms.**
- **Women who had general health problems were also more likely to have high depressive symptoms.**
- **Women with high depressive symptoms reported more health care access problems.**

Women's Caregiving Roles

Women, more than men, fill the role of caring for sick or disabled relatives—in addition to fulfilling work and child-rearing responsibilities. Caregiving responsibilities appear to fall on women uniformly, regardless of income, race, or even marital

---

[4]The depression scale was based on a series of questions concerning how frequently the respondent felt a certain way in the previous week. Responses to statements such as "I felt depressed," "My sleep was restless," "I had crying spells," "I enjoyed life," "I felt sad," or "I felt that people disliked me" were summed up for a total score on depression. Three categories of depression were created that were based on the distribution of scores for all respondents: Low (0–2), Moderate (3–5), and High (6–18).

status. The extent of their responsibilities, however, does vary with family resources. In addition, women providing this care often have their own health problems.

- **Overall, 6 percent of adults surveyed said they were caring for a sick or disabled relative.** In 1998, 9 percent of women were caring for a sick family member, compared with 4 percent of men. Women with annual incomes below the national median of $35,000 were as likely as women above the median to be caregivers (11% vs. 9%).
- **Most women caregivers were in their prime years of employment and child rearing.** Caregiving responsibilities may take a particular toll on women who are already balancing work and family demands. Women of all ages were providing caregiving to sick or disabled family members, although a somewhat higher percentage of women ages 45 to 64 (13%) were fulfilling a caregiving role than were women ages 18 to 29 (7%), 30 to 44 (10%) and 65 and older (7%).
- **Although women in different income groups were equally likely to fulfill a caregiving role, lower-income women faced a greater time commitment and economic toll.** Heavy time burdens are associated with caregiving. Forty-three percent of all women with caregiving responsibilities in 1998 were providing 20 hours or more of care per week. Time burdens were most intense for lower-income women: 52 percent of women with incomes below $35,000 were providing 20 hours or more of care per week, compared with 29 percent of women with incomes above $35,000.
- **The demands of caregiving may take a toll on caregivers' health and well-being.** Often the caregiver herself is in need of care. More than half (54%) of women caregivers had one or more chronic health conditions, compared with two-fifths (41%) of other women. Caregivers also reported higher rates of mental health concerns: 51 percent reported high depressive symptoms—a far higher proportion than the 38 percent of women not currently caring for sick or disabled relatives who reported these symptoms.
- **Women caregivers were also twice as likely to report problems getting the health care they need for themselves.** Compared with other women, women who were caring for sick or disabled family members were twice as likely not to receive needed care (16% vs. 8%) and not to fill a prescription because of cost (26% vs. 13%). One of four caregivers also reported difficulty getting needed care, compared with one-sixth of other women (16%).

The Link Between Health and Economic Security for Working-Age Women

Overall, a strong, negative pattern emerges when comparing women's health status across income groups: the lower a woman's family income, the greater her risk for physical and mental health problems. Among working-age women (ages 18–64), those with family incomes in the bottom half of the income distribution are significantly more likely than higher-income women to have a chronic health condition or disability, depressive symptoms, a diagnosis of depression, and to be in generally poor health.[5]

At the same time, lower-income women have the most difficulty gaining access to needed health care. Women in the bottom fourth of the household income distribution ($16,000 or less) are three times more likely to experience problems getting care when needed and not to have a regular doctor than are women with incomes in the top quarter of the income distribution (above $50,000).

- **Low-income women were at particularly high risk for chronic health problems.** Based on reports of physician diagnoses of four health conditions—hypertension, heart disease, diabetes, and arthritis—low-income women were at notably greater risk for chronic disease than higher-income women. Two of five women ages 18 to 64 with incomes of $16,000 or less reported a physician diagnosis of at least one of these four chronic diseases, or of having cancer in the past five years—a rate 50 percent higher than that for women with incomes above $50,000 (42% vs. 27%).
- **Low-income women were also at high risk for having a disability that limited their participation in routine activities.** Among women ages 18 to 64, one of four (25%) with incomes of $16,000 or less had a disability or handicap preventing them from participating fully in school, work, or other activities, compared with 14 percent of all women and 9 percent of women with incomes above $50,000. This steep gradient of disability and income indicates the negative impact that restrictions on work can have on family standards of living.
- **As with physical health indicators, low-income women were at higher risk for having depressive symptoms and a diagnosis of depression or anxiety.** More than half of low-income women ages 18 to 64 (55%) exhibited high levels of depressive symptoms, compared with 30 percent of women with incomes above $50,000. Similarly, low-income women were more than twice as likely to report a physician diagnosis of depression or anxiety than were upper-income women (26% vs. 12%).
- **Reflecting their generally lower incomes, African American, Hispanic, and Asian American women were also at relatively high risk for health problems.** One of four minority women ages 18 to 64—including 21 percent of African American, 28 percent of Hispanic, and 23 percent of Asian American women—rated her health as fair or poor, compared with 12 percent of white women. Although some measures of chronic disease rates are fairly

---

[5]This section of the report focuses on working-age women (18–64) to control for the impact of aging on declining health and income. However, the negative relationship of income and health persists among women age 65 and older as well.

consistent across racial groups, African American women were more likely to report a physician diagnosis in the past 5 years of hypertension or diabetes than did women in other racial or ethnic groups.

- **Lower-income women were more likely to have problems getting health care when needed and to lack basic primary care.**
- **Health care access barriers were notable for minority women under age 65 across an array of indicators.**

An Increasing Proportion of Low- and Modest-Income Working-Age Women are Uninsured

Health insurance is critical to facilitate access to health care and protect the financial security of women and their families. Among all women ages 18 to 64, nearly one of four is either uninsured (18%) or spent a time without health insurance in the past year (8%). Despite a strong economy, uninsured rates for 1998 have increased since 1993, with the steepest rises concentrated among lower-income and Hispanic women.

Analysis of women's health care experiences by insurance status found that gaps in coverage, as well as being uninsured, contributes to access difficulties and barriers to needed care. Women who are insured now but have had a gap in coverage in the past year encounter difficulties in getting needed health care at rates remarkably similar to those for currently uninsured women.

- **Uninsured rates increased in the past five years, particularly for low- and modest-income women.** In 1998, 18 percent of women ages 18 to 64 were uninsured when surveyed. The proportion of working-age women without insurance was up from the rate of 14 percent reported in 1993, despite five years of economic growth. Increases were concentrated among low- and modest wage women. As of 1998, 35 percent of women under age 65 with incomes of $16,000 or less were uninsured—up from 29 percent in 1993. A similar increase—from 15 percent in 1993 to 21 percent in 1998—occurred for women with incomes from $16,001 to $35,000.
- **The largest increases in uninsured rates occurred among Hispanic women under age 65.** In 1998, two of five (42%) Hispanic women ages 18 to 64 were uninsured, compared with one of three (33%) in 1993. Hispanic women were three times as likely to be uninsured as white women (13%); African American (23%) and Asian American (25%) women were nearly twice as likely to be uninsured as white women.
- **Erosion of job-based health insurance accounted for some of the increase in the uninsured.** Working-age women were heavily dependent on employer-based health insurance coverage, including coverage through their husbands' jobs. By 1998, 64 percent of women ages 18 to 64 reported being insured through an employer, a decline from 66 percent in 1993. In total, 34 percent of working-age women reported having insurance through their own

employer and 21 percent through their spouse's employer; 9 percent had double coverage through both their jobs and their husbands' jobs—down from 15 percent in 1993.

- **Including those who had a gap in health insurance coverage, one of four women were uninsured for a time during 1998. A significant majority of women who were uninsured at some point in that year were full-time workers or married to full-time workers and living on below-median incomes.** In addition to the 18 percent who were uninsured when surveyed, 8 percent of women ages 18 to 64 reported a time when they did not have insurance during the past year—bringing to 26 percent the total proportion of working-age women who were uninsured for a time during 1998. Eight of 10 women who were uninsured for a period in 1998 worked or were married to a worker: most were in full-time working families (68%). Seven of 10 women who had a time uninsured (70%) were living on incomes of $16,000 or less (39%) or from $16,001 to $35,000 (31%).

- **The risk of being uninsured for a period of time in the past year was greatest among women in the bottom half of the income distribution.** Nearly half (48%) of women ages 18 to 64 with incomes of $16,000 or less had been uninsured for a time, as had one-third of women with incomes from $16,001 to $35,000.

- **Being uninsured for a period of time in the past year steeply increased the risk of going without needed health care or having difficulties obtaining health care when needed.** Currently uninsured women ages 18 to 64 were three times more likely than women who had been continuously insured to have gone without needed care during the year (22% vs. 6%) or not to have filled a prescription because of cost (31% vs. 10%). Women who were currently insured but had had a gap in health insurance coverage during the past year were also at high risk for going without needed care during the year. Indeed, rates of health care access problems among women with a gap in coverage were remarkably similar to rates of access difficulties reported by currently uninsured women. Both groups of women were at high overall risk for difficulties getting care when needed: 29 percent of women with a gap in coverage and 50 percent of currently uninsured women said it was extremely, very, or somewhat difficult to get care when needed.

SUMMARY

Women's health has received increased attention since the early 1990s. Federal health agencies now have offices of women's health, and women's health concerns have become a focus of major biomedical and clinical research funded by the National Institutes of Health. Many states and localities have established task forces on women's health as well. While these efforts have great benefits, *The Commonwealth Fund 1998 Survey of Women's Health* points to the need for a continued, concerted, and more concentrated focus on ensuring that women's unique needs are understood and addressed.

The increase in uninsured women, lack of progress in raising preventive care rates, low rates of physician counseling on healthy behaviors, and women's strong caregiving roles all underscore this need. In addition, high rates of reported violence and abuse and the strong link between violence and negative health consequences call for better efforts and awareness on the part of health care professionals to identify women who are victims of violence, provide them with adequate support services, and improve their access to necessary physical and psychological health services.

ABOUT THE AUTHORS

Karen Scott Collins, MD, MPH, is Assistant Vice President at The Commonwealth Fund in New York, New York. She is responsible for developing the Fund's work on health care quality and managed care, women's health, minority health, and child health and development. She serves as Director of the Minority Health Program and is a board member of Grantmakers in Health.

Cathy Schoen is Vice President for Research and Evaluation at The Commonwealth Fund, with continuing responsibilities for the Fund's work on health care coverage and access, and the Task Force on the Future of Health Insurance for Working Americans. She is the author and coauthor of many publications on health care coverage and quality issues.

Susan Joseph, MPH, is a Senior Associate at Global Strategies Group, a market research and political consulting firm, where she is an analyst in their public affairs and political practice. Prior to that position she was a Program Associate at The Commonwealth Fund, working on projects related to women's health and advancing the well-being of elderly people.

Lisa Duchon, PhD, MPA, is Deputy Director of Research and Evaluation at The Commonwealth Fund and serves as a Senior Policy and Research Adviser. Her particular focus is the analysis of economic and financing issues related to Medicare and Medicaid, as well as incremental initiatives to expand coverage and access to health care.

Elizabeth Simantov, PhD, is Senior Research Analyst in The Commonwealth Fund's Research and Evaluation Department. Prior to joining the Fund in 1998, she was an Adjunct Lecturer in Economics at Hunter College.

Michele Yellowitz, MPP, is Program Associate at The Commonwealth Fund and works primarily on projects to develop the capacities of children and young people.

ARTICLE 5

MEDICARE: A WOMEN'S ISSUE

Dorothy P. Rice

Medicare is a health insurance program for older Americans and for persons with disabilities. The elderly population in the United States is expanding, and women age 65 and over continue to outnumber men. They comprise a majority of older Medicare beneficiaries, outnumbering elderly men three to two at ages 85 and over (Kaiser Family Foundation, 1999). Women's greater representation in the Medicare program is a result of demographics—women live longer than men and rely on Medicare for more years than men. Despite their increased longevity, many of these women live in poverty, report overall poor health, and suffer from high rates of chronic conditions. Older women also use more health care services and, as a result of gaps in Medicare coverage, spend significant portions of their incomes on health care, including prescription medications and long-term care services. Despite these limitations, Medicare has contributed to improving the overall health of older women and, as such, the proposed options for preservation and reform of Medicare must be understood as a women's issue.

DEMOGRAPHICS: WHY THE FOCUS ON OLDER WOMEN?

Women have a greater reliance on Medicare as a function of demographics; women live longer than men. At birth, women's life expectancy is 79.4 years, almost six years longer than for men. At age 65, women can expect to rely on Medicare for 19.2 years compared with 15.9 years for men. At age 75, life expectancy for women is 12.1 years and 9.9 years for men (NCHS, 1999, p. 139). Because of their increased longevity, there are greater numbers of women in the Medicare-eligible population. Women comprise 59 percent of all Medicare enrollees 65 years of age and over and 72 percent of those aged 85 and over (NCHS, 1999, p. 308). The increasing number of persons in these age ranges magnifies the effect of this age distribution. In 1995, there were 19.9 million women aged 65 and older; by 2020, the number of women is projected to increase to 29.4 million, and by 2040 to 40.8 million women (Bureau of the Census, 1996). In 1995, women age 65 and over comprised 14.8 percent of the total female population. By 2040 women in this age group will comprise 21.6 percent of the total female population.

HEALTH STATUS: HOW DOES THE HEALTH OF WOMEN STACK UP?

Heart disease remains the leading cause of death in women age 65 and over, followed by malignant neoplasms and cerebrovascular diseases (Hoyert, et al., 1999). However, women's health is determined less by mortality than by health conditions and morbidity which impact quality of life. Among female Medicare beneficiaries in 1996, 60 percent reported having arthritis, 54 percent hypertension, 37 percent heart disease, 27 percent incontinence, and 21 percent osteoporosis or a broken hip (Kaiser Family Foundation, 1999). Additionally, a greater number of women than men reported having more than one of these conditions—73 percent of women reported having two or more chronic conditions compared with 65 percent of men.

The existence of these chronic conditions directly affects the health status of elderly women. Among all women beneficiaries, 43 percent rate their health as excellent or very good, 31 percent good, and 25 percent fair or poor. Among women beneficiaries age 85 and older, the percentage rating their health as excellent or very good declined to 31 percent, 32 percent good, but those rating their health as fair or poor increased to 37 percent (MCBS, 1996).

The health status of women is affected not only by longevity and health conditions, but also by socioeconomic status. In an analysis by the Urban Institute of the 1995 MCBS, 29 percent of all women reported fair or poor health. However, of women under 100 percent of poverty, 43 percent rated their health as fair or poor; at 101–200 percent of poverty and over 200 percent of poverty, 31 percent and 20 percent rated their health as fair or poor, respectively (Neuman, 1999).

ECONOMICS: HOW DO THEY INFLUENCE HEALTH?

Annual income, reliance on Social Security benefits, and poverty rates are important factors that may affect the amount, type, and distribution of health services used by Medicare beneficiaries. As persons age, they tend to leave the labor force or to work fewer hours. When they retire, their pensions are generally lower than their prior earnings. Thus, there is a declining income for older persons. The lower incomes of the elderly are associated with factors over which they have little control: their sex and race, the health and survival of their spouses, their health, their ability to work, and their educational attainment (which is strongly associated with lifetime earnings).

Both women's health and incomes decline with age. In fact, older women are twice as likely as older men to be poor. In 1996, 30 percent of women and 16 percent of men age 65 to 84 had annual incomes under $10,000. For those aged 85 and older, 55 percent of the women compared with 27 percent of the men reported an annual income of less than $10,000 (MCBS, 1996). Among all female Medicare beneficiaries in 1996, 33% reported an annual income greater than $25,000 compared with only 12 percent of females age 85 and older. Of the five million beneficiaries below the poverty level of $7,740 in 1996, almost seven out of ten were women.

LIVING ARRANGEMENTS AND WIDOWHOOD: HOW ARE THEY RELATED?

The living arrangements of elderly female Medicare beneficiaries are important in understanding women's economic status. Not only do women live longer than men, they tend to marry older men, and they are unlikely to remarry once widowed. In 1997, one third of women 65 to 74 years of age and over three fifths of those 75 years and over were widowed. In contrast, less than one tenth of men aged 65 to 74 years and one quarter aged 75 and over were widowed (Bureau of the Census, 1998). The disparity in the marital status of older men and women results in significant differences in their living arrangements. In 1994, three out of four elderly men were married and living with their wives, but only two fifths of elderly women were married and living with their husbands (Rice, 1996).

MEDICARE BENEFIT PAYMENTS: RELATIONSHIP TO HEALTH STATUS AND INCOME

Medicare benefit payments per enrollee increase with age, rising from $2,574 for those 65 years to $6,666 for those 85 years and over in 1996 (NCHS, 1999, table 135). Not surprisingly, Medicare expenditures per enrollee are inversely related to health status, with the highest expenditures of $11,739 for those in poor health and only $2,134 for those reporting excellent health. Medicare benefit payments are also inversely related to income, with payments for women declining from a high of $6,271 for those with incomes under $10,000 to $3,576 for those with incomes $25,000 and over (MCBS, 1996). It is clear that poor health is related to high use of medical services and high expenditures for medical care.

GAPS IN MEDICARE COVERAGE: IMPACT ON OUT-OF-POCKET EXPENSES

Medicare is not a comprehensive program. It was designed in 1965 to cover and pay for acute care for the elderly. It has been clearly oriented toward acute care; long-term nursing home care and outpatient drugs are not covered. These gaps in coverage affect both men and women, but women are disproportionately affected because they are older and sicker and require more medical and long-term care than men. Out-of-pocket payments include a high deductible for inpatient care, payments for Medicare and supplementary insurance premiums, and payments for non-covered services such as prescriptions, eyeglasses, and hearing aids. These limitations result in higher out-of-pocket expenses for older women compared to older men.

Ironically, although women have lower annual incomes, they have greater out-of-pocket health care costs. Women on Medicare spend a greater share of their incomes on health care than men. Out-of pocket health care spending for medical care comprises 22 percent of women's income compared with 17 percent for men. Among older women, those reporting "fair or poor" health spend 28 percent of their income for health care, and for those below the poverty level, women spend an unacceptable 53 percent of their income on health care. (Neuman, 1999).

OUTPATIENT PRESCRIPTION DRUGS: AN UNCOVERED MEDICARE BENEFIT

Most women on Medicare use prescription drugs, the costs of which contribute to their high out-of-pocket costs. Of 22 million women beneficiaries, 78 percent of women used prescription drugs on a regular basis, according to a 1997 survey of Medicare beneficiaries conducted jointly by the Kaiser Family Foundation and The Commonwealth Fund. Of those who used prescription drugs, almost half (46 percent) paid less than $25 a month. However, 14 percent spent between $51 and $100 and 15 percent spent over $100 a month on prescription drugs (Neuman, 1999).

A more recent study by AARP estimated that noninstitutionalized beneficiaries spent, on average, $410 out-of-pocket on prescription drugs in 1999, or about 4 percent of their income, and women spend slightly more out-of-pocket than men (Gibson, 1999). Examining out-of-pocket spending as a percent of income for both men and women, shows that beneficiaries with the lowest incomes spend the highest share of their income out-of-pocket on drugs. As shown in Table 1 (Gibson et al., 1999), beneficiaries with incomes below 100% of poverty spend almost one-tenth (9 percent) of their income out-of-pocket on drugs, and almost one third (30 percent) of their income on all health spending. These estimates clearly show drug spending is a significant burden for those with the lowest incomes.

Adding prescription drug coverage to the Medicare program would have a substantial impact on the costs of the program, as well as to the financial well-being of many of its beneficiaries. Studies suggest that broadening Medicare coverage to include prescription drugs could add between 7.2 percent and 10 percent to Medicare costs (Dummit, 1999). The policy dilemma is that, on the one hand, Medicare's lack of a prescription drug benefit may impede access to certain treatment advances; on the other hand, the cost implications of including a prescription drug benefit will be substantial.

TABLE 1

Income as % of Poverty	Distribution of Beneficiaries	Average Out-of-Pocket Spending		Average Out-of-Pocket Spending as % of Income	
		Health Care	Drugs	Health Care	Drugs
<100%	10%	$1,615	$310	30%	9%
100–135%	9%	$2,090	$415	24%	6%
135–200%	18%	$2,340	$445	23%	5%
200–400%	38%	$2,445	$425	17%	3%
400%+	24%	$2,700	$405	11%	2%

LONG-TERM CARE: LIMITED COVERAGE UNDER MEDICARE

Long-term care refers to a broad range of services for people who, because of a chronic illness or disability, need personal assistance with activities of daily living (ADLs)—bathing, eating, dressing, getting in and out of a chair or bed, and using the toilet. Medicare covers home health care, but has limited coverage for nursing home care. Only the first 100 days are covered for nursing home, with a copayment after 20 days. However, long-term care goes beyond formal home health and nursing home care; long-term care involves the provision of a range of social and medical services and is provided in a variety of institutional, community, and home settings. Family and friends provide the majority of long-term care on an informal basis and three out of four caregivers are women.

Most Medicare beneficiaries with long-term care needs are women. In 1995, 65 percent of those with long-term care needs were women (Neuman, 1990). Most common long-term care needs for assistance in ADLs do not require skilled help, and, therefore, are not generally covered by Medicare or private health insurance. Medicaid does cover skilled nursing home care, but most elderly women do not qualify for Medicaid benefits. Without private health insurance or public coverage, the high cost of long-term care is unaffordable for most Americans, especially older poor women.

Private long-term care insurance currently pays for less than 7% of all long-term care costs. The average cost of nursing home care exceeded $47,000 per year in 1996. As of 1996, close to five million long-term care insurance policies were sold in the United States. The cost of long-term care insurance varies dramatically according to age of the consumer at the time of the policy. At age 65, the annual premium for a long-term care policy that provides $100 per day for nursing home coverage and $50 per day for home care coverage costs $980; with nonforfeiture and lifetime 5 percent compounded inflation protection, the same policy would cost $2,432 annually (Kassner, 1999).

In 1996, Congress passed the Health Insurance Portability and Accountability Act (HIPAA) that provided favorable tax treatment to "federally qualified" long-term care insurance policies. Individuals who are covered by tax qualified policies are allowed to deduct their premiums, up to a maximum limit depending on age. At ages 61 to 70, the maximum deduction is $2,050, provided the taxpayer itemizes deductions and has medical costs in excess of 7.5 percent of adjusted gross income.

President Clinton has proposed a long-term care initiative, in which the main element is a new tax credit of up to $1,000 for eligible people with long-term care needs, their spouses, and caregivers. The other three parts of the initiative would create a new program offering information, counseling, and respite services to caregivers; establish optional private long-term care insurance for federal employees; and provide information to Medicare beneficiaries to help them choose among their options for obtaining and financing long-term care services. The White House estimates the cost of the initiative would be $6.2 billion over five years, of which nearly 90% would be for the tax credit (Komisar and Feder, 1999).

PRESERVING MEDICARE: IS IT WORTH IT?

Although Medicare is not a comprehensive program, it is important to recognize the positive impact the program has had on the health of older women. Despite faults, Medicare is a program that works for a limited number of needs. It has achieved nearly universal coverage and despite current strains on the system it has successfully absorbed growth from 19.5 million in 1967 to 33.4 million elderly and 5 million disabled in 1997 (NCHS, 1999, table 134). Unlike other private insurance coverage, Medicare coverage cannot be discontinued as a result of a health condition or loss of employment. Medicare has resulted in improved access to care, improved economic status of the elderly, and a higher quality of life for the elderly and disabled populations. Contrary to the popular perception of governmental inefficiencies, the administrative costs for Medicare have been remarkably low, at less than 3 percent. Finally, Medicare has provided an important source of support for hospitals, medical education, and research.

The Medicare Hospital Trust Fund is expected to be depleted of funds by 2015. There is clearly a pressing need to address the issue of preservation and/or reform. The National Bipartisan Commission on the Future of Medicare discussed a number of proposals to radically change the structure of Medicare from a publicly administered program to a voucher system or a premium support system. In a voucher system, the government partially subsidizes the elderly and disabled to purchase health insurance plans in a competitive market. Although the Commission could not obtain enough votes to recommend the voucher proposal, it is still being discussed as a possible approach to Medicare cost containment in the future.

The premium support system has been criticized for the following reasons: it will destroy the traditional Medicare that most beneficiaries prefer; it will shift costs to those least able to afford them; administrative expenses will rise; it will move Medicare beneficiaries into HMOs against their preferences; private voucher programs will be confusing to elderly and disabled; and quality of care may be affected. Most importantly, this proposal will not solve Medicare's fiscal problems; Medicare beneficiaries will be forced to assume the burden of ever-increasing health care costs (Bodenheimer, 1999).

Another proposal to restructure the Medicare program is to gradually raise the eligibility age from 65 to 67 years. This policy would increase the number of uninsured Americans at a time when the nation's uninsured population is already rising.

Women themselves recognize the importance of preserving Medicare. In a 1998 survey conducted by The Kaiser Family Foundation and the Harvard School of Public Health, 82 percent of the women interviewed rated preserving Medicare as "very important," 15% as "somewhat important" and only 3 percent as "not important" or "don't know" (Neuman. 1999).

Because Medicare is a women's issue, it is important to understand how the policy changes under consideration will affect older women. Key issues for women include: understanding the implications of proposed reforms for women with low incomes and chronic conditions, assuring the adequacy and affordability of benefits, improving the financial protections for low-income beneficiaries, and addressing fiscal challenges to preserve Medicare for the future.

RESTRUCTURING MEDICARE: WHAT ARE THE OPTIONS?

A three-stage proposal is presented to protect, improve, and expand Medicare. This proposal is equitable for beneficiaries and will ensure Medicare's fiscal health for the future (Bodenheimer, 1999):

1. **Establish a budget for the program.** Average annual growth in Medicare dropped from 17 percent in the 1970s to 12 percent in the 1980s to 10 percent in the years 1993 to 1996, and to only 1.5 percent from 1997 to 1998. If a budget is placed upon the entire Medicare program, the growth in the program expenditures can be contained.
2. **Improve Medicare by adding prescription drug coverage and long-term care to the budgeted Medicare program.** As noted above, these proposals would add to Medicare costs.
3. **Expand the improved and budgeted Medicare program to the entire population.** This proposal would provide health insurance to the 43 million Americans currently without health insurance. Expanding Medicare to the entire population cushions the financial impact on Medicare created by the

retirement of the large baby boomer population, the oldest members of which will begin turning age 65 in 2011.

The United States is the richest country in the world. Ample revenues are available from progressive taxes, the federal budget surplus, and transfers from other governmental programs to finance the improvement and expansion of Medicare.

CONCLUSION

Medicare costs will continue to rise, and consequently changes and reforms will be proposed to restrain costs. Because of their higher dependence on Medicare, their lower overall economic status, and need for expanded rather than restricted coverage, women are at risk for the greatest negative impact of these changes. It is critical that we find solutions that take into account the financial, health, and long-term care needs of elderly women.

ACKNOWLEDGMENT

The author gratefully acknowledges the assistance of Tracy Weitz in the preparation of this article.

ABOUT THE AUTHOR

Dorothy P. Rice, BA, is Professor Emeritus and Recalled, Department of Social and Behavioral Sciences and Institute for Health & Aging, University of California, San Francisco.

REFERENCES

Bodenheimer T, Grumbach K, Livingston B, McCanne DR, Oberlander J, Rice DP, Rosenau PV. *Rebuilding Medicare for the 21st Century: A Challenge for the Medicare Commission and Congress.* The National Campaign to Protect, Improve, and Expand Medicare. San Francisco, February 1999.

Bureau of the Census. Population projections of the United States by age, sex, race, and Hispanic origin: 1995 to 2050. *Current Population Reports,* P25-1130. Washington, DC, 1996.

Dummit, LA. *Medicare: Considerations for Adding a Prescription Drug Benefit.* Testimony before the Committee on Finance, U.S. Senate. U.S. General Accounting Office, GAO/T-HEHS-99-153. Washington, DC, June 23, 1999.

522   *Women's Health and Aging*

Gibson M, Brangan N, Gross D, Caplan C. *How Much Are Medicare Beneficiaries Paying Out-of-Pocket for Prescription Drugs?* AARP Public Policy Institute. Washington, DC, 1999.

Hoyert DL, Kochanek KD, Murphy SL. Deaths: final data for 1997. *National Vital Statistics Reports.* National Center for Health Statistics. Hyattsville, MD, June 30, 1999; 47(19):1–37.

Kaiser Family Foundation. *The Medicare Program: Women and Medicare.* The Kaiser Medicare Policy Project. Washington, DC, May 1999.

Kassner E. Long-term care insurance. *Fact Sheet.* AARP Public Policy Institute. Washington, DC, May 1999.

Komisar HL, Feder J. The President's proposed long-term care initiative: background and issues. *Policy Brief.* The Commonwealth Fund. New York, July 1999.

Medicare Current Beneficiary Survey (MCBS). Health Care Financing Administration. Unpublished tabulations from the 1996 survey, 1996.

National Center for Health Statistics (NCHS). *Health, United States. 1999 with Health and Aging Chartbook.* HHS publication number (PHS) 99–1232. U.S. Government Printing Office. Washington, DC, 1999.

Neuman, P. *Why Medicare Is a Women's Issue: Chart Pack.* The Kaiser Family Foundation. Washington, DC, May 5, 1999.

Rice DP. Beneficiary profile: yesterday, today, and tomorrow. *Health Care Financing Review* 1996; 18(18): 23–46.

Article 6

Aging and Gender: A New Voice on the Women's Health Agenda

Carroll L. Estes and Tracy A. Weitz

INTRODUCTION

The current models for health care delivery, financing, and policy fail to meet the needs of women in general, and older women in particular. The complex interaction of medical, social, and economic factors that affect women's wellness requires a new paradigm that bridges the gap between those who are concerned about aging issues and those concerned about women's health. A new paradigm must also take account of the institutional structures and relations that greatly influence the economic security of women and the ability to access health resources as they age.

The current women's health agenda is the result of independent and isolated efforts in the areas of aging, health, and women's issues. To "bridge the gap," old questions need to be examined in new ways, and new questions need to be asked about old assumptions. In this article, we begin this endeavor by advancing four interrelated themes: (1) there is a gendered relationship between socioeconomic structures and health over time; (2) there are gender-specific implications of health care financing and policy; (3) there is a gender bias in the medical disease-based medical model of health; and (4) there are health consequences to the gendered nature of caregiving.

BACKGROUND

Women comprise an increasing segment of the aging population. O'Rand (1996) argues that the older population of the United States is undergoing a feminization. In 1997, 59 percent of persons 65 years of age and over were women. The sex ratio is higher with age; 71% of persons 85 years of age and over were women (DHHS, 1999). In 1997, the life expectancy was 79.4 years for women and 73.6 years for men. Under current mortality conditions, women who survive to age 65 can on average expect to live to age 84, and women who survive to age 85 can on average anticipate living to age 92 (DHHS, 1999). Despite their increased longevity, older women live under more compromised circumstances than those experienced by men. In general, older women are more likely than men to live in poverty, have less access to a secure retirement, and pay an increased percentage of their income on out-of-pocket health care costs. Likewise, women play substantially different social roles than men and those roles directly impact their health and economic well-being. Women are also more likely than men to suffer from chronic conditions and disabilities that limit their quality of life (Rice & Michel, 1998).

In order to meet the needs of this feminized aging population, the leadership of the aging movement and the women's health movement must work together to build a paradigm of health that promotes the wellness of older women. The current hesitancy to look at aging issues from a gendered perspective and the historical focus of women's health on reproductive issues have hindered this union and deferred to a disease-based medical model agenda for prevention.

Despite recent acknowledgements that aging is a women's issue (AAWH, DHHS, & WHO, 1999), discussions surrounding aging continue to lack a gender-lens and confound the difference between the issues that affect both women and men. Fearful of excluding men, advocates have sought to adopt gender-neutral language and agendas. While the role of poverty in health has received attention, the unique aspects of women's poverty as they age remain unexplored. Only minimal attention has been paid to the ways in which policy implications under discussion uniquely affect women (Shaw, Zuckerman, & Hartman, 1998). For example, current efforts to reform Social Security will affect men and women in distinct and different ways (Estes, 1998; Smeeding, Estes, & Glasse, 1999). When, on rare occasions, these differences are explored, policy makers are accused of political pandering, instead of being recognized for highlighting the potential adverse impacts on vulnerable populations (Toner, 1999).

The women's health movement has historically focused on the reproductive health issues unique to women (Ussher, 1992). In fact, the phrase "maternal-child health" is often used synonymously with women's health (Weisman, 1998). Concerns about access to abortion, family planning, prenatal care, and infant mortality dominate the forefront of women's health. While the graying of the baby-boomers has resulted in an expanded interest in midlife women, the current onslaught of welfare reform and abortion restriction legislation has forced advocates to continue to maintain their focus on traditional reproductive health issues.

For both women and older persons, the health agenda has been developed around the disease-based medical model of prevention through medical intervention. By focusing on the treatment and elimination of disease rather than focusing on the well-being of older women, health is constructed in biological terms only. Social, economic, and political factors that also affect the wellness of older women are often excluded. Feminist scholars suggest that this focus on disease prevention pathologizes the aging process (Lock, 1998).

BRIDGING AGING, GENDER, AND HEALTH: A NEW PARADIGM FOR OLDER WOMEN'S HEALTH

In the Introduction, we suggested four interrelated themes that could provide a foundation for a new paradigm that recognizes the complexities of the medical, social, and economic factors that affect older women's health.

Articulating the Gender-Dependent Relationship Between Socioeconomic Structure and Health

A growing body of evidence indicates that socioeconomic status (SES) is a strong predictor of health, regardless of access to medical care. SES continues to be a remarkably robust indicator of rates of illness and death (Williams & Collins, 1995), and numerous studies and reviews have demonstrated this conclusion (Adler et al., 1994; Adler, Boyce, Chesney, Folkman, & Syme, 1993; Adler & Coriell, 1997; Krieger, Rowley, Herman, Avery, & Phillips, 1993; Lantz et al., 1998). Krieger and colleagues argue that the increasing social inequalities in health in the United States, coupled with growing inequalities in income and wealth, have refocused attention on social class as a key determinant of population health (Krieger, Williams, & Moss, 1997). The relationship between SES and health occurs at every socioeconomic level and for a broad range of SES indicators, and cannot be accounted for simply by classic risk factors such as diet and smoking (Adler et al., 1993). The relationship is so strong that each level of SES is associated with better health outcomes. This occurrence, although not completely understood, is referred to as the "SES gradient in health status" (Adler et al., 1994; Adler et al., 1993).

Given the well-established relationship and the existence of the SES gradient, it is critical to view women's economic situations as a component of their health. Currently, the two poorest groups in the United States are women raising children alone and women over sixty-five living alone (Doress-Worters & Siegal, 1994). Understanding the commonalties that influence the economic situations of these two populations of women is the first step to developing public policies that benefit women across the lifespan. For these two groups of women, the economic status is conditioned by gendered work patterns and by social and political policies that link women's economic security to that of men (Estes, 2000; Harrington Meyer, 1996).

The Role of Gendered Work Patterns in Women's Economic Security. Almost three-quarters of the nation's elderly poor are women (SSA, 1998; SSA & Grad, 1998) and according to future projections by ICF, Inc., by the year 2020 poverty among older people will be almost exclusively poverty among older women (Alone, 1987, as quoted in Friedman, 1994). Lower lifetime earnings produce lower retirement income and higher poverty for older women (Estes & Michel, 1998). Older women's income from all sources is on average 56 percent of that for older men. The median personal income for women 65 or over is $9,355, and the median income for men 65 or older is $16,484, 1.8 times higher than women's income

(Stone & Griffith, 1998). Of female beneficiaries age 85 and older, 55 percent have annual incomes under $10,000, compared to only 27 percent of men the same age (HCFA, 1996). The poverty for women of color is a result of the triple threat of race, gender, and age. More than half of all African-American women over age 75 are poor or near poor (Dalaker & Naifeh, 1998). African-American women age 65 or older have a poverty rate of 28.9 percent, compared to 22.2 percent for African-American men (Council, 1998). Hispanic women have a poverty rate of 28.1 percent compared to 23.6 percent for Hispanic men (Council, 1998). Reasons for the economic reality of all women include gender-biased economic structures such as the methodology used to calculate Social Security, work patterns that differ between men and women, and women's reduced access to other retirement income.

Social Security is the primary source of income for older women, and more women than men are dependent on Social Security as their sole source of income (Estes, 1998). Paradoxically, women receive substantially less, on average, per month than men. For example, in December 1997, women received 75 percent of monthly OASDI (Old Age, Survivors, and Disability Insurance) benefits on average compared with men: $629 for women and $841 for men (SSA, 1998). In 1995, women age 65 and over averaged $6,971 in Social Security Benefits ($727 below poverty for aged individuals) while men averaged $9,376 (Stone & Griffith, 1998).

The current equation used to calculate Social Security benefits is affected by the patterns of women's participation in the labor market. Overall, women are more likely than men to work in the unpaid labor market, thereby receiving no credit toward Social Security, called "zero years" in the workforce in calculating the formula that determines benefits. Additionally, as a result of caregiving responsibilities for both children and adults, women have more "zero years" in the calculation of their Social Security benefits than do men (Ross, 1997). Women average seven "zero years" in the labor force under Social Security compared to just two and a half years for men (Smeeding, 1999). Under the benefit calculation methodology, women are penalized by the Social Security system for their time out of the labor force to provide caregiving (Stone, Cafferata, & Sangl, 1987).

For those women in the paid work force, discrepancies still exist. Women still make only 74.1 cents to every dollar earned by men (NCPE, 1999). Women of color experience the highest wage gap. For each dollar earned by a white male: African-American women earn 62.6 cents; Hispanic women earn 53.9 cents; and white women earn 71.9 cents (NCPE, 1999). Since Social Security benefits are calculated as a function of earned income and years in the workforce, women are again disadvantaged under the system. Because of their lower income, even if they have no "zero years" in the workforce, women still receive lower Social Security payments, on average, than men.

Access to other retirement income to supplement Social Security is needed to mitigate the impact of this inequity. Unfortunately, because of differences in the types of jobs women and men obtain in the marketplace, and the disparity of benefits associated with those jobs, women are also less likely to be offered private pensions (Housnell, 1998). Men are two times more likely to have pension coverage than women (Hennesey, 1997). Also, because private pensions are linked to paid employment, caregiving substantially shapes women's access to a secure retirement. This is another reason women lag behind in retirement income. Even for women with access to pension plans, their greater life expectancy means that they must spread their savings and retirement income over significantly more years on average than men. In 1995, the average pension for women was $6,684 per year. For men the average was almost double: $11,460 (Security, 1999).

Marital status also is key. Being non-married in old age (widowed, divorced, separated, or never married) renders a woman much more vulnerable to poverty when compared with a married older woman (Estes & Michel, 1998). The mean proportion of income that non-married women receive from Social Security is 72 percent. Fifty percent of non-married women rely on Social Security for 80 percent of their income, and one in four non-married women age 65 and older rely on Social Security for 100 percent. In contrast, married couples receive 55 percent of their income from Social Security (SSA & Grad, 1998). Marital status is also predictive of having pension coverage. However, non-married women are more compromised than similar status men. In 1996, 44 percent of non-married men 65 or older had pension coverage, in comparison to 33 percent of non-married women 65 or older (SSA & Grad, 1998). The statistics are even worse for women of color; only 23 percent of African-American non-married women and just 13 percent of Hispanic non-married women received private pension income (SSA & Grad, 1998).

The women's health movement must understand that the role of SES in health is not solely a function of a woman's present economic situation, but of her past and future SES. The agenda of the women's health movement must include a life-course perspective. Currently, the women's health movement is arguing for greater workplace accommodation and flexibility in supporting women in childbearing and reproduction. While these are worthwhile and positive agendas, the long-term implications for the health of older women (by reducing the contribution to Social Security, increasing the number of "zero years", and limiting access to other retirement pensions and savings) must be addressed within the same policy discussion. Pushing for financial support and job security for women to "take time off" for caregiving is inadequate to promote the long-term economic security and the health of older women, because it fails to provide credit toward Social Security or access to private pensions. Likewise, dependence on a spouse's retirement or Social Security is an inadequate solution and dangerously problematic to a woman's economic security.

Linking Women's Economic Security to Men.   The threat of poverty associated with being an older woman is not simply a consequence of longer life. When a woman is married over a long period of time, there is greater stability and security in income (Shaw et al., 1998). In 1996, the median annual income for unmarried elderly women alone was $10,859 compared to $14,007 for unmarried elderly men (SSA & Grad, 1998). Poverty for women is either created or accelerated by widowhood and divorce. Eighty percent of all widows in poverty become poor only after their husbands die (Burkhauser & Smeeding, 1994), and divorced older women have higher poverty rates than widows of the same age (Harrington Meyer, 1996). Widowed older women have a poverty rate of 18 percent, compared with 11.4 percent for widowed men; divorced women have a poverty rate of 22.2 percent compared to 15 percent for divorced men (Council, 1998). Unfortunately, since women have a longer life expectancy than men and many women marry men older than themselves, seven out of ten baby-boom women will outlive their husbands, and many can expect to be widowed for 15 to 20 years. Compared with men, elderly women are three times more likely to be widowed (SSA, 1998).

Women also have a higher probability of being divorced. From 1970 to 1997, the proportion of married women declined from 81.4 percent to 67.9 percent. Much of this change is attributable to higher rates of divorce, although an increase has also occurred in the number of never-married women (Urban Institute, 1999, as reported by Steuerle, 1999). The effects of change in marital status were demonstrated by Shaw et al., who examined a group of women over a nine-year time span and found that poverty was relatively rare and did not increase among women who were married at both times in their study. However, the rate of poverty was substantially higher for women whose marital status had changed over the course of the study (Shaw et al., 1998). Married older women have a four to five times lower poverty rate (4.6 percent) than non-married older women (18 to 22.2 percent) (Council, 1998). Projected increases in the number of divorced, widowed, separated, and never-married women will result in greater economic hardship for older women in general (Estes & Michel, 1998).

The structures that promote women's dependence on men to minimize their threat of poverty are not limited to affecting older women. Recently, there has been increased attention to the need to reduce "unmarried births." Statistics on unmarried births have replaced the policy focus on "teenage pregnancy" (Besharov & Zinsmeister, 1987; Brownstein, 1994; Fulwood, 1993; LAT, 1996; Vobejda, 1995), and because of the national discomfort with abortion, "unmarried" has replaced "unintended" as the marker for federal and state initiatives (Holmes, 1996; NYT, 1998). While this subtle change may not appear to be of importance to those interested in "aging issues," the change is reflective of the same structural issues that link women's economic security to men. The rationale behind the concern about unmarried births is grounded in arguments about the rates of poverty for these families (Besharov & Zinsmeister, 1987). However, rather than addressing the economic structures that perpetuate women's poverty, this rhetorical focus shifts the blame for poverty to the absence of the male. This rationale is similar to the plight of older women whose poverty is attributable to the death or divorce of a spouse. Again, rather than addressing the fundamental political and economic structures that produce women's poverty, blame can be assigned to the absence of the husband. In framing the problem in this manner, the solution to both scenarios is the necessary presence of the man in the woman's life. Marriage for younger women, and continuing marriage and longevity for the husbands of older women, are therefore made the reigning factors for women's economic security. In understanding the similarities that underlie these two issues for women at opposite ends of the life course, those interested in women's health and older women can begin to address the fundamental structural causes of women's poverty, rather than seeking prevention of that poverty solely through continued or increased dependency on men.

Addressing the Gender-Specific Implications of Health Care Financing and Policy

As with the overall economic structure, the current policy and financing system for both public and private health care is extraordinarily problematic for older women. On the public side, women are more dependent than men on Medicare for coverage (Rice & Michel, 1998), and on the private side, employer-based insurance continues to link access to health care to marital status and formal paid employment (Harrington Meyer, 1996). Additionally, both the public and the private models of health care financing fail to include a long-term care policy, which is critical to the health and well-being of older women (Estes, Swan, & Associates, 1993).

The Gender-Specific Limitations of Medicare and Employer-Based Insurance. The majority of Medicare recipients are women, and because of their longer survival older women depend on Medicare for an average of 15 years compared with 7 years for older men (Butler, 1996). In 1996, 59 percent of all Medicare beneficiaries were women (Rice & Michel, 1998). In 1997, 70 percent of Medicare beneficiaries were women 85 or older (HCFA, 1998).

Although older women have greater need for Medicare coverage, the system is designed to address acute illnesses which are more common in men. Medicare is not intended to cover care for chronic illness, although older women suffer disproportionately from these conditions (Hoffman & Rice, 1996). As such, older women spend an average of 22 percent of their incomes on medical expenses, compared to 17 percent for older men (AARP & Lewin-VHI, 1999). Significantly, these costs jumped 115 percent for older women and 107 percent for older men, respectively, during the early 1990s (O'Rand & Aging, 1994). For people ages 85 and older, out-of-pocket costs jumped nearly 200 percent during the same period. The compromised health status of older women and particularly of low-income older women has further negative effects on economic status, as out-of-pocket health costs are inversely related to the ability to pay for them. Low-income individuals spend 37 percent of household income on out-of-pocket costs, while high-income individuals spend just 15 percent of household income (AARP & Lewin-VHI, 1994). Older women of color bear a higher proportion of out-of-pocket health care costs than older white males and females (Wallace, 1998).

Prescription drugs and long-term care are the highest out-of-pocket expenses (Estes & Michel, 1998). Eight of 10 Medicare beneficiaries regularly use prescription medications, which are now an integral component of medical care (Schoen, Neuman, Kitchman, Davis, & Rowland, 1998). Older women suffer disproportionately from chronic conditions that require greater use of prescription medications.

Likewise, therapeutic prevention strategies are more frequently recommended for women, also resulting in higher out-of-pocket costs for older women. As a result most women on Medicare, 17 million, use prescription drugs regularly; 29 percent spend over $50 a month for this purpose (Schoen et al., 1998). Traditional Medicare does not cover outpatient prescription drugs, and only half of beneficiaries with a private supplement have coverage for their medications (Project, 1999). As a result, those with high monthly costs put themselves at financial risk or must forego needed medication (Schoen, et al., 1998).

Ironically the women's health movement has taken on the issue of prescription drugs within a completely separate sphere. Fueled by the blatant inequity between coverage of Viagra and the lack of coverage for contraceptives, women's health advocates have campaigned for "contraceptive parity" (Trafford, 1998). Legislative solutions have focused predominately on funding by HMOs. Because of the historical reproductive health focus of the women's movement, this fight has remained separate from discussions about the substantial needs of older women for prescription drug coverage. Joining the activism for contraceptive parity with those pushing for prescription drug coverage under Medicare will lead to a more comprehensive approach regarding access to and coverage of prescription drugs for all women.

When viewed as a population-specific issue, the debate over coverage for prescription drugs obscures the larger issue of lack of insurance coverage for health care in general. Between 1989 and 1997, the number of people without health insurance increased by 10.1 million to 43.4 million (Carrasquillo, Himmelstein, Woolhandler, & Bor, 1999). The percentage of uninsured women also increased while Medicaid enrollment dropped as a result of cutbacks generated by welfare reform (Carrasquillo, et al., 1999). The 1998 Commonwealth Fund Survey found that among women ages 18 to 64 nearly one of four is either uninsured (18 percent) or spent time without health insurance in the past year (8 percent). The proportion of working-age women without insurance also increased, especially for women earning low to modest wages. As of 1998, 35 percent of women under age 65 with incomes of $16,000 or less were uninsured, up from 29 percent in 1993. The greatest increases in uninsured rates were among low-income and Hispanic women. In 1998, 42 percent of Latina women ages 18 to 64 were uninsured in comparison to 13 percent of white non-Latina women (Collins et al., 1999). It is important to highlight the role race/ethnicity plays in insurance status for women at all ages. Under Medicare, only 2 percent of the elderly women in California are uninsured; however, 7 percent of the Latina elderly and 4 percent of the elderly Asian and Pacific Islander women have no health insurance coverage (Wyn & Martin, 1998).

While access to health coverage for uninsured women has been an important agenda item for the women's movement, the priority has been narrowly focused on increasing coverage for pregnant women and children. To the credit of those pushing this agenda, the fight for expanded coverage of prenatal care has been remarkably successful. The importance of insurance in access to and use of prenatal care is well established. The uniqueness of the duty to provide insurance coverage of prenatal care for all women was demonstrated in an opinion poll of health care executives on access to care. While few respondents supported any universal health care entitlement, two-fifths thought the government should underwrite prenatal care (Weil, 1987). Unfortunately, recent efforts to limit prenatal care for immigrants has forced advocates to prioritize retaining this limited scope of coverage rather than expanding health care coverage to non-pregnant women.

Those concerned with aging have begun to address deficiencies in Medicare coverage for beneficiaries by focusing on maintaining current benefits and expanding access to supplemental insurance to cover additional benefits such as prescription drugs. There are currently a number of national debates underway about how to "save" Medicare (Day, 1998; Fronstin & Copeland, 1997; Fuchs, 1999; Gundling, 1997; McKusick, 1999; Serafini, 1997; Wilensky, 1996). A central theme of these discussions is cutting costs, expanding managed care, and expanding services through supplemental private insurance (Oberlander, 1997). Many proposed changes may mean even higher out-of-pocket costs, which will disproportionately affect women who are less able to pay (Project, 1999). In addition, access to supplemental insurance is limited and influenced by gender, race/ethnicity, and socioeconomic status. In California, access to private coverage to supplement Medicare is most common among white women (56 percent) and least common for Latinas (11 percent) (Wyn & Martin, 1998). Similar to the efforts described above for prenatal advocates, advocates for older women have had to remain focused on maintenance of current benefits and expansion within a very narrow agenda rather addressing larger gaps in coverage.

In maintaining a bipolar focus on reproductive-aged women and Medicare-eligible women, advocates fail to adequately address the overall deficiency of the piecemeal insurance structure. By coalescing efforts pushing for health coverage of pregnant women and efforts working to preserve Medicare, an agenda for comprehensive health care coverage can be forged. Without such an approach, efforts to improve health care will focus on small improvements to the current market-based system rather than more broad-based approaches such as universal health coverage (Blumenthal, 1999).

The Gender-Specific Impact of the Lack of a Long-Term Care Policy. Even the solution of universal health care coverage across the lifespan will be inadequate to fully address the health needs of older women. The current reimbursement model for both public and private insurance fails to include sufficient coverage for long-term care for which elderly women have a disproportionate need (Estes & Swan, 1993). Medicare, the universal elder health policy, does not cover long-term care, and thus it can be said that the U.S. policy on long-term care is gendered in multiple ways largely to the detriment of women. Women are both the users and the providers of long-term care, and thus failure to address long-term care disproportionately falls on women (Project, 1999).

In 1996, three-quarters of the residents in long-term care facilities (skilled nursing homes, intermediate care facilities, retirement homes, and institutions for the mentally retarded) were women, and women made up two-thirds of the home health care users and over half of hospice patients (Rice & Michel, 1998). At the age of 65, a woman has a one in three chance of residing in a nursing home for a year or more during her remaining years, compared with an older man's one in seven chance. Women's chances for entering a nursing home are 52 percent compared with 30 percent for men (Kemper & Murtaugh, 1991). Marital status again plays a role; nearly two-thirds of all current nursing home residents were widowed, with female residents twice as likely to be widowed as male residents (DHHS, 1999).

In addition to having a greater need for long-term care, the labor of long-term care, largely informal, is predominately provided by women, without pay and with negative consequences. Women are 75 percent of the caregivers, 80 percent of whom provide unpaid care twenty-four hours per day, seven days per week (O'Rand & Aging, 1994). The "typical" caregiver is in her mid-forties (Caregiving & AARP, 1997), but 25 percent are between the ages of 65 and 74 and 10 percent are 75 and over (Estes, et al., 1998). A 1997 study found that the midrange estimate for the economic value of informal caregiving was $196 billion (Arno, Levine, & Memmott, 1999). Women care providers, ironically, often outlive anyone to care for them and then are required to "spend down" into poverty in order to qualify for public assistance through Medicaid. Thus, although women often provide care to others at no economic cost, they are required to pay for the care they receive in old age.

The government's refusal to provide a publicly financed universal long-term care policy is borne unequally across gender lines. Devolution and increased state-level responsibility for long-term care makes women dependent on 50 state governors and legislatures. The result is a fragmented and unequal policy across the different states. As discussed in their work, Estes and Linkins view this fragmentation as "the race to the bottom." Because states are in competition with each other for capital and labor, there is economic incentive to eliminate, rather than enhance, coverage of long-term care. Ultimately, it is women who experience the impact of these negative incentives (Estes & Linkins, 1997; revised and printed in Lee, Estes, & Close, 1997).

Unfortunately, Medicare coverage for long-term care does not appear to be on the agenda of advocates, despite the high potential to benefit the health of older women. Likewise, the issue of long-term care has been virtually ignored by the women's health movement. Long-term care must be viewed as an intergenerational issue, and efforts to develop a gender-neutral healthcare financing policy must include sufficient coverage for long-term care.

Moving From a Disease Focus to a Gender-Appropriate Model of Prevention

Even before requiring more intensive long-term care, older women report greater functional disability than do men, as well as poorer health status, which limits their quality of life (Hoffman & Rice, 1996). Enhancing women's quality of life requires understanding the unique impact of disability and chronic illness on women and developing a gender-appropriate approach to prevention. Under the current "infectious disease" mode of health care, metaphors and structures support dramatic cures and lifesaving interventions, thus leaving less sensational efforts that ameliorate chronic illness or enhance functional status and quality of life to struggle for attention (Bierman & Clancy, 1999; Verbrugge & Jette, 1994). Addressing these quality of life issues requires moving beyond the disease-based medical model focus of the current health care model to develop a new gender-appropriate model of prevention.

Chronic Conditions and Disabilities.   Regardless of race and age, women spend about twice as many years disabled before death as their male counterparts (La Croix, Newton, Leveille, & Wallace, 1997). Disability greatly influences functional well-being by limiting individuals' abilities to perform certain tasks of daily living. Researchers group these tasks into two categories: 1) essential activities of daily living (ADL), such as bathing, eating, and dressing; and 2) the more complex instrumental activities of daily living (IADL), such as making meals, shopping, or cleaning. In 1995 among the noninstitutionalized population 70 years of age and over, 10 percent of women and 7 percent of men were unable to do one or more ADL, and about 23 percent of women and 13 percent of men could not do IADLs without help (DHHS, 1999). According to 1994 data, the percentage of women needing help or supervision with IADLs more than doubles across each 10-year age category for women: from 6.3 percent to 15.7 percent to 40.8 percent of women aged 65 to 74, 75 to 84, and 85 and older, respectively. In each age group, the rates of disability among women exceed those among men (Guralnik, Leveille, Hirsch, Ferrucci, & Fried, 1997). In addition, as discussed previously, the need to reside in a nursing home, perhaps the most serious form of loss of independence, is also substantially greater among women than men aged 75 and older (Guralnik, et al., 1997).

Much of women's increased disability is related to the higher prevalence and number of chronic conditions among women. Of the more than 60 chronic conditions monitored by the National Health Interview Survey, almost two-thirds occur with more frequency in women, while only four conditions occur more frequently in men and the remainder are equal (Adams & Marano, 1995). Nine out of ten women aged 65 and over report one or more chronic conditions, and almost three out of four have two or more conditions. Among women age 85 and over, 97 percent have one or more conditions and 90 percent report two or more conditions (Estes & Michel, 1998).

There is a significant relationship between chronic conditions and out-of-pocket health expenses. Older women who classify their health status as poor or fair spend 28 percent of their income out-of-pocket compared to women with excellent health who spend 17 percent of their income out-of-pocket (AARP & Lewin-VHI, 1999). Moreover, men spend about five percentage points less than women at every level of health from excellent to poor (AARP & Lewin-VHI, 1999). Likewise, older women who have one or more severe limitations in their activities of daily living spend one-third of their income out-of-pocket compared to 20 percent for women with no limitations in their activities of daily living. In contrast, men with one or more functional limitations in activities of daily living spend only 29 percent of their income out-of-pocket. It is important to note that these figures do not include the costs of nursing homes or home health care expenses that are significant and would substantially raise the calculation of out-of-pocket expenses, especially for women (AARP & Lewin-VHI, 1999).

Current Prevention Approaches. Chronic conditions are most effectively addressed through prevention of disease rather than treatment, and thus efforts to reduce chronic conditions in women must include a discussion of prevention. Although the rise in managed care has helped shift the health care focus from dramatic treatment to prevention, the recommended approaches for prevention remain inadequate. Among current prevention strategies, medical care interventions remain at the center of the discussion: screening receives the most attention among policy makers, and therapeutic options have received the greatest endorsement from the health care field.

Under current legislation, the Centers for Disease Control funds a national initiative on breast and cervical cancer screening at a substantial annual cost. While these funds have been critical to the diagnosis of many cancers and potential cancers in women (MMWR, 1996), the program has helped perpetuate a disease-focused medical model approach to prevention. Based on the success of this model in increasing rates of screening, states are considering financial support for bone mass testing for women without insurance coverage. This type of policy making is referred to as "body parts legislation," and the approach often pits health care advocates against one another in the fight for limited public resources and creates impediments to the development of an overall comprehensive approach to prevention. In both of these funding approaches, although screening tests are covered, there is no financial support for diagnosis and treatment that must accompany screening if health outcomes are to improve. Thus the full range of services needed for prevention remain unaddressed.

Within the policy formulation for these programs experts have examined and debated the age of the women who are eligible for the service. This focus has been limited to a discussion about the age at which women should start obtaining screening services. Little to no attention is paid to the issue of the age at which screening is no longer needed or when the risks outweigh the benefits. For example, the debate over mammograms focuses on extending informed decision-making and patient choice to women 40 to 50 years old and leaves the decision about when to stop screening to the provider (Blustein & Weiss, 1998). The decision about whether a 90-year-old woman would benefit from a screening mammography is not predicated on the same informed decision-making model. Likewise, public education campaigns for mammography stress an annual exam every year after a woman reaches the age of 50. There is no mention of the appropriate age to stop receiving screening, and as a result women experience highly varied levels of advice from health care providers.

The second focus of prevention has been the routine use of therapeutic options such as hormone replacement therapy (HRT). Once only a treatment for menopausal symptoms, HRT is now used as a prevention strategy for numerous diseases that increase as a woman ages (e.g., heart disease.) The limitations of HRT were illuminated when the results of the first large randomized control trial of HRT were released in the summer of 1999. The Heart Estrogen Replacement Study (HERS) was a trial of HRT for secondary prevention of coronary heart disease. Contrary to the anticipated results, HERS documented no improvement for women on HRT and a slight increase in risk of other negative outcomes (Barrett-Connor & Stuenkel, 1999; Hulley, et al., 1998). Coupled with data suggesting an increased risk of breast cancer in women utilizing long-term HRT, women's health advocates have been increasingly concerned about the routine use of HRT for prevention (Network, 2000). Despite this hesitation, newer data on the potential of HRT in reducing the progression of Alzheimer's disease, continues to create increased pressure for the routine use of HRT (Genazzani & Gambacciani, 1999). Other studies of designer estrogens (or SERMS) have also been touted as prevention options for women. Raloxifene, as a prevention strategy for osteoporosis, and even potentially breast cancer, has received the most media attention (Apgar, 1999; Cummings, et al., 1999; Jordan & Morrow, 1999). In addition to the initiation of new trials, women's health advocates await the results of other large studies of primary prevention, including the much-anticipated Women's Health Initiative. Unfortunately, these studies will generate more, rather than fewer, questions. Women will continue to need alternatives to therapeutic approaches, and even where appropriate these approaches to prevention will need the lifestyle and social support of other prevention components, including exercise, nutrition, and stress reduction.

This focus on new therapeutic options for prevention has fueled pressures at the national level to increase the inclusion of women into clinical trials for federally funded research. Despite the importance of this agenda for all women, women over age 75 still remain almost universally excluded from studies because of comorbidity or other access barriers, as well as strict age criteria (Bugeja, Kumar, & Banerjee, 1997). What we know about the diagnosis and treatment of health conditions that disproportionately affect this age group has come almost exclusively from studies on men or younger women (Goodwin, 1999). This dependence on a medical solution has also resulted in less research attention to explicate the societal mechanisms and sociocultural forces that might explain the origin, manifestation, acceleration, and prevention of specific disease and chronic conditions (Estes & Close, 1993; revised and reprinted in Lee et al., 1997).

For both screening and pharmacology, access to health care services is required. Since both of these approaches are targeted at the perimenopausal or recently menopausal woman, it is important to examine access more closely. Uninsured status rates are increasing for all women, and the lack of health insurance is a serious problem for persons aged 55 to 64 (Powell-Griner, Bolen, & Bland, 1999). It is estimated that 2.5 million Americans aged 55 to 64 are uninsured and that almost 1 million of these individuals are in fair or poor health (Davis, Rowland, Altman, Collins, & Morris, 1995). The current health care system, which ties access to affordable health insurance to employment and marital status with a working husband, places women at a disadvantage (Harrington Meyer, 1996). Midlife women are more likely to be unemployed, work part-time, or be employed in jobs that do not offer benefits. Also, because these women represent the age of the "typical caregiver" (Caregiving & AARP, 1997), they are more likely than men to be out of the paid labor force and engaged in unpaid caregiving for others. Women's access to health insurance during these years is therefore highly dependent on a spouse, which makes women vulnerable to losing coverage in the event of separation, divorce, or death (AOA, 1998). Due to increases in the divorce rate, women's access to coverage is increasingly susceptible to change.

An Expanded Prevention Approach.   The biomedicalization of aging, which focuses on the organic pathology amenable to medical intervention, has resulted in the conceptualization of old age as a disease, aging as a medical problem, and palliation of the aging process as a venerable goal (Estes & Close, 1993; revised and reprinted in Lee, et al., 1997). Lost in the prevention emphasis on early diagnosis (through screening) and therapeutics (e.g., HRT) are the considerable sociopolitical impediments to actualizing prevention. Paradoxically, chronic conditions may be mediated more by life-course experience associated with sociostructural location than by genetic, biologic, or even behavioral factors (Estes & Close, 1993; revised and reprinted in Lee et al., 1997). Developing a gender-appropriate approach to prevention requires recognizing that many major determinants of health lie outside the health care system (Marmor, Barer, & Evans, 1994).

Utilizing the traditional disease-based medical model for prevention model illuminates this limitation. The National Osteoporosis Foundation (NOF) recommends four components of a strategy to prevent osteoporosis: a balanced diet rich in calcium and vitamin D; weight-bearing exercise; a healthy lifestyle with no smoking and limited alcohol intake; and bone density testing and medications when appropriate (NOF, 1998). Legislative policy solutions are being sought to mandate the latter strategy: required HMO coverage of bone scans and implementation of quality indicators mandating counseling on HRT. However, mandates and regulations are insufficient to encourage adoption of the other three strategies. Full actualization will result only from expanding the disease-based medical model prevention approach to incorporate environmental and personal behavioral factors. Prevention requires moving beyond the language of patient compliance to address sociopolitical and economic issues that mitigate adoption of prevention recommendations.

It is documented that many older women consume too little calcium to sustain their physiologic requirements (La Croix, et al., 1997). Supplemental calcium is recommended at an additional cost to the individual woman. While this expense is nominal on a daily basis, over time it is one example of the type of expenses that create additional economic strain on older women. Over-the-counter expenses are in addition to the out-of-pocket expenses associated with the prescription drugs offered as a component of the medical model of prevention (e.g., HRT). Should prescription drug coverage under Medicare become a reality, the financial incentives to utilize prescription rather than over-the-counter alternatives reinforce this hierarchy of the disease-based medical model.

Regular physical activity has been shown to have many health benefits; it can reduce the risk of certain chronic diseases, appears to relieve symptoms of depression, helps to maintain independent living, and enhances overall quality of life (DHHS, 1996). Overall, women over age 65 are less likely to exercise than men (DHHS, 1999), and adoption of regular exercise as a prevention strategy is mitigated by women's life circumstances. Because they limit recreational and personal activities, caregiving responsibilities have a negative impact on a woman's ability to incorporate exercise into her daily routine. Poverty also plays a role in fitness. Safety is often compromised for older women living in poverty, thus limiting access to low-cost exercise alternatives (e.g., neighborhood walking). Safety concerns, however, are not limited to women in poverty, as older women have been found to be far more fearful of crime and respond by restricting their activities outside their homes (AOA, 1998). To successfully increase exercise among women, a community-based solution to address safety and a societal-based solution to address caregiving are requisite. It is not enough to educate women about the importance of exercise.

The gender-specific nature of smoking further illustrates this dynamic. Smoking has been shown to be a risk factor for most poor health outcomes. However, smoking usually starts at a young age as the result of a social environment that targets women. Those concerned about older women must give serious attention to the rise in smoking among young women. Girls are now equally or more likely than boys to smoke, depending on age (Fund, 1997). The reasons for the rise of smoking among young women are complex, but several characteristics have been identified. One of the most common reasons given for smoking among girls is the desire to be thin. The main reason given for not quitting is fear of weight gain (Ernster, 1985; French & Perry, 1996; Wiseman, Turco, Sunday, & Halmi, 1998). The role of the beauty myth in the health of young girls is a well-established issue on the women's agenda, with focused attention on eating disorders.

However, the relationship to the social role of older women is underdeveloped. Aging activists argue that the lack of attention to the issues of older women is directly related to cultural stereotypes of aging in which older women experience a loss of attractiveness and social value. Unfortunately, ageism is not gender-neutral, and our society has a strong prejudice against older women (Bentov, Smith, Laskin Siegal, & Doress-Worters, 1994). Women are labeled "old" at an earlier age than men (Slater, 1995), and their "old" status is reflective of their physical appearance and loss of usefulness to men (Lee, 1998). Women are complimented for "not looking their age," and plastic surgery for women over 50 is an expanding industry. This desire for youth, when linked to the culture of "thinness" that dominates the youth culture, creates an environment that encourages young girls to smoke. Although it is not the goal of social construction, it is the inevitable result.

Efforts addressing the issue of smoking must be conscious of not reinforcing social messages about the status of women and girls. The historical reasons for the higher percentage of men smoking include social norms about what "good girls" did and did not do. Messages to not smoke must be infused with positive advancement for women and focused on health and empowerment rather than on perpetuation of women's subordination. Likewise it must address the underlying gender bias of ageism.

Acknowledging the Health Effect of the Gendered Nature of Caregiving

Women maintain a particular status in society, in the labor market, and in the family; public policies reinforce and entrench these roles (Estes, 2000). Women play a unique role as societies' caregivers. Nearly two-thirds of caregivers of the elderly are themselves older women, many of whom are caring for both children and older family members. Caregiving is a complex and profoundly women's issue. It reflects some of what is best about being a woman: compassion and concern for others. However, the extent to which women engage in caregiving across the lifespan has a direct impact on their own health. Caregiving affects women's long-term economic security, and these negative economic consequences compound the deleterious health consequences of informal caregiving (Association, 1996; Stone, et al., 1987).

Higher rates of stress and depression, use of prescription drugs, lack of attention to personal health conditions, and participation in fewer social and recreational activities are frequently reported for caregivers (Almberg, Jansson, Grafstreom, & Winblad, 1998; Buckwalter, et al., 1999; George, 1984; Martire, Stephens, & Atienza, 1997; Schulz, et al., 1997; Wilcox & King, 1999). The higher use of prescription drugs among this group again highlights the need for a comprehensive approach for medication coverage for women across the lifespan. Also, since depression has been shown to affect the maintenance of health behaviors needed for prevention (i.e., proper diet and exercise), understanding the role of caregiving in development of the gender-appropriate prevention strategy is also imperative.

As with other issues, caregiving is examined in separate spheres of policy making. Child care is viewed as a "woman's" issue, and eldercare is viewed as an "aging" issue. Lost in these two discussions are the women caring for a spouse or a family member of the same age, in addition to the numerous women caring for multiple individuals or generations. Without addressing caregiving in its totality, which includes understanding the gendered nature of the responsibilities, policy solutions will remain elusive.

The desire to maintain caregiving as an individual responsibility is closely linked to the economic structure of our society. There is substantial economic incentive for the government to maintain caregiving as an individual expense rather than a societal expense. Consequently, policy makers continue to press for more family (i.e., women's) responsibility in the care of older persons. The ideological revolution of the Reagan and Bush presidencies helped to entrench the notion of the family as primacy for caregiving, thereby justifying shifting social responsibilities to the private sector (Estes, 1992; revised and reprinted in Lee et al., 1997). In reinforcing the notion of the role of the family in caring for elders, the public sector is released from obligation to pay for or provide the care. This primacy of family (i.e., unpaid women) as caregiver of choice is being repeated in the discourse about childcare. As reflected in the language of a governmental fact sheet ". . .the grandmother is the primary caregiver, offering these children the opportunity to grow up in stable homes and communities among their family and friends" (AOA, 1998). Again, the preference for individual-based solutions (even those supported by tax credits such as President Clinton's 1999 proposed legislation) abdicates the public sector from responsibility for developing a universal and adequate solution to the need. Understanding caregiving through gender and across the lifecourse will promote solutions that address the disproportionate burden of caregiving on women.

CONCLUSION

Because of the complexity of the issues, the traditional disease-based medical model for health, and the separation of women's health from concerns about aging, the issue of older women's health and wellness has been missing from the public agenda. This chapter develops a new agenda regarding older women's health and advocates for a bridging of the work done on behalf of women's health and older women. Older women's health represents a complex interplay of medical, social, and economic factors that cannot be understood in isolation. Successfully addressing the needs of older women's health requires the participation of both those interested in women's health and those concerned about aging issues to create a new agenda grounded in four tenets: (1) there is a gendered relationship between socioeconomic structures and health over time; (2) there are gender-specific implications of health care financing and policy; (3) there is a gender bias in the disease-based medical model of health; and (4) there are health consequences to the gendered nature of caregiving.

ABOUT THE AUTHORS

Carroll L. Estes, PhD, is Professor of Sociology at the Institute for Health and Aging, where she was first and founding director, and in the Department of Social and Behavioral Sciences, School of Nursing, at the University of California, San Francisco. Author of *The Aging Enterprise* and seven other books, she is former president of the Gerontological Society of America, the American Society of Aging, and the Association for Gerontology in Higher Education.

Tracy A. Weitz, MPA, is Center Manager of the UCSF National Center of Excellence in Women's Health, San Francisco, California.

REFERENCES

AARP, & Lewin-VHI, I. (1994). *Aging Baby Boomers: How Secure Is Their Economic Future?* Washington, DC: Forecasting and Environment Scanning Department.

AARP, & Lewin-VHI, I. (1999). *Out-of-Pocket Spending on Health Care by Women Age 65 and Over in Fee-for-Service Medicare: 1998 Projections.* Washington, DC: Public Policy Institute.

AAWH, DHHS, & WHO. (1999). *Healthy Aging, Healthy Living—START NOW!* (Resource Booklet). Washington, DC: American Association for World Health, US Department of Health & Human Services, Pan American Health Organization, World Health Organization.

Adams, P., & Marano, M. (1995). *Current estimates from the National Health Interview Survey:* National Center for Health Statistics, Vital Health Statistics.

Adler, N. E., Boyce, T., Chesney, M. A., Cohen, S., Folkman, S., Kahn, R. L., & Syme, S. L. (1994). Socioeconomic status and health. The challenge of the gradient. *American Psychologist, 49*(1), 15–24.

Adler, N. E., Boyce, W. T., Chesney, M. A., Folkman, S., & Syme, S. L. (1993). Socioeconomic inequalities in health. No easy solution. *Journal of the American Medical Association, 269*(24), 3140–5.

Adler, N. E., & Coriell, M. (1997). Socioeconomic status and women's health. In S. J. Gallant & G. Puryear Keita, et al. (Eds.), *Health Care for Women: Psychological, Social and Behavioral Influences* (pp. 11–23 of xxvii, 439). Washington, DC: American Psychological Association.

Almberg, B., Jansson, W., Grafstreom, M., & Winblad, B. (1998). Differences between and within genders in caregiving strain: a comparison between caregivers of demented and non-caregivers of non-demented elderly people. *Journal of Advanced Nursing, 28*(4), 849–58.

Alone, T. C. F. C. o. E. P. L. (1987). *Old, Alone and Poor: A Plan for Reducing Poverty among Elderly People Living Alone.* New York: The Commonwealth Fund.

AOA. (1998). *Older Women: A Diverse and Growing Population* (Fact Sheet). Washington, DC: Administration on Aging.

Apgar, B. (1999). Is raloxifene the answer to the HRT story? *American Family Physician, 60*(4), 1092, 1095.

Arno, P. S., Levine, C., & Memmott, M. M. (1999). The economic value of informal caregiving. *Health Affairs, 18*(2), 182–8.

Association, A. s. (1996). *An Exploration of the Plight of an Alzheimer's Caregiver.*

Barrett-Connor, E., & Stuenkel, C. (1999). Hormones and heart disease in women: Heart and Estrogen/Progestin Replacement Study in perspective. *Journal of Clinical Endocrinology and Metabolism, 84*(6), 1848–53.

Bentov, M., Smith, D., Laskin Siegal, D., & Doress-Worters, P. B. (1994). Aging and Well-Being. In P. B. Doress-Worters & D. L. Siegal (Eds.), *The New Ourselves Growing Older* (pp. 3–21). New York, NY: Simon & Schuster.

Besharov, D. J., & Zinsmeister, K. (1987, May 3). Unwed moms are white, too; once again the conventional wisdom has it wrong. *Washington Post,* B5.

Bierman, A. S., & Clancy, C. M. (1999). Women's health, chronic disease, and disease management: new words and old music? *Women's Health Issues,* 9(1), 2–17; discussion 30–41.

Blumenthal, D. (1999, June 17). Health care reform at the close of the 20th century. *New England Journal of Medicine, 340,* 1916.

Blustein, J., & Weiss, L. J. (1998). The use of mammography by women aged 75 and older: factors related to health, functioning, and age. *Journal of the American Geriatrics Society, 46*(8), 941–6.

Brownstein, R. (1994, July 14). Welfare reformers confront out-of-wedlock births: panel shows bipartisan resolve to reduce pregnancies by unmarried aid recipients. *Los Angeles Times,* A15.

Buckwalter, K. C., Gerdner, L., Kohout, F., Hall, G. R., Kelly, A., Richards, B., & Sime, M. (1999). A nursing intervention to decrease depression in family caregivers of persons with dementia. *Archives of Psychiatric Nursing, 13*(2), 80–8.

Bugeja, G., Kumar, A., & Banerjee, A. K. (1997). Exclusion of elderly people from clinical research: a descriptive study of published reports. *British Medical Journal (Clinical Research Ed.), 315*(7115), 1059.

Burkhauser, R. V., & Smeeding, T. M. (1994). *Social Security Reform: A Budget Neutral Approach to Reducing Older Women's Disproportionate Risk of Poverty* (Policy Brief 2). Syracuse, NY: Maxwell School Center for Policy Research.

Caregiving, N. A. f., & AARP. (1997). *Family Caregiving in the US.* Washington, DC: American Association for Retired Persons.

Carrasquillo, O., Himmelstein, D. U., Woolhandler, S., & Bor, D. H. (1999). Trends in health insurance coverage, 1989–1997. *International Journal of Health Services, 29*(3), 467–83.

Collins, K. S., Schoen, C., Joseph, S., Duchon, L., Simantov, E., & Yellowitz, M. (1999). *Health concerns across a woman's lifespan: The Commonwealth Fund 1998 Survey of Women's Health.* New York: The Commonwealth Fund.

Council, N. E. (1998, October 27). *Women and Retirement Security.* Paper presented at the Interagency Working Group on Social Security.

Cummings, S. R., Eckert, S., Krueger, K. A., Grady, D., Powles, T. J., Cauley, J. A., Norton, L., Nickelsen, T., Bjarnason, N. H., Morrow, M., Lippman, M. E., Black, D., Glusman, J. E., Costa, A., & Jordan, V. C. (1999). The effect of raloxifene on risk of breast cancer in postmenopausal women: results from the MORE randomized trial. Multiple Outcomes of Raloxifene Evaluation. *Journal of the American Medical Association, 281*(23), 2189–97.

Dalaker, J., & Naifeh, M. (1998). *Poverty in the United States: 1997.* Washington, DC: Bureau of the Census, Current Population Reports.

Davis, K., Rowland, D., Altman, D., Collins, K. S., & Morris, C. (1995). Health insurance: the size and shape of the problem. *Inquiry, 32*(2), 196–203.

Day, B. (1998). How the private sector can save Medicare. *Hospital Quarterly, 1*(3), 64–8.

DHHS. (1996). *Physical Activity and Health: A report of the Surgeon General.* Atlanta, GA: U.S. Department of Health and Human Services, Centers for Disease Control and Prevention, National Center for Chronic Disease Prevention an Health Promotion.

DHHS. (1999). *Health, United States, 1999: Health and Aging Chartbook* (DHHS PHS 99–1232–1). Hyattsville, MD: Department of Health and Human Services (DHHS).

Doress-Worters, P. B., & Siegal, D. L. (1994). *The New Ourselves, Growing Older: Women Aging with Knowledge and Power.* New York: Simon & Schuster.

Ernster, V. L. (1985). Mixed messages for women: a social history of cigarette smoking and advertising. *New York State Journal of Medicine, 85*(7), 335–340.

Estes, C., & Michel, M. (1998). *Social Security and Women* (Fact Sheet). San Francisco: Institute for Health and Aging, UCSF.

Estes, C., Swan, J., & Associates, a. (1993). *The Long Term Care Crisis.* Newbury Park, CA: Sage Publications.

Estes, C. L. (1992, September 19, 1992). *Privatization, the Welfare State, and Aging: The Reagan–Bush Legacy.* Paper presented at the 21st Annual Conference of the British Society of Gerontology, University of Kent at Canterbury.

Estes, C. L. (1998). *Social Security and the Older Woman* (Congressional Briefing). Washington, DC: Organized by the Older Women's League for the Economic Security Task Force, National Council of Women's Organizations.

Estes, C. L. (2000). From gender to the political economy of ageing. *The European Journal of Social Quality, 2*(1).

Estes, C. L., & Close, L. (1993). Public policy and long-term care. In R. P. Abcles, H. C. Gift, & M. G. Ory (Eds.), *Aging and Quality of Life* (pp. 310–335). New York: Springer Publishing Company.

Estes, C. L., Linkins, K., Lynch, M., Newcomer, R., Rice, D., & Rummelsburg, J. (1998). *The Future of Health and Health Care for the Elderly: Trends, Issues, and Assumptions.* San Francisco: Institute of Health and Aging, UCSF.

Estes, C. L., & Linkins, K. W. (1997). Race to the bottom? The challenge facing long-term care. In P. R. Lee, C. L. Estes, & L. Close (Eds.), *The Nation's Health* (fifth ed., pp. 229–236). Boston: Jones and Bartlett.

Estes, C. L., & Swan, J. H. (1993). No care zone and social policy. In C. L. Estes & I. V. Red (Eds.), *The Long Term Care Crisis: Trapped in the No Care Zone.* Newbury Park, CA: Sage Publications.

French, S. A., & Perry, C. L. (1996). Smoking among adolescent girls: prevalence and etiology. *Journal of the American Medical Women's Association, 51*(1–2), 25–8.

Friedman, E. (1994). *An Unfinished Revolution: Women and Health Care in America.* New York: United Hospital Fund of New York.

Fronstin, P., & Copeland, C. (1997). Medicare on life support: will it survive? *Ebri Issue Brief* (189), 1–22.

Fuchs, V. R. (1999). Health care for the elderly: how much? Who will pay for it? *Health Affairs, 18*(1), 11–21.

Fulwood, S., III. (1993, July 14). Out-of-wedlock births rise sharply among most groups. *Los Angeles Times,* A1.

Fund, C. (1997). *Facts on Risky Behaviors. The Commonwealth Fund Survey of the Health of Adolescent Girls:* The Commonwealth Fund.

Genazzani, A. R., & Gambacciani, M. (1999). Hormone replacement therapy: the perspectives for the 21st century. *Maturitas, 32*(1), 11–17.

George, L. K. (1984). The burden of caregiving: How much? What kind? For whom? *Advances in Research, 8.*

Goodwin, J. S. (1999). Geriatrics and the limits of modern medicine. *New England Journal of Medicine, 340*(16), 1283–5.

Gundling, R. (1997). Additional spending reductions necessary to save Medicare. *Healthcare Financial Management, 51*(8), 90.

Guralnik, J. M., Leveille, S. G., Hirsch, R., Ferrucci, L., & Fried, L. P. (1997). The impact of disability in older women. *Journal of the American Medical Women's Association, 52*(3), 113–20.

Harrington Meyer, M. (1996). Making claims as workers or wives: the distribution of Social Security benefits. *American Sociological Review, 61*(June), 449–465.

HCFA. (1996). *Medicare Current Beneficiary Survey.* Washington, DC: Health Care Financing Administration.

HCFA. (1998). *A Profile of Medicare Chart Book.* Washington, DC: Office of Strategic Planning, Health Care Financing Administration.

Hennesey, M. (1997). *Women and Pensions.* Paper presented at the Gerontological Society of America, Chicago.

Hoffman, C., & Rice, D. (1996). *Chronic Illness.* Princeton, NJ: Robert Wood Johnson Foundation.

Holmes, S. A. (1996, Oct 5). U.S. reports drop in rate of births to unwed women; fewer teen-age mothers; health agency sees decline as part of a general easing of troubling social trends. *New York Times,* 1(N), 1(L).

Housnell, C. (1998). *What Every Woman Needs to Know about Money and Retirement* (Booklet): Women's Institute for a Secure Retirement.

Hulley, S., Grady, D., Bush, T., Furberg, C., Herrington, D., Riggs, B., & Vittinghoff, E. (1998). Randomized trial of estrogen plus progestin for secondary prevention of coronary heart disease in postmenopausal women. Heart and Estrogen/Progestin Replacement Study (HERS) Research Group. *Journal of the American Medical Association, 280*(7), 605–13.

Jordan, V. C., & Morrow, M. (1999). Raloxifene as a multifunctional medicine? Current trials will show whether it is effective in both osteoporosis and breast cancer. *British Medical Journal (Clinical Research Ed.), 319*(7206), 331–2.

Kemper, P., & Murtaugh, C. (1991). Lifetime use of nursing home care. *New England Journal of Medicine, 324*(9), 595–600.

Krieger, N., Rowley, D. L., Herman, A. A., Avery, B., & Phillips, M. T. (1993). Racism, sexism, and social class: implications for studies of health, disease, and well-being. *American Journal of Preventive Medicine, 9*(6, Suppl), 82–122.

Krieger, N., Williams, D. R., & Moss, N. E. (1997). Measuring social class in US public health research: concepts, methodologies, and guidelines. *Annual Review of Public Health, 18,* 341–78.

La Croix, A. Z., Newton, K. M., Leveille, S. G., & Wallace, J. (1997). Healthy aging. A women's issue. *Western Journal of Medicine, 167*(4), 220–32.

Lantz, P. M., House, J. S., Lepkowski, J. M., Williams, D. R., Mero, R. P., & Chen, J. (1998). Socioeconomic factors, health behaviors, and mortality: results from a nationally representative prospective study of US adults. *Journal of the American Medical Association, 279*(21), 1703–8.

LAT. (1996, Oct 8). An encouraging downswing: a national drop in unwed births needs to be sustained. *Los Angeles Times,* B6.

Lee, C. (1998). *Women's Health: Psychological and Social Perspectives.* Newbury Park, CA: Sage Publications.

Lee, P. R., Estes, C. L., & Close, L. (Eds.). (1997). *The Nation's Health.* Boston: Jones and Bartlett.

Lock, M. (1998). Anomalous women and political strategies for aging societies. In S. S. e. al. (Ed.), *The Politics of Women's Health: Exploring Agency and Autonomy* (vol. 178–204). Philadelphia: Temple University Press.

Marmor, T. R., Barer, M. L., & Evans, R. G. (1994). The determinants of a population's health: what can be done to improve a democratic nation's health status. In R. G. Evans, M. L. Barer, & T. R. Marmor (Eds.), *Why Are Some People Healthy and Others Not? The Determinants of Health of Populations* (pp. 217–230). New York: A. de Gruyter.

Martire, L. M., Stephens, M. A., & Atienza, A. A. (1997). The interplay of work and caregiving: relationships between role satisfaction, role involvement, and caregivers' well-being. *Journals of Gerontology. Series B, Psychological Sciences and Social Sciences, 52*(5), S279–89.

McKusick, D. (1999). Demographic issues in Medicare reform. *Health Affairs, 18*(1), 194–207.

MMWR. (1996). Update: National Breast and Cervical Cancer Early Detection Program—July 1991–September 1995. *Morbidity and Mortality Weekly Report, 45*(23), 484–7.

NCPE. (1999). *The Wage Gap: 1997* (Fact Sheet). Washington, DC: National Committee on Pay Equity.

Network, N. W. s. H. (2000). *Taking Hormones and Women's Health: Choices, Risks and Benefits.* Washington, DC.

NOF. (1998). *Physician's Guide to Prevention and Treatment of Osteoporosis.* Washington, DC: National Osteoporosis Foundation.

NYT. (1998, March 3). Rules set in effort to reduce some births. *New York Times,* A14(N), A14(L).

Oberlander, J. B. (1997). Managed care and Medicare reform. *Journal of Health Politics, Policy and Law,* 22(2), 595–631.

O'Rand, A. (1996). The cumulative stratification of the life course. In R. Binstock & L. George (Eds.), *Handbook of Aging and the Social Sciences* (pp. 188–207). New York: Academic Press.

O'Rand, A., & Aging, N. A. o. (1994). *The Vulnerable Majority: Older Women in Transition* (Advisory Panel Report): Syracuse University.

Powell-Griner, E., Bolen, J., & Bland, S. (1999). Health care coverage and use of preventive services among the near elderly in the United States. *American Journal of Public Health,* 89(6), 882–6.

Project, T. M. P. T. K. M. P. (1999). *Women and Medicare.* Washington, DC: The Kaiser Family Foundation.

Rice, D., & Michel, M. (1998). *Women and Medicare* (Fact Sheet). San Francisco: Institute for Health and Aging, UCSF, for the Henry J. Kaiser Family Foundation and OWL: The Voice of Midlife and Older Women.

Ross, J. (1997). *Social Security Reform: Implications for Women's Retirement Income* (Report to the Ranking Minority Member, Subcommittee on Social Security, Committee on Ways & Means, House of Representatives). Washington, DC: U.S. GAO.

Schoen, C., Neuman, P., Kitchman, M., Davis, K., & Rowland, D. (1998). *Medicare Beneficiaries: A Population at Risk* (Findings from the Kaiser/Commonwealth 1997 Survey of Medicare Beneficiaries): Kaiser Family Foundation.

Schulz, R., Newsom, J., Mittelmark, M., Burton, L., Hirsch, C., & Jackson, S. (1997). Health effects of caregiving: the caregiver health effects study. An ancillary study of the Cardiovascular Health Study. *Annals of Behavioral Medicine,* 19(2), 110–6.

Security, A. D. S. (1999). *Making Sense of Social Security: A Discussion Starter.* Washington, DC: The Pew Charitable Trusts.

Serafini, M. W. (1997). Brave new world. *National Journal,* 29(33), 1636–9.

Shaw, L., Zuckerman, D., & Hartman, H. (1998). *The Impact of Social Security Reform on Women* (Report). Washington, DC: Institute for Women's Policy Research.

Slater, R. (1995). *The psychology of growing old: looking forward.* Philadelphia: Open University Press.

Smeeding, T. (1999). *Social Security Reform and Older Women: Improving the System.* Syracuse, NY: Syracuse University Press.

Smeeding, T., Estes, C. L., & Glasse, L. (1999). *Social Security Reform and Older Women: Improving the System* (Report for the Task Force on Women). Washington, DC: The Gerontological Society of America.

SSA. (1998). *Fast Facts & Figures about Social Security.* Washington, DC: Office of Research, Evaluation and Statistics, Social Security Administration.

SSA, & Grad, S. (1998). *Income of the Population 55 or Older, 1996.* Washington, DC: Office of Research, Evaluation, and Statistics, Social Security Administration.

Steuerle, E. (1999). *The Treatment of the Family and Divorce in the Social Security Program.* Washington, DC: US Senate Special Committee on Aging.

Stone, A., & Griffith, J. (1998). *Older Women: The Economics of Aging.* Women's Research & Education Institute.

Stone, R., Cafferata, G., & Sangl, J. (1987). Caregivers of the frail elderly: a national profile. *The Gerontologist, 27,* 616–627.

Toner, R. (1999, Sept 13). The debate on aid for the elderly focuses on women; face of aging is female; both parties appeal to them, and use them, in lobbying on safety-net programs. *New York Times,* A1(N), A1(L).

Trafford, A. (1998, May 19). Viagra and the other sex pill. *Washington Post,* 6.

Ussher, J. M. (1992). Reproductive rhetoric and the blaming of the body. In P. Nicolson, J. M. Ussher, & J. Campling (Eds.), *The Psychology of Women's Health and Health Care* (pp. 31–61). Houndmills, Basingstoke, Hampshire, UK: Macmillan.

Verbrugge, L. M., & Jette, A. M. (1994). The disablement process. *Social Science and Medicine, 38*(1), 1–14.

Vobejda, B. (1995, Sept 22). Teen births decline; out-of-wedlock rate levels off. *Washington Post,* A1.

Wallace, S. e. a. (1998). The consequences of color-blind health policy. *The Stanford Law Review, 9*(2), 340–341.

Weil, P. (1987). Opinions of health care executives on access to care. *Hospital and Health Services Administration, 32*(4), 421–37.

Weisman, C. S. (1998). *Women's Health Care: Activist Traditions and Institutional Change.* Baltimore: Johns Hopkins University Press.

Wilcox, S., & King, A. C. (1999). Sleep complaints in older women who are family caregivers. *Journals of Gerontology. Series B, Psychological Sciences and Social Sciences, 54*(3), 189–98.

Wilensky, G. (1996). What it will take to save Medicare (interview by Michael Pretzer). *Medical Economics, 73*(11), 153–4, 157–8, 160.

Williams, D., & Collins, C. (1995). *US Socioeconomic and Racial Differences in Health: Patterns and Explanations* (vol. 21).

Wiseman, C. V., Turco, R. M., Sunday, S. R., & Halmi, K. A. (1998). Smoking and body image concerns in adolescent girls. *International Journal of Eating Disorders, 24*(4), 429–33.

Wyn, R., & Martin, R. (1998). *Women at Risk in California: A Chartbook on Health Insurance Coverage and Access to Care.* The Regents on the University of California.

RECOMMENDED READING

CHAPTER 1

Breslow, L. The Future of Public Health: Prospects in the United States for the 1990s. *Annual Review of Public Health* 1990; *11*:1–28.

Collins, K.S., Hall, A., and Neuhaus, C. *U.S. Minority Health: A Chartbook.* New York: The Commonwealth Fund, May 1999.

Duffy, J. *The Sanitarians: A History of Public Health.* Chicago, IL: University of Illinois Press, 1990.

Fee, E. The Origins and Development of Public Health in the United States. In: *Oxford Textbook of Public Health (2nd ed.).* W. Holland, R. Detels, G. Knox 3:3–22. New York: Oxford Medical Publications. pp. 657, 1991.

McGinnis, J.M., and Lee, Philip R. Healthy People 2000 at mid decade. *Journal of the American Medical Association* 1995; *273*(14):1123–1129.

Pamuk, E., Makuc, D., Heck, K., Reuben, C., and Lochnen, K. *Socioeconomic Status and Health Chartbook, Health, United States, 1998.* Hyattsville, MD: National Center for Health Statistics, pp. 3–20 (Highlights), 1998.

Lee, Philip R. Keynote Address: State of the Nation's Health. *Bulletin of the New York Academy of Medicine* 1995; *72*(Winter Supplement 2):552–569.

U.S. Department of Health and Human Services. *Healthy People 2010: Understanding and Improving Health.* Washington, DC: U.S. Department of Health and Human Services, Government Printing Office, 2000. To access Healthy People 2010 documents online, visit: http://www.health.gov/healthypeople/

CHAPTER 2

Adler, N.E., Boyce, T. McChesney, M.A., Folkman, S., and Syme, L. Socioeconomic Inequalities in Health. No Easy Solutions. *JAMA* 1993; *239:*3140–3145.

Bunker, J.P., Frazier, H.S., and Mosteller, F. Improving Health: Measuring Effects of Medical Care. *Milbank Quarterly* 1994; *2:*225–58.

Bunker, J.P. Medicine Matters after All. *Journal of the Royal College of Physicians* (London), 1995; *29:*105–12.

Evans, R.G., and Stoddart, G. Producing Health, Consuming Health Care. *Social Science and Medicine* 1990; *31* (12):1347–1363.

Evans, R.G., Barer, M.L., and Marmor, T.R. (eds). *Why Are Some People Healthy and Others Not? The Determinants of Health of Populations.* New York: Aldine De Gruyter, 1994.

Jefferys, M. Social Inequalities in Health: Do they diminish with age? *American Journal of Public Health* 1996; *86:*474–475.

Kaplan, G.A., Pamuk E.R., Lynch, JW, Cohen RD, Balfour JL. Inequality in Income and Mortality in the United States: Analysis of Mortality and Potential Pathways. *British Medical Journal* 1996; *312:*999–1003.

Krieger, Williams, and Moss. Measuring Social Class in U.S. Public Health Research: Concepts, Methodologies, and Guidelines. *Annual Review of Public Health* 1997; *18:*341–378.

Kuh, Diana and Ben-Shlomo, Yoav. (eds.). *A Life Course Approach to Chronic Disease Epidemiology.* New York: Oxford University Press, 1997.

McGinnis, J.M., and Lee, P.R. Healthy People 2000 at mid Decade. *Journal of the American Medical Association* 1995; *273:*1123–1129.

McKeown. T. *The Role of Medicine: Dream, Mirage, or Nemesis?* Princeton, NJ: Princeton University Press, 1979.

Marmot, M.G., Davey Smith, G., Stansfeld, S., Patel, C., North, F., Head, J., White, I., Brunner, E., and Feeney, A. Health Inequalities and Social Class. Abridged from *The Lancet,* 1991; *337:*1387–1392, under the original title "Health Inequalities among British Civil Servants: The Whitehall II Study."

Newacheck, P., Jameson, W.J., and Halfon, N. Health Status and Income: The Impact of Poverty on Child Health. *Journal of School Health* 1994; *64:*229–233.

Paffenbarger, R.S., Hyde, R.T., Wing, A.L., et al. The Association of Changes in Physical Activity Level and Other Lifestyle Characteristics with Mortality Among Men. *The New England Journal of Medicine* 1993; *328:*538–545.

Pate, R.R., Pratt, M.S., Blair, N. et al. Physical Activity and Public Health: A Recommendation from the Centers for Disease Control and Prevention and the American College of Sports Medicine. *Journal of the American Medical Association* 1995; 273:402–407, 1995.

Power, C., and Hertzman, C. Social and Biological Pathways Linking Early Life and Adult Disease. *British Medical Bulletin* 1997; 53(1):210–221.

U.S. Department of Health and Human Services. *Surgeon General's Report on Promoting Health/Preventing Disease: Objectives for the Nation in the U.S. Public Health Service.* Public Health Service, Washington, DC, 1980.

U.S. Department of Health and Human Services. *Surgeon General's Report on Nutrition and Health. Public Health Service.* Public Health Service, Washington, DC, 1988.

U.S. Department of Health and Human Services. *The Health Consequences of Smoking: Nicotine Addiction. A Report of the Surgeon General.* Public Health Service, Washington, DC. 88-8406, 1988.

U.S. Department of Health and Human Services. *Healthy People 2000: National Health Promotion and Disease Prevention Objectives.* Washington, DC: Public Health Service, 1990.

Waitzman, N.J., and Smith, K.R. Phantom of the Area: Poverty, Residence and Mortality in the U.S. Presented at the Forum on Social and Economic Disparities in Health and Health Care, Salt Lake City, UT, 1996.

Wilkinson, R.G. Income Distribution and Life Expectancy. *British Medical Journal* 1992; *304:*165–168.

Williams, D.R., and Collins, C. U.S. Socioeconomic and Racial Differences in Health: Patterns and Explanations. *Annual Review of Sociology* 1995; *21:*349–386, 1995.

CHAPTER 3

Estes, Carroll L. *The Aging Enterprise: A Critical Examination of Social Policies and Services for the Aged.* San Francisco: Jossey-Bass Publishers, 1979.

Glied, Sherry. *Chronic Condition: Why Health Reform Fails.* Cambridge, MA: Harvard University Press, 1997.

Hackney, Robert B. *Rethinking Health Care Policy: The New Politics of State Regulation.* Washington, DC: Georgetown University Press, 1998.

Kindon, J.W. *Agendas, Alternatives, and Public Policies (2nd ed.).* New York: HarperCollins, 1995.

Lee, Philip R., and Benjamin, A.E. Health Policy and the Politics of Health Care. Abridged from S.J. Williams & P.R. Torrens (eds.). *Introduction to Health Services,* (4th ed.). Albany, NY: Delmar Publishers, 1993.

Longest, B.B. *Health Policymaking in the United States.* (2nd ed.). Chicago: Health Administration Press, 1998.

Skocpol, Theda. *Boomerang: Clinton's Health Security Effort and Turn Against Government in U.S. Politics.* New York: W.W. Norton & Company, 1996.

CHAPTER 4

Fuchs, V.R. Economics, values, and health care reform. *American Economic Review* 1996; *86:*1–24.

Kassirer, J.E. Managed Care and the Morality of the Marketplace. *NEJM* 1995; *333:*50–52.

Rawls, J. *A Theory of Justice.* Cambridge, MA: The Belknap Press of Harvard University Press, 1971.

CHAPTER 5

Cater, D., and Lee, PR. (eds.). *Politics of Health.* Huntington, NY: Robert E. Krieger, 1979.

Estes, C.L. "Privatization, the Welfare State, and Aging: The Reagan-Bush Legacy." Abidged from a paper presented at the 21st Annual Conference of the British Society of Gerontology, University of Kent at Canterbury, September 19, 1992.

Johnson, H., and David, S. *The System: The American Way of Politics at the Breaking Point,* Epilogue: The System. Boston: Little, Brown & Company, pp. 637–658, 1996, 1997.

Nestle, M. Food Lobbies, The Food Pyramid and U.S. Nutrition Policy. *International Journal of Health Services* 1993; *23:*483–496.

CHAPTER 6

Afifi, A.A., & Breslow, L. The Maturing Paradigm of Public Health. *Annual Review of Public Health,* 1994; *15:*223–235.

American Cancer Society. (No. 98-1152). On Writ of Certiorari to the United States Court of Appeals for the Fourth Circuit in the Supreme Court of the United States, Food and Drug Administration et al. Petitioners v. Brown and Williamson Tobacco Group Corporation et al. Respondents. Milbank, Tweed Hadley and McCloy, LLP, pp. 1–25.

Breslow, L. The Future of Public Health: Prospects in the United States for the 1990s. *Annual Review of Public Health* 1990; *11:*1–28.

Breslow, L. From Disease Prevention to Health Promotion. *Journal of the American Medical Association* 1999; *281*(11):1030–1033.

Centers for Disease Control and Prevention. Achievements in Public Health, 1900–1999: Changes in the Public Health System. *MMWR* December 24, 1999; *48*(50):1141–1147.

Centers for Disease Control and Prevention. Achievements in Public Health, 1900–1999: Family Planning. *MMWR* December 3, 1999; *48*(47):1073–1080.

Centers for Disease Control and Prevention. Achievements in Public Health, 1900–1999: Tobacco Use—United States, 1900–1999. *MMWR* November 5, 1999; *48*(43):986–993.

Centers for Disease Control and Prevention. Achievements in Public Health, 1900–1999: Fluoridation of Drinking Water to Prevent Dental Caries. *MMWR* October 22, 1999; *48*(41):933–940.

Centers for Disease Control and Prevention. Achievements in Public Health, 1900–1999: Safer and Healthier Foods. *MMWR* October 15, 1999; *48*(40):905–913.

Centers for Disease Control and Prevention. Achievements in Public Health, 1900–1999: Healthier Mothers and Babies. *MMWR* October 1, 1999; *48*(38):849–858.

Centers for Disease Control and Prevention. Impact of Vaccines Universally Recommended for Children—United States, 1900–1998. *MMWR* 1999; *48:*243–248.

Centers for Disease Control and Prevention. Achievements in Public Health, 1900–1999: Improvements in Workplace Safety—United States, 1900–1999. *MMWR* 1999; *48:*461–469.

Coates, T.J., and Collins, C. *HIV Prevention: We Don't Need to Wait for a Vaccine.* San Francisco: USCF AIDS Research Institute and Center for AIDS Prevention Studies (CAPS), Department of Medicine, University of California, San Francisco, 1999: 3–14.

Fielding, J.E. Public Health in the Twentieth Century: Advances and Challenges. *Annual Review of Public Health* 1999; *20:*xiii–xxix.

Glantz, S.A. Preventing Tobacco Use—the Youth Access Trap. *American Journal of Public Health* 1996; *86:*156–158.

Institute of Medicine (IOM). *The Future of Public Health:* Summary and Recommendations. Washington, DC: National Academy Press, 1988.

Lasker, R.D., and The Committee on Medicine and Public Health. *Medicine and Public Health: The Power of Collaboration.* Chicago: Health Administration Press, 1997.

Lee, P.R., and Paxman, D. Reinventing Public Health. *Annual Review of Public Health* 1997; *18:*1–35.

Louis Harris and Associates, Inc. *Preventive Care and Physician Counseling.* New York: The Commonwealth Fund, May 1999.

U.S. Preventive Services Task Force. *Guide to Clinical Preventive Services.* Alexandria, VA: International Medical Publishing, 1996.

CHAPTER 7

Baxter, R.J., and Mechanic, RE. Status of Local Health Care Safety Net. *Health Affairs* 1997; *16:*7–22.

Berk, M.L., C.L. Schur, & J.C. Cantor. Ability to Obtain Health Care: Recent Estimates of the Robert Wood Johnson Foundation National Access to Care Survey. *Health Affairs* 1995; *14:*138–146.

Blendon, R., Benson, J., Brodie, M., Altman, D., James, M., and Hugick, L. Voters and Health Care in the 1998 Election. *JAMA* 1999; *279:189–194.*

Davis, K. Incremental coverage of the uninsured. *Journal of the American Medical Association* 1996; *276*(10):831–832.

Donalen, K., Blendon, R.J., Hill, C.A., Hoffman, C., Rowland, D., Frankel, M., and Altman, D. Whatever Happened to the Health Insurance Crisis in the United States? *Journal of the American Medical Association* 1996; *276*(16):1346–1350.

Estes, C.L., Harrington, C., and Pellow, D.N. Medical Industrial Complex. *Encyclopedia of Sociology* (to be published).

Friedman, E. The Uninsured: From Dilemma to Crisis. Abridged from *Journal of the American Medical Association* 1991; *265*:2491–2495.

Halfon, N., Inkelas, M., and Wood, D. (1995). Nonfinancial Barriers to Care for Children and Youth. *Annual Review of Public Health* 1995; *16*:447–472.

Harris, Louis and Associates, Inc. Trade-offs & Choices: Health Policy Options for the 1990s: A Survey. Conducted for Metropolitan Life Insurance Company. New York: Metropolitan Life Insurance Company, 1990.

The Kaiser Commission on the Future of Medicaid. Legislative Summary: "State Children's Health Insurance Program." Menlo Park, CA: The Henry J. Kaiser Family Foundation, December 1997.

Levit, K., Cowan, C., Braden, B., Stiller, J., Sensenig, A., Lazenby, H. National Health Expenditures in 1997: More Slow Growth. *Health Affairs (Millwood)* 1998; *17*(6):99–110.

Reinhardt, U.E. Providing Access to Health Care and Controlling Costs: The Universal Dilemma. Reprinted by permission of the author in *The Nation's Health* (4th ed., pp. 263–278), 1994.

Robinson, J.C. The Dynamics and Limits of Corporate Growth in Health Care. *Health Affairs* 1996; *15*(2):155–169.

Salmon, J.W. A Perspective on the Corporate Transformation of Health Care. *International Journal of Health Services* 1995; *25*(1):11–42.

Starr, Paul. *The Social Transformation of American Medicine.* United States: Basic Books, 1982.

CHAPTER 8

Aaron, H.J., and Reischauer, R.D. The Medicare Reform Debate; What is the next step? *Health Affairs* 1995; Winter.

Culbertson, R., and Lee, P.R. Medicare and physician autonomy. *Health Care Financing Review,* 1997.

Enthoven, A.C., and Singer, S.J. Market-Based Reform: What to Regulate and By Whom. *Health Affairs* (Spring) 1995;105–119.

Etheredge, Lynn. Purchasing Medicare Prescription Drug Benefits. *Health Affairs:* 1999; *18*:7–19.

Fox, P.D., Etheredge, L. & Jones, S.B. Addressing the Needs of Chronically Ill Persons under Medicare. *Health Affairs* (March/April) 1996; 144–150.

Fuchs, Victor R. Health Care For The Elderly: How Much? Who Will Pay For It? *Health Affairs* January/February 1999; *18*(1):11–20.

Gluck, M.E. A Medicare Prescription Drug Benefit. Medicare Brief. No. 1, National Academy of Social Insurance, 1999.

Johnson, H., and Broder, D.S. The System: *The American way of Politics at the Breaking Point.* Boston: Little, Brown, 1996.

The Kaiser Commission on the Future of Medicaid. Medicaid and Long Term Care. Menlo Park, CA: The Henry J. Kaiser Family Foundation, February 1996.

The Kaiser Medicare Policy Project. *Medicare + Choice.* Menlo Park, CA: The Henry J. Kaiser Family Foundation, July 1998.

Moon, M., and Davis, K. Preserving and Strengthening Medicare. *Health Affairs* 1995; *14*(4):31–46.

Rosenbaum, S., and Shin, P. Medicaid Managed Care: Opportunities and Challenges for Minority Americans. Menlo Park, CA: The Henry J. Kaiser Family Foundation, 1998.

Vladeck, B.C. Plenty of Nothing—A Report from the Medicare Commission. *NEJM* 1999; *340:*1503–1506.

CHAPTER 9

Boyle, P.J., and Callahan, D. Minds and Hearts: Priorities in Mental Health services. *Hastings Center Report* 1993; *23*(5):S3.

Ellwood, P.M., and Enthoven, A. "Responsible Choices": The Jackson Hole Group Plan for Health Reform. *Health Affairs* (Summer) 1995; 24–39.

Enthoven, A.C., and Kronick, R. (1991). Universal Health Insurance through Incentive Reform. *JAMA* 1991; *265*(19):2532–2536.

Feder, J., and Moon, M. Managed Care for the Elderly: A Threat or Promise? *Generations* 1996; *20*(20):42–46.

Grumbach, K. et al. Primary Care Physicians' Experience of Financial Incentive in Managed-Care Systems. *The New England Journal of Medicine* 1998; *339:*1516–1521.

Luft, Harold S. Modifying Managed Competition to Address Cost and Quality. *Health Affairs* 1996; *15*(1):23–48.

Remler, D. et al. What do Managed Care Plans Do to Affect Care? Results from a Survey of Physicians. *Inquiry* 1997; Fall *34:*196–204.

Robinson, J.C. The Future of Managed Care Organization. *Health Affairs* (March/April 1999) *18:*6–24.

Robinson, J.C., and Casalino, L.P. The Growth of Medical Groups Paid Through Capitation in California. *NEJM* 1995; *333*(25):1684–1687.

Schwartz, J.S. The Role of Cost Effectiveness in Defining Managed Care. Philadelphia: Leonard Davis Institute, School of Medicine and the Wharton School, University of Pennsylvania, 1997, p. 6.

CHAPTER 10

Bindman, A.B., Grumbach, K., Osmond, D., Komary, M., Vranizan, K., Lurie, N., Billings, J., and Stewart, A. Preventable Hospitalizations and Access to Health Care. *JAMA* 1995; *274:*305–311.

Eddy, D.M. Performance Measurement: Problems and Solutions. *Health Affairs (Millwood)* 1998; *17*(4):7–25.

Friedman, M.A. Issues in Measuring and Improving Health Care Quality. *Health Care Financing Review* Summer 1995; *16*(4).

Grumbach, K., Anderson, G.M., Luft, H.S., Roos, L.L., and Brook, R. Regionalization of Cardiac Surgery in the United States and Canada: Geographic Access, Choice, and Outcomes. *JAMA* 1995; *274:*1282–1288.

Kohn, L., Corrigan, J., Donaldson, M., (eds.) and Committee on Quality of Health Care in America. *To Err is Human: Building a Safer Health System.* New York; Institute of Medicine, 2000.

Leape, LL. Error in Medicine. *JAMA* 1994; *272:*1851–1857.

Leape, L.L., Woods, D.D., Hatlie, M.J., Kizer, K.W., Schroeder, S.A., and Lundberg, G.D. Promoting Patient Safety by Preventing Medical Error. *JAMA* 1998; *280:*1444–1447.

Miller, R.H., and Luft, H.S. Does Managed Care Lead to Better or Worse Quality of Care? *Health Affairs* 1997; *16:*7–23.

Sackett, D.L., Rosenberg, W.C., Muir Gray, J.A., Haynes, R.B., Richardson, W.S. Evidence Based Medicine: What It Is and What It Isn't. *British Medical Journal* 1996; *312:*71–72.

Special compilation: "New Initiatives and Approaches in Health Care Quality" (10 articles). *Health Care Financing Review.* Summer 1995; 16(4).

Wennberg, J.E. Future Directions for Small Area Variations. *Medical Care* 1993; *31*(5):YS75–80, Supplement.

CHAPTER 11

Collins, K.S., Schoen, C., Joseph, S., Duchon, L., Simantov, E., and Yellowitz, M. *Health Concerns Across a Woman's Lifespan: The Commonwealth Fund 1998 Survey of Women's Health.* New York: The Commonwealth Fund, 1999.

Estes, C.L., and Close, L. Public Policy and Long Term Care. In Lee, P.R., Estes, C.L., and Close, L. (eds.). *The Nation's Health* (5th ed.) Boston: Jones and Bartlett Publishers, 1997: 177–191.

Friedland, R.B., and Summer, L. "Demography is not Destiny." Washington, DC: National Academy on an Aging Society. Gerontological Society of America, 1999.

Harrington, Meyer, M. Making Claims as Workers or Wives: The Distribution of Social Security Benefits. *American Sociological Review* 1996; *61*(June):449–465.

Lee, C. Women's health: Psychological and Social Perspectives. Thousand Oaks, CA: Sage, 1998.

Minkler, M., and Estes, C.L., (eds.). *Critical Gerontology and the New Political Economy of Aging.* Amityville, NY: Baywood, 1998.

NCHS. *Health, United States. 1999 with Health And Aging Chartbook.* Washington, DC: National Center for Health Statistics, 1999.

NIH. *Agenda for Research on Women's Health for the 21st Century: A Report of the Task Force on NIH Health Research for the 21st Century.* Vol. 1. Bethesda, MD: U.S. Department of Health and Human Services, Public Health Service, National Institutes of Health. NIH Publication No. 99-4386, 1999.

Walker, A. "Public Policy and Theories of Aging: Constructing and Reconstructing Old Age." In: Handbook of Theories of Aging, V.L. Bengston and K.W. Schaie, (eds.). New York: Springer, 1999: 361–378.

Weisman, C.S. Women's Health Care: Activist Traditions and Institutional Change. Baltimore, MD: Johns Hopkins University Press, 1998.

Wetle, T. Aging is a Women's Issue. *Journal of the American Medical Women's Association* 1997; *52*(3):98, 106.

Williams, D., and Collins, C. In: U.S. Socioeconomic and Racial Differences in Health: Patterns and Explanations, J. Hagan and K. Cook (eds.). *Annual Review of Sociology,* 1995; *21.*

INDEX

California Public Employees' Retirement
  System, 333
Campbell, Jennifer A., as contributor, 313–320
Canadian Task Force on the Periodic Health
  Examination (CTFPHE), 250
Cancer
  as cause of death, 14, 18, 50, 233, 248
  diagnosis, 14
  environmental factors, 22–23
  incidence of, 21
  mortality rates, 4–5, 21–23, 25–26
    sex differences, 21
  screening programs, 479, 496–497, 534
  survival rates, 23
Cardiovascular disease (CVD). *See* Heart
  disease
Caregiving
  community care, 134–135, 147
  women's role as caregiver, 504, 508–509,
    535, 538–539
Carotid endarterectomy, efficacy of, 456
Cataract surgery, 51
Catastrophic Coverage Act, 357
Census Bureau (U.S.)
  current population surveys, 318–320
  employer-sponsored health insurance, 331
  uninsured, number of, 309, 323
  uninsured children, 324–325
Center for Control of Malaria in War Areas, 264
Centers for Disease Control and Prevention
  (CDC)
  AIDS studies, gender bias, 492
  breast and cervical cancer screening
    program, 496, 534
  factors influencing premature mortality, 50
  health policy implementation, 98
  healthy days measures, 35
  heart disease and stroke, 240–246
  history and establishment of, 88, 264
  infectious disease control, 233–239
  motor vehicle safety, 228–232
  public health achievements, 225–226
Cerebrovascular disease (stroke)
  as cause of death, 50, 240
  diagnosis, 14
  mortality rates, 5, 18, 21, 25
    class vs. race differentials, 80
    decline in, 226, 240–246, 248
  prevention, 248
  treatment, 51
Cervical cancer, 248, 479, 503
Chartbook on Minority Health
  (Commonwealth Fund), 5

Childbed fever, prevention, 60
Children. *See also* Infant and child mortality
  health care for children with disabilities, 148
  kiddie-care proposals, 199–200
  lead poisoning, 280, 282
  Medicaid eligibility expansion, 106
  role of Medicaid, 408–411
  uninsured, 147, 199–200, 310, 313, 316,
    324–325
  uninsured, by state, 325
Children's Health Insurance Program (CHIP).
  See State Children's Health Insurance
  Program (CHIP)
Cholera
  exposure to *bacillus,* 60
  outbreaks of, 3, 4, 10, 234, 265
Cholesterol
  and diet, 243
  as risk factor for coronary heart disease, 242
Christian Coalition, 189, 196
Chromosomal diseases, 62
Chronic and degenerative diseases, as causes
  of death, 18–23
Chronic obstructive pulmonary disease, 18, 50,
  492
Cigarette smoking. *See also* Tobacco use
  as cause of death, 248
  decline in, 21, 242
  government intervention, 68
  health risks from, 20–22
  high rate among women, 503, 506, 537–538
  nicotine addiction, 492
  prevention programs, 537–538
    gender bias in, 491–492
  and socioeconomic status, 6
Citizens for Long-Term Care (CLTC), 212
Civil Rights Act, 101, 345, 486
Class. *See* Social class
Clinical medicine
  advances in, 11–12
  shifts in clinical services, 280–282
Clinical preventive services, 5, 221, 247–262
  barriers to, 248–249
  disease focused vs. gender-appropriate
    model of prevention, 532–538
  historical perspective, 249–250
  improving delivery of, 255
  perspectives on importance of public health,
    283–284
  physical examination, 249–250
  and private health insurance benefits,
    280–282
  research agenda, 254–255

gender and racial bias, 470, 491
government assistance, 190
in preventive medicine, 254–255
on socioeconomic inequalities in health,
69–70
women's health issues, 496
Medical savings accounts (MSAs), 194,
200–201, 419
Medical-Industrial Complex, 137, 306
Medicalists, health reform proposals, 124–125
Medicare
beneficiaries
dual eligibles, 405
low-income, 403, 404fig.
benefit payments, 516
benefits, 351–354
budgetary controls, 192
characteristics of, changes in, 341–342
clinical preventive services benefits, 280
costs, 119
eligibility, 351
enactment of, 95, 101–102, 188, 190, 264,
341, 349
expansion of, 98
expenditures, projected growth in, 350fig.
federal budget and, 187
financing and revenues, 351, 354
future of, 345–346, 359
gaps in coverage. *See* Medigap insurance
gender-specific limitations of, 529–531
HMO enrollment, 344–345
home health care cuts, 208
literature review, 345–346
long-term care coverage limited, 518–519
mammography screening benefit, 496
managed care options, 311, 321, 327, 344,
345, 405–406
prescription drug benefits, 322, 326–327,
379–388
preservation and value of, 519–520
quality of care, 358
regulations, 98
report on, 349–361
Republican Party proposals, 194
role of Medicaid, 404–405
scope of the program, 351
supplement medical insurance (Part B), 352
as a women's health issue, 471, 514–522
Medicare + Choice program, 311, 321, 327,
345, 381, 383, 384, 431, 433
Medicare claims payment, 354–358
administration, 353–354
allocation of payments, 355fig.

customary, prevailing, and reasonable (CPR)
system, 344, 355
diagnosis-related groups (DRGs) for hospitals,
166, 172, 343, 344, 355–356, 371
fee schedule for physicians, 103, 308, 343,
344, 352, 357–358, 431
fee-for-service (FFS) system, 144, 342,
354–355, 364, 367–368, 386, 419, 506
participants payments, 352–353
prospective payment system for hospitals,
355–357, 368
resource-based relative value-scale
(RBRVS), 344, 357, 368, 371
services billed by physicians, 356fig.
Medicare Commission. *See* National Bipartisan
Commission on the Future of Medicare
Medicare Hospital Trust Fund, 519
Medicare Peer Review Organization (PRO)
program, 358, 418, 437, 444
Medicare reform, 363–378
legislation, 90, 109
program budget proposal, 370–376
proposals for spending reduction, 105–106
restructuring options, 520–521
voucher system, 364–369
Medicine and public health, 262–301
barriers to collaborations, 269–271
clinical services shifts, 280–282
consolidation and partnerships, 288–290
curative vs. preventive approach to, 273
economic and performance pressures, 286–288
financing streams, 284–286
government reforms, impact of, 278
health care costs, impact of, 276–279
historical relationship between, 263–268
historical timeline, 264fig.
models of health collaboration, 291–296,
294fig.
new opportunities for interaction, 268–269
patient population shifts, 279–280
perspectives on the importance of public
health, 283–284
science and health policies, impact of,
271–274
as separate and independent health sectors,
274–276
Medigap insurance, 306, 322, 326–327, 380,
383, 431, 517
Meningitis, 59, 235
Mental illness
federal treatment programs, 88
state treatment programs, 95
as women's health issue, 492